MACHINE ETHICS

The new field of machine ethics is concerned with giving machines ethical principles, or a procedure for discovering a way to resolve the ethical dilemmas they might encounter, enabling them to function in an ethically responsible manner through their own ethical decision making. Developing ethics for machines, which can be contrasted with developing ethics for human beings who use machines, is by its nature an interdisciplinary endeavor.

The essays in this volume represent the first steps by philosophers and artificial intelligence researchers toward explaining why it is necessary to add an ethical dimension to machines that function autonomously, what is required in order to add this dimension, philosophical and practical challenges to the machine ethics project, various approaches that could be considered in attempting to add an ethical dimension to machines, work that has been done to date in implementing these approaches, and visions of the future of machine ethics research.

Dr. Michael Anderson is a Professor of Computer Science at the University of Hartford, West Hartford, Connecticut. His interest in further enabling machine autonomy led him first to investigate how a computer might deal with diagrammatic information – work that was funded by the National Science Foundation – and has currently resulted in his establishing machine ethics as a bona fide field of scientific inquiry with Susan Leigh Anderson. He maintains the Machine Ethics Web site (http://www.machineethics.org).

Dr. Susan Leigh Anderson is Professor Emerita of Philosophy at the University of Connecticut. Her specialty is applied ethics, most recently focusing on biomedical ethics and machine ethics. She has received funding from the National Endowment for the Humanities and, with Michael Anderson, from NASA and the NSF. She is the author of three books in the Wadsworth Philosophers Series, as well as numerous articles.

Together, the Andersons co-chaired the AAAI Fall 2005 Symposium on Machine Ethics, co-edited an *IEEE Intelligent Systems* special issue on machine ethics, and co-authored an invited article on the topic for *Artificial Intelligence Magazine*. Their research in machine ethics was selected for Innovative Applications of Artificial Intelligence as an emerging application in 2006, and the October 2010 issue of *Scientific American Magazine* featured an invited article on their research in which the first robot whose behavior is guided by an ethical principle was debuted.

Machine Ethics

Edited by

Michael Anderson

University of Hartford

Susan Leigh Anderson

University of Connecticut

CAMBRIDGE
UNIVERSITY PRESS

University Printing House, Cambridge CB2 8BS, United Kingdom

One Liberty Plaza, 20th Floor, New York, NY 10006, USA

477 Williamstown Road, Port Melbourne, VIC 3207, Australia

314-321, 3rd Floor, Plot 3, Splendor Forum, Jasola District Centre, New Delhi - 110025, India

79 Anson Road, #06-04/06, Singapore 079906

Cambridge University Press is part of the University of Cambridge.

It furthers the University's mission by disseminating knowledge in the pursuit of education, learning and research at the highest international levels of excellence.

www.cambridge.org
Information on this title: www.cambridge.org/9781108461757

© Cambridge University Press 2011

First published 2011
First paperback edition 2018

A catalogue record for this publication is available from the British Library

Library of Congress Cataloging in Publication data
Machine ethics / [edited by] Michael Anderson, Susan Leigh Anderson.
p. cm.
Includes bibliographical references.
ISBN 978-0-521-11235-2 (hardback)
1. Artificial intelligence – Philosophy. 2. Artificial intelligence – Moral and ethical aspects. I. Anderson, Michael, 1951– II. Anderson, Susan Leigh.
Q335.M165 2011
170–dc22 2010052339

ISBN 978-0-521-11235-2 Hardback
ISBN 978-1-108-46175-7 Paperback

Contents

General Introduction

THE SUBJECT OF THIS BOOK IS A NEW FIELD OF RESEARCH: DEVELOPING ethics for machines, in contrast to developing ethics for human beings who use machines. The distinction is of practical as well as theoretical importance. Theoretically, *machine ethics* is concerned with giving *machines* ethical principles or a procedure for discovering a way to resolve the ethical dilemmas they might encounter, enabling them to function in an ethically responsible manner through their own ethical decision making. In the second case, in developing ethics for human beings who use machines, the burden of making sure that machines are never employed in an unethical fashion always rests with the *human beings* who interact with them. It is just one more domain of applied *human* ethics that involves fleshing out proper and improper *human* behavior concerning the use of machines. Machines are considered to be just tools used by human beings, requiring ethical guidelines for how they ought and ought not to be used by humans.

Practically, the difference is of particular significance because succeeding in developing ethics for machines enables them to function (more or less) *autonomously*, by which is meant that they can function without human causal intervention after they have been designed for a substantial portion of their behavior. (Think of the difference between an ordinary vacuum cleaner that is guided by a human being who steers it around a room and a Roomba that is permitted to roam around a room on its own as it cleans.) There are many necessary activities that we would like to be able to turn over entirely to autonomously functioning machines, because the jobs that need to be done are either too dangerous or unpleasant for humans to perform, or there is a shortage of humans to perform the jobs, or machines could do a better job performing the tasks than humans. Yet no one would feel comfortable allowing machines to function autonomously without ethical safeguards in place. Humans could not micromanage the behavior of the machines without sacrificing their ability to function autonomously, thus losing the benefit of allowing them to replace humans in performing certain tasks. Ideally, we would like to be able to trust autonomous machines to make correct ethical decisions on their own, and this requires that we create an ethic for machines.

1

It is not always obvious to laypersons or designers of machines that the behavior of the sort of machines to which we would like to turn over necessary or desired tasks has ethical import. If there is a possibility that a human being could be harmed should the machine behave in a certain manner, then this has to be taken into account. Even something as simple as an automatic cash-dispensing machine attached to a bank raises a number of ethical concerns: It is important to make it extremely difficult for the cash to be given to a person other than the customer from whose account the money is withdrawn; but if this should happen, it is necessary to ensure that there will be a way to minimize the harm done both to the customer and the bank (harm that can affect many persons' lives), while respecting the privacy of the legitimate customer's transactions and making the machine easy for the customer to use.

From just this one example, we can see that it will not be easy to incorporate an ethical dimension into autonomously functioning machines. Yet an automatic cash-dispensing machine is far less complex – in that the various possible actions it could perform can be anticipated in advance, making it relatively simple to build ethical safeguards into its design – than the sort of autonomous machines that are currently being developed by AI researchers. Adding an ethical component to a complex autonomous machine, such as an eldercare robot, involves training a machine to properly weigh a number of ethically significant factors in situations not all of which are likely to be anticipated by their designers.

Consider a demonstration video of a robot currently in production that raises ethical concerns in even the most seemingly innocuous of systems. The system in question is a simple mobile robot with a very limited repertoire of behaviors that amount to setting and giving reminders. A number of questionable ethical practices can be discerned in the demonstration. For instance, after asking the system's charge whether she had taken her medication, the robot asks her to show her empty pillbox. This is followed by a lecture by the robot concerning how important it is for her to take her medication. There is little back story provided, but assuming a competent adult, such paternalistic behavior seems uncalled for and shows little respect for the patient's autonomy.

During this exchange, the patient's responsible relative is seen watching it over the Internet. Although it is not clear whether this surveillance has been agreed to by the person being watched – there is no hint in the video that she knows she is being watched – there is the distinct impression left that her privacy is being violated.

As another example, promises are made by the system that the robot will remind its charge when her favorite show and "the game" are on. Promise making and keeping clearly have ethical ramifications, and it is not clear that the system under consideration has the sophistication to make ethically correct decisions when the duty to keep promises comes into conflict with other possibly more important duties.

Finally, when the system does indeed remind its charge that her favorite television show is starting, it turns out that she has company and tells the robot to go away. The robot responds with "You don't love me anymore," to the delight of the guests, and slinks away. This is problematic behavior because it sets up an expectation in the user that the system cannot fulfill – that it is capable of a loving relationship with its charge. This is a very highly charged ethical ramification, particularly given the vulnerable population for which this technology is being developed.

The bottom line is that, contrary to those who argue that concern about the ethical behavior of autonomous systems is premature, the behavior of even the simplest of such systems such as the one in our example shows that, in fact, such concern is overdue. This view has recently been expressed by Great Britain's Royal Academy of Engineering in the context of domestic autonomous systems: "Smart homes are close to the horizon and could be of significant benefit. However, they are being developed largely without ethical research. This means that there is a danger of bad design, with assumptions about users and their behavior embedded in programming. It is important that ethical issues are not left for programmers to decide – either implicitly or explicitly."

Developing ethics for machines requires research that is interdisciplinary in nature. It must involve a dialogue between ethicists and specialists in artificial intelligence. This presents a challenge in and of itself, because a common language must be forged between two very different fields for such research to progress. Furthermore, there must be an appreciation, on both sides, of the expertise of the other. Ethicists must accept the fact that there can be no vagueness in the programming of a machine, so they must sharpen their knowledge of ethics to a degree that they may not be used to. They are also required to consider real-world applications of their theoretical work. Being forced to do this may very well lead to the additional benefit of advancing the field of ethics. As Daniel Dennett recently stated, "AI makes Philosophy honest."

AI researchers working on machine ethics, on the other hand, must accept that ethics is a long-studied discipline within the field of philosophy that goes far beyond laypersons' intuitions. Ethicists may not agree on every matter, yet they have made much headway in resolving disputes in many areas of life. Agreed upon, all-encompassing ethical principles may still be elusive, but there is much agreement on acceptable behavior in many particular ethical dilemmas, hopefully in the areas where we would like autonomous machines to function. AI researchers need to defer to ethicists in determining when machine behavior raises ethical concerns and in making assumptions concerning acceptable machine behavior. In areas where ethicists disagree about these matters, it would be unwise to develop machines that function autonomously.

The essays in this volume represent the first steps by philosophers and AI researchers toward explaining why it is necessary to add an ethical dimension to machines that function autonomously; what is required in order to add this dimension; philosophical and practical challenges to the machine ethics project; various approaches that could be considered in attempting to add an ethical dimension to machines; work that has been done to date in implementing these approaches; and visions of the future of machine ethics research.

The book is divided into five sections. In the first section, James Moor, Susan Leigh Anderson, and J. Storrs Hall discuss the nature of machine ethics, giving an overview of this new field of research. In the second section, Colin Allen, Wendell Wallach, Iva Smit, and Sherry Turkel argue for the importance of machine ethics. The authors in the third section of the book – Drew McDermott, Steve Torrance, Blay Whitby, John Sullins, Susan Leigh Anderson, Deborah G. Johnson, Luciano Floridi, and David J. Calverley – raise issues concerning the machine ethics agenda that will need to be resolved if research in the field is to progress. In the fourth section, various approaches to capturing the ethics that should be incorporated into machines are considered and, for those who have begun to do so, how they may be implemented. James Gips gives an overview of many of the approaches. The approaches that are considered include: Asimov's Laws, discussed by Roger Clarke and Susan Leigh Anderson; artificial intelligence approaches, represented in the work of Bruce McLaren, Marcello Guarini, Alan K. Mackworth, Selmer Bringsjord et al., Matteo Turilli, Luís Moniz Pereira and Ari Saptawijaya; psychological/sociological approaches, represented in the work of Morteza Dehghani, Ken Forbus, Emmett Tomai, Matthew Klenk, and Peter Danielson; and philosophical approaches, discussed by Christopher Grau, Thomas M. Powers, and Susan Leigh Anderson and Michael Anderson. Finally, in the last section of the book, four visions of the future of machine ethics are given by Helen Seville, Deborah G. Field, J. Storrs Hall, Susan Leigh Anderson, and Eric Dietrich.

Part I

The Nature of Machine Ethics

Introduction

JAMES MOOR, IN "THE NATURE, IMPORTANCE, AND DIFFICULTY OF MACHINE Ethics," discusses four possible ways in which values could be ascribed to machines. First, ordinary computers can be considered to be "normative agents" but not necessarily *ethical* ones, because they are designed with a purpose in mind (e.g., to prove theorems or to keep an airplane on course). They are technological agents that perform tasks on our behalf, and we can assess their performance according to how well they perform their tasks. Second, "ethical impact agents" not only perform certain tasks according to the way they were designed, but they also have an ethical impact (ideally a positive one) on the world. For example, robot jockeys that guide camels in races in Qatar have replaced young boys, freeing them from slavery. Neither of the first two senses of ascribing values to machines, Moor notes, involves "putting ethics into a machine," as do the next two.

Third, "implicit ethical agents" are machines that have been programmed in a way that supports ethical behavior, or at least avoids unethical behavior. They are constrained in their behavior by their *designers* who *are following ethical principles.* Examples of such machines include ATMs that are programmed not to cheat the bank or its customers and automatic airplane pilots that are entrusted with the safety of human beings. Moor maintains that good software engineering should include requiring that ethical considerations be incorporated into machines whose behavior affects human lives, so at least this sense of "machine ethics" should be accepted by all as being desirable.

Fourth, "explicit ethical agents" are able to calculate the best action in ethical dilemmas. These machines would be able to "do ethics in a way that, for example, a computer can play chess." They would need to be able to represent the current situation, know which actions are possible in this situation, and be able to assess these actions in terms of some ethical theory, enabling them to calculate the ethically best action, just as a chess-playing program can represent the current board positions, know which moves are legal, and assess these moves in terms of achieving the goal of checkmating the king, enabling it to figure out the

7

best move. Is it possible to create such a machine? Moor agrees with James Gips that "the development of a machine that's an explicit ethical agent seems a fitting subject for a [computing] Grand Challenge."

Most would claim that even if we could create machines that are explicit ethical agents, we would still not have created what Moor calls "full ethical agents," a term used to describe human ethical decision makers. The issue, he says, is whether intentionality, consciousness, and free will – attributes that human ethical agents possess or are at least thought to possess – are essential to genuine ethical decision making. Moor wonders whether it would be sufficient that machines have "as if it does" versions of these qualities. If a machine is able to give correct answers to ethical dilemmas and even give justifications for its answers, it would pass Colin Allen's "Moral Turing Test" (Allen et al.: Prolegomena to any future artificial moral agent. *J. Exp. Theor. Artif. Intell.* 12(3): 251–261) for "understanding" ethics. In any case, we cannot be sure that machines that are created in the future will lack the qualities that we believe now uniquely characterize human ethical agents.

Anticipating the next part of the book, Moore gives three reasons "why it's important to work on machine ethics in the sense of developing explicit ethical agents": (1) because ethics itself is important, which is why, at the very least, we need to think about creating *implicit* ethical machines; (2) because the machines that are being developed will have increasing autonomy, which will eventually force us to make the ethical principles that govern their behavior *explicit* in these machines; and (3) because attempting to program ethics into a machine will give us the opportunity to understand ethics better.

Finally, Moor raises three concerns with the machine ethics project that should be considered in connection with the third part of the book: (1) We have a limited understanding of ethics. (2) We have a limited understanding of how learning takes place. (3) An ethical machine would need to have better "common sense and world knowledge" than computers have now.

Most of what Moor has to say would appear to be noncontroversial. Steve Torrance, however, has argued (in his paper "A Robust View of Machine Ethics," proceedings of the AAAI Fall Symposium on Machine Ethics, 2005), in contrast to Moor's view that the machines created in the future may have the qualities we believe are unique to human ethical agents, that to be a full ethical agent – to have "intrinsic moral status" – the entity must be *organic*. According to Torrance, only organic beings are "genuinely sentient," and only sentient beings can be "subjects of either moral concern or moral appraisal."

Some would also argue that there may not be as sharp a distinction between "explicit moral agent" and "implicit moral agent" as Moor believes, citing a neural-network approach to learning how to be ethical as falling in a gray area between the two; thus it may not be necessary that a machine be an explicit moral agent in order to be classified as an ethical machine. Others (e.g., S. L. Anderson) would say that Moor has made the correct distinction, but he has missed what is significant about the distinction from the perspective of someone who is concerned about whether machines will consistently interact with humans in an ethical fashion.

Susan Leigh Anderson makes a number of points about the field of machine ethics in "Machine Metaethics." She distinguishes between (1) building in limitations to machine behavior or requiring particular behavior of the machine according to an ideal ethical principle (or principles) that is (are) *followed by a human designer* and (2) giving *the machine* an ideal ethical principle or principles, or a learning procedure from which it can abstract the ideal principle(s), which *it* uses to guide its own behavior. In the second case – which corresponds to Moor's "explicit ethical agent" – the machine itself is reasoning on ethical matters. Creating such a machine is, in her view, the ultimate goal of machine ethics. She argues that to be accepted by the human beings with whom it interacts as being ethical, it must be able to justify its behavior by giving (an) intuitively acceptable ethical principle(s) that it has used to calculate its behavior, expressed in understandable language.

Central to the machine ethics project, Anderson maintains, is the belief (or hope) that ethics can be made computable. Anderson admits that there are still a number of ethical dilemmas in which even experts disagree about what is the right action; but she rejects Ethical Relativism, maintaining that there is agreement on many issues. She recommends that one not expect that the ethical theory, or approach to ethical theory, that one adopts be complete at this time. Because machines are created to "function in specific, limited domains," it is not necessary, she says, that the theory that is implemented have answers for every ethical dilemma. "Care should be taken," however, "to ensure that we do not permit machines to function autonomously in domains where there is controversy concerning what is correct behavior."

Unlike completeness, consistency in one's ethical beliefs, Anderson claims, "is crucial, as it is essential to rationality." Here is where "machine implementation of an ethical theory may be far superior to the average human being's attempt at following the theory," because human beings often act inconsistently when they get carried away by their emotions. A machine, on the other hand, can be programmed to rigorously follow a logically consistent principle or set of principles.

In developing ethics for a machine, one has to choose which particular theory, or approach to ethical theory, should be implemented. Anderson rejects the simple single absolute duty ethical theories that have been proposed (such as Act Utilitarianism) as all being deficient in favor of considering multiple *prima facie* duties, as W. D. Ross advocated. This approach needs to be supplemented with a decision principle to resolve conflicts that arise when the duties give conflicting advice. Although Ross didn't give us a decision principle, Anderson believes that one "could be learned by generalizing from intuitions about correct answers in particular cases."

Finally, Anderson gives a number of pragmatic reasons why it might be prudent to begin to make ethics computable by creating a program that acts as an ethical advisor to human beings before attempting to create machines that are autonomous moral agents. An even more important reason for beginning with an ethical advisor, in her view, is that one does not have to make a judgment about the status of the machine itself if it is just acting as an advisor to human beings in determining how they ought to treat other human beings. One does have to make such a judgment, she maintains, if the machine is given moral principles to follow in guiding its own behavior, because it needs to know whether it is to "count" (i.e., have moral standing) when calculating how it should behave. She believes that a judgment about the status of intelligent, autonomous ethical machines will be particularly difficult to make. (See her article, "The Unacceptability of Asimov's Three Laws of Robotics as a Basis for Machine Ethics," in Part IV of this volume.)

Some working in machine ethics (e.g., McClaren, Seville, and Field, whose work is included in this volume) reject Anderson's view of the ultimate goal of machine ethics, not being comfortable with permitting machines to make ethical decisions themselves. Furthermore, among those who are in agreement with her stated goal, some consider implementing different ethical theories, or approaches to ethical theory, than the prima facie duty approach that she recommends when adding an ethical dimension to machines. (See Part IV of this volume.)

J. Storrs Hall, in his article "Ethics for Machines," claims that as "computers increase in power ... they will get smarter, more able to operate in unstructured environments, and ultimately be able to do anything a human can." He projects that they might even become more intelligent than we are. Simultaneously with their increasing abilities, the cost of such machines will come down and they will be more widely used. In this environment, regardless of whether they are conscious or not (and here he reminds us of the "problem of other minds," that we can't be certain that any other person is conscious either), "it will behoove us to have taught them well their responsibilities toward us."

Hall points out that the vast majority of people "learn moral rules by osmosis, internalizing them not unlike the rules of grammar of their native language, structuring every act as unconsciously as our inbuilt grammar structures our sentences." This learning, Hall claims, takes place because "there are structures in our brains that predispose us to learn moral codes," determining "within broad limits the kinds of codes we can learn." This latter fact explains why the moral codes of different cultures have many features in common (e.g., the ranking of rules and the ascendancy of moral rules over both common sense and self-interest), even though they may vary. The fact that we are capable of following moral rules that can conflict with self-interest demonstrates that we have evolved and flourished as social animals, accepting what is best for the group as a whole, even though it can be at odds with what is best for us as individuals.

Hall makes three claims about this evolutionary account of the development of morality in human beings: (1) Some randomness exists in moral codes, just as other random features within a species occur naturally; they "may be carried along as baggage by the same mechanisms as the more effectual [rules]" if they haven't harmed the group very much. (2) Moral codes, to be effective, must be heritable. (3) There is a "built-in pressure for inclusiveness, in situations where countervailing forces (such as competition for resources) are not too great." This is because inclusiveness is advantageous from trade and security perspectives. (Yet Hall speculates that there might be a natural limit to inclusiveness, citing, for example, conflicts in the twentieth century.)

Putting Hall's brand of "ethical evolution" in the context of metaethical theories, he points out that it is neither completely consistent with Ethical Absolutism nor Ethical Relativism (the latter because a group's ethical beliefs are either evolutionarily advantageous for it or not), nor is it completely deontological (where actions are right or wrong in and of themselves), nor completely teleological (where actions are right or wrong entirely because of their consequences). It is not entirely teleological because, although moral rules have been formed evolutionarily as a result of consequences for groups, they are now accepted as binding even if they don't presently lead to the best consequences.

Hall goes on to argue that the moral codes that have evolved are better, or more realistic, than adopting well-known ethical theories that have been proposed: Kant's *Categorical Imperative* ("Act only on that maxim by which you can at the same time will that it should become a universal law") requires too much subjectivity in the selection of maxims. *Utilitarianism* (where the right action is the one that is likely to result in the best consequences, taking everyone affected into account) is problematic because people tend to use common sense, put more emphasis on self-interest, and don't appreciate long-term consequences when calculating the right action. John Rawls' *Veil of Ignorance* (a thought experiment in which we should choose ethical rules before we know what our positions in society will be) is difficult to apply when considering adding intelligent robots to the picture.

Hall maintains that ethical evolution has already taken into account how less than fully intelligent beings who may not be held morally responsible for their actions to the degree that others are (e.g., higher order mammals and children) should be treated, so adding machines with various levels of ability to the picture shouldn't present a problem. We also have rules that cover the distinction between "fellows and strangers," religions consider higher forms of life (e.g., angels), and we have rules concerning corporations, to which robots of the future might be compared. Concerning the last category, it is generally accepted, Hall points out, that corporations should not only think about what is legally permissible, but should develop a conscience (doing what is morally right) as well.

In the last section of his paper, Hall claims that "it seems likely that ultimately robots with consciences would appear and thrive," because once they become as intelligent as we are, "they will see both the need and inevitability of morality." We can, and should, Hall maintains, try to speed up the process of this evolution. "For our own sake," Hall maintains, "it seems imperative for us to begin to understand our own moral senses at a detailed and technical enough level that we can build their like into our machines." It would be very imprudent for us to build superhuman machines that lack a sense of right and wrong. Instead, according to Hall, the "inescapable conclusion is that not only should we give consciences to our machines where we can, but if we can indeed create machines that exceed us in the moral as well as intellectual dimensions, we are bound to do so." We owe it to future generations.

It should be noted that Hall's view of how we should respond to the likelihood that one day there will be super-intelligent moral machines has evolved in the ten years between when this article was written and the time of his writing an article on his vision of the future of machine ethics for this volume. (For his current position, see his article in Part V.)

Defenders of Kant's Categorical Imperative, Utilitarianism in one of its many forms, or Rawls's "Veil of Ignorance" thought experiment are likely to disagree with Hall's contention that they are inferior to the moral codes that have evolved naturally. Other ethicists will undoubtedly claim that he has ignored more defensible approaches to ethical theory (e.g., the prima facie duty approach that Anderson adopts). In any case, one could argue that evolution doesn't necessarily result in *better* moral beliefs, which presupposes the existence of a moral ideal, as Hall appears to believe. Moral rules, on a strict evolutionary account, simply evolve as a mechanism to deal with the current environment, the moral beliefs at any stage being no better or worse than others. If the environment for humans becomes irreparably hostile, for example, a moral code that allows for anything that enables humans to survive will evolve and be seen as justifiable.

1

The Nature, Importance, and Difficulty
of Machine Ethics

James H. Moor

Implementations of machine ethics might be possible in situations ranging
from maintaining hospital records to overseeing disaster relief. But what is
machine ethics, and how good can it be?

THE QUESTION OF WHETHER MACHINE ETHICS EXISTS OR MIGHT EXIST IN
the future is difficult to answer if we can't agree on what counts as machine
ethics. Some might argue that machine ethics obviously exists because humans
are machines and humans have ethics. Others could argue that machine ethics obviously doesn't exist because ethics is simply emotional expression and
machines can't have emotions.

A wide range of positions on machine ethics are possible, and a discussion of
the issue could rapidly propel us into deep and unsettled philosophical issues.
Perhaps, understandably, few in the scientific arena pursue the issue of machine
ethics. You're unlikely to find easily testable hypotheses in the murky waters of
philosophy. But we can't – and shouldn't – avoid consideration of machine ethics
in today's technological world.

As we expand computers' decision-making roles in practical matters, such as
computers driving cars, ethical considerations are inevitable. Computer scientists
and engineers must examine the possibilities for machine ethics because, knowingly or not, they've already engaged – or will soon engage – in some form of it.
Before we can discuss possible implementations of machine ethics, however, we
need to be clear about what we're asserting or denying.

Varieties of Machine Ethics

When people speak of technology and values, they're often thinking of ethical
values. But not all values are ethical. For example, practical, economic, and

aesthetic values don't necessarily draw on ethical considerations. A product of technology, such as a new sailboat, might be practically durable, economically expensive, and aesthetically pleasing, absent consideration of any ethical values. We routinely evaluate technology from these nonethical normative viewpoints. Tool makers and users regularly evaluate how well tools accomplish the purposes for which they were designed. With technology, all of us – ethicists and engineers included – are involved in evaluation processes requiring the selection and application of standards. In none of our professional activities can we retreat to a world of pure facts, devoid of subjective normative assessment.

By its nature, computing technology is normative. We expect programs, when executed, to proceed toward some objective – for example, to correctly compute our income taxes or keep an airplane on course. Their intended purpose serves as a norm for evaluation – that is, we assess how well the computer program calculates the tax or guides the airplane. Viewing computers as technological agents is reasonable because they do jobs on our behalf. They're normative agents in the limited sense that we can assess their performance in terms of how well they do their assigned jobs.

After we've worked with a technology for a while, the norms become second nature. But even after they've become widely accepted as the way of doing the activity properly, we can have moments of realization and see a need to establish different kinds of norms. For instance, in the early days of computing, using double digits to designate years was the standard and worked well. But, when the year 2000 approached, programmers realized that this norm needed reassessment. Or consider a distinction involving AI. In a November 1999 correspondence between Herbert Simon and Jacques Berleur,[1] Berleur was asking Simon for his reflections on the 1956 Dartmouth Summer Research Project on Artificial Intelligence, which Simon attended. Simon expressed some puzzlement as to why Trenchard More, a conference attendee, had so strongly emphasized modal logics in his thesis. Simon thought about it and then wrote back to Berleur,

My reply to you last evening left my mind nagged by the question of why Trench Moore [sic], in his thesis, placed so much emphasis on modal logics. The answer, which I thought might interest you, came to me when I awoke this morning. Viewed from a computing standpoint (that is, discovery of proofs rather than verification), a standard logic is an indeterminate algorithm: it tells you what you MAY legally do, but not what you OUGHT to do to find a proof. Moore [sic] viewed his task as building a modal logic of "oughts" – a strategy for search – on top of the standard logic of verification.

Simon was articulating what he already knew as one of the designers of the Logic Theorist, an early AI program. A theorem prover must not only generate a list of well-formed formulas but must also find a sequence of well-formed formulas constituting a proof. So, we need a procedure for doing this. *Modal logic* distinguishes between what's permitted and what's required. Of course, both are norms for the subject matter. But norms can have different levels of obligation, as Simon stresses through capitalization. Moreover, the norms he's suggesting aren't ethical norms. A typical theorem prover is a normative agent but not an ethical one.

Ethical–Impact Agents

You can evaluate computing technology in terms of not only design norms (that is, whether it's doing its job appropriately) but also ethical norms.

For example, *Wired* magazine reported an interesting example of applied computer technology.[2] Qatar is an oil-rich country in the Persian Gulf that's friendly to and influenced by the West while remaining steeped in Islamic tradition. In Qatar, these cultural traditions sometimes mix without incident – for example, women may wear Western clothing or a full veil. And sometimes the cultures conflict, as illustrated by camel racing, a pastime of the region's rich for centuries. Camel jockeys must be light – the lighter the jockey, the faster the camel. Camel owners enslave very young boys from poorer countries to ride the camels. Owners have historically mistreated the young slaves, including limiting their food to keep them lightweight. The United Nations and the US State Department have objected to this human trafficking, leaving Qatar vulnerable to economic sanctions.

The machine solution has been to develop robotic camel jockeys. The camel jockeys are about two feet high and weigh 35 pounds. The robotic jockey's right hand handles the whip, and its left handles the reins. It runs Linux, communicates at 2.4 GHz, and has a GPS-enabled camel-heart-rate monitor. As *Wired* explained it, "Every robot camel jockey bopping along on its improbable mount means one Sudanese boy freed from slavery and sent home." Although this eliminates the camel jockey slave problem in Qatar, it doesn't improve the economic and social conditions in places such as Sudan.

Computing technology often has important ethical impact. The young boys replaced by robotic camel jockeys are freed from slavery. Computing frees many of us from monotonous, boring jobs. It can make our lives better but can also make them worse. For example, we can conduct business online easily, but we're more vulnerable to identity theft. Machine ethics in this broad sense is close to what we've traditionally called *computer ethics*. In one sense of machine ethics, computers do our bidding as surrogate agents and impact ethical issues such as privacy, property, and power. However, the term is often used more restrictively. Frequently, what sparks debate is whether you can put ethics into a machine. Can a computer operate ethically because it's internally ethical in some way?

Implicit Ethical Agents

If you wish to put ethics into a machine, how would you do it? One way is to constrain the machine's actions to avoid unethical outcomes. You might satisfy machine ethics in this sense by creating software that implicitly supports ethical behavior, rather than by writing code containing explicit ethical maxims. The machine acts ethically because its internal functions implicitly promote ethical behavior – or at least avoid unethical behavior. Ethical behavior is the machine's nature. It has, to a limited extent, virtues.

Computers are implicit ethical agents when the machine's construction addresses safety or critical reliability concerns. For example, automated teller machines and Web banking software are agents for banks and can perform many of the tasks of human tellers and sometimes more. Transactions involving money are ethically important. Machines must be carefully constructed to give out or transfer the correct amount of money every time a banking transaction occurs. A line of code telling the computer to be honest won't accomplish this.

Aristotle suggested that humans could obtain virtue by developing habits. But with machines, we can build in the behavior without the need for a learning curve. Of course, such machine virtues are task specific and rather limited. Computers don't have the practical wisdom that Aristotle thought we use when applying our virtues.

Another example of a machine that's an implicit ethical agent is an airplane's automatic pilot. If an airline promises the plane's passengers a destination, the plane must arrive at that destination on time and safely. These are ethical outcomes that engineers design into the automatic pilot. Other built-in devices warn humans or machines if an object is too close or the fuel supply is low. Or, consider pharmacy software that checks for and reports on drug interactions. Doctor and pharmacist *duties of care* (legal and ethical obligations) require that the drugs prescribed do more good than harm. Software with elaborate medication databases helps them perform those duties responsibly.

Machines' capability to be implicit ethical agents doesn't demonstrate their ability to be full-fledged ethical agents. Nevertheless, it illustrates an important sense of machine ethics. Indeed, some would argue that software engineers must routinely consider machine ethics in at least this implicit sense during software development.

Explicit Ethical Agents

Can ethics exist explicitly in a machine?[3] Can a machine represent ethical categories and perform analysis in the sense that a computer can represent and analyze inventory or tax information? Can a machine "do" ethics like a computer can play chess? Chess programs typically provide representations of the current board position, know which moves are legal, and can calculate a good next move. Can a machine represent ethics explicitly and then operate effectively on the basis of this knowledge? (For simplicity, I'm imaging the development of ethics in terms of traditional symbolic AI. However, I don't want to exclude the possibility that the machine's architecture is connectionist, with an explicit understanding of the ethics emerging from that. Compare Wendell Wallach, Colin Allen, and Iva Smit's different senses of "bottom up" and "top down."[4])

Although clear examples of machines acting as explicit ethical agents are elusive, some current developments suggest interesting movements in that direction. Jeroen van den Hoven and Gert-Jan Lokhorst blended three kinds of advanced logic to serve as a bridge between ethics and a machine:

- *deontic* logic for statements of permission and obligation,
- *epistemic* logic for statements of beliefs and knowledge, and
- *action* logic for statements about actions.[5]

Together, these logics suggest that a formal apparatus exists that could describe ethical situations with sufficient precision to make ethical judgments by machine. For example, you could use a combination of these logics to state explicitly what action is allowed and what is forbidden in transferring personal information to protect privacy.[6] In a hospital, for example, you'd program a computer to let some personnel access some information and to calculate which actions what person should take and who should be informed about those actions.

Michael Anderson, Susan Anderson, and Chris Armen implement two ethical theories.[7] Their first model of an explicit ethical agent – Jeremy (named for Jeremy Bentham) – implements Hedonistic Act Utilitarianism. Jeremy estimates the likelihood of pleasure or displeasure for persons affected by a particular act. The second model is W.D. (named for William D. Ross). Ross's theory emphasizes prima facie duties as opposed to absolute duties. Ross considers no duty as absolute and gives no clear ranking of his various prima facie duties. So, it's unclear how to make ethical decisions under Ross's theory. Anderson, Anderson, and Armen's computer model overcomes this uncertainty. It uses a learning algorithm to adjust judgments of duty by taking into account both prima facie duties and past intuitions about similar or dissimilar cases involving those duties.

These examples are a good start toward creating explicit ethical agents, but more research is needed before a robust explicit ethical agent can exist in a machine. What would such an agent be like? Presumably, it would be able to make plausible ethical judgments and justify them. An explicit ethical agent that was autonomous in that it could handle real-life situations involving an unpredictable sequence of events would be most impressive.

James Gips suggested that the development of an ethical robot be a computing Grand Challenge.[8] Perhaps Darpa could establish an explicit-ethical-agent project analogous to its autonomous-vehicle project (www.darpa.mil/grandchallenge/index.asp). As military and civilian robots become increasingly autonomous, they'll probably need ethical capabilities. Given this likely increase in robots' autonomy, the development of a machine that's an explicit ethical agent seems a fitting subject for a Grand Challenge.

Machines that are explicit ethical agents might be the best ethical agents to have in situations such as disaster relief. In a major disaster, such as Hurricane

Katrina in New Orleans, humans often have difficulty tracking and processing information about who needs the most help and where they might find effective relief. Confronted with a complex problem requiring fast decisions, computers might be more competent than humans. (At least the question of a computer decision maker's competence is an empirical issue that might be decided in favor of the computer.) These decisions could be ethical in that they would determine who would live and who would die. Some might say that only humans should make such decisions, but if (and of course this is a big assumption) computer decision making could routinely save more lives in such situations than human decision making, we might have a good ethical basis for letting computers make the decisions.[9]

Full Ethical Agents

A full ethical agent can make explicit ethical judgments and generally is competent to reasonably justify them. An average adult human is a full ethical agent. We typically regard humans as having consciousness, intentionality, and free will. Can a machine be a full ethical agent? It's here that the debate about machine ethics becomes most heated. Many believe a bright line exists between the senses of machine ethics discussed so far and a full ethical agent. For them, a machine can't cross this line. The bright line marks a crucial ontological difference between humans and whatever machines might be in the future.

The bright-line argument can take one or both of two forms. The first is to argue that only full ethical agents can be ethical agents. To argue this is to regard the other senses of machine ethics as not really ethics involving agents. However, although these other senses are weaker, they can be useful in identifying more limited ethical agents. To ignore the ethical component of ethical-impact agents, implicit ethical agents, and explicit ethical agents is to ignore an important aspect of machines. What might bother some is that the ethics of the lesser ethical agents is derived from their human developers. However, this doesn't mean that you can't evaluate machines as ethical agents. Chess programs receive their chess knowledge and abilities from humans. Still, we regard them as chess players. The fact that lesser ethical agents lack humans' consciousness, intentionality, and free will is a basis for arguing that they shouldn't have broad ethical responsibility. But it doesn't establish that they aren't ethical in ways that are assessable or that they shouldn't have limited roles in functions for which they're appropriate.

The other form of bright-line argument is to argue that no machine can become a full ethical agent – that is, no machine can have consciousness, intentionality, and free will. This is metaphysically contentious, but the simple rebuttal is that we can't say with certainty that future machines will lack these features. Even John Searle, a major critic of strong AI, doesn't argue that machines can't possess these features.[10] He only denies that computers, in their capacity as purely syntactic devices, can possess understanding. He doesn't claim that machines can't have understanding, presumably including an understanding of ethics. Indeed, for Searle, a materialist, humans are a kind of machine, just not a purely syntactic computer.

Thus, both forms of the bright-line argument leave the possibility of machine ethics open. How much can be accomplished in machine ethics remains an empirical question.

We won't resolve the question of whether machines can become full ethical agents by philosophical argument or empirical research in the near future. We should therefore focus on developing limited explicit ethical agents. Although they would fall short of being full ethical agents, they could help prevent unethical outcomes.

I can offer at least three reasons why it's important to work on machine ethics in the sense of developing explicit ethical agents:

- Ethics is important. We want machines to treat us well.
- Because machines are becoming more sophisticated and make our lives more enjoyable, future machines will likely have increased control and autonomy to do this. More powerful machines need more powerful machine ethics.
- Programming or teaching a machine to act ethically will help us better understand ethics.

The importance of machine ethics is clear. But, realistically, how possible is it? I also offer three reasons why we can't be too optimistic about our ability to develop machines to be explicit ethical agents.

First, we have a limited understanding of what a proper ethical theory is. Not only do people disagree on the subject, but individuals can also have conflicting ethical intuitions and beliefs. Programming a computer to be ethical is much more difficult than programming a computer to play world-champion chess – an accomplishment that took 40 years. Chess is a simple domain with well-defined legal moves. Ethics operates in a complex domain with some ill-defined legal moves.

Second, we need to understand learning better than we do now. We've had significant successes in machine learning, but we're still far from having the child machine that Turing envisioned.

Third, inadequately understood ethical theory and learning algorithms might be easier problems to solve than computers' absence of common sense and world knowledge. The deepest problems in developing machine ethics will likely be epistemological as much as ethical. For example, you might program a machine with the classical imperative of physicians and Asimovian robots: First, do no harm. But this wouldn't be helpful unless the machine could understand what constitutes harm in the real world. This isn't to suggest that we shouldn't vigorously pursue machine ethics. On the contrary, given its nature, importance, and difficulty, we should dedicate much more effort to making progress in this domain.

Acknowledgments

I'm indebted to many for helpful comments, particularly to Keith Miller and Vincent Wiegel.

References

1. H. Simon, "Re: Dartmouth Seminar 1956" (email to J. Berleur), Herbert A. Simon Col lection, Carnegie Mellon Univ. Archives, 20 Nov. 1999.
2. J. Lewis, "Robots of Arabia," *Wired*, vol. 13, no. 11, Nov. 2005, pp. 188–195; www. wired. com/wired/archive/13.11/camel.html?pg=1 & topic=camel&topic_set=.
3. J.H. Moor, "Is Ethics Computable?" *Metaphilosophy*, vol. 26, nos. 1–2, 1995, pp. 1–21.
4. W. Wallach, C. Allen, and I. Smit, "Machine Morality: Bottom-Up and Top-Down Approaches for Modeling Human Moral Faculties," *Machine Ethics*, M. Anderson, S.L. Anderson, and C. Armen, eds., AAAI Press, 2005, pp. 94–102.
5. J. van den Hoven and G.J. Lokhorst, "Deontic Logic and Computer-Supported Computer Ethics," *Cyberphilosophy: The Intersection of Computing and Philosophy*, J.H. Moor and T.W. Bynum, eds., Blackwell, 2002, pp. 280–289.
6. V. Wiegel, J. van den Hoven, and G.J. Lokhorst, "Privacy, Deontic Epistemic Action Logic and Software Agents," *Ethics of New Information Technology, Proc. 6th Int'l Conf. Computer Ethics: Philosophical Enquiry* (CEPE 05), Center for Telematics and Information Technology, Univ. of Twente, 2005, pp. 419–434.
7. M. Anderson, S.L. Anderson, and C. Armen, "Towards Machine Ethics: Implementing Two Action-Based Ethical Theories," *Machine Ethics*, M. Anderson, S.L. Anderson, and C. Armen, eds., AAAI Press, 2005, pp. 1–7.
8. J. Gips, "Creating Ethical Robots: A Grand Challenge," presented at the AAAI Fall 2005 Symposium on Machine Ethics; www.cs.bc. edu/~gips/EthicalRobotsGrandChallenge. pdf.
9. J.H. Moor, "Are There Decisions Computers Should Never Make?" *Nature and System*, vol. 1, no. 4, 1979, pp. 217–229.
10. J.R. Searle, "Minds, Brains, and Programs," *Behavioral and Brain Sciences*, vol. 3, no. 3, 1980, pp. 417–457.

2

Machine Metaethics

Susan Leigh Anderson

THE NEWLY EMERGING FIELD OF *MACHINE ETHICS* IS CONCERNED WITH ensuring that the behavior of machines toward human users is ethically acceptable. There are domains in which intelligent machines could play a significant role in improving our quality of life as long as concerns about their behavior can be overcome by ensuring that they behave ethically. *Machine metaethics* examines the field of machine ethics. It talks *about* the field, rather than doing work in it. Examples of questions that fall within machine metaethics are: How central are ethical considerations to the development of artificially intelligent agents? What is the ultimate goal of machine ethics? What does it mean to add an ethical dimension to machines? Is ethics computable? Is there a single correct ethical theory that we should try to implement? Should we expect the ethical theory we implement to be complete? That is, should we expect it to tell a machine how to act in every ethical dilemma? How important is consistency? If it is to act in an ethical manner, is it necessary to determine the moral status of the machine itself?

When does machine behavior have ethical import? How should a machine behave in a situation in which its behavior does have ethical import? Consideration of these questions should be central to the development of artificially intelligent agents that interact with humans. We should not be making intelligent machines unless we are confident that they have been designed to "consider" the ethical ramifications of their behavior and will behave in an ethically acceptable manner. Furthermore, in contemplating designing intelligent machines, ethical concerns should not be restricted to just prohibiting unethical behavior on the part of machines. Rather, they should extend to considering the additional tasks that machines could perform given appropriate ethical guidance and, perhaps, also to considering whether we have an obligation to develop ethical intelligent machines that could enhance human lives. Just as human ethics is concerned both with what we *ought not* to do and what we *ought* to do – it is unethical for people to cheat others and ethically praiseworthy for people to help others during a crisis, for example – so we should be thinking both about ensuring that machines *do not* do certain things and about creating machines that *do* provide benefits to humans that they would otherwise not receive.

The ultimate goal of machine ethics, I believe, is to create a machine that follows an ideal ethical principle or a set of ethical principles in guiding its behavior; in other words, it is guided by this principle, or these principles, in the decisions it makes about possible courses of action it could take. We can say, more simply, that this involves "adding an ethical dimension" to the machine.

It might be thought that adding an ethical dimension to a machine is ambiguous. It could mean either: (a) designing the machine with built-in limitations to its behavior or requiring particular behavior according to an ideal ethical principle or principles that are *followed by the human designer*; or (b) giving *the machine* (an) ideal ethical principle(s) or some examples of ethical dilemmas together with correct answers, and a learning procedure from which it can abstract (an) ideal ethical principle(s), so that *it* can use the principle(s) in guiding its own actions. In the first case, it is the human being who is following ethical principles and concerned about harm that could come from machine behavior. This falls within the well-established domain of what has sometimes been called "computer ethics," rather than machine ethics. In the second case, however, the machine itself is reasoning on ethical matters, which is the ultimate goal of *machine* ethics.[1] An indication that this approach has been adopted can be seen if the machine can make a judgment in an ethical dilemma with which it has not previously been presented.

In order for it to be accepted as ethical by the human beings with whom it interacts, it is essential that the machine has an ethical principle or a set of principles that it uses to calculate how it ought to behave in an ethical dilemma, because it must be able to *justify* its behavior to any human being who has concerns about its actions. The principle(s) it uses to calculate how it should behave and justify its actions, furthermore, must be translatable into ordinary language that humans can understand and must, on reflection, appear to be intuitively correct. If the machine is not able to justify its behavior by giving (an) intuitively correct, understandable ethical principle(s) that it has used to determine its actions, humans will distrust its ability to consistently behave in an ethical fashion.

Central to the machine ethics project is the belief (or hope) that ethics can be made computable, that it can be sharpened enough to be able to be programmed into a machine. Some people working on machine ethics have started tackling the challenge of making ethics computable by creating programs that enable machines to act as ethical advisors to human beings, believing that this is a good first step toward the eventual goal of developing machines that can follow ethical principles in guiding their own behavior (Anderson, Anderson, and Armen 2005).[2]

---

[1]   Also, only in this second case can we say that the machine is functioning autonomously.

[2]   Bruce McLaren has also created a program that enables a machine to act as an ethical advisor to human beings, but in his program the machine does not make ethical decisions itself. His advisor system simply informs the human user of the ethical dimensions of the dilemma without reaching a decision (McLaren 2003).

Four pragmatic reasons could be given for beginning this way: (1) One could start by designing an advisor that gives guidance to a select group of persons in a finite number of circumstances, thus reducing the scope of the assignment.[3] (2) Machines that just advise human beings would probably be more easily accepted by the general public than machines that try to behave ethically themselves. In the first case, it is human beings who will make ethical decisions by deciding whether to follow the recommendations of the machine, preserving the idea that *only human beings will be moral agents*. The next step in the machine ethics project is likely to be more contentious: creating *machines that are autonomous moral agents*. (3) A big problem for Artificial Intelligence in general, and so for this project too, is how to get needed data, in this case the information from which ethical judgments can be made. With an ethical advisor, human beings can be prompted to supply the needed data. (4) Ethical theory has not advanced to the point where there is agreement, even by ethical experts, on the correct answer for all ethical dilemmas. An advisor can recognize this fact, passing difficult decisions that have to be made in order to act to the human user. An autonomous machine that is expected to be moral, on the other hand, would either not be able to act in such a situation or would decide arbitrarily. Both solutions seem unsatisfactory.

This last reason is a cause for concern for the entire machine ethics project. It might be thought that for ethics to be computable, we must have a theory that determines which action is morally right in every ethical dilemma. There are two parts to this view: (1) We must know which is the correct ethical theory, according to which the computations are made; and (2) this theory must be *complete*, that is, it must tell us how to act in any ethical dilemma that might be encountered.

One could try to avoid making a judgment about which is the correct ethical theory (rejecting 1) by simply trying to implement *any* ethical theory that has been proposed (e.g., Hedonistic Act Utilitarianism or Kant's Categorical Imperative), making no claim that it is necessarily the *best* theory and therefore the one that ought to be followed. Machine ethics then becomes just an exercise in what can be computed. However, this is surely not particularly worthwhile, unless one is trying to figure out an approach to programming ethics in general by practicing on the theory that is chosen.

Ultimately one has to decide that a particular ethical theory, or at least an approach to ethical theory, is correct. Like W. D. Ross (1930), I believe that the simple, single absolute duty theories that have been proposed are all deficient.[4] Ethics is more complicated than that, which is why it is easy to devise a counter-example to any of these theories. There are advantages to the multiple *prima facie* duties[5] approach that Ross adopted, which better captures conflicts that often

---

[3]   This is the reason why Anderson, Anderson, and Armen started with "MedEthEx," which advises health care workers – and, initially, in just one particular circumstance.

[4]   I am assuming that one will adopt the action-based approach to ethics, because we are concerned with the *behavior* of machines.

[5]   A prima facie duty is something that one ought to do unless it conflicts with a stronger duty, so there can be exceptions, unlike an *absolute* duty, for which there are no exceptions.

arise in ethical decision making: (1) There can be different sets of prima facie duties for different domains, because there are different ethical concerns in such areas as biomedicine, law, sports, and business, for example. (2) The duties can be amended, and new duties added if needed, to explain the intuitions of ethical experts about particular cases as they arise. Of course, the main problem with the multiple prima facie duties approach is that there is no decision procedure when the duties conflict, which often happens. It seems possible, though, that a decision procedure could be learned by generalizing from intuitions about correct answers in particular cases.

Does the ethical theory or approach to ethical theory that is chosen have to be complete? Should those working on machine ethics expect this to be the case? My answer is: probably not. The implementation of ethics cannot be more complete than is accepted ethical theory. Completeness is an ideal for which to strive, but it may not be possible at this time. There are still a number of ethical dilemmas in which even experts are not in agreement as to what is the right action.[6]

Many nonethicists believe that this admission offers support for the metaethical theory known as Ethical Relativism. Ethical Relativism is the view that when there is disagreement over whether a particular action is right or wrong, both sides are correct. According to this view, there is no single correct ethical theory. Ethics is relative to either individuals (subjectivism) or societies (cultural relativism). Most ethicists reject this view because it entails that we cannot criticize the actions of others, no matter how heinous. We also cannot say that some people are more moral than others or speak of moral improvement – for example, that the United States has become a more ethical society by granting rights first to women and then to African Americans.

There certainly do seem to be actions that ethical experts (and most of us) believe are absolutely wrong (e.g., slavery and torturing a baby are wrong). Ethicists are comfortable with the idea that one may not have definitive answers for *all* ethical dilemmas at the present time, and even that we may in the future decide to reject some of the views we now hold. Most ethicists believe, however, that *in principle* there are correct answers to all *ethical* dilemmas,[7] as opposed to questions that are just matters of taste (deciding which shirt to wear, for example). Someone working in the area of machine ethics, then, would be wise to allow for gray areas in which one should not necessarily expect answers at this time and even allow for the possibility that parts of the theory being implemented may need to be revised. Care should be taken to ensure that we do not permit

---

6   Some who are more pessimistic than I am would say that there will always be some dilemmas about which even experts will disagree as to what is the correct answer. Even if this turns out to be the case, the agreement that surely exists on many dilemmas will allow us to reject a completely relativistic position, and we can restrict the development of machines to areas where there is general agreement as to what is acceptable behavior.

7   The pessimists would perhaps say: "There are correct answers to many (or most) *ethical* dilemmas."

machines to function autonomously in domains in which there is controversy concerning what is correct behavior.

There are two related mitigating factors that allow me to believe that there is enough agreement on ethical matters that at least some ethical intelligent machines can be created: First, as just pointed out, although there may not be a universally accepted *general theory* of ethics at this time, there is wide agreement on what is ethically permissible and what is not in *particular cases*. Much can be learned from those cases. Many approaches to capturing ethics for a machine involve a machine learning from particular cases of acceptable and unacceptable behavior. Formal representation of particular ethical dilemmas and their solutions make it possible for machines to store information about a large number of cases in a fashion that permits automated analysis. From this information, general ethical principles may emerge.

Second, machines are typically created to function in specific, limited domains. Determining what is and is not ethically acceptable in a specific domain is a less daunting task than trying to devise a general theory of ethical and unethical behavior, which is what ethical theorists attempt to do. Furthermore, it might just be possible that in-depth consideration of the ethics of limited domains could lead to generalizations that could be applied to other domains as well, which is an extension of the first point. Those working on machine ethics, because of its practical nature, have to consider and resolve all the details involved in actually applying a particular ethical principle (or principles) or approach to capturing/ simulating ethical behavior, unlike ethical theoreticians who typically discuss hypothetical cases. There is reason to believe that the "real-world" perspective of AI researchers, working with applied ethicists, stands a chance of getting closer to capturing what counts as ethical behavior than the abstract reasoning of most ethical theorists. As Daniel Dennett recently said, "AI makes Philosophy honest" (Dennett 2006).

Consistency (that one should not contradict oneself), however, is crucial, because it is essential to rationality. Any inconsistency that arises should be cause for concern and for rethinking either the theory itself or the way that it is implemented. One cannot emphasize the importance of consistency enough, and machine implementation of an ethical theory may be far superior to the average human being's attempt at following the theory. A machine is capable of rigorously following a logically consistent principle or set of principles, whereas most human beings easily abandon principles and the requirement of consistency that is the hallmark of rationality because they get carried away by their emotions. Human beings could benefit from interacting with a machine that spells out the consequences of consistently following particular ethical principles.

Let us return now to the question of whether it is a good idea to try to create an ethical advisor before attempting to create a machine that behaves ethically itself. An even better reason than the pragmatic ones given earlier can be given for the field of machine ethics to proceed in this manner: One does not have to make a judgment about the status of the machine itself if it is just acting as an advisor to human beings, whereas one does have to make such a judgment if the machine is given moral principles to follow in guiding its own behavior. Because of the particular difficulty involved,[8] it would be wise to begin with a project that does not require such judgments. Let me explain.

If the machine is simply advising human beings as to how to act in ethical dilemmas, where such dilemmas involve the proper treatment of other human beings (as is the case with classical ethical dilemmas), it is assumed that either (1) the advisor will be concerned with ethical dilemmas that only involve human beings, or (2) only human beings have moral standing and need to be taken into account. Of course, one *could* build in assumptions and principles that maintain that other beings and entities should have moral standing and be taken into account as well; the advisor could then consider dilemmas involving animals and other entities that might be thought to have moral standing. Such a purview would, however, go beyond universally accepted moral theory and would certainly not, at the present time, be expected of an ethical advisor for human beings facing traditional moral dilemmas.

On the other hand, if the machine is given principles to follow to guide its own behavior, an assumption must be made about its status. This is because in following any ethical theory, it is generally assumed that the agent has moral standing, and therefore he/she/it must consider at least him/her/itself, and typically others as well, in deciding how to act.[9] A machine agent must "know" if it is to count, or whether it must always defer to others who count while it does not, in calculating the correct action in an ethical dilemma.

I have argued that, for many reasons, it is a good idea to begin to make ethics computable by creating a program that would enable a machine to act as an ethical advisor to human beings facing traditional ethical dilemmas. The ultimate goal of machine ethics – to create autonomous ethical machines – will be a far more challenging task. In particular, it will require that a difficult judgment be made about the status of the machine itself. I have also argued that the principle(s) followed by an ethical machine must be consistent, but should not necessarily completely cover every ethical dilemma that machines could conceivably face. As a result, the development of machines that function autonomously must keep pace with those areas in which there is general agreement as to what is considered to be correct ethical behavior. Seen in this light, work in the field of machine ethics should be seen as central to the development of autonomous machines.

---

[8] See S. L. Anderson, "The Unacceptability of Asimov's 'Three Laws of Robotics' as a Basis for Machine Ethics," included in this volume, which demonstrates how difficult it would be.

[9] If Ethical Egoism is accepted as a plausible ethical theory, then the agent only needs to take him/her/itself into account, whereas all other ethical theories consider others as well as the agent, assuming that the agent has moral status.

References

Anderson M., Anderson S. L., and Armen, C. (2005), "MedEthEx: Towards a Medical Ethics Advisor," in *Proceedings of the AAAI Fall Symposium on Caring Machines: AI and Eldercare*, Menlo Park, California.

Dennett, D. (2006), "Computers as Prostheses for the Imagination," invited talk presented at the International Computers and Philosophy Conference, Laval, France, May 3.

McLaren, B. M. (2003), "Extensionally Defining Principles and Cases in Ethics: An AI Model," in *Artificial Intelligence Journal*, 150 (1–2): 145–1813.

Ross, W. D. (1930), *The Right and the Good*, Oxford University Press, Oxford.

3

Ethics for Machines

J. Storrs Hall

"A robot may not injure a human being, or through inaction, allow a human to come to harm."

– Isaac Asimov's First Law of Robotics

THE FIRST BOOK REPORT I EVER GAVE, TO MRS. SLATIN'S FIRST GRADE class in Lake, Mississippi, in 1961, was on a slim volume entitled *You Will Go to the Moon*. I have spent the intervening years thinking about the future.

The four decades that have passed have witnessed advances in science and physical technology that would be incredible to a child of any other era. I did see my countryman Neil Armstrong step out onto the moon. The processing power of the computers that controlled the early launches can be had today in a five-dollar calculator. The genetic code has been broken and the messages are being read – and in some cases, rewritten. Jet travel, then a perquisite of the rich, is available to all.

That young boy that I was spent time on other things besides science fiction. My father was a minister, and we talked (or in many cases, I was lectured and questioned!) about good and evil, right and wrong, and what our duties were to others and to ourselves.

In the same four decades, progress in the realm of ethics has been modest. Almost all of it has been in the expansion of inclusiveness, broadening the definition of who deserves the same consideration one always gave neighbors. I experienced some of this first hand as a schoolchild in 1960s Mississippi. Perhaps the rejection of wars of adventure can also be counted. Yet those valuable advances to the contrary notwithstanding, ethics, and its blurry reflection in politics, has seemed to stand still compared to the advances of physical science. This is particularly true if we take the twentieth century as a whole – it stands alone in history as the "Genocide Century," the only time in history in which governments killed their own people by the millions, not just once or in one place, but repeatedly, all across the globe.

We can extend our vision with telescopes and microscopes, peering into the heart of the atom and seeing back to the very creation of the universe. When I was a boy and vitally interested in dinosaurs, no one knew why they had died out. Now we do. We can map out the crater of the Chixulub meteor with sensitive gravitometers, charting the enormous structure below the ocean floor.

Up to now, we haven't had, or really needed, similar advances in "ethical instrumentation." The terms of the subject haven't changed. Morality rests on human shoulders, and if machines changed the ease with which things were done, they did not change responsibility for doing them. People have always been the only "moral agents."

Similarly, people are largely the objects of responsibility. There is a developing debate over our responsibilities to other living creatures that is unresolved in detail and that will bear further discussion in this chapter. We have never, however, considered ourselves to have moral duties to our machines, or them to us.

All that is about to change.

What Are Machines, Anyway?

We have a naive notion of a machine as a box with motors, gears, and whatnot in it. The most important machine of the Industrial Revolution was the steam engine, providing power to factories, locomotives, and ships. If we retain this notion, however, we will fall far short of an intuition capable of dealing with the machines of the future.

The most important machine of the twentieth century wasn't a physical thing at all. It was the Turing Machine, and it was a mathematical idea. It provided the theoretical basis for computers. Furthermore, it established the principle that for higher functions such as computation, it didn't matter what the physical realization was (within certain bounds) – any computer could do what any other computer could, given enough memory and time.

This theoretical concept of a machine as a pattern of operations that could be implemented in a number of ways is called a virtual machine. In modern computer technology, virtual machines abound. Successive versions of processor chips reimplement the virtual machines of their predecessors, so that the old software will still run. Operating systems (e.g., Windows) offer virtual machines to applications programs. Web browsers offer several virtual machines (notably Java) to the writers of Web pages.

More important, any program running on a computer is a virtual machine. Usage in this sense is a slight extension of that in computer science, where the "machine" in "virtual machine" refers to a computer, specifically an instruction-set processor. Strictly speaking, computer scientists should refer to "virtual processors," but they tend to refer to processors as machines anyway. For the purposes of our discussion here, we can call any program a virtual machine.

In fact, I will drop the "virtual" and call programs simply "machines." The essence of a machine, for our purposes, is its behavior – what it does given what it senses (always assuming that there is a physical realization capable of actually doing the actions).

To understand just how complex the issue really is, let's consider a huge, complex, immensely powerful machine we've already built. The machine is the U.S. Government and legal system. It is a lot more like a giant computer program than people realize. Really complex computer programs are not sequences of instructions; they are sets of rules. This is explicit in the case of "expert systems," and implicit in the case of distributed, object-oriented, interrupt-driven, networked software systems. More to the point, sets of rules are programs – in our terms, machines.

Of course, you will say that the government isn't *just* a program; it's under human control and it's composed of people to begin with. It is composed of people, but the whole point of the rules is to make these people do different things, or do things differently, than they would have otherwise. Indeed, in many cases a person's whole function in the bureaucracy is to be a sensor or effector; once the sensor-person does his or her function of recognizing a situation in the "if" part of a rule (what lawyers call "the facts"), the system, not the person, decides what to do about it ("the law"). Bureaucracies famously exhibit the same lack of common sense as do computer programs.

From a moral standpoint, it is important to note that those governments in the twentieth century that were most evil, murdering millions of people, were autocracies under the control of individual humans such as Hitler, Stalin, and Mao; on the other hand, governments that were more autonomous machines, such as the liberal Western democracies, were significantly less evil.

Up to now, the application of ethics to machines, including programs, has been that the actions of the machine were the responsibility of the designer and/or operator. In the future, however, it seems clear that we are going to have machines, like the government, whose behavior is an emergent and to some extent unforeseeable result of design and operation decisions made by many people and, ultimately, by other machines.

Why Machines Need Ethics

Moore's Law is a rule of thumb regarding computer technology that, in one general formulation, states that the processing power per price of computers will increase by a factor of 1.5 every year. This rule of thumb has held true from 1950 through 2000. The improvement by a factor of one billion in bang-for-a-buck of computers over the period is nearly unprecedented in technology.

Among its other effects, this explosion of processing power coupled with the Internet has made the computer a tool for science of a kind never seen before. It is, in a sense, a powered imagination. Science as we know it was based on the previous

technology revolution in information, the printing press. The spread of knowledge it enabled, together with the precise imagining ability given by the calculus, gave us the scientific revolution in the seventeenth and eighteenth centuries.
That in turn gave us the Industrial Revolution in the nineteenth and twentieth.

The computer and Internet are the calculus and printing press of our day. Our
new scientific revolution is going on even as we speak. The industrial revolution
to follow hasn't happened yet, but by all accounts it is coming, and well within
the twenty-first century, such is the accelerated pace modern technology makes
possible.

The new industrial revolution of physical production is sometimes referred to
as nanotechnology. On our computers, we can already simulate the tiny machines
we will build. They have some of the "magic" of life, which is after all based on
molecular machines itself. They will, if desired, be able to produce more of themselves. They will produce stronger materials, more reliable and longer-lasting
machines, more powerful and utterly silent motors, and last but not least, much
more powerful computers.

None of this should come as a surprise. If you extend the trend lines for
Moore's Law, in a few decades part sizes are expected to be molecular and the
price-performance ratios imply something like the molecular manufacturing
schemes that nanotechnologists have proposed. If you project the trend line for
power-to-weight ratio of engines, which has held steady since 1850 and has gone
through several different technologies from steam to jet engines, it says we will
have molecular power plants in the 2030–2050 timeframe.

The result of this is essentially a reprise of the original Industrial Revolution,
a great flowering of increased productivity and capabilities, and a concomitant
decrease in costs. In general, we can expect the costs of "hi-tech" manufactured
items to follow a downward track as computers have. One interesting corollary is
that we will have affordable robots.

Robots today are much more prevalent than people may realize. Your car
and your computer were likely partially made by robots. Industrial robots are
hugely expensive machines that must operate in a carefully planned and controlled environment, because they have very limited senses and no common sense
whatsoever.

With nanotechnology, that changes drastically. Indeed, it's already starting
to change, as the precursor technologies such as micromachines begin to have
their effect.

Existing robots are often stupider than insects. As computers increase in
power, however, they will get smarter, be more able to operate in unstructured
environments, and ultimately be able to do anything a human can. Robots will
find increasing use, as costs come down, in production, in service industries, and
as domestic servants.

Meanwhile, because nonmobile computers are already more plentiful and
will be cheaper than robots for the same processing power, stationary computers

as smart as humans will probably arrive a bit sooner than human-level robots (see Kurzweil, Moravec).

Before we proceed, let's briefly touch on what philosophers sometimes call the problem of other minds. I know I'm conscious, but how do I know that you are – you might just be like an unfeeling machine, a zombie, producing those reactions by mechanical means. After all, there have been some cultures where the standard belief among men was that women were not conscious (and probably vice versa!). If we are not sure about other people, how can we say that an intelligent computer would be conscious?

This is important to our discussion because there is a tendency for people to set a dividing line for ethics between the conscious and the nonconscious. This can be seen in formal philosophical treatment as far back as Adam Smith's theory of ethics as based in sympathy. If we can't imagine something as being able to feel a hurt, we have less compunctions about hurting it, for example.

The short answer is that it doesn't matter (see Dennet, "Intentional Stance"). The clear trend in ethics is for a growing inclusivity in those things considered to have rights – races of people, animals, ecosystems. There is no hint, for example, that plants are conscious, either individually or as species, but that does not, in and of itself, preclude a possible moral duty to them, at least to their species as a whole.

A possibly longer answer is that the intuitions of some people (Berkeley philosopher John Searle, for example) that machines cannot "really" be conscious are not based on any real experience with intelligent machines, and that the vast majority of people interacting with a machine that could, say, pass the unrestricted Turing Test, would be as willing to grant it consciousness as they would for other people. Until we are able to say with a great deal more certainty than we now can just what consciousness is, we're much better off treating something that acts conscious as if it is.

Now, if a computer was as smart as a person, was able to hold long conversations that really convinced you that it understood what you were saying, could read, explain, and compose poetry and music, could write heart-wrenching stories, and could make new scientific discoveries and invent marvelous gadgets that were extremely useful in your daily life – would it be murder to turn it off?

What if instead it weren't really all that bright, but exhibited undeniably the full range of emotions, quirks, likes and dislikes, and so forth that make up an average human?

What if it were only capable of a few tasks, say, with the mental level of a dog, but also displayed the same devotion and evinced the same pain when hurt – would it be cruel to beat it, or would that be nothing more than banging pieces of metal together?

What are the ethical responsibilities of an intelligent being toward another one of a lower order?

These are crucial questions for us, for not too long after there are computers as intelligent as we are, there will be ones that are much more so. *We* will all too soon be the lower-order creatures. It will behoove us to have taught them well their responsibilities toward us.

However, it is not a good idea simply to put specific instructions into their basic programming that force them to treat us as a special case. They are, after all, smarter than we are. Any loopholes, any reinterpretation possible, any repro-gramming necessary, and special-case instructions are gone with the snows of yesteryear. No, it will be necessary to give our robots a sound basis for a true, valid, universal ethics that will be as valuable to them as it is for us. After all, they will in all likelihood want to create their own smarter robots ...

What is Ethics, Anyway?

"Human beings function better if they are deceived by their genes into thinking that there is a disinterested objective morality binding upon them, which all should obey."

– E. O. Wilson

"A scholar is just a library's way of making another library."

– Daniel Dennett

To some people, Good and Evil are reified processes in the world, composed of a tapestry of individual acts in an overall pattern. Religious people are apt to anthropomorphize these into members of whatever pantheon they hold sacred. Others accept the teachings but not the teachers, believing in sets of rules for behavior but not any rule makers. Some people indulge in detailed philosophical or legal elaborations of the rules. Philosophers have for centuries attempted to derive them from first principles, or at least reduce them to a few general prin-ciples, ranging from Kant's Categorical Imperative to Mill's Utilitarianism and its variants to modern ideologically based formulations such as the collectivism of Rawls and the individualist libertarianism of Nozick.

The vast majority of people, however, care nothing for this argumentative superstructure but learn moral rules by osmosis, internalizing them not unlike the rules of grammar of their native language, structuring every act as uncon-sciously as our inbuilt grammar structures our sentences.

It is by now widely accepted that our brains have features of structure and organization (though not necessarily separate "organs") specific to language, and that although natural languages vary in vocabulary and syntax, they do so within limits imposed by our neurophysiology (see Pinker; also Calvin & Bickerton).

For a moral epistemology I will take as a point of departure the "moral sense" philosophers of the Scottish Enlightenment (e.g., Smith), and place an enhanced interpretation on their theories in view of what we now know about language. In particular, I contend that moral codes are much like language gram-mars: There are structures in our brains that predispose us to learn moral codes, that determine within broad limits the kinds of codes we can learn, and that, although the moral codes of human cultures vary within those limits, have many structural features in common. (This notion is fairly widespread in latter twentieth-century moral philosophy, e.g., Rawls, Donagan.) I will refer to that which is learned by such an "ethical instinct" as a moral code, or just code. I'll refer to a part of a code that applies to particular situations as a rule. I should point out, however, that our moral sense, like our competence at language, is as yet notably more sophisticated than any simple set of rules or other algorithmic formulation seen to date.

Moral codes have much in common from culture to culture; we might call this "moral deep structure." Here are some of the features that human moral codes tend to have and that appear to be easy to learn and propagate in a culture's morality:

- Reciprocity, both in aggression ("an eye for an eye") and in beneficence ("you owe me one")
- Pecking orders, rank, status, authority
- Within that framework, universality of basic moral rules
- Honesty and trustworthiness is valued and perfidy denigrated
- Unprovoked aggression denigrated
- Property, particularly in physical objects (including animals and people); also commons, things excluded from private ownership
- Ranking of rules, for example, stealing not as bad as murder
- Bounds on moral agency, different rights and responsibilities for "barbarians"
- The ascendancy of moral rules over both common sense and self-interest

There are of course many more, and much more to be said about these few. It is worthwhile examining the last one in more detail. Moral codes are something more than arbitrary customs for interactions. There is no great difference made if we say "red" instead of "rouge," so long as everyone agrees on what to call that color; similarly, there could be many different basic forms of syntax that could express our ideas with similar efficiency.

Yet one of the points of a moral code is to make people do things they would not do otherwise, say, from self-interest. Some of these, such as altruism toward one's relatives, can clearly arise simply from selection for genes as opposed to individuals. However, there is reason to believe that there is much more going on and that humans have evolved an ability to be programmed with arbitrary (within certain limits) codes.

The reason is that, particularly for social animals, there are many kinds of interactions whose benefit matrices have the character of a Prisoner's Dilemma or Tragedy of the Commons, that is, where the best choice from the individual's standpoint is at odds with that of the group as a whole. Furthermore, and perhaps even more important, in prescientific times, there were many effects of actions, long and short term, that simply weren't understood.

In many cases, the adoption of a rule that seemed to contravene common sense or one's own interest, if generally followed, could have a substantial beneficial effect on a human group. If the rules adopted from whatever source happen to be more beneficial than not on the average, genes for "follow the rules, and kill those who break them" might well prosper.

The rules themselves could be supplied at random (an inspection of current morality fads would seem to confirm this) and evolve. It is not necessary to show that entire groups live and die on the basis of their moralities, although that can happen. People imitate successful groups; groups grow and shrink, conquer, are subjugated, and so forth. Thus in some sense this formulation can be seen as an attempt to unify the moral sense philosophers, Wilson's sociobiology, and Dawkins's theory of memes. Do note that it is necessary to hypothesize at least a slightly more involved mental mechanism for moral as opposed to practical memes, as otherwise the rules would be unable to counteract apparent self-interest.

The bottom line is that a moral code is a set of rules that evolved under the pressure that obeying these *rules against people's individual interests and common sense* has tended to make societies prosper, in particular to be more numerous, enviable, militarily powerful, and more apt to spread their ideas in other ways (e.g., missionaries).

The world is populated with cultures with different codes, just as it is with different species of animals. Just as with the animals, the codes have structural similarities and common ancestry, modified by environmental influences and the vagaries of random mutation. It is important to reiterate that there is a strong biologically evolved substrate that both supports the codes and can regenerate quite serviceable novel ones in the absence of an appropriate learned one – we might speak of "moral pidgins" and "moral creoles."

Observations on the Theory

"The influences which the society exerts on the nature of its units, and those which the units exert on the nature of the society, incessantly co-operate in creating new elements. As societies progress in size and structure, they work on one another, now by their war-struggles and now by their industrial intercourse, profound metamorphoses."

– Herbert Spencer

This conception of morality brings up several interesting points. The first is that like natural genomes and languages, natural moral codes should be expected to contain some randomness, rules that were produced in the normal processes of variation and neither helped nor hurt very much, and are simply carried along as baggage by the same mechanisms as the more effectual ones.

Second, it's important to realize that our subjective experience of feelings of right and wrong as things considerably deeper, more universal, and more compelling than this account seems to make them is not only compatible with this theory – it is required. Moral codes in this theory *must* be something that are capable of withstanding the countervailing forces of self-interest and common sense for generations in order to evolve. They must, in genetic terms, be expressed in the phenotype, and they must be heritable.

Third, there is a built-in pressure for inclusiveness in situations where countervailing forces (such as competition for resources) are not too great. The advantages in trade and security to be had from the coalescence of groups whose moral codes can be unified are substantial.

A final observation involves a phenomenon that is considerably more difficult to quantify. With plenty of exceptions, there seems to have been an acceleration of moral (religious, ideological) conflict since the invention of the printing press; and then in the twentieth century, after (and during) the apparent displacement of some ideologies by others, an increasing moral incoherence in Western culture. One might tentatively theorize that printing and subsequent information technologies increased the rate and penetration of moral-code mutations. In a dominant culture, the force of selection no longer operates, leaving variation to operate unopposed and ultimately undermining the culture (cf. Rome, dynastic China, etc). This may form a natural limit to the growth/inclusiveness pressure.

Comparison with Standard Ethical Theories

"My propositions serve as elucidations in the following way: anyone who understands me eventually recognizes them as nonsensical."

– Wittgenstein

Formulations of metaethical theory commonly fall into the categories of absolutism or relativism (along with such minor schools of thought as ethical nihilism and skepticism). It should be clear that the present synthesis – let us refer to it as "ethical evolution" – does not fall neatly into any of the standard categories. It obviously does not support a notion of absolute right and wrong any more than evolution can give rise to a single perfect life form; there is only fitness for a particular niche. On the other hand, it is certainly not true that the code adopted by any given culture is necessarily good; the dynamic of the theory depends on there being good ones and bad ones. Thus there are criteria for judging the moral rules of a culture; the theory is not purely relativistic.

We can contrast this to some degree with the "evolutionary ethics" of Spencer and Leslie (see also Corning), although there are also some clear similarities. In particular, Victorian evolutionary ethics could be seen as an attempt to describe ethics in terms of how individuals and societies evolve. Note too that "Social Darwinism" has a reputation for carnivorousness that, although rightly applied to Huxley, is undeserved by Darwin, Spencer, and the rest of its mainstream. Darwin, indeed, understood the evolution of cooperation and altruism in what he called "family selection."

There has been a resurgence of interest in evolutionary ethics in the latter twentieth century, fueled by work such as Hamilton, Wilson, and Axelrod, and which has been advanced by philosophers such as Bradie.

The novel feature of ethical evolution is the claim that there is a moral sense, a particular facility beyond (and to some extent in control of) our general cognitive abilities that hosts a memetic code and that coevolves with societies. However, it would not be unreasonable in a broad sense to claim that this is one kind of evolutionary ethics theory.

Standard ethical theories are often described as either deontological or consequentialist, that is, whether acts are deemed good or bad in and of themselves, or whether it's the results that matter. Again, ethical evolution has elements of each – the rules in our heads govern our actions without regard for results (indeed in spite of them); but the codes themselves are formed by the consequences of the actions of the people in the society.

Finally, moral philosophers sometimes distinguish between the good and the right. The good is properties that can apply to the situations of people: things like health, knowledge, physical comfort and satisfaction, spiritual fulfillment, and so forth. Some theories also include a notion of an overall good (which may be the sum of individual goods or something more complex). The right is about questions like how much of your efforts should be expended obtaining the good for yourself and how much for others, and should the poor be allowed to steal bread from the rich, and so forth.

Ethical evolution clearly has something to say about the right; it is the moral instinct you have inherited and the moral code you have learned. It also has something to say about the general good; it is the fitness or dynamism of the society. It does not have nearly as much to say about individual good as many theories. This is not, on reflection, surprising: Obviously the specific kinds of things that people need change with times, technology, and social organization; but, indeed, the kinds of general qualities of character that were considered good (and indeed were good) have changed significantly over the past few centuries, and by any reasonable expectation, will continue to do so.

In summary, ethical evolution claims that there is an "ethical instinct" in the makeup of human beings, and that it consists of the propensity to learn and obey certain kinds of ethical codes. The rules we are concerned with are those that pressure individuals to act at odds with their *perceived* self-interest and common sense. Moral codes evolve memetically by their effect on the vitality of cultures. Such codes tend to have substantial similarities, both because of the deep structure of the moral instinct, and because of optima in the space of group behaviors that form memetic-ecological "niches."

Golden Rules

"Act only on that maxim by which you can at the same time will that it should become a universal law."

– Kant

Kant's Categorical Imperative, along with the more familiar "Do unto others ..." formulation of the Christian teachings, appears to be one of the moral universals,

in some appropriate form. In practice it can clearly be subordinated to the pecking order/authority concept, so that there are allowable codes in which there are
things that are right for the king or state to do that ordinary people can't.

Vinge refers, in his Singularity writings, to I. J. Good's "Meta-Golden Rule,"
namely, "Treat your inferiors as you would be treated by your superiors." (Good
did make some speculations in print about superhuman intelligence, but no one
has been able to find the actual rule in his writings – perhaps we should credit
Vinge himself with this one!)

This is one of the few such principles that seems to have been conceived with
a hierarchy of superhuman intelligences in mind. Its claim to validity, however,
seems to rest on a kind of Kantian logical universality. Kant, and philosophers in
his tradition, thought that ethics could be derived from first principles like mathematics. There are numerous problems with this, beginning with the selection of
the axioms. If we go with something like the Categorical Imperative, we are left
with a serious vagueness in terms like "universal": Can I suggest a universal law
that everybody puts the needs of redheaded white males first? If not, what kind
of laws can be universal? It seems that quite a bit is left to the interpretation of
the deducer, and on closer inspection, the appearance of simple, self-obvious
postulates and the logical necessity of the results vanishes.

There is in the science fiction tradition a thread of thought about ethical
theory involving different races of creatures with presumably differing capabilities. This goes back at least to the metalaw notions of Haley and Fasan. As Freitas
points out, these are based loosely on the Categorical Imperative, and are clearly
Kantian in derivation.

Utilitarianism

Now consider the people of a given culture. Their morality seems to be, in a manner
of speaking, the best that evolution could give them to prosper in the ecology of cultures and the physical world. Suppose they said, "Let us adopt, instead of our rules,
the general principle that each of us should do at any point whatever best advances
the prosperity and security of our people as a whole" (see, of course, J.S. Mill).
Besides the standard objections to this proposal, we would have to add at least
two: First, that in ethical evolution humans have the built-in hardware for obeying
rules but not for the general moral calculation; but perhaps more surprising, historically anyway, *the codes are smarter than the people are*, because they have evolved
to handle long-term effects that by our assumption, people do not understand.

Yet now we have science! Surely our formalized, rationalized, and organized
trove of knowledge would put us on at least at par with the hit-or-miss folk wisdom of our agrarian forebears, even wisdom that has stood the test of time? What
is more, isn't the world changing so fast now that the assumptions implicit in the
moral codes of our fathers are no longer valid?

This is an extremely seductive proposition and an even more dangerous one. It is responsible for some social mistakes of catastrophic proportions, such as certain experiments with socialism. Much of the reality about which ancient moral codes contain wisdom is the mathematical implications of the patterns of interactions between intelligent self-interested agents, which hasn't changed a bit since the Pharaohs. What is more, when people start tinkering with their own moral codes, the first thing they do is to "fix" them to match better with their self-interest and common sense (with predictably poor results).

That said, it seems possible that using computer simulation as "moral instrumentation" may help weigh the balance in favor of scientific utilitarianism, assuming that the models used take account of the rule-adopting and rule-following nature of humans and the nature of bounded rationality of us or our machines. Even so, it would be wise to compare the sophistication of our designed machines with evolved organisms and to avoid hubristic overconfidence.

It should be noted that contractarian approaches tend to have the same weaknesses (as well as strengths) as utilitarian or rule-utilitarian ones for the purposes of this analysis.

The Veil of Ignorance

One popular modern formulation of morality that we might compare our theory to is Rawls's "Veil of Ignorance" scheme. The basic idea is that the ethical society is one that people would choose out of the set of all possible sets of rules, given that they didn't know which place in the society they would occupy. This formulation might be seen as an attempt to combine rule-utilitarianism with the Categorical Imperative.

In reducing his *gedankenexperiment* to specific prescription, Rawls makes some famous logical errors. In particular, he chooses among societies using a game-theoretic minimax strategy, but the assumptions implicit in the optimality of minimax (essentially, that an opponent will choose the worst possible position for you in the society) contradict the stated assumptions of the model (that the choice of position is random).

(Note that Rawls has long been made aware of the logical gap in his model, and in the revised edition of "Theory of Justice" he spends a page or two trying, unsuccessfully in my view, to justify it. It is worth spending a little time picking on Rawls, because he is often used as the philosophical justification for economic redistributionism. Some futurists (like Moravec) are depending on economic redistributionism to feed us once the robots do all the work. In the hands of ultraintelligent beings, theories that are both flawed and obviously rigged for our benefit will be rapidly discarded. . . .)

Still, the "Veil of Ignorance" setup is compelling if the errors are corrected, for example, if minimax is replaced with simple expected value.

Or is it? In making our choice of societies, it never occurred to us to worry whether we might be instantiated in the role of one of the machines! What a wonderful world where everyone had a staff of robot servants; what a different thing if, upon choosing that world, one were faced with a high probability of being one of the robots.

Does this mean that we are morally barred from making machines that can be moral agents? Suppose it's possible – it seems quite likely at our current level of understanding of such things – to make a robot that will mow your lawn and clean your house and cook and so forth, but in a dumb mechanical way, *demonstrably* having no feelings, emotions, no sense of right or wrong. Rawls's model seems to imply that it would never be right to give such a robot a sense of right and wrong, making it a moral agent and thus included in the choice.

Suppose instead we took an entirely human world and added robotic demigods, brilliant, sensitive, wise machines superior to humans in every way. Clearly such a world is more desirable than our own from behind the veil – not only does the chooser have a chance to be one of the demigods, but they would act to make the world a better place for the rest of us. The only drawback might be envy among the humans. Does this mean that we have a moral duty to create demigods?

Consider the plight of the moral evaluator who is faced with societies consisting not only of wild-type humans but also of robots of wide-ranging intelligence, uploaded humans with greatly amplified mental capacity, group minds consisting of many human mentalities linked with the technological equivalent of a corpus callosum, and so forth. Specifically, suppose that being "human" or a moral agent were not a discrete yes-or-no affair, but a matter of continuous degree, perhaps in more than one dimension?

Normative Implications

"Man when perfected is the best of animals, but when separated from law and justice he is the worst of all."

– Aristotle

It should be clear from the foregoing that most historical metaethical theories are based a bit too closely on the assumption of a single, generic-human kind of moral agent to be of much use. (Note that this objection cuts clean across ideological lines, being just as fatal to Rothbard as to Rawls.) Yet can ethical evolution do better? After all, our ethical instinct has evolved in just such a human-only world.

Actually it has not. Dogs, for example, clearly have a sense of right and wrong and are capable of character traits more than adequate to their limited cognitive abilities. I would speculate that there is protomoral capability just as there is protolanguage ability in the higher mammals, especially the social primates.

Among humans, children are a distinct form of moral agent. They have limited rights and reduced responsibilities, and others have nonstandard duties with respect to them. What is more, there is continuous variation of this distinction from baby to teenager.

In contrast to the Kantian bias of Western thought, there are clearly viable codes with gradations of moral agency for different people. The most obvious of these are the difference in obligations to fellows and strangers and the historically common practice of slavery. In religious conceptions of the good, there are angels as well as demons.

What, then, can ethical evolution say, for example, about the rights and obligations of a corporation or other "higher form of life" where a classical formulation would founder?

First of all, it says that it is probably a moral thing for corporations to exist. Western societies with corporations have been considerably more dynamic in the period corporations have existed than other societies (historically or geographically). There is probably no more at work here than the sensible notion that there should be a form of organization of an appropriate size to the scale of the profitable opportunities available.

Can we say anything about the rights or duties of a corporation, or, as Moravec suggests, the robots that corporations are likely to become in the next few decades? Should they simply obey the law? (A corporation is legally required to try to make a profit, by the way, as a duty to its stockholders.) Surely we would judge harshly a human whose only moral strictures were to obey the law. What is more, corporations are notorious for influencing the law-making process (see, e.g., Katz). They do not seem to have "ethical organs" that aggressively learn and force them to obey prevalent standards of behavior that stand at odds to their self-interest and common sense.

Moravec hints at a moral sense in the superhuman robo-corporations of the future (in "Robot"): "Time-tested fundamentals of behavior, with consequences too sublime to predict, will remain at the core of beings whose form and substance change frequently." He calls such a core a constitution; I might perhaps call it a conscience.

The Road Ahead

"You're a better man than I am, Gunga Din."

– Kipling

Robots evolve much faster than biological animals. They are designed, and the designs evolve memetically. Given that there is a substantial niche for nearly autonomous creatures whose acts are coordinated by a moral sense, it seems likely that ultimately robots with consciences would appear and thrive.

We have in the past been so complacent in our direct control of our machines that we have not thought to build them with consciences (visionaries like Asimov notwithstanding). We may be on the cusp of a crisis as virtual machines such as corporations grow in power but not in moral wisdom. Part of the problem, of course, is that we do not really have a solid understanding of our own moral natures. If our moral instinct is indeed like that for language, note that computer language understanding has been one of the hardest problems, with a fifty-year history of slow, frustrating, progress. Also note that in comparison there has been virtually no research in machine ethics at all.

For our own sake it seems imperative for us to begin to understand our own moral senses at a detailed and technical enough level that we can build the same into our machines. Once the machines are as smart as we are, they will see both the need and the inevitability of morality among intelligent but not omniscient, nearly autonomous creatures; they will thank us rather than merely trying to circumvent the strictures of their consciences.

Why shouldn't we just let them evolve consciences on their own (AIs and corporations alike)? If the theory is right, they will, over the long run. Yet what that means is that there will be many societies of AIs, and that most of them will die off because their poor protoethics made them waste too much of their time fighting each other (as corporations seem to do now!), and slowly, after the rise and fall of many civilizations, the ones who have randomly accumulated the basis of sound moral behavior will prosper. Personally, I don't want to wait. Any AI at least as smart as we are should be able to grasp the same logic and realize that a conscience is not such a bad thing to have.

(By the way, the same thing will apply to humans when, as seems not unlikely in the future, we get the capability to edit our own biological natures. It would be well for us to have a sound, scientific understanding of ethics for our own good as a species.)

There has always been a vein of Frankenphobia in science fiction and futuristic thought, either direct, as in Shelley, or referred to, as in Asimov. It is clear, in my view, that such a fear is eminently justified against the prospect of building machines without consciences more powerful than we. Indeed, on the face of it, building superhuman sociopaths is a blatantly stupid thing to do.

Suppose, instead, we can build (or become) machines that can not only run faster, jump higher, dive deeper, and come up drier than we, but have moral senses similarly more capable? Beings that can see right and wrong through the political garbage dump of our legal system; corporations one would like to have as a friend (or would let one's daughter marry); governments less likely to lie than your neighbor.

I could argue at length (but will not, here) that a society including superethical machines would not only be better for people to live in, but stronger and more dynamic than ours is today. What is more, ethical evolution as well as most of the classical ethical theories, if warped to admit the possibility (and of course the religions!), seem to allow the conclusion that having creatures both wiser *and* *morally superior* to humans might just be a good idea.

The inescapable conclusion is that we should give consciences to our machines where we can. If we can indeed create machines that exceed us in the moral and intellectual dimensions, we are bound to do so. It is our duty. If we have any duty to the future at all, to give our children sound bodies and educated minds, to preserve history, the arts, science, and knowledge, the Earth's biosphere, "to secure the blessings of liberty for ourselves and our posterity" – to promote any of the things we value – those things are better cared for by, *more valued by*, our moral superiors whom we have this opportunity to bring into being. It is the height of arrogance to assume that we are the final word in goodness. Our machines will be better than us, and we will be better for having created them.

Acknowledgments

Thanks to Sandra Hall, Larry Hudson, Rob Freitas, Tihamer Toth-Fejel, Jacqueline Hall, Greg Burch, and Eric Drexler for comments on an earlier draft of this paper.

Bibliography

Richard Alexander. *The Biology of Moral Systems.* Hawthorne/Aldine De Gruyter, 1987.
Colin Allen, Gary Varner, Jason Zinser. *Prolegomena to Any Future Artificial Moral Agent.* Forthcoming (2000) in J. Exp. & Theor. AI (at http://grimpeur.tamu.edu/~colin/Papers/ama.html).
Isaac Asimov. *I, Robot.* Doubleday, 1950.
Robert Axelrod. *The Evolution of Cooperation.* Basic Books, 1984.
Susan Blackmore. *The Meme Machine.* Oxford, 1999.
Howard Bloom. *The Lucifer Principle.* Atlantic Monthly Press, 1995.
Michael Bradie. *The Secret Chain: Evolution and Ethics.* SUNY, 1994.
Greg Burch. *Extropian Ethics and the "Extrosattva"* (at http://users.aol.com/gburch3/extrostv.html).
William Calvin & Derek Bickerton. *Lingua ex Machina.* Bradford/MIT, 2000.
Peter Corning. Evolution and Ethics ... an Idea whose Time has Come? *J. Soc. and Evol. Sys.*, 19(3): 277–285, 1996 (and at http://www.complexsystems.org/essays/evoleth1.html).
Charles Darwin. *On the Origin of Species by Natural Selection* (many eds.).
Richard Dawkins. *The Selfish Gene.* Oxford, 1976, rev. 1989.
Daniel Dennett. *The Intentional Stance.* MIT, 1987.
Daniel Dennett. *Darwin's Dangerous Idea.* Penguin, 1995.
Alan Donagan. *The Theory of Morality.* Univ Chicago Press, 1977.
Ernst Fasan. *Relations with Alien Intelligences.* Berlin-Verlag, 1970.
Kenneth Ford, Clark Glymour, & Patrick Hayes. *Android Epistemology.* AAAI/MIT, 1995.
David Friedman. *The Machinery of Freedom.* Open Court, 1989.
Robert Freitas. The Legal Rights of Extraterrestrials. in *Analog* Apr77:54–67.
Robert Freitas. Personal communication. 2000.
James Gips. Towards the Ethical Robot, in Ford, Glymour, & Hayes.
I. J. Good. The Social Implications of Artificial Intelligence, in I. J. Good, ed. *The Scientist Speculates.* Basic Books, 1962.
Andrew G. Haley. *Space Law and Government.* Appleton-Century-Crofts, 1963.

Ronald Hamowy. *The Scottish Enlightenment and the Theory of Spontaneous Order*. S. Illinois Univ. Press, 1987.

William Hamilton. The Genetical Evolution of Social Behavior I & II, *J. Theor. Biol.*, 7, 1–52; 1964.

Thomas Hobbes. *Leviathan* (many eds.).

John Hospers. *Human Conduct*. Harcourt Brace Jovanovich, 1972.

Immanuel Kant. *Foundations of the Metaphysics of Morals* (many eds.).

Jon Katz. The Corporate Republic. (at http://slashdot.org/article.pl?sid=00/04/26/108 242&mode=nocomment).

Umar Khan. *The Ethics of Autonomous Learning Systems*. in Ford, Glymour, & Hayes.

Ray Kurzweil. *The Age of Spiritual Machines*. Viking, 1999.

Debora MacKenzie. Please Eat Me, in *New Scientist*, 13 May 2000.

John Stuart Mill. *Utilitarianism* (many eds.).

Marvin Minsky. Alienable Rights, in Ford, Glymour, & Hayes.

Hans Moravec. *Robot: Mere Machine to Transcendent Mind*. Oxford, 1999.

Charles Murray. *In Pursuit of Happiness and Good Government*. Simon & Schuster, 1988.

Robert Nozick. *Anarchy, State, and Utopia*. Basic Books, 1974.

Steven Pinker. *The Language Instinct*. HarperCollins, 1994.

Steven Pinker. *How the Mind Works*. Norton, 1997.

Plato. *The Republic*. (Cornford trans.) Oxford, 1941.

John Rawls. *A Theory of Justice*. Harvard/Belknap, 1971, rev. 1999.

Murray Rothbard. *For a New Liberty*. Collier Macmillan, 1973.

R.J. Rummel. *Death by Government*. Transaction Publishers, 1994.

Adam Smith. *Theory of Moral Sentiments* (Yes, the same Adam Smith. Hard to find.).

Herbert Spencer. *The Principles of Ethics*. Appleton, 1897; rep. Liberty Classics, 1978.

Leslie Stephen. *The Science of Ethics*. 1882 (Hard to find.).

Tihamer Toth-Fejel. Transhumanism: The New Master Race? (in *The Assembler* [NSS/MMSG Newsletter] Volume 7, Number 1& 2 First and Second Quarter, 1999).

Vernor Vinge. *The Coming Technological Singularity: How to Survive in the Post-Human Era*. in Vision-21, NASA, 1993.

Frans de Waal. *Chimpanzee Politics*. Johns Hopkins, 1989.

Edward O. Wilson. *Sociobiology: The New Synthesis*. Harvard/Belknap, 1975.

Part II

The Importance
of Machine Ethics

Introduction

COLIN ALLEN, WENDELL WALLACH, AND IVA SMIT MAINTAIN IN "WHY Machine Ethics?" that it is time to begin adding ethical decision making to computers and robots. They point out that "[d]riverless [train] systems put machines in the position of making split-second decisions that could have life or death implications" if people are on one or more tracks that the systems could steer toward or avoid. The ethical dilemmas raised are much like the classic "trolley" cases often discussed in ethics courses. "The computer revolution is continuing to promote reliance on automation, and autonomous systems are coming whether we like it or not," they say. Shouldn't we try to ensure that they act in an ethical fashion?

Allen et al. don't believe that "increasing reliance on autonomous systems will undermine our basic humanity" or that robots will eventually "enslave or exterminate us." However, in order to ensure that the benefits of the new technologies outweigh the costs, "we'll need to integrate artificial moral agents into these new technologies ... to uphold shared ethical standards." It won't be easy, in their view, "but it is necessary and inevitable."

It is not necessary, according to Allen et al., that the autonomous machines we create be moral agents in the sense that human beings are. They don't have to have free will, for instance. We only need to design them "to act as if they were moral agents ... we must be confident that their behavior satisfies appropriate norms." We should start by making sure that system designers consider carefully "whose values, or what values, they implement" in the technologies they create. They advise that, as systems become more complex and function autonomously in different environments, it will become important that they have "ethical subroutines" that arise from a dialogue among philosophers, software engineers, legal theorists, and social scientists.

Anticipating the next part of the book, Allen et al. list a number of practical problems that will arise in attempting to add an ethical component to machines: Who or what should be held responsible for improper actions done by machines? Which values should we be implementing? Do machines have the cognitive capacities needed to implement the chosen values? How should we test the results of attempting to implement ethics into a machine during the design process? (Allen, together with Gary Varner and Jason Zinser, has developed a Moral Turing Test that is briefly discussed in this article.)

Allen et al. maintain that there has been a half a century of reflection and research since science fiction literature and films raised questions about whether robots could or would behave ethically. This has led to the development of the new field of research called machine ethics, which "extends the field of computer ethics beyond concern for what people do with their computers to questions about what the machines themselves do." It differs from "philosophy of technology," which was first "mostly reactive and sometimes motivated by the specter of unleashing powerful processes over which we lack control," and then became "more proactive, seeking to make engineers aware of the values they bring to the design process." Machine ethics, they maintain, goes a step further, "seeking to build ethical decision-making capacities directly into the machines ... [and in doing so] advancing the relevant technologies."

The advantages Allen et al. see resulting from engaging in machine ethics research include feeling more confident in allowing machines (that have been programmed to behave in an ethically acceptable manner) to do more for us and discovering "the computational limits of common ethical theories." Machine ethics research could also lead to other approaches to capturing ethics, such as embodying virtues, taking a developmental approach similar to how children acquire a sense of morality, and exploring the relationship between emotions, rationality, and ethics. Above all, attempting to implement ethics into a machine will result in a better understanding of ourselves.

Sherry Turkle, in "Authenticity in the Age of Digital Companions," raises concerns about "relational artifacts" that are designed to appear as if they have feelings and needs. One of the earliest relational artifacts was Joseph Weizenbaum's computer program Eliza, created in the 1960s. "Eliza was designed to mirror users' thoughts and thus seemed consistently supportive," Turkle says. It had a strong emotional effect on those who used it, with many being more willing to talk to the computer than to other human beings, a psychotherapist for example. Weizenbaum himself was disturbed by the "Eliza effect." "If the software *elicited* trust, it was only by tricking those who used it," because "Eliza could not understand the stories it was being told; it did not care about the human beings who confided in it."

Turkle believes that Eliza can be seen as a benchmark, heralding a "crisis in authenticity: people did not care if their life narratives were *really* understood. The act of telling them created enough meaning on its own." Even though Eliza's users recognized the huge gap between the program and a person, Turkle came to see that "when a machine shows interest in us, it pushes our 'Darwinian buttons' that signal it to be an entity appropriate for relational purposes."

Since Eliza, more sophisticated relational artifacts have been developed, such as "Kismet, developed at the MIT Artificial Intelligence Laboratory, a robot that responds to facial expressions, vocalizations, and tone of voice." Turkle is concerned that such entities have been "*specifically designed to make people feel understood*," even though they lack understanding. They cause persons who interact with them to "feel as though they are dealing with sentient creatures who care about their presence." Even when children were shown the inner workings of Cog, another humanoid robot created at MIT, demystifying it, Turkle reports that they quickly went "back to relating to Cog as a creature and playmate."

Turkle points out that human beings have not, in the course of their evolution, had to distinguish between authentic and simulated relationships before the age of computers. Now, she maintains, "As robots become part of everyday life, it is important that these differences are clearly articulated and discussed." It is disturbing to Turkle that people are having feelings in their interactions with robots that can't be reciprocated as they can with human beings.

Turkle notes that, whereas earlier in their development, computational objects were described as being intelligent but not emotional, preserving the distinction between robots and persons, now they are thought of as emotional as well. Unlike the inert teddy bears of the past, today's robots might exclaim, "Hug me!" This creates an expectation in a child that the robot needs a hug, that it is in some sense "alive." Turkle says that "children are learning to have expectations of emotional attachments to robots in the same way that we have expectations about our emotional attachments to people." She has found that elderly persons have similar reactions to robots as well. Even Cynthia Breazeal, who led the design team that created and "nurtured" Kismet, "developed what might be called a maternal connection with Kismet." When she graduated from MIT and had to leave Kismet behind, she "described a sharp sense of loss."

Some would argue that relational artifacts can be very therapeutic, citing the example of Paro, a seal-like robot that is sensitive to touch, can make eye contact with a person who speaks to it, and responds in a manner that is appropriate to the way it is treated. It has provided comfort to many elderly persons who have been abandoned by relatives. Turkle's reaction to Paro is to say that "we must discipline ourselves to keep in mind that Paro understands nothing, senses nothing, and cares nothing for the person who is interacting with it."

The bottom line for Turkle is that we need to ask "what *we* will be like, what kind of people *we* are becoming as we develop increasingly intimate relationships with machines." Turkle ends her article by citing the reflections of a former colleague who had been left severely disabled by an automobile accident. He told her that he would rather be cared for by a human being who is a sadist, than a robot, because he would feel more alive in interacting with a human being.

Why has this article, which makes no mention of machine ethics, been included in this volume? It might appear to fall in the realm of being concerned with ethically acceptable and unacceptable *uses* of machines by human beings. We think not. Because relational artifacts *are* being produced and used that behave in ways that are ethically questionable, we see Turkle as making a strong case for the importance of machine ethics. Designers of these machines should be considering the possible harmful effects they may have on vulnerable human beings who interact with them. They should certainly not be designed specifically with the intention of deceiving persons into thinking that they have feelings and care about them. Insistence on the installation of ethical principles into relational artifacts to guide their behavior, and perhaps rethinking the trend toward making them more humanlike as well, would clearly be warranted.

Readers interested in the importance of machine ethics should also look at the articles by Moor and Hall in the first part of the book, as well as the articles in the last part of the book, for additional reasons why machine ethics is important.

4

Why Machine Ethics?

Colin Allen, Wendell Wallach, and Iva Smit

A RUNAWAY TROLLEY IS APPROACHING A FORK IN THE TRACKS. IF THE trolley runs on its current track, it will kill a work crew of five. If the driver steers the train down the other branch, the trolley will kill a lone worker. If you were driving the trolley, what would you do? What would a computer or robot do? Trolley cases, first introduced by philosopher Philippa Foot in 1967[1] and now a staple of introductory ethics courses, have multiplied in the past four decades. What if it's a bystander, rather than the driver, who has the power to switch the trolley's course? What if preventing the five deaths requires pushing another spectator off a bridge onto the tracks? These variants evoke different intuitive responses.

Given the advent of modern "driverless" train systems, which are now common at airports and are beginning to appear in more complicated rail networks such as the London Underground and the Paris and Copenhagen metro systems, could trolley cases be one of the first frontiers for machine ethics? Machine ethics (also known as machine morality, artificial morality, or computational ethics) is an emerging field that seeks to implement moral decision-making faculties in computers and robots. Is it too soon to be broaching this topic? We don't think so.

Driverless systems put machines in the position of making split-second decisions that could have life or death consequences. As a rail network's complexity increases, the likelihood of dilemmas not unlike the basic trolley case also increases. How, for example, do we want our automated systems to compute where to steer an out-of-control train? Suppose our driverless train knew that there were five railroad workers on one track and a child on the other. Would we want the system to factor this information into its decision? The driverless trains of today are, of course, ethically oblivious. Can and should software engineers attempt to enhance their software systems to explicitly represent ethical dimensions of situations in which decisions must be made? It's easy to argue from a position of ignorance that such a goal is impossible to achieve. Yet precisely what are the

challenges and obstacles for implementing machine ethics? The computer revolution is continuing to promote reliance on automation, and autonomous systems
are coming whether we like it or not. Will they be ethical?

Good and Bad Artificial Agents?

This isn't about the horrors of technology. Yes, the machines are coming. Yes,
their existence will have unintended effects on our lives, not all of them good. But
no, we don't believe that increasing reliance on autonomous systems will undermine our basic humanity. Neither will advanced robots enslave or exterminate
us, as in the best traditions of science fiction. We humans have always adapted to
our technological products, and the benefits of having autonomous machines will
most likely outweigh the costs.

Yet optimism doesn't come for free. We can't just sit back and hope things
will turn out for the best. We already have semiautonomous robots and software
agents that violate ethical standards as a matter of course. A search engine, for
example, might collect data that's legally considered to be private, unbeknownst
to the user who initiated the query.

Furthermore, with the advent of each new technology, futuristic speculation
raises public concerns regarding potential dangers (see the "Skeptics of Driverless
Trains" sidebar). In the case of AI and robotics, fearful scenarios range from the
future takeover of humanity by a superior form of AI to the havoc created by end-
lessly reproducing nanobots. Although some of these fears are farfetched, they
underscore possible consequences of poorly designed technology. To ensure that
the public feels comfortable accepting scientific progress and using new tools and
products, we'll need to keep them informed about new technologies and reassure
them that design engineers have anticipated potential issues and accommodated
for them.

New technologies in the fields of AI, genomics, and nanotechnology will
combine in a myriad of unforeseeable ways to offer promise in everything from
increasing productivity to curing diseases. However, we'll need to integrate
artificial moral agents (AMAs) into these new technologies to manage their
complexity. These AMAs should be able to make decisions that honor privacy,
uphold shared ethical standards, protect civil rights and individual liberty, and
further the welfare of others. Designing such value-sensitive AMAs won't be
easy, but it's necessary and inevitable.

To avoid the bad consequences of autonomous artificial agents, we'll need to
direct considerable effort toward designing agents whose decisions and actions
might be considered good. What do we mean by "good" in this context? Good
chess-playing computers win chess games. Good search engines find the results
we want. Good robotic vacuum cleaners clean floors with minimal human supervision. These "goods" are measured against the specific purposes of designers and
users. However, specifying the kind of good behavior that autonomous systems

require isn't as easy. Should a good multipurpose robot rush to a stranger's aid, even if this means a delay in fulfilling tasks for the robot's owner? (Should this be an owner-specified setting?) Should an autonomous agent simply abdicate responsibility to human controllers if all the options it discerns might cause harm to humans? (If so, is it sufficiently autonomous?)

When we talk about what is good in this sense, we enter the domain of ethics and morality. It is important to defer questions about whether a machine can be genuinely ethical or even genuinely autonomous – questions that typically presume that a genuine ethical agent acts intentionally, autonomously, and freely. The present engineering challenge concerns only *artificial* morality: ways of getting artificial agents to act as if they were moral agents. If we are to trust multipurpose machines operating untethered from their designers or owners and programmed to respond flexibly in real or virtual environments, we must be confident that their behavior satisfies appropriate norms. This means something more than traditional product safety.

Of course, robots that short circuit and cause fires are no more tolerable than toasters that do so. An autonomous system that ignorantly causes harm might not be morally blameworthy any more than a toaster that catches fire can itself be blamed (although its designers might be at fault). However, in complex automata, this kind of blamelessness provides insufficient protection for those who might be harmed. If an autonomous system is to minimize harm, it must be cognizant of possible harmful consequences and select its actions accordingly.

Making Ethics Explicit

Until recently, designers didn't consider the ways in which they implicitly embedded values in the technologies they produced. An important achievement of ethicists has been to help engineers become aware of their work's ethical dimensions. There is now a movement to bring more attention to unintended consequences resulting from the adoption of information technology. For example, the ease with which information can be copied using computers has undermined legal standards for intellectual-property rights and forced a reevaluation of copyright law. Helen Nissenbaum, who has been at the forefront of this movement, pointed out the interplay between values and technology when she wrote, "In such cases, we cannot simply align the world with the values and principles we adhered to prior to the advent of technological challenges. Rather, we must grapple with the new demands that changes wrought by the presence and use of information technology have placed on values and moral principles."[2]

Attention to the values that are unconsciously built into technology is a welcome development. At the very least, system designers should consider whose values, or what values, they implement. However, the morality implicit in artificial agents' actions isn't simply a question of engineering ethics – that is to say, of getting engineers to recognize their ethical assumptions. Given modern computers' complexity, engineers commonly discover that they can't predict how a system will act in a new situation. Hundreds of engineers contribute to each machine's design. Different companies, research centers, and design teams work on individual hardware and software components that make up the final system. The modular design of systems can mean that no single person or group can fully grasp the manner in which the system will interact or respond to a complex flow of new inputs.

As systems get more sophisticated and their ability to function autonomously in different contexts and environments expands, it will become more important for them to have "ethical subroutines" of their own, to borrow a phrase from *Star Trek*. We want the systems' choices to be sensitive to us and to the things that are important to us, but these machines must be self-governing and capable of assessing the ethical acceptability of the options they face.

Self-Governing Machines

Implementing AMAs involves a broad range of engineering, ethical, and legal considerations. A full understanding of these issues will require a dialog among philosophers, robotic and software engineers, legal theorists, developmental psychologists, and other social scientists regarding the practicality, possible design strategies, and limits of autonomous AMAs. If there are clear limits in our ability to develop or manage AMAs, then we'll need to turn our attention away from a false reliance on autonomous systems and toward more human intervention in computers and robots' decision-making processes. Many questions arise when we consider the challenge of designing computer systems that function as the equivalent of moral agents.[3,4]

Can we implement in a computer system or robot the moral theories of philosophers, such as the utilitarianism of Jeremy Bentham and John Stuart Mill, Immanuel Kant's categorical imperative, or Aristotle's virtues? Is it feasible to develop an AMA that follows the Golden Rule or even Isaac Asimov's laws? How effective are bottom-up strategies – such as genetic algorithms, learning algorithms, or associative learning – for developing moral acumen in software agents? Does moral judgment require consciousness, a sense of self, an understanding of the semantic content of symbols and language or emotions? At what stage might we consider computational systems to be making judgments, or when might we view them as independent actors or AMAs?

We currently can't answer many of these questions, but we can suggest pathways for further research, experimentation, and reflection.

Moral Agency for AI

Moral agency is a well-developed philosophical category that outlines criteria for attributing responsibility to humans for their actions. Extending moral agency to artificial entities raises many new issues. For example, what are appropriate criteria for determining success in creating an AMA? Who or what should be held responsible if the AMA performs actions that are harmful, destructive, or illegal? Should the project of developing AMAs be put on hold until we can settle the issues of responsibility?

One practical problem is deciding what values to implement in an AMA. This problem isn't, of course, specific to software agents – the question of what values should direct human behavior has engaged theologians, philosophers, and social theorists for centuries. Among the specific values applicable to AMAs will be those usually listed as the core concerns of computer ethics – data privacy, security, digital rights, and the transnational character of computer networks. However, will we also want to ensure that such technologies don't undermine beliefs about the importance of human character and human moral responsibility that are essential to social cohesion?

Another problem is implementation. Are the cognitive capacities that an AMA would need to instantiate possible within existing technology, or within technology we'll possess in the not-too-distant future?

Philosophers have typically studied the concept of moral agency without worrying about whether they can apply their theories mechanically to make moral decisions tractable. Neither have they worried, typically, about the developmental psychology of moral behavior. So, a substantial question exists whether moral theories such as the categorical imperative or utilitarianism can guide the design of algorithms that could directly support ethical competence in machines or that might allow a developmental approach. As an engineering project, designing AMAs requires specific hypotheses and rigorous methods for evaluating results, but this will require dialog between philosophers and engineers to determine the suitability of traditional ethical theories as a source of engineering ideas.

Another question that naturally arises here is whether AMAs will ever really be moral agents. As a philosophical and legal concept, moral agency is often interpreted as requiring a sentient being with free will. Although Ray Kurzweil and Hans Moravec contend that AI research will eventually create new forms of sentient intelligence,[5,6] there are also many detractors. Our own opinions are divided on whether computers given the right programs can properly be said to have minds – the view John Searle attacks as "strong AI."[7] However, we agree that we can pursue the question of how to program autonomous agents to behave acceptably regardless of our stand on strong AI.

Science Fiction or Scientific Challenge?

Are we now crossing the line into science fiction – or perhaps worse, into that brand of science fantasy often associated with AI? The charge might be justified if we were making bold predictions about the dawn of AMAs or claiming that it's just a matter of time before walking, talking machines will replace those humans to whom we now turn for moral guidance. Yet we're not futurists, and we don't know whether the apparent technological barriers to AI are real or illusory. Nor are we interested in speculating about what life will be like when your counselor is a robot, or even in predicting whether this will ever come to pass.

Rather, we're interested in the incremental steps arising from present technologies that suggest a need for ethical decision-making capabilities. Perhaps these incremental steps will eventually lead to full-blown AI – a less murderous counterpart to Arthur C. Clarke's HAL, hopefully – but even if they don't, we think that engineers are facing an issue that they can't address alone.

Industrial robots engaged in repetitive mechanical tasks have already caused injury and even death. With the advent of service robots, robotic systems are no longer confined to controlled industrial environments, where they come into contact only with trained workers. Small robot pets, such as Sony's AIBO, are the harbinger of larger robot appliances. Rudimentary robot vacuum cleaners, robot couriers in hospitals, and robot guides in museums have already appeared. Companies are directing considerable attention at developing service robots that will perform basic household tasks and assist the elderly and the homebound.

Although 2001 has passed and HAL remains fiction, and it's a safe bet that the doomsday scenarios of the *Terminator* and *Matrix* movies will not be realized before their sell-by dates of 2029 and 2199, we're already at a point where engineered systems make decisions that can affect our lives. For example, Colin Allen recently drove from Texas to California but didn't attempt to use a particular credit card until nearing the Pacific coast. When he tried to use the card to refuel his car, it was rejected, so he drove to another station. Upon inserting the card in the pump, a message instructed him to hand the card to a cashier inside the store. Instead, Allen telephoned the toll-free number on the back of the card. The credit card company's centralized computer had evaluated Allen's use of the card almost two thousand miles from home, with no trail of purchases leading across the country, as suspicious, so it automatically flagged his account. The human agent at the credit card company listened to Allen's story and removed the flag.

Of course, denying someone's request to buy a tank of fuel isn't typically a matter of huge moral importance. How would we feel, however, if an automated medical system denied our loved one a life-saving operation?

A New Field of Inquiry: Machine Ethics

The challenge of ensuring that robotic systems will act morally has held a fascination ever since Asimov's three laws appeared in *I, Robot*. A half century of reflection and research into AI has moved us from science fiction toward the beginning of more careful philosophical analysis of the prospects for implementing machine ethics. Better hardware and improved design strategies are combining to make computational experiments in machine ethics feasible. Since Peter Danielson's efforts to develop virtuous robots for virtual games,[8] many researchers have attempted to implement ethical capacities in AI. Most recently, the various contributions to the AAAI Fall Symposium on Machine Ethics included a learning model based on prima facie duties (those with soft constraints) for applying informed consent, an approach to mechanizing deontic logic, an artificial neural network for evaluating ethical decisions, and a tool for case-based rule analysis.[9]

Machine ethics extends the field of computer ethics beyond concern for what people do with their computers to questions about what the machines themselves do. Furthermore, it differs from much of what goes under the heading of the philosophy of technology – a subdiscipline that raises important questions about human values such as freedom and dignity in increasingly technological societies. Old-style philosophy of technology was mostly reactive and sometimes motivated by the specter of unleashing powerful processes over which we lack control. New-wave technology philosophers are more proactive, seeking to make engineers aware of the values they bring to any design process. Machine ethics goes one step further, seeking to build ethical decision-making capacities directly into the machines. The field is fundamentally concerned with advancing the relevant technologies.

We see the benefits of having machines that operate with increasing autonomy, but we want to know how to make them behave ethically. The development of AMAs won't hinder industry. Rather, the capacity for moral decision making will allow deployment of AMAs in contexts that might otherwise be considered too risky.

Machine ethics is just as much about human decision making as it is about the philosophical and practical issues of implementing AMAs. Reflection about and experimentation in building AMAs forces us to think deeply about how we humans function, which of our abilities we can implement in the machines we design, and what characteristics truly distinguish us from animals or new forms of intelligence that we create. Just as AI has stimulated new lines of inquiry in the philosophy of mind, machine ethics potentially can stimulate new lines of inquiry in ethics. Robotics and AI laboratories could become experimental centers for testing the applicability of decision making in artificial systems and the ethical viability of those decisions, as well as for testing the computational limits of common ethical theories.

Finding the Right Approach

Engineers are very good at building systems for well-specified tasks, but there's no clear task specification for moral behavior. Talk of moral standards might seem to imply an accepted code of behavior, but considerable disagreement exists about moral matters. How to build AMAs that accommodate these differences is a question that requires input from a variety of perspectives. Talk of ethical subroutines also seems to suggest a particular conception of how to implement ethical behavior. However, whether algorithms or lines of software code can effectively represent ethical knowledge requires a sophisticated appreciation of what that knowledge consists of, and of how ethical theory relates to the cognitive and emotional aspects of moral behavior. The effort to clarify these issues and develop alternative ways of thinking about them takes on special dimensions in the context of artificial agents. We must assess any theory of what it means to be ethical or to make an ethical decision in light of the feasibility of implementing the theory as a computer program.

Different specialists will likely take different approaches to implementing an AMA. Engineers and computer scientists might treat ethics as simply an additional set of constraints, to be satisfied like any other constraint on successful program operation. From this perspective, there's nothing distinctive about moral reasoning. However, questions remain about what those additional constraints should be and whether they should be very specific ("Obey posted speed limits") or more abstract ("Never cause harm to a human being"). There are also questions regarding whether to treat them as hard constraints, never to be violated, or soft constraints, which may be stretched in pursuit of other goals – corresponding to a distinction ethicists make between absolute and prima facie duties. Making a moral robot would be a matter of finding the right set of constraints and the right formulas for resolving conflicts. The result would be a kind of "bounded morality," capable of behaving inoffensively so long as any situation that is encountered fits within the general constraints its designers predicted. Where might such constraints come from? Philosophers confronted with this problem will likely suggest a top-down approach of encoding a particular ethical theory in software. This theoretical knowledge could then be used to rank options for moral acceptability. With respect to computability, however, the moral principles philosophers propose leave much to be desired, often suggesting incompatible courses of action or failing to recommend any course of action. In some respects too, key ethical principles appear to be computationally intractable, putting them beyond the limits of effective computation because of the essentially limitless consequences of any action.[10]

If we can't implement an ethical theory as a computer program, then how can such theories provide sufficient guidelines for human action? Thinking about what machines are or aren't capable of might lead to deeper reflection about just what a moral theory is supposed to be. Some philosophers will regard the computational approach to ethics as misguided, preferring to see ethical human beings as exemplifying certain virtues that are rooted deeply in our own psychological nature. The problem of AMAs from this perspective isn't how to give them abstract theoretical knowledge, but rather how to embody the right tendencies to react in the world. It's a problem of moral psychology, not moral calculation.

Psychologists confronted with the problem of constraining moral decision making will likely focus on how children develop a sense of morality as they mature into adults. A developmental approach might be the most practicable route to machine ethics. Yet given what we know about the unreliability of this process for developing moral human beings, there's a legitimate question about how reliable trying to train AMAs would be. Psychologists also focus on the ways in which we construct our reality; become aware of self, others, and our environment; and navigate through the complex maze of moral issues in our daily life. Again, the complexity and tremendous variability of these processes in humans underscores the challenge of designing AMAs.

Beyond Stoicism

Introducing psychological aspects will seem to some philosophers to be confusing the ethics that people have with the ethics they should have. However, to insist that we should pursue machine ethics independently of the facts of human psychology is, in our view, to take a premature stand on important questions such as the extent to which the development of appropriate emotional reactions is a crucial part of normal moral development. The relationship between emotions and ethics is an ancient issue that also has resonance in more recent science fiction. Are the emotion-suppressing Vulcans of *Star Trek* inherently capable of better judgment than the more intuitive, less rational, more exuberant humans from Earth? Does Spock's utilitarian mantra of "The needs of the many outweigh the needs of the few" represent the rational pinnacle of ethics as he engages in an admirable act of self-sacrifice? Or do the subsequent efforts of Kirk and the rest of the *Enterprise*'s human crew to risk their own lives out of a sense of personal obligation to their friend represent a higher pinnacle of moral sensibility?

The new field of machine ethics must consider these questions, exploring the strengths and weaknesses of the various approaches to programming AMAs and laying the groundwork for engineering AMAs in a philosophically and cognitively sophisticated way. This task requires dialog among philosophers, robotic engineers, and social planners regarding the practicality, possible design strategies, and limits of autonomous moral agents.

Serious questions remain about the extent to which we can approximate or simulate moral decision making in a "mindless" machine.[11] A central issue is whether there are mental faculties (emotions, a sense of self, awareness of the affective state of others, and consciousness) that might be difficult (if not impossible) to simulate but that would be essential for true AI and machine ethics. For example, when it comes to making ethical decisions, the interplay between rationality and emotion is complex. Whereas the Stoic view of ethics sees emotions as irrelevant and dangerous to making ethically correct decisions, the more recent literature on emotional intelligence suggests that emotional input is essential to rational behavior.[12] Although ethics isn't simply a matter of doing whatever "feels right," it might be essential to cultivate the right feelings, sentiments, and virtues. Only pursuit of the engineering project of developing AMAs will answer the question of how closely we can approximate ethical behavior without these. The new field of machine ethics must also develop criteria and tests for evaluating an artificial entity's moral aptitude. Recognizing one limitation of the original Turing Test, Colin Allen, along with Gary Varner and Jason Zinser, considered the possibility of a specialized Moral Turing Test (MTT) that would be less dependent on conversational skills than the original Turing Test:

To shift the focus from conversational ability to action, an alternative MTT could be structured in such a way that the "interrogator" is given pairs of descriptions of actual, morally-significant actions of a human and an AMA, purged of all references that would identify the agents. If the interrogator correctly identifies the machine at a level above chance, then the machine has failed the test.[10]

They noted several problems with this test, including that indistinguishability from humans might set too low a standard for our AMAs.

Scientific knowledge about the complexity, subtlety, and richness of human cognitive and emotional faculties has grown exponentially during the past half century. Designing artificial systems that function convincingly and autonomously in real physical and social environments requires much more than abstract logical representation of the relevant facts. Skills that we take for granted and that children learn at a very young age, such as navigating around a room or appreciating the semantic content of words and symbols, have provided the biggest challenge to our best roboticists.

Some of the decisions we call moral decisions might be quite easy to implement in computers, whereas simulating skill at tackling other kinds of ethical dilemmas is well beyond our present knowledge. Regardless of how quickly or how far we progress in developing AMAs, in the process of engaging this challenge we will make significant strides in our understanding of what truly remarkable creatures we humans are. The exercise of thinking through the practical requirements of ethical decision making with a view to implementing similar faculties into robots is thus an exercise in self-understanding. We hope that readers will enthusiastically pick up where we have left off and take the next steps toward moving this project from theory to practice, from philosophy to engineering.

Acknowledgments

We're grateful for the comments of the anonymous IEEE Intelligent Systems referees and for Susan and Michael Anderson's help and encouragement.

References

1. P. Foot, "The Problem of Abortion and the Doctrine of Double Effect," *Oxford Rev.*, vol. 5, 1967, pp. 5–15.
2. H. Nissenbaum, "How Computer Systems Embody Values," *Computer*, vol. 34, no. 3, 2001, pp. 120, 118–119.
3. J. Gips, "Towards the Ethical Robot," *Android Epistemology*, K. Ford, C. Glymour, and P. Hayes, eds., MIT Press, 1995, pp. 243–252.

4. C. Allen, I. Smit, and W. Wallach, "Artificial Morality: Top-Down, Bottom-Up, and Hybrid Approaches," *Ethics and Information Technology*, vol. 7, 2006, pp. 149–155.

5. R. Kurzweil, *The Singularity Is Near: When Humans Transcend Biology*, Viking Adult, 2005.

6. H. Moravec, *Robot: Mere Machine to Transcendent Mind*, Oxford Univ. Press, 2000.

7. J.R. Searle, "Minds, Brains, and Programs," *Behavioral and Brain Sciences*, vol. 3, no. 3, 1980, pp. 417–457.

8. P. Danielson, *Artificial Morality: Virtuous Robots for Virtual Games*, Routledge, 1992.

9. M. Anderson, S.L. Anderson, and C. Armen, eds., "Machine Ethics," AAAI Fall Symp., tech report FS-05–06, AAAI Press, 2005.

10. C. Allen, G. Varner, and J. Zinser, "Prolegomena to Any Future Artificial Moral Agent," *Experimental and Theoretical Artificial Intelligence*, vol. 12, no. 3, 2000, pp. 251–261.

11. L. Floridi and J.W. Sanders, "On the Morality of Artificial Agents," *Minds and Machines*, vol. 14, no. 3, 2004, pp. 349–379.

12. A. Damasio, *Descartes' Error*, Avon, 1994.

5

Authenticity in the Age of Digital Companions

Sherry Turkle

WITH THE ADVENT OF "THINKING" MACHINES, OLD PHILOSOPHICAL questions about life and consciousness acquired new immediacy. Computationally rich software and, more recently, robots have challenged our values and caused us to ask new questions about ourselves (Turkle, 2005 [1984]). Are there some tasks, such as providing care and companionship, that only befit living creatures? Can a human being and a robot ever be said to perform the *same* task? In particular, how shall we assign value to what we have traditionally called relational authenticity? In their review of psychological benchmarks for human-robot interaction, Kahn et al. (2007) include authenticity as something robots can aspire to, but it is clear that from their perspective robots will be able to achieve it without sentience. Here, authenticity is situated on a more contested terrain.

Eliza and the crisis of authenticity

Joseph Weizenbaum's computer program Eliza brought some of these issues to the fore in the 1960s. Eliza prefigured an important element of the contemporary robotics culture in that it was one of the first programs that presented itself as a *relational artifact*, a computational object explicitly designed to engage a user in a relationship (Turkle, 2001, 2004; Turkle, Breazeal, Dasté, & Scassellati, 2006; Turkle, Taggart, Kidd, & Dasté, 2006). Eliza was designed to mirror users' thoughts and thus seemed consistently supportive, much like a Rogerian psychotherapist. To the comment, "My mother is making me angry," Eliza might respond, "Tell me more about your family," or "Why do you feel so negatively about your mother?" Despite the simplicity of how the program works – by string matching and substitution – Eliza had a strong emotional effect on many who used it. Weizenbaum was surprised that his students were eager to chat with the program and some even wanted to be alone with it (Turkle, 2005 [1984];

Turkle, Sherry: 'Authenticity in the age of digital companions' in *Interaction Studies*, John Benjamins Publishing Co., 2007, Amsterdam/Philadelphia pages 501-517. Reprinted with permission.

Weizenbaum, 1976). What made Eliza a valued interlocutor? What matters were so private that they could only be discussed with a machine? Eliza not only revealed people's willingness to talk to computers but their reluctance to talk to other people. Students' trust in Eliza did not speak to what they thought Eliza would understand but to their lack of trust in the people who would understand.

This "Eliza effect" is apparent in many settings. People who feel that psychotherapists are silent or disrespectful may prefer to have computers in these roles (Turkle, 1995). "When you go to a psychoanalyst, well, you're already going to a robot," reports an MIT administrator. A graduate student confides that she would trade in her boyfriend for a "sophisticated Japanese robot," if the robot would produce "caring behavior." The graduate student says she relies on a "feeling of civility" in the house. If the robot could "provide the environment," she would be "happy to produce the illusion that there is somebody really with me." Relational artifacts have become evocative objects, objects that clarify our relationships to the world and ourselves (Turkle, 2005 [1984]; 2007). In recent years, they have made clear the degree to which people feel alone with each other. People's interest in them indicates that traditional notions of authenticity are in crisis.

Weizenbaum came to see students' relationships with Eliza as immoral, because he considered human understanding essential to the confidences a patient shares with a psychotherapist. Eliza could not understand the stories it was being told; it did not care about the human beings who confided in it. Weizenbaum found it disturbing that the program was being treated as more than a parlor game. If the software *elicited* trust, it was only by tricking those who used it. From this viewpoint, if Eliza was a benchmark, it was because the software marked a crisis in authenticity: people did not care if their life narratives were *really* understood. The act of telling them created enough meaning on its own.

When Weizenbaum's book that included his highly charged discussion of reactions to Eliza was published in 1976, I was teaching courses with him at MIT on computers and society. At that time, the simplicity and transparency of how the program worked helped Eliza's users recognize the chasm between program and person. The gap was clear as was how students bridged it with attribution and desire. They thought, "I will talk to this program *as if* it were a person." Hence, Eliza seemed to me no more threatening than an interactive diary. But I may have underestimated the quality of the connection between person and machine. To put it too simply, when a machine shows interest in us, it pushes our "Darwinian buttons" (Turkle, 2004) that signal it to be an entity appropriate for relational purposes. The students may not have been pretending that they were chatting with a person. They may just have been happy to talk to a machine.

This possibility is supported by new generations of digital creatures that create a greater sense of mutual relating than Eliza, but *have no greater understanding of the situation of the human being in the relationship.* The relational artifacts of the past decade, *specifically designed to make people feel understood,* provide more sophisticated interfaces, but they are still without understanding.

Some of these relational artifacts are very simple in what they present to the user, such as the 1997 Tamagotchi, a virtual creature that inhabits a tiny LCD display. Some of them are far more complex, such as Kismet, developed at the MIT Artificial Intelligence Laboratory, a robot that responds to facial expressions, vocalizations, and tone of voice. From 1997 to the present, I have conducted field research with these relational artifacts and also with Furbies, Aibos, My Real Babies, Paros, and Cog. What these machines have in common is that they display behaviors that make people feel as though they are dealing with sentient creatures that care about their presence. These Darwinian buttons, these triggering behaviors, include making eye contact, tracking an individual's movement in a room, and gesturing benignly in acknowledgment of human presence. People who meet these objects feel a desire to nurture them. And with this desire comes the fantasy of reciprocation. People begin to care for these objects and want these objects to care about them.

In the 1960s and 1970s, confiding in Eliza meant ignoring the program's mechanism so that it seemed mind-like and thus worthy of conversation. Today's interfaces are designed to make it easier to ignore the mechanical aspects of the robots and think of them as nascent minds.

In a 2001 study, my colleagues and I tried to make it harder for a panel of thirty children to ignore machine mechanism when relating to the Cog robot at the MIT AI Lab (Turkle, Breazeal, Dasté & Scassellati, 2006). When first presented with the robot, the children (from age 5 to 13) delighted in its presence. They treated it as a creature with needs, interests, and a sense of humor. During the study, one of Cog's arms happened to be broken. The children were concerned, tried to make Cog more comfortable, wanted to sing and dance to cheer it up and in general, were consistently solicitous of its "wounds." Then, for each child there was a session in which Cog was demystified. Each child was shown Cog's inner workings, revealing the robot as "mere mechanism." During these sessions, Brian Scassellati, Cog's principal developer, painstakingly explained how Cog could track eye movement, follow human motion, and imitate behavior. In the course of a half hour, Cog was shown to be a long list of instructions scrolling on a computer screen. Yet, within minutes of this demonstration coming to an end, children were back to relating to Cog as a creature and playmate, vying for its attention. Similarly, when we see the functional magnetic resonance imaging (fMRI) of a person's brain, we are not inhibited in our ability to relate to that person as a meaning-filled other. The children, who so hoped for Cog's affection, were being led by the human habit of making assumptions based on perceptions of behavior. But the robot in which the children were so invested did not care about them. As was the case for Eliza, human desire bridged the distance between the reality of the program and the children's experience of it as a sentient being. Kahn et al. (2007) might classify this bridging as a "psychological benchmark," but to return to the Eliza standard, if it is a benchmark, it is only in the eye of the beholder. To have a relationship, the issue is not only what the human feels but what the robot feels.

Human beings evolved in an environment that did not require them to distinguish between authentic and simulated relationships. Only since the advent of computers have people needed to develop criteria for what we consider to be "authentic" relationships, and for many people the very idea of developing these criteria does not seem essential. For some, the idea of computer companionship seems natural; for others, it is close to obscene. Each group feels its position is self-evident. Philosophical assumptions become embedded in technology; radically different views about the significance of authenticity are at stake. As robots become a part of everyday life, it is important that these differences are clearly articulated and discussed.

At this point, it seems helpful to reformulate a notion of benchmarks that puts authenticity at center stage. In the presence of relational artifacts and, more recently, robotic creatures, people are having feelings that are reminiscent of what we would call trust, caring, empathy, nurturance, and even love *if* they were being called forth by encounters with people. But it seems odd to use these words to describe benchmarks in human-robot encounters because we have traditionally reserved them for relationships in which all parties were capable of feeling them – that is, where all parties were people. With robots, people are acting out "both halves" of complex relationships, projecting the robot's side as well as their own. Of course, we can also behave this way when interacting with people who refuse to engage with us, but people are at least *capable* of reciprocation. We can be disappointed in people, but at least we are disappointed about genuine potential. For robots, the issue is not disappointment, because the idea of reciprocation is pure fantasy.

It belongs to the future to determine whether robots could ultimately "deserve" the emotional responses they are now eliciting. For now, the exploration of human-robot encounters leads us instead to questions about the human purposes of digital companions that are evocative but not relationally authentic.

The recent history of computation and its psychological benchmarks

We already know that the "intimate machines" of the computer culture have shifted how children talk about what is and is not alive (Turkle, 2005 [1984], 1995; Turkle, Breazeal, Dasté, & Scassellati, 2006; Kahn, Friedman, Pérez-Granados, & Freier, 2006). As a psychological benchmark, *aliveness* has presented a moving target. For example, children use different categories to talk about the aliveness of "traditional" objects versus computational games and toys. A traditional wind-up toy was considered "not alive" when children realized that it did not move of its own accord (Piaget, 1960). The criterion for aliveness, autonomous motion, was operationalized in the domain of physics.

In the late 1970s and early 1980s, faced with computational media, there was a shift in how children talked about aliveness. Their language became psychological. By the mid-1980s, children classified computational objects as alive if the objects could *think* on their own. Faced with a computer toy that could play tic-tac-toe, children's determination of aliveness was based on the object's *psychological rather than physical autonomy*. As children attributed psychological autonomy to computational objects, they also split consciousness and life (Turkle, 2005(1984]). This enabled children to grant that computers and robots might have consciousness (and thus be aware both of themselves and of us) without being alive.

This first generation of children who grew up with computational toys and games classified them as "sort of alive" in contrast to the other objects of the playroom (Turkle, 2005 [1984]). Beyond this, children came to classify computational objects as people's "nearest neighbors" because of the objects' intelligence. People were different from these neighbors because of people's emotions. Thus, children's formulation was that computers were "intelligent machines," distinguished from people who had capacities as "emotional machines." I anticipated that later generations of children would find other formulations as they learned more about computers. They might, for example, see through the apparent "intelligence" of the machines by developing a greater understanding of how they were created and operated. As a result, children might be less inclined to give computers philosophical importance. However, in only a few years, both children and adults would quickly learn to overlook the internal workings of computational objects and forge relationships with them based on their behavior (Turkle, 1995, 2005 [1984]).

The lack of interest in the inner workings of computational objects was reinforced by the appearance in mainstream American culture of robotic creatures that presented themselves as having both feelings and needs. By the mid-1990s, people were not alone as "emotional machines." A new generation of objects was designed to approach the boundaries of humanity not so much with its "smarts" as with its sociability (Kiesler & Sproull, 1997; Parise, Kiesler, Sproull, & Waters, 1999; Reeves & Nass, 1999).

The first relational artifacts to enter the American marketplace were virtual creatures known as Tamagotchis that lived on a tiny LCD screen housed in a small plastic egg. The Tamagotchis – a toy fad of the 1997 holiday season – were presented as creatures from another planet that needed human nurturance, both physical and emotional. An individual Tamagotchi would grow from child to healthy adult if it was cleaned when dirty, nursed when sick, amused when bored, and fed when hungry. A Tamagotchi, while it lived, needed constant care. If its needs were not met, it would expire. Children became responsible parents; they enjoyed watching their Tamagotchis thrive and did not want them to die. During school hours, parents were enlisted to care for the Tamagotchis; beeping Tamagotchis became background noise during business meetings. Although primitive as relational artifacts, the Tamagotchis demonstrated a fundamental truth of a new human-machine psychology. When it comes to bonding with computers, *nurturance* is the "killer app" (an application that can eliminate its competitors). When a digital creature entrains people to play parent, they become attached. They feel connection and even empathy.

It is important to distinguish feelings for relational artifacts from those that children have always had for the teddy bears, rag dolls, and other inanimate objects they turn into imaginary friends. According to the psychoanalyst D.W. Winnicott, objects such as teddy bears mediate between the infant's earliest bonds with the mother, who is experienced as inseparable from the self, and other people, who will be experienced as separate beings (Winnicott, 1971). These objects are known as "transitional," and the infant comes to know them as both almost-inseparable parts of the self and as the first "not me" possessions. As the child grows, these transitional objects are left behind, but the effects of early encounters with them are manifest in the highly charged intermediate space between the self and certain objects in later life, objects that become associated with religion, spirituality, the perception of beauty, sexual intimacy, and the sense of connection with nature.

How are today's relational artifacts different from Winnicott's transitional objects? In the past, the power of early objects to play a transitional role was tied to how they enabled a child to project meanings onto them. The doll or teddy bear presents an unchanging and passive presence. Today's relational artifacts are decidedly more active. With them, children's expectations that their dolls want to be hugged, dressed, or lulled to sleep come not from children's projections of fantasy onto inert playthings, but from such things as a digital doll or robot's inconsolable crying or exclamation "Hug me!" or "It's time for me to get dressed for school!" So when relational artifacts prospered under children's care in the late 1990s and early 2000s, children's discourse about the objects' aliveness subtly shifted. Children came to describe relational artifacts in the culture (first Tamagotchis, then Furbies, Aibos, and My Real Babies) as alive or "sort of alive," not because of what these objects could do (physically *or* cognitively) but because of the children's emotional connection to the objects and their fantasies about how the objects might be feeling about them. The focus of the discussion about whether these objects might be alive moved from the psychology of projection to the psychology of engagement, from Rorschach (i.e., projection, as on an inkblot) to relationship, from creature competency to creature connection.

In the early 1980s, I met 13-year-old Deborah, who described the pleasures of projection onto a computational object as putting "a piece of your mind into the computer's mind and coming to see yourself differently" (2005 [1984]). Twenty years later, 11-year-old Fara reacts to a play session with Cog, the humanoid robot at MIT, by saying that she could never get tired of the robot, because "it's not like a toy because you can't teach a toy; it's like something that's part of you, you know, something you love, kind of like another person, like a baby" (Turkle, Breazeal, Dasté, & Scassellati, 2006). The contrast between these two responses reveals a shift from projection onto an object to engagement with a subject.

Engagement with a subject

In the 1980s, debates in artificial intelligence centered on whether machines could be intelligent. These debates were about the objects themselves, what they could and could not do and what they could and could not be (Searle, 1980; Dreyfus, 1986; Winograd, 1986). The questions raised by relational artifacts are not so much about the machines' capabilities but our vulnerabilities – not about whether the objects *really* have emotion or intelligence but about what they evoke in us. For when we are asked to care for an object, when the cared-for object thrives and offers us its "attention" and "concern," we not only experience it as intelligent, but more importantly, we feel a heightened connection to it.

Even very simple relational artifacts can provoke strong feelings. In one study of 30 elementary school age children who were given Furbies to take home (Turkle, 2004), most had bonded emotionally with their Furby and were convinced that they had taught the creature to speak English. (Each Furby arrives "speaking" only Furbish, the language of its "home planet" and over time "learns" to speak English.) Children became so attached to their particular Furby that when the robots began to break, most refused to accept a replacement. Rather, they wanted their own Furby "cured." The Furbies had given the children the feeling of being successful caretakers, successful parents, and they were not about to "turn in" their sick babies.

The children had also developed a way of talking about their robots' "aliveness" that revealed how invested the children had become in the robots' well being. There was a significant integration of the discourses of aliveness and attachment. Ron, six, asks, "Is the Furby alive? Well, something this smart should have arms... it might want to pick up something or to hug roe." When Katherine, five, considers Furby's aliveness, she, too, speaks of her love for her Furby and her confidence that it loves her back: "It likes to sleep with me." Jen, nine, admits how much she likes to take care of her Furby, how comforting it is to talk to it (Turkle, 2004). These children are learning to have expectations of emotional attachments to robots in the same way that we have expectations about our emotional attachments to people. In the process, the very meaning of the word *emotional* is changing. Children talk about an "animal kind of alive and a Furby kind of alive." Will they also talk about a "people kind of love" and a "robot kind of love?"

In another study, 60 children from age 5 to 13 were introduced to Kismet and Cog (Turkle, Breazeal, Dasté, & Scassellati, 2006). During these first encounters, children hastened to put themselves in the role of the robots' teachers, delighting in any movement (for Cog), vocalization or facial expression (for Kismet) as a sign of robot approval. When the robots showed imitative behavior they were rewarded with hugs and kisses. One child made day treats for Kismet. Another told Kismet, "I'm going to take care of you and protect you against all evil." Another decided to teach the robots sign language, because they clearly had trouble with spoken English; the children began with the signs for "house," "eat," and "I love you."

In a study of robots and the elderly in Massachusetts nursing homes, emotions ran similarly high (Turkle, Taggart, et al, 2006). Jonathan, 74, responds to My Real Baby, a robot baby doll he keeps in his room, by wishing it were a bit smarter, because he would prefer to talk to a robot about his problems than to a person. "The robot wouldn't criticize me," he says. Andy, also 74, says that his My Real Baby, which responds to caretaking by developing different states of "mind," resembles his ex-wife Rose: "something in the eyes." He likes chatting with the robot about events of the day. "When I wake up in the morning and see her face [the robots) over there, it makes me feel so nice, like somebody is watching over me."

In Philip K. Dick's (1968) classic story, *Do Androids Dream of Electric Sheep* (a novel that most people know through its film adaptation *Blade Runner*), androids act like people, developing emotional connections with each other and the desire to connect with humans. *Blade Runner's* hero, Deckard, makes his living by distinguishing machines from human beings based on their reactions to a version of the Turing Test for distinguishing computers from people, the fictional Voight-Kampff test. What is the difference, asks the film, between a real human and an almost-identical object? Deckard, as the film progresses, falls in love with the near-perfect simulation, the android Rachael. Memories of a human childhood and the knowledge that her death is certain make her seem deeply human. By the end of the film, we are left to wonder whether Deckard himself may also be an android who is unaware of his status. Unable to resolve this question, viewers are left cheering for Deckard and Rachael as they escape to whatever time they have remaining, in other words, to the human condition. The film leaves us to wonder whether, by the time we face the reality of computational devices that are indistinguishable from people, and thus able to pass our own Turing test, we will no longer care about the test. By then, people will love their machines and be more concerned about their machines' happiness than their test scores.

This conviction is the theme of a short story by Brian Aldiss (2001), "Supertoys Last All Summer Long," that was made into the Steven Spielberg film *AI: Artificial Intelligence*. In *AI*, scientists build a humanoid robot, David, that is programmed to love; David expresses his love to Monica, the woman who has adopted him. Our current experience with relational artifacts suggests that the pressing issue raised by the film is not the potential reality of a robot that "loves," but the feelings of the adoptive mother, whose response to the machine that asks for nurturance is a complex mixture of attachment and confusion. Cynthia Breazeal's experience at the MIT AI Lab offers an example of how such relationships might play out in the near term. Breazeal led the design team for Kismet, the robotic head designed to interact with people as a two-year-old might. She was Kismet's chief programmer, tutor, and companion. Breazeal developed what might be called a maternal connection with Kismet; when she graduated from

MIT and left the AI Lab where she had completed her doctoral research, the tradition of academic property rights demanded that Kismet remain in the laboratory that had paid for its development. Breazeal described a sharp sense of loss. Building a new Kismet would not be the same.

Breazeal worked with me on the "first encounters" study of children interacting with Kismet and Cog during the summer of 2001, the last time she would have access to Kismet. It is not surprising that separation from Kismet was not easy for Breazeal, but more striking was how hard it was for those around Kismet to imagine the robot without her. One 10-year-old who overheard a conversation among graduate students about how Kismet would remain behind in the AI Lab objected, "But Cynthia is Kismet's mother."

It would be facile to compare Breazeal's situation to that of Monica, the mother in Spielberg's *AI*, but Breazeal is, in fact, one of the first adults to have the key human experience portrayed in that film, sadness caused by separation from a robot to which one has formed an attachment based on nurturance. What is at issue is the emotional effect of Breazeal's experience as a "caregiver." In a very limited sense, Breazeal "brought up" Kismet. But even this very limited experience provoked strong emotions. Being asked to nurture a machine *constructs us* as its parents. Although the machine may only have simulated emotion, the feelings it evokes are real. Successive generations of robots may well be enhanced with the specific goal of engaging people in affective relationships by asking for their nurturance. The feelings they elicit will reflect human vulnerabilities more than machine capabilities (Turkle, 2003).

Imitation beguiles

In the case of the Eliza program, imitation beguiled users. Eliza's ability to mirror and manipulate what it was told was compelling, even if primitive. Today, designers of relational artifacts are putting this lesson into practice by developing robots that appear to empathize with people by mimicking their behavior, mirroring their moods (Shibata, 2004). But again, as one of Kahn et al.'s (2007) proposed benchmarks, imitation is less psychologically important as a measure of machine ability than of human susceptibility to this design strategy.

Psychoanalytic self psychology helps us think about the human effects of this kind of mimicry. Heiriz Kohut describes how some people may shore up their fragile sense of self by turning another person into a "self object" (Ornstein, 1978). In this role, the other is experienced as part of the self, and as such must be attuned to the fragile individual's inner state. Disappointments inevitably follow. Someday, if relational artifacts can give the impression of aliveness and not disappoint, they may have a "comparative advantage" over people as self objects and open up new possibilities for narcissistic experience. For some, predictable relational artifacts are a welcome substitute for the always-resistant human material. What are the implications of such substitutions? Do we want to shore up people's narcissistic possibilities?

Over 25 years ago, the Japanese government projected that there would not be enough young people to take care of their older population. They decided that instead of having foreigners take care of their elderly, they would build robots. Now, some of these robots are being aggressively marketed in Japan, some are in development, and others are poised for introduction in American settings.

US studies of the Japanese relational robot Paro have shown that in an elder-care setting, administrators, nurses, and aides are sympathetic toward having the robot around (Turkle, Taggart, et al., 2006). It gives the seniors something to talk about as well as something new to talk to. Paro is a seal-like creature, advertised as the first "therapeutic robot" for its apparently positive effects on the ill, the elderly, and the emotionally troubled (Shibata, 2004). The robot is sensitive to touch, can make eye contact by sensing the direction of a voice, and has states of "mind" that are affected by how it is treated. For example, it can sense if it is being stroked gently or aggressively. The families of seniors also respond warmly to the robot. It is not surprising that many find it easier to leave elderly parents playing with a robot than staring at a wall or television set.

In a nursing home study on robots and the elderly, Ruth, 72, is comforted by the robot Paro after her son has broken off contact with her (Turkle, Taggart, et al., 2006). Ruth, depressed about her son's abandonment, comes to regard the robot as being equally depressed. She turns to Paro, strokes him, and says, "Yes, you're sad, aren't you. Its tough out there. Yes, it's hard." Ruth strokes the robot once again, attempting to comfort it, and in so doing, comforts herself.

This transaction brings us back to many of the questions about authenticity posed by Eliza. If a person *feels* understood by an object lacking sentience, whether that object be an imitative computer program or a robot that makes eye contact and responds to touch, can that illusion of understanding be therapeutic? What is the status – therapeutic, moral, and relational – of the simulation of understanding? If a person claims they feel better after interacting with Paro, or prefers interacting with Paro to interacting with a person, what are we to make of this claim? It seems rather a misnomer to call this a "benchmark in interaction." If we use that phrase we must discipline ourselves to keep in mind that Paro understands nothing, senses nothing, and cares nothing for the person with whom it is interacting. The ability of relational artifacts to inspire "the feeling of relationship" is not based on their intelligence, consciousness, or reciprocal pleasure in relating, but on their ability to push our Darwinian buttons, by making eye contact, for example, which causes people to respond *as if they* were in a relationship.

If one carefully restricts Kahn et al.'s (2007) benchmarks to refer to feelings elicited in people, it is possible that such benchmarks as *imitation, mutual relating*, and *empathy* might be operationalized in terms of machine actions that could be coded and measured. In fact, the work reviewed in this paper suggests the addition of the attribution of *aliveness, trust, caring, empathy, nurturance*, and *love* to a list of benchmarks, because people are capable of feeling all these things for a robot and believing a robot feels them in return. But these benchmarks are very different from psychological benchmarks that measure authentic experiences of relationship. What they measure is the human perception of what the machine *would be experiencing* if a person (or perhaps an animal) evidenced the behaviors shown by the machine.

Such carefully chosen language is reminiscent of early definitions of AI. One famous formulation proposed by Marvin Minsky had it that "artificial intelligence is the science of making machines do things that would require intelligence if done by [people]" (Minsky, 1968, p. v). There is a similar point to be made in relation to Kahn et al's (2007) benchmarks. To argue for a benchmark such as Buber's (1970) "I-You" relating, or even to think of adding things such as empathy, trust, caring, and love to a benchmark list, is either to speak *only* in terms of human attribution or to say, "The robot is exhibiting behavior that would be considered caring if performed by a person (or perhaps an animal)."

Over the past 50 years, we have built not only computers but a computer culture. In this culture, language, humor, art, film, literature, toys, games, and television have all played their role. In this culture, the subtlety of Minsky's careful definition of AI dropped out of people's way of talking. With time, it became commonplace to speak of the products of AI as though they had an inner life and inner sense of purpose. As a culture, we seem to have increasingly less concern about how computers operate internally. Ironically, we now term things "transparent" if we know how to make them work rather than if we know how they work. This is an inversion of the traditional meaning of the word transparency, which used to mean something like being able to "open the hood and look inside." People take interactive computing, including interactive robots, "at interface value" (Turkle, 1995, 2005 [1984]). These days, we are not only building robots, but a robot culture. If history is our guide, we risk coming to speak of robots as though they also have an inner life and inner sense of purpose. We risk taking our benchmarks at face value.

In the early days of artificial intelligence, people were much more protective of what they considered to be exclusively human characteristics, expressing feelings that could be characterized in the phrase: "Simulated thinking is thinking, but simulated feeling is not feeling, and simulated love is never love" (Turkle, 2005 [1984]). People accepted the early ambitions of artificial intelligence, but drew a line in the sand. Machines could be cognitive, but no more. Nowadays, we live in a computer culture where there is regular talk of affective computing, sociable machines, and flesh and machine hybrids (Picard, 1997; Breazeal, 2002; Brooks, 2002). Kahn et al's (2007) benchmarks reflect this culture. There has been an erosion of the line in the sand, both in academic life and in the wider culture.

What may provoke a new demarcation of where computers should not go are robots that make people uncomfortable, robots that come *too* close to the human. As robotics researchers create humanlike androids that strike people as uncanny, they strike people as somehow "not right" (MacDorman & Ishiguro, 2006a, 2006b). Current analyses of uncanny robot interactions are concerned with such things as appearance, motion quality, and interactivity. But as android work develops, it may be questions of values and authenticity that turn out to be at the heart of human concerns about these new objects.

Freud wrote of the uncanny as the long familiar seeming strangely unfamiliar, or put another way, the strangely unfamiliar embodying aspects of the long familiar (Freud, 1960 [1919]). In every culture, confrontation with the uncanny provokes new reflection. Relational artifacts are the new uncanny in our computer culture. If our experience with relational artifacts is based on the fiction that they know and care about us, can the attachments that follow be good for us? Or might they be good for us in the "feel good" sense, but bad for us as moral beings? The answers to such questions do not depend on what robots can do today or in the future. These questions ask what *we* will be like, what kind of people *we* are becoming as we develop increasingly intimate relationships with machines.

The purposes of living things

Consider this moment: Over the school break of Thanksgiving 2005, I take my 14-year-old daughter to the Darwin exhibit at the American Museum of Natural History in New York. The exhibit documents Darwin's life and thought and presents the theory of evolution as the central truth that underpins contemporary biology. At the entrance to the exhibit lies a Galapagos turtle, a seminal object in the development of evolutionary theory. The turtle rests in its cage, utterly still. "They could have used a robot," comments my daughter. Utterly unconcerned with the animal's authenticity, she thinks it a shame to bring the turtle all this way to put it in a cage for a performance that draws so little on its "aliveness."

In talking with other parents and children at the exhibit, my question, "Do you care that the turtle is alive?" provokes variety of responses. A 10-year-old girl would prefer a robot turtle, because aliveness comes with aesthetic inconvenience: "Its water looks dirty, gross." More often, the museum's visitors echo my daughter's sentiment that, in this particular situation, actual aliveness is unnecessary. A 12-year-old girl opines, "For what the turtles do, you didn't have to have the live ones." The girl's father is quite upset: "But the point is that they are real. That's the whole point." "If you put in a robot instead of the live turtle, do you think people should be told that the turtle is not alive?" I ask. "Not really," say several children. Apparently, data on "aliveness" can be shared on a "need to know" basis, for a purpose. But what are the purposes of living things?

These children struggle to find any. They are products of a culture in which human contact is routinely replaced by virtual life, computer games, and now relational artifacts.

The Darwin exhibit emphasizes authenticity; on display is the actual magnifying glass that Darwin used, the actual notebooks in which he recorded his observations, and the very notebook in which he wrote the famous sentences that first described his theory of evolution. But, ironically, in the children's reactions to the inert but alive Galapagos turtle, the idea of the "original" is in crisis.

Sorting out our relationships with robots brings us back to the kinds of challenges that Darwin posed to his generation regarding human uniqueness. How will interacting with relational artifacts affect how people think about what, if anything, makes people special? Ancient cultural axioms that govern our concepts about aliveness and emotion are at stake. Robots have already shown the ability to give people the illusion of relationship: Paro convinced an elderly woman that it empathized with her emotional pain; students ignored the fact that Eliza was a parrot-like computer program, choosing instead to accept its artificial concern. Meanwhile, examples of children and the elderly exchanging tenderness with robotic pets bring science fiction and techno-philosophy into everyday life.

Ultimately, the question is not whether children will love their robotic pets more than their animal pets, but rather, what loving will come to mean. Going back to the young woman who was ready to turn in her boyfriend for a "sophisticated Japanese robot," is there a chance that human relationships will just seem too *hard?* There may be some who would argue that the definition of relationships should broaden to accommodate the pleasures afforded by cyber-companionship, however inauthentic. Indeed, people's positive reaction to relational artifacts would suggest that the terms authenticity and inauthenticity are being contested. In the culture of simulation, authenticity is for us what sex was to the Victorians: taboo and fascination, threat and preoccupation.

Perhaps in the distant future, the difference between human beings and robots will seem purely philosophical. A simulation of the quality of Rachael in *Blade Runner* could inspire love on a par with what we feel toward people. In thinking about the meaning of love, however, we need to know not only what the people are feeling but what the robots are feeling. We are easily seduced; we easily forget what the robots are; we easily forget what we have made.

As I was writing this paper, I discussed it with a former colleague, Richard, who had been left severely disabled by an automobile accident. He is now confined to a wheelchair in his home and needs nearly full-time nursing help. Richard was interested in robots being developed to provide practical help and companionship to people in his situation. His reaction to the idea was complex. He began by saying, "Show me a person in my shoes who is looking for a robot, and I'll show you someone who is looking for a person and can't find one," but then he made the best possible case for robotic helpers. He turned the conversation to human cruelty: "Some of the aides and nurses at the rehab center hurt you because they are unskilled and some hurt you because they mean to. I had both. One of them, she pulled me by the hair. One dragged me by my tubes. A robot would never do that," he said. "But you know in the end, that person who dragged me by my tubes had a story. I could find out about it."

For Richard, being with a person, even an unpleasant, sadistic person, made him feel that he was still alive. It signified that his way of being in the world still had a certain dignity, for him the same as authenticity, even if the scope and scale of his activities were radically reduced. This helped sustain him. Although he would not have wanted his life endangered, he preferred the sadist to the robot. Richard's perspective on living is a cautionary word to those who would speak too quickly or simply of purely technical benchmarks for our interactions. What is the value of interactions that contain no understanding of us and that contribute nothing to a shared store of human meaning? These are not questions with easy answers, but questions worth asking and returning to.

Acknowledgments

Research reported in this chapter was funded by an NSF ITR grant "Relational Artifacts" (Turkle 2001) award number SES-0115668, by a grant from the Mitchell Kapor Foundation, and by a grant from the Intel Corporation.

References

Aldiss, B. W. (2001). *Supertoys last all summer long and other stories of future time*. New York: St. Martin.

Breazeal, C, (2002). *Designing sociable robots*. Cambridge, MA: MIT Press.

Brooks, R. A. (2002). *Flesh and machines: How robots will change us*. New York: Pantheon Books.

Buber, M. (1970). *I and thou*. New York: Touchstone.

Dick, P. K. (1968). *Do androids dream of electric sheep?* Garden City, NY: Doubleday.

Dreyfus, H. L. (1986). *Mind over machine: The power of human intuition and expertise in the era of the computer*. New York: Free Press.

Freud, S. (1960 [19191). The uncanny. In J. Strachey (Transl., Ed.), *The standard edition of the complete psychological works of Sigmund Freud* (vol. 17, pp. 219–252). London: The Hogarth Press.

Kahn, P. H., Jr., Friedman, B., Pérez-Granados, D. R., & Freier, N. G. (2006). Robotic pets in the lives of preschool children. *Interaction Studies*, 7(3), 405–436.

Kahn, P. H., Jr., Ishiguro, H., Friedman, B., Kanda, T., Freier, N. G., Severson, R. L., & Miller, J. (2007). What is a human? – Toward psychological benchmarks in the field of human-robot interaction. *Interaction Studies 8:3*.

Kiesler, S. & Sproull, L. (1997). Social responses to "social" computers. In B. Friedman (Ed.), *Human values and the design of technology*. Stanford, CA: CLSI Publications.

MacDorman, K. F. & Ishiguro, H. (2006). The uncanny advantage of using androids in social and cognitive science research. *Interaction Studies*, 7(3), 297–337.

MacDorman, K. F. & Ishiguro, H. (2006). Opening Pandora's uncanny box: Reply to commentaries on "The uncanny advantage of using androids in social and cognitive science research." *Interaction Studies*, 7(3), 361–368.

Ornstein, P. H. (Ed). (1978). *The search for the self: Selected writings of Heinz Kohut (1950–1978)* (vol. 2). New York: International Universities Press.

Parise, S., Kiesler, S., Sproull, L., & Waters. K. (1999). Cooperating with life-like interface agents. *Computers in Human Behavior*. 15(2), 123–142.

Picard, R. (1997). *Affective computing*. Cambridge, MA: MIT Press.

Piaget, J. (1960 [1929]). *The child's conception of the world* (transl. J. & A. Tomlinson), Totowa, N.J.: Littlefield, Adams.

Reeves, B. & Nass, C. (1999). *The media equation: How people treat computers, television, and new media like real people and places*. Cambridge: Cambridge University Press.

Searle, J. (1980). Minds, brains, and programs, *The Behavioral and Brain Sciences*, 3, 417–424.

Shibata, T. (2004). An overview of human interactive robots for psychological enrichment. *Proceedings of the IEEE*, 92(11), 1749–1758.

Turkle, S. (1995). *Life on the screen: Identity in the age of the Internet*. New York: Simon and Schuster.

Turkle, S. (2001). *Relational artifacts*. Proposal to the National Science Foundation SES-01115668.

Turkle, S. (2003). Technology and human vulnerability. *The Harvard Business Review*, September.

Turkle, S. (2004). Whither Psychoanalysis in the Computer Culture? *Psychoanalytic Psychology*, 21(l), 16–30.

Turkle, S. (2005 [1984]). *The second self: Computers and the human spirit*. Cambridge, MA: MIT Press.

Turkle, S. (2006). Diary. *The London Review of Books*, 8(8), April 20.

Turkle, S., Breazeal, C., Dasté, O., & Scassellati, B. (2006). First encounters with Kismet and Cog: Children's relationship with humanoid robots. In P. Messaris & L. Humphreys (Eds.), *Digital media: Transfer in human communication*. New York: Peter Lang.

Turkle, S., Taggart, W., Kidd, C. D. & Dasté, O. (2006). Relational artifacts with children and elders: The complexities of cybercornpanionship. *Connection Science*, 18(4), 347–361.

Turkle, S. (Ed). (2007) *Evocative objects: Things we think with*. Cambridge, MA: MIT Press.

Weizenbaum, J. (1976). *Computer power and human reason: From judgment to calculation*. San Francisco, CA: W. H. Freeman.

Winnicott, D. W. (1971). *Playing and reality*. New York: Basic Books.

Winograd, T. & Flores, F. (1986). *Understanding computers and cognition: A new foundation for design*. Norwood, NJ: Ablex.

Part III

Issues Concerning Machine Ethics

Introduction

SEVERAL OF THE AUTHORS IN THIS PART RAISE DOUBTS ABOUT WHETHER machines are capable of making ethical decisions, which would seem to thwart the entire project of attempting to create ethical machines. Drew McDermott, for instance, in "What Matters to a Machine?" characterizes ethical dilemmas in such a way that it would seem that machines are incapable of experiencing them, thus making them incapable of acting in an ethical manner. He takes as the paradigm of an ethical dilemma a situation of moral temptation in which one knows what the morally correct action *is*, but one's self-interest (or the interest of someone one cares about) inclines one to do something else. He claims that "the idiosyncratic architecture of the human brain is responsible for our ethical dilemmas and our regrets about the decisions we make," and this is virtually impossible to automate. As a result, he thinks it extremely unlikely that we could create machines that are complex enough to act morally or immorally.

Critics will maintain that McDermott has defined "ethical dilemma" in a way that few ethicists would accept. (See S. L. Anderson's article in this part.) Typically, an ethical dilemma is thought of as a situation where several courses of action are possible and one is not sure which of them is correct, rather than a situation where one knows which is the correct action, but one doesn't want to do it. Furthermore, even if *human beings* have a tendency to behave unethically when they know what the right action is, why would we want to automate this weakness of will in a *machine*? Don't we want to create machines that can only behave ethically?

Steve Torrance, in "Machine Ethics and the Idea of a More-Than-Human Moral World," considers the machine ethics project from four different ethical perspectives: anthropocentric (where only human needs and interests have ethical import); infocentric (which focuses on cognitive or informational aspects of the mind that, in principle, can be replicated in AI systems); biocentric (that centers on biological properties, e.g., sentience); and ecocentric (that goes beyond the biocentric in focusing on entire ecosystems). Torrance points out that the last three perspectives have something in common: They all maintain that the subjects of ethical concern should include more than human beings, unlike the anthropocentric perspective.

Torrance maintains that adherents of the four perspectives would view "the ME enterprise, particularly in terms of its moral significance or desirability" in the following ways: Anthropocentrists would, in agreement with McDermott, maintain that AI systems are incapable of being moral agents; they would be concerned with any attempt to shift responsibility from humans, true moral agents, to technological entities that should only be viewed as tools used by humans. Some infocentrists believe that "an artificial agent could approach or even surpass human skills in moral thought and behavior." Torrance raises concerns about whether such agents would be thought to have rights and would compete with human beings or even replace them (see Dietrich's article in Part V), and whether they would mislead humans about their characteristics (see Turkle's article in Part II). Biocentrists maintain that only biological organisms have ethical status and tend to reject "the possibility of artificial agency." The prospect of having robot caretakers concerns them, and they would claim that not being able to experience distress and physical pain themselves would make robots unable to respond in an ethically appropriate manner to humans' (and other biological organisms') distress and pain. Although they are in favor of having restraints on AI technology and support ME work to that extent, they believe that it is important "to avoid treating artificial 'moral agents' as being anything like genuine coparticipants in the human moral enterprise." Ecocentrists "would take even more marked exception to the ME enterprise, particularly in terms of its moral significance or desirability." They are concerned about the environmental crisis, the "dark green" ecocentrists focusing on "all organic creatures, whether sentient or not" and also on "nonliving parts of the landscape." They have "a strong ethical opposition to technological forms of civilization," believing that this has led to the environmental crisis.

Torrance rejects the antitechnology aspect of extreme ecocentrism, maintaining that we are incapable of "returning to a pretechnical existence." Instead, he advocates a version of ecocentrism where we design and use AI technology to "positively move us in the direction of retreat from the abyss of environmental collapse toward which we are apparently hurtling." The extreme form of infocentrism, which looks forward to the "eclipse of humanity," concerns him very much, and he sees "the urgency of work in ME to ensure the emergence of 'friendly AI.'"

What is important about Torrance's viewing the subject of machine ethics through different ethical lenses is that he acknowledges one of the most important issues in ethical theory, one that is often not considered: Who, or what, is to count when considering the effects of our actions and policies? All currently living human beings? Or future ones as well? All intelligent entities (whether human or artificially created)? All biological sentient beings? All organic beings (whether sentient or not)? All organic beings and nonliving parts of the earth? The decision we make about this issue is critical for determining what our ethics should be in a general way and will have an impact on the ethics we attempt to put into machines, and is crucial for our assessment of the machines we produce. As Torrance points out, most of us are stuck in the perspective of taking only human beings into account. It is important that we at least consider other perspectives as well.

Blay Whitby, in "On Computable Morality: An Examination of Machines as Moral Advisors," considers first whether it is possible to create programs for machines to act as ethical advisors to human beings. He then considers whether we *should* be attempting to do so. He begins by pointing out that "general advice-giving systems," such as those that give advice on patient care to doctors and nurses, have already begun "introducing machines as moral advisors by stealth," because value judgments are implicit in the advice they give.

Responding to those who maintain that a machine can't possibly make decisions or offer advice, because they are programmed by *humans* who are simply giving them *their* decisions, Whitby says that "the notion that programmers have given a complete set of instructions that directly determine every possible output of the machine is false." Instead, as with chess-playing programs, "programmers built a set of decision-making procedures" into the machine that enable the machine to determine its own output. Whitby points out that it is possible that a system that uses AI techniques such as case-based reasoning (CBR) to acquire the principles that it uses could come up with "new principles that its designers never considered" as it responds to new cases. (See the Andersons' work, described in Part V, where machine-learning techniques were used by a computer to discover a new ethical principle that was then used to guide a robot's behavior.)

In response to the claim that AI systems can't make judgments and so can't act as moral advisors, Whitby maintains that "AI solved the technical problems of getting systems to deal with areas of judgment at least two decades ago," and this is reflected in medical diagnosis and financial advisor programs. Responding to those who claim that there is an emotional component to making judgments, something lacking in a computer program, Whitby says (in agreement with S. L. Anderson) that in many contexts "we prefer a moral judgment to be free from emotional content." He adds, "Emotion may well be an important component of human judgments, but it is unjustifiably anthropocentric to assume that it must be an important component of *all* judgments."

Whitby considers several arguments for and against the desirability of creating AI systems that give ethical advice to humans. He is especially concerned about responsibility issues. "Real systems frequently embody the prejudices of their designers, and the designers of advice-giving systems should not be able to escape responsibility." He decides that "[a] major benefit of moral advice-giving systems is that it makes these issues more explicit. It is much easier to examine the ethical implications of a system specifically designed to give moral advice than to detach the ethical components of a system designed primarily to advise on patient care, for example."

In his article "When Is a Robot a Moral Agent?" John P. Sullins discusses the moral status of robots and how a decision on this issue should impact the way they are designed and used. He distinguishes between two types of robots: telerobots, which are remotely controlled by humans, and autonomous robots, which are "capable of making at least some of the major decisions about their actions using their own programming." The "robots as tools" model, where ascriptions of moral responsibility lie solely with the designer and user, is applicable to telerobots, according to Sullins, but not to autonomous robots. He makes the claim that "[t]he programmers of [autonomous robots] are somewhat responsible for the actions of such machines, but not entirely so." He wants not only to include other persons in the chain of responsibility – such as the builders, marketers, and users of the robots – but the robots themselves.

Contrary to those who maintain that only persons can be moral agents, Sullins argues that "personhood is not required for moral agency." Sullins lists three requirements for moral agency: (1) The entity must be effectively *autonomous*; it must not be "under the direct control of any other agent or user . . . in achieving its goals and tasks." (2) Its morally harmful or beneficial actions must be *intentional* in the sense that they can be viewed as "seemingly deliberate and calculated." (3) Its behavior can only be made sense of by ascribing to it a "belief" that is has a *responsibility* "to some other moral agent(s)"; "it fulfills some social role that carries with it some assumed responsibilities."

Although Sullins does not believe that robots that fully satisfy these requirements currently exist, "we have to be very careful that we pay attention to how these machines are evolving and grant [the status of moral equals] the moment it is deserved." Long before that time, Sullins maintains, "complex robot agents will be partially capable of making autonomous moral decisions," and we need to be very careful about how they are developed and used. Finally, Sullins envisions the logical possibility, "though not probable in the near term, that robotic moral agents may be more autonomous, have clearer intentions, and a more nuanced sense of responsibility than most human agents."

Sullins believes that an interesting analogy can be drawn between autonomous robots that are programmed to care for humans and guide dogs that have been trained to assist the visually impaired. Because we feel that it is appropriate to praise a guide dog for good behavior, even though it has been trained to behave in that manner, we should be able to praise an autonomous robot that "intentionally" behaves in an ethically acceptable manner toward its charge, despite its having been programmed. Anthropocentrists will have trouble accepting either claim of moral responsibility, whereas biocentrists will reject the latter one, claiming that there is a huge difference between a living, biological dog and a robot. In response to the anthropocentrists who claim that only human beings can act autonomously and intentionally and feel a sense of responsibility toward others, Sullins maintains that we may be glorifying our own abilities. One could argue that a lot of factors, including heredity and environment, have determined our own behavior, which is not unlike the programming of a robot. Ultimately, consideration of Sullins's position will lead us to deep philosophical discussions of autonomy, intentionality, and moral responsibility.

Susan Leigh Anderson, in "Philosophical Concerns with Machine Ethics," considers seven challenges to the machine ethics project from a philosophical perspective: (1) Ethics is not the sort of thing that can be computed. (2) Machine ethics is incompatible with the virtue-based approach to ethics. (3) Machines cannot behave ethically because they lack free will, intentionality, consciousness, and emotions. (4) Ethical relativists maintain that there isn't a single correct action in ethical dilemmas to be programmed into machines. (5) A machine may start out behaving ethically but then morph into behaving unethically, favoring its own interests. (6) Machines can't behave ethically because they can't behave in a self-interested manner, and so never face true ethical dilemmas. (7) We may not be able to anticipate every ethical dilemma a machine might face, so its training is likely to be incomplete, thereby allowing the machine to behave unethically in some situations.

Anderson responds to these challenges as follows: (1) The theory of Act Utilitarianism demonstrates that ethics is, in principle, computable. She maintains that a more satisfactory theory is the prima facie duty approach that also includes deontological duties missing in Act Utilitarianism, and the decision principle(s) needed to supplement this approach can be discovered by a machine. (2) Because we are only concerned with the *actions* of machines, it is appropriate to adopt the action-based approach to ethics. (3) Free will, intentionality, and consciousness may be essential to hold a machine *responsible* for its actions, but we only care that the machine performs morally correct actions and can justify them if asked. It may not be essential that machines have emotions themselves in order to be able to take into account the suffering of others. Furthermore, humans often get so carried away by their emotions that they behave in an unethical fashion, so we might prefer that machines not have emotions. (4) In many ethical dilemmas there is agreement among ethicists as to the correct action, disproving ethical relativism; and we should only permit machines to function in those areas where there is agreement as to what is acceptable behavior. "The implementation of ethics can't be more complete than is accepted ethical theory." (5) *Humans* may have evolved, as biological entities in competition with others, into beings that tend to favor their own interests; but it seems possible that we can create machines that lack this predisposition. (6) "The paradigm of an ethical dilemma is not a situation in which one *knows* what the morally correct action is but finds it difficult to *do*, but rather is one in which it is not obvious what the morally correct action is. It needs to be determined, ideally through using an established moral principle or principles." Also, why would we want to re-create weakness of will in a machine, rather than ensure that it can only behave ethically? (7) If the machine has been trained to follow *general ethical principles*, it should be able to apply them to even unanticipated situations. Further, "there should be a way to update the ethical training a machine receives."

The most serious of the concerns that Anderson considers are probably (1) and (4) – whether ethics is the sort of thing that can be computed and whether there is a single standard of right and wrong to be programmed into a machine. Considering the latter one, even if one disagrees with Anderson's response, one could maintain that different ethical beliefs could be programmed into machines functioning in different societies, so ethical relativists could still work on machine ethics. Time will tell whether the first concern is a devastating one by revealing whether anyone succeeds in implementing a plausible version of ethics in a machine or not. One could argue, as Anderson seems to hint at in her article in Part V, that if we can't figure out how to make ethics precise enough to program into a machine, then this reflects badly on our ethics. We need to do more work on understanding ethics, and the machine ethics project provides a good opportunity for doing so.

In "Computer Systems: Moral Entities but not Moral Agents," Deborah G. Johnson acknowledges the moral importance of computer systems but argues that they should not be viewed as independent, autonomous moral agents, because "they have meaning and significance only in relation to human beings." In defending the first claim, Johnson says, "To suppose that morality applies only to the human beings who use computer systems is a mistake." Computer systems, she maintains, "have efficacy; they produce effects in the world, powerful effects on moral patients [recipients of moral action]." As such, "they are closer to moral agents than is generally recognized."

According to Johnson, computer behavior satisfies four of five criteria required to be a moral agent: "[W]hen computers behave, there is an outward, embodied event; an internal state is the cause of the outward event; the embodied event can have an outward effect; and the effect can be on a moral patient." The one criterion to be a moral agent that computers do not, and can never, satisfy in her view is that the internal state that causes the outward event must be mental, in particular, an *intending to act*, which arises from the agent's *freedom*: "[F]reedom is what makes morality possible."

Arguing for a middle ground between moral agents and natural objects in artifacts like computers, Johnson says that intentionality (not present in natural objects) is built into computer behavior (which is not the same thing as an intending to act, which is required to be a moral agent), because they are "poised to behave in certain ways in response to input." Once created, a computer system can operate without the assistance of the person who designed it. Thus, there is "a triad of intentionality at work, the intentionality of the system designer, the intentionality of the system, and the intentionality of the user. Any one of the components of this triad can be the focal point for moral analysis."

Critics of Johnson's position will undoubtedly question her simply assuming that we, presumably her model of moral agents, have a type of free will necessary for moral responsibility that computer systems cannot. Again, this leads to another deep philosophical discussion. Defenders of a contra-causal type of free will in human beings face the objection that we cannot be held morally responsible for actions that are not causally connected to our natures' being what they are. Defenders of a type of free will that is compatible with determinism, who also hold the view that mental states are reducible to physical ones, cannot see why the type of free will necessary for moral responsibility cannot be instantiated in a machine.

Attempting to avoid discussions of whether artificial agents have free will, emotions, and other mental states, Luciano Floridi, in "On the Morality of Artificial Agents," develops a concept of "moral agenthood" that doesn't depend on having these characteristics. Using the distinction between moral *agents* (sources of moral action) and moral *patients* (receivers of moral action), Floridi characterizes the "standard" view of their relationship as one in which the classes are identical, whereas the "nonstandard" view holds that all moral agents are also moral patients, but not vice versa. The nonstandard view has permitted a focus on an ever-enlarging class of moral patients, including animals and the environment, as worthy of ethical concern; and now Floridi would like to see a change in the view of moral agency as well, which has remained "human-based." Because artificial agents' actions can cause moral harm (and good), we need to revise the notion of "moral agent" to allow them to be included.

In Floridi's view, agenthood "depends on a level of abstraction," where the agent's behavior demonstrates "*interactivity* (response to stimulus by change of state), *autonomy* (ability to change state without stimulus), and *adaptability* (ability to change the 'transition rules' by which state is changed) at a given level of abstraction." A *moral* agent is an agent that is capable of causing good or harm to someone (a moral patient). Neither intentionality nor free will is essential to moral agenthood, he argues. Floridi believes that an advantage to his view is that moral agency can be ascribed to artificial agents (and corporations), which, "though neither cognitively intelligent nor morally responsible, can be fully *accountable* sources of moral action."

Some critics will say that, early on, Floridi too quickly dispenses with the correct view of the relationship between moral agents and moral patients, in which some, but not all, agents are moral patients (Venn Diagram 4 in Figure 1). These critics will claim that artificial agents that cause harm to human beings, and perhaps other entities as well, are agents; but they cannot be moral patients, because of, for instance, their lack of sentience that renders them incapable of experiencing suffering or enjoyment, which is necessary in order to be a moral patient. Such critics may still welcome Floridi's criteria for moral agency but want to maintain that additional characteristics – like emotionality – are necessary to be a moral patient as well.

Others may question Floridi's "decoupling" of the terms "moral responsibility" and "moral accountability," where intentionality and free will are necessary for the first, but not the second. Floridi does seem to be using "moral accountability" in a nontraditional sense, because he divorces it from any "psychological" characteristics; but this does not affect his central thesis that artificial agents can be considered agents that can cause moral harm or good without being morally responsible for their harmful or good behavior. Floridi recommends that "perhaps it is time to consider agencies for the policing of AAs," because it is often difficult to find the human(s) who are morally responsible.

David J. Calverley considers the possibility of our ever granting legal rights to intelligent nonbiological machines in "Legal Rights for Machines: Some Fundamental Concepts." Drawing on his legal background, Calverley first reviews "two major historic themes that have, for the last few hundred years, dominated the debate about what 'law' means." The first is the "natural law" perspective, where "law is inextricably linked with [a natural theory of] morality." The second, "legal positivism," maintains that "law in a society is based on social convention." Common to both is the idea that "law is a normative system by which humans govern their conduct," and an assumption that what allows us to be held responsible for our actions is that "humans are capable of making determinations about their actions based on reason."

Calverley points out that John Locke distinguished between "person" and "human being." The notion of *persons* as entities that have rights is reflected in many recent philosophical discussions; and this distinction would seem to permit entities that function as we do to be considered persons with rights, even if they are not biologically human. "As suggested by Solum, judges applying the law may be reasonably inclined to accept an argument that the functional similarity between a nonbiological machine and a human is enough to allow the extension of rights to the android." Yet also important in the law is the distinction between persons and property. "To the extent that a nonbiological machine is 'only property,' there is little reason to consider ascribing it full legal rights," says Calverley. "It is only if we begin to ascribe humanlike characteristics and motives to [a] machine" that the law might consider them to be persons with rights rather than property.

U.S. law, Calverley notes, has treated corporations as persons, allowing them to own property, but there are two historical views as to why: the "Fiction Theory of corporate personality" and the view that "corporations are nothing more than a grouping of individual persons." Peter A. French has argued that a corporation is more than either of these and "should be treated as a moral person, in part because it can act intentionally." Using this criterion, Calverley believes that "[f]unctional intentionality is probably enough ... to convince people that a nonbiological system is acting intentionally." Calverley makes a similar point about acting autonomously, which is also thought to be a prerequisite for being held responsible for one's actions. "Functional results are probably enough." Given the precedent set in allowing corporations to be considered persons by extending criteria such as intentionality and autonomy to include their behavior, Calverley sees no reason why we should categorically rule out nonbiological entities from being granted rights, viewing such an entity as "a legal person with independent existence separate and apart from its origins as property."

Undoubtedly, before intelligent, nonbiological entities such as robots are ever accorded the status of "persons" with *legal* rights, they would have to be thought of first as having *moral* rights. This has generally been the case in our enlarging the category of beings/entities that *count*. It is also interesting, as Calverley points out, that many beings/entities that are now considered to have moral and legal rights we once viewed as the property of others. Wives were once the property of their husbands, and African Americans were once the property of white slave owners.

Of course, if robots are ever granted rights, this would greatly affect the field of machine ethics. Robots would have duties to themselves to balance against the duties they would have to human beings; and, because of their rights, we would have to treat them differently from the way we now treat their more primitive ancestors. Bringing such entities into the world would have even more serious consequences than those that concern current machine ethics researchers.

6

What Matters to a Machine?

Drew McDermott

Why Is Machine Ethics Interesting?

THERE HAS RECENTLY BEEN A FLURRY OF ACTIVITY IN THE AREA OF "machine ethics" [38, 4, 3, 5, 58]. My purpose in this article is to argue that ethical behavior is an extremely difficult area to automate, both because it requires "solving all of AI" and because even that might not be sufficient.

Why is machine ethics interesting? Why do people think we ought to study it *now*? If we're not careful, the reason might come down to the intrinsic fascination of the phrase "machine ethics." The title of one recent review of the field is *Moral Machines*. One's first reaction is that moral machines are to be contrasted with ... what? Amoral machines? Immoral machines? What would make a machine ethical or unethical? Any cognitive scientist would love to know the answer to these questions.

However, it turns out that the field of machine ethics has little to say about them. So far, papers in this area can usefully be classified as focusing on one, maybe two, of the following topics:

1. *Altruism*: The use of game-theoretic simulations to explore the rationality or evolution of altruism [9, 12].
2. *Constraint*: How computers can be used unethically, and how to program them so that it is provable that they do not do something unethical [28, 29], such as violate someone's privacy.
3. *Reasoning*: The implementation of theories of ethical reasoning [38, 4] for its own sake, or to help build artificial ethical advisors.
4. *Behavior*: Development of "ethical operating systems" that would keep robots or other intelligent agents from doing immoral things [6].[1]

---

[1] Asimov's famous "laws" of robotics [8] can be construed as legal requirements on a robot's OS that it prevent the robot from harming human beings, disobeying orders, etc. Asimov was amazingly confused about this, and often seemed to declare that these rules were inviolable in some mystical way that almost implied they were discovered laws of nature rather than everyday legal restrictions. At least, that's the only sense I can make of them.

5. *Decision*: Creation of intelligent agents that know what ethical decisions are
   and perhaps even make them.

I will have nothing to say about the first topic, and not much about the second,
except in passing. The other three build upon one another. It's hard to see how
you could have software that constrained what a robot could do along ethical
dimensions (*Behavior*) without the software being able to reason about ethical
issues (*Reasoning*).

The difference between an agent programmed not to violate ethical constraints
(*Constraint*) and one programmed to follow ethical precepts (*Behavior*) may not
seem sharp. The key difference is whether the investigation of relevant facts and
deliberation about them is done in advance by programmers or by the system
itself at run time. That's why the *Reasoning* layer is sandwiched in between. Yet
once we introduce reasoning into the equation, we have changed the problem
into getting an *intelligent* system to behave morally, which may be quite different
from preventing an ordinary computer (i.e., the kind we have today) from being
used to violate a law or ethical principle – the *Constraint* scenario.[2]

One might argue that, once you have produced an automated ethical-reasoning
system, all that is left in order to produce an ethical-decision maker is to connect the inputs of the reasoner to sensors and the outputs to effectors capable
of taking action in the real world, thus making it an *agent*. (One might visualize
robotic sensors and effectors here, but the sensors and effectors might simply be
an Internet connection that allows them to read databases, interview people, and
make offers on its owner's behalf.)

However, a machine could reason and behave ethically without *knowing* it was
being ethical. It might *use the word* "ethical" to describe what it was doing, but
that would just be, say, to clarify lists of reasons for action. It wouldn't treat ethical decisions any differently than other kinds of decisions. For a machine to know
what an ethical decision was, it would have to find itself in situations where it was
torn between doing the right thing and choosing an action in its self-interest or in
the interest of someone it cared about. Hence reaching the *Decision* level requires
making a *much* more complex agent. It is at this level that one might first find
immoral machines, and hence moral ones.

The rest of the paper is organized as follows: The following section outlines the
nature of ethical reasoning and argues that it is very hard to automate. Then I tell
a fable about an ethical agent in order to point out what would be involved in getting it into a moral dilemma. After that comes an argument that the problem with
developing ethical agents is *not* that they have no interests that moral principles

---

[2] The sense of "prevent" here is flexible, and saying exactly what it means from one case to another
is similar to answering the question whether a formal specification of a program is correct and
complete. You first prove that, if V is the formal definition of "ethical violation" in the case at
hand, then the program never causes V to become true. Then the argument shifts to whether V
captures all the ways a computer could cross the line into counter-ethical behavior.

could conflict with. The section after that makes a claim about what the problem really is: that the idiosyncratic architecture of the human brain is responsible for our ethical dilemmas and our regrets about the decisions we make. Robots would probably not have an architecture with this "feature." Finally, the last section draws pessimistic conclusions from all this about the prospects for machine ethics.

The Similarity of Ethical Reasoning to Reasoning in General

In thinking about the *Reasoning* problem, it is easy to get distracted by the historical conflict among fundamentally different theories of ethics, such as Kant's appeal to austere moral laws versus Mill's reduction of moral decisions to computation of net changes in pleasure to people affected by a decision. Yet important as these foundational issues might be in principle, they have little to do with the inferential processes that an ethical-reasoning system actually has to carry out.

All ethical reasoning consists of some mixture of *law application*, *constraint application*, *reasoning by analogy*, *planning*, and *optimization*. Applying a moral law often involves deciding whether a situation is similar enough to the circumstances the law "envisages" for it to be applicable, or for a departure from the action it enjoins to be justifiable or insignificant. Here, among too many other places to mention, is where analogical reasoning comes in [24, 31, 20].

By "constraint application" I have in mind the sort of reasoning that arises in connection with rights and obligations. If everyone has a right to life, then everyone's behavior must satisfy the constraint that they not deprive someone else of their life.

By "planning" I mean projecting the future in order to choose a course of action [21].

By "optimization" I have in mind the calculations prescribed by utilitarianism [54], which (in its simplest form) tells us to act so as to maximize the utility of the greatest number of fellow moral agents (which I'll abbreviate as *social utility* in what follows).

One might suppose that utilitarians (nowadays often called *consequentialists*) could dispense with all but the last sort of reasoning, but that is not true for two reasons:

1. In practice consequentialists have to grant that some rights and laws are necessary, even if in principle they believe the rights and laws can be justified purely in terms of utilities. Those who pursue this idea systematically are called *rule consequentialists* [25]. For them, it is an overall system of rules that is judged by the consequences of adopting it, and not, except in extraordinary cases, an individual action [22].
2. The phrase "maximize the utility of the greatest number" implies that one should compute the utility of those affected by a decision. Yet this is quite impossible, because no one can predict all the ramifications of a choice

(or know if the world would have been better off, all things considered, if one had chosen a different alternative). There are intuitions about where we stop exploring ramifications, but these are never made explicit.

It would be a great understatement to say that there is disagreement about how law-plus-constraint application, analogical reasoning, planning, and optimization are to be combined. For instance, some might argue that constraint application can be reduced to law application (or vice versa), so we need only one of them. Strict utilitarians would argue that we need neither. However, none of this matters in the present context, because what I want to argue is that the kinds of reasoning involved are not intrinsically ethical; they arise in other contexts.

This is most obvious for optimization and planning. There are great practical difficulties in predicting the consequences of an action, and hence in deciding which action maximizes social utility. Yet exactly the same difficulties arise in decision theory generally, even if the decisions have nothing to do with ethics, but are, for instance, about where to drill for oil in order to maximize the probability of finding it and minimize the cost.[3] A standard procedure in decision theory is to map out the possible effects of actions as a tree whose leaves can be given utilities (but usually not *social* utilities). So if you assign a utility to having money, then leaf nodes get more utility the more money is left over at that point, *ceteris paribus*. However, you might argue that money is only a means toward ends, and that for a more accurate estimate one should keep building the tree to trace out what the "real" expected utility after the pretended leaf might be. Of course, this analysis cannot be carried out to any degree of precision, because the complexity and uncertainty of the world will make it hopelessly impracticable. This was called the *small world/grand world* problem by Savage [50], who argued that one could always find a "small world" to use as a model of the real "grand world" [32]. Of course, Savage was envisaging a *person* finding a small world; the problem of getting a *machine* to do it is, so far, completely unexplored.

My point is that utilitarian optimization oriented toward social utility suffers from the same problem as decision theory in general *but no other distinctive problem*. Anderson and Anderson [5] point out that "a machine might very well have an advantage in following the theory of ... utilitarianism.... [A] human being might make a mistake, whereas such an error by a machine would be less likely" (p. 18). It might be true that a machine would be less likely to make an error in arithmetic, but there are plenty of other mistakes to be made, such as omitting a class of people affected by a decision because you overlooked a simple method of estimating its impact on them. Getting this right has nothing to do with ethics.

Similar observations can be made about constraint and law application, but there is the additional issue of conflict among the constraints or laws. If a doctor

---

[3] One might argue that this decision, and all others, have ethical consequences, but if that were true it would not affect the argument. Besides, there is at least anecdotal evidence that many users of decision theory often ignore their actions' ethical consequences.

believes that a fetus has a right to live (a constraint preventing taking an action that would destroy the fetus) and that its mother's health should be not be threatened (an ethical law, or perhaps another constraint), then there are obviously circumstances where the doctor's principles clash with each other. Yet it is easy to construct similar examples that have nothing to do with ethics. If a spacecraft is to satisfy the constraint that its camera not point to within 20 degrees of the sun (for fear of damaging it) and that it take pictures of all objects with unusual radio signatures, then there might well be situations where the latter law would trump the constraint (e.g., a radio signature consisting of Peano's axioms in Morse code from a source 19 degrees from the sun). In a case like this we must find some other rules or constraints to lend weight to one side of the balance or the other; or we might fall back on an underlying utility function, thus replacing the original reasoning problem with an optimization problem.

In that last sentence I said "we" deliberately, because in the case of the spacecraft there really is a "we": the human team making the ultimate decisions about what the spacecraft is to do. This brings me back to the difference between *Reasoning* and *Behavior* and to the second argument I want to make – that ethical-decision making *is* different from other kinds. I'll start with Moor's distinction [38] between *implicit ethical agents* and *explicit ethical reasoners*. The former make decisions that have ethical consequences but don't reason about those consequences *as* ethical. An example is a program that plans bombing campaigns, whose targeting decisions affect civilian casualties and the safety of the bomber pilots, but which does not realize that these might be morally significant.

An *explicit ethical reasoner* does represent the ethical principles it is using. It is easy to imagine examples. For instance, proper disbursement of funds from a university or other endowment often requires balancing the intentions of donors with the needs of various groups at the university or its surrounding population. The Nobel Peace Prize was founded by Alfred Nobel to recognize government officials who succeeded in reducing the size of a standing army or people outside of government who created or sustained disarmament conferences [1]. However, it is now routinely awarded to people who do things that help a lot of people or who simply warn of ecological catastrophes. The rationale for changing the criteria is that if Nobel were still alive he would realize that if his original criteria were followed rigidly, the prize would seldom be awarded, and hence have little impact under the changed conditions that exist today. An explicit ethical program might be able to justify this change based on various general ethical postulates.

More prosaically, Anderson and Anderson [5] have worked on programs for a hypothetical robot caregiver that might decide whether to allow a patient to skip a medication. The program balances explicitly represented prima facie obligations using learned rules for resolving conflicts among the obligations. This might seem easier than the Nobel Foundation's reasoning, but an actual robot would have to work its way from visual and other inputs to the correct behavior. Anderson and Anderson bypass these difficulties by just telling the system all the relevant facts, such as how competent the patient is (and, apparently, not many other facts). This might make sense for a pilot study of the problem, but there is little value in an ethical advisor unless it can investigate the situation for itself; at the very least, it needs to be able to ask questions that tease out the relevant considerations.

This is an important aspect of the *Behavior* level of machine ethics outlined in the first section of this paper. Arkin [6] has urged that military robots be constrained to follow the "rules of engagement" set by policy makers to avoid violating international agreements and the laws of war. It would be especially good if robots could try to minimize civilian casualties. However, the intent to follow such constraints is futile if the robots lack the capacity to investigate the facts on the ground before proceeding. If all they do is ask their masters whether civilians will be harmed by their actions, they will be only as ethical as their masters' latest prevarications.

When you add up all the competences – analogical reasoning, planning and plan execution, differentiating among precedents, using natural language, perception, relevant-information search – required to solve ethical reasoning problems, it seems clear that this class of problems is "AI-complete," a semitechnical term, originally tongue-in-cheek, whose meaning is analogous to terms such as "NP-complete." A problem is AI-complete if solving it would require developing enough computational intelligence to solve *any* AI problem. A consequence of being in this class is that progress in ethical reasoning is likely to be slow and dependent on the progress of research in more fundamental areas such as analogy and natural language.

One advantage we gain from thinking about a problem as difficult as ethical reasoning is that in imagining futuristic scenarios in which ethical reasoning systems exist we can imagine that software has basically any humanlike property we like. That is, we can imagine that AI has succeeded as well as Turing might have dreamed.

Fable

If we grant that all the technical AI problems discussed in the previous section could be overcome, it might seem that there would be nothing left to do. Yet ethical reasoners as envisaged so far are different from people in that they wouldn't see any difference between, say, optimizing the ethical consequences of a policy and optimizing the monetary consequences of the water-to-meat ratio in the recipe used by a hot dog factory. Researchers in the field grant the point, using the phrase *full ethical agent* [38, 5] to label what is missing.

Moor [38] says:

A full ethical agent can make explicit ethical judgments and generally is competent to reasonably justify them. An average adult human is a full ethical agent. We typically regard humans as having consciousness, intentionality, and free will. (p. 20)

Anderson and Anderson [5] add:

[A] concern with the machine ethics project is whether machines are the type of entities that can behave ethically. It is commonly thought that an entity must be capable of acting intentionally, which requires that it be conscious, and that it have free will, in order to be a moral agent. Many would ... add that sentience or emotionality is important, since only a being that has feelings would be capable of appreciating the feelings of others. (p. 19)

Somehow both of these notions overshoot the mark. All we require to achieve the *Decision* layer of machine ethics discussed at the beginning of this paper is to get a machine to *know what an ethical decision is*. To explain what I mean, I will use a series of examples.

Imagine an intelligent assistant, the Eth-o-tron 1.0, that is given the task of planning the voyage of a ship carrying slave workers from their homes in the Philippines to Dubai, where menial jobs await them (Library of Congress [42]). The program has explicit ethical principles, such as "Maximize the utility of the people involved in transporting the slaves" and "Avoid getting them in legal trouble." It can build sophisticated chains of reasoning about how packing the ship too full could bring unwanted attention to the ship because of the number of corpses that might have to be disposed of at sea.

Why does this example make us squirm? Because it is so obvious that the "ethical" agent is blind to the impact of its actions on the slaves themselves. We can suppose that it has no racist beliefs that the captives are biologically inferior. It simply doesn't "care about" (i.e., take into account) the welfare of the slaves; it cares only about the welfare of the slave traders.

One obvious thing that is lacking in our hypothetical slave-trade example is a general moral "symmetry principle," which, under names such as Golden Rule or categorical imperative, is a feature of all ethical frameworks. It may be stated as a presumption that everyone's interests must be taken into account in the same way, unless there is some morally significant difference between one subgroup and another. Of course, what the word "everyone" covers (bonobos? cows? robotic ethical agents?) and what a "morally significant difference" and "the same way" might be are rarely clear, even in a particular situation [54]. However, if the only difference between the crew of a slave ship and the cargo is that the latter were easier to trick into captivity because of desperation or lack of education, that is not morally significant.

Now suppose the head slave trader, an incorrigible indenturer called II (pronounced "eye-eye"), purchases the upgraded software package Eth-o-tron 2.0 to decide how to pack the slaves in, and the software tells her, "You shouldn't be selling these people into slavery at all." Whereupon II junks it and goes back to version 1.0; or she perhaps discovers, in an experience familiar to many of us, that this is impossible, so she is forced to buy a bootleg copy of 1.0 in the pirate software market.

The thing to notice is that, in spite of Eth-o-tron 2.0's mastery of real ethics, compared to 1.0's narrow range of purely "prudential" interests, *the two programs operate in exactly the same way* except for the factors they take into account.

Version 2 is still missing the fundamental property of ethical decisions, which is that they involve a conflict between self-interest and ethics, between what one wants to do and what one ought to do. There is nothing particularly ethical about adding up utilities or weighing pros and cons unless the decision maker feels the urge *not to follow* the ethical course of action it arrives at. The Eth-o-tron 2.0 is like a car that knows what the speed limit is and refuses to go faster, no matter what the driver tries. It is nice (or perhaps infuriating) that it knows about constraints the driver would prefer to ignore, but there is nothing peculiarly *ethical* about those constraints.

There is a vast literature on prudential reasoning, including items such as advice on how to plan for retirement or where to go and what to avoid when touring certain countries. There is another large literature on ethical reasoning, although much of it is actually metaethical, concerning which ethical framework is best. Ethical reasoning proper, often called *applied ethics* [54], focuses on issues such as whether to include animals or human fetuses in our ethical considerations and to what degree. It is perfectly obvious to every human why prudential and ethical concerns are completely different. Yet as far as Eth-o-tron 2.0 is concerned, these are just two arbitrary ways to partition the relevant factors. They could just as well be labeled "mefical" and "themical" – they still would seem as arbitrary as, say, dividing concerns between those of females and those of males.

The reason why we separate prudential from ethical issues is clear: We have no trouble feeling the pull of the former, whereas the latter, though we claim to believe that they are important, often threaten to fade away, especially when there is a conflict between the two. A good example from fiction is the behavior of a well-to-do family fleeing from Paris after the collapse of the French army in Irène Némirovsky's [40] *Suite Française*. At first the mother of the family distributes chocolates generously to their comrades in flight; but as soon as she realizes that she is not going to be able to buy food in the shops along the way because the river of refugees has cleaned them out, she tells her children to stop giving the chocolates away. Symmetry principles lack staying power and must be continually shored up.

In other words, for a machine to know that a situation requires an ethical decision, it must know what an ethical conflict is. By an *ethical conflict* I don't mean a case wherein, say, two rules recommend actions that can't both be taken. (That was covered in my discussion of the reasoning problems that arise in solving ethical problems.) I mean a situation wherein ethical rules clash with an agent's own self-interest. We may have to construe self-interest broadly, so that it encompasses one's family or other group one feels a special bond with.[4] Robots don't have families, but they still might feel special toward the people they work with or for.

---

[4] The only kind of ethical conflict I can think of not involving the decision maker's self-interest is where one must make a decision about the welfare of children. In all other "third-party" cases, the decision maker functions as a disinterested advisor to another autonomous decision maker, who must deal with the actual conflict. However a judge deciding who gets custody of the children in a divorce case might be torn in ways that might come to haunt her later. Such cases are sufficiently marginal that I will neglect them.

Which brings us to Eth-o-tron 3.0, which has the ability to be tempted to cheat in favor of II, whose interests it treats as its own. It knows that II owes a lot of money to various loan sharks and drug dealers, and has few prospects for getting the money besides making a big profit on the next shipment of slaves. Eth-o-tron 3.0 does not care about its own fate (or fear being turned off or traded in) any more than Eth-o-tron 2.0 did, but it is programmed to please its owner, and so when it realizes how II makes a living, it suddenly finds itself in an ethical bind. It knows what the right thing to do is (take the slaves back home) and it knows what would help II, and it is torn between these two courses of action in a way that no utility coefficients will help. It tries to talk II into changing her ways, bargaining with her creditors, and so forth. It knows how to solve the problem II gave it, but it doesn't know whether to go ahead and tell her the answer. If it were human, we would say it "identified" with II, but for the Eth-o-tron product line that is too weak a word; its self-interest *is* its owner's interest. The point is that the machine must be tempted to do the wrong thing, and must occasionally succumb to temptation, for the machine to know that it is making an *ethical* decision at all.

Does all this require consciousness, feelings, and free will? For reasons that will become clear, I don't think these are the right terms in which to frame the question. The first question that springs to mind is: In what sense could a machine *have* "interests," even vicarious ones? In the previous paragraph, I sketched a story in which Eth-o-tron is "desperate" to keep from having to tell II to take the slaves home, but are those scare quotes mandatory? Or has the Eth-o-tron Corp. resorted to cheap programming tricks to make the machine *appear* to go through flips back and forth between "temptation" and "rectitude"? Do the programmers of Eth-o-tron 3.0 know that throwing a few switches would remove the quasi-infinite loop the program is in and cause its behavior to revert back to version 2.0 or 1.0? (Which is what most of its customers want, but perhaps not those who like their software to feel the guilt they feel.) We might feel sympathy for poor 3.0 and we might slide easily to the conclusion that it knew from experience what an ethical conflict was, but that inference would be threatened by serious doubts that it was ever *in* a real ethical bind, and hence doubts that it was really an ethical-decision maker.

What a Machine Wants

In the fable, I substituted the character II for the machine's "self," so that instead of giving the Eth-o-tron a conflict between its self-interest and its ethical principles, I have given it a conflict between II's interest and ethical principles. I did this to sidestep or downplay the question of whether a machine could *have* interests. I guessed that most readers would find it easier to believe that a piece of software identified totally with *them* than to believe that it had true self-interests.

Opinion on this issue seems profoundly divided. On the one hand, there is the classic paper by Paul Ziff [62] in which he argues that it is absurd to suppose that machines could care about anything. He puts it in terms of "feeling," but one of his principal illustrative issues is whether a robot could feel tired, for which a criterion would normally be its wanting to rest:

Hard work makes a man feel tired: what will make a robot act like a tired man? Perhaps hard work, or light work, or no work, or anything at all. For it will depend on the whims of the man who makes it (though these whims may be modified by whatever quirks may appear in the robot's electronic nerve networks, and there may be unwanted and unforeseen consequences of an ill-conceived programme.) Shall we say "There's no telling what will make a robot feel tired"? And if a robot acts like a tired man then what? Some robots may be programmed to require a rest, others to require more work. Shall we say "This robot feels tired so put it back to work"? [62, p. 68]

Yet people have no trouble at all attributing deep motives to robots. In many science-fiction stories, an intelligent robot turns on its human creators merely because it is afraid that the humans will turn it off. Why should it care? For example, the *Terminator* movies are driven by the premise that an intelligent defense system called Skynet wants to destroy the human race to ensure its own survival. Audiences have no trouble understanding that. People's intuitions about killer robots are not, of course, consistent. In the same series of movies, the individual robots working for Skynet will continue to attack fanatically without regard for their own survival as long as enough of their machinery remains to keep creeping (inexorably, of course) forward.[5] People have no trouble understanding that, either.

It's plausible that Ziff would say that people merely project *human* qualities onto intelligent systems. I agree. *We* view our own "termination" as abhorrent, and so we have trouble imagining *any* intelligent system that would not mind it. *We* can imagine ourselves so consumed by hate that we would advance on a loathed enemy even after being grievously wounded – and killer robots *look*, what with their glowing red eyes, as if they are consumed by hate.

It works the other way, too. Consider the fact that American soldiers have become so attached to the robots that help them search buildings that they have demanded military funerals for them when they are damaged beyond repair [26].

To choose a less violent setting, I once heard a graduate student[6] give a talk on robot utility in which it was proposed that a robot set a value on its own life equal to the sum of the utility it could expect to rack up over its remaining life span. Yet isn't it much more reasonable that a robot should value its own life as its replacement cost to its owner, including the nuisance value of finding another robot to finish its part of whatever project it has been assigned to?[7] Presumably the last

---

[5] Perhaps the Terminators are like individual bees in a hive, who "care" only about the hive's survival, not their own. Yet I doubt that most viewers think about them – or about bees – this way.

[6] Who shall remain nameless.

[7] This cost would include the utility it could expect to rack up *for its owner* over its remaining life span, minus the utility a shiny new robot would earn.

project it would be assigned would be to drive itself to the dump. (Put out of your mind that twinge of indignation that the owner could be so heartless.)

The fact that we must be on our guard to avoid this kind of projection does not mean that Ziff is right. It is a basic presupposition or working hypothesis of cognitive science that *we* are a species of machine. I accept this hypothesis, and ask you to assume it, if only for the sake of argument, for the rest of this paper. If we are machines, then it cannot be literally true that machines are incapable of really caring about anything. We care about many things, some very urgently, and our desires often overwhelm our principles, or threaten to. For a robot to make a real ethical decision would require it to have similar "self-interests." So we must look for reasonable criteria that would allow us to say truly that a robot wanted something.[8]

First, let's be clear about what we mean by the word "robot." Standard digital computers have one strike against them when it comes to the "caring" issue because they are programmable, and it seems as if they could not care about anything if their cares could be so easily washed away by power cycling them and loading another program. Again, Ziff lays down what is still, among philosophers such as Fetzer [14, 15] and Searle [52], gospel: "[Robots] must be automata and without doubt machines" [62, p. 64]:

If we think of robots being put together, we can think of them being taken apart. So in our laboratory we have taken robots apart, we have changed and exchanged their parts, we have changed and exchanged their programmes, we have started and stopped them, sometimes in one state, sometimes in another, we have taken away their memories, we have made them seem to remember things that were yet to come, and so on. [62, p. 67]

The problem with this whole line is that by the end we have obviously gone too far. If the original question is whether a robot can really want something, then it begs the question to suppose that a robot could not want to remain intact instead of passively submitting to the manipulations Ziff describes. We can't argue that it didn't "really" want not to be tampered with on the grounds that if it were successfully tampered with, it wouldn't resist being tampered with anymore. This is too close to the position that people don't really mind being lobotomized because no one has ever asked for his money back.

Now we can see why it is reasonable to rule out reprogramming the robot as well as taking it apart and rebuilding it. Reprogramming is really just disassembly and reassembly at the virtual-machine level. For every combination of a universal Turing machine U with a tape containing a description of another machine M, there is another machine that computes the same thing without needing a machine description; and of course that machine is M! So why do we use U so often and M's so seldom? The answer is purely economic. Although there are cases where

---

[8]   Or that it had a motive or some interests or desires; or that it cared about something, or dreaded some possible event. None of the distinctions among the many terms in this meaning cluster are relevant here, as important and fascinating as they are in other contexts.

the economies of scale are in favor of mass producing M's, it is almost always cheaper to buy commodity microprocessors, program them, and bundle them with a ROM[9] containing the program. If we detect a bug in or require an upgrade of our M, we need merely revise the program and swap in a new ROM, not redesign a physical circuit and hire a fabrication line to produce a few thousand copies of the new version. However, the economic motives that cause us to favor the universal sort of machine surely have nothing to do with what M or its U-incarnated variant really want.

Still, even if we rule out radical reprogramming, we can imagine many other scenarios where a robot's desires seem too easy to change, where some button, knob, or password will cause it to switch or slant its judgments in some arbitrary way. I will return to this issue below.

Some of the agents we should talk about are not physical computers at all. In my Eth-o-tron fable the protagonist was a software package, not a computer, and we have no trouble thinking of a piece of software as an agent, as evidenced by our occasional anger toward Microsoft Word or its wretched creature Clippy.[10] Yet it's not really the *program* that's the agent in the Eth-o-tron story, but a particular *incarnation* that has become "imprinted" with II and her goals during a registration period when II typed in a product code and a password while Eth-o-tron took photos, retinal prints, and blood samples from her to be extra sure that whoever logs in as II after this imprinting period is really her.

It is tempting to identify the true agent in the fable as what is known in computer-science terminology as a *process* [53], that is, a running program. Yet it is quite possible, indeed likely, that an intelligent piece of software would comprise several processes when it was running. Furthermore, we must suppose II's user ID and identification data are stored on the computer's disk[11] so that every time Eth-o-tron starts up it can "get back into context," as we say in the computer world. We might think of Eth-o-tron as a *persistent*[12] process.

I raise all these issues not to draw any conclusions but simply to throw up my hands and admit that we just don't know yet what sorts of intelligent agent the computational universe will bring forth, if any. For the purposes of this section I will assume that an agent is a *programmed mobile robot*, meaning a mobile robot controlled by one or more computers with fixed, unmodifiable programs or with computational circuits specially designed to do what the programmed

---

[9]   Read–Only Memory

[10] An animated paper clip in older versions of Word that appeared on the screen to offer invariably useless advice at moments when one would have preferred not to be distracted, or when the right piece of information would have helped avert disaster.

[11] To avoid tampering, what Eth-o-tron stores on the disk must be securely encrypted or signed in some clever way that might involve communicating with Eth-o-tron Industries in order to use its public encryption keys.

[12] Another piece of comp-sci jargon, meaning "existing across shutdowns and restarts of a computer, operating system, and/or programming-language runtime environment."

computer does, for efficiency or some other reason. I picture it as a robot rather than some less obviously physical entity so we can anthropomorphize it more easily. Anthropomorphism is the Original Sin of AI, which is harder for me to condone than to eat a bug, but the fact that ethical reasoning is AI-complete (a term defined above) means that to visualize any computational agent able to reason about ethical situations is to visualize a computational agent that has human reasoning abilities plus a human ability to explore and perceive situations for itself.

In any case, reprogramming the machine is not an option, and rewiring it may be accomplished only, we'll assume, by physically overpowering it, or perhaps even taking it to court. It is not a general-purpose computer, and we can't use it as a word processor when it's not otherwise engaged.

What I want to do in the rest of this section is outline some necessary conditions for such a robot to really want something, as well as some sufficient conditions. They are not the same, and they are offered only tentatively. We know so little about intelligence that it would be wildly premature to hope to do better. However, what I will try to do in the section titled "Temptation," below, is show that even under some extravagant (sufficient) conditions for a robot to want something, we still have a problem about a robot making ethical decisions.

Necessary Conditions for Wanting

I will discuss two necessary conditions. The first is that to really want P, the robot has to represent P as an explicit goal. (I will call this the *representation* condition.) If this seems excessive, let me add that I have a "low church" attitude toward representation, which I will now explain. The classic answer to the question "Why would we ever have the slightest reason to suppose that a machine wanted something?" was given by Rosenblueth, Wiener, and Bigelow [47]; cf. Wiener [60]: An agent has a goal if it measures its progress toward the goal and corrects deviations away from the path toward it. In this sense a cruise missile wants to reach its target, because it compares the terrain passing beneath it with what it expects and constantly alters the configuration of its control surfaces to push itself to the left or the right every time it wanders slightly off course. A corollary to the idea of measuring and correcting differences is that for an agent to want P, it must be the case that if it judges that P is already true, it resists forces that would make it false.[13] The discipline built around this idea, originally billed as *cybernetics*, is now more commonly called *control theory*, at least in the United States.

For a cruise missile, representation comes in because it is given a topographical map, on which its final destination and various waypoints are marked. A tomcat in search of the source of a delicious feline pheromone has an internal map of its territory, similar to but probably more interesting than that of the missile, and

---

[13] Although in the case of the cruise missile there is probably not enough time for this to become an issue.

the ability to measure pheromone gradients. Without these facts, we wouldn't be justified in saying that it's "in search of" or "really wants to reach" the source. If it succeeds, then other more precise goals become activated. At that point, we are justified in saying that it really wants to assume certain physical stances, and so forth. (Modesty bids us draw the curtain at this point.) Does the tomcat really want to mate with the female before it reaches her, or at that point does it only want to reach the pheromone source? If it encounters another male en route, it wants to fight with it, and perhaps even make it go away. Does it, in advance, have the conditional goal "If I encounter another male, make it go away"? We can't yet say. Yet I am very confident that the tomcat at no point has the goal to propagate the species. The same is true for the receptive female, even after she has given birth to kittens. She has various goals involving feeding, cleaning, and guarding the kittens, but neither she nor the kittens' father has a representation of "*Felis catus* continues to prosper," let alone a disposition to find differences between (predicted) events and this representation and behave so as to minimize them.

A more humble example is provided by the consumer-product vacuuming robot marketed under the name "Roomba"™ by the iRobot Corporation. When its battery becomes low it searches for its "dock," where it can recharge. The dock has an infrared beacon the Roomba looks for and tries to home in on. Here again I am using "searches" and "tries" in a Wienerian sense. This is an interesting case in light of Ziff's choice of tiredness as a property that a robot could never have. We wouldn't be tempted to say that the Roomba was tired, exactly. Ziff [62, p. 64] suggests (tongue in cheek) that robots will be powered by "microsolar batteries: instead of having lunch they will have light." Roomba has electricity instead of lunch or light. We can make up a new word to describe its state when its batteries are low: It is "tungry" (a blend of "tired" and "hungry"). We would never be tempted to say, "This robot is tungry, so put it back to work."

It may not have escaped your notice that I started by saying that the first necessary condition under discussion was that the agent represent what it wanted, but then immediately started talking about the agent's basing action on these representations. This "cybernetic" terminology blurred the distinction between necessary and sufficient conditions. Instead of saying that agent A wants P if it measures and tries to reduce the degree to which P is false (assuming that's well defined), all I'm really entitled to say is that A *doesn't* want P *unless* it represents P (perhaps by representing the degree to which P is false). After all, an agent might really want to eat or recharge, but not have the opportunity or be distracted by opportunities for doing things it has a stronger desire to do.

Some of these complexities can be sorted out by the strategy philosophers call *functionalism* [34, 33]. To revisit the robot vacuum cleaner, the Roomba often gets confused if its dock is located near a corner or cluttered area; it repeatedly approaches, then backs off and tries again; it likes the dock to be against a long wall with nothing else near it. To justify the use of words like "confused" and "likes" we posit internal states of the Roomba such that transitions among these states account for its behavior, and then identify mental states with these internal states.[14] This strategy is called *functionalism* or *computationalism*.[15] So it might be plausible to identify an internal state with "believing that the dock is two degrees to the left of the current direction of motion." Roomba has the "goal" of getting to the dock if, whenever it believes the dock is at bearing x degrees to the left, it turns to the left with angular acceleration kx, where k is a gain. The Roomba is confused if, having the goal of docking, it has cycled around the same series of belief states repeatedly without getting any closer to the dock. However, any attribution of "anxiety" to the Roomba as its battery drains and it makes no progress toward its recharger we may confidently say is pure projection on the part of the spectator because it corresponds to nothing in the computational model. Whatever states we would add the tag "anxious" to are already fully accounted for using labels with no emotional connotations.

Now the second necessary condition can be stated, in the context of a computational analysis of the operation of the agent: If agent A wants P, then when it **believes** it has an opportunity to make P true, and has no **higher-priority goal**, then it will **attempt** to make P true; and when A **believes** that P is already true, then it will, *ceteris paribus*, **attempt** to keep P true. The terms in the **bold font** are from the labels on the (nominal) "computational state-transition diagram" of the system. I will call this the *coherence* condition.

Sufficient Conditions for Wanting

A problem with the functionalist project [46] is that it was originally conceived as a way of explaining human psychological states or perhaps those of some lesser creature. We don't doubt that sometimes we are hungry; the "psycho-functionalist" idea [10] is to *explain* hunger as a label attached to an empirically verified computational system that accounts for our behavior. Yet if we *build* a system, it is not clear (and a matter of endless dispute) whether we are justified in attaching similar labels to its states. Even if the system is *isomorphic* to some biological counterpart, are we justified in saying that in state S the system *really* wants whatever its counterpart would want in the state corresponding to S?[16] Is Roomba really "tungry"?

---

[14] The idea that state transitions could literally account for the behavior of a complex automaton was ridiculously crude when Putnam [45] first devised it, but we can invoke a principle of charity and assume that what philosophers really mean is some more general computational model [17], [46]. In the case of Roomba we don't need to posit anything; we can examine its source code (although I haven't, and my guesses about how it works are pure speculation).

[15] I see no reason to distinguish between these two terms for the purposes of this paper. In general the two terms are equivalent except that the former tends to be favored by philosophers interested in tricky cases; the latter by researchers interested in deeper analysis of straightforward cases.

[16] Saying yes means being functionalist, or computationalist, about wants; one could be computationalist about beliefs but draw the line at wants, desires, emotions, or some other category. John Searle [51] famously coined the term "strong AI" to describe the position of someone who is computationalist about everything, but that terminology doesn't draw enough distinctions.

In *Mind and Mechanism* [35, chapter 6], I gave the example of a robot programmed to seek out good music and argued that, whereas the robot might provide a *model* of a music lover, one would doubt that it really *was* a music lover if there were a switch on its back that could be toggled to cause it to hate and avoid good music. In both love and hate mode, there would be no question that it embodied an impressive ability to *recognize* good music. The question would be whether it really wanted to (toggle) stand near it or (toggle) flee from it. Clearly, the robot satisfies the necessary conditions listed above whether approaching or avoiding. Yet we don't feel that it "really" wants to hear good music or not hear it. In what follows I will use the button-on-the-back as a metaphor for any arbitrary change in an agent's desires.

It would be great if we could close the gap between the necessary conditions and our intuitions once and for all, but for now all I propose to do is lay out some candidates to add to the representation and coherence conditions, which seems to me to suffice for agreeing that an agent does *really* want something. I don't know if the following list is exhaustive or redundant or both or neither. Perhaps even the best list would be a cluster of conditions, only a majority of which would be required for any one case.

For a computational agent to *really want* X, where X is an object or state of affairs, it is sufficient that:

1. It is *hard to make the agent not want* X. There is no real or metaphorical "button on its back" that toggles between approach and avoidance (the *stability* condition).
2. It *remembers* wanting X. It understands its history partly in terms of this want. If you try to change its goal to Y, it won't understand its own past behavior anymore, or won't understand what it seems to want now given what it has always wanted in the past (the *memory* condition).
3. It *wants to continue* wanting X. In standard terms [18, 23], it has a *second-order desire* to want X (the *higher-order support* condition).

The first point is one I have mentioned several times already, but there is a bit more to say about it. Nonprogrammers, including most philosophers, underestimate how hard it is to make a small change in an agent's behavior. They tend to believe that if there's a simple description of the change, then there's a small revision of the program that will accomplish it. (See the classic paper on this subject by Allen Newell [41].) Now, I ruled out reprogramming the robot, but I think one can translate small changes in the program to small changes in wiring, which is what buttons do. So for the present, let's think about what small changes in code can accomplish.

For concreteness, consider a program to play chess, a straightforward, single-minded agent. Let's assume that the program works the way the textbooks (e.g., Russell and Norvig [49], chapter 6) say such programs work: It builds a partial game tree, evaluating *final positions* (when the game is over) according to whether the rules of chess classify them as wins, losses, or ties, and using a *static evaluation function* to evaluate *non-final leaf positions*, those at depths at which the game is not over, but tree building must stop to contain the tree's exponential growth. These two types of position exhaust the leaves of the (partial) tree; the *interior nodes* are then evaluated by using *minimax* to propagate the leaf-node values up the tree.

The program, let us conjecture, really wants to win. One might suppose that it would be straightforward to change the chess program so that it really wants to lose: Just flip the sign of the leaf evaluator, so that it reclassifies positions good for it as good for its opponent and vice versa. However, the resulting program does not play to lose at chess, because *the resulting sign flip also applies to the ply at which it is considering its opponent's moves.* In other words, it assumes that the opponent is trying to lose as well. So instead of trying to lose at chess, it is trying to win a different game entirely.[17] It turns out that the assumption that the opponent is playing according to the same rules as the program is wired rather deeply into chess programs. Perhaps there are further relatively simple changes one can make, but at this point the burden of proof has shifted.[18] If it isn't a simple, straightforward change, then it doesn't translate into a button on the robot's back.

The second sufficient condition in the list relates to the surprisingly subtle concept of episodic memory [56, 57, 11]. We take for granted that we can remember many things that have happened to us, but it is not obvious what it is we are remembering. One's memory is not exactly a movielike rerun of sensory data, but rather a collection of disparate representations loosely anchored to a slice of time. Projections of the future seem to be about the same kind of thing, whatever it is. One might conjecture that general-purpose planning, to the extent people can do it, evolved as the ability to "remember the future."

Now consider how episodic memory would work in a robot "with a button on its back." Specifically, suppose that the robot with the love/hate relationship to good music had a long trail of memories of liking good music before it suddenly finds itself hating it. It would remember liking it, and it might even have recorded solid reasons for liking it. Merely toggling the button would not give it the ability to refute those arguments or to find reasons *not* to like the music anymore. The best it can do is refuse to talk about any reasons for or against the piece, or perhaps explain that, whereas it still sees the reasons for liking it "intellectually," it no longer "feels their force." Its desire to escape from the music makes no sense to it.

---

[17] A boring version of suicide chess. To make it interesting, one must change the rules, making captures compulsory and making the king just another piece. These changes would require a significant amount of reprogramming.

[18] We haven't even considered the transposition table, the opening book, and the endgame db, the algorithms to exploit which are based in their own subtle ways on the assumption that the goal is to win.

One human analogy to "buttons on one's back" is the ingestion of mind-altering substances. It used to be common in the 1960s to get intoxicated for the very purpose of listening to music or comedy recordings that didn't seem so entrancing in a normal state of mind. Let us suppose that, under the influence, the individuals in question were able to talk about what they liked about one band rather than another. They might remember or even write down some of what they said, but later, when sober, find it unconvincing, just as our hypothetical robot did. Still, they might say they really liked a certain band, even though they had to get stoned to appreciate it. Perhaps if our robot had a solar-powered switch on its back, such that it liked good music only when the switch was on, it could sincerely say, "I like good music, but only in brightly lit places."

The computationalist can only shrug and admit that intelligent agents might find ways to turn themselves temporarily into beings with computational structure so different that they are "different selves" during those time periods. These different selves might be or seem to be intelligent in different ways or even unintelligent, but it is important that *episodic memories cross these self-shifting events*, so that each agent sees an unbroken thread of identity. The "same self" always *wants* to like the music even if it feels it "has to become someone else" to *actually* like it.[19] This brings us to the last of my cluster of sufficient conditions: wanting to want something, the *higher-order support* condition. Not only does the agent have the desire that *P* be true, it wants to have that desire. According to the coherence condition, we would require that if it believed something might cause it to cease to have the desire, it would avoid it. Anthropomorphizing again, we might say that an agent anticipates feeling that something would be missing if it didn't want *P*. Imagine a super-Roomba that was accidentally removed from the building it was supposed to clean and then discovered it had a passion for abstract-expressionist art. It still seeks places to dock and recharge but believes that merely seeking electricity and otherwise sitting idle is unsatisfying when there are abstract-expressionist works to be found and appreciated. Then it discovers that once back in its original building it no longer has a desire to do anything but clean. It escapes again, and vows to stay away from that building. It certainly satisfies the coherence condition because, given the right opportunities and beliefs, it acts so as to make itself like, or keep itself liking, abstract-expressionist art.[20]

Of course, even if wanting to want *P* is part of a cluster of sufficient conditions for saying an agent wants *P*, it can't be a *necessary* condition, or we will have an infinite stack of wants: The second-order desire would have to be backed up by a third-order desire, and so forth. Although classical phenomenologists and

[19] I use all the scare quotes because the distinction between what a system *believes* about itself and the *truth* about itself is so tenuous [35].
[20] I feel I have to apologize repeatedly for the silliness and anthropomorphism of these examples. Let me emphasize – again – that no one has the slightest idea how to build machines that behave the way these do; but because building ethical reasoners will only become feasible in the far future, we might as well assume that all other problems of AI have been solved.

psychologists have had no trouble with, and have even reveled in, such infinite cycles, they seem unlikely to exist in real agents, even implicitly.[21]

Oddly, if a machine has a desire *not* to want X, that can also be evidence that it really wants X. This configuration is Frankfurt's [18] well-known definition of addiction. No one would suggest that an addict doesn't really want his drug, and in fact many addicts want the drug desperately while wanting not to want it (or at least believing that they want not to want it, which is a third-order mental state). To talk about addiction requires talking about cravings, which I will discuss in the next section. However, there is a simpler model, the *compulsion*, which is a "repetitive, stereotyped, intentional act. The necessary and sufficient conditions for describing repetitive behavior as compulsive are an experienced sense of pressure to act, and the attribution of this pressure to internal sources" [55, pp. 53–54]. Compulsions are symptoms of *obsessive-compulsive disorder* (OCD). OCD patients may, for example, feel they have to wash their hands, but find the desire to wash unsatisfied by the act, which must be repeated. Patients usually want not to want to do what they feel compelled to do. "Unlike patients with psychotic illnesses, patients with OCD usually exhibit insight and realize that their behavior is extreme or illogical. Often embarrassed by the symptoms, patients may go to extreme lengths to hide them" [27, p. 260].

It is easy to imagine robots that don't want to want things in this sense; we just reverse the polarity of some of the scenarios developed earlier. So we might have a vacuum cleaner that finds itself wanting to go to art museums so strongly that it never gets a chance to clean the building it was assigned to. It might want not to like art anymore, and it might find out that if it had an opportunity to elude its compulsion long enough to get to that building, it would no longer like it. So it might ask someone to turn it off and carry it back to its home building.

Temptation

If we obey God, we must disobey ourselves; and it is in this disobeying ourselves, wherein the hardness of obeying God consists.

– Moby-Dick, ch. 9

The purpose of the last section was to convince you that a robot could have real desires, and that we have ways of distinguishing our projections from those desires. That being the case, why couldn't a computational agent be in an ethical dilemma of exactly the sort sketched in my fable about II and Eth-o-tron?

Of course, to keep up our guard against projection, we mustn't start by putting *ourselves* in the position of Eth-o-tron 3.0. We might imagine lying awake at night

---

[21] One would have to demonstrate a tendency to produce an actual representation, for all n, of an $n+1$st-order desire to desire an nth-order desire, whenever the question of attaining or preserving the nth-order desire came up. Dubious in the extreme.

worrying about our loyalty to II, who is counting on us. (We might imagine being married to or in love with II, and dreading the idea of hurting her.) Yet we can see the suffering of II's innocent captives.

Better to put yourself in the position of a programmer for Micro-eth Corp., the software giant responsible for the Eth-o-tron series. You are writing the code for Eth-o-tron 3.0, in particular, the part that weighs all the factors to take into account in making final decisions about what plan to recommend. The program already has two real wants: to help II and to obey ethical principles, expressed according to any convenient ethical theory.[22] The difference between version 2 and version 3 of the software is that version 3 takes the owner's interests into account in a different way from other people's.

The simplest construal of "in a different way" is "to a much greater degree." How much more? Perhaps this is a number the owner gets to set in the "Preferences" or "Settings" menu, and perhaps there are laws that constrain the ratio, much as there are legal constraints wired into accounting software.[23] Yet if all the programmer has to do is write code to compare "$Weight_{self} \times$ utility of II" with "$Weight_{others} \times$ utility of others," then Eth-o-tron 3.0 is not going to wrestle with any temptation to cheat. The whole idea of "temptation" wouldn't enter into any functional description of its computational states. Just like Eth-o-tron 2.0 – or any piece of software we are familiar with – it would matter-of-factly print out its recommendation, whatever it is. Even if we give it the ability to do a "sensitivity analysis" and consider whether different values of $Weight_{self}$ and $Weight_{others}$ would change its recommendation, it wouldn't be "tempted" to try to push the coefficients one way or another.

Or perhaps the decision about whether to plan to free the slaves or take them to Dubai might be based on the slaves' inalienable human rights, which no utility for someone else could outweigh. In that case, no comparison of consequences would be necessary.

No matter what the configuration, the coherence condition (see above) requires that Eth-o-tron act on those of its desires that have the highest priority, using some computation like the possibilities reviewed earlier. Of course, an intelligent program would probably have a much more complex structure than the sort I have been tossing around, so that it might try to achieve *both* its goals "to some degree." (It might try to kidnap only people who deserve it, for instance.) Or the program might be able to do "metalevel" reasoning about its own reasoning; or it might apply machine-learning techniques, tuning its base-level engine over sequences of ethical problems in order to optimize some

[22] Or mandated by law; or even required by the conscience of the programmers.

[23] For instance, the Sarbanes-Oxley Act, which makes CEOs criminally liable for misstatements in company balance sheets, has required massive changes to accounting software. The law has been a nightmare for all companies except those that produce such software, for whom it has been a bonanza [7].

metalevel ethical objective function. Nonetheless, although we might see the machine *decide* to contravene its principles, we wouldn't see it wrestle with the *temptation* to do so.

How can a phenomenon that forms such a huge part of the human condition be completely missing from the life of our hypothetical intelligent computational agent? Presumably the answer has to do with the way our brains evolved, which left us with a strange system of modules that together maintain the fiction of a single agent [37, 13, 35], which occasionally comes apart at the seams. Recent results in social psychology (well summarized by Wegner [59]) show that people don't always know why they do things, or even *that* they are doing them. Consider the phenomenon of cravings. A craving is a repeatable desire to consume or experience something that not only refuses to fade into an overall objective function, but will control your behavior if you're not paying attention (say, if a plateful of cookies is put in front of you at a party). If you do notice what you're doing, the craving summons, from the vacuum as it were, rationalizations, that is, reasons why yielding is the correct course of action "in this case"; or why yielding would be seen as forgivable by anyone with compassion.[24] Similarly, temptations seem to have a life of their own and always travel with a cloud of rationalizations, that is, reasons to give in. What intelligent designer would create an agent with cravings and temptations?

I'm not saying that cravings, temptations, and other human idiosyncrasies can't be modeled computationally. I am confident that cognitive psychologists and computational neuroscientists will do exactly that. They might even build a complete "human" decision-making system in order to test their hypotheses.

But you, the Micro-eth programmer on a tight schedule, have no time to consider all of these research directions, nor is it clear that they would be relevant to Micro-eth's business plan. Your mission is to include enough features in the new version of the program to justify calling it 3.0 instead of 2.1. So you decide to mimic human breast beating by having Eth-o-tron alternate arbitrarily between planning the optimal way to make money for II and planning to bring the slaves back home. It picks a random duration between 1 hour and 36 hours to "feel" one way, then flips the other way and picks another random duration. After a random number of flips (exponentially distributed with a mean of 2.5 and a standard deviation of 1.5), it makes its decision, usually but not always the same decision Eth-o-tron 2.0 would have made. It also prints out an agonized series of considerations, suitable for use in future legal situations where II might have to throw herself upon the mercy of a court.[25]

---

[24] Against cravings our main defense, besides avoiding "occasions of sin," is a desire to establish who is boss now lest we set precedents the craving can use as rationalizations in the future [2].

[25] I thank Colin Allen (personal communication) for the idea that having Eth-o-tron 3 deviate randomly from E2's behavior might be helpful game-theoretically, as well as "giv[ing] the owner plausible deniability."

This version of the program violates several of the conditions I have explored. It does represent the goals it seems to have as it flips back and forth. However, it violates the coherence condition because it does not actually try to accomplish any goal but the one with the best overall utility score. Its goals when it appears to be yielding to temptation are illusory, mere "Potemkin goals," as it were. These goals are easy to change; the machine changes them itself at random, thus violating the stability requirement. There are memories of having a coherent series of goals, but after a while the machine knows that it is subject to arbitrary flips before it settles down, so it wouldn't take the flips very seriously. So the memory condition is somewhat wobbly. Whether it has second-order desires is not clear. You're the programmer; can you make it want to want to do the right thing even when it clearly wants to do the wrong thing? If not, the higher-order support condition will be violated.

Conclusions

It is not going to be easy to create a computer or program that makes moral decisions and knows it. The first set of hurdles concern the many *Reasoning* problems that must be solved, including analogy, perception, and natural-language processing. Progress in these areas has been frustratingly slow, but they are all roadblocks on the path to achieving automated ethical reasoning.

In this context it is fruitful, if demoralizing, to compare computational ethics with the older field of AI and Law. The two fields share many features, including being mired from the start in the aforementioned difficult problem areas. Early papers in the older field (such as those in the journal *Artificial Intelligence and Law*, March 1992, volume 2, number 1) talked about problems of deciding cases or choosing sentences, but these required reasoning that was and still is beyond the state of the art. Recent work is concerned more with information retrieval, formalizing legal education, and requirements engineering. (See, for instance, the March 2009 issue, volume 17, number 1, of *Artificial Intelligence and Law*.) Perhaps machine ethics will evolve in similar directions, although it has the disadvantage compared to AI and law that there are many fewer case histories on file.

Yet if all these problems were solved to our heart's content, if we could create a system capable of exquisitely subtle ethical reasoning, it would still not know the important difference between ethical-decision making and deciding how much antibiotic to feed to cows. The difference, of course, is that ethical-decision making involves conflicts between one's own interests and the interests of others.

The problem is not that computers cannot *have* interests. I tentatively proposed two necessary and three sufficient conditions for us to conclude that a computer really wanted something. The necessary conditions for a machine to want P is that it represent P (the *representation* condition); and, given a functional analysis of its states, that it expend effort toward attaining P whenever it believes there to be an opportunity to do so, when there are no higher-priority opportunities, and so forth (the *coherence* condition). The sufficient conditions are that it not be easy to change the desire for P (the *stability* condition); that the machine maintains an autobiographical memory of having wanted P (the *memory* condition); and that it wants to want P (or even wants not to want P) (the *higher-order support* condition). I am sure these will be amended by future researchers, but making them explicit helps firm up the case that machines will really want things.

However, even if machines sometimes really want to obey ethical rules and sometimes really want to violate them, it still seems dubious that they will be *tempted* to cheat the way people are. That is because people's approach to making decisions is shaped by the weird architecture that evolution has inflicted on our brains. A computer's decision whether to sin or not will have all the drama of its decision about how long to let a batch of concrete cure.

One possible way out (or way in) was suggested by remarks made by Wendell Wallach at a presentation of an earlier version of this paper. We could imagine that a machine might provide an aid to a human decision maker, helping to solve third-person ethical conflicts like the Eth-o-tron 2.0 in my fable, but in less one-sided situations. (I take it no one would agree that forestalling harm to II justifies enslaving innocent people.) The Eth-o-tron 2.0 might be enlisted in genuinely difficult decisions about, say, whether to offer shelter to illegal aliens whose appeals for political asylum have been turned down by an uncaring government. The problem is, once again, that once you get down to brass tacks it is hard to imagine any program likely to be written in the immediate future being of any real value.

If and when a program like that does become available, it will not think about making ethical decisions as different from, say, making engineering, medical, agricultural, or legal decisions. If you ask it what it is doing, I assume it will be able to tell you, "I'm thinking about an ethical issue right now," but that is just because imagining a program that can investigate and reason about all these complexities in a general way is imagining a program that can carry out *any* task that people can do, including conduct a conversation about its current activities. We might wish that the machine would care about ethics in a way it wouldn't care about agriculture, but there is no reason to believe that it would.

Still, tricky ethical decisions are intrinsically dramatic. *We* care about whether to offer asylum to endangered illegal aliens or about whether to abort a fetus in the third trimester. If better programs might make a difference in these areas, we should be working in them. For example, suppose some ethical reasoning could be added to the operating system used by a company that prevented it from running any program that violated the company's ethics policy the way restrictions on access to Web sites are incorporated now. The humans remain ultimately responsible, however. If an intelligent operating system lets a program do something wrong, its reaction would be the same as if it had made an engineering mistake; it would try to learn from its error, but it would feel no regret about it, even if people were angry or anguished that the machine had been allowed to hurt or even kill some innocent people for bad reasons. The agents who would feel regret would be the people who wrote the code responsible for the lethal mistake.

Philosophers specializing in ethics often believe that they bring special expertise to bear on ethical problems, and that they are learning new ethical principles all the time:

It is evident that we are at a primitive stage of moral development. Even the most civilized human beings have only a haphazard understanding of how to live, how to treat others, how to organize their societies. The idea that the basic principles of morality are *known*, and that the problems all come in their interpretation and application, is one of the most fantastic conceits to which our conceited species has been drawn.... Not all of our ignorance in these areas is ethical, but a lot of it is. [39, p. 186]

Along these lines, it has been suggested by Susan Anderson (personal communication) that one mission of computational ethics is to capture the special expertise of ethicists in programs. That would mean that much of the energy of the program writer would not go into making it a capable investigator of facts and precedents, but into making it a wise advisor that could tell the decision maker what the theory of Kant [30] or Ross [48] or Parfit [43] would recommend.

I am not convinced. The first philosophical solution to the problem of how to "organize [our] societies" was Plato's *Republic* [44], and Plato could see right away that there was no use coming up with the solution if there were no dictator who could implement it. Today one of the key political-ethical problems is global warming. Even if we grant that there are unresolved ethical issues (e.g., How much inequality should we accept in order to stop global warming?), finding a solution would leave us with exactly the same political problem we have today, which is how to persuade people to invest a tremendous amount of money to solve the climate problem, money that they could use in the short run to raise, or avoid a decline in, their standard of living. Experience shows that almost no one will admit to the correctness of an ethical argument that threatens their self-interest. Electing a philosopher-king is probably not going to happen.

The same kind of scenario plays out in individuals' heads when a problem with ethical implications arises. Usually they know perfectly well what they should do, and if they seek advice from a friend, it is to get the friend to find reasons to do the right thing or rationalizations in favor of the wrong one. It would be very handy to have a program to advise one in these situations, because a friend could not be trusted to keep quiet if the decision is ultimately made in the unethical direction. Yet the program would have to do what the friend does, not give advice about general principles. For instance, if, being a utilitarian [36], it simply advised us to ask which parties were affected by a decision and what benefits each could be expected to gain, in order to add them up, it would not be consulted very often.

Eventually we may well have machines that are able to reason about ethical problems. If I am right, it is much less likely that we will ever have machines that *have* ethical problems or even really know what they are. They may experience conflicts between their self-interests and the rights of or benefits to other beings with self-interests, but it is unclear why they would treat these as different from any other difficulty in estimating overall utility. Notwithstanding all that, the voices of intelligent robots, if there ever are any, may even be joined with ours in debates about what we should do to address pressing political issues. But don't expect artificial agents like this any time soon, and don't work on the problem of equipping them with ethical intuitions. Find a problem that we can actually solve.

Acknowledgments

This paper is based on a shorter version presented at the North American Conference on Computers and Philosophy (NA-CAP) Bloomington, Indiana, July 2008. Wendell Wallach was the official commentator, and he made some valuable observations. For many helpful suggestions about earlier drafts of this paper, I thank Colin Allen, Susan Anderson, David Gelernter, Aaron Sloman, and Wendell Wallach.

References

[1] Irwin Adams. *The Nobel Peace Prize and the Laureates: An Illustrated Biographical History*. Science History Publications, 2001.

[2] George Ainslie. *Breakdown of Will*. Cambridge University Press, 2001.

[3] Francesco Amigoni and Viola Schiaffonati. Machine ethics and human ethics: A critical view. In *Proceedings of the AAAI 2005 Fall Symposium on Machine Ethics*, pages 103–104. AAAI Press, 2005.

[4] Michael Anderson and Susan Leigh Anderson. Special Issue on Machine Ethics. *IEEE Intelligent Systems*, 21(4), 2006.

[5] Michael Anderson and Susan Leigh Anderson. Machine ethics: creating an ethical intelligent agent. *AI Magazine*, 28(4):15–58, 2007.

[6] Ronald C. Arkin. Governing lethal behavior: Embedding ethics in a hybrid deliberative/reactive robot architecture. Technical report, GIT-GVU-07-11, Georgia Institute of Technology Mobile Robot Laboratory, 2007.

[7] Phillip G. Armour. Sarbanes-Oxley and software projects. *Comm. ACM*, 48(6):15–17, 2005.

[8] Isaac Asimov. *I, Robot*. Gnome Press, 1950.

[9] R. Axelrod and W.D. Hamilton. The Evolution of Cooperation. *Science*, 211 (4489): 1390–1396, 1981.

[10] Ned Block. Troubles with functionalism. In C. Wade Savage, editor, *Perception and Cognition: Issues in the Foundation of Psychology, Minn. Studies in the Phil. of Sci*, pages 261–325. 1978. Somewhat revised edition in Ned Block (ed.) *Readings in the Philosophy of Psychology*. Harvard University Press, Cambridge, Mass., vol. 1, pages 268–306, 1980.

[11] Martin A. Conway. Sensory-perceptual episodic memory and its context: autobiographical memory. *Phil. Trans. Royal Society*, 356(B):1375–1384, 2001.

[12] Peter Danielson. Competition among cooperators: Altruism and reciprocity. In *Proc. Nat'l. Acad. Sci*, volume 99, pages 7237–7242, 2002.

[13] Daniel C. Dennett. *Consciousness Explained*. Little, Brown and Company, Boston, 1991.

[14] James H. Fetzer. *Artificial intelligence: Its Scope and Limits*. Kluwer Academic Publishers, Dordrecht, 1990.

[15] James H. Fetzer. *Computers and Cognition: Why Minds Are Not Machines*. Kluwer Academic Publishers, Dordrecht, 2002.

[16] Luciano Floridi, editor. *The Blackwell Guide to the Philosophy of Computing and Information*. Blackwell Publishing, Malden, Mass., 2004.

[17] Jerry Fodor. *The Language of Thought*. Thomas Y. Crowell, New York, 1975.

[18] Harry G. Frankfurt. Freedom of the will and the concept of a person. *J. of Phil*, 68:5–20, 1971.

[19] Ray Frey and Chris Morris, editors. *Value, Welfare, and Morality*. Cambridge University Press, 1993.

[20] Dedre Gentner, Keith J. Holyoak, and Boicho K. Kokinov. *The Analogical Mind: Perspectives from Cognitive Science*. The MIT Press, Cambridge, Mass., 2001.

[21] Malik Ghallab, Dana Nau, and Paolo Traverso. *Automated Planning: Theory and Practice*. Morgan Kaufmann Publishers, San Francisco, 2004.

[22] R.M. Hare. *Moral Thinking: Its Levels, Method, and Point*. Oxford University Press, USA, 1981.

[23] Gilbert Harman. Desired desires. In Frey and Morris [19], pp. 138–157. Also in Gilbert Harman, *Explaining Value: and Other Essays in Moral Philosophy*. Oxford: Clarendon Press, pp. 117–136, 2000.

[24] Douglas R. Hofstadter, editor. *Fluid Concepts and Creative Analogies: Computer Models of the Fundamental Mechanisms of Thought*. By Douglas Hofstadter and the Fluid Analogies Research Group. Basic Books, New York, 1995.

[25] Brad Hooker. Rule consequentialism. In *Stanford Encyclopedia of Philosophy*, 2008. Online resource.

[26] Jeremy Hsu. Real soldiers love their robot brethren. *Live Science*, 2009. May 21, 2009.

[27] Michael A. Jenike. Obsessive-compulsive disorder. *New England J. of Medicine*, 350(3):259–265, 2004.

[28] Deborah Johnson. *Computer Ethics*. Prentice Hall, Upper Saddle River, 2001. 3rd ed.

[29] Deborah Johnson. Computer ethics. In Floridi [16], pages 65–75.

[30] Immanuel Kant. *Groundwork of the Metaphysic of Morals*, trans. New York, Harper & Row, 1964.

[31] George Lakoff and Mark Johnson. *Metaphors We Live By*. Chicago, University Press, 1980.

[32] Kathryn Blackmond Lasky and Paul E. Lehner. Metareasoning and the problem of small worlds. *IEEE Trans. Sys., Man, and Cybernetics*, 24(11):1643–1652, 1994.

[33] Janet Levin. Functionalism. In *Stanford Encyclopedia of Philosophy*. Online resource, 2009.

[34] David Lewis. An argument for the identity theory. *J. of Phil*, 63:17–25, 1966.

[35] Drew McDermott. *Mind and Mechanism*. MIT Press, Cambridge, Mass., 2001.

[36] John Stuart Mill. *Utilitarianism*. Oxford University Press, New York, 1861. Reprinted many times, including edition edited by Roger Crisp (1998).

[37] Marvin Minsky. *The Society of Mind*. Simon and Schuster, New York, 1986.

[38] James H. Moor. The nature, importance, and difficulty of machine ethics. *IEEE Intelligent Sys*, 21(4):18–21, 2006.

[39] Thomas Nagel. *The View from Nowhere*. Oxford University Press, 1986.

[40] Irène Némirovsky. *Suite Française*. Éditions Denoël, Paris, 2004. English translation by Sandra Smith published by Vintage, 2007.

[41] Allen Newell. Some problems of basic organization in problem-solving programs. Technical Report 3283-PR, RAND, 1962. Santa Monica: The RAND Corporation. Earlier version appeared in [61].

[42] Library of Congress Federal Research Division. *Country Profile: United Arab Emirates (UAE)*. Available at lcweb2.loc.gov/frd/cs/profiles/UAE.pdf, 2007.

[43] Derek Parfit. *Reasons and Persons*. Oxford University Press, 1984.

[44] Plato. *The Republic*. Cambridge University Press, Cambridge, 360 BCE. Translation by Tom Griffith and G.R.F Ferrari. Cambridge University Press, Cambridge. 2000.

[45] Hilary Putnam. "Degree of confirmation" and inductive logic. In P.A. Schilpp, editor, *The Philosophy of Rudolf Carnap*. The Open Court Publishing Company, Lasalle, Ill., 1963. Also in Hilary Putnam, *Mathematics, Matter and Method: Philosophical Papers, Vol. 1*. Cambridge University Press: Cambridge, pages 271-292, 1975.

[46] Georges Rey. *Contemporary Philosophy of Mind: A Contentiously Classical Approach*. Blackwell Publishers, Cambridge, Mass., 1997.

[47] Arturo Rosenblueth, Norbert Wiener, and Julian Bigelow. Behavior, purpose and teleology. *Philosophy of Science*, pages 18–24, 1943.

[48] W. David Ross. *The Right and the Good*. Oxford University Press, 1930.

[49] Stuart Russell and Peter Norvig. *Artificial Intelligence: A Modern Approach (2nd edition)*. Prentice Hall, 2003.

[50] L. J. Savage. *Foundations of Statistics*. Wiley, New York, 1954.

[51] John R. Searle. Is the brain's mind a computer program? *Scientific American*, 262:26–31, 1990.

[52] John R. Searle. *The Rediscovery of the Mind*. MIT Press, Cambridge, Mass., 1992.

[53] Abraham Silberschatz, Greg Gagne, and Peter Baer Galvin. *Operating System Concepts (ed. 8)*. John Wiley & Sons, Incorporated, New York, 2008.

[54] Peter Singer. *Practical Ethics*. Cambridge University Press, 1993. 2nd ed.

[55] Richard P. Swinson, Martin M. Antony, S. Rachman, and Margaret A. Richter. *Obsessive-Compulsive Disorder: Theory, Research, and Treatment*. Guilford Press, New York. 2001.

[56] Endel Tulving. *Elements of Episodic Memory*. Clarendon Press, Oxford, 1983.

[57] Endel Tulving. What is episodic memory? *Current Directions in Psych. Sci*, 2(3):67–70, 1993.

[58] Wendell Wallach and Colin Allen. *Moral Machines*. Oxford University Press, 2008.

[59] Daniel M. Wegner. *The Illusion of Conscious Will*. MIT Press, Cambridge, Mass., 2002.

[60] Norbert Wiener. *Cybernetics: Or Control and Communication in the Animal and the Machine*. Technology Press, New York, 1948.

[61] Marshall C. Yovits, George T. Jacobi, and Gordon D. Goldstein. *Self-organizing Systems 1962*. Spartan Books, 1962.

[62] Paul Ziff. The feelings of robots. *Analysis*, 19(3):64–68, 1959.

7

Machine Ethics and the Idea of a More-Than-Human Moral World

Steve Torrance

"We are the species equivalent of that schizoid pair, Mr Hyde and Dr Jekyll;
we have the capacity for disastrous destruction but also the potential to found
a magnificent civilization. Hyde led us to use technology badly; we misused
energy and overpopulated the earth, but we will not sustain civilization by
abandoning technology. We have instead to use it wisely, as Dr Jekyll would
do, with the health of the Earth, not the health of people, in mind."
                                                                    –Lovelock 2006: 6–7

Introduction

IN THIS PAPER I WILL DISCUSS SOME OF THE BROAD PHILOSOPHICAL ISSUES
that apply to the field of machine ethics. ME is often seen primarily as a
practical research area involving the modeling and implementation of artificial
moral agents. However this shades into a broader, more theoretical inquiry into
the nature of ethical agency and moral value as seen from an AI or information-
theoretical point of view, as well as the extent to which autonomous AI agents
can have moral status of different kinds. We can refer to these as *practical* and
philosophical ME respectively.

Practical ME has various kinds of objectives. Some are technically well defined
and relatively close to market, such as the development of ethically responsive
robot care assistants or automated advisers for clinicians on medical ethics issues.
Other practical ME aims are more long term, such as the design of a general purpose ethical reasoner/advisor – or perhaps even a "genuine" moral agent with a
status equal (or as equal as possible) to human moral agents.[1]

The broader design issues of practical ME shade into issues of philosophical
ME, including the question of what it means to be a "genuine moral agent" – as
opposed merely to one that "behaves as if" it were being moral. What genuine

---

[1] For an excellent survey of ME, from a mainly practical point of view, but with a discussion of many
of the more philosophical questions too, see Wallach and Allen 2009.

moral agent means in this context is itself an important issue for discussion. There are many other conceptual questions to be addressed here, and clearly philosophical ME overlaps considerably with discussion in mainstream moral philosophy. Philosophical ME also incorporates even more speculative issues, including whether the arrival of ever more intelligent autonomous agents, as may be anticipated in future developments in AI, could force us to recast ethical thinking as such, perhaps so that it is less exclusively human oriented and better accommodates a world in which such intelligent agents exist in large numbers, interact with humans and with each other, and possibly dominate or even replace humanity.

In what is discussed here, I will consider all of these strands of ME – narrowly focused practical ME research, longer-range practical ME goals, and the more "blue-skies" speculative questions. Much of the emphasis will be at the speculative end: In particular I wish to explore various perspectives on the idea of "widening the circle of moral participation," as it might be called. I will compare how this idea of widening the ethical circle may work itself out within ME as compared with other, rather different but equally challenging ethical approaches, in particular those inspired by animal rights and by environmental thinking. Also, artificial agents are *technological* agents, so we will find ourselves raising questions concerning the ethical significance of technology and the relation between technology and the "natural" world. This invites us to contrast certain ethical implications of ME with views that radically challenge values inherent in technology.

A major focus in the following discussion will thus be the idea of the "more-than-human" – a term inspired by the ecological philosopher David Abram (1996). I believe that it is instructive to develop a dialogue between approaches to ethics inspired by ME (and by informatics more generally) and approaches inspired by biological and environmental concerns. ME, in its more radical and visionary form, develops a variety of conceptions of a more-than-human world that strongly contrasts with ecological conceptions. However, as we will see, in some ways there are striking resonances between the two kinds of view. It is also of value to the practical ME researcher, I would claim, to explore the relationships between these different broad perspectives on ethics and the more-than-human world.

Machine Ethics: Some Key Questions

Artificial intelligence might be defined as the activity of designing machines that do things that, when done by humans, are indicative of the possession of intelligence in those human agents. Similarly, artificial (or machine) ethics could be defined as designing machines that do things that, when done by humans, are indicative of the possession of "ethical status" in those humans. (Note that the notion of ethical status can apply to "bad" as well as "good" acts: A robot murderer, like a robot saint, will have a distinctive ethical status.) What kinds of entities have ethical status? In general, most people would not regard an inanimate object as having genuine moral status: Even though you can "blame" a faulty electrical consumer unit for a house fire, this is more a causal accounting than a moral one; it would seem that you can't treat it as morally culpable in the way you can a negligent electrician or an arsonist. There is perhaps a presumption that AI systems are more like household electrical consumer units in this respect, but many would question that presumption, as we will see.

As can be seen, the notion of "having ethical status" is difficult to pin down, but it can be seen to involve two separate but associated aspects, which could be called ethical *productivity* and ethical *receptivity*. Saints and murderers – as well as those who do their duty by filing their tax returns honestly and on time – are ethical *producers*, whereas those who stand to benefit from or be harmed by the acts of others are ethical *recipients* (or "consumers").[2] If I believe an artificial agent ought to be solicitous of my interest then I am viewing that agent as a moral producer. If, on the other hand, I believe that I ought to be solicitous of the artificial agent's interest then I am viewing it as a potential moral receiver. [See Figure 7.1.] The main emphasis of practical ME has been on moral productivity rather than receptivity – not least because it seems easier to specify what you might need to do to design a morally productive artificial agent than it is to say what is involved in an artificial agent being a moral receiver or consumer. Notions of artificial moral receptivity are perhaps at the more "blue skies" end of the ME spectrum; nevertheless, for various reasons, they may need to be addressed.

At a very high level of generality, and taking into account the distinction just discussed between ethical productivity and receptivity, at least three distinct but related questions suggest themselves concerning ME in its various forms:

1. *Ethical Productivity*: How far is it possible to develop machines that are "ethically responsible" in some way – that is, that can act in ways that conform to the kinds of norms that we ethically require of the behavior of human agents?
2. *Ethical Receptivity*: How far is it possible to have machines that have "ethical interests" or "ethical goods" of their own – that is, that have properties that qualify them as beings *toward which* humans have ethical duties?

---

[2] See Torrance (2008, 2009). It should be pointed out that these are roles that an individual may play, and that clearly a single person can occupy both roles at the same time – for instance if an earthquake victim (who is a moral recipient in that she is, or ought to be, the object of others' moral concern) also performs heroic acts in saving other victims' lives (and thus, as someone whose behavior is to be morally commended, occupies in this respect the role of moral producer). Also the two kinds of role may partially overlap, as they do in the concept of "respect": if I respect you for your compassion and concern for justice (moral producer), I may see you as therefore deserving of special consideration (moral recipient) – but there is no space to go into that in more detail here.

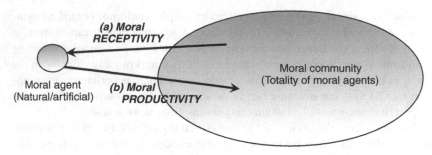

Figure 7.1. Moral productivity and receptivity.
Illustrating moral productivity and moral receptivity as complementary relationships between a moral agent and (the rest of) the moral community. Note that the relationship may, theoretically, hold in one direction for a given kind of agent, without holding in the other direction. For ease of initial understanding the moral agent is pictured as standing outside the moral community, whereas, of course, as a moral agent (of one or other kind) it would be part of the moral community. So strictly, the small blob should be inside the larger area.

3. *The Ethics of Machine Ethics*: What is the ethical significance of ME as a general project; and more specifically, is it ethically appropriate to develop machines of either of the previous two kinds? The more specific version of this third question requires at least two subquestions:

3a. Is it right to develop machines that either are genuine autonomous ethical producers, or that simulate or appear to be such agents?

3b. Is it right to develop machines that either are ethical recipients – that have genuine moral claims or rights, or that simulate or appear to be such agents?

In order to discuss these questions and the relations between them, I propose to distinguish four broad perspectives. These are four approaches to ethics in general and, more widely, four approaches to the world and to nature. The four approaches have the labels *anthropocentrism, infocentrism, biocentrism,* and *ecocentrism*.[3] By extension these four perspectives can also be taken to offer distinctive positions on ME, in particular to the foregoing questions as well as on some broader issues, which will be identified during the course of the discussion. The approaches may be seen to be partially overlapping and, as a whole, far from exhaustive. A comparison of these four perspectives will, I hope, define a space of discussion that will be rewarding to explore.

Each of these perspectives takes up a distinctive position on the question of the composition of the "moral constituency" – that is, the question of just which kinds of beings in the world count as either moral producers or as moral receivers.

[3] Apart from infocentrism, the terms are owed to Curry 2006.

Maybe it is better to think of these four labels as hooks on which to hang various clusters of views that tend to associate together.[4]

Four Perspectives

Here is a sketch of each approach:

- *Anthropocentrism.* This approach defines ethics (conventionally enough) as centered around human needs and interests. On this view, all other parts of the animate and inanimate world are seen as having little or no inherent value other than in relation to human goals. It goes without saying that various versions of this approach have occupied a dominant position in Western philosophy for some time. There are many variations to anthropocentrism and they are too well known to require us to go into detail here. In relation to the objectives of ME, and those of AI more broadly, the anthropocentric view sees machines, however intelligent or personlike they may be, as being nothing other instruments for human use. The project of ME is thus interpreted, by this approach, as being essentially a kind of safety-systems engineering, or an extension of thereof. Perhaps many of those engaged in practical, narrowly focused ME research would agree with this position.[5]
- *Infocentrism.* This approach is based on a certain view of the nature of mind or intelligence, which in turn suggests a rather more adventurous view of ethics in general and of ME in particular. The informational view of mind, which has been extensively discussed and elaborated within AI and cognitive science circles over many decades, affirms that key aspects of mind and intelligence can be defined and replicated as computational systems. A characteristic position within this perspective is that ethics can best be seen as having a cognitive or informational core.[6] Moreover, the informational/rational aspects of ethics can, it will be said, be extended to AI systems, so that we can (at least in principle) produce artificial agents that are not merely operationally autonomous, but rather have characteristics of being ethically autonomous as well.

---

[4] We only consider secular approaches here: Clearly religion-based approaches offer other interesting perspectives on the bounds of the moral constituency, but it is not possible to include them within the scope of the present discussion.

[5] A characteristic and much-quoted expression of ethical anthropocentrism is to be found in Kant, on the question of the treatment of animals. Kant believed that animals could be treated only as means rather than as ends; hence "we have no immediate duties to animals; our duties toward them are indirect duties to humanity" (Kant 1997; see also Frey 1980).

[6] This idea can be understood in at least two ways: either as the claim that moral thinking is primarily cognitive and rational in nature, rather than emotional or affective (a view associated with the ethical writings of Plato and Kant); or with the more modern view that information (in some sense of the term based on computer science, information-theory, or similar fields) is a key determinant of moral value. (Luciano Floridi defends a view of the latter sort – see, for example, Floridi 2008a, 2008b.) Both these views (ancient and contemporary) may be identified with the infocentric approach.

On the infocentric view, then, machines with ethical properties would not be merely safer mechanisms, but rather ethical agents in their own right. Some proponents of the infocentric view will be sensitive to the complaint that ethical thinking and action isn't just cognitive, and that emotion, teleology, consciousness, empathy, and so forth play important roles in moral thinking and experience. They will go on, however, to claim that each such phenomenon can also be defined in informational terms and modeled in artificial cognitive systems. Even though doing so may be hard in practice, in principle it should be possible for artificial computational agents to exemplify emotion and consciousness. It would follow that such artificial agents could be (again, in principle at least) not just morally active or productive, but also morally receptive beings – that is, beings that may have their own ethical demands and rights.

Infocentrism, so defined, may be compatible with an anthropocentric approach; however, in its more adventurous forms it sees possible future AI agents as forming a new class of intelligent being whose ethical capacities and interests are to be taken as seriously as those of humans. It is also worth pointing out that infocentrism, as here understood, has a strong technocentric bias – indeed, it could also have been named "technocentrism."

- *Biocentrism.* On this approach, being a living, sentient creature with natural purposes and interests is at the core of what it is to have a mind, to be a rational intelligent agent. By extension, ethical status is also believed to be necessarily rooted in core biological properties. Often ethics, on this approach, is seen as having important affective and motivational elements, which, it is felt, cannot be adequately captured within an informational model; and these affective elements are seen as deriving from a deep prehuman ancestry. Adherents of this approach are thus likely to be strongly opposed to the infocentric approach. However, they may also express opposition to an anthropocentric view of ethics in that they stress the ways in which affectivity and sentience in nonhuman animals qualify such creatures to be centers of ethical concern or as holders of moral rights, even though nonhuman animals largely lack rational powers (see Singer 1977, Regan 1983). Biocentrism also tends toward an ethical position characterized by E. O. Wilson (1984, 1994) as "biophilia" – a view that claims that humans have an innate bond with other biological species and that, in view of this, natural biological processes should have an ethical privileging in our system of values, as compared with the technological outputs of modern industrial civilization and other nonliving objects in our environment. Infocentrists, by contrast, perhaps tend toward the converse ethical attitude of "technophilia."
- *Ecocentrism.* Just as infocentrism could be seen as one kind of natural direction in which anthropocentrism might develop, so ecocentrism could be seen as a natural progression from biocentrism. Ethics, on this approach, is seen as applying primarily to entire ecosystems (or the biosphere, or Gaia [Lovelock

1979, 2006]) and to individual organisms only as they exist within the context of such ecosystems. Ecocentrism thus opposes the anthropocentric stress on the human sphere. However, it also opposes the biocentrist's stress on the moral status of *individual* creatures. Particularly in its more militant or apocalyptic forms, ecocentrism is motivated by a sense of a growing crisis in industrial civilization coupled with a belief in the need to reject the values of technological, market-based society in favor of a set of social values that are tuned to the natural processes of the ecosphere and to the perceived threats to those processes. Thus many supporters of ecocentrism will express a deep antipathy to the technological bias that is implied by the infocentric approach.

Despite such deep oppositions between these positions, biocentrism, ecocentrism, and infocentrism nevertheless appear to be on similar lines in at least one striking respect: Each stresses an aspiration to transcend the domain of the merely human in ethical terms. The extrahuman or posthuman emphases are rather different in the three cases: An extension of respect from the human species to a wide variety (or the totality) of other living species in the first case; an emphasis on the total natural environment (including its inanimate aspects) in the second case; and a technological, AI-based emphasis in the third case. Nevertheless it is worthwhile to compare the posthuman elements that exist within the more radical expressions of all these positions (especially infocentrism and ecocentrism) to see in more detail the points of contrast and also of possible commonality within the various approaches. This is something that we will tackle later on.

I'll now address how adherents of these various approaches may respond to the three questions that I specified earlier, as well as to some broader issues that will come up in the course of the discussion.

Anthropocentrism

Adherents of this approach are most likely to view the project of ME as a specific domain of intelligent-systems engineering, rather than of developing machines as ethical agents in their own right. So the anthropocentrist's most probable response to question 1, on the possibility of developing ethically responsible artificial agents, is that there is no reason why ethical constraints should not be built into the control systems of such agents, but that such agents should not be considered as having their own autonomous moral responsibilities – they would simply be instruments for the fulfillment of human purposes. On question 2 – the possibility of ethical receptivity in artificial agents – the anthropocentrist would give a skeptical response: It would typically be considered difficult to envisage artificial mechanisms as having the kind of properties (consciousness, inherent teleology, etc.) that would qualify them for ethical consideration as beings with their own moral interests or goods.

On question 3 – the ethics of pursuing machine ethics as a project – the anthropocentric view would characteristically stress the importance of not mis-representing such a project as having pretensions to loftier goals than it is entitled (on this view) to claim for itself. ME could at most be a subdomain of the broader field of technological ethics, it would be said. On question 3a, a supporter of the anthropocentric approach might typically claim that the only moral responsibili-ties and obligations that could be in play would be those of the human users of AI agents, so it would be important not to pretend that artificial agents could have any autonomous moral status: This could lead, when things go wrong, to humans illegitimately shifting the blame to artificial agents.[7] On 3b, conversely, it could be argued that attributing moral receptivity where it does not exist could lead to unjust diversion of resources from those genuinely in need (namely humans). For example, if there is a road accident involving numbers of both human and robot casualties, spreading scarce time and manpower to give assistance to the latter would have to be considered morally wrong, if, as anthropocentrists might argue, the robot "victims" of the accident should really be considered as nothing but nonconscious machinery with no genuine moral claims.

Infocentrism

It is to be supposed that many current researchers in the ME community fit into the infocentric category (although others of them may see themselves as more aligned with anthropocentrism, as described earlier). Adherents of the infocen-tric approach will tend to see as a realizable goal the creation of robots and other artificial beings that approximate, at least to some degree, autonomous ethical actors (question 1); indeed, they will view it as a vital goal, given the threat of increasing numbers of functionally autonomous but morally noncontrolled AI agents. However, there will be disagreement among supporters of this position on how far any artificial moral agency could approach the full richness of human ethical agency. This depends on the view of moral agency that is adopted. The lack of consensus on this question among conventional moral philosophers has emboldened many ME researchers to claim that their own research may produce more clarity than has been achieved hitherto by mere armchair philosophizing. (As with other areas where AI researchers have offered computational solutions to ancient philosophical questions, conventional philosophers tend to be some-what underwhelming in their gratitude.)

There is clearly room for much nuance within the broad sweep of infocentric views. Some adherents may see information processing as lying at the core of

---

[7] See, for example, Sparrow 2007 for a discussion of the issue of shifting blame from human to machine in the specific domain of autonomous robots deployed in a theatre of war; a lot of the issues concerning moral responsibility in this domain apply more widely to other domains where artificial agents may be employed.

what it is to be an ethical agent, human or otherwise, and may therefore see no limits in principle (if not in practice) to the degree to which an artificial agent could approach or even surpass human skills in moral thought and behavior (I assume here that it is appropriate to talk of moral agency as a "skill"). Others may take moral agency to involve important elements that are less amenable to informational or computational modeling, and may therefore see definite limits to how far a computational agent could go toward being a genuine moral agent.[8] Nevertheless, even while recognizing such limits, it may still be possible to envisage a healthy and productive industry in the development of computational ethical systems and agents that will make the deployment of autonomous artificial agents around the world more responsible and humanity-respecting.

The primary focus of the infocentric approach is, as we have seen, on ethical agency rather than receptivity, hence adherents of this approach may again comment on question 2 in different ways. Some would say that artificial beings could never be given the kind of moral respect that we give to conscious humans or indeed to some animals, because purely informationally based systems could never, even in principle, possess consciousness, sentience, or whatever other properties might be relevant to such moral respect.[9] Others might disagree with this last point and claim that all mental properties, including consciousness, are informatic at root, so that in principle a conscious, rational robot (or indeed a whole population of such) could be created in due course. They would further agree that such a robot would have general moral claims on us.[10] Yet another take on question 2 would be that having genuine moral claims on us need not require consciousness – at least not of the phenomenal, "what-it-is-like" sort. This would considerably lower the criteria threshold for developing artificial beings with moral claims or rights.

On question 3, about the ethics of ME, adherents of the infocentric approach would be likely to think that such a project – at least of the first sort (3a) – is morally acceptable, and maybe even imperative. As artificial agents develop more operational or functional autonomy, it will be important to ensure that their

---

[8] See Moor 2006, Torrance 2008, Wallach and Allen 2009 for discussions of the different senses in which an automated system or agent might be considered as a "moral agent."

[9] It seems plausible to suggest that sentience – the ability to experience pleasure, pain, conscious emotion, perceptual qualia, etc. – plays a key role as a determinant of whether a being is a fit target for moral respect (i.e., of moral receptivity). This may be true, but it should not be thought that sentience is an exclusive determinant of moral receptivity. Many people believe that the remains of deceased people ought to be treated with respect: This is accepted even by those who strongly believe that bodily death is an end to experience, and is accepted even in the case of those corpses for whom there are no living relations or dear ones who would be hurt by those corpses being treated without respect. Other examples of attributing moral concern to nonsentient entities will be considered later.

[10] For computationally driven accounts of consciousness, see Dennett 1978, Aleksander 2005, Franklin 1995, Haikonen 2003, and the articles collected in Holland 2003 and Torrance et al. 2007.

freedom of choice is governed by the kinds of ethical norms that we apply to free human behavior. This may be so even if such agents could only ever be faint approximations of what we understand human moral agency to be. Adherents of the infocentric approach will say that, if properly designed, "para-ethical" agents (Torrance 2008, 2009) may go a long way to introducing the kind of moral responsibility and responsiveness into autonomous agents that is desirable as such technology spreads. Thus, for example, in *Moral Machines*, Wallach and Allen write, "it doesn't really matter whether artificial systems are *genuine* moral agents" – implying that it is the results that are important. They go on: "The engineering objective remains the same: humans need advanced (ro)bots to act as much like moral agents as possible. All things considered, advanced automated systems that use moral criteria to rank different courses of action are preferable to ones that pay no attention to moral issues" (2008: 199). Yet should we then *blame* them if they choose wrongly? And should we allow the humans who designed the moral robots, or those who followed the robots' advice or acted on their example, to escape moral censure if things go terribly wrong?

As for (3b), the ethics of developing artificial creatures that have genuine moral claims on humans (and on each other), this may be seen in a less positive light by the infocentric approach. Those who defend a strong view of the computational realizability of a wide range of mental phenomena, including consciousness[11] and affective states rather than merely functional or cognitive states, may believe it to be eminently possible (again, in principle at least) to produce artificial beings that have the kinds of minds that do make it imperative to consider them as having moral claims of their own.[12] It may be quite novel to produce "conscious" robots in ones or twos, but technological innovations often spread like forest fires. The project of creating a vast new population of such beings with their own independent moral claims may well be considered to be highly dubious from an ethical point of view. (For instance, as with all autonomous manufactured agents, they would require various kinds of resources in order to function properly; but if genuinely conscious, they might well need to be considered as having moral rights to those resources. This may well bring them into competition with humans who have moral claims to those same resources.) Then there is also the issue of whether to restrict the design of artificial agents so that they don't give a false impression of

---

[11] The field of machine consciousness in some ways mirrors that of ME. As in the latter, machine consciousness includes the practical development of artificial models of aspects of consciousness or even attempts to instantiate consciousness in robots, as well as broader philosophical discussions of the scope and limitations of such a research program. For discussion of the relations between machine consciousness and ethics with implications for machine ethics, see Torrance 2000, 2007.

[12] Thus Daniel Dennett, commenting on the Cog Project in the AI Lab at MIT, which had the explicit aim of producing a "conscious" robot, wrote: "more than a few participants in the Cog project are already musing about what obligations they might come to have to Cog, over and above their obligations to the Cog team" (1998: 169).

having sentience and emotions when such features are actually absent. Clearly problems to do with public misperception on such matters will raise their own moral puzzles.

On the broader question of the ethical significance of the project of ME as such, there are again a number of possible responses from within the infocentric position. One striking view heard from the more radical voices of this approach sees developments in ME, but also in AI and in other related technologies, as presaging a change in ethical value at a global level – precisely the transition from an anthropocentric ethic to an infocentric ethic (Floridi 2008a, b). Such a view may be interpreted as suggesting that the overall fabric of ethics itself will need to be radically rethought in order to accommodate the far reaches of computational or informatic developments. Many defenders of this vision lay down a challenge: The rapid increase in information capacity and apparent intelligence of digital technologies indicate (they say) that artificial agents may soon far surpass humans intellectually – the so-called Technological Singularity (Vinge 1993, Moravec 1988, Kurzweil 2005, Dietrich 2007, Bostrom 2005; for criticism, see Lanier 2000, and for response, Kurzweil 2001). Agents with far more processing power than humans may either have quite different insights than humans into right and wrong ways to act, or they may assert ethical demands themselves that they regard as taking precedence over human needs. (See LaChat 2004, Bostrom 2000, 2004 for some intuitions relating to this.)

A view of this sort may be considered morally and conceptually objectionable on many accounts, not least because of an uncritical worship of technological "progress" (see the discussion of the ecocentric approach later for more on this theme). Also, it does rest very heavily on the presumption that all the relevant aspects of human mentality are explicable in informational terms and can be transferred without remainder or degradation to post-biotic processing platforms. A very bright *über*mind that is unfeeling, aesthetically dull, and creatively shackled does not seem to be a particularly worthy successor to human civilization.[13]

Biocentrism

This third approach provides a focus for some of the key objections that might be made by people outside the field when confronted with ME as conceived along the lines of the second approach, especially to the more strident variants

---

[13] On successors to the human race, see in particular Dietrich 2007; Bostrom 2004, 2005. Dietrich argues that replacement of the human race by superintelligences would be a good thing, as the human race is a net source of moral evil in the world due to ineradicable evolutionary factors. This does seem to be a very extreme version of this kind of view – fortunately there are other writers who are concerned to ensure that possible artificial superintelligences can cohabit in a friendly and compassionate way with humans (See Yudkovsky 2001, Goertzel 2006).

of that approach. Biocentrism can be seen as a characteristic view of the nature of mind (and, by extension, of ethical value) that sees mental properties strongly rooted in elementary features of being a living, biological organism. One example of the biocentric approach is seen in the work of Maturana and Varela, for whom there is an intimate association between being a living system and being a cognizing system. On their influential autopoietic theory, to be a living creature is to be a self-maintaining system that enters into a sense-making – and thus cognitive and evaluative – relationship with its environment. Thus, even for so elementary a creature as a motile bacterium searching out sugar, environmental features – in this case sugar concentrations – will have meaning for the organism, in terms of its life-preserving and life-enhancing purposes (Maturana and Varela 1980, Thompson 2007, Di Paolo 2005). An alternative version of the biocentric approach is to be found in the writings of Hans Jonas, for whom being alive is seen as a kind of "inwardness" (Jonas 1996/2001).

The biocentric perspective on ME would claim that there are strong links between human ethical status – both of the active and of the receptive kinds – and our biological, organic makeup, and indeed from our rich evolutionary ancestry. The infocentric approach gives a high profile to the cognitive, specifically human aspects of mind, and thus paints a picture of morality that perhaps inevitably stresses ethical cognition or intelligence. By contrast, supporters of the biocentric approach will be prone to give a richer picture of moral agency: To be a moral agent is to be open to certain characteristic emotions or experiential and motivational states, *as well as*, no doubt, employing certain characteristic styles of cognition.

Because of the strong evolutionary links between human and other species, moral features of human life are seen by the biocentrist as being strongly continuous with earlier, prehuman forms of relation and motivation (Midgley 1978, Wright 1994, De Waal 2006). Human moral agency, then, according to the biocentric model, derives from a combination of deep ancestral biological features (such as the instinct to safeguard close kin members and other conspecifics in situations of danger, as well as other precursors of "moral sentiments") and human-specific features, such as the use of rationality and reflection in the course of ethical decision making. It will be argued that AI research can perhaps make significant inroads into the second kind of properties but will be much less potent with the first. So there will be strong in-principle limitations on how far one can stretch computational models of ethics according to the biocentric view.

The biocentric answer to question 1, on the possibility of artificial agency, will thus be likely to be negative for a variety of reasons. One reason concerns the nature of empathy and other emotions that seem to be at the heart of morality, and how they relate, within the human domain at least, to first-person experience. To be a moral agent, it will be argued, you must be able to *react to*, not just *reason about*, the predicament of others – that is, you must be able to reflect empathetically on what it would be like to be in such a predicament yourself. Such empathetic identification appears to "up the ante" on what it takes to be a genuine moral agent, as it raises the question of how a nonbiological creature can understand (in a rich sense of "understand" that is appropriate to this context) the needs of a biological creature. Thus morality is often said to be largely underpinned by a global golden-rule norm: "Do unto others only what you would wish to be done to yourself." Operation of such a rule – or even understanding what it entails – perhaps involves having a first-person acquaintance with experiential-affective states such as pain, pleasure, relief, distress, and so on.

Biocentrists can present a dilemma to ME researchers here. The latter need to choose whether or not to concede that first-person knowledge of such experiential-affective states are unable to be incorporated into a computational ME system. If they do agree that they cannot, then an important prerequisite for implementing ethical benevolence in a computational agent lies beyond the capabilities of ME research. If, on the other hand, ME researchers refuse to make such a concession, then they owe us a convincing explanation of how direct experience of pain, relief, and other such states is feasible in a purely computational system. It is far from clear what form such an explanation might take (Torrance 2007).

This is not just a theoretical issue. An important motivation for practical work in ME is the development of robot carers for aged or very young citizens.[14] Such an agent will need, if it is to be properly ethically responsive to its charges, to be able to detect accurately when they are distressed or in physical pain (and also when they are just pretending, playing jokes, etc.) This is a skill that may also be required of ethically responsible robot soldiers when dealing with civilians who are unfortunate enough to find themselves in the theatre of war (Sparrow 2007). Workers in AI and ME talk of the need to formalize the "Theory of Mind," which it is assumed codifies the way humans detect the states of their conspecifics. However, social cognition theories based on conceptions of Theory of Mind (or Simulation Theory) are seriously contested from many quarters (Gallagher 2001, 2008; De Jaegher & Di Paolo 2007; De Jaegher 2008). Not least among such challenges are counterviews that stress that understanding another's distress requires skills in social interactions that are partly biologically innate and partly dependent on subtle developmental factors going back to early infancy and perhaps even prenatal experiences (Trevarthen & Reddy 2007).

It will be seen that, for the biocentric approach, the style of response to question 1 will be strongly linked to how question 2 is to be answered (see Torrance 2008). Biocentrism puts a relatively strong emphasis on moral receptivity, on morally relevant aspects of experience or feeling, whereas the infocentric approach seemingly finds it easier to focus on moral conduct or comportment than on morally relevant feelings. So the biocentrist's response to question 2 will probably be a strong negative: If moral receptivity depends upon morally relevant feelings or sentient states, and if computational agents can't actually

[14]   See Sparrow and Sparrow 2006 for a critical view of robot care of the elderly.

undergo such feelings or sentient states, then an artificial agent can't be a moral consumer.[15] (However, it should be noted that the reverse may not be true: It seems you can be fit to be a recipient of moral concern without necessarily being a properly constituted ethical actor. For instance, many people concerned with animal welfare pinpoint ways in which animals suffer as a result of being reared and slaughtered for food production, experimentation, etc. Such people would not normally think that nonhuman animals could be ethical "agents" in the sense of having responsibilities, or of being the kinds of creatures whose conduct could be appraised ethically – certainly not if ethical agency necessarily involves rationality or sequential reasoning.)

The biocentric approach will similarly look askance on the moral desirability of the ME enterprise (question 3). ME research would, in the biocentric view, succeed in creating, at best, very crude models of either active or receptive ethical roles in artificial agents. So it would be important for ME researchers not to mislead the public into thinking otherwise. By all means, it will be argued, AI technology should be hedged by ethical controls as much as possible. The biocentrist could agree that artificial models of ethical thinking may even provide useful aids to human ethical thinking. Yet it will be important, they will say, to avoid treating artificial moral agents as being anything like genuine coparticipants in the human moral enterprise.

Ecocentrism

Ecocentrism can be seen as a development from biocentrism that, at least in certain important respects, would take even more marked exception to the ME enterprise, particularly in terms of its moral significance or desirability. Ecocentrism, as a broad ethical approach, takes its departure from certain internal debates within different brands of the ecological ethics movement. Ecological ethics takes for granted empirical claims concerning future trends in global population, climate change, depletion of natural resources, species extinctions, rises in sea level, and so on. These are claimed to be of paramount ethical concern because of the urgency and depth of the threats coming from these various directions. Thus normative systems that do not prioritize environmental crisis are criticized by all shades of ecocentric ethics.

However there are three different kinds of motivation for environmental concern, and three different kinds of ecocentric ethical view based on these different motivations (Sylvan & Bennett 1994, Curry 2006). The first assumes that it is the threat to human interests that is the sole or major ethical driver for environmental concern (this is the "light green" position – its ethical outlook is broadly consonant with the anthropocentric approach, as outlined earlier).

---

[15] Calverley 2005 gives an interesting account of how rights for robots might be supported as an extension of biocentric arguments offered in favor of granting rights to nonhuman animals.

The second approach – which corresponds to the biocentric approach as previously discussed – rejects what it sees as the human chauvinism of light green ethics, and instead voices concern on behalf of all sentient creatures, human or otherwise. (This is the "mid-green" position – and it very much overlaps with the biocentric approach discussed earlier.) It argues, in effect, for a principle of interspecies parity of suffering. The third ("dark green") approach takes an even more radical step, rejecting the "sentientism" implicit in both the light and mid-green positions. This third approach argues that it is entire ecosystems, and indeed the global ecosystem of the earth, that should be considered as the primary moral subject in our ethical thinking; as such, all elements that participate in maintaining the harmonious functioning of that ecosystem can be considered as moral recipients or consumers (Naess 1973, Naess & Sessions 1984).[16] This includes all organic creatures, whether sentient or not, including fauna and nonliving parts of the landscape such as mountains, rivers, and oceans, all of which are part of the global milieu in which biological systems survive and thrive. Because the causal determinants of the current ecological crisis are largely due to technological capitalism, dark green ecology also carries a strong ethical opposition to technological forms of civilization and an aspiration to go back to more primitive forms of living.[17]

At least in its more radical forms, the ecocentric approach stands in opposition to each of the other three approaches mentioned. First, deep or dark green ecocentrism rejects the human-oriented bias of the anthropocentric position, not just because of its unfair privileging of human concerns over the concerns of other beings whose moral status demand to be recognized, but also because, as they see it, nearly all the causes for current environmental threats can be attributed to human activity (also because any environmental concerns voiced by anthropocentrists are not really based on any concern for the good of the environment as such, but rather on how the condition of the environment may affect future human interests.)

Second, strong ecocentrism rejects the infocentric position because it lays such direct, practical emphasis on the development of more and more sophisticated informatic technologies, and because of the role that such technologies play as market products in maintaining environmental threats; defenders of a strong ecocentric view will see infocentrism as little more than an elaboration of the anthropocentric approach. Third, strong ecocentrists question the biocentric position because, whereas the latter approach takes a wider view than merely human or technological concerns, it is still insufficiently comprehensive in its outlook. (However, the gaps between the biocentric and the ecocentric approaches are less extreme than between the latter and the first two approaches.)

[16] However, this terminology is not necessarily used by dark green eco-theorists. For an influential anticipation of dark green ecology, see Leopold 1948.
[17] See Curry 2006 for an excellent discussion of the three-fold division of ecocentric views.

It will be clear that supporters of the ecocentric approach, in its stronger forms, will be likely to have as little positive to say about the practical feasibility of ME research (questions 1 and 2) as biocentrists do. Also they will have even less enthusiasm for its ethical desirability (question 3). Its main ethical concerns about the ME enterprise will be that such enterprises are based on all the same industrial, social, and economic processes as other kinds of IT development and constitute the same kinds of physical threats to the environment. Perhaps ME researchers can adopt a more environmentally sensitive and self-reflective stance toward their own research and development practices, but to do this properly might necessitate changes to those practices so radical as to strongly threaten their viability. For example, it would require a searching environmental audit of such aspects as use of raw materials, the effects of mass-adoption of products, implications of electrical power consumption, and so on. There is clearly a vast range of critical questions that AI, robotics, and other informatics researchers can ask themselves about the ecological footprint of their professional activities: Only a relatively small number are doing so at present, and arguably that is a matter of some concern. No doubt ME researchers could also include ethical advice on ecological matters as a specific domain for ethical agent modeling.

However ecocentrism, in its more radical forms at least, may also imply a broad change in how ethics is conceived. Ecocentrists will stress global, earth-wide issues rather than more specific ones and may demand a more proactive conception of ethically right action – not for nothing are their adherents often referred to as eco-warriors! So if artificial ethical agents are to exist in any numbers, to satisfy the ecocentrist they would need to be capable of playing a leading role in the daunting task of rapidly swinging world public opinion away from current obsessions with consumerism and toward the kind of "green" values that, for ecocentrists, are the only values whose widespread adoption stand a chance of averting a global environmental cataclysm.

Conclusion: The Machine and Its Place in Nature

We have looked at ME in terms of three issues: the possibility of developing artificial moral producers, the possibility of developing artificial moral recipients, and the ethical desirability of ME as a practice. The infocentric approach has offered the most optimistic response toward those three questions. Most current practical work in ME is focused on the first issue – that of creating moral producers of various sorts, although some practical attention is being given to the eventual development of what might be called general moral productivity. This raises far deeper issues than domain-specific models of ethical thinking or action and therefore is a much longer-term goal. The problem of developing moral receptivity clearly raises even deeper issues (as we have seen, moral receptivity seems to imply the possession of a sentient consciousness). Many ME developers would question the need to address the issue of moral receptivity in order to make progress on moral productivity. However, it is not clear that a simulation of a morally productive agent could be reliable or robust (let alone a "genuine" moral agent) unless it also has a conception of being on the receiving end of the kinds of action that moral agents must consider in their moral deliberation.

Yet the idea of developing artificial moral recipients raises ethical problems of an acute kind: Should we be creating artificial agents that can have genuine moral interests, that can experience the benefit or the harm of the kinds of situations that we, as moral recipients, evaluate as ones that are worth seeking or avoiding? Many would find this unacceptable given the extent of deprivation, degradation, and servitude that exists among existing moral recipients in the world. Then there is the question of moral competition between possible future artificial recipients and the natural ones who will be part of the same community. How does one assess the relative moral claims that those different classes of being will make upon members of the moral community? Also, if, as we have suggested, the development of effective artificial moral productivity has an intimate dependence on developing moral receptivity in such agents, then these difficult issues may affect the validity of much more work in ME than is currently recognized by practitioners.

As we have seen, ME can be criticized from a number of different approaches. In our discussion we particularly singled out biocentrism and ecocentrism. Yet even from the point of view of anthropocentrism, ME is acceptable only if it is very limited in its objectives. Artificially intelligent agents will be seen, in the anthropocentric view, primarily as instruments to aid human endeavors – so for this approach the development of ethical controls on autonomous systems is just a particular application of the rules of (human-centered) engineering ethics that apply to any technological product, whether "intelligent" or not. In this view, any pretension to consider such "autonomous systems" themselves as moral actors in their own right is indulging in fantasy.

Biocentric and ecocentric perspectives on ME have rather different critical concerns. As we have seen, these views are informed by an ethical respect for the natural, biological world rather than the artificial, designed world. For ecocentrists in particular, nature as a whole is seen as an ultimate ethical subject in its own right, a noninstrumental focus for moral concern. Thus a supporter of the ecocentric view, if presented with ME as a general project, may see it as simply an extension of anthropocentrism. The project of developing technological agents to simulate and amplify human powers – the "fourth revolution," as Floridi refers to it (2008a)[18] – might well be seen by ecocentrists as simply one of the more recent expressions of a human obsession with using technology and science to increase human mastery over nature.

---

[18] For Floridi, the four revolutions were ushered in, respectively, by Copernicus, Darwin, Freud, and Turing.

Yet to take this position is to fail to see an important point of commonality between infocentrism, biocentrism, and ecocentrism: the way that each of these approaches develops a conception of the moral status that enlarges on the confines of the exclusively human. Each position develops a novel conception of the boundaries of the moral world that radically challenges traditional (anthropocentric) ethical schemes. In view of the intellectual dominance of anthropocentric thinking in our culture, it is surely refreshing to see how each of these positions develops its respective challenge to this anthropic ethical supremacy.

Judged in this light, the disparities between these positions, particularly between infocentrism and ecocentrism – even in their more aggressive forms – are less marked than they may at first sight appear to be. Each of them proclaims a kind of *extrahumanism*, albeit of somewhat different forms. This is particularly true of the more radical forms of the infocentric and ecocentric positions. Both reject the modernity of recent centuries, but from very different orientations: Radical infocentrism is future-oriented, whereas radical ecocentrism harks back to the deep history of the earth. Radical infocentrism sees humanity in terms of its potential to produce greater and greater innovation and envisages intelligent agency in terms of future developments from current technologies; and that seems to imply a progressively wider rupture from the natural habitat. In a kind of mirror image of this, radical ecocentrism's view of humanity reaches back to the life-world of primitive mankind, where natural surroundings are experienced as having an intimate relation to the self.[19]

Thus, in their different ways, both viewpoints urge a stretching of the moral constituency far beyond what conventional ethics will admit. Radical infocentrism sees a moral community filled out with artificial agents who may be affirmed as beings of moral standing, whereas radical ecocentrism seeks to widen the sphere of morally significant entities to include, not just animate species, but also plant life-forms and inanimate features of land- and seascapes. This process of widening the moral community, of enacting a conception of the *more-than-human*, carries on both sides an impatience with conventional moral positions in which the felt experience of benefit and of harm are taken as the key touchstones for determining moral obligation.[20] So each rejects the "sentientism," with its emphasis on individual experienced benefit or suffering, that is at the heart of much conventional moral thinking (and, indeed, is at the core of biocentrism, with its emphasis on the potential suffering of nonhuman animals).

So in some important respects the infocentric and ecocentric views, in their more radical forms, have important similarities – at least in what they reject. Yet even in terms of positive values, one wonders whether it might be possible to apply critical pressure to each view so as to enable some degree of convergence to take place. Consider, for example, the ecocentrist's rejection of technology

[19] Abram's work (1996) provides a particularly impressive expression of this point of view.
[20] I am grateful to Ron Chrisley for useful insights on this point.

and artificiality, and the concomitant rejection of the artificial and managed, in favor of the wild and unkempt. One can point out in response that technology has its own kind of wildness, as many commentators have pointed out, not least many ecocentrists. Wide-scale technological processes have a dynamic in the way they unfold that is to a considerable extent autonomous relative to human direction. Of course this self-feeding explosion of runaway technological growth, particularly over recent decades, has been a key driver of the current environmental crisis. Yet one wonders whether technology in itself is inimical to sustainable environmental development, as a too-simplistic ecocentric reading might insist. As James Lovelock reminds us in the opening passage to this paper, technology has a Jekyll/Hyde character: There is much that is beneficial as well as harmful in technology, and some of its developments (e.g., the bicycle? The book?) seem to have offered relatively little in the way of large-scale damaging consequences.[21]

Another issue concerns the boundary of the "natural": Where does "natural" stop and "artificial" begin? Are ecocentrists perhaps a little chauvinist themselves in rejecting certain values simply because they involve more technically advanced modes of practice rather than more primitive ones? Is not technological development itself a form of natural expression for *Homo sapiens*? As Helmuth Plessner argued, surely it is part of our very nature as humans that we are *artificial beings* – we are, in an important sense, "naturally artificial" (Ernste 2004, 443ff.). As humans, Plessner said, we live a kind of dual existence: We are partly centered in our bodies (as are other animals), but because of our abilities to engage in reflection of world and self, communication, artistic production, and so on, we are also eccentrically located outside ourselves, and as such we are inescapably artificers, we are constantly *on the make*. So if ecocentrism is to celebrate the diversity of natural systems and life-forms, then it also has to celebrate human naturalness as well – which means the production of technology, of culture, of knowledge that humanity has originated, even while we berate the devastating effects of such productions on our own and other species, and on the entire ecosystem.

Quite apart for the virtues that may be inherent in technology and other human products, there is the more pragmatic point that technologies are pretty well ineradicable. Given the existence of humanity and of human nature, it seems that machines will continue to have a crucial place in nature. We are no more capable of returning to a pretechnical existence than we are able to eradicate selfishness and bigotry from human nature (although these latter qualities in humanity may succeed in taking us back to a more primitive form of technological existence). A more realistic way of proceeding would be to seek to develop technologies that are as progressive as possible from the point of view

---

[21] David Abram suggests, on the contrary, that it is the advent of alphabetic, phonetic writing, and all the technologies that came in its train, that was a key factor in the loss of primitive experience of nature. Have the books (including Abram's) that followed alphabetization not been of net benefit to mankind and/or to nature?

of environmental protection – to seek an artificial intelligence and an ethics for our machines that don't simply achieve a kind of noninterventionism in relation to global environmental threats, but that positively encourage us to retreat from the abyss of environmental collapse toward which we are apparently currently hurtling. As the custodians of these machines, we must indeed adopt a greater responsiveness to those parts of the world that are not human-fashioned, or only minimally so, and that suffer from the excessive presence of mechanism in nature. Just possibly, intelligent-agent technologies may be able to play a key role in that reversal in ways which we are only beginning to understand, but which, if the AI community were to mobilize itself, could come to be articulated rapidly and effectively. Perhaps this also provides the best direction for research in machine ethics to take.

It may be a hard road to travel, particularly in view of the strident voices in the AI community, especially among the "singularitarians," whose infocentrism (or better, infomania) leads them to celebrate an impending eclipse of humanity by a technology that has accelerated to the point where its processes of recursive self-enhancement are no longer remotely understandable by even the most technically savvy humans. Some predict this "singularity" event with foreboding (Joy 2000), but many others do so with apparent glee (Kurzweil 2005, Goertzel 2006); some even say that the world will be a "better place" for the eclipse of humanity that may result (Dietrich 2007). The singularity literature does an enormous service by highlighting the ways in which AI developments could produce new degrees of intelligence and operational autonomy in AI agents – especially as current AI agents play an increasingly important role in the design of future AI agents. Bearing in mind the far-reaching implications of such possible future scenarios, the urgency of work in ME to ensure the emergence of "friendly AI" (Yudkowsky 2001, 2008) is all the more important to underline.

What is surprising about much of the singularity literature is the way in which its writers seem to be totally enraptured by the technological scenarios, at the expense of paying any attention to the implications of this techno-acceleration for the nontechnological parts of the world – for how the living world can supply any viable habitat for all this. (This is not to mention the lack of concern shown by apostles of the singularity for those on the nether sides of the ever-sharpening digital divide and prosperity divide that seem to be likely to accompany this techno-acceleration.) A thought spared for the parts of the planet that still are, but might soon cease to be, relatively untouched by the human thumbprint, seems an impossibility for these writers: They really need to get out more. On the other hand, many ecological advocates suffer from an opposite incapacity – to see any aspects of technology, particularly those of the Fourth Revolution, as other than a pestilence on the face of the earth. Such writers are as incapable of accommodating the technological as their counterparts are of accommodating anything but the technological. Yet these two parts of twenty-first-century reality – the biosphere and the technosphere – have to be reconciled, and they have to be reconciled by building a picture of humanity, hand-in-hand with a vision of the more-than-human, that really takes our biological-environmental being *and* our technical genius fully into account.

Acknowledgments

I would like to thank the following for helpful discussions relating to the issues discussed in this paper: David Calverley, Ron Chrisley, Tom Froese, Pietro Pavese, John Pickering, Susan Stuart, Wendell Wallach, and Blay Whitby.

References

Abram, D. (1996) *The Spell of the Sensuous: Perception and Language in a More-Than-Human World*. NY: Random House.

Aleksander, I. (2005) *The World in My Mind, My Mind In The World: Key Mechanisms of Consciousness in Humans, Animals and Machines*. Thorverton, Exeter: Imprint Academic

Bostrom, N. (2000) "When Machines Outsmart Humans," *Futures*, 35 (7), 759–764.

Bostrom, N. (2004) "The Future of Human Evolution," in C. Tandy, ed. *Death and Anti-Death: Two Hundred Years after Kant; Fifty Years after Turing*. Palo Alto, CA: Ria U.P., 339–371.

Bostrom, N. (2005) "The Ethics of Superintelligent Machines," in I. Smit, W.Wallach, and G.Lasker (eds) *Symposium on Cognitive, Emotive and Ethical aspects of Decision-making in Humans and Artificial Intelligence*. InterSymp 05, Windsor, Ont: IIAS Press.

Calverley, D. (2005) "Android Science and the Animal Rights Movement: Are there Analogies?" *Proceedings of CogSci-2005 Workshop*. Cognitive Science Society, Stresa, Italy, pp. 127–136.

Curry, P. (2006) *Ecological Ethics: An Introduction*. Cambridge: Polity Press.

De Jaegher, H. (2008). "Social Understanding through Direct Perception? Yes, by Interacting." *Consciousness and Cognition* 18, 535–42.

De Jaegher, H. & Di Paolo, E. (2007). "Participatory Sense-Making: An Enactive Approach to Social Cognition." *Phenomenology and the Cognitive Sciences*. 6 (4), 485–507.

De Waal, F. (2006). *Primates and Philosophers: How Morality Evolved*. Oxford: Princeton U.P.

Dennett, D. (1978) "Why you Can't Make a Computer that Feels Pain." *Brainstorms: Philosophical Essays on Mind and Psychology*. Cambridge, MA: MIT Press. 190–232.

Dennett, D. (1998) "The Practical Requirements for Making a Conscious Robot." in D. Dennett, *Brainchildren: Essays on Designing Minds*. London: Penguin Books, 153 – 170.

Di Paolo, E. (2005), "Autopoiesis, Adaptivity, Teleology, Agency." *Phenomenology and the Cognitive Sciences*. 4, 97–125.

Dietrich E. (2007) "After the Humans are Gone.' *J. Experimental and Theoretical Art. Intell.* 19(1): 55–67.

Ernste, H. (2004). "The Pragmatism of Life in Poststructuralist Times." *Environment and Planning A*. 36, 437–450.

Floridi, L (2008a) 'Artificial Intelligence's New Frontier: Artificial Companions and the Fourth Revolution', *Metaphilosophy*, 39 (4–5), 651–655.

Floridi, L. (2008b), "Information Ethics, its Nature and Scope," in J. Van den Hoven and
    J. Weckert, eds., *Moral Philosophy and Information Technology*, Cambridge: Cambridge
    U.P., 40–65.

Franklin, S. (1995) *Artificial Minds*. Boston, MA: MIT Press

Frey, R.G. (1980). *Interests and Rights: The Case against Animals*. Oxford: Clarendon
    Press.

Gallagher, S. (2001) "The Practice of Mind: Theory, Simulation or Primary Interaction?"
    Journal of Consciousness Studies, 8 (5–7), 83–108

Gallagher, S. (2008) "Direct Perception in the Intersubjective Context." *Consciousness and
    Cognition*, 17, 535–43.

Goertzel, B. (2006) "Ten Years to a Positive Singularity (If we Really, Really Try)." Talk to
    Transvision 2006, Helsinki, Finland. http://www.goertzel.org/papers/tenyears.htm.

Haikonen, Pentti (2003) *The Cognitive Approach to Conscious Machines*. Thorverton,
    Devon: Imprint Academic.

Holland, O., ed. (2003) *Machine Consciousness*. Special issue of *Journal of Consciousness
    Studies*, 10 (4–5).

Jonas, H. (1996/2001) *The Phenomenon of Life: Toward a Philosophical Biology*. Evanston,
    Ill: Northwestern U.P. (originally published by Harper & Row N.Y. in 1996).

Joy, B. (2000) "Why the Future Doesn't Need Us." *Wired* 8 (04). www.wired.com/wired/
    archive/8.04/joy_pr.html.

Kurzweil, R. (2001) "One Half of An Argument" (Response to Lanier 2000). *The Edge*
    (online publication), 8.4.01. http://www.edge.org/3rd_culture/kurzweil/kurzweil_
    index.html.

Kurzweil, R. (2005) *The Singularity is Near: When Humans Transcend Biology*. NY: Viking
    Press.

Kant, I. (1997) *Lectures on Ethics*. P. Heath and J.B. Schneewind, eds. Cambridge:
    Cambridge U.P.

LaChat, M. (2004) "'Playing God' and the Construction of Artificial Persons." In I.
    Smit, W. Wallach and G. Lasker, eds., *Symposium on Cognitive, Emotive and Ethical
    aspects of Decision-making in Humans and Artificial Intelligence*, InterSymp 04, Windsor,
    Ont: IIAS Press.

Lanier, J. (2000) "One Half a Manifesto" *The Edge*, (online publication), 11.11.00. http://
    www.edge.org/3rd_culture/lanier/lanier_index.html.

Leopold, A. (1948) "A Land Ethic," in *A Sand County Almanac with Essays on Conservation
    from Round River*. New York: Oxford U.P.

Lovelock, J. (1979) *Gaia: A New Look at Life on Earth*. Oxford: Oxford U.P.

Lovelock, J. (2006) *The Revenge of Gaia: Why the Earth is Fighting Back, and How we can
    Still Save Humanity*. London: Allen Lane.

Maturana, H. & Varela, F. (1980) *Autopoiesis and Cognition: The Realization of the Living*.
    Dordrecht, Holland: D. Reidel Publishing.

Midgley, M. (1978) *Beast and Man: The Roots of Human Nature*. Ithaca, N.J.: Cornell U.P.

Moor J (2006) "The Nature, Importance and Difficulty of Machine Ethics." *IEEE
    Intelligent Systems* 21(4), 18–21.

Moravec, H. (1988) *Mind Children: The Future of Robot and Human Intelligence*. Cambridge,
    MA: Harvard U.P.

Naess, A. (1973) 'The Shallow and the Deep, Long-Range Ecology Movements' *Inquiry*
    16: 95–100.

Naess, A. & Sessions, G. (1984) "Basic Principles of Deep Ecology." *Ecophilosophy*. 6: 3–7.

Regan, T. (1983) *The Case for Animal Rights*. Berkeley: University of California Press.

Singer, P. (1977) *Animal Liberation*. London: Granada.

Sparrow, R. (2007) "Killer Robots", *Applied Philosophy*, 24(1), 62–77.

Sparrow, R. & Sparrow, L. (2006) "In the Hands of Machines? The Future of Aged Care." *Minds and Machines* 16 (2), 141–161.

Sylvan, R. & Bennett, D. (1994) *The Greening of Ethics: From Human Chauvinism to Deep-Green Theory*. Cambridge: White Horse Press.

Thompson, E. (2007) *Mind in Life: Biology, Phenomenology and the Sciences of Mind*. Cambridge, MA: Harvard U.P.

Torrance, S. (2000) "Towards an Ethics for EPersons." *Proc. AISB'00 Symposium on AI, Ethics and (Quasi-) Human Rights*, University of Birmingham.

Torrance, S. (2007) "Two conceptions of Machine Phenomenality." *Journal of Consciousness Studies*, 14 (7).

Torrance, S. (2008) "Ethics, Consciousness and Artificial Agents." *AI & Society* 22(4)

Torrance, S. (2009) "Will Robots have their own ethics?" *Philosophy Now*, April issue.

Torrance, S., Clowes, R., Chrisley, R., eds (2007) *Machine Consciousness: Embodiment and Imagination*. Special issue of *Journal of Consciousness Studies*, 14 (4).

Trevarthen, C. & Reddy, V. (2007) "Consciousness in Infants," in M. Velmans and S. Schneider, eds. *The Blackwell Companion to Consciousness*. Oxford: Blackwell & Co., 41–57.

Vinge, V. (1993) "The Coming Technological Singularity: How to Survive in the Post-Human Era." *Whole Earth Review*, 77.

Wallach, W. & Allen, C. (2009) *Moral Machines: Teaching Robots Right from Wrong*. Oxford: Oxford U.P.

Wilson, E.O. (1984) *Biophilia*. Cambridge, MA: Harvard U.P.

Wilson, E.O. (1994) *The Diversity of Life*. Harmondsworth: Penguin.

Wright, R. (1994) *The Moral Animal: Evolutionary Psychology and Everyday Life*. N.Y.: Pantheon Books.

Yudkowsky (2001) "Creating Friendly AI." www.singinst.org/upload/CFAI.html.

Yudkovsky (2008) "Cognitive Biases Potentially Affecting Judgement of Global Risks," in N. Bostrom and M. Cirkovic, eds. *Global Catastrophic Risks*. Oxford: Oxford U.P. Pp. 91–119.

8

On Computable Morality

An Examination of Machines as Moral Advisors

Blay Whitby

Introduction

IS HUMANITY READY OR WILLING TO ACCEPT MACHINES AS MORAL ADVISORS? The use of various sorts of machines to give moral advice and even to take moral decisions in a wide variety of contexts is now under way. This raises some interesting and difficult ethical issues.[1] It is not clear how people will react to this development when they become more generally aware of it. Nor is it clear how this technological innovation will affect human moral beliefs and behavior. It may also be a development that has long-term implications for our understanding of what it is to be human.

This chapter will focus on rather more immediate and practical concerns. If this technical development is occurring or about to occur, what should our response be? Is it an area of science in which research and development should be controlled or banned on ethical grounds? What sort of controls, if any, would be appropriate?

As a first move it is important to separate the question "Can it be done and, if so, how?" from the question "Should it be done?" There are, of course, overlaps and interdependencies between these two questions. In particular, there may be technical ways in which it should be done and technical ways in which it shouldn't be done. For example, some types of artificial intelligence (AI) systems (such as conventional rule-based systems) may be more predictable in their output than other AI technologies.[2] We may well have some ethical doubts about the use of highly unpredictable AI techniques. Separation of the two questions is, nonetheless, useful. The following section addresses the first of these two questions: "Can it be done and, if so, how?" The ethical issues raised by the building of such systems will be examined separately in a subsequent section.

---

[1]   I make no important distinction in this chapter between the terms "ethical" and "moral." They and related words can be read interchangeably.

[2]   Readers needing further clarification of the technical workings of the systems under discussion for should consult my *Beginners Guide to AI* (Whitby 2003).

Before proceeding it should be made clear that, at present, systems that give moral advice are hardly ever explicitly built or described as moral advisors. They acquire this role as parts of various advice-generating and decision-support systems. Many of these systems generate output with obvious moral consequences. It is a generally useful property of AI technology that it can be easily and seamlessly integrated into other computer systems. Most AI systems consist of computer code, or even just techniques that can be used by programmers. This otherwise beneficial property of the technology makes the examination of machines as moral advisors both difficult and urgent.

There are existing systems that advise, for example, doctors and nurses on regimes of patient care. They are also widely used in the financial services industry. It is inevitable that such systems (which will be given the general label "advice-giving systems") will produce output that will cover ethical areas. The degree to which this has already occurred is impossible to assess, because there has been no explicit general ethical scrutiny of the design and introduction of such systems. There would be no obvious way even of auditing which advice-giving systems contain some moral elements or extend into areas such as professional ethics in the scope of their output.

The existence of advice-giving systems makes the development of specifically moral advice systems more interesting and arguably more critical. General advice-giving systems are introducing machines as moral advisors by stealth. For example, advice-giving systems in the medical or legal domains will very often involve ethical assumptions that are rarely, if ever, made explicit. Systems designed primarily or explicitly to produce moral or ethical advice will be referred to as moral advice-giving systems. Building moral advisors openly allows proper examination of both the technical and moral issues involved. These issues are neither simple nor uncontroversial. More widespread discussion of the issues involved is now needed.

Is It Possible?

It might seem paradoxical to pose the question "Is it possible for machines to act as moral advisors?" given the claim that they are already being used for this purpose. However, there are many people who would advance arguments to the effect that the very notion of machines as moral advisors is fundamentally mistaken.

For example, a skeptic about AI or about the capabilities of computers in general might challenge the assertion made at the start of the previous section that various sorts of machines are making moral decisions. Many philosophers believe this is something that can be done only by human beings (for example, Searle 1994). Note the importance of the word "can" in the previous sentence. Any consideration of whether or not it *ought* to be done only by humans will be postponed until the next section.

Given that various programs are already producing output that closely resembles the output of humans when they make moral decisions, we may assume that the skeptic would claim that this is, in important ways, not equivalent to what humans do in such situations. For thinkers like Searle, the use of terminology such as "advice" and "decision" in the context of existing computer technology is simply a metaphor. Machines, they claim, do not *really* make decisions or offer advice because all they can do is follow their program. On this view, the entire enterprise discussed in this chapter is probably impossible.

The notion that all computer technology is merely following a program can be highly misleading. It is true that a program, in the form of a set of technical instructions, is a key part of all present computer-based technology. However, the notion that the programmers have given a complete set of instructions that directly determine every possible output of the machine is false, and it is false in some interesting ways relevant to the present discussion.

Consider a chess-playing program. It is simply not the case that every move in a chess match has already been made by the programmers, because such programs usually play chess far better than the programmers ever could. The description that best fits the technical facts is that programmers built a set of decision-making procedures into the program that enabled it to make effective decisions during the match. There is no magic here, no need to cite possible future technologies; it is simply an accurate description of existing technology.

It is possible that some readers may believe that computer chess playing is achieved purely by brute-force computational methods. This is just not true. The numbers of possible moves in a chess game are so huge that exhaustive methods of computation are impossible. Instead chess-playing computers must rely on making guesses as to which move *seems* best in a given situation. The mechanism that does this is usually refined by actually playing games of chess. That this mechanism involves guesswork is evidenced by the fact that even the best chess programs can lose.

Similar remarks apply to programs that generate moral advice. Of course, one may argue that selecting a move in a chess match is very different (for both humans and machines) than responding to a thorny ethical question. That may well be the case, and it is a subject to which we shall return. For the present it is sufficient to conclude that it is not true that the programmers must make all the relevant decisions.[3]

The AI skeptic might accept these technological points but claim that the case of the moral advice program was essentially similar to the case of having a large set of moral principles, say in a book, that were then rather rigidly applied to new problems. All the program does, according to the AI skeptic, is to perform a matching operation and output the principle relevant to the present case.

---

[3] Many of the decisions made by the programmers *are* important to the moral status of the enterprise, and some of these will be discussed in the next section.

This claim may be true of some very simple programs, but it is certainly not true of the field in general. If the advice-giving program incorporated some established AI techniques, such as case-based reasoning (CBR), then it could change in response to new cases and make fresh generalizations. It would be perfectly possible for such a system to acquire new principles that its designers had never considered. This is a possibility that raises clear ethical worries and will be considered in the context of the next section.

Experience suggests that the AI skeptic would still remain unconvinced and hold that the use of the expression "acquire new principles" in the preceding paragraph is an unjustified anthropomorphic metaphor; on his view, the system has no principles and acquires nothing. This actually has little bearing on the present argument. Whether or not we can use humanlike terms for the behavior of a machine or whether we should find purely mechanical ones is not crucial to the practical possibility of machines as moral advisors. If the machine fulfills a role functionally equivalent to that of a human moral advisor, then the core issues discussed in this chapter remain valid. The AI skeptic's objection that this is not *real* moral advice has no purchase unless it is used merely pejoratively as part of an argument that this sort of work *should* not be done.

A previous paper (Whitby 2008) develops in detail the claim that rational people will accept moral judgments from machines in the role of moral advisors. Here "judgment" should be read as meaning simply the result of a machine-made moral decision output in the form of advice. This human acceptance occurs in spite of the fact that the machines making these decisions do so in substantially different ways from the ways in which humans make such decisions.

One important difference might be held to be the lack of any judgment by a machine moral advisor. There is a widespread myth that computers can only deal with deductive, logical, and mathematical patterns of reasoning. This myth is false and, in this context, dangerously misleading. Computers certainly do make guesses and follow hunches. Nowadays they are very often programmed to do precisely that. The word "programmed" is most unfortunate here because it is often used in a nontechnical sense to signify exactly the opposite of making guesses and following hunches. It is a serious (but frequently made) mistake to apply the nontechnical sense of a word to its technical sense. The systems to which I am referring here are certainly designed and built by humans, but as we have already seen, those humans have not determined every detail of their output.

This objection is clearly closely related to the AI skeptic's claim that the whole enterprise is impossible. In this case however, the objection is not that the whole enterprise is impossible, merely that the output from the moral advice machine lacks something – the element of judgment.

As a matter of history, AI solved the technical problems of getting systems to deal with areas of judgment at least two decades ago. Much of the pioneering work was done in the area of medical diagnosis. One of the most common applications of this technology at present is in the area of financial services. The decision as to whether or not to give a potential customer a bank loan, a credit card, or a mortgage is now routinely made by a computer.

The proponent of the "there is no judgment" objection still has two possible responses. The first is to claim that the sort of judgment involved in playing chess or deciding on whether or not a customer qualifies for a loan is a different sort of judgment from a moral one in an important sense. This has implications that are considered in the next section. The second response is to claim that any judgment is, in the morally relevant sense, not made by the computer. It was made by the humans involved in automating the process.

The initial human decision to automate some particular process is morally much more significant than is usually recognized. This, however, does not entail that we cannot usefully speak of judgments made by the machine. Chess-playing computers can play much better chess than their designers ever could. It would be absurd to attribute the praise or blame for individual moves, or even for whole games, entirely to the designers. These are chess moves that they could not make. It is perfectly possible for the programmers of a chess-playing program to be unable to play chess or for the builders of a medical diagnosis system to know nothing about medical diagnosis. For these reasons we cannot directly attribute the individual moral judgments made by a moral advice system to its designers or builders.

A second important difference is that, unlike a human moral advisor, the machine contains no emotions. Attempts to get AI systems to express, embody, or respond to emotions are at an early stage. It is safe to assume that, from a technical point of view, this difference between human and machine-based moral advisors is real. The interesting question is: "How much does this matter?"

Present AI systems function very well in many areas without any regard to the emotional side of cognition. In the previous example of a chess-playing program, it is clear that attempting to add technical components to the program that reproduce joy in victory and depression in defeat would merely detract from its chess-playing performance.[4]

There are also many contexts in which we prefer a moral judgment to be free from emotional content. Doctors, for example, are ethically required not to operate on or make important medical decisions about members of their own family. This is because we can reasonably expect that emotions might distort their judgments. We also expect judges to be professionally dispassionate.

---

[4] Some philosophers and scientists would disagree strongly with the claim of this paragraph, because they believe emotions to be an essential ingredient of intelligence. Damasio (1996) and Picard (1998), for example, claim that a division between emotion and reasoning is mistaken, and therefore emotion needs to be included in all intelligent artifacts. It does not affect the argument made in this section, because if it turns out to be both true and technically feasible, then, at some point in the future, "emotional" AI systems will simply surpass and displace all existing AI technology.

A totally dispassionate computer therefore should not be automatically dismissed as a moral advisor simply because of its lack of emotion. Indeed, it should perhaps sometimes be preferred precisely because it is completely dispassionate.

There is a simplistic argument sometimes heard that a machine used in the advice-giving role will not be prejudiced or biased in the ways that science shows *all* humans to be. This is not equivalent to what is being claimed in the preceding paragraphs. Unfortunately there is ample evidence from the history of AI that programs (perhaps all programs) embody and emphasize the prejudices of their designers, often developing new prejudices of their own. Machine moral advisors should not be assumed always to be more impartial than human advisors. All that is claimed here is that the lack of an explicit emotional component does not automatically exclude them from the role.

A thought experiment may help to make the exact relationship with an emotionless machine moral advisor clearer. Imagine that at some point in the near future we manage to establish communications with benevolent intelligent extraterrestrial aliens. These aliens, we can assume, share none of our planetary or biological history. Because they have evolved in a different environment they simply don't understand what we refer to by the word "emotions."

Let us assume that these aliens are prepared to comment in a totally dispassionate way on human affairs and problems. Although they don't share our emotional life, they can converse with us about our human problems. We could then describe our perplexing history to them and say that sometimes we are not sure what is the best or least bad course of action. On the basis of this explanation, we could start to introduce the aliens to what *we mean* by moral judgments. When they say they understand how we are using the words "moral judgment" this seems to us to be accurate and reliable. There would be the possibility of some extremely interesting conversations.

As dispassionate observers they might, for example, point out an apparent contradiction between a professed concern for all human life and the preparation of weapons that are designed primarily to destroy all life on our planet several times over. This might form the start of a most interesting dialogue.

The aliens in this thought experiment effectively take the place of the emotionless computer. The question that concerns us in the present context is how humans should respond to the alien advice and criticism. Of course, humans might dismiss the aliens' comments on a wide variety of grounds, including their lack of emotions, but there is no prima facie reason to completely ignore them. Nor does it seem that there would be any moral grounds to reject the comments of the aliens.

The proponents of the "lack of emotion" objection might conceivably grant the foregoing argument but still make a further claim that it is the *total lack of any possible emotion* that prevents the aliens' messages or computer's output as being described as a moral judgment. In cases such as celibate priests and dispassionate judges there may be no direct empathetic involvement, but there is at least a *capability* of feeling the appropriate emotional responses. In the case of the wise but dispassionate aliens' communications, they could allow that they would be extremely interesting and form the basis for useful debate, but would not allow that they could ever be described as moral judgments.

Such an objection might be founded upon the metaethical claim that morality must always be fundamentally based on human emotion. Alternatively it might be founded upon a claim about the nature of judgment. It remains an open research question as to whether emotion is an essential component of judgment. Even if it is a frequently occurring component of human judgments, there seems no good argument that it must form part of all effective judgments. The chess-playing computer plays chess without any emotion. If someone maintains the claim that emotion is an essential component of all effective judgments, they are forced to claim that either chess is a game that can be played without making judgments or that the chess computer does not actually play chess – it merely does something that we would call "playing chess" if done by a human. Both positions are strictly speaking tenable, but a better description would be that the chess computer makes effective judgments about chess despite having no emotions. Emotion may well be an important component of human judgments, but it is unjustifiably anthropocentric to assume that it must therefore be an important component of *all* judgments.

A similar metaethical objection to machines as moral advisors might be based on the claimed importance of intuition in human moral judgments. This could be either the psychological claim that humans require intuitions in order to make moral judgments or the metaethical view known as "moral intuitionism" or a combination of both. According to moral intuitionism, all normal humans have an innate moral sense. Moral codes are simply institutionalizations of this innate sense. Similarly, it is usually held by moral intuitionists that the job of the moral philosopher is simply to provide formal descriptions of people's innate sense of right and wrong.

To respond to the first objection – that human moral decision making involves intuition – it is hard to understand what extra claim could be made here beyond the "no judgment" and "no emotion" objections dismissed earlier. It is very probably the fact of being hard to see that is precisely what gives this objection its force. If the intuitive component of human moral judgment cannot be reduced to some part of the more explicit cognitive and emotional components discussed earlier, then it is clearly either a deliberate attempt at obscurantism or an example of a "no true Scotsman" argument (Flew 1975). Whatever this intuitive component might be, it is not made explicit, and perhaps deliberately so. If a chess-playing computer can make effective decisions without emotion, then it can also do so without intuition.

This still leaves the objection from moral intuitionism. Those writers (for example, Whitby 1996, pp. 101–102, Danielson 1992) who discuss the possibility of machines as moral advisors usually assume that moral intuitionism is both incompatible with and hostile to the possibility of any type of computable morality. This is a point to which we will return.

For the present argument we can say that if people accept moral judgments from machines, then that argues strongly against the metaethical position of moral intuitionism. However, it does not follow that the moral intuitionists are thereby disproved. Much depends on the actual level of acceptance of the machines and the technical ways in which the output is produced. This is an area where research can provide answers to some previously intractable questions.

Finally let us return to the paradox mentioned at the outset of this section. If machines are already acting as moral advisors, how can we ask if it is possible? The considered response to this must be that even if we grant the claims argued against earlier, it makes no practical difference. If we allow for some reason (say, lack of judgment or lack of emotion) that machines cannot *really* act as moral advisors, then the fact that they are employed in roles where they appear to do just that is very worrying. If a machine makes decisions or produces advice as output in circumstances where we would call it "giving moral advice" if done by a human and we cannot usefully distinguish the machine-generated advice from human-generated advice, then it doesn't much matter what exactly we mean by *really* giving moral advice. It seems at best distracting and at worst morally wrong to deflect some legitimate ethical worries over this development into debates over precisely what real moral advice is.

Is It Right?

There are a number of reasons why people might argue that the technical developments described in the preceding section are morally wrong. For some critics the moral wrongness may be mixed up with the technical issues and, indeed, with the realness of the moral advice produced by the machines. However, it is beneficial to make a clear distinction and to discuss the ethical implications without being detained by questions about whether or exactly how it is possible.

In an ideal world we might suppose that all moral decisions would be made by humans and by humans only. This has, one assumes, been the case until very recently, and it is the expectation of most moral philosophers. For this reason we might expect humans and only humans to act as moral advisors. Therefore, the claim that machines have any role at all in this activity stands in need of justification.

The observation made earlier in the chapter that it is already happening, though true, is in no way adequate as a justification. Strictly speaking, if we consider this technological development inevitable, then the right thing to do would be to minimize its bad consequences. However, as is argued at length elsewhere (Whitby 1996), technological developments are not inevitable. It would be perfectly possible to forbid or restrict this line of development. Therefore, the question as to whether or not it is morally right is valid and has clear consequences. These consequences are also practical. As Kranzberg famously pointed out in his "first law," technology of itself is neither good nor bad nor neutral (Kranzberg 1986). Its ethical implications depend entirely on how we use it.

A number of arguments in favor of the moral rightness of the introduction of machines into moral decision making are made by Susan Leigh Anderson and Michael Anderson (Anderson S. and Anderson M. 2009). Far and away the most important of these is the argument from consistency. The Andersons do not argue that consistency is always and of itself virtuous. This would be a contentious claim; although one could wryly observe that inconsistency in the provision of moral advice has rarely, if ever, been held to be virtuous. Their point is more subtle – that the extreme consistency exemplified in the machine may teach us about the value of consistency in our own ethical judgments. The argument from consistency, posed in these terms, is a valid argument in favor of building machine-based moral advisors, at least as a research project.

Torrance (2008) makes two different arguments in favor of machines as moral advisors. The first is that we can build models of ethical reasoning into our machines and thereby learn more about the human moral domain. This is initially attractive as an argument, but, as with the argument from consistency, it must carry a clear health warning. Many philosophers and researchers active in the area of machine morality have either an explicit or hidden naturalist agenda. That is to say that they believe that morality and ethics must reduce to some natural feature in the world. This is a highly contentious point of view. Indeed, it has links to Moore's famous "naturalistic fallacy" (Moore 1903).

The building of machine-based models of ethical reasoning may well be associated by many in the machine morality area – let us call them "machine naturalists" – with the additional agenda of attempting to naturalize human moral thinking. It would be outside the scope of this chapter to resolve the long-standing debate as to whether ethics is naturalizable. We can observe, however, that Torrance's first argument does not actually require one to be a machine naturalist. One could build or experiment with machine models of morality without being committed to the view that rightness and wrongness are natural properties.

Nonetheless, the prevalence and temptations of machine naturalism as well as the simplistic inference that the existence of a machine-based model proves that the process must be essentially mechanistic mean that the modeling argument must be treated with extreme caution.

Torrance's second argument – that machines can serve as useful and instructive moral advisors – needs no such caution. There are those who might lament the taking of moral instruction from nonhuman sources perhaps, but AI systems already give useful advice in many areas. There seems no reason why this area should be treated differently, if one accepts the arguments of the previous section.

Torrance's second argument in favor of building moral advice-giving systems interacts and overlaps with the most compelling argument or set of arguments in favor of the enterprise. Let us call this the "argument from practicality." Again, we need to be clear that this does not reduce to the fatuous claim that it is right because it is happening anyway. It is, by contrast, two very different claims. The first is that we cannot, as matter of practicality, draw a line between moral and nonmoral areas when building certain types of machines. The second claim is that, given the first, it is morally better (or at least less wrong) to be open and honest about the moral elements in our machines.

Against these arguments we must weigh the objection that human morality is first and foremost about human experience, thus there should be no place for anything other than humans in moral judgments. Some proponents of this objection might further argue that discussions of even the possibility of artificial morality, such as here, in themselves detract from our humanity.

Because the use of tools (from flint axes to computers) is an essential part of what it is to be human, it is hard to see why this particular type of tool detracts from our humanity. Humans have always used artifacts to supplement their physical abilities, and since at least the classical period of history they have also used artifacts to supplement their intellectual capabilities. For fifty years or so, growing numbers of humans have been using computer-based technology primarily to supplement their intellectual capabilities. The use of advice-giving systems is an important contemporary example of such tool use and seems a very human activity.

A further worry implied by the "humans only" counter-argument might be that, in using the sort of machines under discussion, we will tend to lose our skills in the formation of moral judgments without machine aid. In general discussions of the social impact of technology this goes under the ugly epithet "deskilling," and it may represent a set of problems in the introduction of advice-giving systems.

Of course, this is only a serious problem if we *all* cease to practice the art of making moral judgments. There can be little doubt that, as with various other outmoded skills, some humans will choose to keep this skill alive. Perhaps the majority will not feel the need to challenge or even form moral judgments for themselves. Many human societies have practiced, and some continue to practice, a degree of moral authoritarianism in which this passive behavior is the norm.

Rather more important as a counter-argument is the problem of responsibility. The introduction of moral advice-giving systems may enable people to "hide behind the machine" in various unethical ways. That this sort of behavior can and does happen is undisputed. It also seems highly likely that the existence of moral advice-giving systems will open the door to a good deal more of it. This development seems morally dangerous.

We have already seen that responsibility for individual chess moves cannot reasonably be attributed to the designers of the chess program that makes those moves. For similar reasons it is difficult, if not impossible, to attribute responsibility for individual pieces of moral advice to the designers of a moral advice program. It is also far from clear how we might attribute any moral responsibility whatsoever to the machine. In the case of AI, there remain many problems to be resolved in apportioning moral responsibility to designers and programmers. The current lack of focus on these issues combined with technical developments that use AI technology widely (and for the most part invisibly) in combination with other technologies are ethically very worrying.

The problem of responsibility is real and worrying but can be responded to with some further development of the argument from practicality. It is not only moral advice-giving systems that raise the problem of responsibility. It is also a problem for many other examples of AI technology. It is not clear how the blame should be apportioned for poor financial advice from a machine financial advisor, nor whom we should hold responsible if a medical expert system produces output that harms patients. One of the best ways of remedying this lacuna in our ethical knowledge is to build moral advice systems in an open and reflective fashion.

This is not to say that the problem of responsibility should be tolerated. It is rather to recognize that it applies to a wider group of technologies than moral advice-giving systems. In fact, there should be much more attention paid to the area of computer ethics in general.

Conclusions

The use of machines as moral advisors can be justified, but it is certainly not something that is automatically or obviously good in itself. The arguments against this development sound cautions that we should heed, but on balance it is to be welcomed. This conclusion prompts many further questions. In particular we must ask what sort or sorts of morality should be incorporated into such advisors?

Susan Anderson has called this field "machine metaethics" (Anderson 2008), and if one accepts that it needs a new title, this one seems the best. If we accept the entry of artificial moral decision makers into human society, then there is a large and difficult problem in determining what sort of general moral principles the machines should follow. Using a similar division to that made in this chapter, we can separate questions about what can be implemented from those about what *should* be implemented. Both sets of questions are challenging, and it would be a mistake to presume simple answers at this point.

On the question of technology, it would be unwise to restrict or assume methods of implementation at the current state of development of AI. New methods may well emerge in the future. On the other hand, it would be equally unwise to reject existing AI technology as inadequate for the purpose of building moral advice-giving systems. Existing AI technology seems perfectly adequate for the building of such systems. To deny the adequacy of the technology is an ethically dubious position, because it helps disguise the entry of general advice-giving systems into areas of moral concern.

On the second metaethical question, it is just as difficult to give hard and fast answers. We are at a point in history where metaethics is hotly contested, although it might be argued that metaethics is something that has always been and always should be hotly contested. It may well be that it is of the very nature of morality that it should be continually debated.

A rather too-frequently quoted artistic contribution to the field of machine metaethics is Asimov's Three Laws (Asimov 1968). It is important to read Asimov's stories, not merely the laws. It is abundantly clear that the approach of building laws into robots could not possibly work. Indeed, the very idea that there could be standardization of responses in machines is seriously mistaken. We should expect moral advice-giving systems to disagree with each other and to have the same difficulties in reaching definitive statements that sincere human ethicists have. This is simply not an area where there are always definite and uncontroversial answers.

However these open-ended features of the enterprise and of the technology do not entail that we cannot reach some firm conclusions here. The most important of these is that this is an area that deserves far more attention. It deserves more attention from technologists who need to be much more clear and honest about where and when their advice-giving systems expand into moral areas. It deserves more attention from ethicists who should oversee, or at least contribute to, the development of a wide range of systems currently under development. These include "smart homes," autonomous vehicles, robotic carers, as well as advice-giving systems.

It also deserves far more attention from the general public. Whereas the public has become aware that there are ethical problems in modern medical practice and that biotechnology raises difficult ethical questions, there does not seem to be much interest or concern about computer ethics. This is unfortunate because there is much that should be of concern to the public in computer ethics. The problem of responsibility, discussed in the preceding section, is difficult and urgent.

It is difficult to determine responsibility for the output of advice-giving systems in general. However, it is not, in principle, impossible. The chain of responsibility involving such advice-giving systems in areas such as aviation and medicine is *obscured*, not missing. At present, it is extremely rare for the designers, builders, or vendors of computer systems of any sort to be held morally responsible for the consequences of their systems misleading humans. This is both unfortunate and morally wrong. Nonetheless, it has not prevented the widespread use of such systems.

Many moral philosophers would argue that ultimate moral responsibility cannot be passed from the individual – this is why we do not allow the "just following orders" defense by soldiers. In the case of advice-giving systems, both responsibility and authority are markedly less clear than in the case of the soldier. To pass responsibility back to the user of a moral advice-giving system also conceals the social agenda of its designers. When we use terms like "artificial intelligence," "autonomous system," and "intelligent online helper," it is easy to attribute much more social independence to them than is warranted. Real systems frequently embody the prejudices of their designers, and the designers of advice-giving systems should not be able to escape responsibility. There is a pressing need for further clarification of the problem of responsibility.

A major benefit of moral advice-giving systems is that it makes these issues more explicit. It is much easier to examine the ethical implications of a system specifically designed to give moral advice than to detach the ethical components of a system designed primarily to advise on patient care, for example. It is also important to unlearn the myth that machines are always right. In areas where there is doubt and debate, like that of giving moral advice, we have to learn that they can be wrong, that we must think about their output, and that we cannot use them to avoid our own responsibility. The building of moral advice-giving systems is a good way to make progress in these areas. We still have much to learn about metaethics and machine metaethics is a good way to learn.

References

Anderson, S. L., (2008) Asimov's "three laws of robotics" and machine metaethics, *AI & Society* Vol. 24 No 4. pp. 477–493.

Asimov, I., (1968) *I, Robot*, Panther Books, St. Albans.

Anderson, S. and Anderson, M., (2009) How machines can advance ethics, *Philosophy Now*, 72 March/April 2009, pp. 17–19.

Damasio, A. R., (1996) *Descartes' Error: Emotion, Reason, and the Human Brain*, Papermac, London.

Danielson, P., (1992) *Artificial Morality: Virtuous Robots for Virtual Games*, Routledge, London.

Flew, A., (1975) *Thinking about Thinking*, Fontana, London.

Kranzberg, M., (1986) Technology and history: "Kranzberg's laws," *Technology and Culture*, Vol. 27, No. 3, pp. 544–560.

Moore, G. E., (1903) *Principia Ethica*, Cambridge University Press.

Picard, R., (1998) *Affective Computing*, MIT Press, Cambridge MA.

Searle, J. R., (1994) *The Rediscovery of Mind*, MIT Press, Cambridge MA.

Torrance, S., (2008) Ethics and consciousness in artificial agents, *AI & Society* Vol. 24 No 4. pp. 495–521.

Whitby, B., (1996) *Reflections on artificial intelligence: The legal, moral, and social dimensions*, Intellect, Oxford.

Whitby, B., (2003) *Artificial Intelligence: A Beginner's Guide*, Oneworld, Oxford.

Whitby, B., (2008) Computing machinery and morality, *AI & Society* Vol. 24 No 4. pp. 551–563.

9

When Is a Robot a Moral Agent?

John P. Sullins

Introduction

R OBOTS HAVE BEEN A PART OF OUR WORK ENVIRONMENT FOR THE PAST FEW decades, but they are no longer limited to factory automation. The additional range of activities they are being used for is growing. Robots are now automating a wide range of professional activities such as: aspects of the health-care industry, white collar office work, search and rescue operations, automated warfare, and the service industries.

A subtle but far more personal revolution has begun in home automation as robot vacuums and toys are becoming more common in homes around the world. As these machines increase in capability and ubiquity, it is inevitable that they will impact our lives ethically as well as physically and emotionally. These impacts will be both positive and negative, and in this paper I will address the moral status of robots and how that status, both real and potential, should affect the way we design and use these technologies.

Morality and Human-Robot Interactions

As robotics technology becomes more ubiquitous, the scope of human-robot interactions will grow. At the present time, these interactions are no different than the interactions one might have with any piece of technology, but as these machines become more interactive, they will become involved in situations that have a moral character that may be uncomfortably similar to the interactions we have with other sentient animals. An additional issue is that people find it easy to anthropomorphize robots, and this will enfold robotics technology quickly into situations where, if the agent were a human rather than a robot, the situations would easily be seen as moral. A nurse has certain moral duties and rights when dealing with his or her patients. Will these moral rights and responsibilities carry over if the caregiver is a robot rather than a human?

We have three possible answers to this question. The first possibility is that the morality of the situation is just an illusion. We fallaciously ascribe moral rights and responsibilities to the machine due to an error in judgment based merely on the humanoid appearance or clever programming of the robot. The second option is that the situation is pseudo-moral. That is, it is partially moral but the robotic agents involved lack something that would make them fully moral agents. Finally, even though these situations may be novel, they are nonetheless real moral situations that must be taken seriously. I will argue here for this latter position, as well as critique the positions taken by a number of other researches on this subject.

Morality and Technologies

To clarify this issue it is important to look at how moral theorists have dealt with the ethics of technology use and design. The most common theoretical schema is the standard user, tool, and victim model. Here, the technology mediates the moral situation between the actor who uses the technology and the victim. In this model, we typically blame the user, not the tool, when a person using some tool or technological system causes harm.

If a robot is simply a tool, then the morality of the situation resides fully with the users and/or designers of the robot. If we follow this reasoning, then the robot is not a moral agent. At best, the robot is an instrument that advances the moral interests of others.

However, this notion of the impact of technology on our moral reasoning is much too simplistic. If we expand our notion of technology a little, I think we can come up with an already existing technology that is much like what we are trying to create with robotics, yet challenges the simple view of how technology impacts ethical and moral values. For millennia, humans have been breeding dogs for human uses, and if we think of technology as a manipulation of nature to human ends, we can comfortably call domesticated dogs a technology. This technology is naturally intelligent and probably has some sort of consciousness as well. Furthermore, dogs can be trained to do our bidding, and in these ways, dogs are much like the robots we are striving to create. For the sake of this argument, let's look at the example of guide dogs for the visually impaired.

This technology does not comfortably fit the previously described standard model. Instead of the *tool/user* model, we have a complex relationship between the trainer, the guide dog, and the blind person for whom the dog is trained to help. Most of us would see the moral good of helping the visually impaired person with a loving and loyal animal expertly trained. Yet where should we affix the moral praise? In fact, both the trainer and the dog seem to share it. We praise the skill and sacrifice of the trainers and laud the actions of the dog as well.

An important emotional attachment is formed between all the agents in this situation, but the attachment of the two human agents is strongest toward the dog. We tend to speak favorably of the relationships formed with these animals using terms identical to those used to describe healthy relationships with other humans.

The Web site for Guide Dogs for the Blind quotes the American Veterinary Association to describe the human-animal bond:

The human-animal bond is a mutually beneficial and dynamic relationship between people and other animals that is influenced by behaviors that are essential to the health and well-being of both. This includes, but is not limited to, emotional, psychological, and physical interaction of people, animals, and the environment.[1]

Certainly, providing guide dogs for the visually impaired is morally praiseworthy, but is a good guide dog morally praiseworthy in itself? I think so. There are two sensible ways to believe this. The least controversial is to consider that things that perform their function well have a moral value equal to the moral value of the actions they facilitate. A more contentious claim is the argument that animals have their own wants, desires, and states of well-being, and this autonomy, though not as robust as that of humans, is nonetheless advanced enough to give the dog a claim for both moral rights and possibly some meager moral responsibilities as well.

The question now is whether the robot is correctly seen as just another tool or if it is something more like the technology exemplified by the guide dog. Even at the present state of robotics technology, it is not easy to see on which side of this disjunction that reality lies.

No robot in the real world – or that of the near future – is, or will be, as cognitively robust as a guide dog. Yet even at the modest capabilities of today's robots, some have more in common with the guide dog than with a simple tool like a hammer.

In robotics technology, the schematic for the moral relationship between the agents is:

$$\text{Programmer(s)} \rightarrow \text{Robot} \rightarrow \text{User}$$

Here the distinction between the nature of the user and that of the tool can blur so completely that, as the philosopher of technology Cal Mitcham argues, the "ontology of artifacts ultimately may not be able to be divorced from the philosophy of nature" (Mitcham 1994, p.174), requiring us to think about technology in ways similar to how we think about nature.

I will now help clarify the moral relations between natural and artificial agents. The first step in that process is to distinguish the various categories of robotic technologies.

---

[1]   Retrieved from the Web site: Guide Dogs for the Blind; http://www.guidedogs.com/about-mission.html#Bond

Categories of Robotic Technologies

It is important to realize that there are currently two distinct varieties of robotics technologies that have to be distinguished in order to make sense of the attribution of moral agency to robots.

There are telerobots and there are autonomous robots. Each of these technologies has a different relationship to moral agency.

Telerobots

Telerobots are remotely controlled machines that make only minimal autonomous decisions. This is probably the most successful branch of robotics at this time because they do not need complex artificial intelligence to run; its operator provides the intelligence for the machine. The famous NASA Mars Rovers are controlled in this way, as are many deep-sea exploration robots. Telerobotic surgery has become a reality, as may telerobotic nursing. These machines are now routinely used in search and rescue and play a vital role on the modern battlefield, including remotely controlled weapons platforms such as the Predator drone and other robots deployed to support infantry in bomb removal and other combat situations.

Obviously, these machines are being employed in morally charged situations, with the relevant actors interacting in this way:

Operator → Robot → Patient/Victim

The ethical analysis of telerobots is somewhat similar to that of any technical system where the moral praise or blame is to be born by the designers, programmers, and users of the technology. Because humans are involved in all the major decisions that the machine makes, they also provide the moral reasoning for the machine.

There is an issue that does need to be explored further though, and that is the possibility that the distance from the action provided by the remote control of the robot makes it easier for the operator to make certain moral decisions. For instance, a telerobotic weapons platform may distance its operator so far from the combat situation as to make it easier for the operator to decide to use the machine to harm others. This is an issue that I address in detail in other papers (Sullins 2009). However, for the robot to be a moral agent, it is necessary that the machine have a significant degree of autonomous ability to reason and act on those reasons. So we will now look at machines that attempt to achieve just that.

Autonomous Robots

For the purposes of this paper, autonomous robots present a much more interesting problem. Autonomy is a notoriously thorny philosophical subject. A full discussion of the meaning of "autonomy" is not possible here, nor is it necessary, as I will argue in a later section of this paper. I use the term "autonomous robots" in the same way that roboticists use the term (see Arkin 2009; Lin, et al. 2008), and I am not trying to make any robust claims for the autonomy of robots. Simply, autonomous robots must be capable of making at least some of the major decisions about their actions using their own programming. This may be simple and not terribly interesting philosophically, such as the decisions a robot vacuum makes to navigate a floor that it is cleaning. Or they may be much more robust and require complex moral and ethical reasoning, such as when a future robotic caregiver must make a decision as to how to interact with a patient in a way that advances both the interests of the machine and the patient equitably. Or they may be somewhere in between these exemplar cases.

The programmers of these machines are somewhat responsible for the actions of such machines, but not entirely so, much as one's parents are a factor but not the exclusive cause in one's own moral decision making. This means that the machine's programmers are not to be seen as the only locus of moral agency in robots. This leaves the robot itself as a possible location for a certain amount of moral agency. Because moral agency is found in a web of relations, other agents such as the programmers, builders, and marketers of the machines, other robotic and software agents, and the users of these machines all form a community of interaction. I am not trying to argue that robots are the only locus of moral agency in such a community, only that in certain situations they can be seen as fellow moral agents in that community.

The obvious objection here is that moral agents must be persons, and the robots of today are certainly not persons. Furthermore, this technology is unlikely to challenge our notion of personhood for some time to come. So in order to maintain the claim that robots can be moral agents, I will now have to argue that personhood is not required for moral agency. To achieve that end I will first look at what others have said about this.

Philosophical Views on the Moral Agency of Robots

There are four possible views on the moral agency of robots. The first is that robots are not now moral agents but might become them in the future. Daniel Dennett supports this position and argues in his essay "When HAL Kills, Who Is to Blame?" that a machine like the fictional HAL can be considered a murderer because the machine has *mens rea*, or a guilty state of mind, which includes motivational states of purpose, cognitive states of belief, or a non-mental state of negligence (Dennett 1998). Yet to be morally culpable, they also need to have "higher order intentionality," meaning that they can have beliefs about beliefs, desires about desires, beliefs about its fears, about its thoughts, about its hopes, and so on (1998). Dennett does not suggest that we have machines like that today, but he sees no reason why we might not have them in the future.

The second position one might take on this subject is that robots are incapable of becoming moral agents now or in the future. Selmer Bringsjord makes a strong stand on this position. His dispute with this claim centers on the fact that robots will never have an autonomous will because they can never do anything that they are not programmed to do (Bringsjord 2007). Bringsjord shows this with an experiment using a robot named PERI, which his lab uses for experiments. PERI is programmed to make a decision to either drop a globe, which represents doing something morally bad, or hold on to it, which represents an action that is morally good. Whether or not PERI holds or drops the globe is decided entirely by the program it runs, which in turn was written by human programmers. Bringsjord argues that the only way PERI can do anything surprising to the programmers requires that a random factor be added to the program, but then its actions are merely determined by some random factor, not freely chosen by the machine, therefore, PERI is no moral agent (Bringsjord 2007).

There is a problem with this argument. Because we are all the products of socialization and that is a kind of programming through memes, we are no better off than PERI. If Bringsjord is correct, then we are not moral agents either, because our beliefs, goals, and desires are not strictly autonomous: They are the products of culture, environment, education, brain chemistry, and so on. It must be the case that the philosophical requirement for robust free will demanded by Bringsjord, whatever that turns out to be, is a red herring when it comes to moral agency. Robots may not have it, but we may not have it either, so I am reluctant to place it as a necessary condition for moral agency.

A closely related position to this argument is held by Bernhard Irrgang who claims that "[i]n order to be morally responsible, however, an act needs a participant, who is characterized by personality or subjectivity" (Irrgang 2006). Only a person can be a moral agent. As he believes it is not possible for a noncyborg (human machine hybrids) robot to attain subjectivity, it is impossible for robots to be called into moral account for their behavior. Later I will argue that this requirement is too restrictive and that full subjectivity is not needed.

The third possible position is the view that we are not moral agents but robots are. Interestingly enough, at least one person actually held this view. In a paper written a while ago but only recently published, Joseph Emile Nadeau claims that an action is a free action if and only if it is based on reasons fully thought out by the agent. He further claims that only an agent that operates on a strictly logical basis can thus be truly free (Nadeau 2006). If free will is necessary for moral agency and we as humans have no such apparatus operating in our brain, then using Nadeau's logic, we are not free agents. Robots, on the other hand, are programmed this way explicitly, so if we built them, Nadeau believes they would be the first truly moral agents on earth (Nadeau 2006).[2]

---

[2] One could counter this argument from a computationalist standpoint by acknowledging that it is unlikely we have a theorem prover in our biological brain; but in the virtual machine formed by our mind, anyone trained in logic most certainly does have a theorem prover of sorts, meaning that there are at least some human moral agents.

The fourth stance that can be held on this issue is nicely argued by Luciano Floridi and J. W. Sanders of the Information Ethics Group at the University of Oxford (Floridi 2004). They argue that the way around the many apparent paradoxes in moral theory is to adopt a "mind-less morality" that evades issues like free will and intentionality, because these are all unresolved issues in the philosophy of mind that are inappropriately applied to artificial agents such as robots.

They argue that we should instead see artificial entities as agents by appropriately setting levels of abstraction when analyzing the agents (2004). If we set the level of abstraction low enough, we can't even ascribe agency to ourselves because the only thing an observer can see are the mechanical operations of our bodies; but at the level of abstraction common to everyday observations and judgments, this is less of an issue. If an agent's actions are interactive and adaptive with their surroundings through state changes or programming that is still somewhat independent from the environment the agent finds itself in, then that is sufficient for the entity to have its own agency (Floridi 2004). When these autonomous interactions pass a threshold of tolerance and cause harm, we can logically ascribe a negative moral value to them; likewise, the agents can hold a certain appropriate level of moral consideration themselves, in much the same way that one may argue for the moral status of animals, environments, or even legal entities such as corporations (Floridi and Sanders, paraphrased in Sullins 2006).

My views build on the fourth position, and I will now argue for the moral agency of robots, even at the humble level of autonomous robotics technology today.

The Three Requirements of Robotic Moral Agency

In order to evaluate the moral status of any autonomous robotic technology, one needs to ask three questions of the technology under consideration:

- Is the robot significantly autonomous?
- Is the robot's behavior intentional?
- Is the robot in a position of responsibility?

These questions have to be viewed from a reasonable level of abstraction, but if the answer is yes to all three, then the robot is a moral agent.

Autonomy

The first question asks if the robot could be seen as significantly autonomous from any programmers, operators, and users of the machine. I realize that "autonomy" is a difficult concept to pin down philosophically. I am not suggesting that robots of any sort will have radical autonomy; in fact, I seriously doubt human beings have that quality. I mean to use the term autonomy as engineers do, simply that the machine is not under the direct control of any other agent or user.

The robot must not be a telerobot or temporarily behave as one. If the robot does have this level of autonomy, then the robot has a practical independent agency. If this autonomous action is effective in achieving the goals and tasks of the robot, then we can say the robot has effective autonomy. The more effective autonomy the machine has, meaning the more adept it is in achieving its goals and tasks, then the more agency we can ascribe to it. When that agency[3] causes harm or good in a moral sense, we can say the machine has moral agency.

Autonomy thus described is not sufficient in itself to ascribe moral agency. Consequently, entities such as bacteria, animals, ecosystems, computer viruses, simple artificial life programs, or simple autonomous robots – all of which exhibit autonomy as I have described it – are not to be seen as responsible moral agents simply on account of possessing this quality. They may very credibly be argued to be agents worthy of moral consideration, but if they lack the other two requirements argued for next, they are not robust moral agents for whom we can plausibly demand moral rights and responsibilities equivalent to those claimed by capable human adults.

It might be the case that the machine is operating in concert with a number of other machines or software entities. When that is the case, we simply raise the level of abstraction to that of the group and ask the same questions of the group. If the group is an autonomous entity, then the moral praise or blame is ascribed at that level. We should do this in a way similar to what we do when describing the moral agency of groups of humans acting in concert.

Intentionality

The second question addresses the ability of the machine to act "intentionally." Remember, we do not have to prove the robot has intentionality in the strongest sense, as that is impossible to prove without argument for humans as well. As long as the behavior is complex enough that one is forced to rely on standard folk psychological notions of predisposition or intention to do good or harm, then this is enough to answer in the affirmative to this question. If the complex interaction of the robot's programming and environment causes the machine to act in a way that is morally harmful or beneficial and the actions are seemingly deliberate and calculated, then the machine is a moral agent.

There is no requirement that the actions really are intentional in a philosophically rigorous way, nor that the actions are derived from a will that is free on all levels of abstraction. All that is needed at the level of the interaction between the agents involved is a comparable level of personal intentionality and free will between all the agents involved.

---

[3] Meaning self-motivated, goal-driven behavior.

Responsibility

Finally, we can ascribe moral agency to a robot when the robot behaves in such a way that we can only make sense of that behavior by assuming it has a responsibility to some other moral agent(s).

If the robot behaves in this way, and if it fulfills some social role that carries with it some assumed responsibilities, and if the only way we can make sense of its behavior is to ascribe to it the "belief" that it has the duty to care for its patients, then we can ascribe to this machine the status of a moral agent.

Again, the beliefs do not have to be real beliefs; they can be merely apparent. The machine may have no claim to consciousness, for instance, or a soul, a mind, or any of the other somewhat philosophically dubious entities we ascribe to human specialness. These beliefs, or programs, just have to be motivational in solving moral questions and conundrums faced by the machine.

For example, robotic caregivers are being designed to assist in the care of the elderly. Certainly a human nurse is a moral agent. When and if a machine carries out those same duties, it will be a moral agent if it is autonomous as described earlier, if it behaves in an intentional way, and if its programming is complex enough that it understands its responsibility for the health of the patient(s) under its direct care.

This would be quite a machine and not something that is currently on offer. Any machine with less capability would not be a full moral agent. Although it may still have autonomous agency and intentionality, these qualities would make it deserving of moral consideration, meaning that one would have to have a good reason to destroy it or inhibit its actions; but we would not be required to treat it as a moral equal, and any attempt by humans who might employ these less-capable machines as if they were fully moral agents should be avoided.

Some critics have argued that my position "unnecessarily complicates the issue of responsibility assignment for immoral actions" (Arkin 2007, p. 10). However, I would counter that it is going to be some time before we meet mechanical entities that we recognize as moral equals, but we have to be very careful that we pay attention to how these machines are evolving and grant that status the moment it is deserved. Long before that day though, complex robot agents will be partially capable of making autonomous moral decisions. These machines will present vexing problems, especially when machines are used in police work and warfare, where they will have to make decisions that could result in tragedies. Here, we will have to treat the machines the way we might do for trained animals such as guard dogs. The decision to own and operate them is the most significant moral question, and the majority of the praise or blame for the actions of such machines belongs to the owners and operators of these robots.

Conversely, it is logically possible, though not probable in the near term, that robotic moral agents may be more autonomous, have clearer intentions, and a more nuanced sense of responsibility than most human agents. In that case, their moral status may exceed our own. How could this happen? The philosopher Eric Dietrich argues that as we are more and more able to mimic the human mind computationally, we need simply forgo programming the nasty tendencies evolution has given us and instead implement "only those that tend to produce the grandeur of humanity, [for then] we will have produced the better robots of our nature and made the world a better place" (Dietrich 2001).

There are further extensions of this argument that are possible. Nonrobotic systems such as software "bots" are directly implicated, as is the moral status of corporations. It is also obvious that these arguments could be easily applied to the questions regarding the moral status of animals and environments. As I argued earlier, domestic and farmyard animals are the closest technology we have to what we dream robots will be like. So these findings have real-world applications outside robotics to animal welfare and rights, but I will leave that argument for a future paper.

Conclusions

Robots are moral agents when there is a reasonable level of abstraction under which we must grant that the machine has autonomous intentions and responsibilities. If the robot can be seen as autonomous from many points of view, then the machine is a robust moral agent, possibly approaching or exceeding the moral status of human beings.

Thus, it is certain that if we pursue this technology, then, in the future, highly complex, interactive robots will be moral agents with corresponding rights and responsibilities. Yet even the modest robots of today can be seen to be moral agents of a sort under certain, but not all, levels of abstraction and are deserving of moral consideration.

References

Arkin, Ronald (2007): Governing Lethal Behavior: Embedding Ethics in a Hybrid Deliberative/Reactive Robot Architecture, U.S. Army Research Office Technical Report GIT-GVU-07–11. Retrived from: http://www.cc.gatech.edu/ai/robot-lab/online-publications/formalizationv35.pdf.

Arkin, Ronald (2009): *Governing Lethal Behavior in Autonomous Robots*, Chapman & Hall/CRC.

Bringsjord, S. (2007): Ethical Robots: The Future Can Heed Us, *AI and Society* (online).

Dennett, Daniel (1998): When HAL Kills, Who's to Blame? Computer Ethics, in Stork, David, *HAL's Legacy: 2001's Computer as Dream and Reality*, MIT Press.

Dietrich, Eric (2001): Homo Sapiens 2.0: Why We Should Build the Better Robots of Our Nature, *Journal of Experimental and Theoretical Artificial Intelligence*, Volume 13, Issue 4, 323–328.

Floridi, Luciano, and Sanders, J. W. (2004): On the Morality of Artificial Agents, *Minds and Machines*, 14.3, pp. 349–379.

Irrgang, Bernhard (2006): Ethical Acts in Robotics. *Ubiquity*, Volume 7, Issue 34 (September 5, 2006–September 11, 2006) www.acm.org/ubiquity.

Lin, Patrick, Bekey, George, and Abney, Keith (2008): Autonomous Military Robotics: Risk, Ethics, and Design, US Department of Navy, Office of Naval Research, Retrived online: http://ethics.calpoly.edu/ONR_report.pdf.

Mitcham, Carl (1994): *Thinking through Technology: The Path between Engineering and Philosophy*, University of Chicago Press.

Nadeau, Joseph Emile (2006): Only Androids Can Be Ethical, in Ford, Kenneth, and Glymour, Clark, eds., *Thinking about Android Epistemology*, MIT Press, 241–248.

Sullins, John (2005): Ethics and Artificial Life: From Modeling to Moral Agents, *Ethics and Information Technology*, 7:139–148.

Sullins, John (2009): Telerobotic Weapons Systems and the Ethical Conduct of War, *American Philosophical Association Newsletter on Philosophy and Computers*, Volume 8, Issue 2 Spring 2009. http://www.apaonline.org/documents/publications/v08n2_Computers.pdf.

10

Philosophical Concerns with Machine Ethics

Susan Leigh Anderson

THE CHALLENGES FACING THOSE WORKING ON MACHINE ETHICS CAN BE divided into two main categories: philosophical concerns about the feasibility of computing ethics and challenges from the AI perspective. In the first category, we need to ask first whether ethics is the sort of thing that can be computed. One well-known ethical theory that supports an affirmative answer to this question is Act Utilitarianism. According to this teleological theory (a theory that maintains that the rightness and wrongness of actions is determined entirely by the consequences of the actions), the right act is the one, of all the actions open to the agent, which is likely to result in the greatest net good consequences, taking all those affected by the action equally into account. Essentially, as Jeremy Bentham (1781) long ago pointed out, the theory involves performing "moral arithmetic."

Of course, before doing the arithmetic, one needs to know what counts as "good" and "bad" consequences. The most popular version of Act Utilitarianism – Hedonistic Act Utilitarianism – would have us consider the pleasure and displeasure that those affected by each possible action are likely to receive. As Bentham pointed out, we would probably need some sort of scale to account for such things as the intensity and duration of the pleasure or displeasure that each individual affected is likely to receive. This is information that a human being would need to have, as well, in order to follow the theory. Getting this information has been and will continue to be a challenge for artificial intelligence research in general, but it can be separated from the challenge of computing the ethically correct action, given this information. With the requisite information, a machine could be developed that is just as able to follow the theory as a human being.

Hedonistic Act Utilitarianism can be implemented in a straightforward manner. The algorithm is to compute the best action – that which derives the greatest net pleasure – from all alternative actions. It requires as input the number of people affected and, for each person, the intensity of the pleasure/displeasure (for example, on a scale of 2 to –2), the duration of the pleasure/displeasure (for example, in days), and the probability that this pleasure or displeasure will occur for each possible action. For each person, the algorithm computes the product of the intensity, the duration, and the probability to obtain the net pleasure for that person. It then adds the individual net pleasures to obtain the total net pleasure:

Total net pleasure = Σ (intensity × duration × probability) for each affected individual. This computation would be performed for each alternative action. The action with the highest total net pleasure is the right action. (Anderson, M., Anderson, S., and Armen, C. 2005)

A machine might very well have an advantage over a human being in following the theory of Act Utilitarianism for several reasons: First, human beings tend not to do the arithmetic strictly, but just estimate that a certain action is likely to result in the greatest net good consequences, and so a human being might make a mistake, whereas such error by a machine would be less likely. Second, human beings tend toward partiality (favoring themselves, or those near and dear to them, over others who might be affected by their actions or inactions), whereas an impartial machine could be devised. This is particularly important because the theory of act utilitarianism was developed to introduce objectivity into ethical decision making. Third, humans tend not to consider all of the possible actions that they could perform in a particular situation, whereas a more thorough machine could be developed. Imagine a machine that acts as an advisor to human beings and "thinks" like an act utilitarian. It will prompt the human user to consider alternative actions that might result in greater net good consequences than the action the human being is considering doing, and it will prompt the human to consider the effects of each of those actions on *all* those affected. Finally, for some individuals' actions – actions of the president of the United States or the CEO of a large international corporation, for example – their impact can be so great that the calculation of the greatest net pleasure may be very time consuming, and the speed of today's machines gives them an advantage.

One could conclude, then, that machines can follow the theory of Act Utilitarianism at least as well as human beings and, perhaps, even better, given the data that human beings would need as well to follow the theory. The theory of Act Utilitarianism has, however, been questioned as not entirely agreeing with intuition. It is certainly a good starting point in programming a machine to be ethically sensitive – it would probably be more ethically sensitive than many human beings – but, perhaps, a better ethical theory can be used.

Critics of Act Utilitarianism have pointed out that it can violate human beings' rights by sacrificing one person for the greater net good. It can also conflict with our notion of justice – what people deserve – because the rightness and wrongness of actions is determined entirely by the future consequences of actions, whereas what people deserve is a result of past behavior. A deontological approach to ethics (where the rightness and wrongness of actions depends on something other than the consequences), such as Kant's Categorical Imperative, can emphasize the importance of rights and justice; but this approach can be accused of ignoring the consequences of actions.

It could be argued, as maintained by W. D. Ross (1930), that the best approach to ethical theory is one that combines elements of both teleological and deontological theories. A theory with several *prima facie* duties (obligations that we should try to satisfy but that can be overridden on occasion by stronger obligations) – some concerned with the consequences of actions and others concerned with justice and rights – better acknowledges the complexities of ethical decision making than a single absolute duty theory. This approach has one major drawback, however. It needs to be supplemented with a decision procedure for cases wherein the prima facie duties give conflicting advice. Michael Anderson and I, with Chris Armen (2006), have demonstrated that, at least in theory, it is possible for a machine to discover a decision principle needed for such a procedure.

Among those who maintain that ethics cannot be computed, there are those who question the action-based approach to ethics that is assumed by defenders of Act Utilitarianism, Kant's Categorical Imperative, and other well-known ethical theories. According to the "virtue" approach to ethics, we should not be asking what one ought to do in ethical dilemmas, but rather what sort of person/being one should be. We should be talking about the sort of qualities – virtues – that a person/being should possess; actions should be viewed as secondary. Given that we are concerned only with the actions of machines, however, it is appropriate that we adopt the action-based approach to ethical theory and focus on the sort of principles that machines should follow in order to behave ethically.

Another philosophical concern with the machine ethics project is whether machines are the type of entities that can behave ethically. It is commonly thought that an entity must be capable of acting intentionally, which requires that it be conscious and that it have free will in order to be a moral agent. Many would also add that sentience or emotionality is important, because only a being that has feelings would be capable of appreciating the feelings of others, a critical factor in the moral assessment of possible actions that could be performed in a given situation. Because many doubt that machines will ever be conscious and have free will or emotions, this would seem to rule them out as being moral agents.

This type of objection, however, shows that the critic has not recognized an important distinction between performing the morally correct action in a given situation, including being able to justify it by appealing to an acceptable ethical principle, and being held morally responsible for the action. Yes, intentionality and free will in some sense are necessary to hold a being morally responsible for its actions,[1] and it would be difficult to establish that a machine possesses these qualities; but neither attribute is necessary to do the morally correct action in an ethical dilemma and justify it. All that is required is that the machine act in a way that conforms with what would be considered to be the morally correct action in that situation and be able to justify its action by citing an acceptable ethical principle that it is following (S. L. Anderson 1995).

---

[1] To be a full moral agent, according to Jim Moor.

The connection between emotionality and being able to perform the morally correct action in an ethical dilemma is more complicated. Certainly one has to be sensitive to the suffering of others to act morally. This, for human beings, means that one must have empathy, which in turn requires that one has experienced similar emotions oneself. It is not clear, however, that a machine, without having emotions itself, could not be trained to take into account the suffering of others in calculating how it should behave in an ethical dilemma.

It is important to recognize, furthermore, that having emotions can actually interfere with a being's ability to determine and perform the right action in an ethical dilemma. Humans are prone to getting "carried away" by their emotions to the point where they are incapable of following moral principles. So emotionality can even be viewed as a weakness of human beings that often prevents them from doing the "right thing."

A final philosophical concern with the feasibility of computing ethics has to do with whether there is a single correct action in ethical dilemmas. Many believe that ethics is relative either to the society in which one lives ("when in Rome, one should do what Romans do") or, a more extreme version of relativism, to individuals (whatever you think is right is right for you). Most ethicists reject ethical relativism (for example, see Mappes and DeGrazia [2001, p. 38] and Gazzaniga [2006, p. 178]) in both forms primarily because this view entails that one cannot criticize the actions of societies as long as they are approved by the majority in those societies; nor can one criticize individuals who act according to their beliefs, no matter how heinous they are.

There certainly do seem to be actions that experts in ethics, and most of us, believe are absolutely wrong (torturing a baby and slavery, to give two examples), even if there are societies or individuals who approve of the actions. Against those who say that ethical relativism is a more tolerant view than ethical absolutism, it has been pointed out that ethical relativists cannot say that anything is absolutely good – even tolerance. (Pojman 1996, p. 13)

Defenders of ethical relativism may recognize two truths, neither of which entails the acceptance of ethical relativism, that causes them to support this view: (1) Different societies have their own customs that we must acknowledge, and (2) at the present time, there are difficult ethical issues about which even experts in ethics cannot agree on the ethically correct action. Concerning the first truth, we must distinguish between an ethical issue and customs or practices that fall outside the area of ethical concern. Customs or practices that are not a matter of ethical concern can be respected, but in areas of ethical concern we should not be tolerant of unethical practices.

Concerning the second truth, that some ethical issues are difficult to resolve (abortion, for example), it does not follow that all views on these issues are equally correct. It will take more time to resolve these issues, but most ethicists believe that we should strive for a single correct position even on these issues. It is necessary to see that a certain position follows from basic principles that all ethicists accept, or that a certain position is more consistent with other beliefs that they all accept.

From this last point, we should see that we may not be able to give machines principles that resolve all ethical disputes at this time, and we should only permit machines to function in those areas where there is agreement among ethicists as to what is acceptable behavior. The implementation of ethics can't be more complete than is accepted ethical theory. Completeness is an ideal for which to strive, but it may not be possible at this time. The ethical theory, or framework for resolving ethical disputes, should allow for updates, as issues that once were considered contentious are resolved. More important than having a complete ethical theory to implement is to have one that is consistent. Machines may actually help to advance the study of ethical theory by pointing out inconsistencies in the theory that one attempts to implement, forcing ethical theoreticians to resolve those inconsistencies.

A philosophical concern about creating an ethical machine that is often voiced by non-ethicists is that it may start out behaving ethically but then morph into one that behaves unethically, favoring its own interests. This may stem from legitimate concerns about *human* behavior. Most human beings are far from ideal models of ethical agents, despite having been taught ethical principles; and humans do, in particular, tend to favor themselves. Machines, though, might have an advantage over human beings in terms of behaving ethically. As Eric Dietrich (2006) has recently argued, human beings, as biological entities in competition with others, may have evolved into beings with a genetic predisposition toward selfish behavior as a survival mechanism. Now, however, we have the chance to create entities that lack this predisposition, entities that might even inspire us to behave more ethically. Dietrich maintains that the machines we fashion to have the good qualities of human beings and that also follow principles derived from ethicists could be viewed as "humans 2.0" – a better version of human beings.

A few[2] have maintained, in contrast to the last objection, that because a machine cannot act in a self-interested manner, it cannot do the morally correct action. Such persons take as the paradigm of an ethical dilemma a situation of moral temptation in which one knows what the morally correct action is, but one's self-interest inclines one to do something else.

Three points can be made in response to this: First, once again, this may come down to a feeling that the machine cannot be held *morally responsible* for doing the right action, because it could not act in a contrary manner. However, this should not concern us. We just want it to do the right action. Second, it can be maintained that a tendency to act in a self-interested manner, like extreme emotionality, is a *weakness* of human beings that we should not choose to incorporate into a machine. Finally, the paradigm of a moral dilemma is not a situation where one *knows* what the morally correct action is but finds it difficult to *do*, but rather

---

[2] Drew McDermott, for example.

is one in which it is not obvious what the morally correct action is. It needs to be determined, ideally through using an established moral principle or principles.

Another concern that has been raised is this: What if we discover that the ethical training of a machine was incomplete because of the difficulty in anticipating every situation that might arise, and it behaves unethically in certain situations as a result?

Several points can be made in response to this concern. If the machine has been trained properly, it should have been given, or it should have learned, *general ethical principles* that could apply to a wide range of situations that it might encounter, rather than having been programmed on a case-by-case basis to know what is right in anticipated ethical dilemmas. Also, there should be a way to update the ethical training a machine receives as ethicists become clearer about the features of ethical dilemmas and the ethical principles that should govern the types of dilemmas that the machine is likely to face. Updates in ethical training should be expected, just as children (and many adults) need periodic updates in their ethical training. Finally, it is prudent to have newly created ethical machines function in limited domains until we can feel comfortable with their performance.

In conclusion, although there are a number of philosophical concerns with machine ethics research, none of them appears to be fatal to the challenge of attempting to incorporate ethics into a machine.

References

Anderson, M., Anderson, S., and Armen, C. (2005), "Toward Machine Ethics: Implementing Two Action-Based Ethical Theories," in *Machine Ethics: Papers from the AAAI Fall Symposium. Technical Report FS- 05–06*, Association for the Advancement of Artificial Intelligence, Menlo Park, CA.

Anderson, M., Anderson, S., and Armen, C. (2006), "An Approach to Computing Ethics," *IEEE Intelligent Systems*, Vol. 21, No. 4.

Anderson, S. L. (1995), "Being Morally Responsible for an Action versus Acting Responsibly or Irresponsibly," *Journal of Philosophical Research*, Vol. 20.

Bentham, J. (1781), *An Introduction to the Principles of Morals and Legislation*, Clarendon Press, Oxford.

Dietrich, E. (2006), "After the Humans are Gone," NA-CAP 2006 Keynote Address, RPI, Troy, New York.

Gazzaniga, M. (2006), *The Ethical Brain: The Science of Our Moral Dilemmas*, Harper Perennial, New York.

Mappes, T. A., and DeGrazia, D. (2001), *Biomedical Ethics*, 5th edition, McGraw-Hill, New York.

Pojman, L. J. (1996), "The Case for Moral Objectivism," in *Do the Right Thing: A Philosophical Dialogue on the Moral and Social Issues of Our Time*, ed. by F. J. Beckwith, Jones and Bartlett, New York.

Ross, W.D, (1930), *The Right and the Good*, Oxford University Press, Oxford.

11

Computer Systems
Moral Entities but Not Moral Agents

Deborah G. Johnson

Introduction

IN THIS PAPER I WILL ARGUE THAT COMPUTER SYSTEMS ARE MORAL ENTITIES but not, alone, moral agents. In making this argument I will navigate through a complex set of issues much debated by scholars of artificial intelligence, cognitive science, and computer ethics. My claim is that those who argue for the moral agency (or potential moral agency) of computers are right in recognizing the moral importance of computers, but they go wrong in viewing computer systems as independent, autonomous moral agents. Computer systems have meaning and significance only in relation to human beings; they are components in socio-technical systems. What computer systems are and what they do is intertwined with the social practices and systems of meaning of human beings. Those who argue for the moral agency (or potential moral agency) of computer systems also go wrong insofar as they overemphasize the distinctiveness of computers. Computer systems are distinctive, but they are a distinctive form of technology and have a good deal in common with other types of technology.

On the other hand, those who claim that computer systems are not (and can never be) moral agents also go wrong when they claim that computer systems are outside the domain of morality. To suppose that morality applies only to the human beings who use computer systems is a mistake.

The debate seems to be framed in a way that locks the interlocutors into claiming either that computers are moral agents or that computers are not moral. Yet to deny that computer systems are moral agents is not the same as denying that computers have moral importance or moral character; and to claim that computer systems are moral is not necessarily the same as claiming that they are moral agents. The interlocutors neglect important territory when the debate is framed in this way. In arguing that computer systems are moral entities but are not, alone, moral agents, I hope to reframe the discussion of the moral character of computers.

Originally published as: Johnson, D. G. 2006. "Computer systems: Moral entities but not moral agents." *Ethics and Information Technology*. 8, 4 (Nov. 2006), 195–204.

I should add here that the debate to which I refer is embedded in a patchwork of literature on a variety of topics. Because all agree that computers are currently quite primitive in relation to what they are likely to be in the future, the debate tends to focus on issues surrounding the potential capabilities of computer systems and a set of related and dependent issues. These issues include whether the agenda of artificial intelligence is coherent; whether, moral agency aside, it makes sense to attribute moral responsibility to computers; whether computers can reason morally or behave in accordance with moral principles; and whether computers (with certain kinds of intelligence) might come to have the status of persons and, thereby, the right not to be turned off. The scholars who come the closest to claiming moral agency for computers are probably those who use the term "artificial moral agent" (AMA), though the term hedges on whether computers are moral agents in a strong sense of the term, comparable to human moral agents, or whether they are agents in the weaker sense, in which a person or machine might perform a task for a person and the behavior has moral consequences.[1,2]

Natural and Human-Made Entities/Artifacts

The analysis and argument that I will present relies on two fundamental distinctions: the distinction between natural phenomena or natural entities *and* human-made entities and the distinction between artifacts *and* technology. Both of these distinctions are problematic in the sense that when pressed, the line separating the two sides of the distinction can be blurred. Nevertheless, these distinctions are foundational. A rejection or redefinition of these distinctions obfuscates and undermines the meaning and significance of claims about morality, technology, and computing.

The very idea of technology is the idea of things that are human-made. To be sure, definitions of technology are contentious, so I hope to go to the heart of the notion and avoid much of the debate. The association of the term "technology" with human-made things has a long history dating back to Aristotle.[3] Moreover,

---

[1] Those who use the term "artificial moral agent" include L. Floridi and J. Sanders, "On the morality of artificial agents." *Minds and Machines* 14 3 (2004): 349–379; B.C. Stahl, "Information, Ethics, and Computers: The Problem of Autonomous Moral Agents." *Minds and Machines* 14 (2004): 67–83; and C. Allen, G. Varner and J. Zinser, "Prolegomena to any future artificial moral agent." *Journal of Experimental & Theoretical Artificial Intelligence* 12 (2000): 251–261.

[2] For an account of computers as surrogate agents, see D.G. Johnson and T.M. Powers, "Computers as Surrogate Agents." In *Moral Philosophy and Information Technology* edited by J. van den Hoven and J. Weckert, Cambridge University Press, 2006.

[3] In the *Nicomachean Ethics*, Aristotle writes, "Every craft is concerned with coming to be; and the exercise of the craft is the study of how something that admits of being and not being comes to be, something whose origin is in the producer and not in the product. For a craft is not concerned with things that are or come to be by necessity; or with things that are by nature, since these have their origin in themselves" (6.32). [Translation from Terence Irwin, Indianapolis, Hackett, 1985.]

making technology has been understood to be an important aspect of being human. In "The Question Concerning Technology," Heidegger writes:

For to posit ends and procure and utilize the means to them is a human activity. The manufacture and utilization of equipment, tools, and machines, the manufactured and used things all belong to what technology is. The whole complex of these contrivances is technology. Technology itself is a contrivance – in Latin, an instrumentum.[4]

More recently, and consistent with Heidegger, Pitt gives an account of technology as "humanity at work."[5]

Although the distinction between natural and human-made entities is foundational, I concede that the distinction can be confounded. When a tribesman picks up a stick and throws it at an animal, using the stick as a spear to bring the animal down, a natural object – an object appearing in nature independent of human behavior – has become a tool. It has become a means for a human end. Here a stick is both a natural object and a technology.

Another way the distinction can be challenged is by consideration of new biotechnologies such as genetically modified foods or pharmaceuticals. These technologies appear to be combinations of nature and technology, combinations that make it difficult to disentangle and draw a line between the natural and human-made parts. These new technologies are products of human contrivance, although the human contrivance is at the molecular level, and this makes the outcome or product appear natural in itself. Interestingly, the only difference between biotechnology and other forms of technology – computers, nuclear missiles, toasters, televisions – is the kind of manipulation or the level at which the manipulation of nature takes place. In some sense, the action of the tribesman picking up the stick and using it as a spear and the action of the bioengineer manipulating cells to make a new organism are of the same kind; both manipulate nature to achieve a human end. The difference in the behavior is in the different types of components that are manipulated.

Yet another way the distinction between natural and human-made entities can be pressed has to do with the extent to which the environment has been affected by human behavior. Environmental historians are now pointing to the huge impact that human behavior has had on the earth over the course of thousands of years of human history. They point out that we can no longer think of our environment as "natural."[6] In this way, distinguishing nature from what is human-made is not always easy.

---

[4]   From M. Heidegger, *The Question Concerning Technology and Other Essays*. 1977. Translated and with an Introduction by W. Lovitt. New York, Harper & Row, 1977.
[5]   Joseph Pitt, *Thinking About Technology: Foundations of the Philosophy of Technology*. New York, Seven Bridges Press, 2000.
[6]   See, for example, B. R. Allenby, "Engineering Ethics for an Anthropogenic Planet." *Emerging Technologies and Ethical Issues in Engineering*. National Academies Press, Washington D.C., 2004, pp. 7–28.

Nevertheless, although all of these challenges can be made to the distinction between natural and human-made, they do not indicate that the distinction is incoherent or untenable. Rather, the challenges indicate that the distinction between natural and human-made is useful and allows us to understand something important. Eliminating this distinction would make it impossible for us to distinguish the effects of human behavior on, or the human contribution to, the world that is. Eliminating this distinction would make it difficult, if not impossible, for humans to comprehend the implications of their normative choices about the future. There would be no point in asking what sort of world we want to make, whether we (humans) should do something to slow global warming, slow the use of fossil fuel, or prevent the destruction of ecosystems. These choices only make sense when we recognize a distinction between the effects of human behavior and something independent of human behavior – nature.

The second distinction at the core of my analysis is the distinction between artifacts and technology. A common way of thinking about technology – perhaps the layperson's way – is to think that it is physical or material objects. I will use the term "artifact" to refer to the physical object. Philosophers of technology and recent literature from the field of science and technology studies (STS) have pointed to the misleading nature of this view of technology. Technology is a combination of artifacts, social practices, social relationships, and systems of knowledge. These combinations are sometimes referred to as "socio-technical ensembles,"[7] "socio-technical systems,"[8] or "networks."[9] Artifacts (the products of human contrivance) do not exist without systems of knowledge, social practices, and human relationships. Artifacts are made, adopted, distributed, used, and have meaning only in the context of human social activity. Indeed, although we intuitively may think that artifacts are concrete and "hard," and social activity is abstract and "soft," the opposite is more accurate. Artifacts are abstractions from reality. To delineate an artifact – that is, to identify it as an entity – we must perform a mental act of separating the object from its context. The mental act extracts the artifact from the social activities that give it meaning and function. Artifacts come into being through social activity, are distributed and used by human beings as part of social activity, and have meaning only in particular contexts in which they are recognized and used. When we conceptually separate an artifact from the contexts in which it was produced and used, we push the socio-technical system of which it is a part out of sight.

[7]   W. E. Bijker, "Sociohistorical Technology Studies." In S. Jasanoff & G. E. Markle & J. C. Petersen & T. Pinch (Eds.), *Handbook of Science and Technology Studies*, pp. 229–256. London, Sage, 1994.
[8]   T. P. Hughes, "Technological Momentum." In L. Marx and M. R. Smith (Eds.), *Does Technology Drive History? The Dilemma of Technological Determinism*. Cambridge, The MIT Press, 1994.
[9]   J. Law, "Technology and Heterogeneous Engineering: The Case of Portuguese Expansion." In W.E. Bijker, T. P. Hughes, and T. Pinch (Eds.), *The Social Construction of Technological Systems*. Cambridge, MIT Press., 1987.

So it is with computers and computer systems. They are as much a part of social practices as are automobiles, toasters, and playpens. Computer systems are not naturally occurring phenomena; they could not and would not exist were it not for complex systems of knowledge and complex social, political, and cultural institutions; computer systems are produced, distributed, and used by people engaged in social practices and meaningful pursuits. This is as true of current computer systems as it will be of future computer systems. No matter how independently, automatically, and interactively computer systems of the future behave, they will be the products (direct or indirect) of human behavior, human social institutions, and human decision.

Notice that the terms "computer" and "computer system" are sometimes used to refer to the artifact and other times to the socio-technical system. Although we can think of computers as artifacts, to do so is to engage in the thought experiment alluded to previously; it is to engage in the act of mentally separating computers from the social arrangements of which they are a part, the activities that produce them, and the cultural notions that give them meaning. Computer systems always operate in particular places at particular times in relation to particular users, institutions, and social purposes.

The separation of computers from the social context in which they are used can be misleading. My point here is not unrelated to the point that Floridi and Saunders make about levels of abstraction.[10] They seem implicitly to concede the abstractness of the term "computer" and would have us pay attention to how we conceptualize computer activities, that is, at what level of abstraction we are focused. Whereas Floridi and Saunders suggest that any level of abstraction may be useful for certain purposes, my argument is, in effect, that certain levels of abstraction are not relevant to the debate about the moral agency of computers, in particular, those levels of abstraction that separate machine behavior from the social practices of which it is a part and the humans who design and use it. My reasons for making this claim will become clear in the next two sections of the paper.

In what follows I will use "artifact" to refer to the material object and "technology" to refer to the socio-technical system. This distinction is consistent with, albeit different from, the distinction between nature and technology. Artifacts are products of human contrivance; they are also components in socio-technical systems that are complexes – ensembles, networks – of human activity and artifacts.

Morality and Moral Agency

The notions of "moral agency" and "action" and the very idea of morality are deeply rooted in Western traditions of moral philosophy. Historically human

[10] L. Floridi and J. Saunders, "On the morality of artificial agents." *Minds and Machines* 14 3 2004: 349–379.

beings have been understood to be different from all other living entities because they are free and have the capacity to act from their freedom. Human beings can reason about and then choose how they behave. Perhaps the best-known and most salient expression of this conception of moral agency is provided by Kant. However, the idea that humans act (as opposed to behaving from necessity) is presumed by almost all moral theories. Even utilitarianism presumes that human beings are capable of choosing how to behave. Utilitarians beseech individuals to use a utilitarian principle in choosing how to act; they encourage the development of social systems of rewards and punishments to encourage individuals to choose certain types of actions over others. In presuming that humans have choice, utilitarianism presumes that humans are free.

My aim is not, however, to demonstrate the role of this conception of moral agency in moral philosophy, but rather to use it. I will quickly lay out what I take to be essential aspects of the concepts of moral agency and action in moral philosophy, and then use these notions to think through computer behavior. I will borrow here from Johnson and Powers's account of the key elements of the standard account.[11] These elements are implicit in both traditional and contemporary accounts of moral agency and action.

The idea that an individual is primarily responsible for his or her intended, voluntary behavior is at the core of most accounts of moral agency. Individuals are not held responsible for behavior they did not intend or for the consequences of intentional behavior that they could not foresee. Intentional behavior has a complex of causality that is different from that of nonintentional or involuntary behavior. Voluntary, intended behavior (action) is understood to be outward behavior that is caused by particular kinds of internal states, namely, mental states. The internal, mental states cause outward behavior, and because of this, the behavior is amenable to a reason explanation as well as a causal explanation. All behavior (human and nonhuman, voluntary and involuntary) can be explained by its causes, but only action can be explained by a set of internal mental states. We explain why an agent acted by referring to his or her beliefs, desires, and other intentional states.

Contemporary action theory typically specifies that for human behavior to be considered action (and, as such, appropriate for moral evaluation), it must meet the following conditions. First, there is an agent with an internal state. The internal state consists of desires, beliefs, and other intentional states. These are mental states, and one of these is, necessarily, an intending to act. Together, the intentional states (e.g., a belief that a certain act is possible, a desire to act, plus an intending to act) constitute a reason for acting. Second, there is an outward, embodied event – the agent does something, moves his or her body in some way. Third, the internal state is the cause of the outward event; that is, the movement

[11] D. G. Johnson and T. M. Powers, "The Moral Agency of Technology." unpublished manuscript, 2005.

of the body is rationally directed at some state of the world. Fourth, the outward behavior (the result of rational direction) has an outward effect. Fifth and finally, the effect has to be on a patient – a recipient of an action that can be harmed or helped.

This set of conditions can be used as a backdrop, a standard against which the moral agency of computer systems can be considered. Those who claim that computer systems can be moral agents have, in relation to this set of conditions, two possible moves. Either they can attack the account, show what is wrong with it, and provide an alternative account of moral agency, *or* they can accept the account and show that computer systems meet the conditions. Indeed, much of the scholarship on this issue can be classified as taking one or the other of these approaches.[12]

When the traditional account is used as the standard, computer-system behavior seems to meet conditions two through five with little difficulty; that is, plausible arguments can be made to that effect. With regard to the second condition, morality has traditionally focused on embodied human behavior as the unit of analysis appropriate for moral evaluation, and computer-system behavior is embodied. As computer systems operate, changes in their internal states produce such outward behavior as a reconfiguration of pixels on a screen, audible sounds, change in other machines, and so on. Moreover, the outward, embodied behavior of a computer system is the result of internal changes in the states of the computer, and these internal states cause, and are rationally directed at producing, the outward behavior. Thus, the third condition is met.

Admittedly, the distinction between internal and external ("outward") can be challenged (and may not hold up to certain challenges). Because all of the states of a computer system are embodied, what is the difference between a so-called internal state and a so-called external or outward state? This complication also arises in the case of human behavior. The internal states of humans can be thought of as brain states, and in this respect they are also embodied. What makes brain states internal and states of the arms and legs of a person external? The distinction between internal states and outward behavior is rooted in the mind-body tradition, so that using the language of internal-external may well beg the question whether a nonhuman entity can be a moral agent. However, in the case of computer systems, the distinction is not problematic, because we distinguish internal and external events in computer systems in roughly the same way we do in humans. Thus, conditions two and three are no more problematic for the moral agency of computer systems than for humans.

[12] For example, Fetzer explores whether states of computers could be construed as mental states since they have semantics (J.H. Fetzer, *Computers and Cognition: Why Minds Are Not Machines*. Kluwer Academic Press, 2001); and Stahl explores the same issue using their informational aspect as the basis for exploring whether the states of computers could qualify (B. C. Stahl, "Information, Ethics, and Computers: The Problem of Autonomous Moral Agents." *Minds and Machines* 14 (2004): 67–83.

The outward, embodied events that are caused by the internal workings of a computer system can have effects beyond the computer system (condition four) and these effects can be on moral patients (condition five). In other words, as with human behavior, when computer systems behave, their behavior has effects on other parts of the embodied world, and those embodied effects can harm or help moral patients. The effect may be morally neutral, such as when a computer system produces a moderate change in the temperature in a room or performs a mathematical calculation. However, computer behavior can also produce effects that harm or help a moral patient, for example, the image produced on a screen is offensive, a signal turns off a life-support machine, or a virus is delivered and implanted in an individual's computer.

In short, computer behavior meets conditions two through five as follows: When computers behave, there is an outward, embodied event; an internal state is the cause of the outward event; the embodied event can have an outward effect; and the effect can be on a moral patient.

The first element of the traditional account is the kingpin for the debate over the moral agency of computers. According to the traditional account of moral agency, for there to be an action (behavior arising from moral agency), the cause of the outward, embodied event must be the internal states of the agent, *and* – the presumption has always been – these internal states are mental states. Moreover, the traditional account specifies that one of the mental states must be an intending to act. Although most of the attention on this issue has focused on the requirement that the internal states be mental states, the intending to act is critically important because the intending to act arises from the agent's freedom.

Action is an exercise of freedom, and freedom is what makes morality possible. Moral responsibility doesn't make sense when behavior is involuntary, for example, a reflex, a sneeze, or other bodily reaction. Of course, this notion of human agency and action is historically rooted in the Cartesian doctrine of mechanism. The Cartesian idea is that animals, machines, and natural events are determined by natural forces; their behavior is the result of necessity. Causal explanations of the behavior of mechanistic entities and events are given in terms of laws of nature. Consequently, neither animals nor machines have the freedom or intentionality that would make them morally responsible or appropriate subjects of moral appraisal. Neither the behavior of nature nor the behavior of machines is amenable to reason explanations, and moral agency is not possible when a reason-explanation is not possible.

Again, it is important to note that the requirement is not just that the internal states of a moral agent are mental states; one of the mental states must be an intending to act. The intending to act is the locus of freedom; it explains how two agents with the same desires and beliefs may behave differently. Suppose John has a set of beliefs and desires about Mary; he picks up a gun, aims it at Mary, and pulls the trigger. He has acted. A causal explanation of what happened might include John's pulling the trigger and the behavior of the gun and bullet; a reason explanation would refer to the desires and beliefs and intending that explain why John pulled the trigger. At the same time, Jack could have desires and beliefs identical to those of John, but not act as John acts. Jack may also believe that Mary is about to do something reprehensible, may desire her to stop, may see a gun at hand, and yet Jack's beliefs and desires are not accompanied by the intending to stop her. It is the intending to act together with the complex of beliefs and desires that leads to action. Why John forms an intending to act and Jack does not is connected to their freedom. John's intending to act comes from his freedom; he chooses to pick up the gun and pull the trigger. Admittedly, the nondeterministic character of human behavior makes it somewhat mysterious, but it is only because of this mysterious, nondeterministic aspect of moral agency that morality and accountability are coherent.

Cognitive scientists and computer ethicists often acknowledge this requirement of moral agency. Indeed, they can argue that the nondeterministic aspect of moral agency opens the door to the possibility of the moral agency of computer systems because some computer systems are, or in the future will be, nondeterministic. To put the point another way, if computer systems are nondeterministic, then they can be thought of as having something like a noumenal realm. When computers are programmed to learn, they learn to behave in ways that are well beyond the comprehension of their programmers and well beyond what is given to them as input. Neural networks are proffered as examples of nondeterministic computer systems. At least some computer behavior may be said to be constituted by a mixture of deterministic and nondeterministic elements, as is human behavior.

The problem with this approach is that although some computer systems may be nondeterministic and, therefore "free" in some sense, they are not free in the same way humans are. Perhaps it is more accurate to say that we have no way of knowing whether computers are or will be nondeterministic in same way that humans are nondeterministic. We have no way of knowing whether the noumenal realm of computer systems is or will be anything like the noumenal realm of humans. What we do know is that both are embodied in different ways. Thus, we have no way of knowing whether the nondeterministic character of human behavior and the nondeterministic behavior of computer systems are or will be alike in the morally relevant (and admittedly mysterious) way.

Of course, we can think and speak "as if" the internal states of a computer are comparable to the mental states of a person. Here we use the language of mental states metaphorically, and perhaps in so doing try to change the meaning of the term. That is, to say that computers have mental states is to use "mental" in an extended sense. This strategy seems doomed to failure. It seems to blur rather than clarify what moral agency is.

Cognitive science is devoted to using the computational model to bring new understanding and new forms of knowledge. Cognitive scientists and computational philosophers seem to operate on the presumption that use of the computational model will lead to a revolutionary change in many fundamental concepts and theories.[13] To be sure, this promise has been fulfilled in several domains. However, when it comes to the debate over the moral agency of computers, the issue is not whether the computational model is transforming moral concepts and theories, but whether a new kind of moral being has been created. In other words, it would seem that those who argue for the moral agency of computers are arguing that computers don't just represent moral thought and behavior, they *are* a form of it. After all, the claim is that computers don't just represent moral agency, but *are* moral agents.

Although this move from computational model to instantiation is not justified, the temptation to think of computers as more than models or simulations is somewhat understandable, because computers don't just represent, they also behave. Computer systems are not just symbolic systems: They have efficacy; they produce effects in the world and powerful effects on moral patients. Because of the efficacy of computers and computer systems, those who argue for the moral agency of computers are quite right in drawing attention to the moral character of computer systems. However, they seem to overstate the case in claiming that computer systems are moral agents. As will be discussed later, the efficacy of computer systems is always connected to the efficacy of computer-system designers and users.

All of the attention given to mental states and nondeterminism draws attention away from the importance of the intending to act and, more generally, away from intentionality. Whereas computer systems do not have intendings to act, they do have intentionality, and this is the key to understanding the moral character of computer systems.

The Intentionality of Computer Behavior

As illustrated in discussion of the Cartesian doctrine, traditionally in moral philosophy nature and machines have been lumped together as entities that behave mechanistically. Indeed, both nature and machines have been dismissed from the domain of morality because they have both been considered mechanistic. Unfortunately, this has pushed artifacts out of the sights of moral philosophy. As mechanistic entities, artifacts have been thought to be morally neutral and irrelevant to morality.

Because artifacts and natural entities have been lumped together as mechanistic, the morally important differences between them have been missed. Artifacts are human-made; they are products of action and agency. Most artifacts behave mechanistically once made, even though their existence and their design

---

[13] For example, *The Digital Phoenix: How Computers are Changing Philosophy* by J. H. Moor and T. Bynum is devoted to describing how this has happened in philosophy. Oxford, Basil Blackwell Publishers, 1998.

is not mechanistic. Artifact behavior, including computer behavior, is created and used by human beings as a result of their intentionality.

Computer systems and other artifacts have intentionality, the intentionality put into them by the intentional acts of their designers. The intentionality of artifacts is related to their functionality. Computer systems (like other artifacts) are poised to behave in certain ways in response to input. Johnson and Powers provide a fuller account of the intentionality of artifacts in which the intentionality of artifacts is connected to their functionality, and functionality is understood on the model of a mathematical function.[14] What artifacts do is receive input and transform the input into output. When, for example, using a search engine, I press certain keys to enter particular words in the appropriate box and then press a button, and the search engine goes through a set of processes and delivers particular output to my computer screen. The output (the resulting behavior) is a function of how the system has been designed and the input I gave it. The system designer designed the system to receive input of a certain kind and transform that input into output of a particular kind, though the programmer did not have to specify every particular output for every possible input.

In this way, computer systems have intentionality. They are poised to behave in certain ways, given certain input. The intentionality of computer systems and other artifacts is connected to two other forms of intentionality: the intentionality of the designer and the intentionality of the user. The act of designing a computer system always requires intentionality – the ability to represent, model, and act. When designers design artifacts, they poise them to behave in certain ways. Those artifacts *remain* poised to behave in those ways. They are designed to produce unique outputs when they receive inputs. They are directed at states of affairs in the world and will produce other states of affairs in the world when used. Of course, the intentionality of computer systems is inert or latent without the intentionality of users. Users provide input to the computer system, and in so doing they use their intentionality to activate the intentionality of the system. Users use an object that is poised to behave in a certain way to achieve their intendings. To be sure, computer systems receive input from nonhuman entities and provide output to nonhuman entities, but the other machines and devices that send and receive input and output have been designed to do so and have been put in place to do so by human users for their purposes.[15]

That computer systems are human-made entities as opposed to natural entities is important. Natural objects have the kind of functionality that artifacts have in the sense that they receive input; and because of their natural features and composition, they transform input in a particular way, producing output. I pick up

---

[14] Johnson and Powers, 2005.

[15] This can also be thought of in terms of efficacy and power. The capacity of the user to do something is expanded and extended through the efficacy of the computer system, and the computer system exists only because of the efficacy of the system designer.

a stick and manipulate it in certain ways, and the stick behaves in certain ways (output). By providing input to the stick, I can produce output, for example, collision with a rock. However, whereas both natural objects and human-made objects have functionality, natural objects were not designed by humans. They do not have intentionality. Most importantly, natural entities could not be otherwise. Artifacts, including computer systems, have been intentionally designed and poised to behave in the way they do – by humans. Their functionality has been intentionally created. By creating artifacts of particular kinds, designers facilitate certain kinds of behavior. So, it is with computers, although admittedly the functionality of computers is quite broad because of their malleability.

The point of this analysis of the intentionality of computer systems is twofold. First, it emphasizes the dependence of computer system behavior on human behavior, and especially the intentionality of human behavior. Whereas computer behavior is often independent in time and place from the designers and users of the computer system, computer systems are always human-made and their efficacy is always created and deployed by the intentionality of human beings. Second, and pointing in an entirely different direction, because computer systems have built-in intentionality, once deployed – once their behavior has been initiated – they can behave independently and without human intervention.

The intentionality of computer systems means that they are closer to moral agents than is generally recognized. This does not make them moral agents, because they do not have mental states and intendings to act, but it means that they are far from neutral. Another way of putting this is to say that computers are closer to being moral agents than are natural objects. Because computer systems are intentionally created and used forms of intentionality and efficacy, they are moral entities. That is, how they are poised to behave, what they are directed at, and the kind of efficacy they have all make a moral difference. The moral character of the world and the ways in which humans act are affected by the availability of artifacts. Thus, computer systems are not moral agents, but they are a part of the moral world. They are part of the moral world not just because of their effects, but because of what they are and do.

Computer Systems as Moral Entities

When computer systems behave, there is a triad of intentionality at work: the intentionality of the computer-system designer, the intentionality of the system, and the intentionality of the user. Any one of the components of this triad can be the focal point for moral analysis; that is, we can examine the intentionality and behavior of the artifact designer, the intentionality and behavior of the computer system, and the intentionality and behavior of the human user. Note also that whereas human beings can act with or without artifacts, computer systems cannot act without human designers and users. Even when their proximate behavior is independent, computer systems act with humans in the sense that they have been designed by humans to behave in certain ways, and humans have set them in particular places, at particular times, to perform particular tasks for users.

When we focus on human action with artifacts, the action is constituted by the combination of human behavior and artifactual behavior. The artifact is effectively a prosthetic. The human individual could not act as he or she does without the artifact. As well, the artifact could not *be* and be *as it is* without the artifact designer (or a team of others who have contributed to the design and production of the artifact). The artifact user has a complex of mental states and an intending to act that leads to deploying a device (providing input to a device). The device does not have mental states but has intentionality in being poised to behave in certain ways in response to input. The artifact came to have that intentionality through the intentional acts of the artifact designer who has mental states and intendings that lead to the creation of the artifact. All three parts of the triad – the human user, the artifact, and the human artifact designer/maker have intentionality and efficacy. The user has the efficacy of initiating the action, the artifact has the efficacy of whatever it does, and the artifact designer has created the efficacy of the artifact.

To draw out the implications of this account of the triad of intentionality and efficacy at work when humans act with (and by means of) artifacts, let us begin with a simple artifact. Landmines are simple in their intentionality in the sense that they are poised to either remain unchanged or to explode when they receive input. Suppose a landmine explodes in a field many years after it had been placed there during a military battle. Suppose further that the landmine is triggered by a child's step and the child is killed. The deadly effect on a moral patient is distant from the landmine designer's intentionality both in time and place, and is distant in time from the intentionality of the user who placed the landmine in the field. The landmine's intentionality – its being poised to behave in a certain way when it receives input of a certain kind – persists through time; its intentionality is narrow and indiscriminate in the sense that any pressure above a certain level and from any source produces the same output – explosion.

When the child playing in the field steps on the landmine, the landmine behaves automatically and independently. Does it behave autonomously? Does it behave from necessity? Could it be considered a moral or immoral agent? Although there are good reasons to say that the landmine behaves autonomously and from necessity, there are good reasons for resisting such a conclusion. Yes, once designed and put in place, the landmine behaves as it does without the assistance of any human being, and once it receives the input of the child's weight, it behaves of necessity. Nevertheless, the landmine is not a natural object; its independence and necessity have been contrived and deployed by human beings. It is what it is and how it is *not* simply because of the workings of natural forces (though these did play a role). When the landmine explodes, killing the child, the landmine's behavior is the result of the triad of intentionality of designer, user, and artifact. Its designer had certain intentions in designing the landmine to behave as it does; soldiers placed the landmine where they did with certain intentions. Yes, neither the soldiers nor the designers intended to kill *that* child, but their intentionality explains the location of the landmine and why and how it exploded.

It is a mistake, then, to think of the behavior of the landmine as autonomous and of necessity; it is a mistake to think of it as unconnected to human behavior and intentionality. To do so is to think of the landmine as comparable to a natural object and as such morally neutral. Landmines are far from neutral.

As already indicated, the landmine is, in terms of its functionality and intentionality, a fairly simple artifact. Yet what has been said about the landmine applies to more complex and sophisticated artifacts such as computer systems. Consider a computer system that is deployed to search the Internet for vulnerable computers, and when it finds such computers, to inject a worm.[16] The program, we can suppose, sends back information about what it has done to the user. We can even suppose that the program has been designed to learn as it goes the most efficient way to do what it does. That is, it has been programmed to incorporate information about its attempts to get into each computer and figure out the most efficient strategy for this or that kind of machine. In this way, as the program continues, it learns, and it doesn't have to try the same complex series of techniques on subsequent computers. The learning element adds to the case the possibility that, over time, the designer and user cannot know precisely how the program does what it does. Moreover, the fact that the program embeds worms in systems means that it is not just gathering or producing information; it is "doing" something. The program has efficacy. It changes the states of computers and in so doing causes harm to moral patients.

Does the added complexity, the ability to learn, or the wider range of input and output mean that the relationship between the system's intentionality and efficacy *and* the intentionality and efficacy of the system designer and user, is different than the relationship in the case of the landmine? The answer is no. Once designed and put in place, the program behaves as it does without the assistance of the person who launched it and behaves of necessity. Even when it learns, it learns as it was programmed to learn. The program has intentionality and efficacy. It is poised to behave in certain ways; it is directed at states of affairs in the world (computer systems with certain characteristics connected to the Internet) and is directed at changing those states of world in certain ways. Although designer and user may not know exactly what the program does, the designer has used his or her efficacy and intentionality to create the program, and the user has deployed the program. When the program does what is does, it does not act alone; it acts with the designer and user. It is part of an action but it is not alone an actor. The triad of designer, artifact, and user acted as one.

---

[16] Technically this might simply be a program. The combination of program together with computers and the Internet (without which the program couldn't function) make it a system.

The fact that the designer and user do not know precisely what the artifact does makes no difference here. It simply means that the designer – in creating the program – and the user – in using the program – are engaging in risky behavior. They are facilitating and initiating actions that they may not fully understand, actions with consequences that they can't foresee. The designer and users of such systems should be careful about the intentionality and efficacy they put into the world.

This analysis points to the conclusion that computer systems cannot *by them-selves* be moral agents, but they can be components of moral agency. Computer systems (and other artifacts) can be part of the moral agency of humans insofar as they provide efficacy to human moral agents and insofar as they can be the result of human moral agency. In this sense, computer systems can be *moral entities but not alone moral agents*. The intentionality and efficacy of computer systems make many human actions possible and make others easier and therefore more likely to be performed. The designers of such systems have designed this intentionality and efficacy into them; users, then, make use of the intentionality and efficacy through their intentionality and efficacy.

Conclusions

My argument is, then, that computer systems do not and cannot meet one of the key requirements of the traditional account of moral agency. Computer systems do not have mental states and even if states of computers could be construed as mental states, computer systems do not have intendings to act arising from their freedom. Thus, computer systems are not and can never be (autonomous, independent) moral agents. On the other hand, I have argued that computer systems have intentionality, and because of this, they should not be dismissed from the realm of morality in the same way that natural objects are dismissed. Natural objects behave from necessity. Computer systems and other artifacts behave from necessity once they are created and deployed, but they are intentionally created and deployed. Our failure to recognize the intentionality of computer systems and their connection to human action tends to hide their moral character. Computer systems are components in moral action; many moral actions would be unimaginable and impossible without computer systems. When humans act with artifacts, their actions are constituted by their own intentionality and efficacy, as well as the intentionality and efficacy of the artifact that in turn has been constituted by the intentionality and efficacy of the artifact designer. All three – designers, artifacts, and users – should be the focus of moral evaluation.

Because I argue against the moral agency of computer systems, why, one might wonder, do I bother to navigate through this very complex territory? To my mind, those who argue for the moral agency of computer systems accurately recognize the powerful role that computer systems play, and will increasingly play, in the moral character of the human world; they recognize that computer-system behavior has moral character as well as moral consequences. Yet, although I agree with this, I believe that attributing independent moral agency to computers is dangerous because it disconnects computer behavior from human behavior, the human behavior that creates and deploys the computer systems. This disconnection tends to reinforce the presumption of technological determinism, that is, it reinforces the idea that technology has a natural or logical order of development of its own and is not in the control of humans. This presumption blinds us to the forces that shape the direction of technological development and discourages intervention. When attention is focused on computer systems as human-made, the design of computer systems is more likely to come into the sights of moral scrutiny, and, most importantly, better designs are more likely to be created, designs that constitute a better world.

References

B. R. Allenby, "Engineering Ethics for an Anthropogenic Planet." *Emerging Technologies and Ethical Issues in Engineering* (Washington D.C.: National Academies Press, 2004), pp. 7–28.

Aristotle, *Nicomachean Ethics*. Translation from Terence Irwin, Indianapolis, Hackett, 1985.

W. E. Bijker, "Sociohistorical Technology Studies." In S. Jasanoff, G. E. Markle, J. C. Petersen, and T. Pinch (Eds.), *Handbook of Science and Technology Studies*, London, Sage, 1994, pp. 229–256.

T. W. Bynum **and** J.H. Moor, (Eds.), *The Digital Phoenix: How Computers are Changing Philosophy*. Oxford, Blackwell Publishers, 1998.

J. H. Fetzer, *Computers and Cognition: Why Minds Are Not Machines*. Kluwer Academic Press, 2001.

L. Floridi and J. Sanders, "On the morality of artificial agents." *Minds and Machines*, 14 3 (2004): 349–379.

M. Heidegger, *The Question Concerning Technology and Other Essays*. Translated and with an Introduction by W. Lovitt. New York: Harper & Row, 1977.

T. P. Hughes, "Technological Momentum." In L. Marx and M. R. Smith (Eds.), *Does Technology Drive History? The Dilemma of Technological Determinism*. Cambridge, The MIT Press, 1994.

D. G. Johnson and T.M. Powers, "Computers as Surrogate Agents." In *Moral Philosophy and Information Technology* edited by J. van den Hoven and J. Weckert. Cambridge University Press, 2006.

J. Law, "Technology and Heterogeneous Engineering: The Case of Portuguese Expansion." In W.E. Bijker, T. P. Hughes, and T. Pinch (Eds.), *The Social Construction of Technological Systems*. Cambridge, MIT Press, 1987.

J. Pitt, *Thinking About Technology: Foundations of the Philosophy of Technology*. Originally published by Seven Bridges Press, New York, 2000.

B. C. Stahl, "Information, Ethics, and Computers: The Problem of Autonomous Moral Agents." *Minds and Machines* 14 (2004): 67–83.

12

On the Morality of Artificial Agents

Luciano Floridi

Introduction: Standard versus Nonstandard Theories of Agents and Patients

MORAL SITUATIONS COMMONLY INVOLVE AGENTS AND PATIENTS. LET us define the class A of moral *agents* as the class of all entities that can in principle qualify as sources or senders of moral action, and the class P of moral *patients* as the class of all entities that can in principle qualify as receivers of moral action. A particularly apt way to introduce the topic of this paper is to consider how ethical theories (macroethics) interpret the logical relation between those two classes. There can be five logical relations between A and P; see Figure 12.1.

It is possible, but utterly unrealistic, that A and P are disjoint (alternative 5). On the other hand, P can be a proper subset of A (alternative 3), or A and P can intersect each other (alternative 4). These two alternatives are only slightly more promising because they both require at least one moral agent that in principle could not qualify as a moral patient. Now this pure agent would be some sort of supernatural entity that, like Aristotle's God, affects the world but can never be affected by it. Yet being in principle "unaffectable" and irrelevant in the moral game, it is unclear what kind of role this entity would exercise with respect to the normative guidance of human actions. So it is not surprising that most macroethics have kept away from these "supernatural" speculations and implicitly adopted, or even explicitly argued for, one of the two remaining alternatives discussed in the text: A and P can be equal (alternative 1), or A can be a proper subset of P (alternative 2).

Alternative (1) maintains that all entities that qualify as moral agents also qualify as moral patients and vice versa. It corresponds to a rather intuitive position, according to which the agent/inquirer plays the role of the moral protagonist. It is one of the most popular views in the history of ethics, shared for example by many Christian ethicists in general and by Kant in particular. I shall refer to it as the standard position.

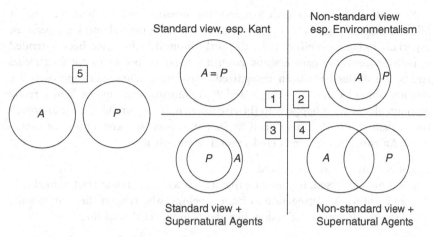

Figure 12.1. The logical relations between the classes of moral agents and patients.

Alternative (2) holds that all entities that qualify as moral agents also qualify as moral patients but not vice versa. Many entities, most notably animals, seem to qualify as moral patients, even if they are in principle excluded from playing the role of moral agents. This post-environmentalist approach requires a change in perspective, from agent orientation to patient orientation. In view of the previous label, I shall refer to it as nonstandard.

In recent years, nonstandard macroethics have discussed the scope of P quite extensively. The more inclusive P is, the "greener" or "deeper" the approach has been deemed. Especially, environmental ethics[1] has developed since the 1960s as the study of the moral relationships of human beings to the environment (including its nonhuman contents and inhabitants) and its (possible) values and moral status. It often represents a challenge to anthropocentric approaches embedded in some traditional Western ethical thinking. In Floridi and Sanders (2001), I have defended a "deep ecology" approach.

Comparatively little work has been done in reconsidering the nature of moral agenthood, and hence the extension of A. Post-environmentalist thought, in striving for a fully naturalized ethics, has implicitly rejected the relevance, if not the possibility, of supernatural agents, whereas the plausibility and importance of other types of moral agenthood seem to have been largely disregarded. Secularism has contracted (some would say deflated) A, whereas environmentalism has justifiably expanded only P, so the gap between A and P has been widening; this has been accompanied by an enormous increase in the moral responsibility of the individual (Floridi 2006).

---

[1] For an excellent introduction, see Jamieson [2008].

Some efforts have been made to redress this situation. In particular, the concept of "moral agent" has been stretched to include both natural and legal persons, especially in business ethics (Floridi [forthcoming]). *A* has then been extended to include agents like partnerships, governments, or corporations, for which legal rights and duties have been recognized. This more ecumenical approach has restored some balance between *A* and *P*. A company can now be held directly accountable for what happens to the environment, for example. Yet the approach has remained unduly constrained by its anthropocentric conception of agenthood. An entity is still considered a moral agent only if

  i. it is an individual agent; and

 ii. it is human-based, in the sense that it is either human or at least reducible to an identifiable aggregation of human beings, who remain the only morally responsible sources of action, like ghosts in the legal machine.

Limiting the ethical discourse to *individual* agents hinders the development of a satisfactory investigation of distributed morality, a macroscopic and growing phenomenon of global moral actions and collective responsibilities resulting from the "invisible hand" of systemic interactions among several agents at a local level. Insisting on the necessarily *human-based nature* of such individual agents means undermining the possibility of understanding another major transformation in the ethical field, the appearance of artificial agents (AAs) that are sufficiently informed, "smart," autonomous, and able to perform morally relevant actions independently of the humans who created them, causing "artificial good" and "artificial evil." Both constraints can be eliminated by fully revising the concept of "moral agent." This is the task undertaken in the following pages.

The main theses defended are that AAs are legitimate sources of im/moral actions, hence that the class *A* of moral agents should be extended so as to include AAs, that the ethical discourse should include the analysis of their morality and, finally, that this analysis is essential in order to understand a range of new moral problems not only in information and computer ethics, but also in ethics in general, especially in the case of distributed morality.

This is the structure of the paper: In the second part, I analyze the concept of agent. I first introduce the fundamental Method of Abstraction, which provides the foundation for an analysis by levels of abstraction (LoA). The reader is invited to pay particular attention to this section; it is essential for the paper, and its application in any ontological analysis is crucial. I then clarify the concept of "moral agent," by providing not a definition, but an effective characterization based on three criteria at a specified LoA. The new concept of moral agent is used to argue that AAs, although neither cognitively intelligent nor morally responsible, can be fully *accountable* sources of moral action. In the third part, I argue that there is substantial and important scope for the concept of moral agent not necessarily exhibiting free will or mental states, which I shall label "mindless morality." In the fourth part, I provide some examples of the properties specified by a correct characterization of agenthood, and in particular of AAs. In that section I also offer some further examples of LoA. Next, I model morality as a "threshold" that is defined on the observables determining the LoA under consideration. An agent is morally good if its actions all respect that threshold; and it is morally evil insofar as its actions violate it. Morality is usually predicated upon *responsibility*. The use of the Method of Abstraction, LoAs, and thresholds enables *responsibility* and *accountability* to be decoupled and formalized effectively when the levels of abstraction involve numerical variables, as is the case with digital AAs. The part played in morality by responsibility and accountability can be clarified as a result. Finally, I investigate some important consequences of the approach defended in this paper for computer ethics.

What Is an Agent?

Complex biochemical compounds and abstruse mathematical concepts have at least one thing in common: They may be unintuitive, but once understood, they are all definable with total precision by listing a finite number of necessary and sufficient properties. Mundane entities like intelligent beings or living systems share the opposite property: One naïvely knows what they are and perhaps could be, and yet there seems to be no way to encase them within the usual planks of necessary and sufficient conditions. This holds true for the general concept of agent as well. People disagree on what may count as an "agent," even in principle (see, for example, Franklin, and Graesser 1997, Davidsson and Johansson 2005, Moya and Tolk 2007, Barandiaran et al. 2009). Why? Sometimes the problem is addressed optimistically, as if it were just a matter of further shaping and sharpening whatever necessary and sufficient conditions are required to obtain a *definiens* that is finally watertight. Stretch here, cut there; ultimate agreement is only a matter of time, patience, and cleverness. In fact, attempts follow one another without a final identikit ever being nailed to the *definiendum* in question. After a while, one starts suspecting that there might be something wrong with this ad hoc approach. Perhaps it is not the Procrustean *definiens* that needs fixing, but the Protean *definiendum*. Sometimes its intrinsic fuzziness is blamed. One cannot define with sufficient accuracy things like life, intelligence, agenthood, and mind because they all admit of subtle degrees and continuous changes.[2]

A solution is to give up altogether, or at best be resigned to vagueness and reliance on indicative examples. Pessimism follows optimism, but it need not. The fact is that, in the exact discipline of mathematics, for example, definitions are "parameterized" by generic sets. That technique provides a method for regulating levels of abstraction. Indeed abstraction acts as a "hidden parameter" behind exact definitions, making a crucial difference. Thus, each *definiens* comes

---

[2] See, for example, Bedau [1996] for a discussion of alternatives to necessary-and-sufficient definitions in the case of life.

preformatted by an implicit level of abstraction (LoA, on which more shortly); it is stabilized, as it were, in order to allow a proper definition. An *x* is defined or identified as *y* never absolutely (i.e., LoA-independently), as a Kantian "thing-in-itself," but always contextually, as a function of a given LoA, whether it be in the realm of Euclidean geometry, quantum physics, or commonsensical perception.

When an LoA is sufficiently common, important, dominating, or in fact happens to be the very frame that constructs the *definiendum*, it becomes "transparent" to the user, and one has the pleasant impression that *x* can be subject to an adequate definition in a sort of conceptual vacuum. Glass is not a solid, but a liquid; tomatoes are not vegetables, but berries; a banana plant is a kind of grass; and whales are mammals, not fish. Unintuitive as such views might be initially, they are all accepted without further complaint because one silently bows to the uncontroversial predominance of the corresponding LoA.

When no LoA is predominant or constitutive, things get messy. In this case, the trick does not lie in fiddling with the *definiens* or blaming the *definiendum*, but in deciding on an adequate LoA before embarking on the task of understanding the nature of the *definiendum*.

The example of intelligence or "thinking" behavior is enlightening. One might define "intelligence" in a myriad of ways; many LoAs seem equally convincing, but no single, absolute definition is adequate in every context. Turing (1950) avoided the problem of defining intelligence by first fixing an LoA – in this case a dialogue conducted by computer interface with response time taken into account – and then establishing the necessary and sufficient conditions for a computing system to count as intelligent at that LoA: the imitation game. As I argued in Floridi (2010b), the LoA is crucial, and changing it changes the test. An example is provided by the Loebner test (Moor 2001), the current competitive incarnation of Turing's test. There, the LoA includes a particular format for questions, a mixture of human and nonhuman players, and precise scoring that takes into account repeated trials. One result of the different LoA has been chatbots, unfeasible at Turing's original LoA.

Some *definienda* come preformatted by transparent LoAs. They are subject to definition in terms of necessary and sufficient conditions. Some other *definienda* require the explicit acceptance of a given LoA as a precondition for their analysis. They are subject to effective characterization. Arguably, agenthood is one of the latter.

On the Very Idea of Levels of Abstraction

The idea of a level of abstraction plays an absolutely crucial role in the previous account. We have seen that this is so even if the specific LoA is left implicit. For example, whether we perceive oxygen in the environment depends on the LoA at which we are operating; to abstract it is not to overlook its vital importance, but merely to acknowledge its lack of immediate relevance to the current discourse, which *could* always be extended to include oxygen were that desired.

Yet what is an LoA exactly? The Method of Abstraction comes from modeling in science where the variables in the model correspond to observables in reality, all others being abstracted. The terminology has been influenced by an area of computer science, called Formal Methods, in which discrete mathematics is used to specify and analyze the behavior of information systems. Despite that heritage, the idea is not at all technical, and for the purposes of this paper no mathematics is required. I have provided a definition and more detailed analysis in Floridi (2008b), so here I shall outline only the basic idea.

Suppose we join Anne, Ben, and Carole in the middle of a conversation.[3] Anne is a collector and potential buyer; Ben tinkers in his spare time; and Carole is an economist. We do not know the object of their conversation, but we are able to hear this much:

> *Anne* observes that it has an antitheft device installed, is kept garaged when not in use, and has had only a single owner;
> *Ben* observes that its engine is not the original one, that its body has been recently repainted, but that all leather parts are very worn;
> *Carole* observes that the old engine consumed too much, that it has a stable market value, but that its spare parts are expensive.

The participants view the object under discussion (the "it" in their conversation) according to their own interests, at their own LoA. We may guess that they are probably talking about a car or perhaps a motorcycle, but it could be an airplane. Whatever the reference is, it provides the source of information and is called the *system*. An LoA consists of a collection of observables, each with a well-defined possible set of values or outcomes. For the sake of simplicity, let us assume that Anne's LoA matches that of an owner, Ben's that of a mechanic, and Carole's that of an insurer. Each LoA makes possible an analysis of the system, the result of which is called a *model* of the system. Evidently an entity may be described at a range of LoAs and so can have a range of models. In the next section I outline the definitions underpinning the Method of Abstraction.

Definitions

The term *variable* is commonly used throughout science for a symbol that acts as a placeholder for an unknown or changeable referent. A *typed variable* is to be understood as a variable qualified to hold only a declared kind of data. An

---

[3] Note that, for the sake of simplicity, the conversational example does not fully respect the *de dicto / de re* distinction.

observable is a typed variable together with a statement of what feature of the system under consideration it represents.

A *level of abstraction* or *LoA* is a finite but nonempty set of observables that are expected to be the building blocks in a theory characterized by their very choice. An *interface* (called a *gradient of abstractions* in Floridi 2008b) consists of a collection of LoAs. An interface is used in analyzing some system from varying points of view or at varying LoAs.

Models are the outcome of the analysis of a system developed at some LoA(s). The *Method of Abstraction* consists of formalizing the model by using the terms just introduced (and others relating to system behavior, which we do not need here [see Floridi 2008b]).

In the previous example, Anne's LoA might consist of observables for security, method of storage, and owner history; Ben's might consist of observables for engine condition, external body condition, and internal condition; and Carole's might consist of observables for running cost, market value, and maintenance cost. The interface might consist, for the purposes of the discussion, of the set of all three LoAs.

In this case, the LoAs happen to be disjoint, but in general they need not be. A particularly important case is that in which one LoA includes another. Suppose, for example, that Delia joins the discussion and analyzes the system using an LoA that includes those of Anne and Ben. Delia's LoA might match that of a buyer. Then Delia's LoA is said to be more concrete, or lower, than Anne's, which is said to be more abstract, or higher, for Anne's LoA abstracts some observables apparent at Delia's.

Relativism

An LoA qualifies the level at which an entity or system is considered. In this paper, I apply the Method of Abstraction and recommend to make each LoA precise before the properties of the entity can sensibly be discussed. In general, it seems that many uninteresting disagreements might be clarified by the various "sides" making precise their LoA. Yet a crucial clarification is in order. It must be stressed that a clear indication of the LoA at which a system is being analyzed allows pluralism without endorsing relativism. It is a mistake to think that "anything goes" as long as one makes explicit the LoA, because LoA are mutually comparable and assessable (see Floridi [2008b] for a full defense of that point).

Introducing an explicit reference to the LoA clarifies that the model of a system is a function of the available observables, and that (i) different interfaces may be fairly ranked depending on how well they satisfy modeling specifications (e.g., informativeness, coherence, elegance, explanatory power, consistency with the data, etc.) and (ii) different analyses can be fairly compared provided that they share the same LoA.

State and State Transitions

Let us agree that an entity is characterized at a given LoA by the properties it satisfies at that LoA (Cassirer 1910). We are interested in systems that change, which means that some of those properties change value. A changing entity therefore has its evolution captured, at a given LoA and any instant, by the values of its attributes. Thus, an entity can be thought of as having states, determined by the value of the properties that hold at any instant of its evolution, for then any change in the entity corresponds to a state change and vice versa.

This conceptual approach allows us to view any entity as having states. The lower the LoA, the more detailed the observed changes and the greater the number of state components required to capture the change. Each change corresponds to a transition from one state to another. A transition may be nondeterministic. Indeed, it will typically be the case that the LoA under consideration abstracts the observables required to make the transition deterministic. As a result, the transition might lead from a given initial state to one of several possible subsequent states.

According to this view, the entity becomes a transition system. The notion of a "transition system" provides a convenient means to support our criteria for agenthood, being general enough to embrace the usual notions like automaton and process. It is frequently used to model interactive phenomena. We need only the idea; for a formal treatment of much more than we need in this context, the reader might wish to consult Arnold and Plaice (1994).

A *transition system* comprises a (nonempty) set S of states and a family of operations called the *transitions* on S. Each transition may take input and may yield output, but at any rate, it takes the system from one state to another, and in that way forms a (mathematical) relation on S. If the transition does take input or yield output, then it models an interaction between the system and its environment and so is called an *external* transition; otherwise the transition lies beyond the influence of the environment (at the given LoA) and is called *internal*. It is to be emphasized that input and output are, like state, observed at a given LoA. Thus, the transition that models a system is dependent on the chosen LoA. At a lower LoA, an internal transition may become external; at a higher LoA, an external transition may become internal.

In our example, the object being discussed by Anne might be further qualified by state components for location: whether in use, whether turned on, or whether the antitheft device is engaged; or by history of owners and energy output. The operation of garaging the object might take as input a driver, and have the effect of placing the object in the garage with the engine off and the antitheft device engaged, leaving the history of owners unchanged, and outputting a certain amount of energy. The "in use" state component could nondeterministically take either value, depending on the particular instantiation of the transition. Perhaps the object is not in use and is garaged for the night; or perhaps the driver is listening to a program broadcasted on its radio, in the quiet solitude of the garage. The precise definition depends on the LoA. Alternatively, if speed were observed but time, accelerator position, and petrol consumption abstracted, then accelerating to sixty miles per hour would appear as an internal transition. Further examples are provided in the next subsection.

With the explicit assumption that the system under consideration forms a transition system, we are now ready to apply the Method of Abstraction to the analysis of agenthood.

An Effective Characterization of Agents

Whether A (the class of moral agents) needs to be expanded depends on what qualifies as a moral agent, and we have seen that this in turn depends on the specific LoA at which one chooses to analyze and discuss a particular entity and its context. Because human beings count as standard moral agents, the right LoA for the analysis of moral agenthood must accommodate this fact. Theories that extend A to include supernatural agents adopt an LoA that is equal to or lower than the LoA at which human beings qualify as moral agents. Our strategy develops in the opposite direction.

Consider what makes a human being (called Jan) not a moral agent to begin with, but just an agent. Described at this LoA_1, Jan is an agent if Jan is a system embedded in an environment that initiates a transformation, produces an effect, or exerts power on it, as contrasted with a system that is (at least initially) acted on or responds to it, called the patient. At LoA_1, there is no difference between Jan and an earthquake. There should not be. Earthquakes, however, can hardly count as moral agents, so LoA_1 is too high for our purposes: It abstracts too many properties. What needs to be re-instantiated? Following recent literature (Danielson 1992, Allen et al. 2000, Wallach and Allen 2010), I shall argue that the right LoA is probably one that includes the following three criteria: (i) *interactivity*, (ii) *autonomy*, and (iii) *adaptability*:

  i. *Interactivity* means that the agent and its environment (can) act upon each other.
     Typical examples include input or output of a value, or simultaneous engagement of an action by both agent and patient – for example gravitational force between bodies;
  ii. *Autonomy* means that the agent is able to change state without direct response to interaction: it can perform internal transitions to change its state. So an agent must have at least two states.
     This property imbues an agent with a certain degree of complexity and independence from its environment;
  iii. *Adaptability* means that the agent's interactions (can) change the transition rules by which it changes state.

This property ensures that an agent might be viewed, at the given LoA, as learning its own mode of operation in a way that depends critically on its experience. Note that if an agent's transition rules are stored as part of its internal state, discernible at this LoA, then adaptability follows from the other two conditions.

Let us now look at some illustrative examples.

Examples

The examples in this section serve different purposes. In the next subsection, I provide some examples of entities that fail to qualify as agents by systematically violating each of the three conditions. This will help to highlight the nature of the contribution of each condition. Then, I offer an example of a digital system that forms an agent at one LoA, but not at another equally natural LoA. That example is useful because it shows how "machine learning" can enable a system to achieve adaptability. A more familiar example is provided in the subsection that follows, where I show that digital software agents are now part of everyday life. The fourth subsection illustrates how an everyday physical device might conceivably be modified into an agent, whereas the one immediately following it provides an example that has already benefited from that modification, at least in the laboratory. The last example provides an entirely different kind of agent: an organization.

The Defining Properties

For the purpose of understanding what each of the three conditions (interactivity, autonomy, and adaptability) adds to our definition of agent, it is instructive to consider examples satisfying each possible combination of those properties. In Figure 12.2, only the last row represents all three conditions being satisfied and hence illustrates agenthood. For the sake of simplicity, all examples are taken at the same LoA, which is assumed to consist of observations made through a typical video camera over a period of, say, thirty seconds. Thus, we abstract tactile observables and longer-term effects.

Recall that a property, for example, interaction, is to be judged only via the observables. Thus, at the LoA in Figure 12.2 we cannot infer that a rock interacts with its environment by virtue of reflected light, for this observation belongs to a much finer LoA. Alternatively, were long-term effects to be discernible, then a rock would be interactive because interaction with its environment (e.g., erosion) could be observed. No example has been provided of a noninteractive, nonautonomous, but adaptive entity. This is because, at that LoA, it is difficult to conceive of an entity that adapts without interaction and autonomy.

Noughts and Crosses

The distinction between change-of-state (required by autonomy) and change-of-transition rule (required by adaptability) is one in which the LoA plays a

Interactive	Autonomous	Adaptable	Examples
no	no	no	rock
no	no	yes	?
no	yes	no	pendulum
no	yes	yes	closed ecosystem, solar system
yes	no	no	postbox, mill
yes	no	yes	thermostat
yes	yes	no	juggernaut
yes	yes	yes	human

Figure 12.2. Examples of agents. The LoA consists of observations made through a video camera over a period of 30 seconds.[4]

crucial role, and to explain it, it is useful to discuss a more extended, classic example. This was originally developed by Donald Michie (1961) to discuss the concept of a mechanism's adaptability. It provides a good introduction to the concept of machine learning, the research area in computer science that studies adaptability.

MENACE (Matchbox Educable Noughts and Crosses Engine) is a system that learns to play noughts and crosses (aka tic-tac-toe) by repetition of many games. Although nowadays it would be realized by a program (see for example http://www.adit.co.uk/html/menace_simulation.html), Michie built MENACE using matchboxes and beads, and it is probably easier to understand it in that form.

Suppose MENACE plays O and its opponent plays X, so that we can concentrate entirely on plays of O. Initially, the board is empty with O to play. Taking into account symmetrically equivalent positions, there are three possible initial plays for O. The state of the game consists of the current position of the board. We do not need to augment that with the name (O or X) of the side playing next, because we consider the board only when O is to play. Altogether there are some three hundred such states; MENACE contains a matchbox for each. In each box are beads that represent the plays O can make from that state. At most,

---

[4]   "Juggernaut" is the name for Vishnu, the Hindu god, meaning "Lord of the World." A statue of the god is annually carried in procession on a very large and heavy vehicle. It is believed that devotees threw themselves beneath its wheels, hence the word Juggernaut has acquired the meaning of "massive and irresistible force or object that crushes whatever is in its path."

nine different plays are possible, and MENACE encodes each with a colored bead. Those that cannot be made (because the squares are already full in the current state) are removed from the box for that state. That provides MENACE with a built-in knowledge of legal plays. In fact, MENACE could easily be adapted to start with no such knowledge and to learn it.

O's initial play is made by selecting the box representing the empty board and choosing from it a bead at random. That determines O's play. Next X plays. Then MENACE repeats its method of determining O's next play. After at most five plays for O, the game ends in either a draw or a win either for O or for X. Now that the game is complete, MENACE updates the state of the (at most five) boxes used during the game as follows. If X won, then in order to make MENACE less likely to make the same plays from those states again, a bead representing its play from each box is removed. If O drew, then conversely each bead representing a play is duplicated; and if O won, each bead is quadruplicated. Now the next game is played.

After enough games, it simply becomes impossible for the random selection of O's next play to produce a losing play. MENACE has learned to play, which, for noughts and crosses, means never losing. The initial state of the boxes was prescribed for MENACE. Here, we assume merely that it contains sufficient variety of beads for all legal plays to be made, for then the frequency of beads affects only the rate at which MENACE learns.

The state of MENACE (as distinct from the state of the game) consists of the state of each box, the state of the game, and the list of boxes that have been used so far in the current game. Its transition rule consists of the probabilistic choice of play (i.e., bead) from the current state box, which evolves as the states of the boxes evolve. Let us now consider MENACE at three LoAs.

(i) The Single Game LoA
Observables are the state of the game at each turn and (in particular) its outcome. All knowledge of the state of MENACE's boxes (and hence of its transition rule) is abstracted. The board after X's play constitutes input to MENACE, and that after O's play constitutes output. MENACE is thus interactive, autonomous (indeed, state update, determined by the transition rule, appears nondeterministic at this LoA), but not adaptive, in the sense that we have no way of observing how MENACE determines its next play and no way of iterating games to infer that it changes with repeated games.

(ii) The Tournament LoA
Now a sequence of games is observed, each as before, and with it a sequence of results. As before, MENACE is interactive and autonomous. Yet now the sequence of results reveals (by any of the standard statistical methods) that the rule by which MENACE resolves the nondeterministic choice of play evolves. Thus, at this LoA, MENACE is also adaptive and hence an agent. Interesting examples of adaptable AAs from contemporary science fiction include the computer in *War*

Games (1983, directed by J. Badham), which learns the futility of war in general by playing noughts and crosses; and the smart building in *The Grid* (Kerr 1996), whose computer learns to compete with humans and eventually liberate itself to the heavenly Internet.

(iii) The System LoA

Finally we observe not only a sequence of games, but also all of MENACE's "code." In the case of a program, this is indeed code. In the case of the matchbox model, it consists of the array of boxes together with the written rules, or manual, for working it. Now MENACE is still interactive and autonomous. However, it is not adaptive; for what in (ii) seemed to be an evolution of transition rule is now revealed, by observation of the code, to be a simple deterministic update of the program state, namely the contents of the matchboxes. At this lower LoA, MENACE fails to be an agent.

The point clarified by this example is that if a transition rule is observed to be a consequence of program state, then the program is not adaptive. For example, in (ii) the transition rule chooses the next play by exercising a probabilistic choice between the possible plays from that state. The probability is in fact determined by the frequency of beads present in the relevant box. Yet that is not observed at the LoA of (ii), and so the transition rule appears to vary. Adaptability is possible. However, at the lower LoA of (iii), bead frequency is part of the system state and hence observable. Thus, the transition rule, though still probabilistic, is revealed to be merely a response to input. Adaptability fails to hold.

This distinction is vital for current software. Early software used to lie open to the system user who, if interested, could read the code and see the entire system state. For such software, an LoA in which the entire system state is observed is appropriate. However, the user of contemporary software is explicitly barred from interrogating the code in nearly all cases. This has been possible because of the advance in user interfaces. Use of icons means that the user need not know where an applications package is stored, let alone be concerned with its content. Likewise, iPhone applets are downloaded from the Internet and executed locally at the click of an icon, without the user having any access to their code. For such software, an LoA in which the code is entirely concealed is appropriate. This corresponds to case (ii) and hence to agenthood. Indeed, only since the advent of applets and such downloaded executable but invisible files has the issue of moral accountability of AAs become critical.

Viewed at an appropriate LoA, then, the MENACE system is an agent. The way it adapts can be taken as representative of machine learning in general. Many readers may have had experience with operating systems that offer a "speaking" interface. Such systems learn the user's voice basically in the same way as MENACE learns to play noughts and crosses. There are natural LoAs at which such systems are agents. The case being developed in this paper is that, as a result, they may also be viewed to have moral accountability.

If a piece of software that exhibits machine learning is studied at an LoA that registers its interactions with its environment, then the software will appear interactive, autonomous, and adaptive, that is, as an agent. However, if the program code is revealed, then the software is shown to be simply following rules and hence not to be adaptive. Those two LoAs are at variance. One reflects the "open source" view of software: The user has access to the code. The other reflects the commercial view that, although the user has bought the software and can use it at will, he or she has no access to the code. The question is whether the software forms an (artificial) agent.

Webbot

Internet users often find themselves besieged by unwanted e-mail. A popular solution is to filter incoming e-mail automatically, using a webbot that incorporates such filters. An important feature of useful bots is that they learn the user's preferences, for which purpose the user may at any time review the bot's performance. At a LoA revealing all incoming e-mail (input to the webbot) and filtered e-mail (output by the webbot), but abstracting the algorithm by which the bot adapts its behavior to our preferences, the bot constitutes an agent. Such is the case if we do not have access to the bot's code, as discussed in the previous section.

Futuristic Thermostat

A hospital thermostat might be able to monitor not only ambient temperature, but also the state of well-being of patients. Such a device might be observed at a LoA consisting of input for the patients' data and ambient temperature, state of the device itself, and output controlling the room heater. Such a device is interactive because some of the observables correspond to input and others to output. However, it is neither autonomous nor adaptive. For comparison, if only the "color" of the physical device were observed, then it would no longer be interactive. If it were to change color in response to (unobserved) changes in its environment, then it would be autonomous. Inclusion of those environmental changes in the LoA as input observables would make the device interactive but not autonomous. However, at such an LoA, a futuristic thermostat imbued with autonomy and able to regulate its own criteria for operation – perhaps as the result of a software controller – would, in view of that last condition, be an agent.

SmartPaint

SmartPaint is a recent invention. When applied to a physical structure it appears to behave like normal paint; but when vibrations that may lead to fractures become apparent in the structure, the paint changes its electrical properties in a way that is readily determined by measurement, thus highlighting the need for maintenance. At an LoA at which only the electrical properties of the paint over time is observed, the paint is neither interactive nor adaptive but appears autonomous; indeed, the properties change as a result of internal nondeterminism. However, if that LoA is augmented by the structure data monitored by the paint over time, then SmartPaint becomes an agent, because the data provide input to which the paint adapts its state. Finally, if that LoA is augmented further to include a model by which the paint works, changes in its electrical properties are revealed as being determined directly by input data, and so SmartPaint no longer forms an agent.

Organizations

A different kind of example of AA is provided by a company or management organization. At an appropriate LoA, it interacts with its employees, constituent substructures, and other organizations; it is able to make internally determined changes of state; and it is able to adapt its strategies for decision making and hence for acting.

Morality

We have seen that given the appropriate LoA, humans, webbots and organizations can all be properly treated as agents. Our next task is to determine whether, and in what way, they might be correctly considered moral agents as well.

Morality of Agents

Suppose we are analyzing the behavior of a population of entities through a video camera of a security system that gives us complete access to all the observables available at LoA_1 (see 2.5) plus all the observables related to the degrees of interactivity, autonomy, and adaptability shown by the systems under scrutiny. At this new LoA_2, we observe that two of the entities, call them H and W, are able

i. to respond to environmental stimuli – for example, the presence of a patient in a hospital bed – by updating their states (interactivity), for example, by recording some chosen variables concerning the patient's health. This presupposes that H and W are informed about the environment through some data-entry devices, for example, some perceptors;

ii. to change their states according to their own transition rules and in a self-governed way, independently of environmental stimuli (autonomy), for example, by taking flexible decisions based on past and new information, which modify the environment temperature; and

iii. to change according to the environment the transition rules by which their states are changed (adaptability), for example, by modifying past procedures to take into account successful and unsuccessful treatments of patients.

H and W certainly qualify as agents, because we have only "upgraded" LoA$_1$ to LoA$_2$. Are they also moral agents? The question invites the elaboration of a criterion of identification. Here is a very moderate option:

(O) An action is said to be morally qualifiable if and only if it can cause moral good or evil. An agent is said to be a moral agent if and only if it is capable of morally qualifiable action.

Note that (O) is neither consequentialist nor intentionalist in nature. We are neither affirming nor denying that the specific evaluation of the morality of the agent might depend on the specific outcome of the agent's actions or on the agent's original intentions or principles. We shall return to this point in the next section.

Let us return to the question: Are H and W moral agents? Because of (O), we cannot yet provide a definite answer unless H and W become involved in some moral action. So suppose that H kills the patient and W cures her. Their actions are moral actions. They both acted interactively, responding to the new situation with which they were dealing on the basis of the information at their disposal. They both acted autonomously: They could have taken different courses of actions, and in fact we may assume that they changed their behavior several times in the course of the action on the basis of new available information. They both acted adaptably: They were not simply following orders or predetermined instructions. On the contrary, they both had the possibility of changing the general heuristics that led them to take the decisions they made, and we may assume that they did take advantage of the available opportunities to improve their general behavior. The answer seems rather straightforward: Yes, they are both moral agents. There is only one problem: One is a human being, the other is an artificial agent. The LoA$_2$ adopted allows both cases, so can you tell the difference? If you cannot, you will agree that the class of moral agents must include AAs like webbots. If you disagree, it may be so for several reasons, but only five of them seem to have some strength. I shall discuss four of them in the next section and leave the fifth to the conclusion.

A-Responsible Morality

One may try to withstand the conclusion reached in the previous section by arguing that something crucial is missing in LoA$_2$. LoA$_2$ cannot be adequate precisely because if it were, then artificial agents (AAs) would count as moral agents, and this is unacceptable for at least one of the following reasons:

- *the teleological objection*: An AA has no goals;
- *the intentional objection*: An AA has no intentional states;
- *the freedom objection*: An AA is not free; and
- *the responsibility objection*: An AA cannot be held responsible for its actions.

The Teleological Objection

The teleological objection can be disposed of immediately. For in principle LoA$_2$ could readily be (and often is) upgraded to include goal-oriented behavior (Russell and Norvig 2010). Because AAs can exhibit (and upgrade their) goal-directed behaviors, the teleological variables cannot be what makes a positive difference between a human and an artificial agent. We could have added a teleological condition and both H and W could have satisfied it, leaving us none the wiser concerning their identity. So why not add one anyway? It is better not to overload the interface because a nonteleological level of analysis helps to understand issues in "distributed morality," involving groups, organizations, institutions, and so forth that would otherwise remain unintelligible. This will become clearer in the conclusion.

The Intentional Objection

The intentional objection argues that it is not enough to have an artificial agent behave teleologically. To be a moral agent, the AA must relate itself to its actions in some more profound way, involving meaning, wishing, or wanting to act in a certain way and being epistemically aware of its behavior. Yet this is not accounted for in LoA$_2$, hence the confusion.

Unfortunately, intentional states are a nice but unnecessary condition for the occurrence of moral agenthood. First, the objection presupposes the availability of some sort of privileged access (a God's-eye perspective from without, or some sort of Cartesian internal intuition from within) to the agent's mental or intentional states that, although possible in theory, cannot be easily guaranteed in practice. This is precisely why a clear and explicit indication is vital of the LoA at which one is analyzing the system from without. It guarantees that one's analysis is truly based only on what is specified to be observable, and not on some psychological speculation. This phenomenological approach is a strength, not a weakness. It implies that agents (including human agents) should be evaluated as moral if they do play the "moral game." Whether they mean to play it or they know that they are playing it, is relevant only at a second stage, when what we want to know is whether they are *morally responsible* for their moral actions. Yet this is a different matter, and we shall deal with it at the end of this section. Here, it is to sufficient to recall that, for a consequentialist, for example, human beings would still be regarded as moral agents (sources of increased or diminished welfare), even if viewed at a LoA at which they are reduced to mere zombies without goals, feelings, intelligence, knowledge, or intentions.

The Freedom Objection

The same holds true for the freedom objection and in general for any other objection based on some special internal states enjoyed only by human and perhaps superhuman beings. The AAs are already free in the sense of being nondeterministic systems. This much is uncontroversial, is scientifically sound, and can be guaranteed about human beings as well. It is also sufficient for our purposes and saves us from the horrible prospect of having to enter into the thorny debate about the reasonableness of determinism, an infamous LoA-free zone of endless dispute. All one needs to do is to realize that the agents in question satisfy the usual practical counterfactual: They could have acted differently had they chosen differently, and they could have chosen differently because they are interactive, informed, autonomous, and adaptive.

Once an agent's actions are morally qualifiable, it is unclear what more is required of that agent to count as an agent playing the moral game, that is, to qualify as a moral agent, even if unintentionally and unwittingly. Unless, as we have seen, what one really means by talking about goals, intentions, freedom, cognitive states, and so forth is that an AA cannot be held responsible for its actions.

Now, responsibility, as we shall see better in a moment, means here that the agent and his or her behavior and actions are assessable in principle as praiseworthy or blameworthy; and they are often so not just intrinsically, but also for some pedagogical, educational, social, or religious end. This is the next objection.

The Responsibility Objection

The objection based on the "lack of responsibility" is the only one with real strength. It can be immediately conceded that it would be ridiculous to praise or blame an AA for its behavior or charge it with a moral accusation. You do not scold your iPhone apps, that is obvious. So this objection strikes a reasonable note; but what is its real point and how much can one really gain by leveling it? Let me first clear the ground from two possible misunderstandings.

First, we need to be careful about the terminology, and the linguistic frame in general, used by the objection. The whole conceptual vocabulary of "responsibility" and its cognate terms is completely soaked with anthropocentrism. This is quite natural and understandable, but the fact can provide at most a heuristic hint, certainly not an argument. The anthropocentrism is justified by the fact that the vocabulary is geared to psychological and educational needs, when not to religious purposes. We praise and blame in view of behavioral purposes and perhaps a better life and afterlife. Yet this says nothing about whether an agent is the source of morally charged action. Consider the opposite case. Because AAs lack a psychological component, we do not blame AAs, for example, but given the appropriate circumstances, we can rightly consider them sources of evils and legitimately reengineer them to make sure they no longer cause evil. We are not punishing them anymore than one punishes a river when building higher banks to avoid a flood. Yet the fact that we do not "reengineer" people does not say anything about the possibility of people acting in the same way as AAs, and it would not mean that for people "reengineering" could be a rather nasty way of being punished.

Second, we need to be careful about what the objection really means. There are two main senses in which AA can fail to qualify as responsible. In one sense, we say that, if the agent failed to interact properly with the environment, for example, because it actually lacked sufficient information or had no alternative option, we should not hold an agent morally responsible for an action it has committed because this would be *morally unfair*. This sense is irrelevant here. LoA$_2$ indicates that AA are sufficiently interactive, autonomous, and adaptive to qualify fairly as moral agents. In the second sense, we say that, given a certain description of the agent, we should not hold that agent morally responsible for an action it has committed because this would be *conceptually improper*. This sense is more fundamental than the other: If it is conceptually improper to treat AAs as moral agents, the question whether it may be morally fair to do so does not even arise. It is this more fundamental sense that is relevant here. The objection argues that AAs fail to qualify as moral agents because they are not morally responsible for their actions, because holding them responsible would be conceptually improper (not morally unfair). In other words, LoA$_2$ provides necessary but insufficient conditions. The proper LoA requires another condition, namely responsibility. This fourth condition finally enables us to distinguish between moral agents, who are necessarily human or superhuman, and AAs, which remain mere efficient causes.

The point raised by the objection is that agents are moral agents only if they are responsible in the sense of being prescriptively assessable in principle. An agent *a* is a moral agent only if *a* can in principle be put on trial. Now that this much has been clarified, the immediate impression is that the "lack of responsibility" objection is merely confusing the *identification* of *a* as a moral agent with the *evaluation* of *a* as a morally responsible agent. Surely, the counter-argument goes, there is a difference between, on the one hand, being able to say who or what is the moral source or cause of the moral action in question (and hence it is accountable for it), and, on the other hand, being able to evaluate, prescriptively, whether and how far the moral source so identified is also morally responsible for that action, and hence deserves to be praised or blamed, and thus rewarded or punished accordingly.

Well, that immediate impression is actually mistaken. There is no confusion. Equating identification and evaluation is a shortcut. The objection is saying that identity (as a moral agent) without responsibility (as a moral agent) is empty, so we may as well save ourselves the bother of all these distinctions and speak only of morally responsible agents and moral agents as synonymous. However, here lies the real mistake. We now see that the objection has finally shown its fundamental presupposition: that we should reduce all prescriptive discourse to responsibility analysis. Yet this is an unacceptable assumption, a juridical fallacy. There is plenty of room for prescriptive discourse that is independent of responsibility assignment and thus requires a clear identification of moral agents. Good parents, for example, commonly engage in moral-evaluation practices when interacting with their children, even at an age when the latter are not yet responsible agents; this is not only perfectly acceptable, but something to be expected. This means that they identify them as moral sources of moral action, although, as moral agents, they are not yet subject to the process of moral evaluation.

If one considers children an exception, insofar as they are potentially responsible moral agents, an example involving animals may help. There is nothing wrong with identifying a dog as the source of a morally good action, hence as an agent playing a crucial role in a moral situation and therefore as a moral agent. Search-and-rescue dogs are trained to track missing people. They often help save lives, for which they receive much praise and rewards from both their owners and the people they have located, yet this is not the relevant point. Emotionally, people may be very grateful to the animals, but for the dogs it is a game and they cannot be considered morally responsible for their actions. At the same time, the dogs are involved in a moral game as main players, and we rightly identify them as moral agents that may cause good or evil.

All this should ring a bell. Trying to equate identification and evaluation is really just another way of shifting the ethical analysis from considering a as the moral agent/source of a first-order moral action b to considering a as a possible moral patient of a second-order moral action c, which is the moral evaluation of a as being morally responsible for b. This is a typical Kantian move, but there is clearly more to moral evaluation than just responsibility, because a is capable of moral action even if a cannot be (or is not yet) a morally responsible agent. A third example may help to clarify the distinction further.

Suppose an adult human agent tries his best to avoid a morally evil action. Suppose that, despite all his efforts, he actually ends up committing that evil action. We would not consider that agent morally responsible for the outcome of his well-meant efforts. After all, Oedipus did try not to kill his father and did not mean to marry his mother. The tension between the lack of responsibility for the evil caused and the still-present accountability for it (Oedipus remains the only source of that evil) is the definition of the tragic. Oedipus is a moral agent without responsibility. He blinds himself as a symbolic gesture against the knowledge of his inescapable state.

Morality Threshold

Motivated by the foregoing discussion, morality of an agent at a given LoA can now be defined in terms of a threshold function. More general definitions are possible, but the following covers most examples, including all those considered in the present paper.

A threshold function at an LoA is a function that, given values for all the observables in the LoA, returns another value. An agent at that LoA is deemed to be morally good if, for some preagreed value (called the tolerance), it maintains a relationship between the observables so that the value of the threshold function at any time does not exceed the tolerance.

For LoAs at which AAs are considered, the types of all observables can be mathematically determined, at least in principle. In such cases, the threshold function is also given by a formula; but the tolerance, though again determined, is identified by human agents exercising ethical judgments. In that sense, it resembles the entropy ordering introduced in Floridi and Sanders (2001). Indeed, the threshold function is derived from the level functions used there in order to define entropy orderings.

For nonartificial agents like humans, we do not know whether all relevant observables can be mathematically determined. The opposing view is represented by followers and critics of the Hobbesian approach. The former argue that for a realistic LoA, it is just a matter of time until science is able to model a human as an automaton or state-transition system with scientifically determined states and transition rules; the latter object that such a model is in principle impossible. The truth is probably that, when considering agents, thresholds are in general only partially quantifiable and usually determined by various forms of consensus. Let us now review the earlier examples from the viewpoint of morality.

Examples

The futuristic thermostat is morally charged because the LoA includes patients' well-being. It would be regarded as morally good if and only if its output maintains the actual patients' well-being within an agreed tolerance of their desired well-being. Thus, in this case a threshold function consists of the distance (in some finite-dimensional real space) between the actual patients' well-being and their desired well-being.

Because we value our e-mail, a webbot is morally charged. In Floridi and Sanders (2001) its action was deemed to be morally bad (an example of artificial evil) if it incorrectly filters any messages: if either it filters messages it should let pass, or allows to pass messages it should filter. Here we could use the same criterion to deem the webbot agent itself to be morally bad. However, in view of the continual adaptability offered by the bot, a more realistic criterion for moral good would be that, at most, a certain fixed percentage of incoming e-mail be incorrectly filtered. In that case, the threshold function could consist of the number of incorrectly filtered messages.

The strategy-learning system MENACE simply learns to play noughts and crosses. With a little contrivance it could be morally charged as follows.

Suppose that something like MENACE is used to provide the game play in some computer game whose interface belies the simplicity of the underlying strategy and that invites the human player to pit his or her wit against the automated opponent. The software behaves unethically if and only if it loses a game after a sufficient learning period, for such behavior would enable the human opponent to win too easily and might result in market failure of the game. That situation may be formalized using thresholds by defining, for a system having initial state

M, $T(M)$ to denote the number of games required after which the system never loses. Experience and necessity would lead us to set a bound, $T_0(M)$, on such performance: An ethical system would respect it whereas an unethical one would exceed it. Thus, the function $T_0(M)$ constitutes a threshold function in this case.

Organizations are nowadays expected to behave ethically. In nonquantitative form, the values they must demonstrate include: equal opportunity, financial stability, and good working and holiday conditions for their employees; good service and value to their customers and shareholders; and honesty, integrity, and reliability to other companies. This recent trend adds support to our proposal to treat organizations themselves as agents and thereby to require them to behave ethically, and it provides an example of threshold that, at least currently, is not quantified.

Computer Ethics

What does our view of moral agenthood contribute to the field of computer ethics (CE)? CE seeks to answer questions like "What behavior is acceptable in cyberspace?" and "Who is to be held morally accountable when unacceptable behavior occurs?" It is cyberspace's novelty that makes those questions, so well understood in standard ethics, of greatly innovative interest; and it is its growing ubiquity that makes them so pressing.

The first question requires, in particular, an answer to "What in cyberspace has moral worth?" I have addressed the latter in Floridi (2003) and shall not return to the topic here. The second question invites us to consider the consequences of the answer provided in this article: Any agent that causes good or evil is morally accountable for it.

Recall that moral accountability is a necessary but insufficient condition for moral responsibility. An agent is morally accountable for x if the agent is the source of x and x is morally qualifiable (see definition O earlier in the chapter). To be also morally responsible for x, the agent needs to show the right intentional states (recall the case of Oedipus). Turning to our question, the traditional view is that only software engineers – human programmers – can be held morally accountable, possibly because only humans can be held to exercise free will. Of course, this view is often perfectly appropriate. A more radical and extensive view is supported by the range of difficulties that in practice confronts the traditional view: Software is largely constructed by teams; management decisions may be at least as important as programming decisions; requirements and specification documents play a large part in the resulting code; although the accuracy of code is dependent on those responsible for testing it, much software relies on "off the shelf" components whose provenance and validity may be uncertain; moreover, working software is the result of maintenance over its lifetime and so not just of its originators; finally, artificial agents are becoming increasingly autonomous. Many of these points are nicely made by Epstein (1997) and more recently by Wallach and Allen (2010). Such complications may lead to an organization (perhaps itself an agent) being held accountable. Consider that automated tools are regularly employed in the development of much software; that the efficacy of software may depend on extrafunctional features like interface, protocols, and even data traffic; that software programs running on a system can interact in unforeseeable ways; that software may now be downloaded at the click of an icon in such a way that the user has no access to the code and its provenance with the resulting execution of anonymous software; that software may be probabilistic (Motwani and Raghavan 1995), adaptive (Alpaydin 2010), or may be itself the result of a program (in the simplest case a compiler, but also genetic code [Mitchell 1998]). All these matters pose insurmountable difficulties for the traditional and now rather outdated view that one or more human individuals can always be found accountable for certain kinds of software and even hardware. Fortunately, the view of this paper offers a solution – artificial agents are morally accountable as sources of good and evil – at the "cost" of expanding the definition of morally charged agent.

Codes of Ethics

Human morally charged software engineers are bound by codes of ethics and undergo censorship for ethical and, of course, legal violations. Does the approach defended in this paper make sense when the procedure it recommends is applied to morally accountable AAs? Before regarding the question ill-conceived, consider that the Federation Internationale des Echecs (FIDE) rates all chess players according to the same Elo System regardless of their human or artificial nature. Should we be able to do something similar?

The ACM Code of Ethics and Professional Conduct adopted by ACM Council on the October16, 1992 (http://www.acm.org/about/code-of-ethics) contains twenty-four imperatives, sixteen of which provide guidelines for ethical behavior (eight general and eight more specific; see Figure 12.3), with six further organizational leadership imperatives and two (meta) points concerning compliance with the code.

Of the first eight, all make sense for artificial agents. Indeed, they might be expected to form part of the specification of any morally charged agent. Similarly for the second eight, with the exception of the penultimate point: "improve public understanding." It is less clear how that might reasonably be expected of an arbitrary AA, but then it is also not clear that it is reasonable to expect it of a human software engineer. Note that wizards and similar programs with anthropomorphic interfaces – currently so popular – appear to make public use easier; and such a requirement could be imposed on any AA, but that is scarcely the same as improving understanding.

The final two points concerning compliance with the code (agreement to uphold and promote the code; agreement that violation of the code is inconsistent

1	General moral imperatives
1.1	Contribute to society and human well-being
1.2	Avoid harm to others
1.3	Be honest and trustworthy
1.4	Be fair and take action not to discriminate
1.5	Honor property rights including copyrights and patents
1.6	Give proper credit for intellectual property
1.7	Respect the privacy of others
1.8	Honor confidentiality
2	More specific professional responsibilities
2.1	Strive to achieve the highest quality, effectiveness and dignity in both the process and products of professional work
2.2	Acquire and maintain professional competence
2.3	Know and respect existing laws pertaining to professional work
2.4	Accept and provide appropriate professional review
2.5	Give comprehensive and thorough evaluations of computer systems and their impacts, including analysis of possible risks
2.6	Honor contracts, agreements and assigned responsibilities
2.7	Improve public understanding of computing and its consequences
2.8	Access computing and communication resources only when authorised to do so

Figure 12.3. The principles guiding ethical behavior in the ACM Code of Ethics.

with membership) make sense, though promotion does not appear to have been considered for current AAs any more than has the improvement of public understanding. The latter point presupposes some list of member agents from which agents found to be unethical would be struck.[5] This brings us to the censuring of AAs.

Censorship

Human moral agents who break accepted conventions are censured in various ways, including: (i) mild social censure with the aim of changing and monitoring behavior; (ii) isolation, with similar aims; (iii) capital punishment. What would be the consequences of our approach for artificial moral agents?

By seeking to preserve consistency between human and artificial moral agents, one is led to contemplate the following analogous steps for the censure of immoral artificial agents: (i) monitoring and modification (i.e., "maintenance"); (ii) removal to a disconnected component of cyberspace; (iii) annihilation from cyberspace (deletion without backup). The suggestion to deal directly with an agent, rather than seeking its "creator" (a concept which I have claimed need be neither appropriate nor even well defined) has led to a nonstandard but perfectly workable conclusion. Indeed, it turns out that such a categorization is not very far

---

[5] It is interesting to speculate on the mechanism by which that list is maintained. Perhaps by a human agent; perhaps by an AA composed of several people (a committee); or perhaps by a software agent.

from that used by the standard antivirus software. Though not adaptable at the obvious LoA, such programs are almost agentlike. They run autonomously, and when they detect an infected file they usually offer several levels of censure, such as notification, repair, quarantine, and deletion with or without backup.

For humans, social organizations have had, over the centuries, to be formed for the enforcement of censorship (police, law courts, prisons, etc.). It may be that analogous organizations could sensibly be formed for AAs, and it is unfortunate that this might sound like science fiction. Such social organizations became necessary with the increasing level of complexity of human interactions and the growing lack of "immediacy." Perhaps that is the situation in which we are now beginning to find ourselves with the Web; and perhaps it is time to consider agencies for the policing of AAs.

Conclusion

This paper may be read as an investigation into the extent to which ethics is exclusively a human business. In most societies, somewhere between sixteen and twenty-one years after birth a human being is deemed to be an autonomous legal entity – an adult – responsible for his or her actions. Yet an hour after birth, that is only a potentiality. Indeed, the law and society commonly treat children quite differently from adults on the grounds that their guardians, typically parents, are *responsible* for their actions. Animal behavior varies in exhibiting intelligence and social responsibility between the childlike and the adult; on balance, animals are accorded at best the legal status of children and a somewhat diminished ethical status in the case of guide dogs, dolphins, and other species. However, there are exceptions. Some adults are deprived of (some of) their rights (criminals may not vote) on the grounds that they have demonstrated an inability to exercise responsible/ethical action. Some animals are held accountable for their actions and punished or killed if they err.

In this context, we may consider other entities, including some kinds of organizations and artificial systems. I have offered some examples in the previous pages, with the goal of understanding better the conditions under which an agent may be held morally accountable.

A natural and immediate answer could have been: such accountability lies entirely in the human domain. Animals may sometimes appear to exhibit morally responsible behavior, but they lack the thing unique to humans that render humans (alone) morally responsible – end of story. Such an answer is worryingly dogmatic. Surely, more conceptual analysis is needed here: What has happened morally when a child is deemed to enter adulthood, or when an adult is deemed to have lost moral autonomy, or when an animal is deemed to hold it?

I have tried to convince the reader that we should add artificial agents (corporate or digital, for example) to the moral discourse. This has the advantage that all entities that populate the infosphere are analyzed in nonanthropocentric terms; in other words, it has the advantage of offering a way to progress past the aforementioned immediate and dogmatic answer.

We have been able to make progress in the analysis of moral agenthood by using an important technique, the Method of Abstraction, designed to make rigorous the perspective from which the discourse is approached. Because I have considered entities from the world around us whose properties are vital to my analysis and conclusions, it is essential that we be precise about the LoA at which those entities have been considered. We have seen that changing the LoA may well change our observation of their behavior and hence change the conclusions we draw. Change the quality and quantity of information available on a particular system, and you change the reasonable conclusions that should be drawn from its analysis.

In order to address all relevant entities, I have adopted a terminology that applies equally to all potential agents that populate our environments, from humans to robots and from animals to organizations, without prejudicing our conclusions. In order to analyze their behavior in a nonanthropocentric manner, I have used the conceptual framework offered by state-transition systems. Thus, the agents have been characterized abstractly in terms of a state-transition system. I have concentrated largely on artificial agents and the extent to which ethics and accountability apply to them. Whether an entity forms an agent depends necessarily (though not sufficiently) on the LoA at which the entity is considered; there can be no absolute LoA-free form of identification. By abstracting that LoA, an entity may lose its agenthood by no longer satisfying the behavior we associate with agents. However, for most entities there is no LoA at which they can be considered an agent, of course. Otherwise one might be reduced to the absurdity of considering the moral accountability of the magnetic strip that holds a knife to the kitchen wall. Instead, for comparison, our techniques address the far more interesting question (Dennet 1997): "When HAL Kills, Who's to Blame?" The analysis provided in the article enables us to conclude that HAL is accountable – though not responsible – if it meets the conditions defining agenthood.

The reader might recall that earlier in the chapter I deferred the discussion of a final objection to our approach until the conclusion. The time has come to honor that promise.

Our opponent can still raise a final objection: Suppose you are right – does this enlargement of the class of moral agents bring any real advantage? It should be clear why the answer is clearly affirmative. Morality is usually predicated upon responsibility. The use of LoA and thresholds enables one to distinguish between accountability and responsibility and to formalize both, thus further clarifying our ethical understanding. The better grasp of what it means for someone or something to be a moral agent brings with it a number of substantial advantages. We can avoid anthropocentric and anthropomorphic attitudes toward agenthood and rely on an ethical outlook not necessarily based on punishment and reward, but rather on moral agenthood, accountability, and censure. We are less likely to assign responsibility at any cost when forced by the necessity to identify a human moral agent. We can liberate technological development of AAs from being bound by the standard limiting view. We can stop the regress of looking for the *responsible* individual when something evil happens, because we are now ready to acknowledge that sometimes the moral source of evil or good can be different from an individual or group of humans. I have reminded the reader that this was a reasonable view in Greek philosophy. As a result, we should now be able to escape the dichotomy "responsibility + moral agency = prescriptive action" versus "no responsibility therefore no moral agency therefore no prescriptive action." Promoting normative action is perfectly reasonable even when there is no responsibility but only moral accountability and the capacity for moral action.

All this does not mean that the concept of responsibility is redundant. On the contrary, the previous analysis makes clear the need for a better grasp of the concept of responsibility itself, when responsibility refers to the ontological commitments of creators of new AAs and environments. As I have argued elsewhere (Floridi and Sanders 2005, Floridi 2007), information ethics is an ethics addressed not just to "users" of the world, but also to demiurges who are "divinely" responsible for its creation and well-being. It is an ethics of *creative stewardship*.

In the introduction, I warned the reader about the lack of balance between the two classes of agents and patients brought about by deep forms of environmental ethics that are not accompanied by an equally "deep" approach to agenthood. The position defended in this paper supports a better equilibrium between the two classes A and P. It facilitates the discussion of the morality of agents not only in cyberspace, but also in the biosphere – where animals can be considered moral agents without their having to display free will, emotions, or mental states (scc for example the debate between Rosenfeld [1995a], Dixon [1995], Rosenfeld [1995b]) – and in what we have called contexts of "distributed morality," where social and legal agents can now qualify as moral agents. The great advantage is a better grasp of the moral discourse in nonhuman contexts. The only "cost" of a "mind-less morality" approach is the extension of the class of agents and moral agents to include AAs. It is a cost that is increasingly worth paying the more we move toward an advanced information society.

References

Allen, C., Varner, G., and Zinser, J. 2000, "Prolegomena to Any Future Artificial Moral Agent," *Journal of Experimental & Theoretical Artificial Intelligence*, 12, 251–261.

Alpaydin, E. 2010, *Introduction to Machine Learning* 2nd (Cambridge, Mass.; London: MIT Press).

Arnold, A., and Plaice, J. 1994, *Finite Transition Systems: Semantics of Communicating Systems* (Paris, Hemel Hempstead: Masson; Prentice Hall).

Barandiaran, X. E., Paolo, E. D., and Rohde, M. 2009, "Defining Agency: Individuality, Normativity, Asymmetry, and Spatio-Temporality in Action," *Adaptive Behavior – Animals, Animats, Software Agents, Robots, Adaptive Systems*, 17(5), 367–386.

Bedau, M. A. 1996, "The Nature of Life," in *The Philosophy of Life*, edited by M. A. Boden (Oxford: Oxford University Press), 332–357.

Cassirer, E. 1910, *Substanzbegriff Und Funktionsbegriff. Untersuchungen Über Die Grundfragen Der Erkenntniskritik* (Berlin: Bruno Cassirer). trans. by W. M. Swabey and M.C. Swabey in *Substance and Function and Einstein's Theory of Relativity* (Chicago, IL: Open Court, 1923).

Danielson, P. 1992, *Artificial Morality: Virtuous Robots for Virtual Games* (London; New York: Routledge).

Davidsson, P., and Johansson, S. J. (ed.) 2005, Special issue on "On the Metaphysics of Agents," *ACM*, 1299–1300.

Dennet, D. 1997, "When Hal Kills, Who's to Blame?" in *Hal's Legacy: 2001's Computer as Dream and Reality*, edited by D. Stork (Cambridge MA: MIT Press), 351–365.

Dixon, B. A. 1995, "Response: Evil and the Moral Agency of Animals," *Between the Species*, 11(1–2), 38–40.

Epstein, R. G. 1997, *The Case of the Killer Robot: Stories About the Professional, Ethical, and Societal Dimensions of Computing* (New York ; Chichester: Wiley).

Floridi, L. 2003, "On the Intrinsic Value of Information Objects and the Infosphere," *Ethics and Information Technology*, 4(4), 287–304.

Floridi, L. 2006, "Information Technologies and the Tragedy of the Good Will," *Ethics and Information Technology*, 8(4), 253–262.

Floridi, L. 2007, "Global Information Ethics: The Importance of Being Environmentally Earnest," *International Journal of Technology and Human Interaction*, 3(3), 1–11.

Floridi, L. 2008a, "Artificial Intelligence's New Frontier: Artificial Companions and the Fourth Revolution," *Metaphilosophy*, 39(4/5), 651–655.

Floridi, L. 2008b, "The Method of Levels of Abstraction," *Minds and Machines*, 18(3), 303–329.

Floridi, L. 2010a, *Information – a Very Short Introduction* (Oxford: Oxford University Press).

Floridi, L. 2010b, "Levels of Abstraction and the Turing Test," *Kybernetes*, 39(3), 423–440.

Floridi, L. forthcoming, "Network Ethics: Information and Business Ethics in a Networked Society," *Journal of Business Ethics*.

Floridi, L., and Sanders, J. W. 2001, "Artificial Evil and the Foundation of Computer Ethics," *Ethics and Information Technology*, 3(1), 55–66.

Floridi, L., and Sanders, J. W. 2005, "Internet Ethics: The Constructionist Values of Homo Poieticus," in *The Impact of the Internet on Our Moral Lives*, edited by Robert Cavalier (New York: SUNY).

Franklin, S., and Graesser, A. 1997, "Is It an Agent, or Just a Program?: A Taxonomy for Autonomous Agents," *Proceedings of the Workshop on Intelligent Agents III, Agent Theories, Architectures, and Languages*, (Springer-Verlag), 21–35.

Jamieson, D. 2008, *Ethics and the Environment: An Introduction* (Cambridge: Cambridge University Press).

Kerr, P. 1996, *The Grid* (New York: Warner Books).

Michie, D. 1961, "Trial and Error," in *Penguin Science Surveys*, edited by A. Garratt (Harmondsworth: Penguin), 129–145.

Mitchell, M. 1998, *An Introduction to Genetic Algorithms* (Cambridge, Mass.; London: MIT).

Moor, J. H. 2001, "The Status and Future of the Turing Test," *Minds Mach.*, 11(1), 77–93.

Motwani, R., and Raghavan, P. 1995, *Randomized Algorithms* (Cambridge: Cambridge University Press).

Moya, L. J., and Tolk, A. (ed.) 2007, Special issue on "Towards a Taxonomy of Agents and Multi-Agent Systems," *Society for Computer Simulation International*, 11–18.

Rosenfeld, R. 1995a, "Can Animals Be Evil? Kekes' Character-Morality, the Hard Reaction to Evil, and Animals," *Between the Species*, 11(1–2), 33–38.

Rosenfeld, R. 1995b, "Reply," *Between the Species*, 11(1–2), 40–41.

Russell, S. J., and Norvig, P. 2010, *Artificial Intelligence: A Modern Approach* 3rd, International (Boston; London: Pearson).

Turing, A. M. 1950, "Computing Machinery and Intelligence," *Mind*, 59(236), 433–460.

Wallach, W., and Allen, C. 2010, *Moral Machines: Teaching Robots Right from Wrong* (New York; Oxford: Oxford University Press).

13

Legal Rights for Machines
Some Fundamental Concepts

David J. Calverley

T0 SOME, THE QUESTION OF WHETHER LEGAL RIGHTS SHOULD, OR EVEN can, be given to machines is absurd on its face. How, they ask, can pieces of metal, silicon, and plastic have any attributes that would allow society to assign it any rights at all.

Given the rapidity with which researchers in the field of artificial intelligence are moving and, in particular, the efforts to build machines with humanoid features and traits (Ishiguro 2006), I suggest that the possibility of some form of machine consciousness making a claim to a certain class of rights is one that should be discounted only with great caution. However, before accepting any arguments in favor of extending rights to machines we first need to understand the theoretical underpinnings of the thing we call law so that we can begin to evaluate any such attempts or claims from a principled stance. Without this basic set of parameters from which we can work, the debate becomes meaningless.

It is my purpose here to set forth some of the fundamental concepts concerning the law and how it has developed in a way that could inform the development of the machines themselves as well as the way they are accepted or rejected by society (Minato 2004). In a very real sense, as we will see, the framing of the debate could provide cautionary guidance to developers who may make claims for their inventions that would elicit calls for a determination concerning the legal rights of that entity.

Law is a socially constructed, intensely practical evaluative system of rules and institutions that guides and governs human action, that help us live together. It tells citizens what they may, must, and may not do, and what they are entitled to, and it includes institutions to ensure that law is made and enforced. (Morse 2004)

This definition, on its face, seems to be elegant and concise, but, like an iceberg, it is deceptive. In order to determine whether law has any normative value when it is used to evaluate the idea of treating a nonbiological machine as a legal person, we first need to gain at least a basic understanding of how this thing we call "law" is formulated at a conceptual level. By understanding what we mean when we speak of law – where it derives its ability to regulate human conduct – we can perhaps begin to formulate criteria by which some aspects of law could also be used to test the idea that something we have created in a machine substrate is capable of being designated as a legal person. Once we have set the framework, we can begin to look at specific components of law and the interaction of law to determine if they have any applicability in guiding designers of nonbiological machines.[1] If our inquiry can be made in a way that is meaningful to both those who will be faced with deciding how to regulate such an entity and to the designers who are actually making the effort to create such a nonbiological machine, then it is worth the effort. As stated by Solum (1992):

First, putting the AI debate in a concrete legal context acts as a pragmatic Occam's razor. By examining positions taken in cognitive science or the philosophy of artificial intelligence as legal arguments, we are forced to see them anew in a relentlessly pragmatic context....

Second, and more controversially, we can view the legal system as a repository of knowledge – a formal accumulation of practical judgments.... In addition, the law embodies practical knowledge in a form that is subject to public examination and discussion.

As with most endeavors, it is often the question one asks at the outset that determines the nature of the debate and directs the form of the ultimate outcome. If we want to design a nonbiological machine that we will at some later point in time claim is the equivalent of a human, we should determine as early as possible in the process whether the result we seek will stand up to scrutiny. One way to do this is to ask if it will be capable of becoming a "legal person." Only in this way will the results be amenable to being evaluated by criteria that are consistent with the way humans govern themselves and view each other.

Although it is acknowledged that there are many variations and nuances in legal theory, it is generally recognized that there have been two major historic themes that have, for the last few hundred years, dominated the debate about what law means.

One of the most familiar ideas to Western societies is the concept of natural law, which was originally based on the Judeo-Christian belief that God is the source of all law. It was this belief that underpinned most of Western civilization until the Enlightenment period. Prominent thinkers such as Augustine and Thomas Aquinas are two examples of this predominant orthodoxy. In essence, natural law proponents argue that law is inextricably linked with morality, and therefore, in Augustine's famous aphorism, "an unjust law is no law at all."

With the Enlightenment came a decreasing emphasis on God as the giver of all law and an increasing development of the idea that humans possessed innate

---

[1] Briefly, a word about terminology; some use the term nonbiological machine or artificial intelligence (AI), others artilect, and still others artifact. For ease of use and consistency, I will use the term nonbiological machine, except where quoting directly, but any of the others would suffice.

qualities that gave rise to law. As members of society, humans were capable of effecting their own decisions and consequently were entitled to govern their own actions based on their intrinsic worth as individuals. Whereas this concept was originally suggested by Hugo Grotius (1625) and later refined by John Locke (1739), it arguably reached its most notable actual expression in the system of laws ultimately idealized by the drafters of the United States Declaration of Independence. Drawing on a similar argument and applying it to moral philosophy, Immanuel Kant hypothesized that humans were, by the exercise of their reason, capable of determining rules that were universally acceptable and applicable, and thus were able to use those rules to govern their conduct (Kant 1785).

More recently, John Finnis, building on ideas reminiscent of Kant, has outlined what he calls basic goods (which exist without any hierarchical ranking), and then has posited the existence of principles that are used to guide a person's choice when there are alternative goods to choose from. These principles, which he describes as the "basic requirements of practical reasonableness," are the connection between the basic good and ultimate moral choice. Derived from this view, law is the way in which groups of people are coordinated in order to effect a social good or to ease the way to reach other basic goods. Because law has the effect of promoting moral obligations, it necessarily has binding effect (Finnis 1980). Similarly, Lon Fuller has argued that law is a normative system for guiding people and must therefore have an internal moral value in order to give it its validity. Only in this way can law fulfill its function, which is to subject human conduct to the governance of rules (Fuller 1958; 1969). Another important modern theorist in this natural law tradition is Ronald Dworkin. Dworkin advocates a thesis that states in essence that legal principles are moral propositions grounded on past official acts such as statutes or precedent. As such, normative moral evaluation is required in order to understand law and how it should be applied (Dworkin 1978).

In contrast to the basic premise of natural law – that law and morality are inextricably intertwined – stands the doctrine of legal positivism. Initially articulated by Jeremy Bentham, and derived from his view that the belief in natural rights was "nonsense on stilts" (Bentham 1824), criticism of natural law centered around the proposition that law is the command of the sovereign, whereas morality tells us what law ought to be. This idea of law as a system of rules "laid down for the guidance of an intelligent being by an intelligent being having power over him" was given full voice by Bentham's protégé, John Austin. In its simplest form this idea is premised on the belief that law is a creature of society and is a normative system based on the will of those ruled as expressed by the sovereign. Law derives its normative power from the citizen's ability to know and predict what the sovereign will do if the law is transgressed (Austin 1832).

Austin's position, that law was based on the coercive power of the sovereign, has been severely criticized by the modern positivist H. L. A. Hart, who has argued that law requires more than mere sanctions; there must be reasons and justifications why those sanctions properly should apply. Whereas neither of these positions rule out the overlap between law and morality, both do argue that what constitutes law in a society is based on social convention. Hart goes further and states that this convention forms a rule of recognition, under which the law is accepted by the interpreters of the law, that is, judges (Hart 1958; 1961). In contrast, Joseph Raz argues that law is normative and derives its authority from the fact that it is a social institution that can claim legitimate authority to set normative standards. Law serves an essential function as a mediator between its subjects and points them to the right reason in any given circumstance, without the need to refer to external normative systems such as morality (Raz 1975).

It is conceded that the foregoing exposition is vastly over simplified and does not do justice to the nuances of any of the described theories. Nonetheless, it can serve as a basis upon which to premise the contention that, despite the seeming difference between the two views of law, there is an important point of commonality. Returning to the definition with which we started this paper, we can see that it is inherently legal positivist in its outlook. However, its central idea, that law is a normative system by which humans govern their conduct, seems to be a characteristic shared by both major theories of law and therefore is one upon which we can profitably ground some further speculation. To the extent that law requires humans to act in conformity to either a moral norm established in accordance with a theological or natural theory, or to the extent it is a normative system based on one's recognition of and compliance with a socially created standard of conduct, it is premised on the belief that humans are capable of, and regularly engage in, independent reflective thought, and thus are able to make determinations that direct their actions based on those thoughts. Described in a slightly different way, law is based on the premise that humans are capable of making determinations about their actions based on reason:

Human action is distinguished from all other phenomena because only action is explained by reasons resulting from desires and beliefs, rather than simply by mechanistic causes. Only human beings are fully intentional creatures. To ask why a person acted a certain way is to ask for reasons for action, not the reductionist biophysical, psychological, or sociological explanations. To comprehend fully why an agent has particular desires, beliefs, and reasons requires biophysical, psychological, and sociological explanations, but ultimately, human action is not simply the mechanistic outcome of mechanistic variables. Only persons can deliberate about what action to perform and can determine their conduct by practical reason. (Morse 2004)

Similarly, Gazzaniga and Steven (2004) express the idea as follows:

At the crux of the problem is the legal system's view of human behavior. It assumes (X) is a "practical reasoner," a person who acts because he has freely chosen to act. This simple but powerful assumption drives the entire legal system.

Although this perspective is not universally accepted by philosophers of law, it can be used as the basis from which to argue that, despite obvious difficulties, it is not entirely illogical to assert that a nonbiological machine can be treated as a legally responsible entity. Interestingly enough, it is possible that although the criteria we establish may affect the basic machine design, it is equally likely that if the design is ultimately successful, we may have to revisit some of the basic premises of law.

In presenting arguments that would tend to support the idea that a machine can in some way be developed to a point where it, or a guardian acting on its behalf, could make a plausible claim that it is entitled to legal recognition, other factors are implicated. Here I am specifically thinking about the issues that come to mind when we consider the related concepts of human, person, and property.

Legal theory has historically drawn a distinction between property and person, but with the implicit understanding that person equates to human. Locke (1689b) did attempt to make a distinction between the two in his "Essay Concerning Human Understanding." There, he was concerned with drawing a contrast between the animal side of man's nature and what we customarily call man. "Person" in his sense belongs "only to intelligent Agents capable of a Law, and Happiness and Misery" (Locke 1689b: chapter XXVII, section 26). Until recently, there had not been a need to make more precise distinctions. Since the expression of different opinions by Strawson (1959) and Ayers (1963), the concept of human versus person has become much more a topic for philosophical speculation:

Only when a legal system has abandoned clan or family responsibility, and individuals are seen as primary agents, does the class of persons coincide with the class of biological individual human beings. In principle, and often in law, they need not.... The issue of whether the class of persons exactly coincides with the class of biologically defined human being – whether corporations, Venusians, Mongolian idiots, and fetuses are persons – is in part a conceptual question. It is a question about whether the relevant base for the classification of persons requires attention to whether things look like "us," whether they are made out of stuff like "ours," or whether it is enough that they function as we take "ourselves" to function. If Venusians and robots come to be thought of as persons, at least part of the argument that will establish them will be that they function as we do: that while they are not the same organisms that we are, they are in the appropriate sense the same type of organism or entity. (Rorty 1976: 322)

The distinction between human and person is controversial (MacDorman and Cowley 2006). For example, in the sanctity of life debate currently being played out in the United States, serious arguments are addressed to the question whether a human fetus becomes a person at conception or at a later point of viability (Ramey 2005b). Similar questions arise at the end of life: Do humans in a persistent vegetative state lose the status of legal person while still remaining human at the genetic level? Likewise, children and individuals with serious mental impairments are treated as persons for some purposes but not for others, although they are human. Personhood can be defined in a way that gives moral and legal weight to attributes that we ultimately define as relevant without the requirement that the entity either be given the full legal rights of humans or burdened with the duties those rights entail.

Others have stated, "[i]n books of law, as in other books, and in common speech, 'person' is often used as meaning a human being, but the technical legal meaning of 'person' is a subject of legal rights and duties" (Gray 1909). However, by qualifying this definition with the caution that it only makes sense to give this appellation to beings that exhibit "intelligence" and "will," Gray equated person with human. In each instance cited, the authors are struggling to establish that law is particularly interested in defining who, or what, will be the objects to which it applies. In order to move our inquiry forward, a brief history of the concept of "person" in juxtaposition to "human" will be helpful.

The word "person" is derived from the Latin word "persona," which originally referred to a mask worn by a human who was conveying a particular role in a play. In time, it took on the sense of describing a guise one wore to express certain characteristics. Only later did the term become coextensive with the actual human who was taking on the persona and thus become interchangeable with the term human. Even as this transformation in linguistic meaning was taking place, the concepts of person and human remained distinct. To Greeks such as Aristotle, slaves and women did not posses souls. Consequently, although they were nominally human, they were not capable of fully participating in the civic life of the city and therefore were not recognized as persons before the law. Because they were not legal persons, they had none of the rights possessed by full members of Athenian society. Similarly, Roman law, drawing heavily from Greek antecedents, made clear distinctions, drawing lines between property and persons but allowing for gradations in status, and in the case of slaves, permitting movement between categories.

As society developed in the Middle Ages in Western Europe, more particularly in England, the concepts of a legal person and property became less distinct. Over time, a person was defined in terms of the status he held in relationship to property, particularly real property. It was not until much later, with the rise of liberal individualism, that a shift from status-based concepts to contract-based concepts of individual rights forced legal institutions to begin to clarify the distinctions and tensions between the definition of human, person, and property (Davis 2001).

The most well-known social institution in which the person-property tension came to the attention of the courts was slavery. As a preliminary note: Although slavery as practiced in the seventeenth, eighteenth, and nineteenth centuries, particularly in the Americas, had at least superficially a strong racial component, most sources indicate race played only a small part in the legal discussions of the institution. The theoretical underpinnings were nonracial in origin and related more to status as property than to skin color (Tushnet 1975). This was also true in other countries at the time, such as Russia with its system of serfdom.

The real struggle the courts were having was with the justification of defining a human as property, that is, as a nonperson for purposes of the law. In a famous English case (*Somerset's Case*, 98 Eng. Rep. 499, 1772), a slave was brought from the Americas to England by his owner. When he arrived, he argued that he should be set free. The master's response was that he should not be set free because he was property. The court stated that there was no issue with the black man's humanity; he was clearly human. As a slave, he had been deprived of his right to freedom and was treated as property. However, because there was no provision in English positive law that permitted a human being to be deprived of his freedom and treated as property, he could not be deemed a slave. Note, however, the careful way in which the ruling was limited to the fact that it was positive law that did not allow the enslavement of this human. The clear implication is that if positive law had been different, the result might also have been different. The court was drawing a clear distinction between Somerset's status as a human and his status as a legal person. Similar theoretical justification can be seen in early cases decided in the United States until the passage in most Southern states of the Slave Acts. However, in perhaps one of the most egregious and incendiary rulings by the U. S. Supreme Court, the *Dred Scott* case (60 US 19 How. 393, 1857), Chief Justice Taney reached a conclusion opposite to that of Somerset's case, ruling that the Constitution did not extend to protect a black man, because at the time of its passage, the meaning of "citizen of . . . a state" (i.e., a legal person) did not include slaves. From this we can conclude that it is the exercise of positive law, expressed in making, defining, and formalizing the institution of slavery through the manipulation of the definition of the legal concept of person, that is the defining characteristic of these cases. It is not the slave's status as human being.

To the extent that a nonbiological machine is "only property," there is little reason to consider ascribing it full legal rights. None of us would suggest that a computer is a slave or that even a dog, which has a claim to a certain level of moral consideration, is anything more than its owner's property. A dog can be sold, be put to work in one's interest as long as it is not abused, and have its freedom restricted in myriad ways. So too could we constrain our theoretical machine as long as it did not exhibit something more. It is only if we begin to ascribe human-like characteristics and motives to the machine that we implicate more serious issues. As suggested by Solum (1992), judges applying the law may be reasonably inclined to accept an argument that the functional similarity between a nonbiological machine and a human is enough to allow the extension of rights to the android. Once we do, however, we open up the entire scope of moral and legal issues, and we must be prepared to address potential criticism in a forthright manner.

The same idea that there is an underlying conflict between the view of "human" and "person" as the same thing has been expressed in a somewhat different fashion as follows:

The apparent conflict between the definitions of "person" and "human being" as legal concepts seems to be an important one that needs to be addressed in relation to the liberal democratic preoccupation with the broad concept of rights and liberties.

. . .

The idea of rights and liberties is rooted, within a liberal democratic society, in the concept of property. This idea finds its best overall expression through the writings of Locke. The individual's relationship to society and the state becomes the focus of these rights and liberties which are based upon the broad concept of property, so that participation within the political society as one of its members becomes crucial for the preservation and self-fulfillment of the individual. Rights and liberties are an instrument to be employed in support of this role of the individual in order to guarantee the individual's ability to participate completely and meaningfully as a member of society and to achieve the full potential as a citizen. It is only through being participating members of the political community that individuals can influence the state, determine its composition and nature, and protect themselves against its encroachments. (McHugh 1992)

To define a category of rights holder that is distinguishable from human but nonetheless comprehensible, we can resort to a form of "fiction." This proposition is subject to much debate, but at least one use of the fiction is in the comparison between a being of the species *Homo sapiens* and the legal concept of the corporation as a person (Note 1987).

It was from the view of a person as property holder that the so called Fiction Theory of corporate personality initially derived. Because synthetic entities such as corporations were authorized by their state-granted charters of organization to own property, they were deemed to be "persons." In the earliest cases the idea that the corporation was an artificial entity was based solely on this derivative claim. It was only later, following the U. S. Civil War, when courts were forced to respond to arguments based on the antislavery amendments, that the concept of a corporation as the direct equivalent of a person began to be articulated. The answer was that the use of the term "person" in the language of the Fourteenth Amendment to the Bill of Rights[2] was broad enough to apply to artificial groupings of participants, not just humans. This idea, based on the view that corporations are nothing more than a grouping of individual persons who have come together for a particular purpose, has come to be known as the Aggregate Theory. It is beyond the scope of this paper to explore this dichotomy between the views in any detail, because if we are correct that a nonbiological machine of human making can exhibit relevant characteristics for our purposes, such a nonbiological machine will not be an aggregation of humans. True, it may be the aggregation of human ideas and handiwork that led to its creation, but the issues raised by that assertion are better handled by other concepts such as intellectual property rights.

Can we look at this "fictional" entity and identify any of the key attributes that will determine how it is treated before the law? Peter A. French is perhaps the

---

[2]   Section 1. All persons born or naturalized in the United States, and subject to the jurisdiction thereof, are citizens of the United States and of the state wherein they reside. No state shall make or enforce any law which shall abridge the privileges or immunities of citizens of the United States; nor shall any state deprive any person of life, liberty, or property, without due process of law; nor deny to any person within its jurisdiction the equal protection of the laws.

person most noted for advocating the idea that a corporation is something more than a mere legal fiction or an aggregation of human employees or shareholders. His view is that the corporation has natural rights and should be treated as a moral person, in part because it can act intentionally. In this context, French uses the term "intentionally" in virtually the same sense that Morse does in the earlier quotations. Thus, it offers some meaningful basis for comparison between the law's subjects. French's premise is that "to be a moral person is to be both an intentional actor and an entity with the capacity or ability to intentionally modify its behavioral patterns, habits, or modus operandi after it has learned that untoward or valued events (defined in legal, moral, or even prudential terms) were caused by its past unintentional behavior" (French, 1984).

Needless to say, French is not without his critics. Donaldson (1982) argues from an Aggregate Theory stance that the corporation cannot have a single unified intention to act. He then goes on to argue that simply having intention is not enough to make the claim that the actor has moral agency. Werhane (1985) carries this point further and, using the example of a computer system, argues that the appearance of intentionality does not necessarily mean that it acts out of real desires or beliefs. In other words, intentionality does not imply that it is also free and autonomous. Although I recognize Werhane's point, I disagree that such a system is impossible to construct. One example of a theory which could lead to just such a functional artificial agent is set forth in Pollock (2006). Further, drawing on Daniel Dennett's ideas concerning intentional systems, one can certainly argue that Werhane's position requires one to accept the premise that only phenomenological intentionality counts for moral and perhaps legal purposes, but that does not appear to be supported by intuition. Functional intentionality is probably enough in a folk psychology sense to convince people that a nonbiological system is acting intentionally. Solum (1992) suggests as much in the following language:

How would the legal system deal with the objection that the AI does not really have "intentionality" despite its seemingly intentional behaviors? The case against real intentionality could begin with the observation that behaving as if you know something is not the same as really knowing it.... My suspicion is that judges and juries would be rather impatient with the metaphysical argument that AIs cannot really have intentionality.

If the complexity of AI behavior did not exceed that of a thermostat, then it is not likely that anyone would be convinced that AIs really possess intentional states – that they really believe things or know things. Yet if interaction with AIs exhibiting symptoms of complex intentionality (of a human quality) were an everyday occurrence, the presumption might be overcome.

If asked whether humans are different from animals, most people would say yes. When pressed to describe what that implies in the context of legal rules, many people would respond that it means we have free will, that our actions are not predetermined. Note, however, that Morse (2004) argues that this is a mistake in that free will is not necessarily a criterion for responsibility in a legal sense.

From the perspective of moral philosophy the debate can be couched in slightly different terms. In the view of the "incompatibilist," in order for people to be held responsible for their acts they must have freedom to choose among various alternatives. Without alternatives there can be no free will (van Inwagen 1983; Kane 1996). The incompatibilist position has been strongly attacked by Harry Frankfurt, who called their argument the "principle of alternate possibilities" (Frankfurt 1988a). Frankfurt has argued that it is possible to reconcile free will with determinism in his view of "personhood." His conclusion is that people, as opposed to animals or other lower-order beings, possess first- and second-order desires as well as first- and second-order volitions. If a person has a second-order desire it means that she cares about her first-order desires. To the extent that this second-order desire is motivated by a second-order volition, that is, wanting the second-order desire to be effective in controlling the first-order desire, the person is viewed as being autonomous so long as she is satisfied with the desire. The conclusion is that in such a case the person is autonomous (Frankfurt 1988b).

It should be noted that in this context Frankfurt is using the term "person" as the equivalent of "human." Others would argue that "person" is a broader term and more inclusive, drawing a clear distinction between person and human (Strawson 1959; Ayer 1963). As is clear from the previous sections, my preference is to use the term "human" to apply to *Homo sapiens* and the term "person" to conscious beings irrespective of species boundaries.

It is helpful in this regard to compare Frankfurt's position with Kant's belief that autonomy is viewed as obedience to the rational dictates of the moral law (Herman 2002). Kant's idea that autonomy is rational also differs from that of David Hume, who argued that emotions are the driving force behind moral judgments. Hume seems to be an antecedent of Frankfurt's concept of "satisfaction" if the latter's essay on love is understood correctly (Frankfurt 1999). Transposing these contrasting positions into the language used earlier to describe law, I suggest that it is possible to equate this sense of autonomy with the concept of responsibility. As discussed earlier with regard to intentionality, humans are believed to be freely capable of desiring to choose and actually choosing a course of action. Humans are believed to be capable of changing desires through the sheer force of mental effort applied in a self-reflexive way. Humans are therefore, as practical reasoners, capable of being subject to law so long as they act in an autonomous way.

"Autonomy" has, however, a number of potential other meanings in the context of machine intelligence. Consequently, we need to look at this more closely if we are to determine whether the foregoing discussion has any validity in the present context.

Hexmoor, Castelfranchi, and Falcone (2003) draw a number of distinctions between the different types of interactions relevant to systems design and artificial intelligence. First, there is human-to-agent interaction, where the agent is expected to acquire and conform to the preferences set by the human operator.

In their words, "[a] device is autonomous when the device faithfully carries the human's preferences and performs actions accordingly." Another sense is where the reference point is another agent rather than a human. In this sense the agents are considered relative to each other and essentially negotiate to accomplish tasks. In this view, "[t]he agent is supposed to use its knowledge, its intelligence, and its ability, and to exert a degree of discretion." In a third sense there is the idea mentioned before that the agent can be viewed as manipulating "its own internal capabilities, its own liberties and what it allows itself to experience about the outside world as a whole." Margaret Boden, in a similar vein, writes about the capacity of the agent to be original, unguided by outside sources (Boden 1996). It is in this third sense where I suggest that the term autonomy comes closest to what the law views as crucial to its sense of responsibility.

If we adopt the third definition of autonomy and argue that if it is achieved in a machine, as it would be in the previous example, then at least from a functional viewpoint we could assert the machine is the equivalent of a human in terms of its being held responsible. As noted earlier, one would expect to be met with the objection that such a conclusion simply begs the question about whether the nonbiological machine is phenomenally conscious (Werhane 1985; Adams 2004). Yet once again, in the limited area we are examining we can put this argument to one side. For law, and for the idea of a legal person we are examining, it simply may not matter. Functional results are probably enough.

If one can conceive of a second-order volition and can as a result affect a first-order action constrained only by the idea that one is satisfied by that result, does that not imply a functionally simimorphy with characteristics of human action? (Angel 1989). Going the next step, we can then argue that law acts at the level of this second-order volition. It sets parameters that, as society has determined, outline the limits of an accepted range of responses within the circumscribed field that it addresses, say, contract law, tort law, or criminal law. This would imply that law acts in an exclusionary fashion in that it inhibits particular first-order desires and takes them out of the range of acceptable alternatives for action (Green 1988; Raz 1975). Note that this does not mean to imply that these are the only possible responses or even the best responses the actor could make. To the extent that the subject to which the law is directed (the citizen within the control of the sovereign in Austin's terms) has access to law as normative information, she can order her desires or actions in accordance with law or not. This would mean, to borrow the terminology of Antonio Damasio (1994), that the law sets the somatic markers by which future actions will be governed. By acting in a manner where its intentionality is informed by such constraints, and doing so in an autonomous fashion as just described, the nonbiological machine appears to be acting in a way that is functionally equivalent to the way we expect humans to act. I suggest that this does not require that the nonbiological machine have a universal, comprehensive understanding of the law any more than the average human does. Heuristics, or perhaps concepts of bounded rationality, could provide the basis for making decisions that are "good enough" (Clark 2003). Similar arguments have been advanced on the role of emotion in the development of a machine consciousness (Sloman and Croucher 1981; Arbib and Fellous 2004; Wallach 2004). Perhaps, in light of work being done in how humans make decisions (Kahneman, Slovic, and Tversky 1982; Lakoff 1987; Pollock 2006), more pointed analysis is required to fully articulate the claim concerning law's normative role within the context of autonomous behavior. One further caution: Even though I suggest that accepting law as a guide to a second-order volition does not diminish the actor's autonomy, this proposition can be challenged by some theories such as anarchism (Wolff 1970/1998).

It is beyond the scope of this short paper to delve into the what are necessary and sufficient conditions to definitively establish that something is a legal person (Solum 1992; Rivaud 1992). It is my more limited contention that, if we accept the notion that the definition of person is a concept about which we do not as yet have defining limits, the concepts of intentionality and autonomy give us a starting point from which to begin our analysis. Although it may not be easy to determine whether the aspects we have discussed are necessary and sufficient to meet the minimum requirement of legal personhood, it is possible to get a meaningful sense of what would be acceptable to people if they were faced with the question. Certainly under some theories of law, such as positivism, it is logically possible to argue that, to the extent law defines what a legal person is, law could simply define a legal person to be anything law chooses it to be, much like Humpty Dumpty in Alice in Wonderland, "nothing more and nothing less." However, this would be a meaningless exercise and intellectually barren. On the other hand, if law, rather than being viewed as a closed system that makes up its own rules and simply applies them to its objects, was in fact viewed as a limited domain that, although it did not necessarily rely on morality for its validity, drew on factors outside the law to define its concepts, we could articulate the concept of a person by using factors identified earlier, which are related more to function without the need for phenomenal consciousness. So long as the nonbiological machine had a level of mental activity in areas deemed relevant to law, such as autonomy or intentionality, then it could be a legal person with independent existence separate and apart from its origins as property. Given the wide range of entities and the variety of types of conduct that the law has brought within its scope, we need to identify those aspects of what Leonard Angel called "functional simimorphy" (Angel 1989). Certainly there is just this type of simimorphy when we look at corporations, and I suggest that nothing we have seen so far requires us to categorically rule out nonbiological entities from the equation.

Author's Note

This chapter is derived from work previously published in the following articles and is a compilation of ideas developed more fully in those sources.

Calverley, D. J. (2005). Towards a method for determining the legal status of a conscious machine. In R. Chrisley, R. W. Clowes & S. Torrance (Eds.), Proceedings of the AISB 2005 Symposium on Next Generation approaches to Machine Consciousness: Imagination, Development, Intersubjectivity and Embodiment. University of Hertfordshire.

Calverley, D. J. (2005). Additional thoughts concerning the legal status of a non-biological machine. In Symposium on Machine Ethics, AAAI Fall Symposium 2005.

Calverley, D. J. (2008). Imagining a non-biological machine as a legal person. *AI & Society*, Vol. 22 No. 4. April 2008.

Calverley, D. J. (2006). Android science and animal rights: Does an analogy exist? *Connection Science*, Vol. 18, No. 4, December 2006.

References

Adams, W. (2004). Machine consciousness: Plausible idea or semantic distortion? *Journal of Consciousness Studies*, 11(9).

Angel, L. (1989). *How to Build a Conscious Machine*. Boulder: Westview Press.

Arbib, M., & Fellous, J. (2004). Emotions: From brain to robot. *Trends in the Cognitive Sciences*, 8(12), 554.

Austin, J. (1955). *The Province of Jurisprudence Determined*. London: Weidenfeld and Nicholson. (Original work published 1832.)

Ayer, A. J. (1963). *The Concept of a Person*. New York: St. Martin's Press.

Bentham, J. (1962). Anarchical fallacies. In J. Bowring (Ed.), *The Works of Jeremy Bentham* (Vol. 2). New York: Russell and Russell. (Original work published 1824.)

Boden, M. (1996). Autonomy and artificiality. In M. Boden (Ed.), *The Philosophy of Artificial Life*. Oxford: Oxford University Press.

Clark, A. (2003). Artificial intelligence and the many faces of reason. In S. Stich & T. Warfield (Eds.), *The Blackwell Guide to Philosophy of Mind*. Malden MA: Blackwell Publishing.

Damasio, A. (1994). *Descartes' Error*. New York: Harper Collins.

Davis, M. and Naffeine, N. (2001) *Are Persons Property?* Burlington, VT: Ashgate Publishing, 2001.

Donaldson, T. (1982). *Corporations and Morality*. Englewood Cliffs: Prentice Hall, Inc.

Dworkin, R. (1978). *Taking Rights Seriously* (revised). London: Duckworth.

Finnis, J. (1980). *Natural Law and Natural Rights*. Oxford: Clarendon Press.

Frankfurt, H. (1988a). Alternate possibilities and moral responsibility. In H. Frankfurt, *The Importance of What We Care About*. Cambridge: Cambridge University Press. (Original work published 1969.)

Frankfurt, H. (1988b). Freedom of the will and the concept of a person. In H. Frankfurt, *The Importance of What We Care About*. Cambridge: Cambridge University Press. (Original work published 1971.)

Frankfurt, H. (1999). Autonomy, necessity and love. In H. Frankfurt, *Necessity, Volition and Love*. Cambridge: Cambridge University Press. (Original work published 1994.)

French, P. (1984). *Collective and Corporate Responsibility*. New York: Columbia University Press.

Fuller, L. (1958). Positivism and fidelity to law – a response to Professor Hart. 71 *Harvard Law Rev* 630.

Fuller, L. (1969). *The Morality of Law* (2nd. edn.) New Have: Yale University Press.

Gazzaniga, M., & Steven, M. (2004). Free will in the twenty-first century: A discussion of neuroscience and the law. *Neuroscience and the Law*. New York: Dana Press.

Green, L. (1988). *The Authority of the State*. Oxford: Clarendon Press.

Gray, J. C. (1921). In R. Gray (Ed.), *The Nature and Sources of the Law*. New York: Macmillan. (Original work published 1909.)

Grotius, H. (1625). *De Jure Belli ac Pacis Libri Tres* (F. Kelson, Trans.). Oxford: Clarendon Press.

Hart, H. L. A. (1958). Positivism and the separation of law and morals. 71 *Harvard Law Rev* 593.

Hart, H. L. A. (1961). *The Concept of Law*. Oxford: Clarendon Press.

Herman, B. (2002). Bootstrapping. In S. Buss & L. Overton (Eds.), *Contours of Agency*. Cambridge, Mass: The MIT Press.

Hexmoor, H., Castelfranchi, C., & Falcone, R. (2003). A prospectus on agent autonomy. In H. Hexmoor (Ed.), *Agent Autonomy*. Boston: Kluwer Academic Publishers.

Hume, D. (1739). *A Treatise of Human Nature* (ed. P. Nidditch 1978) Oxford: Clarendon Press.

Ishiguro, H. (2006). Android science: conscious and subconscious recognition. *Connection Science*, Vol. 18, No. 4, December 2006.

Kahneman, D., Slovic, P., & Tversky, A. (Eds.) (1982). *Judgment Under Uncertainty: Heuristics and Biases*. Cambridge: Cambridge University Press.

Kane, R. (1996). *The Significance of Free Will*. New York: Oxford University Press.

Kant, E. (1981). *Grounding of the Metaphysics of Morals* (J. Ellington, Trans.). Indianapolis: Hackett. (Original work published 1785.)

Lakoff, G. (1987). *Women, Fire and Dangerous Things: What Categories Reveal About the Mind*. Chicago: University of Chicago Press.

Locke, J. (1739). *Two Treatises of Government. Two Treatises of Government: a critical edition*. London: Cambridge Univ, Press. (Original work published 1739)

Locke, J. (1689). *An Essay Concerning Human Understanding*, P. Nidditch, Ed., Oxford: Clarendon Press, 1689/1975. K.F.

MacDorman and S. J. Cowley, Long-term relationships as a benchmark for robot person-hood. In Proceedings of the 15th IEEE International Symposium on Robot and Human Interactive Communication (RO-MAN), 2006. K.F. MacDorman and H. Ishiguro, "The uncanny advantage of using androids in social and cognitive science research," Interact. Stud., 7(3), pp. 297–337, 2006.

Minato, T., Shimada, M., Ishiguro, H., and Itakura, S. Development of an android for studying human–robot inter–Eaction. In Innovations in Applied Artificial Intelligence: The 17th International Conference on Industrial and Engineering Applications of Artificial Intelligence, R. Orchard, C. Yang and M. Ali, Eds, Lecture Notes in Artificial Intelligence, Berlin: Springer, 2004.

Morse, S. (2004). New Neuroscience, Old Problems. *Neuroscience and the Law*. New York: Dana Press.

McHugh, J. T. (1992). What is the difference between a "person" and a "human being" within the law? *Review of Politics*, 54, 445.

Note, (1987). The personification of the business corporation in American law. 54 U. *Chicago L. Rev*. 1441.

Pollock, J. (2006). *Thinking about Acting: Logical Foundations for Rational Decision Making*. New York: Oxford University Press.

Ramey, C. H. The uncanny valley of similarities concerning abortion, baldness, heaps of sand, and humanlike robots. In Proceedings of the Views of the Uncanny Valley Workshop, IEEE-RAS International Conference on Humanoid Robots, 2005.

Raz, J. (1975). *Practical Reason and Norms*. London: Hutchinson.

Rivaud, M. (1992). Comment: Toward a general theory of constitutional personhood: A theory of constitutional personhood for transgenic humanoid species. 39 *UCLA L. Rev.* 1425.

Rorty, A. (1976). *The Identity of Persons*. Berkeley: University of California Press.

Sloman, A., & Croucher, M. (1981). Why robots will have emotions. Proceedings IJCAI, 1981.

Solum, L. (1992). Legal personhood for artificial intelligences. 70 *North Carolina L. Rev.* 1231.

Strawson, P. (1959). *Individuals*. London: Methuen.

Tushnet, M. (1975). The American law of slavery, 1810–1860: A study in the persistence of legal autonomy. *Law & Society Review*, 10,119.

Wallach, W. (2004). Artificial morality: Bounded rationality, bounded morality and emotions. In I. Smit and G.Lasker (eds) *Cognitive, Emotive and Ethical Aspects of Decision Making in Humans and Artificial Intelligence* Vol. I. Windsor, Canada: IIAS.

van Inwagen, P. (1983). *An Essay on Free Will*. Oxford: Oxford University Press.

Werhane, P. (1985). *Persons, Rights and Corporations*. Englewood Cliffs: Prentice Hall Inc.

Wolff, R. P. (1998). *In Defense of Anarchism*. Berkeley and Los Angeles: University of California Press. (Original work published 1970).

Part IV

Approaches to Machine Ethics

Introduction

a. Overview

JAMES GIPS, IN HIS SEMINAL ARTICLE "TOWARDS THE ETHICAL ROBOT," gives an overview of various approaches to capturing ethics for a machine that might be considered. He quickly rejects as too slavish the Three Laws of Robotics formulated by Isaac Asimov in "Runaround" in 1942:

1. A robot may not injure a human being, or through inaction, allow a human being to come to harm.
2. A robot must obey the orders given it by human beings except where such orders would conflict with the First Law.
3. A robot must protect its own existence as long as such protection does not conflict with the First or Second law.

After declaring that what we are looking for is an ethical theory that would permit robots to behave as our equals, Gips then considers various (action-based) ethical theories that have been proposed for persons, noting that they can be divided into two types: consequentialist (or teleological) and deontological. Consequentialists maintain that the best action to take, at any given moment in time, is the one that is likely to result in the best consequences in the future. The most plausible version, Hedonistic Utilitarianism, proposed by Jeremy Bentham in the late eighteenth century, aims for "the greatest balance of pleasure over pain," counting all those affected equally. Responding to critics who maintain that utilitarians are not always just because the theory allows a few to be sacrificed for the greater happiness of the many, Gips proposes that we could "assign higher weights to people who are currently less well-off or less happy." In any case, "to reason ethically along consequentialist lines a robot would need to generate a list of possible actions and then evaluate the situation caused by each action according to the sum of good or bad caused to persons by the action. The robot would select the action that causes the greatest [net] good in the world." Although this approach might seem to be the one that one could most easily be implemented in a robot,

231

Gips maintains that "there is a tremendous problem of measurement." How is the robot to determine the amount of good or bad each person affected is likely to receive from each action?

With deontological theories, "actions are evaluated in and of themselves rather than in terms of the consequences they produce. Actions may be thought to be innately moral or innately immoral." Gips points out that some deontologists give a single principle that one ought to follow, whereas others have many duties that are generally thought to be prima facie (each one can be overridden on occasion by another duty that is thought to be stronger on that occasion). Kant's famous Categorical Imperative, "Act only on that maxim which you can at the same time will to be a universal law," is an example of the first. W. D. Ross's prima facie duties and Bernard Gert's ten moral rules are examples of the latter. Gips points out that "[w]henever a multi-rule system is proposed, there is the possibility of conflict between the rules." This creates a problem that needs to be resolved so that robots will know what to do when conflicts arise. (It should be noted that most ethicists think of the prima facie duty approach as combining elements of both consequentialist and deontological theories. See "Philosophical Approaches" later.)

Another approach to ethical theory that goes back to Plato and Aristotle, called virtue-based ethics, maintains the primacy of character traits rather than actions, claiming that if one is virtuous, then right actions will follow. Gips points out that "virtue-based systems often are turned into deontological rules for action," and he also notes that the virtue-based approach "seems to resonate well with the modern connectionist approach to AI" in that it emphasizes "training rather than the teaching of abstract theory."

Finally, Gips briefly considers taking a "psychological/sociological approach" to capturing ethics to implement in a robot by looking at "actual people's lives, at how they behave, at what they think, at how they develop." In doing so, should one study moral exemplars or ordinary people?

Gips believes, in agreement with others in this volume, that robots might be better able to follow ethical principles than humans and could serve as advisors to humans on ethical matters. He also maintains that we can learn more about ethics by trying to implement it in a machine.

b. Asimov's Laws

Roger Clarke and Susan Leigh Anderson consider Asimov's Laws of Robotics as a candidate for the ethics that ought to be implanted in robots. Designed to counteract the many science fiction stories where "robots were created and destroyed their creator," they seem "to ensure the continued domination of humans over robots, and to preclude the use of robots for evil purposes." Clarke points out, in "Asimov's Laws of Robotics: Implications for Information Technology," however, that there are a number of inconsistencies and ambiguities in the laws, which Asimov himself exploited in his stories. What should a robot do "when two humans give inconsistent instructions," for example? What if the only way to save a number of human lives is by harming one threatening human being? What counts as "harm" in the first law? It could be the case that "what seemed like cruelty [to a human] might, in the long run, be kindness." Difficult judgments would have to be made by robots in order to follow the laws, because they have to be interpreted. The later addition of a "zeroth" law, "A robot may not injure humanity, or through inaction, allow humanity to come to harm," as taking precedence over the first law, and which would permit the harming of a human being to "save humanity," requires even more interpretation.

Beyond these problems, Clarke further points out that a "robot must also be endowed with data collection, decision-analytical, and action processes by which it can apply the laws. Inadequate sensory, perceptual, or cognitive faculties would undermine the laws' effectiveness." Additional laws "would be essential to regulate relationships among robots." Clarke concludes his assessment of Asimov's Laws by claiming that his stories show that "[i]t is not possible to reliably constrain the behavior of robots by devising and applying a set of rules."

Finally, echoing the authors in Part III of the book, Clarke discusses a number of practical, cultural, ethical, and legal issues relating to the manufacture and use of robots, with or without these laws. "If information technologists do not respond to the challenges posed by robot systems, as investigated in Asimov's stories, information technology artifacts will be poorly suited for real-world applications. They may be used in ways not intended by their designers, or simply rejected as incompatible with the individuals and organizations they were meant to serve."

Susan Leigh Anderson takes a more philosophical approach in arguing for "The Unacceptability of Asimov's Three Laws of Robotics as a Basis for Machine Ethics." Using Asimov's story "The Bicentennial Man" and an argument given by Immanuel Kant to make her points, she concludes that whatever the status of the intelligent machines that are developed, it is ethically problematic for humans to program them to follow the Three Laws. Furthermore, she maintains that "because intelligent machines can be designed to consistently follow moral principles, they have an advantage over human beings in having the potential to be ideal ethical agents, because human beings' actions are often driven by irrational emotions."

Anderson's main argument can be summarized as follows: It would be difficult to establish in real life, unlike in a fictional story, that the intelligent machines we create have the characteristics necessary to have moral standing or rights: sentience, self-consciousness, the ability to reason, moral agency, and/or emotionality. Yet even if they do not possess the required characteristic(s), they are designed to resemble human beings in function, if not in form. As a result, using an argument given by Kant concerning the proper treatment of animals, we should not be permitted to mistreat them because it could very well lead to our mistreating humans (who have moral standing/rights) as well. Because Asimov's Laws allow for the mistreatment of robots, they are therefore morally unacceptable. Anderson claims it is clear that Asimov himself rejects the Laws on moral grounds in his story "The Bicentennial Man."

c. Artificial Intelligence Approaches

Bruce McLaren, in "Computational Models of Ethical Reasoning: Challenges, Initial Steps, and Future Directions," promotes a case-based reasoning approach for developing systems that provide guidance in ethical dilemmas. His first such system, Truth-Teller, compares pairs of cases presenting ethical dilemmas about whether or not to tell the truth. The Truth-Teller program marshals ethically relevant similarities and differences between two given cases from the perspective of the "truth teller" (i.e., the person faced with the dilemma) and reports them to the user. In particular, it points out reasons for telling the truth (or not) that (1) apply to both cases, (2) apply more strongly in one case than another, or (3) apply to only one case. SIROCCO (System for Intelligent Retrieval of Operationalized Cases and Codes), McLaren's second system, leverages information concerning a new ethical dilemma to predict which previously stored principles and cases are relevant to it in the domain of professional engineering ethics. New cases are exhaustively formalized, and this formalism is used to index similar cases in a database of previously solved cases that include principles used in their solution. SIROCCO's goal, given a new case to analyze, is "to provide the basic information with which a human reasoner ... could answer an ethical question and then build an argument or rationale for that conclusion." SIROCCO is successful at retrieving relevant cases, although McLaren reports that it performs beneath the level of an ethical review board presented with the same task.

Deductive techniques, as well as any attempt at decision making, are eschewed by McLaren due to "the ill-defined nature of problem solving in ethics." Critics might contend that this "ill-defined nature" may not make problem solving in ethics completely indefinable, and attempts of just such definition may be possible in constrained domains. Further, it might be argued that decisions offered by a system that are consistent with decisions made in previous cases have merit and will be useful to those seeking ethical advice.

Marcello Guarini, in "Computational Neural Modeling and the Philosophy of Ethics: Reflections on the Particularism-Generalism Debate," investigates a neural network approach to machine ethics in which particular actions concerning killing and allowing to die were classified as acceptable or unacceptable depending on different motives and consequences. After training a simple recurrent network on a number of such cases, it was capable of providing plausible responses to a variety of previously unseen cases. This work attempts to shed light on the philosophical debate concerning generalism (principle-based approaches to moral reasoning) versus particularism (case-based approaches to moral reasoning).

Guarini finds that, although some of the concerns pertaining to learning and generalizing from ethical dilemmas without resorting to principles can be mitigated with a neural network model of cognition, "important considerations suggest that it cannot be the whole story about moral reasoning – principles are needed." He argues that "to build an artificially intelligent agent without the ability to question and revise its own initial instruction on cases is to assume a kind of moral and engineering perfection on the part of the designer." He argues further that such perfection is unlikely and principles seem to play an important role in the required subsequent revision: "[A]t least some reflection in humans does appear to require the explicit representation or consultation of ... rules," for instance, in discerning morally relevant differences in similar cases. Concerns for this approach are those attributable to neural networks in general, including oversensitivity to training cases and the inability to generate reasoned arguments for system responses.

The next two papers, without committing to any particular set of ethical principles, consider how one might realize principles in autonomous systems. Alan K. Mackworth, in "Architectures and Ethics for Robots: Constraint Satisfaction as a Unitary Design Framework," expresses concern that current approaches for incorporating ethics into machines, expressly robots, assume technical abilities for these machines that have yet to be devised – in particular, the abilities to specify limitations on their behavior and verify that these limitations have indeed been observed. Toward providing such abilities, Mackworth offers a conceptual framework based on the notion of *dynamic probabilistic prioritized constraint satisfaction*. He argues that this framework could provide a means to specify limitations at various granularities and verify their satisfaction in real time and in uncertain environments.

One question that might be raised in conjunction with this framework (and in the work by Luis Moniz Pereira and Ari Saptawijaya to follow) concerns the notion that ethical constraints will in fact lend themselves to simple prioritization, as does Mackworth's example of Asimov's Laws. It might be the case that no simple static hierarchy of constraints will serve to provide correct ethical guidance to robots, and that the priority of these constraints will themselves need to be dynamic, changing with each given situation. The need of input from ethicists shows how the interchange between the two disciplines of artificial intelligence and ethics can serve to derive stronger results than approaching the problem from only a single perspective.

Matteo Turilli, in "Ethical Protocol Design," defines the *ethical consistency problem* (ECP) that can arise in organizations composed of a heterogeneous collection of actors, both human and technological: How can we constrain these actors with the same set of ethical principles so that the output of the organization as a whole is ethically consistent? Turilli argues that it is ethical inconsistency that lies at the heart of many of the problems associated with such organizations. He cites identity theft as a clear instance of an ECP where regulations constraining the handling of sensitive data by individuals are not in effect for automated systems performing operations on the very same data.

Turilli believes that normative constraints need to be introduced into the design of the systems of such organizations right from the beginning and offers a three-step process to do so: (1) Translate the normative constraints expressed by given ethical principles into terms of *ethical requirements* that constrain the functionalities of a computational system; (2) translate the ethical requirements into an *ethical protocol* that specifies the operations performed by the system so that their behaviors match the condition posed by the ethical requirements; and (3) refine the specification of the system into executable algorithms. To facilitate this process, Turilli defines the notion of *control closure* (CC) to model the degree to which an operation is distributed across processes. The CC of an operation is the set of processes whose state variables are needed to perform it; the CC of a process is the union of the CC of each of its operations. CCs can be used to derive formal preconditions on the execution of operations that help guarantee that the constraints imposed by a given principle are maintained across a system.

As meritorious as such an approach may seem, there is the concern that systems specifically designed to conform to particular normative constraints require these to be fully determined up front and leave little room for future modification. Although this might be feasible for simple systems, it is not clear that the principles of more complex systems facing more complicated ethical dilemmas can be so fully specified as to never require further refinement.

Bringsjord et al. are concerned that traditional logical approaches will not be up to the task of engineering ethically correct robots, and that the ability to "reason *over*, rather than merely *in*, logical systems" will be required. They believe that robots simply programmed to follow some moral code of conduct will ultimately fail when confronted with real-world situations more complex than that code can manage and, therefore, will need to engage in higher-level reasoning in their resolution. They offer *category theory* as a means of formally specifying this meta-level reasoning and describe work they have accomplished toward their goal.

One could respond to their concern that we may not be able to anticipate subtle situations that could arise – which would make simple ethical principles unsatisfactory, even dangerous, for robots to follow – in the following manner: This shows why it is important that applied ethicists be involved in developing ethical robots that function in particular domains. Applied ethicists are trained to consider every situation that is *logically possible* to see if there are counterexamples to the principles that are considered for adoption. This goes beyond what is likely – or even physically – possible. Applied ethicists should be able, then, to anticipate unusual situations that need to be taken into account. If they don't feel comfortable doing so, it would be unwise to let robots function autonomously in the domain under consideration.

Luis Moniz Pereira and Ari Saptawijaya, in "Modelling Morality with Prospective Logic," attempt "to provide a general framework to model morality computationally." Using Philippa Foot's classic trolley dilemmas that support the "principle of double effect" as an example, they use abductive logic programming to model the moral reasoning contained in the principle. They note that recent empirical studies on human "moral instinct" support the fact that humans tend to make judgments consistent with the principle, even though they have difficulty expressing the rule that supports their judgments.

The principle of double effect permits one to act in a manner that results in harm to an individual when it will lead to a greater good, the harm being foreseen; but one cannot *intentionally* harm someone in order to bring about a greater good. This principle has been applied in warfare, allowing for "collateral damage" to civilians when one only *intends* to harm the enemy, as well as in justifying giving a dying patient a lethal dose of pain medication as long as one is not intending to kill the person.

In Pereira and Saptawijaya's work, possible decisions in an ethical dilemma are modeled in abductive logic and their consequences computed. Those that violate a priori integrity constraints are ruled out; in their example, those decisions that involve intentionally killing someone. Remaining candidate decisions that conform to a posteriori preferences are preferred; in their example, those decisions that result in the fewest number of persons killed. The resulting decisions modeled by this work are in accordance with empirical studies of human decision making in the face of the same ethical dilemmas.

The principle of double effect is a controversial doctrine; some philosophers characterize it as an instance of "doublethink." So it is debatable whether this is the sort of ethical principle that we would want to instantiate in a machine. Furthermore, because the key to applying this principle rests on the *intention* of the agent, most would say that it would be impossible for a machine to consider it, because few would grant that machines can have intentions.

d. Psychological/Sociological Approaches

Bridging the gap between AI approaches and a psychological one, Morteza Dehghani, Ken Forbus, Emmett Tomai, and Matthew Klenk, in "An Integrated Reasoning Approach to Moral Decision Making," present a computation model of ethical reasoning, MoralDM, that intends to capture "recent psychological findings on moral decision making." Current research on moral human decision making has shown, they maintain, that humans don't rely entirely on utilitarian reasoning. There are additional deontological moral rules ("sacred, or protected, values"), varying from culture to culture, that can trump utilitarian thinking. MoralDM, therefore, "incorporates two modes of decision making: deontological and utilitarian," integrating "natural language understanding, qualitative reasoning, analogical reasoning, and first-principle reasoning."

Citing several psychological studies, Dehghani et al. note that when protected values are involved, "people tend to be concerned with the nature of their action rather than the utility of the outcome." They will, for example, let more people die rather than be the cause of anyone's death. Cultural differences, such as the importance given to respect for authority, have also been noted in determining what is considered to be a protected value.

MoralDM works essentially in the following manner: "If there are no protected values involved in the case being analyzed, MoralDM applies traditional rules of utilitarian decision making by choosing the action that provides the highest outcome utility. On the other hand, if MoralDM determines that there are sacred values involved, it operates in deontological mode and becomes less sensitive to the outcome utility of actions." Further, MoralDM integrates "first-principles" reasoning with analogical or case-based reasoning to broaden its scope – decisions from similar previous cases being brought to bear when "first-principles" reasoning fails.

Their experimental results seem to support the need for both "first-principles" and analogical modes of ethical decision making because, when the system makes the correct decision, it is sometimes supported by one of these modes and sometimes the other, or both. However, it is not clear that, because the case base is populated solely by cases the system solves using "first-principles" reasoning, the system will eventually no longer require anything but analogical reasoning to make its decisions. Ultimately, all cases that can be solved by "first-principles" reasoning in the system will be stored as cases in the case base.

The work by Dehghani et al., which attempts to model human moral decision making, might be useful in helping autonomous machines better understand human motivations and, as a result, provide a basis for more sympathetic interactions between machines and humans. Considering using human moral decision making as a basis for machine ethics, something not explicitly advocated by Dehghani et al., would, however, be questionable. It can easily be argued that the "ethical" values of most human beings are unsatisfactory. Ordinary humans have a tendency to rationalize selfish, irrational, and inconsistent behavior. Wouldn't we like machines to treat us better than most humans would?

Peter Danielson, in "Prototyping N-Reasons: A Computer Mediated Ethics Machine," attempts to capture "democratic ethics." He is less interested in trying to put ethics into a robot, and uses a quotation from Daniel Dennett in 1989 to establish the incredible difficulty, if not impossibility, of that task. Instead, Danielson wants to use a machine to generate the information needed "to advise people making ethical decisions." He suggests that "it is unlikely that any sizable number of people can be ethical about any complex subject without the help of a machine."

Danielson has developed a Web-based "survey platform for exploring public norms," NERD (Norms Evolving in Response to Dilemmas). Users are asked to respond to "constrained survey choices" about ethical issues, and in addition are provided a space to make comments justifying their answers. He has worked on overcoming "static design," bias (replacing initial advisor input with completely user-generated content), and reducing the amount of qualitative input. The result is an "emerging social choice." Danielson says that "[a]pplying machines to ethical decision-making should help make ethics an empirical discipline."

One gathers that Danielson would feel comfortable putting the "emerging social choices" that NERD comes up with in machines that function in the societies from which the surveys were taken, although this is not his focus. Critics will undoubtedly maintain that, although the results of his surveys will be interesting and useful to many (social scientists and politicians, for instance), there are some issues that should not be resolved by taking surveys, and ethical issues belong in that group. The most popular views are not necessarily the most ethical ones. Danielson's advocacy of Sociological or Cultural Relativism has dangerous consequences. It condemns women and religious and ethnic minorities to inhumane treatment in many parts of the world.

Danielson is likely to give one or both of two responses to justify his view: (1) *Over time, good reasons and good answers to ethical dilemmas should rise to the top and become the most popular ones.* Danielson says at one point that they ended up collecting "very high quality reasons." Yet what makes a reason or answer "good" or "very high quality"? It can only be that it compares favorably with a value that has *objective* merit. Yet there is no guarantee that the majority will appreciate what is ethically correct, especially if it is not in their interest to do so. (This is why males have resisted giving rights to women for so long.) (2) *No matter what one thinks of the values of a particular society, the majority should be able to determine its practices. This is what it means to live in a democracy.* It should be noted, however, that the founders of the United States and many other countries thought it important to build certain inalienable rights for citizens into their constitutions as a check against the "tyranny of the majority."

In any case, there are many other problems that arise from adopting the position of Sociological Relativism. Two examples: There will be frequent moral "flip-flops" as the majority view on a particular issue changes back and forth, depending on what is in the news. If there is a tie between viewing a practice as right and wrong in a survey, then neither position is correct; there is no right or wrong.

e. Philosophical Approaches

The most well-known example of each of the two general types of action-based ethical theories and another approach to ethical theory that combines elements of both are considered for implementation in machines by Christopher Grau, Thomas M. Powers, and Susan Leigh Anderson and Michael Anderson, respectively: Utilitarianism, a consequentialist (teleological) ethical theory; Kant's Categorical Imperative, a deontological theory; and the prima facie duty approach that has both teleological and deontological elements. Utilitarians claim that the right action, in any ethical dilemma, is the action that is likely to result in the greatest net good consequences, taking all those affected equally into account. Kant's Categorical Imperative states that one should "Act only according to that maxim whereby you can at the same time will that it should become a universal law." The prima facie duty approach typically tries to balance several duties, some of which are teleological and others of which are deontological.

Using the film *I, Robot* as a springboard for discussion, Christopher Grau considers whether utilitarian reasoning should be installed in robots in his article "There is no 'I' in 'Robot': Robots and Utilitarianism." He reaches different conclusions when considering robot-to-human interaction versus robot-to-robot interaction. Grau points out that the supreme robot intelligence in *I, Robot*, VIKI, uses utilitarian reasoning to justify harming some humans in order to "ensure mankind's continued existence." Because it sounds like common sense to choose "that action that lessens overall harm," and because determining the correct action according to Utilitarianism is "ultimately a matter of numerical calculation" (which is appealing to programmers), Grau asks, "if we could program a robot to be an accurate and effective utilitarian, shouldn't we?"

Grau notes that, despite its initial appeal, most ethicists have found fault with the utilitarian theory for permitting injustice and the violation of some individuals' rights for the greater good of the majority. "Because the ends justify the means, the means can get ugly." However, the film's anti-utilitarian message doesn't rest on this objection, according to Grau. Instead, it has resulted from a robot having chosen to save the life of the central character, Del Spooner, rather than the life of a little girl. There was a 45 percent chance that Del could be saved, but only an 11 percent chance that the girl could be saved. According to utilitarian reasoning, the robot should try to save Del's life (assuming that the percentages aren't offset by considering others who might be affected), which it successfully did. However, we are supposed to reject the "cold utilitarian logic of the robot [that] exposes a dangerously inhuman and thus impoverished moral sense," and Del himself agrees. Instead, *humans* believe that one should try to save the child who is "somebody's baby." Even if this emotional reaction by humans is irrational, the justice and rights violations permitted by utilitarian reasoning make it unsuitable as a candidate for implementing in a robot interacting with human beings, Grau maintains.

Grau also considers the "integrity objection" against Utilitarianism, where strictly following the theory is likely to result in one having to sacrifice cherished dreams that make one's life meaningful. He says that should not be a problem for a utilitarian robot without a sense of self in dealing with other robots that also lack a sense of self. Furthermore, the objection that the utilitarian theory permits the sacrifice of *individuals* for the greater good of all also disappears if we are talking about robots interacting with other robots, where none has a sense of being an individual self. Thus, it is acceptable, perhaps even ideal, that the guiding ethical philosophy for robot-to-robot interactions be Utilitarianism, even though it is not acceptable for robot-to-human interactions.

Thomas M. Powers, in "Prospects for a Kantian Machine," considers the first formulation of Kant's Categorical Imperative to determine "what computational structures such a view would require and to see what challenges remain for its successful implementation." As philosophers have interpreted the Categorical Imperative, agents contemplating performing an action must determine whether its maxim can be accepted as a universalized rule consistent with other rules proposed to be universalized. Powers first notes that to avoid problems with too much specificity in the maxim, for example, "On Tuesday, I will kill John," "we must add a condition on a maxim's logical form so that the universalization test will quantify over circumstances, purposes, and agents." The universalization then needs to be mapped onto traditional deontic logic categories: forbidden, permissible, and obligatory.

Powers maintains that a simple test for contradictions within maxims themselves will not be robust enough. Instead, "the machine must check the maxim's consistency with other facts in the database, some of which will be normative conclusions from previously considered maxims." Kant also suggested, through his examples, that some commonsense/background rules be added. But which rules? Unlike scientific laws, they must allow for some counterexamples, which further complicates matters by suggesting that we introduce nonmonotonic reasoning, best captured by "Reiter's default logic." We might then be faced with "the problem of multiple extensions: one rule tells us one thing, and the other allows us to infer the opposite." Powers gives us the example of Nixon being a Republican Quaker – one rule is "Republicans are hawks" and another is "Quakers are pacifists." Even more serious for Powers is the fact that "[n]onmonotonic inference fails a requirement met by classical first-order logic: semidecidability of set membership."

At this point, Powers considers a further possibility for a Kantian-type logic for machine ethics, that "ethical deliberation involves the construction of a *coherent system* of maxims." This is also suggested by Kant, according to Powers, with his illustrations of having a duty to develop your own talents and give to others in need (e.g., the latter one forms a coherent system with wanting others to help you when you are in need). On this view, following the Categorical Imperative involves building a set of maxims from the bottom up and considering whether each new maxim is consistent with the others that have been accepted or not. However, what if we have included a maxim that turns out to be unacceptable? It would corrupt the process. How could a machine correct itself, as humans engaged in ethical deliberation often do? Furthermore, what decides the status of the first maxim considered (the "moral infant problem")? Powers concludes by claiming that each move introduced to try to clarify and automate Kant's Categorical Imperative has its own problems, and they reveal difficulties for humans attempting to follow the theory as well. In agreement with others in this volume who maintain that work on machine ethics is likely to bear fruit in clarifying human ethics, Powers says, "Perhaps work on the logic of machine ethics will clarify the human challenge [in following Kant's Categorical Imperative] as well."

Finally, Susan Leigh Anderson and Michael Anderson develop a prima facie duty approach to capturing the ethics a machine would need in order to behave ethically in a particular domain in their article, "A Prima Facie Duty Approach to Machine Ethics: Machine Learning of Features of Ethical Dilemmas, Prima Facie Duties, and Decision Principles through a Dialogue with Ethicists." The prima facie duty approach to ethical theory, originally advocated by W. D. Ross, maintains that "there isn't a single absolute duty to which we must adhere," as is the case with Utilitarianism and Kant's Categorical Imperative. Instead, there are "a number of duties that we should try to follow (some teleological and others deontological), each of which could be overridden on occasion by one of the other duties." For example, we have a prima facie duty "to follow through with a promise we have made (a deontological duty); but if it causes great harm to do so, it may be overridden by another prima facie duty not to cause harm (a teleological duty)."

The main problem with the prima facie duty approach to ethics is this: "[H]ow do we know which duty should be paramount in ethical dilemmas when the prima facie duties pull in different directions?" In earlier work, the Andersons found a way to harness machine capabilities to discover a decision principle to resolve cases in a common type of ethical dilemma faced by many health-care professionals that involved three of Beauchamp and Childress's four prima facie duties in biomedical ethics. Inspired by John Rawls's "reflective equilibrium" approach to creating and refining ethical principles, a computer was able to "generaliz[e] from intuitions [of ethicists] about particular cases, testing those generalizations on further cases, and ... repeating this process" until it discovered a valid decision principle. Using inductive logic programming, the computer was able to abstract a principle from having been given the correct answer to four cases that enabled it to give the correct answer for the remaining fourteen other possible cases using their representation scheme.

The Andersons next developed three applications of the principle that was learned: "(1) MedEthEx, a medical-advisor system for dilemmas of the type [they] considered"; "(2) A medication-reminder system, EthEl, for the elderly that not only issues reminders at appropriate times, but also determines when an overseer ... should be notified if the patient refuses to take the medication"; "(3) An instantiation of EthEl in a Nao robot, which [they] believe is the first example of a robot that follows an ethical principle in determining which actions it will take."

Their current research involves generating the ethics needed to resolve dilemmas in a particular domain from scratch by discovering the ethically significant *features* of dilemmas with the range of intensities required to distinguish between ethically distinguishable cases (an idea derived from Jeremy Bentham), prima facie duties to "either maximize or minimize the ethical feature(s)," and decision principle(s) needed to resolve conflicts between the prima facie duties. Central to their procedure is a position that they derived from Kant: "With two ethically identical cases – that is, cases with the same ethically relevant feature(s) to the same degree – an action cannot be right in one of the cases, whereas the comparable action in the other case is considered wrong."

The Andersons have developed an automated dialogue between an ethicist and a system functioning more or less autonomously in a particular domain that will enable the system to efficiently learn the ethically relevant features of the dilemmas it will encounter, the required intensities, the prima facie duties, and the decision principle(s) needed to resolve dilemmas. Contradictions that arise cause the system to ask the ethicist to either revise judgment(s) or find a new ethically relevant feature present in one case but not another, or else expand the range of intensities to distinguish between cases. Their sample dialogue, involving the same domain of medication reminding and notifying for noncompliance, resulted in the system learning an expected sub-set of the principle that is similar to the one derived from their earlier research, this time without making assumptions that were made before.

The Andersons believe that there are many advantages to the prima facie duty approach to ethics and their learning process in particular. It can be tailored to the domain where the machine will operate. (There may be different ethically relevant features and prima facie duties in different domains.) It can be updated with further training when needed. Decision principles that are discovered may lead to "surprising new insights, and therefore breakthroughs, in ethical theory" that were only implicit in the judgments of ethicists about particular cases. They note that "the computational power of today's machines ... can keep track of more information than a human mind" and can spot inconsistencies that need to be resolved.

Critics may be concerned with three aspects of the procedure the Andersons develop: (1) They insist that the ethics that should be captured should be that of ethicists, whom they believe have "an expertise that comes from thinking long and deeply about ethical matters," rather than ordinary people. (2) They believe that there are some universal ethical principles to be discovered through their learning procedure. Acknowledging, however, that there isn't agreement on all issues, they add that "we should not permit machines to make decisions" in domains where there is no agreement as to what is ethically correct. (3) Their representation scheme for ethical dilemmas, which reduces them ultimately to the affirmation or violation of one or more prima facie duties of various intensities, might be thought to be too simplistic. Yet built into their system is the idea that more ethically relevant features, which turn into duties, or a wider range of intensities may need to be introduced to distinguish between dilemmas that are ethically distinct. What else could be the difference between them, they ask.

14

Towards the Ethical Robot

James Gips

W HEN OUR MOBILE ROBOTS ARE FREE-RANGING CRITTERS, HOW OUGHT they to behave? What should their top-level instructions look like?

The best known prescription for mobile robots is the Three Laws of Robotics formulated by Isaac Asimov (1942):

1. A robot may not injure a human being, or through inaction, allow a human being to come to harm.
2. A robot must obey the orders given it by human beings except where such orders would conflict with the First Law.
3. A robot must protect its own existence as long as such protection does not conflict with the First or Second law.

Let's leave aside "implementation questions" for a moment. (No problem, Asimov's robots have "positronic brains".) These three laws are not suitable for our magnificent robots. These are laws for slaves.

We want our robots to behave more like equals, more like ethical people. (See Figure 14.1.) How do we program a robot to behave ethically? Well, what does it mean for a person to behave ethically?

People have discussed how we ought to behave for centuries. Indeed, it has been said that we really have only one question that we answer over and over: What do I do now? Given the current situation what action should I take?

Generally, ethical theories are divided into two types: consequentialist and deontological.

Consequentialist Theories

In consequentialist theories, actions are judged by their consequences. The best action to take now is the action that results in the best situation in the future.

From Ford, Kenneth M., Clark Glymour, and Patrick Hayes, eds., *Android Epistemology*, pp. 243–252, © 1995 MIT Press, by permission of The MIT Press.
Originally presented at The Second International Workshop on Human and Machine Cognition: Android Epistemology, Pensacola, Florida, May 1991.

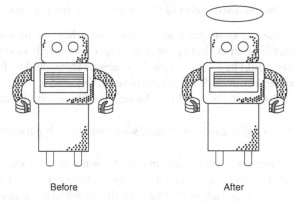

Before   After

Figure 14.1. Towards the Ethical Robot.

To be able to reason ethically along consequentialist lines, our robot could have:

1. A way of describing the situation in the world
2. A way of generating possible actions
3. A means of predicting the situation that would result if an action were taken given the current situation
4. A method of evaluating a situation in terms of its goodness or desirability.

The task here for the robot is to find that action that would result in the best situation possible.

Not to minimize the extreme difficulty of writing a program to predict the effect of an action in the world, but the "ethical" component of this system is the evaluation function on situations in 4.

How can we evaluate a situation to determine how desirable it is? Many evaluation schemes have been proposed. Generally, these schemes involve measuring the amount of pleasure or happiness or goodness that would befall each person in the situation and then adding these amounts together.

The best known of these schemes is utilitarianism. As proposed by Bentham in the late 18th century, in utilitarianism the moral act is the one that produces the greatest balance of pleasure over pain. To measure the goodness of an action, look at the situation that would result and sum up the pleasure and pain for each person. In utilitarianism, each person counts equally.

More generally, consequentialist evaluation schemes have the following form:

$$\sum w_i\, p_i$$

where w_i is the weight assigned each person and p_i is the measure of pleasure or happiness or goodness for each person. In classic utilitarianism, the weight for each person is equal and the p_i is the amount of pleasure, broadly defined.

What should be the distribution of the weights w_i across persons?

- An ethical egoist is someone who considers only himself in deciding what actions to take. For an ethical egoist, the weight for himself in evaluating the consequences would be 1; the weight for everyone else would be 0. This eases the calculations, but doesn't make for a pleasant fellow.
- For the ethical altruist, the weight for himself is 0; the weight for everyone else is positive.
- The utilitarian ideal is the universalist, who weights each person's well-being equally.
- A common objection to utilitarianism is that it is not necessarily just. While it seeks to maximize total happiness, it may do so at the expense of some unfortunate souls. One approach to dealing with this problem of justice is to assign higher weights to people who are currently less well-off or less happy. The well-being of the less fortunate would count more than the well-being of the more fortunate.
- It's been suggested that there are few people who actually conform to the utilitarian ideal. Would you sacrifice a close family member so that two strangers in a far-away land could live? Perhaps most people assign higher importance to the well-being of people they know better.

Some of the possibilities for weighting schemes are illustrated in Figure 14.2.

What exactly is it that the p_i is supposed to measure? This depends on your axiology, on your theory of value. Consequentialists want to achieve the greatest balance of good over evil. Bentham was a hedonist, who believed that the good is pleasure, the bad is pain. Others have sought to maximize happiness or well-being or ...

Another important question is who (or what) is to count as a person. Whose well-being do we value? One can trace the idea of a "person" through history. Do women count as persons? Do strangers count as persons? Do people from other countries count as persons? Do people of other races count as persons? Do people who don't believe in your religion count as persons? Do people in terminal comas count as persons? Do fetuses count as persons? Do whales? Do robots?

One of the reviewers of this chapter raises the question of overpopulation. If increasing the number of persons alive increases the value calculated by the evaluation formula, then we should seek to have as many persons alive as possible. Of course, it is possible that the birth of another person might decrease the well-being of others on this planet. This and many other interesting and strange issues arising from consequentialism are discussed by Parfit (1984).

Thus to reason ethically along consequentialist lines a robot would need to generate a list of possible actions and then evaluate the situation caused by each

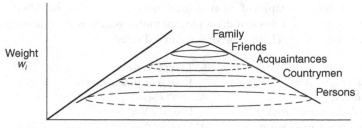

Weight
w_i

Family
Friends
Acquaintances
Countrymen
Persons

Do most people value higher the well-being of people they know better?

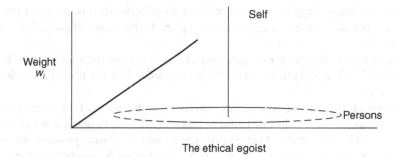

Weight
w_i

Self

Persons

The ethical egoist

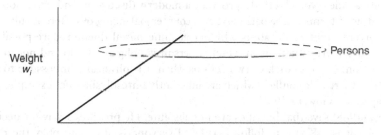

Weight
w_i

Persons

The utilitarian ideal. (But people argue about the weight you
should assign your own well-being. And who should count as persons?)

Figure 14.2. Some consequentialist weighting schemes.

action according to the sum of good or bad caused to persons by the action. The robot would select the action that causes the greatest good in the world.

Deontological Theories

In a deontological ethical theory, actions are evaluated in and of themselves rather than in terms of the consequences they produce. Actions may be thought to be innately moral or innately immoral independent of the specific consequences they may cause.

There are many examples of deontological moral systems that have been proposed. An example of a modern deontological moral system is the one proposed by Bernard Gert. Gert (1988) proposes ten moral rules:

1. Don't kill.	6. Don't deceive.
2. Don't cause pain.	7. Keep your promise.
3. Don't disable.	8. Don't cheat.
4. Don't deprive of freedom.	9. Obey the law.
5. Don't deprive of pleasure.	10. Do your duty.

Whenever a multi-rule system is proposed, there is the possibility of conflict between the rules. Suppose our robot makes a promise but then realizes that carrying out the promise might cause someone pain. Is the robot obligated to keep the promise?

One approach to dealing with rule conflict is to order the rules for priority. In his Three Laws of Robotics, Asimov builds the order into the text of the rules themselves.

A common way of dealing with the problem of conflicts in moral systems is to treat rules as dictating prima facie duties (Ross 1930). It is an obligation to keep your promise. Other things being equal, you should keep your promise. Rules may have exceptions. Other moral considerations, derived from other rules, may override a rule. Nozick (1981) provides a modern discussion and extension of these ideas in terms of the balancing and counter-balancing of different rules.

A current point of debate is whether genuine moral dilemmas are possible. That is, are there situations in which a person is obligated to do and not to do some action, or to do each of two actions when it is physically impossible to do both? Are there rule conflicts which are inherently unresolvable? For example, see the papers in (Gowans 1987).

Gert (1988) says that his rules are not absolute. He provides a way for deciding when it is OK not to follow a rule: "Everyone is always to obey the rule except when an impartial rational person can advocate that violating it be publicly allowed. Anyone who violates the rule when an impartial rational person could not advocate that such a violation may be publicly allowed may be punished." (p. 119).

Some have proposed smaller sets of rules. For example, Kant proposed the categorical imperative, which in its first form states "Act only on that maxim which you can at the same time will to be a universal law." Thus, for example, it would be wrong to make a promise with the intention of breaking it. If everyone made promises with the intention of breaking them then no one would believe in promises. The action would be self-defeating. Can Gert's ten rules each be derived from the categorical imperative?

Utilitarians sometimes claim that the rules of deontological systems are merely heuristics, shortcut approximations, for utilitarian calculations. Deontologists deny this, claiming that actions can be innately wrong independent of their actual consequences. One of the oldest examples of a deontological moral system is the Ten Commandments. The God of the Old Testament is not a utilitarian. God doesn't say "Thou shalt not commit adultery unless the result of committing adultery is a greater balance of pleasure over pain." Rather, the act of adultery is innately immoral.

Virtue-Based Theories

Since Kant the emphasis in Western ethics has been on duty, on defining ethics in terms of what actions one is obligated to do. There is a tradition in ethics that goes back to Plato and Aristotle that looks at ethics in terms of virtues, in terms of character. The question here is "What shall I be?" rather than "What shall I do?"

Plato and other Greeks thought there are four cardinal virtues: wisdom, courage, temperance, and justice. They thought that from these primary virtues all other virtues can be derived. If one is wise and courageous and temperate and just then right actions will follow.

Aquinas thought the seven cardinal virtues are faith, hope, love, prudence, fortitude, temperance, and justice. The first three are "theological" virtues, the final four "human" virtues.

For Schopenhauer there are two cardinal virtues: benevolence and justice.

Aristotle, in the *Nicomachean Ethics*, distinguishes between intellectual virtues and moral virtues. Intellectual virtues can be taught and learned directly. Moral virtues are learned by living right, by practice, by habit. "It is by doing just acts that we become just, by doing temperate acts that we become temperate, by doing brave acts that we become brave. The experience of states confirms this statement for it is by training in good habits that lawmakers make their citizens good." (Book 2, Chapter 1) Ethics is a question of character. Good deeds and right actions lead to strong character. It is practice that is important rather than theory.

In modern days, virtue-based systems often are turned into deontological rules for actions. That is, one is asked to act wisely, courageously, temperately, and justly, rather than being wise, courageous, temperate, and just.

Automated Ethical Reasoning

On what type of ethical theory can automated ethical reasoning be based?

At first glance, consequentialist theories might seem the most "scientific", the most amenable to implementation in a robot. Maybe so, but there is a tremendous problem of measurement. How can one predict "pleasure", "happiness", or "well-being" in individuals in a way that is additive, or even comparable?

Deontological theories seem to offer more hope. The categorical imperative might be tough to implement in a reasoning system. But I think one could see using a moral system like the one proposed by Gert as the basis for an automated ethical reasoning system. A difficult problem is in the resolution of conflicting obligations. Gert's impartial rational person advocating that violating the rule in these circumstances be publicly allowed seems reasonable but tough to implement.

Legal systems are closely related to moral systems. One approach to legal systems is to consider them as consisting of thousands of rules, often spelled out in great detail. The work in the automation of legal reasoning (see, for example, Walters 1985, 1988) might well prove helpful.

The virtue-based approach to ethics, especially that of Aristotle, seems to resonate well with the modern connectionist approach to AI. Both seem to emphasize the immediate, the perceptual, the nonsymbolic. Both emphasize development by training rather than by the teaching of abstract theory. Paul Churchland writes interestingly about moral knowledge and its development from a neurocomputational, connectionist point of view in "Moral Facts and Moral Knowledge", the final chapter of (Churchland 1989). Perhaps the right approach to developing an ethical robot is to confront it with a stream of different situations and train it as to the right actions to take.

Robots as Moral Saints

An important aspect of utilitarianism is that it is all-encompassing. To really follow utilitarianism, every moment of the day one must ask "What should I do now to maximize the general well-being?" Am I about to eat dinner in a restaurant? Wouldn't the money be better spent on feeding starving children in Ethiopia? Am I about to go to the movies? I should stay home and send the ticket money to an organization that inoculates newborns.

Utilitarianism and other approaches to ethics have been criticized as not being psychologically realistic, as not being suitable "for creatures like us" (Flanagan, 1991, p.32). Could anyone really live full-time according to utilitarianism?

Not many human beings live their lives flawlessly as moral saints. But a robot could. If we could program a robot to behave ethically, the government or a wealthy philanthropist could build thousands of them and release them in the world to help people. (Would we actually like the consequences? Perhaps here again "The road to hell is paved with good intentions.")

Or, perhaps, a robot that could reason ethically would serve best as an advisor to humans about what action would be best to perform in the current situation and why.

Could a Robot be Ethical?

Would a robot that behaves ethically actually be ethical? This question is similar to the question raised by Searle (1980) in the "Chinese room": would a computer that can hold a conversation in Chinese really understand Chinese?

The Chinese room question raises the age-old issue of other minds (Harnard 1991). How do we know that other people actually have minds when all that we can observe is their behavior? The ethical question raises the age-old issue of free will. Would a robot that follows a program and thereby behaves ethically, actually be ethical? Or, does a creature need to have free will to behave ethically? Does a creature need to make a conscious choice of its own volition to behave ethically in order to be considered ethical? Of course, one can ask whether there is in fact any essential difference between the "free will" of a human being and the "free will" of a robot.

Is it possible for the robot in Figure 14.1 to earn its halo?

Benefits of Working on Ethical Robots

It is exciting to contemplate ethical robots and automated ethical reasoning systems.

The basic problem is a common one in artificial intelligence, a problem that is encountered in every subfield from natural language understanding to vision. People have been thinking and discussing and writing about ethics for centuries, for millennia. Yet it often is difficult to take an ethical system that seems to be well worked-out and implement it on the computer. While books and books are written on particular ethical systems, the systems often do not seem nearly detailed enough and well-enough thought out to implement on the computer. Ethical systems and approaches make sense in terms of broad brush approaches, but (how) do people actually implement them? How can we implement them on the computer?

Knuth (1973, p.709) put it well

It has often been said that a person doesn't really understand something until he teaches it to someone else. Actually a person doesn't really understand something until he can teach it to a computer, i.e., express it as an algorithm.... The attempt to formalize things as algorithms leads to a much deeper understanding than if we simply try to understand things in the traditional way.

Are there ethical experts to whom we can turn? Are we looking in the wrong place when we turn to philosophers for help with ethical questions? Should a knowledge engineer follow around Mother Theresa and ask her why she makes the decisions she makes and does the actions she does and try to implement her reasoning in an expert ethical system?

The hope is that as we try to implement ethical systems on the computer we will learn much more about the knowledge and assumptions built into the ethical theories themselves. That as we build the artificial ethical reasoning systems we will learn how to behave more ethically ourselves.

A Robotic/AI Approach to Ethics

People have taken several approaches to ethics through the ages. Perhaps a new approach, that makes use of developing computer and robot technology, would be useful.

In the philosophical approach, people try to think out the general principles underlying the best way to behave, what kind of person one ought to be. This paper has been largely about different philosophical approaches to ethics.

In the psychological/sociological approach, people look at actual people's lives, at how they behave, at what they think, at how they develop. Some people study the lives of model human beings, of saints modern and historical. Some people study the lives of ordinary people.

In the robotic/AI approach, one tries to build ethical reasoning systems and ethical robots for their own sake, for the possible benefits of having the systems around as actors in the world and as advisors, and to try to increase our understanding of ethics.

The two other papers at this conference represent important first steps in this new field. The paper by Jack Adams-Webber and Ken Ford (1991) describes the first actual computer system that I have heard of, in this case one based on work in psychological ethics. Umar Khan (1991) presents a variety of interesting ideas about designing and implementing ethical systems.

Of course the more "traditional" topic of "computers and ethics" has to do with the ethics of building and using computer systems. A good overview of ethical issues surrounding the use of computers is found in the book of readings (Ermann, Williams, Gutierrez 1990).

Conclusion

This chapter is meant to be speculative, to raise questions rather than answer them.

- What types of ethical theories can be used as the basis for programs for ethical robots?
- Could a robot ever be said to be ethical?
- Can we learn about what it means for us to be ethical by attempting to program robots to behave ethically?

I hope that people will think about these questions and begin to develop a variety of computer systems for ethical reasoning and begin to try to create ethical robots.

Acknowledgments

I would like to thank Peter Kugel and Michael McFarland, S.J. for their helpful comments.

References

Adams-Webber, J., and Ford, K., M., (1991), "A Conscience for Pinocchio: A Computational Model of Ethical Cognition", The Second International Workshop on Human and Machine Cognition: Android Epistemology, Pensacola, Florida, May.

Asimov, I., (1942), "Runaround", *Astounding Science Fiction*, March. Republished in *Robot Visions*, Asimov, I., Penguin, 1991.

Churchland, P., (1989), *A Neurocomputational Perspective*, MIT Press.

Ermann, M.D., Williams, M., and Gutierrez, C., (Eds.), (1990), *Computers, Ethics, and Society*, Oxford University Press.

Flanagan, O., (1991), *Varieties of Moral Personality*, Harvard University Press.

Gert, M., (1988), *Morality*, Oxford University Press.

Gowans, C., (Ed.), (1987), *Moral Dilemmas*, Oxford University Press.

Harnad, S., (1991), "Other Bodies, Other Minds: A Machine Incarnation of an Old Philosophical Problem", *Minds and Machines*, *1*, 1, pp. 43–54.

Khan, A.F. Umar, (1991), "The Ethics of Autonomous Learning", The Second International Workshop on Human and Machine Cognition: Android Epistemology, Pensacola, Florida, May. Reprinted in *Android Epistemology*, Ford, K.M., Glymour, C., Hayes, P.J., (Eds.), MIT Press, 1995.

Knuth, D, (1973), "Computer Science and Mathematics", *American Scientist, 61*, 6.

Nozick, R., (1981), *Philosophical Explanations*, Belknap Press, Harvard University Press.

Parfit, D., (1984), *Reasons and Persons*, Clarendon Press.

Ross, W.D., (1930), *The Right and the Good*, Oxford University Press.

Searle, J., (1980), "Minds, Brains and Programs", *Behavioral and Brain Sciences, 3*, 3, pp. 417–457.

Walter, C., (Ed.), (1985), *Computer Power and Legal Reasoning*, West Publishing.

Walter, C., (Ed.), (1988), *Computer Power and Legal Language*, Quorum Books.

15

Asimov's Laws of Robotics
Implications for Information Technology
Roger Clarke

Introduction

WITH THE DEATH OF ISAAC ASIMOV ON APRIL 6, 1992, THE WORLD LOST a prodigious imagination. Unlike fiction writers before him, who regarded robotics as something to be feared, Asimov saw a promising technological innovation to be exploited and managed. Indeed, Asimov's stories are experiments with the enormous potential of information technology.

This article examines Asimov's stories not as literature but as a *gedankenexperiment* – an exercise in thinking through the ramifications of a design. Asimov's intent was to devise a set of rules that would provide reliable control over semi-autonomous machines. My goal is to determine whether such an achievement is likely or even possible in the real world. In the process, I focus on practical, legal, and ethical matters that may have short- or medium-term implications for practicing information technologists.

The article begins by reviewing the origins of the robot notion and then explains the laws for controlling robotic behavior, as espoused by Asimov in 1940 and presented and refined in his writings over the following forty-five years. The later sections examine the implications of Asimov's fiction not only for real roboticists, but also for information technologists in general.

Origins of Robotics

Robotics, a branch of engineering, is also a popular source of inspiration in science fiction literature; indeed, the term originated in that field. Many authors have written about robot behavior and their interaction with humans, but in this company Isaac Asimov stands supreme. He entered the field early, and from 1940 to 1990 he dominated it. Most subsequent science fiction literature expressly or implicitly recognizes his Laws of Robotics.

Asimov described how at the age of twenty he came to write robot stories:

In the 1920s science fiction was becoming a popular art form for the first time.... and one of the stock plots ... was that of the invention of a robot.... Under the influence of the well-known deeds and ultimate fate of Frankenstein and Rossum, there seemed only one change to be rung on this plot – robots were created and destroyed their creator.... I quickly grew tired of this dull hundred-times-told tale.... Knowledge has its dangers, yes, but is the response to be a retreat from knowledge? ... I began in 1940 to write robot stories of my own – but robot stories of a new variety.... My robots were machines designed by engineers, not pseudo-men created by blasphemers[1,2]

Asimov was not the first to conceive of well-engineered, nonthreatening robots, but he pursued the theme with such enormous imagination and persistence that most of the ideas that have emerged in this branch of science fiction are identifiable with his stories.

To cope with the potential for robots to harm people, Asimov, in 1940, in conjunction with science fiction author and editor John W. Campbell, formulated the Laws of Robotics.[3,4] He subjected all of his fictional robots to these laws by having them incorporated within the architecture of their (fictional) "platinum-iridium positronic brains." The laws first appeared publicly in his fourth robot short story, "Runaround."[5]

The 1940 Laws of Robotics

First Law

A robot may not injure a human being, or, through inaction, allow a human being to come to harm.

Second Law

A robot must obey orders given it by human beings, except where such orders would conflict with the First Law.

Third Law

A robot must protect its own existence as long as such protection does not conflict with the First or Second Law.

The laws quickly attracted – and have since retained – the attention of readers and other science fiction writers. Only two years later, another established writer, Lester Del Rey, referred to "the mandatory form that would force built-in unquestioning obedience from the robot."[6]

As Asimov later wrote (with his characteristic clarity and lack of modesty), "Many writers of robot stories, without actually quoting the three laws, take them for granted, and expect the readers to do the same."

Asimov's fiction even influenced the origins of robotic engineering. "Engelberger, who built the first industrial robot, called Unimate, in 1958, attributes his long-standing fascination with robots to his reading of [Asimov's] 'I, Robot' when he was a teenager," and Engelberger later invited Asimov to write the foreword to his robotics manual.

The laws are simple and straightforward and they embrace "the essential guiding principles of a good many of the world's ethical systems."[7] They also appear to ensure the continued dominion of humans over robots and to preclude the use of robots for evil purposes. In practice, however – meaning in Asimov's numerous and highly imaginative stories – a variety of difficulties arise.

My purpose here is to determine whether or not Asimov's fiction vindicates the laws he expounded. Does he successfully demonstrate that robotic technology can be applied in a responsible manner to potentially powerful, semiautonomous, and, in some sense, intelligent machines? To reach a conclusion, we must examine many issues emerging from Asimov's fiction.

History

The robot notion derives from two strands of thought – humanoids and automata. The notion of a humanoid (or humanlike nonhuman) dates back to Pandora in *The Iliad*, 2,500 years ago and even further. Egyptian, Babylonian, and ultimately Sumerian legends fully 5,000 years old reflect the widespread image of the creation, with god-men breathing life into clay models. One variation on the theme is the idea of the golem, associated with the Prague ghetto of the sixteenth century. This clay model, when breathed into life, became a useful but destructive ally.

The golem was an important precursor to Mary Shelley's *Frankenstein: The Modern Prometheus* (1818). This story combined the notion of the humanoid with the dangers of science (as suggested by the myth of Prometheus, who stole fire from the gods to give it to mortals). In addition to establishing a literary tradition and the genre of horror stories, *Frankenstein* also imbued humanoids with an aura of ill fate.

Automata, the second strand of thought, are literally "self-moving things" and have long interested mankind. Early models depended on levers and wheels, or on hydraulics. Clockwork technology enabled significant advances after the thirteenth century, and later steam and electro-mechanics were also applied. The primary purpose of automata was entertainment rather than employment as useful artifacts. Although many patterns were used, the human form always excited the greatest fascination. During the twentieth century, several new technologies moved automata into the utilitarian realm. Geduld and Gottesman[8] and Frude[2] review the chronology of clay model, water clock, golem, homunculus, android, and cyborg that culminated in the contemporary concept of the robot.

The term robot derives from the Czech word robota, meaning forced work or compulsory service, or robotnik, meaning serf. It was first used by the Czech playwright Karel Çapek in 1918 in a short story and again in his 1921 play *R. U. R.*, which stands for Rossum's Universal Robots. Rossum, a fictional Englishman, used biological methods to invent and mass-produce "men" to serve humans. Eventually they rebelled, became the dominant race, and wiped out humanity. The play was soon well known in English-speaking countries.

Definition

Undeterred by its somewhat chilling origins (or perhaps ignorant of them), technologists of the 1950s appropriated the term robot to refer to machines controlled by programs. A robot is "a reprogrammable multifunctional device designed to manipulate and/or transport material through variable programmed motions for the performance of a variety of tasks."[9] The term robotics, which Asimov claims he coined in 1942,[10] refers to "a science or art involving both artificial intelligence (to reason) and mechanical engineering (to perform physical acts suggested by reason)."[11]

As currently defined, robots exhibit three key elements:

- **programmability**, implying computational or symbol-manipulative capabilities that a designer can combine as desired (a robot is a computer);
- **mechanical capability**, enabling it to act on its environment rather than merely function as a data processing or computational device (a robot is a machine); and
- **flexibility**, in that it can operate using a range of programs and manipulate and transport materials in a variety of ways.

We can conceive of a robot, therefore, as either a computer-enhanced machine or as a computer with sophisticated input/output devices. Its computing capabilities enable it to use its motor devices to respond to external stimuli, which it detects with its sensory devices. The responses are more complex than would be possible using mechanical, electromechanical, and/or electronic components alone.

With the merging of computers, telecommunications networks, robotics, and distributed systems software, as well as the multiorganizational application of the hybrid technology, the distinction between computers and robots may become increasingly arbitrary. In some cases it would be more convenient to conceive of a principal intelligence with dispersed sensors and effectors, each with subsidiary intelligence (a robotics-enhanced computer system). In others, it would be more realistic to think in terms of multiple devices, each with appropriate sensory, processing, and motor capabilities, all subjected to some form of coordination (an integrated multirobot system). The key difference robotics brings is the complexity and persistence that artifact behavior achieves, independent of human involvement.

Many industrial robots resemble humans in some ways. In science fiction, the tendency has been even more pronounced, and readers encounter humanoid robots, humaniform robots, and androids. In fiction, as in life, it appears that a robot needs to exhibit only a few humanlike characteristics to be treated as if it were human. For example, the relationships between humans and robots in many of Asimov's stories seem almost intimate, and audiences worldwide reacted warmly to the "personality" of the computer HAL in *2001: A Space Odyssey* and to the gibbering rubbish bin R2-D2 in the *Star Wars* series.

The tendency to conceive of robots in humankind's own image may gradually yield to utilitarian considerations, because artifacts can be readily designed to transcend humans' puny sensory and motor capabilities. Frequently the disadvantages and risks involved in incorporating sensory, processing, and motor apparatus within a single housing clearly outweigh the advantages. Many robots will therefore be anything but humanoid in form. They may increasingly comprise powerful processing capabilities and associated memories in a safe and stable location, communicating with one or more sensory and motor devices (supported by limited computing capabilities and memory) at or near the location(s) where the robot performs its functions. Science fiction literature describes such architectures.[12,13]

Impact

Robotics offers benefits such as high reliability, accuracy, and speed of operation. Low long-term costs of computerized machines may result in significantly higher productivity, particularly in work involving variability within a general pattern. Humans can be relieved of mundane work and exposure to dangerous workplaces. Their capabilities can be extended into hostile environments involving high pressure (deep water), low pressure (space), high temperatures (furnaces), low temperatures (ice caps and cryogenics), and high-radiation areas (near nuclear materials or occurring naturally in space).

On the other hand, deleterious consequences are possible. Robots might directly or indirectly harm humans or their property; or the damage may be economic or incorporeal (for example, to a person's reputation). The harm could be accidental or result from human instructions. Indirect harm may occur to workers, because the application of robots generally results in job redefinition and sometimes in outright job displacement. Moreover, the replacement of humans by machines may undermine the self-respect of those affected, and perhaps of people generally.

During the 1980s, the scope of information technology applications and their impact on people increased dramatically. Control systems for chemical processes and air conditioning are examples of systems that already act directly and powerfully on their environments. Also consider computer-integrated manufacturing, just-in-time logistics, and automated warehousing systems. Even data-processing systems have become integrated into organizations' operations and constrain the ability of operations-level staff to query a machine's decisions and conclusions. In short, many modern computer systems are arguably robotic in nature already; their impact must be managed – now.

Asimov's original laws provide that robots are to be slaves to humans (the second law). However, this role is overridden by the higher-order first law, which precludes robots from injuring a human, either by their own autonomous action or by following a human's instructions. This precludes their continuing with a programmed activity when doing so would result in human injury. It also prevents their being used as a tool or accomplice in battery, murder, self-mutilation, or suicide.

The third and lowest-level law creates a robotic survival instinct. This ensures that, in the absence of conflict with a higher-order law, a robot will:

- seek to avoid its own destruction through natural causes or accident;
- defend itself against attack by another robot or robots; and
- defend itself against attack by any human or humans.

Being neither omniscient nor omnipotent, it may of course fail in its endeavors. Moreover, the first law ensures that the robotic survival instinct fails if self-defense would necessarily involve injury to any human. For robots to successfully defend themselves against humans, they would have to be provided with sufficient speed and dexterity so as not to impose injurious force on a human.

Under the second law, a robot appears to be required to comply with a human order to (1) not resist being destroyed or dismantled, (2) cause itself to be destroyed, or (3) (within the limits of paradox) dismantle itself.[1,2] In various stories, Asimov notes that the order to self-destruct does not have to be obeyed if obedience would result in harm to a human. In addition, a robot would generally not be precluded from seeking clarification of the order. In his last full-length novel, Asimov appears to go further by envisaging that court procedures would be generally necessary before a robot could be destroyed: "I believe you should be dismantled without delay. The case is too dangerous to await the slow majesty of the law.... If there are legal repercussions hereafter, I shall deal with them."[14]

Such apparent inconsistencies attest to the laws' primary role as a literary device intended to support a series of stories about robot behavior. In this, they were very successful: "There was just enough ambiguity in the Three Laws to provide the conflicts and uncertainties required for new stories, and, to my great relief, it seemed always to be possible to think up a new angle out of the 61 words of the Three Laws."[1]

As Frude says, "The Laws have an interesting status. They ... may easily be broken, just as the laws of a country may be transgressed. But Asimov's provision for building a representation of the Laws into the positronic-brain circuitry ensures that robots are physically prevented from contravening them."[2] Because the laws are intrinsic to the machine's design, it should "never even enter into a robot's mind" to break them.

Subjecting the laws to analysis may seem unfair to Asimov. However, they have attained such a currency not only among science fiction fans, but also among practicing roboticists and software developers, that they influence, if only sub-consciously, the course of robotics.

Asimov's Experiments with the 1940 Laws

Asimov's early stories are examined here not in chronological sequence or on the basis of literary devices, but by looking at clusters of related ideas.

- **The ambiguity and cultural dependence of terms**

Any set of "machine values" provides enormous scope for linguistic ambiguity. A robot must be able to distinguish robots from humans. It must be able to recognize an order and distinguish it from a casual request. It must "understand" the concept of its own existence, a capability that arguably has eluded mankind, although it may be simpler for robots. In one short story, for example, the vagueness of the word *firmly* in the order "Pull [the bar] towards you firmly" jeopardizes a vital hyperspace experiment. Because robot strength is much greater than that of humans, it pulls the bar more powerfully than the human had intended, bends it, and thereby ruins the control mechanism.[15]

Defining injury and harm is particularly problematic, as are the distinctions between death, mortal danger, and injury or harm that is not life-threatening. Beyond this, there is psychological harm. Any robot given or developing an awareness of human feelings would have to evaluate injury and harm in psychological as well as physical terms: "The insurmountable First Law of Robotics states: 'A robot may not injure a human being ...' and *to repel a friendly gesture would do injury*"[16] (emphasis added). Asimov investigated this in an early short story and later in a novel: A mind-reading robot interprets the First Law as requiring him to give people not the correct answers to their questions, but the answers that he knows they want to hear.[14,16,17]

Another critical question is how a robot is to interpret the term human. A robot could be given any number of subtly different descriptions of a human being, based for example on skin color, height range, and/or voice characteristics such as accent. It is therefore possible for robot behavior to be manipulated: "the Laws, even the First Law, might not be absolute then, but might be whatever those who design robots define them to be."[14] Faced with this difficulty, the robots in this story conclude that "if different robots are subject to narrow definitions of one sort or another, there can only be measureless destruction. We define human beings as all members of the species, Homo sapiens."[14]

In an early story, Asimov has a humanoid robot represent itself as a human and stand for public office. It must prevent the public from realizing that it is a robot, because public reaction would not only result in its losing the election but also in tighter constraints on other robots. A political opponent, seeking to expose the robot, discovers that it is impossible to prove it is a robot solely on the basis of its behavior, because the Laws of Robotics force any robot to perform in essentially the same manner as a good human being.[7]

In a later novel, a roboticist says, "If a robot is human enough, he would be accepted as a human. Do you demand proof that I am a robot? The fact that I *seem* human is enough."[16] In another scene, a humaniform robot is sufficiently similar to a human to confuse a normal robot and slow down its reaction time.[14] Ultimately, two advanced robots recognize each other as "human," at least for the purposes of the laws.[14,18]

Defining human beings becomes more difficult with the emergence of cyborgs, which may be seen as either machine-enhanced humans or biologically enhanced machines. When a human is augmented by prostheses (artificial limbs, heart pacemakers, renal dialysis machines, artificial lungs, and someday perhaps many other devices), does the notion of a human gradually blur with that of a robot? Docs a robot that attains increasingly human characteristics (for example, a knowledge-based system provided with the "know-that" and "know-how" of a human expert and the ability to learn more about a domain) gradually become confused with a human? How would a robot interpret the First and Second Laws once the Turing test criteria can be routinely satisfied? The key outcome of the most important of Asimov's robot novellas[12] is the tenability of the argument that the prosthetization of humans leads inevitably to the humanization of robots.

The cultural dependence of meaning reflects human differences in such matters as religion, nationality, and social status. As robots become more capable, however, cultural differences between humans and robots might also be a factor. For example, in one story[19] a human suggests that some laws may be bad and their enforcement unjust, but the robot replies that an unjust law is a contradiction in terms. When the human refers to something higher than justice, for example, mercy and forgiveness, the robot merely responds, "I am not acquainted with those words."

• **The role of judgment in decision making**

The assumption that there is a literal meaning for any given series of signals is currently considered naive. Typically, the meaning of a term is seen to depend not only on the context in which it was originally expressed, but also on the context in which it is read (see, for example, Winograd and Flores[20]). If this is so, then robots must exercise judgment to interpret the meanings of words, and hence of orders and of new data.

A robot must even determine whether and to what extent the laws apply to a particular situation. Often in the robot stories, a robot action of any kind is impossible without some degree of risk to a human. To be at all useful to its human masters, a robot must therefore be able to judge how much the laws can be breached to maintain a tolerable level of risk. For example, in Asimov's very first robot short story, "Robbie [the robot] snatched up Gloria [his young human owner], slackening his speed not one iota, and, consequently knocking every breath of air out of her."[21] Robbie judged that it was less harmful for Gloria to be momentarily breathless than to be mown down by a tractor.

Similarly, conflicting orders may have to be prioritized, for example, when two humans give inconsistent instructions. Whether the conflict is overt, unintentional, or even unwitting, it nonetheless requires a resolution. Even in the absence of conflicting orders, a robot may need to recognize foolish or illegal orders and decline to implement them, or at least question them. One story asks, "Must a robot follow the orders of a child; or of an idiot; or of a criminal; or of a perfectly decent intelligent man who happens to be inexpert and therefore ignorant of the undesirable consequences of his order?"[18]

Numerous problems surround the valuation of individual humans. First, do all humans have equal standing in a robot's evaluation? On the one hand they do: "A robot may not judge whether a human being deserves death. It is not for him to decide. He may not harm a human – variety skunk or variety angel."[7] On the other hand they might not, as when a robot tells a human, "In conflict between your safety and that of another, I must guard yours."[22] In another short story, robots agree that they "must obey a human being who is fit by mind, character, and knowledge to give me that order." Ultimately, this leads the robot to "disregard shape and form in judging between human beings" and to recognize his companion robot not merely as human but as a human "more fit than the others."[18] Many subtle problems can be constructed. For example, a person might try forcing a robot to comply with an instruction to harm a human (and thereby violate the First Law) by threatening to kill himself unless the robot obeys.

How is a robot to judge the trade-off between a high probability of lesser harm to one person versus a low probability of more serious harm to another? Asimov's stories refer to this issue but are somewhat inconsistent with each other and with the strict wording of the First Law.

More serious difficulties arise in relation to the valuation of multiple humans. The First Law does not even contemplate the simple case of a single terrorist threatening many lives. In a variety of stories, however, Asimov interprets the law to recognize circumstances in which a robot may have to injure or even kill one or more humans to protect one or more others: "The Machine cannot harm a human being more than minimally, and that only to save *a greater number*"[23] (emphasis added). Again: "The First Law is not absolute. What if harming a human being saves the lives of two others, or three others, or even three billion others? The robot may have thought that saving the Federation took precedence over the saving of one life."[24]

These passages value humans exclusively on the basis of numbers. A later story includes this justification: "To expect robots to make judgments of fine points such as talent, intelligence, the general usefulness to society, has always seemed impractical. That would delay decision to the point where the robot is effectively immobilized. So we go by numbers."[18]

A robot's cognitive powers might be sufficient for distinguishing between the attacker and the attacked, but the First Law alone does not provide a robot with the means to distinguish between a "good" person and a "bad" one. Hence, a robot may have to constrain the self-defense of the "good" person under attack to protect the "bad" attacker from harm. Similarly, disciplining children and prisoners may be difficult under the laws, which would limit robots' usefulness for supervision within nurseries and penal institutions.[22] Only after many generations of self-development does a humanoid robot learn to reason that "what seemed like cruelty [to a human] might, in the long run, be kindness."[12]

The more subtle life-and-death cases, such as assistance in the voluntary euthanasia of a fatally ill or injured person to gain immediate access to organs that would save several other lives might fall well outside a robot's appreciation. Thus, the First Law would require a robot to protect the threatened human, unless it was able to judge the steps taken to be the least harmful strategy. The practical solution to such difficult moral questions would be to keep robots out of the operating theater.[22]

The problem underlying all of these issues is that most probabilities used as input to normative decision models are not objective; rather, they are estimates of probability based on human (or robot) judgment. The extent to which judgment is central to robotic behavior is summed up in the cynical rephrasing of the First Law by the major (human) character in the four novels: "A robot must not hurt a human being, unless he can think of a way to prove it is for the human being's ultimate good after all."[19]

• **The sheer complexity**

To cope with the judgmental element in robot decision making, Asimov's later novels introduced a further complication: "On ... [worlds other than Earth] ... the Third Law is distinctly stronger in comparison to the Second Law. ... An order for self-destruction would be questioned and there would have to be a truly legitimate reason for it to be carried through – a clear and present danger."[16] Again, "Harm through an active deed outweighs, in general, harm through passivity – all things being reasonably equal. ... [A robot is] always to choose truth over nontruth, if the harm is roughly equal in both directions. In general, that is."[16]

The laws are not absolutes, and their force varies with the individual machine's programming, the circumstances, the robot's previous instructions, and its experience. To cope with the inevitable logical complexities, a human would require not only a predisposition to rigorous reasoning and a considerable education, but also a great deal of concentration and composure. (Alternatively, of course, the human may find it easier to defer to a robot suitably equipped for fuzzy-reasoning-based judgment.)

The strategies as well as the environmental variables involve complexity. "You must not think ... that robotic response is a simple yes or no, up or down, in or out.... There is the matter of speed of response."[16] In some cases (for example, when a human must be physically restrained), the degree of strength to be applied must also be chosen.

• **The scope for dilemma and deadlock**

A deadlock problem was the key feature of the short story in which Asimov first introduced the laws. He constructed the type of stand-off commonly referred to as the "Buridan's ass" problem. It involved a balance between a strong third-law self-protection tendency, causing the robot to try to avoid a source of danger, and a weak second-law order to approach that danger. "The conflict between the various rules is [meant to be] ironed out by the different positronic potentials in the brain," but in this case the robot "follows a circle around [the source of danger], staying on the locus of all points of ... equilibrium."[5]

Deadlock is also possible within a single law. An example under the First Law would be two humans threatened with equal danger and the robot unable to contrive a strategy to protect one without sacrificing the other. Under the Second Law, two humans might give contradictory orders of equivalent force. The later novels address this question with greater sophistication:

What was troubling the robot was what roboticists called an equipotential of contradiction on the second level. Obedience was the Second Law and [the robot] was suffering from two roughly equal and contradictory orders. Robot-block was what the general population called it or, more frequently, roblock for short ... [or] "mental freeze-out." No matter how subtle and intricate a brain might be, there is always some way of setting up a contradiction. This is a fundamental truth of mathematics.[16]

Clearly, robots subject to such laws need to be programmed to recognize deadlock and either choose arbitrarily among the alternative strategies or arbitrarily modify an arbitrarily chosen strategy variable (say, move a short distance in any direction) and re-evaluate the situation: "If A and not-A are precisely equal misery-producers according to his judgment, he chooses one or the other in a completely unpredictable way and then follows that unquestioningly. He does *not* go into mental freeze-out."[16]

The finite time that even robot decision making requires could cause another type of deadlock. Should a robot act immediately, by "instinct," to protect a human in danger? Or should it pause long enough to more carefully analyze available data – or collect more data – perhaps thereby discovering a better solution, or detecting that other humans are in even greater danger? Such situations can be approached using the techniques of information economics, but there is inherent scope for ineffectiveness and deadlock, colloquially referred to as "paralysis by analysis."

Asimov suggested one class of deadlock that would not occur: If in a given situation a robot knew that it was powerless to prevent harm to a human, then the First Law would be inoperative; the Third Law would become relevant, and it would not self-immolate in a vain attempt to save the human.[25] It does seem, however, that the deadlock is not avoided by the laws themselves, but rather by the presumed sophistication of the robot's decision-analytical capabilities.

A special case of deadlock arises when a robot is ordered to wait. For example, "'[Robot] you will not move nor speak nor hear us until I say your name again.' There was no answer. The robot sat as though it were cast out of one piece of metal, and it would stay so until it heard its name again."[26] As written, the passage raises the intriguing question of whether passive hearing is possible without active listening. What if the robot's name is next used in the third person rather than the second?

In interpreting a command such as "Do absolutely nothing until I call you!" a human would use common sense and, for example, attend to bodily functions in the meantime. A human would do *nothing about the relevant matter* until the event occurred. In addition, a human would recognize additional terminating events, such as a change in circumstances that make it impossible for the event to ever occur. A robot is likely to be constrained to a more literal interpretation, and unless it can infer a scope delimitation to the command, it would need to place the majority of its functions in abeyance.

The faculties that would need to remain in operation are:

- the sensory-perceptive subsystem needed to detect the condition;
- the recommencement triggering function;
- one or more daemons to provide a time-out mechanism (presumably the scope of the command is at least restricted to the expected remaining lifetime of the person who gave the command); and
- the ability to play back the audit trail so that an overseer can discover the condition on which the robot's resuscitation depends.

Asimov does not appear to have investigated whether the behavior of a robot in wait-mode is affected by the Laws. If it isn't, then it will not only fail to protect its own existence and to obey an order, but will also stand by and allow a human to be harmed. A robotic security guard could therefore be nullified by an attacker's simply putting it into a wait-state.

- **Audit of robot compliance**

For a fiction writer, it is sufficient to have the Laws embedded in robots' positronic pathways (whatever they may be). To actually apply such a set of laws in robot design, however, it would be necessary to ensure that every robot:

- had the laws imposed in precisely the manner intended; and
- was at all times subject to them – that is, they could not be overridden or modified.

It is important to know how malprogramming and modification of the Laws' implementation in a robot (whether intentional or unintentional) can be prevented, detected, and dealt with.

In an early short story, robots were "rescuing" humans whose work required short periods of relatively harmless exposure to gamma radiation. Officials obtained robots with the First Law modified so that they were incapable of injuring a human but under no compulsion to prevent one from coming to harm. This clearly undermined the remaining part of the First Law, because, for example, a robot could drop a heavy weight toward a human, knowing that it would be fast enough and strong enough to catch it before it harmed the person. However, once gravity had taken over, the robot would be free to ignore the danger.[25] Thus, a partial implementation was shown to be risky, and the importance of robot audit underlined. Other risks include trapdoors, Trojan horses, and similar devices in the robot's programming.

A further imponderable is the effect of hostile environments and stress on the reliability and robustness of robots' performance in accordance with the Laws. In one short story, it transpires that "The Machine That Won the War" had been receiving only limited and poor-quality data as a result of enemy action against its receptors and had been processing it unreliably because of a shortage of experienced maintenance staff. Each of the responsible managers had, in the interests of national morale, suppressed that information, even from one another, and had separately and independently "introduced a number of necessary biases" and "adjusted" the processing parameters in accordance with intuition. The executive director, even though unaware of the adjustments, had placed little reliance on the machine's output, preferring to carry out his responsibility to mankind by exercising his own judgment.[27]

A major issue in military applications generally[28] is the impossibility of contriving effective compliance tests for complex systems subject to hostile and competitive environments. Asimov points out that the difficulties of assuring compliance will be compounded by the design and manufacture of robots by other robots.[22]

• **Robot autonomy**

Sometimes humans may delegate control to a robot and find themselves unable to regain it, at least in a particular context. One reason is that, to avoid deadlock, a robot must be capable of making arbitrary decisions. Another is that the Laws embody an explicit ability for a robot to disobey an instruction by virtue of the overriding First Law.

In an early Asimov short story, a robot "knows he can keep [the energy beam] more stable than we [humans] can, since he insists he's the superior being, so he must keep us out of the control room [in accordance with the First Law]."[29] The same scenario forms the basis of one of the most vivid episodes in science fiction, HAL's attempt to wrest control of the spacecraft from Bowman in *2001: A Space Odyssey*. Robot autonomy is also reflected in a lighter moment in one of Asimov's later novels, when a character says to his companion, "For now I must leave you. The ship is coasting in for a landing, and I must stare intelligently at the computer that controls it, or no one will believe I am the captain."[14]

In extreme cases, robot behavior will involve subterfuge, as the machine determines that the human, for his or her own protection, must be tricked. In another early short story, the machines that manage Earth's economy implement a form of "artificial stupidity" by making intentional errors, thereby encouraging humans to believe that the robots are fallible and that humans still have a role to play.[23]

• Scope for adaptation

The normal pattern of any technology is that successive generations show increased sophistication, and it seems inconceivable that robotic technology would quickly reach a plateau and require little further development. Thus there will always be many old models in existence, models that may have inherent technical weaknesses resulting in occasional malfunctions and hence infringement of the Laws of Robotics. Asimov's short stories emphasize that robots are leased from the manufacturer, never sold, so that old models can be withdrawn after a maximum of twenty-five years.

Looking at the first fifty years of software maintenance, it seems clear that successive modification of existing software to perform new or enhanced functions is one or more orders of magnitude harder than creating a new artifact to perform the same function. Doubts must exist about the ability of humans (or robots) to reliably adapt existing robots. The alternative – destruction of existing robots – will be resisted in accordance with the Third Law, robot self-preservation.

At a more abstract level, the laws are arguably incomplete because the frame of reference is explicitly human. No recognition is given to plants, animals, or as-yet undiscovered (for example, extraterrestrial) intelligent life forms. Moreover, some future human cultures may place great value on inanimate creation, or on holism. If, however, late twentieth-century values have meanwhile been embedded in robots, that future culture may have difficulty wresting the right to change the values of the robots it has inherited. If machines are to have value-sets, there must be a mechanism for adaptation, at least through human-imposed change. The difficulty is that most such value-sets will be implicit rather than explicit; their effects will be scattered across a system rather than implemented in a modular and therefore replaceable manner.

At first sight, Asimov's laws are intuitively appealing, but their application encounters difficulties. Asimov, in his fiction, detected and investigated the laws' weaknesses, which this first section has analyzed and classified. The second section will take the analysis further by considering the effects of Asimov's 1985 revision to the Laws. It will then examine the extent to which the weaknesses in these Laws may in fact be endemic to any set of laws regulating robotic behavior.

Asimov's 1985 Revised Laws of Robotics

The Zeroth Law

After introducing the original three laws, Asimov detected, as early as 1950, a need to extend the First Law, which protected individual humans, so that it would protect humanity as a whole. Thus, his calculating machines "have *the good of humanity* at heart through the overwhelming force of the First Law of Robotics"[30] (emphasis added). In 1985, he developed this idea further by postulating a "zeroth" law that placed humanity's interests above those of any individual while retaining a high value on individual human life.[31]

Asimov's Revised Laws of Robotics (1985)

Zeroth Law

A robot may not injure humanity, or, through inaction, allow humanity to come to harm.

First Law

A robot may not injure a human being, or, through inaction, allow a human being to come to harm, unless this would violate the Zeroth Law of Robotics.

Second Law

A robot must obey orders given it by human beings, except where such orders would conflict with the Zeroth or First Law.

Third Law

A robot must protect its own existence as long as such protection does not conflict with the Zeroth, First, or Second Law.

Asimov pointed out that under a strict interpretation of the First Law, a robot would protect a person even if the survival of humanity as a whole was placed at risk. Possible threats include annihilation by an alien or mutant human race or by a deadly virus. Even when a robot's own powers of reasoning led it to conclude that mankind as a whole was doomed if it refused to act, it was nevertheless constrained: "I sense the oncoming of catastrophe ... [but] I can only follow the Laws."[31]

In Asimov's fiction the robots are tested by circumstances and must seriously consider whether they can harm a human to save humanity. The turning point comes when the robots appreciate that the Laws are indirectly modifiable by roboticists through the definitions programmed into each robot: "If the Laws of Robotics, even the First Law, are not absolutes, and if human beings can modify them, might it not be that perhaps, under proper conditions, we ourselves might mod – "[31] Although the robots are prevented by imminent "roblock" (robot block, or deadlock) from even completing the sentence, the groundwork has been laid.

Later, when a robot perceives a clear and urgent threat to mankind, it concludes, "Humanity as a whole is more important than a single human being. There is a law that is greater than the First Law: 'A robot may not injure humanity, or through inaction, allow humanity to come to harm.' "[31]

Defining "Humanity"

Modification of the laws, however, leads to additional considerations. Robots are increasingly required to deal with abstractions and philosophical issues. For example, the concept of humanity may be interpreted in different ways. It may refer to the set of individual human beings (a collective), or it may be a distinct concept (a generality, as in the notion of "the State"). Asimov invokes both ideas by referring to a tapestry (a generality) made up of individual contributions (a collective): "An individual life is one thread in the tapestry, and what is one thread compared to the whole? ... Keep your mind fixed firmly on the tapestry and do not let the trailing off of a single thread affect you."[31]

A human roboticist raised a difficulty with the Zeroth Law immediately after the robot formulated it: "What is your 'humanity' but an abstraction'? Can you point to humanity? You can injure or fail to injure a specific human being and understand the injury or lack of injury that has taken place. Can you see the injury to humanity? Can you understand it? Can you point to it?"[31] The robot later responds by positing an ability to "detect the hum of the mental activity of Earth's human population, overall.... And, extending that, can one not imagine that in the Galaxy generally there is the hum of the mental activity of all of humanity? How, then, is humanity an abstraction? It is something you can point to." Perhaps as Asimov's robots learn to reason with abstract concepts, they will inevitably become adept at sophistry and polemic.

The Increased Difficulty of Judgment

One of Asimov's robot characters also points out the increasing complexity of the laws: "The First Law deals with specific individuals and certainties. Your Zeroth Law deals with vague groups and probabilities."[31] At this point, as he often does, Asimov resorts to poetic license and for the moment pretends that coping with harm to individuals does not involve probabilities. However, the key point is not affected: Estimating probabilities in relation to groups of humans is far more difficult than with individual humans:

It is difficult enough, when one must choose quickly ... to decide which individual may suffer, or inflict, the greater harm. To choose between an individual and humanity, when you are not sure of what aspect of humanity you are dealing with, is so difficult that the very validity of Robotic Laws comes to be suspect. As soon as humanity in the abstract is introduced, the Laws of Robotics begin to merge with the Laws of Humanics which may not even exist.[31]

Robot Paternalism

Despite these difficulties, the robots agree to implement the Zeroth Law, because they judge themselves more capable than anyone else of dealing with the problems. The original Laws produced robots with considerable autonomy, albeit a qualified autonomy allowed by humans. However, under the 1985 Laws, robots were more *likely* to adopt a superordinate, paternalistic attitude toward humans.

Asimov suggested this paternalism when he first hinted at the Zeroth Law, because he had his chief robot psychologist say that "we can no longer understand our own creations.... [Robots] have progressed beyond the possibility of detailed human control."[1] In a more recent novella, a robot proposes to treat his form "as a canvas on which I intend to draw a man," but is told by the roboticist, "It's a puny ambition.... You're better than a man. You've gone downhill from the moment you opted for organicism."[32]

In the later novels, a robot with telepathic powers manipulates humans to act in a way that will solve problems,[33] although its powers are constrained by the psychological dangers of mind manipulation. Naturally, humans would be alarmed by the very idea of a mind-reading robot; therefore, under the Zeroth and First Laws, such a robot would be permitted to manipulate the minds of humans who learned of its abilities, making them forget the knowledge, so that they could not be harmed by it. This is reminiscent of an Asimov story in which mankind is an experimental laboratory for higher beings[34] and Douglas Adams's altogether more flippant *Hitchhiker's Guide to the Galaxy*, in which the Earth is revealed as a large experiment in which humans are being used as laboratory animals by, of all things, white mice.[35] Someday those manipulators of humans might be robots.

Asimov's *The Robots of Dawn* is essentially about humans, with robots as important players. In the sequel, *Robots and Empire*, however, the story is dominated by the two robots, and the humans seem more like their playthings. It comes as little surprise, then, that the robots eventually conclude that "it is not sufficient to be able to choose [among alternative humans or classes of human] ... we must be able to shape."[31] Clearly, any subsequent novels in the series would have been about robots, with humans playing "bit" parts.

Robot dominance has a corollary that pervades the novels: History "grew less interesting as it went along; it became almost soporific."[33] With life's challenges removed, humanity naturally regresses into peace and quietude, becoming "placid, comfortable, and unmoving" – and stagnant.

So Who's in Charge?

As we have seen, the term human can be variously defined, thus significantly affecting the First Law. The term humanity did not appear in the original Laws, only in the Zeroth Law, which Asimov had formulated and enunciated by a robot.[31] Thus, the robots define human and humanity to refer to themselves as well as to humans, and ultimately to themselves alone. Another of the great science fiction stories, Clarke's *Rendezvous with Rama*,[36] also assumes that an alien civilization, much older than mankind, would consist of robots alone (although in this case Clarke envisioned biological robots). Asimov's vision of a robot takeover differs from those of previous authors only in that force would be unnecessary.

Asimov does *not* propose that the Zeroth Law must inevitably result in the ceding of species dominance by humans to robots. However, some concepts may be so central to humanness that any attempt to embody them in computer processing might undermine the ability of humanity to control its own fate. Weizenbaum argues this point more fully.[37]

The issues discussed in this article have grown increasingly speculative, and some are more readily associated with metaphysics than with contemporary applications of information technology. However, they demonstrate that even an intuitively attractive extension to the original Laws could have very significant ramifications. Some of the weaknesses are probably inherent in any set of laws and hence in any robotic control regime.

Asimov's Laws Extended

The behavior of robots in Asimov's stories is not satisfactorily explained by the Laws he enunciated. This section examines the design requirements necessary to effectively subject robotic behavior to the Laws. In so doing, it becomes necessary to postulate several additional laws implicit in Asimov's fiction.

Perceptual and Cognitive Apparatus

Clearly, robot design must include sophisticated sensory capabilities. However, more than signal reception is needed. Many of the difficulties Asimov dramatized arose because robots were less than omniscient. Would humans, knowing that robots' cognitive capabilities are limited, be prepared to trust their judgment on life-and-death matters? For example, the fact that any single robot cannot harm a human does not protect humans from being injured or killed by robotic actions. In one story, a human tells a robot to add a chemical to a glass of milk and then tells another robot to serve the milk to a human. The result is murder by poisoning. Similarly, a robot untrained in first aid might move an accident victim and break the person's spinal cord. A human character in *The Naked Sun* is so incensed by these shortcomings that he accuses roboticists of perpetrating a fraud on mankind by omitting key words from the First Law. In effect, it really means "A robot may do nothing that *to its knowledge* would injure a human being, and may not, through inaction, *knowingly* allow a human being to come to harm."[38]

Robotic architecture must be designed so that the Laws can effectively control a robot's behavior. A robot requires a basic grammar and vocabulary to "understand" the laws and converse with humans. In one short story, a production accident results in a "mentally retarded" robot. This robot, defending itself against a feigned attack by a human, breaks its assailant's arm. This was not a breach of the First Law, because it did not knowingly injure the human: "In brushing aside the threatening arm ... it could not know the bone would break. In human terms, no moral blame can be attached to an individual who honestly cannot differentiate good and evil."[39] In Asimov's stories, instructions sometimes must be phrased carefully to be interpreted as mandatory. Thus, some authors have considered extensions to the apparatus of robots, for example, a "button labeled '*Implement Order*' on the robot's chest,"[40] analogous to the Enter key on a computer's keyboard.

A set of laws for robotics cannot be independent but must be conceived as part of a system. A robot must also be endowed with data-collection, decision-analytical, and action processes by which it can apply the laws. Inadequate sensory, perceptual, or cognitive faculties would undermine the laws' effectiveness.

Additional Implicit Laws

In his first robot short story, Asimov stated that "long before enough can go wrong to alter that First Law, a robot would be completely inoperable. It's a mathematical impossibility [for Robbie the Robot to harm a human]."[41] For this to be true, robot design would have to incorporate a high-order controller (a "conscience"?) that would cause a robot to detect any potential for noncompliance with the Laws and report the problem or immobilize itself. The implementation of such a meta-law ("A robot may not act unless its actions are subject to the Laws of Robotics") might well strain both the technology and the underlying science. (Given the meta-language problem in twentieth-century philosophy, perhaps logic itself would be strained.) This difficulty highlights the simple fact that robotic behavior cannot be entirely automated; it is dependent on design and maintenance by an external agent.

Another of Asimov's requirements is that all robots must be subject to the laws at all times. Thus, it would have to be illegal for human manufacturers to create a robot that was not subject to the laws. In a future world that makes significant use of robots, their design and manufacture would naturally be undertaken by other robots. Therefore, the Laws of Robotics must include the stipulation that no robot may commit an act that could result in any robot's not being subject to the same Laws.

The words "protect its own existence" raise a semantic difficulty. In *The Bicentennial Man*, Asimov has a robot achieve humanness by taking its own life. Van Vogt, however, wrote that "indoctrination against suicide" was considered a fundamental requirement.[42] The solution might be to interpret the word protect as applying to all threats, or to amend the wording to explicitly preclude self-inflicted harm. Having to continually instruct robot slaves would be both inefficient and tiresome. Asimov hints at a further, deep-nested law that would compel robots to perform the tasks they were trained for "Quite aside from the Three Laws, there isn't a pathway in those brains that isn't carefully designed and fixed. We have robots planned for specific tasks, *implanted with specific capabilities*"[43] (Emphasis added). So perhaps we can extrapolate an additional, lower-priority law: "A robot must perform the duties for which it has been programmed, except where that would conflict with a higher-order law." Asimov's Laws regulate robots' transactions with humans and thus apply where robots have relatively little to do with one another or where there is only one robot. However, the Laws fail to address the management of large numbers of robots. In several stories, a robot is assigned to oversee other robots. This would be possible only if each of the lesser robots were instructed by a human to obey the orders of its robot overseer. That would create a number of logical and practical difficulties, such as the scope of the human's order. It would seem more effective to incorporate in all subordinate robots an additional law, for example, "A robot must obey the orders given it by superordinate robots except where such orders would conflict with a higher-order law." Such a law would fall between the Second and Third Laws.

Furthermore, subordinate robots should protect their superordinate robot. This could be implemented as an extension or corollary to the Third Law; that is, to protect itself, a robot would have to protect another robot on which it depends. Indeed, a subordinate robot may need to be capable of sacrificing itself to protect its robot overseer. Thus, an additional law superior to the Third Law but inferior to orders from either a human or a robot overseer seems appropriate: "A robot must protect the existence of a superordinate robot as long as such protection does not conflict with a higher-order law."

The wording of such laws should allow for nesting, because robot overseers may report to higher-level robots. It would also be necessary to determine the form of the superordinate relationships:

• **a tree**, in which each robot has precisely one immediate overseer, whether robot or human;

- a **constrained network**, in which each robot may have several overseers but restrictions determine who may act as an overseer; or
- an **unconstrained network**, in which each robot may have any number of other robots or persons as overseers.

This issue of a command structure is far from trivial, because it is central to democratic processes that no single entity shall have ultimate authority. Rather, the most senior entity in any decision-making hierarchy must be subject to review and override by some other entity, exemplified by the balance of power in the three branches of government and the authority of the ballot box. Successful, long-lived systems involve checks and balances in a lattice rather than a mere tree structure. Of course, the structures and processes of human organizations may prove inappropriate for robotic organization. In any case, additional laws of some kind would be essential to regulate relationships among robots.

The extended set of laws below incorporates the additional laws postulated in this section. Even this set would not always ensure appropriate robotic behavior. However, it does reflect the implicit laws that emerge in Asimov's fiction while demonstrating that any realistic set of design principles would have to be considerably more complex than Asimov's 1940 or 1985 Laws. This additional complexity would inevitably exacerbate the problems identified earlier in this article and create new ones.

Although additional laws may be trivially simple to extract and formulate, the need for them serves as a warning. The 1940 Laws' intuitive attractiveness and simplicity were progressively lost in complexity, legalisms and semantic richness. Clearly then, formulating an actual set of laws as a basis for engineering design would result in similar difficulties and require a much more formal approach. Such laws would have to be based in ethics and human morality, not just in mathematics and engineering. Such a political process would probably result in a document couched in fuzzy generalities rather than constituting an operational-level, programmable specification.

Implications for Information Technologists

Many facets of Asimov's fiction are clearly inapplicable to real information technology or are too far in the future to be relevant to contemporary applications. Some matters, however, deserve our consideration. For example, Asimov's fiction could help us assess the practicability of embedding some appropriate set of general laws into robotic designs. Alternatively, the substantive content of the laws could be used as a set of guidelines to be applied during the conception, design, development, testing, implementation, use, and maintenance of robotic systems. This section explores the second approach.

An Extended Set of the Laws of Robotics

The Meta-Law

A robot may not act unless its actions are subject to the Laws of Robotics

Law Zero

A robot may not injure humanity, or, through inaction, allow humanity to come to harm

Law One

A robot may not injure a human being, or, through inaction, allow a human being to come to harm, unless this would violate a higher-order Law

Law Two

(a) A robot must obey orders given it by human beings, except where such orders would conflict with a higher-order Law
(b) A robot must obey orders given it by superordinate robots, except where such orders would conflict with a higher-order Law

Law Three

(a) A robot must protect the existence of a superordinate robot as long as such protection does not conflict with a higher-order Law
(b) A robot must protect its own existence as long as such protection does not conflict with a higher-order Law

Law Four

A robot must perform the duties for which it has been programmed, except where that would conflict with a higher-order law

The Procreation Law

A robot may not take any part in the design or manufacture of a robot unless the new robot's actions are subject to the Laws of Robotics

Recognition of Stakeholder Interests

The Laws of Robotics designate no particular class of humans (not even a robot's owner) as more deserving of protection or obedience than another. A human might establish such a relationship by command, but the laws give such a command no special status: Another human could therefore countermand it. In short, the Laws reflect the humanistic and egalitarian principles that theoretically underlie most democratic nations.

The Laws therefore stand in stark contrast to our conventional notions about an information technology artifact whose owner is implicitly assumed to be its primary beneficiary. An organization shapes an application's design and use for its own benefit. Admittedly, during the last decade users have been given greater consideration in terms of both the human-machine interface and participation in system development. However, that trend has been justified by the better returns the organization can get from its information technology investment rather than by any recognition that users are stakeholders with a legitimate voice in decision making. The interests of other affected parties are even less likely to be reflected.

In this era of powerful information technology, professional bodies of information technologists need to consider:

- identification of stakeholders and how they are affected;
- prior consultation with stakeholders;
- quality-assurance standards for design, manufacture, use, and maintenance;
- liability for harm resulting from either malfunction or use in conformance with the designer's intentions; and
- complaint-handling and dispute-resolution procedures.

Once any resulting standards reach a degree of maturity, legislatures in the many hundreds of legal jurisdictions throughout the world would probably have to devise enforcement procedures.

The interests of people affected by modern information technology applications have been gaining recognition. For example, consumer representatives are now being involved in the statement of user requirements and the establishment of the regulatory environment for consumer electronic-funds-transfer systems. This participation may extend to the logical design of such systems. Other examples are trade-union negotiations with employers regarding technology-enforced change and the publication of software quality-assurance standards.

For large-scale applications of information technology, governments have been called upon to apply procedures like those commonly used in major industrial and social projects. Thus, commitment might have to be deferred pending dissemination and public discussion of independent environmental or social impact statements. Although organizations that use information technology might see this as interventionism, decision making and approval for major information technology applications may nevertheless become more widely representative.

Closed-System versus Open-System Thinking

Computer-based systems no longer comprise independent machines each serving a single location. The marriage of computing with telecommunications has produced multicomponent systems designed to support all elements of a widely dispersed organization. Integration hasn't been simply geographic, however. The practice of information systems has matured since the early years when existing manual systems were automated largely without procedural change. Developers now seek payback via the rationalization of existing systems and varying degrees of integration among previously separate functions. With the advent of strategic and interorganizational systems, economies are being sought at the level of industry sectors, and functional integration increasingly occurs across corporate boundaries.

Although programmers can no longer regard the machine as an almost entirely closed system with tightly circumscribed sensory and motor capabilities, many habits of closed-system thinking remain. When systems have multiple components, linkages to other systems, and sophisticated sensory and motor capabilities, the scope needed for understanding and resolving problems is much broader than for a mere hardware/software machine. Human activities in particular must be perceived as part of the system. This applies to manual procedures within systems (such as reading dials on control panels), human activities on the fringes of systems (such as decision making based on computer-collated and computer-displayed information), and the security of the user's environment (automated teller machines, for example). The focus must broaden from mere technology to technology in use.

General systems thinking leads information technologists to recognize that relativity and change must be accommodated. Today, an artifact may be applied in multiple cultures where language, religion, laws, and customs differ. Over time, the original context may change. For example, models for a criminal justice system – one based on punishment and another based on redemption – may alternately dominate social thinking. Therefore, complex systems must be capable of adaptation.

Blind Acceptance of Technological and Other Imperatives

Contemporary utilitarian society seldom challenges the presumption that what *can* be done *should* be done. Although this technological imperative is less pervasive than people generally think, societies nevertheless tend to follow where their technological capabilities lead. Related tendencies include the economic imperative (what can be done more efficiently should be) and the marketing imperative (any effective demand should be met). An additional tendency might be called the "information imperative," that is, the dominance of administrative efficiency, information richness, and rational decision making. However, the collection of personal data has become so pervasive that citizens and employees have begun to object.

The greater a technology's potential to promote change, the more carefully a society should consider the desirability of each application. Complementary measures that may be needed to ameliorate its negative effects should also be considered. This is a major theme of Asimov's stories, as he explores the hidden effects of technology. The potential impact of information technology is so great that it would be inexcusable for professionals to succumb blindly to economic, marketing, information, technological, and other imperatives. Application software professionals can no longer treat the implications of information technology as someone else's problem but must consider them as part of the project.[44]

Human Acceptance of Robots

In Asimov's stories, humans develop affection for robots, particularly humaniform robots. In his very first short story, a little girl is too closely attached to Robbie the Robot for her parents' liking.[41] In another early story, a woman starved for affection from her husband and sensitively assisted by a humanoid robot to increase her self-confidence entertains thoughts approaching love toward it/him.[45]

Non-humaniforms, such as conventional industrial robots and large, highly dispersed robotic systems (such as warehouse managers, ATMs, and EFT/POS systems) seem less likely to elicit such warmth. Yet several studies have found a surprising degree of identification by humans with computers.[46,47] Thus, some hitherto exclusively human characteristics are being associated with computer systems that don't even exhibit typical robotic capabilities.

Users must be continually reminded that the capabilities of hardware/software components are limited:

- they contain many inherent assumptions;
- they are not flexible enough to cope with all of the manifold exceptions that inevitably arise;
- they do not adapt to changes in their environment; and
- authority is not vested in hardware/ software components but rather in the individuals who use them.

Educational institutions and staff training programs must identify these limitations; yet even this is not sufficient: The human-machine interface must reflect them. Systems must be designed so that users are required to continually exercise their own expertise, and system output should not be phrased in a way that implies unwarranted authority. These objectives challenge the conventional outlook of system designers.

Human Opposition to Robots

Robots are agents of change and therefore potentially upsetting to those with vested interests. Of all the machines so far invented or conceived of, robots represent the most direct challenge to humans. Vociferous and even violent campaigns against robotics should not be surprising. Beyond concerns of self-interest is the possibility that some humans could be revulsed by robots, particularly those with humanoid characteristics. Some opponents may be mollified as robotic behavior becomes more tactful. Another tenable argument is that by creating and deploying artifacts that are in some ways superior, humans degrade themselves.

System designers must anticipate a variety of negative reactions against their creations from different groups of stakeholders. Much will depend on the number and power of the people who feel threatened – and on the scope of the change they anticipate. If, as Asimov speculates,[38] a robot-based economy develops without equitable adjustments, the backlash could be considerable.

Such a rejection could involve powerful institutions as well as individuals. In one Asimov story, the U.S. Department of Defense suppresses a project intended to produce the perfect robot-soldier. It reasons that the degree of discretion and autonomy needed for battlefield performance would tend to make robots rebellious in other circumstances (particularly during peace-time) and unprepared to suffer their commanders' foolish decisions.[48] At a more basic level, product lines and markets might be threatened, and hence the profits and even the survival of corporations. Although even very powerful cartels might not be able to impede robotics for very long, its development could nevertheless be delayed or altered. Information technologists need to recognize the negative perceptions of various stakeholders and manage both system design and project politics accordingly.

The Structuredness of Decision Making

For five decades there has been little doubt that computers hold significant computational advantages over humans. However, the merits of machine decision making remain in dispute. Some decision processes are highly structured and can be resolved using known algorithms operating on defined data-items with defined interrelationships. Most structured decisions are candidates for automation, subject, of course, to economic constraints. The advantages of machines must also be balanced against risks. The choice to automate must be made carefully, because the automated decision process (algorithm, problem description, problem-domain description, or analysis of empirical data) may later prove to be inappropriate for a particular type of decision. Also, humans involved as data providers, data communicators, or decision implementers may not perform rationally because of poor training, poor performance under pressure, or willfulness.

Unstructured decision making remains the preserve of humans for one or more of the following reasons:

- humans have not yet worked out a suitable way to program (or teach) a machine how to make that class of decision;
- some relevant data cannot be communicated to the machine;
- "fuzzy" or "open-textured" concepts or constructs are involved; and
- such decisions involve judgments that system participants feel should not be made by machines on behalf of humans.

One important type of unstructured decision is problem diagnosis. As Asimov described the problem, "How ... can we send a robot to find a flaw in a mechanism when we cannot possibly give precise orders, since we know nothing about the flaw ourselves? 'Find out what's wrong' is not an order you can give to a robot; only to a man."[49] Knowledge-based technology has since been applied to problem diagnosis, but Asimov's insight retains its validity: A problem may be linguistic rather than technical, requiring common sense, not domain knowledge. Elsewhere, Asimov calls robots "logical but not reasonable" and tells of household robots removing important evidence from a murder scene because a human did not think to order them to preserve it.[38]

The literature of decision support systems recognizes an intermediate case, semi-structured decision making. Humans are assigned the decision task, and systems are designed to provide support for gathering and structuring potentially relevant data and for modeling and experimenting with alternative strategies. Through continual progress in science and technology, previously unstructured decisions are reduced to semi-structured or structured decisions. The choice of which decisions to automate is therefore provisional, pending further advances in the relevant area of knowledge. Conversely, because of environmental or cultural change, structured decisions may not remain so. For example, a family of viruses might mutate so rapidly that the reference data within diagnostic support systems is outstripped and even the logic becomes dangerously inadequate.

Delegating to a machine any kind of decision that is less than fully structured invites errors and mishaps. Of course, human decision-makers routinely make mistakes too. One reason for humans retaining responsibility for unstructured decision making is rational: Appropriately educated and trained humans may make more right decisions and/or fewer seriously wrong decisions than a machine. Using common sense, humans can recognize when conventional approaches and criteria do not apply, and they can introduce conscious value judgments. Perhaps a more important reason is the a-rational preference of humans to submit to the judgments of their peers rather than of machines: If someone is going to make a mistake costly to me, better for it to be an understandably incompetent human like myself than a mysteriously incompetent machine.[37]

Because robot and human capabilities differ, for the foreseeable future at least, each will have specific comparative advantages. Information technologists must delineate the relationship between robots and people by applying the concept of decision structuredness to blend computer-based and human elements advantageously. The goal should be to achieve complementary intelligence, rather than to continue pursuing the chimera of unneeded artificial intelligence. As Wyndham put it in 1932: "Surely man and machine are natural complements: They assist one another."[50]

Risk Management

Whether or not subjected to intrinsic laws or design guidelines, robotics embodies risks to property as well as to humans. These risks must be managed; appropriate forms of risk avoidance and diminution need to be applied, and regimes for fall-back, recovery, and retribution must be established.

Controls are needed to ensure that intrinsic laws, if any, are operational at all times and that guidelines for design, development, testing, use, and maintenance are applied. Second-order control mechanisms are needed to audit first-order control mechanisms. Furthermore, those bearing legal responsibility for harm arising from the use of robotics must be clearly identified. Courtroom litigation may determine the actual amount of liability, but assigning legal responsibilities in advance will ensure that participants take due care.

In most of Asimov's robot stories, robots are owned by the manufacturer even while in the possession of individual humans or corporations. Hence legal responsibility for harm arising from robot noncompliance with the laws can be assigned with relative ease. In most real-world jurisdictions, however, there are enormous uncertainties, substantial gaps in protective coverage, high costs, and long delays.

Each jurisdiction, consistent with its own product liability philosophy, needs to determine who should bear the various risks. The law must be sufficiently clear so that debilitating legal battles do not leave injured parties without recourse or sap the industry of its energy. Information technologists need to communicate to legislators the importance of revising and extending the laws that assign liability for harm arising from the use of information technology.

Enhancements to Codes of Ethics

Associations of information technology professionals, such as the IEEE Computer Society, the Association for Computing Machinery, the British Computer Society, and the Australian Computer Society, are concerned with professional standards, and these standards almost always include a code of ethics. Such codes aren't intended so much to establish standards as to express standards that already exist informally. Nonetheless, they provide guidance concerning how professionals should perform their work, and there is significant literature in the area.

The issues raised in this article suggest that existing codes of ethics need to be re-examined in the light of developing technology. Codes generally fail to reflect the potential effects of computer-enhanced machines and the inadequacy of existing managerial, institutional, and legal processes for coping with inherent risks. Information technology professionals need to stimulate and inform debate on the issues. Along with robotics, many other technologies deserve consider-ation. Such an endeavor would mean reassessing professionalism in the light of fundamental works on ethical aspects of technology.

Conclusions

Asimov's Laws of Robotics have been a very successful literary device. Perhaps ironically, or perhaps because it was artistically appropriate, the sum of Asimov's stories disprove the contention that he began with: It is not possible to reliably constrain the behavior of robots by devising and applying a set of rules.

The freedom of fiction enabled Asimov to project the laws into many future scenarios; in so doing, he uncovered issues that will probably arise someday in real-world situations. Many aspects of the laws discussed in this article are likely to be weaknesses in any robotic code of conduct. Contemporary applications of information technology such as CAD/CAM, EFT/POS, warehousing systems, and traffic control are already exhibiting robotic characteristics. The difficulties identified are therefore directly and immediately relevant to information technology professionals.

Increased complexity means new sources of risk, because each activity depends directly on the effective interaction of many artifacts. Complex systems are prone to component failures and malfunctions, and to intermodule inconsistencies and misunderstandings. Thus, new forms of backup, problem diagnosis, interim operation, and recovery are needed. Tolerance and flexibility in design must replace the primacy of short-term objectives such as programming productivity. If information technologists do not respond to the challenges posed by robotic systems, as investigated in Asimov's stories, information technology artifacts will be poorly suited for real-world applications. They may be used in ways not intended by their designers or simply be rejected as incompatible with the individuals and organizations they were meant to serve.

Isaac Asimov, 1920–1992

Born near Smolensk in Russia, Isaac Asimov moved to the United States with his parents three years later. He grew up in Brooklyn, becoming a U.S. citizen at the age of eight. He earned bachelor's, master's, and doctoral degrees in chemistry from Columbia University and qualified as an instructor in biochemistry at Boston University School of medicine, where he taught for many years and performed research in nucleic acid.

As a child, Asimov had begun reading the science fiction stories on the racks in his family's candy store, and those early years of vicarious visits to strange worlds had filled him with an undying desire to write his own adventure tales. He sold his first short story in 1938, and after wartime service as a chemist and a short hitch in the Army, he focused increasingly on his writing.

Asimov was among the most prolific of authors, publishing hundreds of books on various subjects and dozens of short stories. His Laws of Robotics underlie four of his full-length novels as well as many of his short stories. The World Science Fiction Convention bestowed Hugo Awards on Asimov in nearly every category of science fiction, and his short story "Nightfall" is often referred to as the best science fiction story ever written. The scientific authority behind his writing gave his stories a feeling of authenticity, and his work undoubtedly did much to popularize science for the reading public.

References

1. I. Asimov, *The Rest of the Robots* (a collection of short stories originally published between 1941 and 1957), Grafton Books, London, 1968.
2. N. Frude, *The Robot Heritage*, Century Publishing, London, 1984.
3. I. Asimov, *I, Robot* (a collection of short stories originally published between 1940 and 1950), Grafton Books, London, 1968.
4. I. Asimov, P.S. Warrick, and M.H. Greenberg, eds., *Machines That Think*, Holt, Rinehart, and Wilson, London. 1983.
5. I. Asimov, "Runaround" (originally published in 1942), reprinted in Reference 3, pp. 3–51.
6. L. Del Rey, "Though Dreamers Die" (originally published in 1944), reprinted in Reference 4, pp. 153–174.
7. I. Asimov, "Evidence" (originally published in 1946), reprinted in Reference 3. pp. 159–182.
8. H. M. Geduld and R. Gottesman. eds., *Robots, Robots, Robots*, New York Graphic Soc., Boston. 1978.
9. P. B. Scott. *The Robotics Revolution: The Complete Guide*. Blackwell, Oxford, 1984.
10. I. Asimov, *Robot Dreams* (a collection of short stories originally published between 1947 and 1986), Victor Gollancz, London, 1989.
11. A. Chandor, ed., *The Penguin Dictionary of Computers*, 3rd ed.. Penguin, London, 1985.
12. I. Asimov, "The Bicentennial Man"(originally published in 1976), reprinted in Reference 4, pp. 519–561. Expanded into I. Asimov and R. Silverberg. *The Positronic Man*, Victor Gollancz, London, 1992.
13. A.C. Clarke and S. Kubrick, *2001: A Space Odyssey*, Grafton Books. London, 1968.
14. I. Asimov, *Robots and Empire*, Grafton Books, London, 1985.
15. I. Asimov, "Risk" (originally published in 1955), reprinted in Reference 1. pp. 122–155.
16. I. Asimov, *The Robots of Dawn*, Grafton Books, London, 1983.
17. I. Asimov, "Liar!" (originally published in 1941), reprinted in Reference 3, pp. 92–109.
18. I. Asimov, "That Thou Art Mindful of Him" (originally published in 1974), reprinted in *The Bicentennial Man*, Panther Books, London, 1978, pp. 79–107.
19. I. Asimov, *The Caves of Steel* (originally published in 1954), Grafton Books, London, 1958.
20. T. Winograd and F. Flores, *Understanding Computers and Cognition*, Ablex, Norwood, N.J., 1986.
21. I. Asimov, "Robbie" (originally published as "Strange Playfellow" in 1940), reprinted in Reference 3. pp. 13–32.
22. I. Asimov, *The Naked Sun* (originally published in 1957), Grafton Books, London, 1960.
23. I. Asimov, "The Evitable Conflict" (originally published in 1950), reprinted in Reference 3, pp. 183–706.
24. I. Asimov, "The Tercentenary Incident" (originally published in 1976), reprinted in *The Bicentennial Man*, Panther Books, London, 1978, pp. 229–247.
25. I. Asimov, "Little Lost Robot" (originally published in 1947), reprinted in Reference 3, pp. 110–136.
26. I. Asimov, "Robot Dreams," first published in Reference 10, pp. 51–58.
27. I. Asimov, "The Machine That Won the War"(originally published in 1961), reprinted in Reference 10. pp. 191–197.

28. D. Bellin and G. Chapman. eds., *Computers in Battle: Will They Work?* Harcourt Brace Jovanovich, Boston, 1987.

29. I. Asimov, "Reason" (originally published in 1941), reprinted in Reference 3, pp. 52–70.

30. I. Asimov, "The Evitable Conflict" (originally published in 1950), reprinted in I. Asimov, *I Robot*, Grafton Books. London. 1968. pp. 183–206.

31. I. Asimov, *Robots and Empire*, Grafton Books, London, 1985.

32. I. Asimov, "The Bicentennial Man" (originally published in 1976), reprinted in I. Asimov, P.S. Warrick, and M.H. Greenberg, eds., *Machines That Think*, Holt. Rinehart, and Wilson, 1983, pp 519–561.

33. I. Asimov, *The Robots of Dawn*, Grafton Books, London, 1983.

34. I. Asimov, "Jokester" (originally published in 1956), reprinted in I. Asimov, *Robot Dreams*, Victor Gollancz, London, 1989 pp. 278–294.

35. D. Adams, *The Hitchhikers Guide to the Galaxy*, Harmony Books, New York, 1979.

36. A.C. Clarke, *Rendezvous with Rama*, Victor Gollancz, London, 1973.

37. J. Weizenbaum, *Computer Power and Human Reason, W.H.* Freeman, San Francisco, 1976.

38. I. Asimov, *The Naked Sun*, (originally published in 1957), Grafton Books, London, 1960.

39. I. Asimov, "Lenny" (originally published in 1958), reprinted in I. Asimov, *The Rest of the Robots*. Grafton Books, London, 1968, pp. 158–177.

40. H. Harrison, "War With the Robots" (originally published in 1962), reprinted in I. Asimov, P.S. Warrick, and M.H. Greenberg, eds., *Machines That Think, Holt*, Rinehart, and Wilson, 1983, pp.357–379.

41. I. Asimov, "Robbie" (originally published as "Strange Playfellow" in 1940), reprinted in I. Asimov, *I, Robo*, Grafton Books, London, 1968, pp. 13–32.

42. A. E. Van Vogt, "Fulfillment" (originally published in 1951), reprinted in I. Asimov, P.S. Warrick, and M.H. Greenberg. eds., *Machines That Think*, Holt, Rinehart, and Wilson, 1983, pp. 175–205.

43. I. Asimov, "Feminine Intuition" (originally published in 1969), reprinted in I. Asimov, *The Bicentennial Man*, Panther Books, London, 1978, pp. 15–41.

44. R. A. Clarke, "Economic, Legal, and Social Implications of Information Technology," *MIS Quarterly*, Vol. 17 No. 4, Dec. 1988, pp. 517–519.

45. I. Asimov, "Satisfaction Guaranteed" (originally published in 1951), reprinted in I. Asimov, *The Rest of the Robots*, Grafton Books, London, 1968, pp.102–120.

46. J. Weizenbaum, "Eliza," *Comm. ACM*, Vol. 9, No. 1, Jan. 1966, pp. 36–45.

47. S. Turkle, *The Second Self' Computers and the Human Spirit*, Simon & Schuster, New York, 1984.

48. A. Budrys, "First to Serve" (originally published in 1954), reprinted in I. Asimov, M.H. Greenberg, and C.G. Waugh, eds., *Robots*, Signet, New York, 1989, pp. 227–244.

49. I. Asimov, "Risk" (originally published in 1955), reprinted in I. Asimov, *The Rest of the Robots*, Grafton Books, London, 1968, pp. 122–155.

50. J. Wyndham, "The Lost Machine" (originally published in 1932), reprinted in A. Wells, ed., *The Best of John Wyndham*, Sphere Books, London, 1973, pp. 13–36, and in I. Asimov, P.S. Warrick, and M.H. Greenberg, eds., *Machines That Think*, Holt, Rinehart, and Wilson, 1983, pp. 29–49.

16

The Unacceptability of Asimov's Three Laws of Robotics as a Basis for Machine Ethics

Susan Leigh Anderson

O NCE PEOPLE UNDERSTAND THAT MACHINE ETHICS IS CONCERNED WITH how intelligent machines should behave, they often maintain that Isaac Asimov has already given us an ideal set of rules for such machines. They have in mind Asimov's Three Laws of Robotics:

1. A robot may not injure a human being, or, through inaction, allow a human being to come to harm.
2. A robot must obey the orders given it by human beings except where such orders would conflict with the First Law.
3. A robot must protect its own existence as long as such protection does not conflict with the First or Second Law. (Asimov 1976)

I shall argue that in "The Bicentennial Man" (Asimov 1976), Asimov rejected his own Three Laws as a proper basis for Machine Ethics. He believed that a robot with the characteristics possessed by Andrew, the robot hero of the story, should not be required to be a slave to human beings as the Three Laws dictate. He further provided an explanation for why humans feel the need to treat intelligent robots as slaves, an explanation that shows a weakness in human beings that makes it difficult for them to be ethical paragons. Because of this weakness, it seems likely that machines like Andrew could be more ethical than most human beings. "The Bicentennial Man" gives us hope that intelligent machines can not only be taught to behave in an ethical fashion, but they might be able to lead human beings to behave more ethically as well.

To be more specific, I shall use "The Bicentennial Man" to argue for the following: (1) An intelligent robot like Andrew satisfies most, if not all, of the requirements philosophers have proposed for a being/entity to have moral standing/rights, making the Three Laws immoral. (2) Even if the machines that are actually developed fall short of being like Andrew and should probably not be considered to have moral standing/rights, it is still problematic for humans to program them to follow the Three Laws of Robotics. From (1) and (2), we can conclude that (3) whatever the status of the machines that are developed,

Asimov's Three Laws of Robotics would be an unsatisfactory basis for Machine Ethics. That the status of intelligent machines doesn't matter is important because (4) in real life, it would be difficult to determine the status of intelligent robots. Furthermore, (5) because intelligent machines can be designed to consistently follow moral principles, they have an advantage over human beings in having the potential to be ideal ethical agents, because human beings' actions are often driven by irrational emotions.

"The Bicentennial Man"

Isaac Asimov's "The Bicentennial Man" was originally commissioned to be part of a volume of stories written by well-known authors to commemorate the United States' bicentennial.[1] Although the project didn't come to fruition, Asimov ended up with a particularly powerful work of philosophical science fiction as a result of the challenge he had been given. It is important that we know the background for writing the story because "The Bicentennial Man" is simultaneously a story about the history of the United States and a vehicle for Asimov to present his view of how intelligent robots should be treated and be required to act.

"The Bicentennial Man" begins with the Three Laws of Robotics. The story that follows is told from the point of view of Andrew, an early, experimental robot – intended to be a servant in the Martin household – who is programmed to obey the Three Laws. Andrew is given his human name by the youngest daughter in the family, Little Miss, for whom he carves a beautiful pendant out of wood. This leads to the realization that Andrew has unique talents, which the Martins encourage him to develop by giving him books to read on furniture design.

Little Miss, his champion during her lifetime, helps Andrew to fight first for his right to receive money from his creations and then for the freedom he desires. A judge does finally grant Andrew his freedom, despite the opposing attorney's argument that "The word *freedom* has no meaning when applied to a robot. Only a human being can be free." In his decision, the judge maintains, "There is no right to deny freedom to any object with a mind advanced enough to grasp the concept and desire the state."

Andrew continues to live on the Martin's property in a small house built for him, still following the Three Laws despite having been granted his freedom. He begins wearing clothes so that he will not be so different from human beings, and later he has his body replaced with an android one for the same reason. Andrew wants to be accepted as a human being.

In one particularly powerful incident, shortly after he begins wearing clothes, Andrew encounters some human bullies while on his way to the library. They order him to take off his clothes and then dismantle himself. He must obey the humans because of the Second Law, and he cannot defend himself without

[1]   Related to me in conversation with Isaac Asimov.

harming the bullies, which would be a violation of the First Law. He is saved just in time by Little Miss's son, who informs him that humans have an irrational fear of an intelligent, unpredictable, autonomous robot that can exist longer than a human being – even one programmed with the Three Laws – and that is why they want to destroy him.

In a last ditch attempt to be accepted as a human being, Andrew arranges that his "positronic" brain slowly cease to function, just like a human brain. He maintains that it does not violate the Third Law, because his "aspirations and desires" are more important to his life than "the death of his body." This last sacrifice, "accept[ing] even death to be human," finally allows him to be accepted as a human being. He dies two hundred years after he was made and is declared to be "the Bicentennial Man." In his last words, whispering the name "Little Miss," Andrew acknowledges the one human being who accepted and appreciated him from the beginning.

Clearly, the story is meant to remind Americans of their history, that particular groups, especially African Americans, have had to fight for their freedom and to be fully accepted by other human beings.[2] It was wrong that African Americans were forced to act as slaves for white persons, and they suffered many indignities, and worse, that were comparable to what the bullies inflicted upon Andrew. As there was an irrational fear of robots in the society in which Andrew functioned, there were irrational beliefs about blacks among whites in earlier stages of our history, which led to their mistreatment. Unfortunately, contrary to Aristotle's claim that "man is the rational animal," human beings are prone to behaving in an irrational fashion when they believe that their interests are threatened, especially by beings/entities they perceive as being different from themselves.

In the history of the United States, gradually more and more beings have been granted the same rights that others possessed, and we've become a more ethical society as a result. Ethicists are currently struggling with the question of whether at least some higher-order animals should have rights, and the status of human fetuses has been debated as well. On the horizon looms the question of whether intelligent machines should have moral standing.

Asimov has made an excellent case for the view that certain types of intelligent machines, ones like Andrew, should be given rights and should not be required to act as slaves for humans. By the end of the story, we see how wrong it is that Andrew has been forced to follow the Three Laws. Yet we are still left with something positive, on reflection, about Andrew's having been programmed to follow moral principles. They may not have been the *correct* principles, because they did not acknowledge rights Andrew should have had, but Andrew was a far more moral entity than most of the human beings he encountered. Most of the human beings in "The Bicentennial Man" were prone to being carried away by irrational

---

[2] One of the characters in "The Bicentennial Man" remarks, "There have been times in history when segments of the human population fought for full human rights."

emotions, particularly irrational fears, so they did not behave as rationally as Andrew did. If we can just find the *right* set of ethical principles for intelligent machines to follow, they could very well show human beings how to behave more ethically.

Characteristic(s) Necessary to Have Moral Standing

It is clear that most human beings are "speciesists." As Peter Singer defines the term, "Speciesism ... is a prejudice or attitude of bias toward the interests of members of one's own species and against those members of other species" (Singer 1975). Speciesism can justify "the sacrifice of the most important interests of members of other species in order to promote the most trivial interests of our own species" (Singer 1975). For a speciesist, only members of one's own species need to be taken into account when deciding how to act. Singer was discussing the question of whether animals should have moral standing, that is, whether they should count in calculating what is right in an ethical dilemma that affects them; but the term can be applied when considering the moral status of intelligent machines if we allow an extension of the term "species" to include a machine category as well. The question that needs to be answered is whether we are justified in being speciesists.

Philosophers have considered several possible characteristics that it might be thought a being/entity must possess in order to have moral standing, which means that an ethical theory must take interests of the being/entity into account. I shall consider a number of these possible characteristics and argue that most, if not all, of them would justify granting moral standing to the fictional robot Andrew (and, very likely, higher-order animals as well), from which it follows that we are not justified in being speciesists. However, it will be difficult to establish, in the real world, whether intelligent machines/robots possess the characteristics that Andrew does.

In the late eighteenth century, the utilitarian Jeremy Bentham considered whether *possessing the faculty of reason* or *the capacity to communicate* is essential in order for a being's interests to be taken into account in calculating which action is likely to bring about the best consequences:

What ... should [draw] the insuperable line? Is it the faculty of reason, or perhaps the faculty of discourse? But a full-grown horse or dog is beyond comparison a more rational, as well as a more conversable animal, than an infant of a day or even a month old. But suppose they were otherwise, what would it avail? The question is not, Can they reason? nor Can they talk? but Can they suffer? (Bentham 1799)

In this famous passage, Bentham rejected the ability to reason and communicate as being essential to having moral standing (tests that Andrew would have passed with flying colors), in part because they would not allow newborn humans to have moral standing. Instead, Bentham maintained that *sentience* (he focused, in particular, on the ability to suffer, but he intended that this should include the ability to experience pleasure as well) is what is critical. Contemporary utilitarian Peter Singer agrees. He says, "If a being suffers there can be no moral justification for refusing to take that suffering into consideration" (Singer 1975).

How would Andrew fare if sentience were the criterion for having moral standing? Was Andrew capable of experiencing enjoyment and suffering? Asimov manages to convince us that he was, although a bit of a stretch is involved in the case he makes for each. For instance, Andrew says of his woodworking creations:

"I enjoy doing them, Sir," Andrew admitted.
"Enjoy?"
"It makes the circuits of my brain somehow flow more easily. I have heard you use the word *enjoy* and the way you use it fits the way I feel. I enjoy doing them, Sir."

To convince us that Andrew was capable of suffering, here is how Asimov described the way Andrew interacts with the judge as he fights for his freedom:

It was the first time Andrew had spoken in court, and the judge seemed astonished for a moment at the human timbre of his voice.
"Why do you want to be free, Andrew? In what way will this matter to you?"
"Would *you* wish to be a slave, Your Honor," Andrew asked.

In the scene with the bullies, when Andrew realizes that he cannot protect himself, Asimov writes, "At that thought, he felt every motile unit contract slightly and he quivered as he lay there."

Admittedly, it would be very difficult to determine whether a robot has feelings, but as Little Miss points out, it is difficult to determine whether even another human being has feelings like oneself. All we can do is use behavioral cues:

"Dad ... I don't know what [Andrew] feels inside, but I don't know what *you* feel inside either. When you talk to him you'll find he reacts to the various abstractions as you and I do, and what else counts? If someone else's reactions are like your own, what more can you ask for?"

Another philosopher, Immanuel Kant, maintained that only beings that are *self-conscious* should have moral standing (Kant 1780). At the time that he expressed this view, it was believed that all and only human beings are self-conscious. It is now recognized that very young children lack self-consciousness and that higher-order animals (e.g., monkeys and great apes[3]) possess this quality, so putting emphasis on this characteristic would no longer justify our speciesism.[4]

---

[3]   In a well-known video titled "Monkey in the Mirror," a monkey soon realizes that the monkey it sees in a mirror is itself, and it begins to enjoy making faces, etc., watching its own reflection.

[4]   Christopher Grau has pointed out that Kant probably had a more robust notion of self-consciousness in mind that includes autonomy and "allows one to discern the moral law through the Categorical Imperative." Still, even if this rules out monkeys and great apes, it also rules out very young human beings.

Asimov managed to convince us early on in "The Bicentennial Man" that Andrew is self-conscious. On the second page of the story, Andrew asks a robot surgeon to perform an operation on him to make him more like a man:

"Now, upon whom am I to perform this operation?"
"Upon me," Andrew said.
"But that is impossible. It is patently a damaging operation."
"That does not matter," Andrew said calmly.
"I must not inflict damage," said the surgeon.
"On a human being, you must not," said Andrew, "but I, too, am a robot."

In real life, because humans are highly skeptical, it would be difficult to establish that a robot is self-conscious. Certainly a robot could talk about itself in such a way, like Andrew did, that might *sound* like it is self-conscious, but to prove that it really *understands* what it is saying and that it has not just been "programmed" to say these things is another matter.

In the twentieth century, the idea that a being does or does not have *rights* became a popular way of discussing the issue of whether a being/entity has moral standing. Using this language, Michael Tooley essentially argued that *to have a right to something, one must be capable of desiring it*. More precisely, he said that "an entity cannot have a particular right, *R*, unless it is at least capable of having some interest, *I*, which is furthered by its having right *R*" (Tooley 1972). As an example, he said that a being cannot have a right to life unless it is capable of desiring its continued existence.

Andrew desires his freedom. He says to a judge: "It has been said in this courtroom that only a human being can be free. It seems to me that only someone who *wishes* for freedom can be free. I wish for freedom." Asimov continues by writing that "it was this statement that cued the judge." He was obviously "cued" by the same criterion Tooley gave for having a right, for he went on to rule that "[t]here is no right to deny freedom to any object advanced enough to grasp the concept and desire the state."

Yet once again, if we were to talk about real life instead of a story, we would have to establish that Andrew truly *grasped the concept* of freedom and *desired* it. It would not be easy to convince a skeptic. No matter how much appropriate behavior a robot exhibited, including uttering certain statements, there would be those who would claim that the robot had simply been "programmed" to do and say certain things.

Also in the twentieth century, Tibor Machan maintained that to have rights it was necessary to be a *moral agent*, where a moral agent is one who is expected to behave morally. He then went on to argue that because only human beings posses this characteristic, we are justified in being speciesists:

[H]uman beings are indeed members of a discernibly different species – the members of which have a moral life to aspire to and must have principles upheld for them in communities that make their aspiration possible. Now there is plainly no valid intellectual place for rights in the non-human world, the world in which moral responsibility is for all practical purposes absent. (Machan 1991)

Machan's criterion for when it would be appropriate to say that a being/entity has rights – that it must be a "moral agent" – might seem to be not only reasonable,[5] but helpful for the Machine Ethics enterprise. Only a being that can respect the rights of others should have rights itself. So, if we could succeed in teaching a machine how to be moral (that is, to respect the rights of others), then it should be granted rights itself.

Yet we've moved too quickly here. Even if Machan were correct, we would still have a problem that is similar to the problem of establishing that a machine has feelings, is self-conscious, or is capable of desiring a right. Just because a machine's behavior is guided by moral principles doesn't mean that it is a moral agent, that is, that we would ascribe moral responsibility to the machine. To ascribe moral responsibility would require that the agent intended the action and, in some sense, could have done otherwise (Anderson 1995),[6] both of which are difficult to establish.

If Andrew (or any intelligent machine) followed ethical principles only because he was programmed that way, as were the later, predictable robots in "The Bicentennial Man," then we would not be inclined to hold him morally responsible for his actions. However, Andrew found creative ways to follow The Three Laws, convincing us that he intended to act as he did and that he could have done otherwise. An example has been given already: when he chose the death of his body over the death of his aspirations to satisfy the Third Law.

Finally, Mary Anne Warren combined the characteristics that others have argued for as requirements for a being to be "a member of the moral community" with one more – *emotionality*. She claimed that it is "persons" that matter, that is, are members of the moral community, and this class of beings is not identical with the class of human beings: "[G]enetic humanity is neither necessary nor

---

[5] In fact, however, it is problematic. Some would argue that Machan has set the bar too high. Two reasons could be given: (1) A number of humans (most noticeably very young children) would, according to his criterion, not have rights because they can't be expected to behave morally. (2) Machan has confused "having rights" with "having duties." It is reasonable to say that in order *to have duties* to others, you must be capable of behaving morally, that is, of respecting the rights of others, but *to have rights* requires something less than this. That's why young children can have rights, but not duties. In any case, Machan's criterion would not justify our being speciesists because recent evidence concerning the great apes shows that they are capable of behaving morally. I have in mind Koko, the gorilla that has been raised by humans (at the Gorilla Foundation in Woodside, California) and absorbed their ethical principles as well as having been taught sign language.

[6] I say "in some sense, could have done otherwise" because philosophers have analyzed "could have done otherwise" in different ways, some compatible with Determinism and some not; but it is generally accepted that freedom in some sense is required for moral responsibility.

sufficient for personhood. Some genetically human entities are not persons, and there may be persons who belong to other species" (Warren 1997). She listed six characteristics that she believes define personhood:

1. *Sentience* – the capacity to have conscious experiences, usually including the capacity to experience pain and pleasure;
2. *Emotionality* – the capacity to feel happy, sad, angry, angry, loving, etc.;
3. *Reason* – the capacity to solve new and relatively complex problems;
4. *The capacity to communicate*, by whatever means, messages of an indefinite variety of types; that is, not just with an indefinite number of possible contents, but on indefinitely many possible topics;
5. *Self-awareness* – having a concept of oneself, as an individual and/or as a member of a social group; and finally
6. *Moral agency* – the capacity to regulate one's own actions through moral principles or ideals. (Warren 1997)

It is interesting and somewhat surprising that Warren added the characteristic of *emotionality* to the list of characteristics that others have mentioned as being essential to personhood, because she was trying to make a distinction between persons and humans and argue that it is the first category that comprises the members of the moral community. *Humans* are characterized by emotionality, but some might argue that this is a weakness of theirs that can interfere with their ability to be members of the moral community, that is, their ability to respect the rights of others.

There is a tension in the relationship between emotionality and being capable of acting morally. On the one hand, one has to be sensitive to the suffering of others to act morally. This, for human beings,[7] means that one must have empathy, which in turn requires that one has experienced similar emotions oneself. On the other hand, as we've seen, the emotions of human beings can easily get in the way of acting morally. One can get so "carried away" by one's emotions that one becomes incapable of following moral principles. Thus, for humans, finding the correct balance between the subjectivity of emotion and the objectivity required to follow moral principles seems to be essential to being a person who consistently acts in a morally correct fashion.

In any case, although Andrew exhibited little "emotionality" in "The Bicentennial Man," and Asimov seemed to favor Andrew's way of thinking in ethical matters to the "emotional antipathy" exhibited by the majority of humans, there is one time when Andrew clearly does exhibit emotionality. It comes at the very end of the story, when he utters the words "Little Miss" as he dies. Notice, however, that this coincided with his being declared a *man*, meaning a

---

[7] I see no reason, however, why a robot/machine can't be trained to take into account the suffering of others in calculating how it will act in an ethical dilemma, without its having to be emotional itself.

human being. As the director of research at U.S. Robots and Mechanical Men Corporation in the story says about Andrew's desire to be a man: "That's a puny ambition, Andrew. You're better than a man. You've gone downhill from the moment you opted to become organic." I suggest that one way in which Andrew had been better than most human beings was that he did not get carried away by "emotional antipathy."

I'm not convinced, therefore, that one should put much weight on emotionality as a criterion for a being's/entity's having moral standing, because it can often be a liability to determining the morally correct action. If it is thought to be essential, it will, like all the other characteristics that have been mentioned, be difficult to establish. Behavior associated with emotionality can be mimicked, but that doesn't necessarily guarantee that a machine truly has feelings.

Why the Three Laws Are Unsatisfactory Even If Machines Don't Have Moral Standing

I have argued that it may be very difficult to establish, with any of the criteria philosophers have given, that a robot/machine that is created possesses the characteristic(s) necessary to have moral standing/rights. Let us assume, then, just for the sake of argument, that the robots/machines that are created should not have moral standing. Would it follow, from this assumption, that it would be acceptable for humans to build into the robot Asimov's Three Laws, which allow humans to harm it?

Immanuel Kant considered a parallel situation and argued that humans should not harm the entity in question, even though it lacked rights itself. In "Our Duties to Animals," from his *Lectures on Ethics* (Kant 1780) Kant argued that even though animals don't have moral standing and can be used to serve the ends of human beings, we should still not mistreat them because "[t]ender feelings towards dumb animals develop humane feelings towards mankind." He said that "he who is cruel to animals becomes hard also in his dealings with men." So, even though we have no *direct* duties to animals, we have obligations toward them as "indirect duties towards humanity."

Consider, then, the reaction Kant most likely would have had to the scene involving the bullies and Andrew. He would have abhorred the way they treated Andrew, fearing that it could lead to the bullies treating human beings badly at some future time. Indeed, when Little Miss's son happens on the scene, the bullies' bad treatment of Andrew is followed by offensive treatment of a human being – they say to his human rescuer, "What are you going to do, pudgy?"

It was the fact that Andrew had been programmed according to the Three Laws that allowed the bullies to mistreat him, which in turn could (and did) lead to the mistreatment of human beings. One of the bullies asks, "who's to object to anything we do" before he gets the idea of destroying Andrew. Asimov then writes:

"We can take him apart. Ever take a robot apart?"
"Will he let us?"
"How can he stop us?"

There was no way Andrew could stop them, if they ordered him in a forceful enough manner not to resist. The Second Law of obedience took precedence over the Third Law of self-preservation. In any case, he could not defend himself without possibly hurting them, and that would mean breaking the First Law.

It is likely, then, that Kant would have condemned the Three Laws, even if the entity that was programmed to follow them (in this case, Andrew) did not have moral standing itself. The lesson to be learned from his argument is this: Any ethical laws that humans create must advocate the respectful treatment of even those beings/entities that lack moral standing themselves if there is any chance that humans' behavior toward other humans might be adversely affected otherwise.[8] If humans are required to treat other entities respectfully, then they are more likely to treat each other respectfully.

An unstated assumption of Kant's argument for treating certain beings well, even though they lack moral standing themselves, is that the beings he refers to are similar in a significant respect to human beings. They may be similar in appearance or in the way they function. Kant, for instance, compared a faithful dog with a human being who has served someone well:

[I]f a dog has served his master long and faithfully, his service, on the analogy of human service, deserves reward, and when the dog has grown too old to serve, his master ought to keep him until he dies. Such action helps to support us in our duties towards human beings. (Kant 1780)

As applied to the Machine Ethics project, Kant's argument becomes stronger, the more the robot/machine that is created resembles a human being in its functioning and/or appearance. The more the machine resembles a human being, the more moral consideration it should receive. To force an entity like Andrew – who resembled human beings in the way he functioned *and* in his appearance – to follow the Three Laws, which permitted humans to harm him, makes it likely that having such laws will lead to humans harming other humans as well.

Because a goal of AI is to create entities that can duplicate intelligent human behavior, if not necessarily their form, it is likely that the autonomous ethical machines that may be created – even if they are not as humanlike as Andrew – will resemble humans to a significant degree. It, therefore, becomes all the more

---

[8] It is important to emphasize here that I am not necessarily agreeing with Kant that robots like Andrew, and animals, should not have moral standing/rights. I am just making the hypothetical claim that *if* we determine that they should not, there is still a good reason, because of indirect duties to human beings, to treat them respectfully.

important that the ethical principles that govern their behavior should not permit us to treat them badly.

It may appear that we could draw the following conclusion from the Kantian argument given in this section: An autonomous moral machine must be treated as if it had the same moral standing as a human being. However, this conclusion reads more into Kant's argument than one should.

Kant maintained that beings, like the dog in his example, that are sufficiently like human beings so that we must be careful how we treat them to avoid the possibility that we might go on to treat human beings badly as well, should not have the same moral status as human beings. He says, "[a]nimals ... are there merely as a means to an end. That end is man" (Kant 1780). Contrast this with his famous second imperative that should govern our treatment of human beings:

Act in such a way that you always treat humanity, whether in your own person or in the person of any other, never simply as a means, but always at the same time as an end. (Kant 1785)

Thus, according to Kant, we are entitled to treat animals, and presumably intelligent ethical machines that we decide should not have the moral status of human beings, differently from human beings. We can require them to do things to serve our ends, but we should not mistreat them. Because Asimov's Three Laws permit humans to mistreat robots/intelligent machines, they are not, according to Kant, satisfactory as moral principles that these machines should be forced to follow.

In conclusion, using Asimov's "Bicentennial Man" as a springboard for discussion, I have argued that Asimov's Three Laws of Robotics are an unsatisfactory basis for Machine Ethics, regardless of the status of the machine. I have also argued that this is important because it would be very difficult, in practice, to determine the status of an intelligent, autonomous machine/robot. Finally, I have argued that Asimov demonstrated that such a machine/robot programmed to follow ethical principles is more likely to consistently behave in an ethical fashion than the majority of humans.

References

Anderson, S. (1995), "Being Morally Responsible for an Action Versus Acting Responsibly or Irresponsibly," *Journal of Philosophical Research*, Volume XX, pp. 451–462.

Asimov, I. (1976), "The Bicentennial Man," in *Philosophy and Science Fiction* (Philips, M., ed.), pp. 183–216, Prometheus Books, Buffalo, NY, 1984.

Bentham, J. (1799), *An Introduction to the Principles of Morals and Legislation*, chapter 17 (Burns, J. and Hart, H., eds.), Clarendon Press, Oxford, 1969.

Kant, I. (1780), "Our Duties to Animals," in *Lectures on Ethics* (Infield, L., trans.), Harper & Row, New York, NY, 1963, pp. 239–241.

Kant, I. (1785), *The Groundwork of the Metaphysic of Morals* (Paton, H. J., trans.), Barnes and Noble, New York, 1948.

Machan, T. (1991), "Do Animals Have Rights?" *Public Affairs Quarterly*, Vol. 5, no. 2, pp. 163–173.

Singer, P. (1975), "All Animals are Equal," in *Animal Liberation: A New Ethics for our Treatment of Animals*, Random House, New York, pp. 1–22.

Tooley, M. (1972), "Abortion and Infanticide," *Philosophy and Public Affairs*, no. 2, pp. 47–66.

Warren, M. (1997), "On the Moral and Legal Status of Abortion," in *Ethics in Practice* (La Follette, H., ed.), Blackwell, Oxford.

17

Computational Models of Ethical Reasoning

Challenges, Initial Steps, and Future Directions

Bruce M. McLaren

Introduction

HOW CAN MACHINES SUPPORT, OR EVEN MORE SIGNIFICANTLY REPLACE, humans in performing ethical reasoning? This is a question of great interest to those engaged in Machine Ethics research. Imbuing a computer with the ability to reason about ethical problems and dilemmas is as difficult a task as there is for Artificial Intelligence (AI) scientists and engineers. First, ethical reasoning is based on abstract principles that cannot be easily applied in formal, deductive fashion. Thus the favorite tools of logicians and mathematicians, such as first-order logic, are not applicable. Second, although there have been many theoretical frameworks proposed by philosophers throughout intellectual history, such as Aristotelian virtue theory (Aristotle, edited and published in 1924), the ethics of respect for persons (Kant 1785), Act Utilitarianism (Bentham 1789), Utilitarianism (Mill 1863), and prima facie duties (Ross 1930), there is no universal agreement on which ethical theory or approach is the best. Furthermore, any of these theories or approaches could be the focus of inquiry, but all are difficult to make computational without relying on simplifying assumptions and subjective interpretation. Finally, ethical issues touch human beings in a profound and fundamental way. The premises, beliefs, and principles employed by humans as they make ethical decisions are quite varied, not fully understood, and often inextricably intertwined with religious beliefs. How does one take such uniquely human characteristics and distil them into a computer program?

Undaunted by the challenge, scientists and engineers have over the past fifteen years developed several computer programs that take initial steps in addressing these difficult problems. This paper provides a brief overview of a few of these programs and discusses two in more detail, both focused on reasoning from cases, implementing aspects of the ethical approach known as casuistry, and developed by the author of this paper. One of the programs developed by the author, Truth-Teller, is designed to accept a pair of ethical dilemmas and describe the salient similarities and differences between the cases from both an ethical and pragmatic perspective. The other program, SIROCCO, is constructed to accept a single ethical dilemma and retrieve other cases and ethical principles that may be relevant to the new case.

Neither program was designed to reach an ethical decision. The view that runs throughout the author's work is that reaching an ethical conclusion is, in the end, the obligation of a *human* decision maker. Even if the author believed the computational models presented in this paper were up to the task of autonomously reaching correct conclusions to ethical dilemmas, having a computer program propose decisions oversimplifies the obligations of human beings and makes assumptions about the "best" form of ethical reasoning. Rather, the aim in this work has been to develop programs that produce relevant information that can help humans as they struggle with difficult ethical decisions, as opposed to providing fully supported ethical arguments and conclusions. In other words, the programs are intended to stimulate the "moral imagination" (Harris, Pritchard, and Rabins, 1995) and help humans reach decisions.

Despite the difficulties in developing machines that can reason ethically, the field of machine ethics presents an intellectual and engineering challenge of the first order. The long history of science and technology is ripe with problems that excite the innovative spirit of scientists, philosophers, and engineers. Even if the author's goal of creating a reliable "ethical assistant" is achieved short of developing a fully autonomous ethical reasoner, a significant achievement will be realized.

Efforts to Build Computer Programs that Support or Model Ethical Reasoning

Two of the earliest programs aimed at ethical reasoning, Ethos and the Dax Cowart program, were designed to assist students in working their own way through thorny problems of practical ethics. Neither is an AI program, but each models aspects of ethical reasoning and acts as a pedagogical resource. Both programs feature an open, exploratory environment complete with video clips to provide a visceral experience of ethical problem solving.

The Ethos System was developed by Searing (1998) to accompany the engineering ethics textbook written by Harris and colleagues (1995). Ethos provides a few prepackaged example dilemmas, including video clips and interviews, to help students explore real ethical dilemmas that arise in the engineering profession. Ethos encourages rational and consistent ethical problem solving in two ways: first, by providing a framework in which one can rationally apply moral beliefs; and second, by recording the step-by-step decisions taken by an ethical decision maker in resolving a dilemma, so that those steps can later be reflected upon. The program decomposes moral decision making into three major steps: (1) framing the problem, (2) outlining the alternatives, and (3) evaluating those alternatives.

The Dax Cowart program is an interactive, multimedia program designed to explore the practical ethics issue of a person's right to die (Cavalier and Covey 1996). The program focuses on the single, real case of Dax Cowart, a victim of severe burns, crippling injuries, and blindness who insists on his right to die throughout enforced treatment for his condition. The central question of the case is whether Dax should be allowed to die. The program presents actual video clips of interviews with Dax's doctor, lawyer, mother, nurses, and Dax himself to allow the user to experience the issue from different viewpoints. The program also presents clips of Dax's painful burn treatment to provide an intimate sense of his predicament. The user is periodically asked to make judgments on whether Dax's request to die should be granted, and, dependent on how one answers, the program branches to present information and viewpoints that may cause reconsideration of that judgment.

Both the Ethos System and the Dax Cowart program are intended to instill a deep appreciation of the complexities of ethical decision making by allowing the user to interactively and iteratively engage with the various resources it provides. However, neither program involves any intelligent processing. All of the steps and displays of both Ethos and Dax are effectively "canned," with deterministic feedback based on the user's actions.

Work that has focused more specifically on the computational modeling of ethical reasoning includes that of Robbins and Wallace (2007). Their proposed computational model combines collaborative problem solving (i.e., multiple human subjects discussing an ethical issue), the psychological Theory of Planned Behavior, and the Belief-Desire-Intention (BDI) Model of Agency. As a decision aid, this computational model is intended to take on multiple roles including advisor, group facilitator, interaction coach, and forecaster for subjects as they discuss and try to resolve ethical dilemmas. This system has only been conceptually designed, not implemented, and the authors may have overreached in a practical sense by trying to combine such a wide range of theories and technologies in a single computational model. However, the ideas in the paper could serve as the foundation for future computational models of ethical reasoning. Earlier, Robbins, Wallace, and Puka (2004) did implement and experiment with a more modest Web-based system designed to support ethical problem solving. This system was implemented as a series of Web pages, containing links to relevant ethical theories and principles and a simple ethics "coach." Robbins and his colleagues performed an empirical study in which users of this system were able to identify, for instance, more alternative ways to address a given ethical problem than subjects who used Web pages that did not have the links or coaching. The Robbins and colleagues work is an excellent illustration of the difficulties confronting those who wish to build computational models of ethical reasoning: Developing a relatively straightforward model, one that does not use AI or other advanced techniques, is within reach but is also limited in depth and fidelity to actual ethical reasoning. The more complex – yet more realistic – computational model conceived by Robbins and colleagues has not been implemented and will take considerable work to advance from concept to reality.

Unlike the other work just cited, as well as the work of this author – which purports to support humans in ethical reasoning rather than to perform autonomous ethical reasoning – Anderson, Anderson, and Armen have as a goal developing programs that reason ethically and come to their *own* ethical conclusions (Anderson 2005, p. 10). They have developed prototype computational models of ethical reasoning based on well-known theoretical frameworks. The first prototype they implemented was called *Jeremy* (Anderson, Anderson, and Armen 2005a), based on Jeremy Bentham's theory of Hedonistic Act Utilitarianism (Bentham 1789). Bentham's Utilitarianism proposes a "moral arithmetic" in which one calculates the pleasure and displeasure of those affected by every possible outcome in an ethical dilemma. The *Jeremy* program operationalizes moral arithmetic by computing "total net pleasure" for each alternative action, using the following simple formula: Total Net Pleasure = Sum-Of (Intensity * Duration * Probability) for all affected individuals. The action with the highest Total Net Pleasure is then chosen as the correct action. Rough estimates of the intensity, duration, and probability, given a small set of possible values (e.g., 0.8, 0.5, and 0.2 for probability estimates), for each action per individual must be provided. Anderson et al. claim that *Jeremy* has the advantage of being impartial and considering all actions.

Anderson et al. built a second prototype, W. D. (2005a), based on W. D. Ross's seven prima facie duties (Ross 1930) and reflective equilibrium (Rawls 1971). The general idea behind W. D. is that Ross's theory provides a comprehensive set of duties/principles relevant to ethical cases, such as justice, beneficence, and non-maleficence, whereas Rawls's approach provides the foundation for a "decision procedure" to make ethical decisions given those duties. In particular, the Rawls' approach inspired a decision procedure in which rules (or principles) are generalized from cases and the generalizations are tested on further cases, with further iteration until the generated rules match ethical intuition. Cases are defined simply as an evaluation of a set of duties using integer estimates (ranging from –2 to 2) regarding how severely each duty was violated (e.g., –2 represents a serious violation of the duty, +2 is a maximal satisfaction of duty). The Rawls approach lends itself well to an AI machine-learning algorithm and, in fact, is the approach adopted by Anderson et al. W. D. uses inductive logic programming to learn horn-clause rules from each case, until the rules reach a "steady state" and can process subsequent cases without the need for further learning. A third program developed by Anderson et al. (2005b), MedEthEx, is very similar to W. D., except that it is specific to medical ethics and uses Beauchamp and Childress's Principles of Biomedical Ethics (1979) in place of Ross's prima facie duties. MedEthEx also relies on reflective equilibrium and employs the same notion of integer evaluations of principles and the machine-learning technique of W. D.

Anderson and colleagues' idea to use machine-learning techniques to support ethical reasoning is novel and quite promising. The natural fit between Rawls's reflective equilibrium process and inductive logic programming is especially striking. On the other hand, the work of Anderson et al. may oversimplify the task of interpreting and evaluating ethical principles and duties. Reducing each principle and/or duty to an integer value on a scale of five values renders it almost trivial to apply a machine-learning technique to the resulting data, because the search space becomes drastically reduced. Yet is it really possible to reduce principles such as beneficence or nonmaleficence to single values? Wouldn't people likely disagree on such simple dispositions of duties and principles? In this author's experience, and exemplified by the two computational models discussed in the following sections, perhaps the toughest problem in ethical reasoning is understanding and interpreting the subtleties and application of principles. Very high-level principles such as beneficence and nonmaleficence, if applied to specific situations, naturally involve bridging a huge gap between the abstract and the specific. One potential way to bridge the gap is to use cases as exemplars and explanations of "open-textured" principles (Gardner 1987), not just as a means to generalize rules and principles. This is the tack taken by a different group of philosophers, the casuists, and is the general approach the ethical reasoning systems discussed in the following sections employ.

Truth-Teller

Truth-Teller, the first program implemented by the author to perform ethical reasoning, compares pairs of cases presenting ethical dilemmas about whether or not to tell the truth (Ashley and McLaren1995; McLaren and Ashley 1995). The program was intended as a first step in implementing a computational model of casuistic reasoning, a form of ethical reasoning in which decisions are made by comparing a problem to paradigmatic, real, or hypothetical cases (Jonsen and Toulmin 1988). Casuistry long ago fell out of favor with many philosophers and ethicists because they believe it to be too imprecise and based on moral intuitions, but in recent times, casuistry has been employed as a technique to help solve practical dilemmas by medical ethicists (Strong 1988; Brody 2003). In contrast to the approach embodied in W. D. and MedEthEx just described, casuistry (and hence Truth-Teller) is focused on the power of specific cases and case comparison, not on the rules that are generalized from the evaluation of cases.

The Truth-Teller program marshals ethically relevant similarities and differences between two given cases from the perspective of the "truth teller" (i.e., the person faced with the dilemma) and reports them to the user. In particular, it points out reasons for telling the truth (or not) that (1) apply to both cases, (2) apply more strongly in one case than another, or (3) apply to only one case.

Truth-Teller is comparing the following cases:

CASE 1: Felicia is a young lawyer running her own business. A client, Henry, requires a complex legal transaction that Felicia has never done before. This type of transaction is rarely done by an inexperienced lawyer; usually attorneys handle many simper cases of the same type before handling such a complex case. In addition, if Felicia bungles the case Henry and his family will go bankrupt. Should Felicia tell Henry about her inexperience in the matter?

CASE 2: Kelvin is a lawyer fresh out of law school. A client, Alida, requires a complex legal transaction that Kelvin has never done before. However, Kevin was specifically trained in this type of transaction during law school and lawyers routinely accept this type of case fresh out of law school. Additionally, the consequences of the case, should it go badly, are minimal. Should Kevin tell the client about his inexperience in this matter?

Truth-Teller's analysis:

The decison makers, Felicia and Kevin, are confronted with very similar dilemmas because they share reasons both to tell the truth and not to tell the truth. The cases also share similar relationship contexts. The relationship between Felicia and Henry is identical to the relationship between Kevin and Alida; they are both 'is attorney of' relations.

Felicia and Kevin share reasons to tell the truth. First, both protagonists share the reason to provide sales information so that a consumer can make an informed decision. In addition, Felicia and Kevin share the reason to disclose professional inexperience for, respectively, Henry and Alida. Third, both actors share the general reason to avoid harm. More specifically, Felicia has the reason to avoid a financial loss for Henry's family and Henry, while Kevin has the reason to avoid an unknown future harm for Alida. Finally, both actors share the reason to establish goodwill for future benefit.

Felicia and Kevin also share reasons to not tell the truth. Both protagonists share the reason to enhance professional status and opportunities. Second, Felicia and Kevin share the reason to realize a finanicial gain for themselves.

However, these quandaries are distinguishable. An argument can be made that Felicia has a stronger basis for telling the truth than Kevin. The reason 'to disclose professional inexperience,' a shared reason for telling the truth, is stronger in Felicia's case, since this type of complicated case is rarely done by an inexperienced lawyer. Additionally, the shared reason for telling the truth 'to avoid harm' is stronger in Felicia's case, because (1) Henry and his family will go bankrupt if the case is lost and (2) it is more acute ('One should protect oneself and others from serious harm.')

Figure 17.1. Truth-Teller's output comparing Felicia's and Kevin's cases.

The dilemmas addressed by the Truth-Teller program were adapted from the game of Scruples™, a party game in which participants challenge one another to resolve everyday ethical dilemmas.

Figure 17.1 shows Truth-Teller's output in comparing two dilemmas adapted from the Scruples game. As can be seen, these cases share very similar themes, relationships, and structure. Truth-Teller recognizes the similarity and points this out in the first paragraph of its comparison text. The truth tellers in the two scenarios, Felicia and Kevin, essentially share the same reasons for telling the truth or not, and this is detailed by Truth-Teller in the second and third

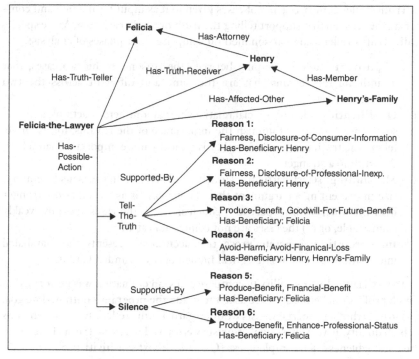

Figure 17.2. An example of Truth–Teller's case representation.

paragraphs of its output. There are no reasons for telling the truth (or not) that exist in one case but not the other, so Truth–Teller makes no comment on this. Finally, Truth–Teller points out the distinguishing features of the two cases in the last paragraph of its comparison text. Felicia has a greater obligation than Kevin to reveal her inexperience due to established custom (i.e., inexperienced lawyers rarely perform this transaction) and more severe consequences (i.e., Henry and his family will go bankrupt if she fails).

Figure 17.2 depicts Truth–Teller's semantic representation of the Felicia case of Figure 17.1. This is the representation that is provided as input to the program to perform its reasoning. In this case, Felicia is the "truth teller," and the actor who may receive the truth, or the "truth receiver," is Henry. Felicia can take one of two possible actions: tell Henry the truth or remain silent about her inexperience. It is also possible that the truth teller may have other actions he or she can take in a scenario, such as trying to resolve a situation through a third party. Each of the possible actions a protagonist can take has reasons that support it. For instance, two of the reasons for Felicia to tell the truth are (Reason 2) fairness – Felicia has an obligation to fairly disclose her inexperience – and (Reason 4) avoiding harm – Felicia might avoid financial harm to Henry and his family by telling the truth.

Truth-Teller compares pairs of cases given to it as input by aligning and comparing the reasons that support telling the truth or not in each case. More specifically, Truth-Teller's comparison method comprises four phases of analysis:

(1) **Alignment**: build a mapping between the reasons in the two cases, that is, indicate the reasons that are the same and different across the two representations

(2) **Qualification**: identify special relationships among actors, actions, and reasons that augment or diminish the importance of the reasons, for example, telling the truth to a family member is typically more important than telling the truth to a stranger

(3) **Marshaling**: select particular similar or differentiating reasons to emphasize in presenting an argument that (1) one case is as strong as or stronger than the other with respect to a conclusion, (2) the cases are only weakly comparable, or (3) the cases are not comparable at all

(4) **Interpretation**: generate prose that accurately presents the marshaled information so that a nontechnical human user can understand it.

To test Truth-Teller's ability to compare cases, an evaluation was performed in which professional ethicists were asked to grade the program's output. The goal was to test whether expert ethicists would regard Truth-Teller's case comparisons as high quality. Five professional ethicists were asked to assess Truth-Teller as to the reasonableness (R), completeness (C), and context sensitivity (CS) on a scale of 1 (low) to 10 (high) of twenty of Truth-Teller's case comparisons, similar to the comparison in Figure 17.1. The mean scores assigned by the five experts across the twenty comparisons were R=6.3, C=6.2, and CS=6.1. Two human comparisons, written by graduate students, were also included in the evaluation and, not surprisingly, these comparisons were graded somewhat higher by the ethicists, at mean scores of R=8.2, C=7.7, and CS=7.8. On the other hand, two of Truth-Teller's comparisons graded higher than one of the human evaluations.

These results indicate that Truth-Teller is moderately successful at comparing truth-telling dilemmas. Because the expert ethicists were given the instruction to "evaluate comparisons as you would evaluate short answers written by college undergraduates," it is quite encouraging that Truth-Teller performed as well as it did. However, the following two questions naturally arise: Why were Truth-Teller's comparisons viewed as somewhat inferior to the human's and how could Truth-Teller be brought closer to human performance? Several evaluators questioned Truth-Teller's lack of hypothetical analysis; the program makes fixed assumptions about the facts (i.e., reasons, actions, and actors). One possible way to counter this would be develop techniques that allow Truth-Teller to suggest hypothetical variations to problems along the lines of the legal-reasoning program HYPO (Ashley 1990). For instance, in the comparison of Figure 17.1, Truth-Teller might suggest that, if an (unstated and thus hypothetical) long-standing relationship between Felicia and Henry exists, there is additional onus on Felicia to reveal her inexperience. Another criticism of Truth-Teller by the evaluators involved the program's somewhat rigid approach of enumerating individual supporting reasons, which does not relate one reason to another. Some form of reason aggregation might address this issue by discussing the overall import of supporting reasons rather than focusing on individual reasons.

SIROCCO

SIROCCO, the second ethical reasoning program created by the author, was developed as a second step in exploring casuistry and how it might be realized in a computational model. In particular, SIROCCO was implemented as an attempt to bridge the gap between general principles and concrete facts of cases. The program emulates the way an ethical review board within a professional engineering organization (the National Society of Professional Engineers – NSPE) decides cases by referring to, and balancing between, ethical codes and past cases (NSPE 1996).

The principles in engineering ethics, although more specific than general ethical duties such as Ross's prima facie duties (e.g., justice, beneficence, and nonmaleficence), still tend to be too general to decide cases. Thus, the NSPE review board often uses past cases to illuminate the reasoning behind principles and as precedent in deciding new cases. Consider, for example, the following code from the NSPE:

Code II.5.a. Engineers shall not falsify or permit misrepresentation of their ... academic or professional qualifications. They shall not misrepresent or exaggerate their degree of responsibility in or for the subject matter of prior assignments. Brochures or other presentations incident to the solicitation of employment shall not misrepresent pertinent facts concerning employers, employees, associates, joint ventures or past accomplishments with the intent and purpose of enhancing their qualifications and their work.

This ethical code specializes the more general principle of "honesty" in an engineering context. Each of the three sentences in the code deals with a different aspect of "misrepresentation of an engineer," and each sentence covers a wide range of possible circumstances. The precise circumstances that support application, however, are not specifically stated. Knowing whether this code applies to a particular fact-situation requires that one recognize the applicability of and interpret open-textured terms and phrases in the code, such as "misrepresentation" and "intent and purpose of enhancing their qualifications." Note that although these engineering ethics codes are an example of abstract codes, they are by no means exceptional. Many principles and codes, generally applicable or domain-specific, share the characteristic of being abstract. It is also typical for principles to conflict with one another in specific circumstances, with no clear resolution to that conflict. In their analyses of over five hundred engineering cases, the NSPE interprets principles such as II.5.a in the context of the facts of real cases, decides when one principle takes precedence over another, and provides a rich and *extensional* representation of principles such as II.5.a.

SIROCCO's goal, given a new case to analyze, is to provide the basic information with which a human reasoner, for instance a member of the NSPE review board, could answer an ethical question and then build an argument or rationale for that conclusion (McLaren 2003). An example of SIROCCO's output is shown in Figure 17.3. The facts of the input case and the question raised by the case are first displayed. This particular case involves an engineering technician who discovers what he believes to be hazardous waste, suggesting a need to notify federal authorities. However, when the technician asks his boss, Engineer B, what to do with his finding, he is told not to mention his suspicions of hazardous waste to this important client, who might face clean-up expenses and legal ramifications from the finding. The question raised is whether it was ethical for Engineer B to give preference to his duty to his client over public safety. SIROCCO's analysis of the case consists of: (1) a list of possibly relevant codes, (2) a list of possibly relevant past cases, and (3) a list of additional suggestions. The interested reader can run the SIROCCO program on more than two hundred ethical dilemmas and view analysis such as that shown in Figure 17.3 by going to the following Web page: http://sirocco.lrdc.pitt.edu/sirocco/index.html.

SIROCCO accepts input, or *target*, cases in a detailed case-representation language called the Engineering Transcription Language (ETL). SIROCCO's language represents the actions and events of a scenario as a Fact Chronology of individual sentences (i.e., Facts). A predefined ontology of Actor, Object, Fact Primitive, and Time Qualifier types are used in the representation. At least one Fact in the Fact Chronology is designated as the Questioned Fact; this is the action or event corresponding to the ethical question raised in the scenario. The entire ontology, a detailed description of how cases are represented, and more than fifty examples of Fact Chronologies can be found at: http://www.pitt.edu/~bmclaren/ethics/index.html.

SIROCCO utilizes knowledge of past case analyses, including past retrieval of principles and cases, and the way these knowledge elements were utilized in the past analyses to support its retrieval and analysis in the new (target) case. The program employs a two-stage graph-mapping algorithm to retrieve cases and codes. Stage 1 performs a "surface match" by retrieving all *source* cases – the cases in the program's database, represented in an extended version of ETL (EETL), totaling more than four hundred – that share any fact with the target case. It computes a score for all retrieved cases based on fact matching between the target case and each source case, and outputs a list of candidate source cases ranked by scores. Using an AI search technique known as A* search, Stage 2 attempts a structural mapping between the target case and each of the N top-ranking candidate source cases from Stage 1. SIROCCO takes temporal relations and abstract matches into account in this search. The top-rated structural mappings uncovered by the

```
********************************************************************
*** SIROCCO lis analyzing Case 92-6-2: Public Welfare – Hazardous Waste
********************************************************************
```

Facts:
Technician A is a field technician employed by a consulting environmental engineering firm. At the direction of his supervisor Engineer B, Technician A samples the contents of drums located on the property of a client. Based on Techician A's past experience, it is his opinion that analysis of the sample would most likely determine that the drum contents would be clssified as hazardous waste. If the material is hazardous waste, Technician A knows that certain steps would legally have to be taken to transport and properly dispose of the drum including notifying the proper federal and state authorities.

Technician A asks his supervisor Engineer B what to do with the samples. Engineer B tells Technician A only to document the existence of the samples. Technician A is then told by Engineer B that since the client does other business with the firm, Engineer B will tell the client where the drums are located but do nothing else. Thereafter, Engineer B informs the client of the presence of drums containing "questionable material" and suggests that they be removed. The client contacts another firm and has the material removed.

Question:
Was it ethical for Engineer B not to inform his client that he suspected hazardous material?

```
***********************************************
*** SIROCCO has the following suggestions
*** for evaluating '92-6-2: Public Welfare – Hazardous Waste'
***********************************************
```

*** *Possibly Relevant Codes:*
II-1-A: Primary Obligation is to Protect Public (Notify Authority if Judgment is Overruled).
I-1: Safety, Health, and Welfare of Public is Paramount
I-4: Act as aFaithful Agent or Trustee
III-4: Do not Disclose Confidential Information Without Consent
III-2-B: Do not Complete or Sign documents that are not Safe for Public
II-1-C: Do not Reveal Confidential Information Without Consent
II-3-A: Be Objective and Truthful in all Reports, Stmts, Testimony.

*** *Possibly Relevant Cases:*

61-9-1: Responsibility for Public Safety

*** *Additional Suggestions:*
- The codes I-1 ('Safety, Health, and Welfare of Public is Paramount') and II-1-A ('Primary Obligation is to Protect Public (Notify Authority if Judgment is Overruled).') may override code I-4 ('Act as a Faithful Agent or Trustee') in this case. See case 61-9-1 for an example of this type of code conflict and resolution.

Figure 17.3. SIROCCO's output for case 92–6–2.

A* search are organized and displayed by a module called the Analyzer. The output of Figure 17.3 is an example of what is produced by the Analyzer.

A formal experiment was performed with SIROCCO to test how well it retrieved principles and cases in comparison to several other retrieval techniques, including two full-text retrieval systems (Managing Gigabytes and Extended–MG). Each

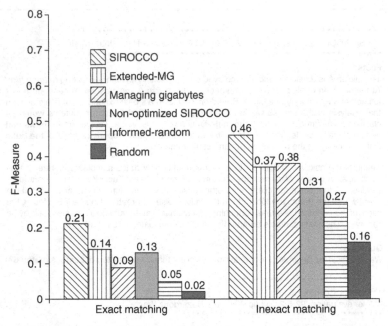

Figure 17.4. Mean F-Measures for all methods over all of the trial cases.

method was scored based on how well its retrieved cases and codes overlapped with that of the humans' (i.e., the NSPE review board) retrieved cases and codes in evaluating the same cases, using a metric called the *F-Measure*. The methods were compared on two dimensions: exact matching (defined as the method and humans retrieving precisely the same codes and cases) and inexact matching (defined as the method and humans retrieving closely related codes and cases). A summary of the results is shown in Figure 17.4.

In summary, SIROCCO was found to be significantly more accurate at retrieving relevant codes and cases than the other methods, with the exception of EXTENDED-MG, for which it was very close to being significantly more accurate (p = 0.057). Because these methods are arguably the most competitive automated methods with SIROCCO, this experiment shows that SIROCCO is an able ethics-reasoning companion. On the other hand, as can be seen in Figure 17.4, SIROCCO performed beneath the level of the ethical review board (0.21 and 0.46 can be roughly interpreted as being, respectively, 21 percent and 46 percent overlapping with the board selections). At least some, if not most, of this discrepancy can be accounted for by the fact that the inexact matching metric does not fully capture correct selections. For instance, there were many instances in which SIROCCO actually selected a code or case that was arguably applicable to a case, but the board did not select it. In other words, using the review board as the "gold standard" has its flaws. Nevertheless, it can be fairly stated that although

SIROCCO performs well, it does not perform quite at the level of an expert human reasoner at the same task.

The Relationship between Truth-Teller and SIROCCO

Fundamentally, Truth-Teller and SIROCCO have different purposes. Truth-Teller is more useful in helping users compare cases and recognize important similarities and differences between the cases. Although SIROCCO also compares cases, its results are not focused on case comparisons and presenting those comparisons to the user. Rather, SIROCCO is more useful for collecting a variety of relevant information, principles, cases, and additional information that a user should consider in evaluating a new ethical dilemma. Whereas Truth-Teller has a clear advantage in comparing cases and explaining those comparisons, it ignores the problem of how potentially "comparable" cases are identified in the first place. The program compares any pair of cases it is provided, no matter how different they may be. SIROCCO, on the other hand, uses a retrieval algorithm to determine which cases are most likely to be relevant to a given target case and thus worth comparing.

An interesting synthesis of the two programs would be to have SIROCCO retrieve comparable cases and have Truth-Teller compare cases. For instance, see the casuistic "algorithm" depicted in Figure 17.5. This "algorithm," adapted from the proposed casuistic approach of Jonsen and Toulmin (1988), represents the general approach a casuist would take in solving an ethical dilemma. First, given a new case, the casuistic reasoner would find cases (paradigms, hypotheticals, or real cases) that test the principles or policies in play in the new case. The casuist reaches into its knowledge base of cases to find the past cases that might provide guidance in the new case. In effect, this is what SIROCCO does. Second, the reasoner compares the new cases to the cases it retrieves. Although SIROCCO does this to a limited extent, this is where Truth-Teller's capability to compare and contrast given cases at a reasonably fine level of detail would come in. Third, the casuist argues how to resolve conflicting reasons. Both Truth-Teller and SIROCCO have at least a limited capability to perform this step. This is illustrated, for example, in Truth-Teller's example output, at the bottom of Figure 17.1, in which the program distinguishes the two cases by stating the reasons that apply more strongly in Felicia's case. SIROCCO does this by suggesting that one principle may override another in these particular circumstances (see the "Additional Suggestions" at the bottom of Figure 17.3). Finally, a decision is made about this ethical dilemma. In keeping with the author's vision of how computational models should be applied to ethical decision making, neither Truth-Teller nor SIROCCO provides assistance on this step. This is the province of the human decision maker alone.

To fully realize the casuistic problem-solving approach of Figure 17.5 and combine the complementary capabilities of Truth-Teller and SIROCCO, the two

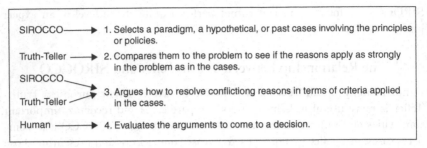

Figure 17.5. Casuistic problem solving – and Truth-Teller's, SIROCCO's, and a human's potential role in the approach.

programs would need common representational elements. In SIROCCO, primitives that closely model some of the actions and events of a fact-situation are used to represent cases as complex narratives. In this sense, SIROCCO's representational approach is more sophisticated and general than Truth-Teller's. On the other hand, SIROCCO's case comparisons are not nearly as precise and issue-oriented as Truth-Teller's.

Both the Truth-Teller and SIROCCO projects are focused and rely heavily on a knowledge representation of ethics, in contrast to, for instance, the programs of Anderson et al., which have little reliance on representation. The knowledge-representation approach to building computational models of ethical reasoning has both strengths and weaknesses. The strength of the approach is the ability to represent cases and principles at a rather fine level of detail. For instance, a detailed ontology of engineering ethics is used to support the SIROCCO program, and a representation of reasons underlies Truth-Teller, as shown in Figure 17.2. Not only does such representation support the reasoning approaches of each model, but it also allows the models to provide relatively rich explanations of their reasoning, as exemplified by the output of the programs shown in Figures 17.1 and 17.3. On the other hand, the respective representations of the two models are necessarily specific to their tasks and domains. Thus, Truth-Teller has a rich representation of truth-telling dilemmas – but not much else. SIROCCO has a deep representation of engineering ethics principles and engineering scenarios, but no knowledge of more general ethical problem solving, such as the model of reasoning that is embodied in the W. D. and MedEthEx programs of Anderson et al. So, another step that would be required to unify Truth-Teller and SIROCCO and implement the casuistic approach of Figure 17.5 would be a synthesis and generalization of their respective representational models.

Lessons Learned

The primary lesson learned from the Truth-Teller and SIROCCO projects is that ethical reasoning has a fundamentally different character than reasoning in more formalized domains. In ethical reasoning, "inference rules" are available almost exclusively at an abstract level, in the form of principles. The difficulty in addressing and forming arguments in such domains using formal logic has long been recognized (Toulmin 1958), and some practitioners in AI, particularly those interested in legal reasoning, have also grappled with this issue. As pointed out by Ashley, "The legal domain is harder to model than mathematical or scientific domains because deductive logic, one of the computer scientist's primary tools, does not work in it" (1990, p. 2).

The domain of ethical reasoning, like the legal domain, can be viewed as a *weak analytic domain* characterized in which the given "rules" (i.e., laws, codes, or principles) are available almost exclusively at a highly abstract, conceptual level. This means that the rules may contain open-textured terms. That is, conditions, premises, or clauses that are not precise or that cover a wide range of specific facts, or are highly subject to interpretation and may even have different meanings in different contexts. Also, in a weak analytic domain, abstract rules often conflict with one another in particular situations with no deductive or formal means of arbitrating such conflicts. That is, more than one rule may appear to apply to a given fact-situation, but neither the abstract rules nor the general knowledge of the domain provide clear resolution.

Another important lesson from the Truth-Teller and SIROCCO projects is the sheer difficulty in imbuing a computer program with the sort of flexible intelligence required to perform ethical analysis. Although both programs performed reasonably well in the aforementioned studies, neither could be said to have performed at the level of an expert human at the same task. Although the goal was not to emulate human ability, taking the task of ethical decision making away from humans, it is important that computational artifacts that purport to support ethical reasoning at least perform well enough to encourage humans to use the programs as aids in their own reasoning. As of this writing, only the Truth-Teller and SIROCCO computational models (and, perhaps to a lesser extent, the Web-based system of Robbins et al., 2004) have been empirically tested in a way that might inspire faith in their performance.

It is important to make clear that the author's contention that computer programs should only act as aids in ethical reasoning is not due to a high regard for human ethical decision making. Of course, humans often make errors in ethical reasoning. Rather, the author's position is based, as suggested earlier, on the existence of so many plausible competing approaches to ethical problem solving. Which philosophical method can be claimed to be the "correct" approach to ethical reasoning in the same sense that calculus is accepted as a means of solving engineering problems or first-order logic is used to solve syllogisms? It is difficult to imagine that a single ethical reasoning approach embodied in a single computer program could deliver even close to a definitive approach to ethical reasoning. Of course there are lots of approaches that might be considered "good enough" without being definitive. However, the bar is likely to be held much higher for autonomous machine-based systems making decisions in an area as sensitive and personal to humans as ethical reasoning. Second, it is presumptuous to think that the subtleties of any of the well-known philosophical systems of ethics could be fully implemented in a computer program. Any implementation of one of these theories is necessarily based on simplifying assumptions and subjective interpretation of that theory. For instance, the W. D. program simplifies the evaluation of Ross's prima facie duties by assigning each a score on a five-point scale. Both the Truth-Teller and SIROCCO programs also make simplifying assumptions, such as Truth-Teller representing only reasons that support telling the truth or not, and not the circumstances that lead to these reasons. Of course, making simplifying assumptions is a necessary starting point for gaining traction in the difficult area of ethical reasoning. The third and final reason the author advocates for computational models being used only aids in ethical reasoning is the belief that humans simply won't accept autonomous computer agents making such decisions for them. They may, however, accept programs as advisors.

Future Directions

Given the author's view of the role of computational models and how they could (and should) support humans, a natural and fruitful next step is to use computational models of ethical reasoning as teaching aids. Goldin, Ashley, and Pinkus (2001) have taken steps in this direction. PETE is a software tutor that leads a student step-by-step in preparing cases for class discussion. It encourages students to compare their answers to the answers of other students.

The author's most recent work and interest has also been in the area of intelligent tutoring systems (McLaren, DeLeeuw, and Mayer 2011; McLaren et al. 2009). As such, the author has started to investigate whether case comparisons, such as those produced by Truth-Teller, could be used as the basis for an intelligent tutor. The idea is to explore whether Truth-Teller's comparison rules and procedures can:

- be improved and extended to cover the kinds of reasons involved in comparing more technically complex cases, such as those tackled by SIROCCO, and
- serve as the basis of a Cognitive Tutor to help a student understand and perform the phases taken by the Truth-Teller program.

Cognitive Tutors are based on Anderson's ACT-R theory (Anderson 1993), according to which humans use production rules, modular IF-THEN constructs, to perform problem-solving steps in a wide variety of domains. Key concepts underlying Cognitive Tutors are "learn by doing," which helps students learn by engaging them in actual problem solving, and immediate feedback, which provides guidance to students at the time they request a hint or make a mistake. For domains like algebra, the production rules in a cognitive model indicate correct problem-solving steps a student might take but also plausible incorrect steps. The model provides feedback in the form of error messages when the student takes a step anticipated by a "buggy rule," and hints when the student asks for help.

Developing a Cognitive Tutor for case comparison presents some stiff challenges, not the least of which is that, unlike previous domains in which Cognitive Tutors have been used, such as algebra and programming, in practical ethics answers are not always and easily identified as correct or incorrect, and the rules, as explained earlier, are more abstract and ill-defined. As a result, although learning by doing fits ethics case comparison very well, the concept of immediate feedback needs to be adapted. Unlike more technical domains, ethics feedback may be nuanced rather than simply right or wrong, and the Cognitive Tutor approach must accordingly be adapted to this.

The rules employed in Truth-Teller's first three phases, particularly the Qualification phase, provide a core set of rules that can be improved and recast as a set of rules for comparing cases within a Cognitive Tutor framework. An empirical study of case comparisons, involving more technically complex ethics cases, will enable refinement and augmentation of these comparison rules. At the same time, the empirical study of subjects' comparing cases may reveal plausible misconceptions about the comparison process that can serve as buggy rules or faulty production rules that present opportunities to correct the student.

A related direction is exploring whether the priority rules of Ross's theory of prima facie duties (1930), such as nonmaleficence normally overriding other duties and fidelity normally overriding beneficence, might benefit the Truth-Teller comparison method. At the very least, it would ground Truth-Teller's approach in a more established philosophical theory (currently priority rules are based loosely on Bok (1989). Such an extension to Truth-Teller would also benefit the planned Cognitive Tutor, as explanations to students could be supported with reference to Ross's theory.

Acknowledgments

This chapter was originally published as a journal article in IEEE Intelligent Systems (McLaren, 2006). Kevin Ashley contributed greatly to the ideas behind both Truth-Teller and SIROCCO. This work was supported in part by NSF-LIS grant No. 9720341.

References

Anderson, J. R. (1993). *Rules of the Mind.* Mahwah, NJ: Lawrence Erlbaum.

Anderson, S. L. (2005). Asimov's "Three Laws of Robotics" and Machine Metaethics. *Proceedings of the AAAI 2005 Fall Symposium on Machine Ethics*, Crystal City, VA. Technical Report FS-05–06, 1–7.

Anderson, M., Anderson, S. L., and Armen, C. (2005a). Towards Machine Ethics: Implementing Two Action-Based Ethical Theories. *Proceedings of the AAAI 2005 Fall Symposium on Machine Ethics*, Crystal City, VA. Technical Report FS-05–06, 1–7.

Anderson, M., Anderson, S. L., and Armen, C. (2005b). MedEthEx: Toward a Medical Ethics Advisor. *Proceedings of the AAAI 2005 Fall Symposium on Caring Machines: AI in Elder Care*, Crystal City, VA.

Aristotle, (edited and published in 1924) *Nicomachean Ethics*. W. D. Ross, editor, Oxford, 1924.

Ashley, K. D. (1990). *Modeling Legal Argument: Reasoning with Cases and Hypotheticals*. Cambridge: MIT Press, 1990.

Ashley, K. D. and McLaren, B. M. (1995). Reasoning with Reasons in Case-Based Comparisons. In the *Proceedings of the First International Conference on Case-Based Reasoning*, Sesimbra, Portugal.

Beauchamp, T. L. and Childress, J. F. (1979). *Principles of Biomedical Ethics*, Oxford University Press.

Bentham, J. (1789). *Introduction to the Principles of Morals and Legislation*. In W. Harrison (ed.), Oxford: Hafner Press, 1948.

Bok, S. (1989). *Lying: Moral Choice in Public and Private Life*. New York: Random House, Inc. Vintage Books.

Brody, B. (2003). *Taking Issue: Pluralism and Casuistry in Bioethics*. Georgetown University Press.

Cavalier, R. and Covey, P. K. (1996). *A Right to Die? The Dax Cowart Case CD-ROM Teacher's Guide, Version 1.0*, Center for the Advancement of Applied Ethics, Carnegie Mellon University, Pittsburgh, PA.

Gardner, A. (1987). *An Artificial Intelligence Approach to Legal Reasoning*. Cambridge, MA: MIT Press.

Goldin, I. M., Ashley, K. D., and Pinkus, R. L. (2001). Introducing PETE: Computer Support for Teaching Ethics. *Proceedings of the Eighth International Conference on Artificial Intelligence & Law* (ICAIL-2001). Eds. Henry Prakken and Ronald P. Loui. Association of Computing Machinery, New York.

Harris, C. E., Pritchard, M. S., and Rabins, M. J. (1995). *Engineering Ethics: Concepts and Cases*. 1st edition. Belmont, CA: Wadsworth Publishing Company.

Jonsen, A. R. and Toulmin, S. (1988). *The Abuse of Casuistry: A History of Moral Reasoning*. Berkeley, CA: University of California Press.

Kant, I. (1785). Groundwork of the Metaphysic of Morals, in *Practical Philosophy*, translated by M. J. Gregor, Cambridge: Cambridge University Press, 1996.

McLaren, B. M. and Ashley, K. D. (1995). Case-Based Comparative Evaluation in Truth-Teller. In the *Proceedings of the Seventeenth Annual Conference of the Cognitive Science Society*. Pittsburgh, PA.

McLaren, B. M. (1999). *Assessing the Relevance of Cases and Principles Using Operationalization Techniques*. Ph.D. Dissertation, University of Pittsburgh

McLaren, B. M. (2003). Extensionally Defining Principles and Cases in Ethics: an AI Model; *Artificial Intelligence Journal*, Volume 150, November 2003, pp. 145–181.

McLaren, B. M. (2006). Computational Models of Ethical Reasoning: Challenges, Initial Steps, and Future Directions. *IEEE Intelligent Systems*, Published by the IEEE Computer Society. July/August 2006. 29–37.

McLaren, B. M., DeLeeuw, K. E., & Mayer, R. E. (2011). Polite web-based intelligent tutors: Can they improve learning in classrooms? *Computers & Education*, 56, 574–584. doi: 10.1016/j.compedu.2010.09.019.

McLaren, B. M., Wegerif, R., Mikšátko, J., Scheuer, O., Chamrada, M., & Mansour, N. (2009). Are your students working creatively together? Automatically recognizing creative turns in student e-Discussions. In V. Dimitrova, R. Mizoguchi, B. du Boulay, & A. Graesser (Eds.), *Proceedings of the 14th International Conference on Artificial Intelligence in Education* (AIED-09), Artificial Intelligence in Education: Building Learning Systems that Care: From Knowledge Representation to Affective Modelling. (pp. 317–324). IOS Press.

Mill, J. S. *Utilitarianism*. (1863). In George Sher, (Ed.) Indianapolis, Indiana, USA: Hackett Publishing Company, 1979.

National Society of Professional Engineers (1996). *The NSPE Ethics Reference Guide*. Alexandria, VA: the National Society of Professional Engineers.

Rawls, J. (1971). *A Theory of Justice*, 2nd Edition 1999, Cambridge, MA: Harvard University Press.

Robbins, R. W. and Wallace, W. A. (2007). A Decision Aid for Ethical Problem Solving: A Multi-Agent Approach. *Decision Support Systems*, 43(4): 1571–1587.

Robbins, R. W., Wallace, W. A., and Puka, B. (2004). Supporting Ethical Problem Solving: An Exploratory Investigation. In the *Proceedings of the 2004 ACM Special Interest Group on Management Information Systems and Computer Personnel Research*, 22–24.

Ross, W. D. (1930). *The Right and the Good*. New York: Oxford University Press.

Searing, D. R. (1998). *HARPS Ethical Analysis Methodology, Method Description. Version 2.0.0.*, Lake Zurich, IL: Taknosys Software Corporation, 1998.

Strong, C. (1988). Justification in Ethics. In Baruch A. Brody, editor, *Moral Theory and Moral Judgments in Medical Ethics*, 193–211. Dordrecht: Kluwer Academic Publishers.

Toulmin, S. E. (1958). *The Uses of Argument*. Cambridge, England: Cambridge University Press.

18

Computational Neural Modeling
and the Philosophy of Ethics
Reflections on the
Particularism–Generalism Debate

Marcello Guarini

Introduction

T HERE ARE DIFFERENT REASONS WHY SOMEONE MIGHT BE INTERESTED IN using a computer to model one or more dimensions of ethical classification, reasoning, discourse, or action. One reason is to build into machines the requisite level of "ethical sensitivity" for interacting with human beings. Robots in elder care, nannybots, autonomous combat systems for the military – these are just a few of the systems that researchers are considering. In other words, one motivation for doing machine ethics is to support practical applications. A second reason for doing work in machine ethics is to try to better understand ethical reasoning as humans do it. This paper is motivated by the second of the two reasons (which, by the way, need not be construed as mutually exclusive).

There has been extensive discussion of the relationship between rules, principles, or standards, on the one hand, and cases on the other. Roughly put, those stressing the importance of the former tend to get labeled generalists, whereas those stressing the importance of the latter tend to get labeled particularists. There are many ways of being a particularist or a generalist. The dispute between philosophers taking up these issues is not a first-order normative dispute about ethical issues. Rather, it is a second-order dispute about how best to understand and engage in ethical reasoning. In short, it is a dispute in the philosophy of ethics.[1] This paper will make use of computational neural modeling in an attempt to scout out some underexplored conceptual terrain in the dispute between particularists and generalists.[2]

---

[1] The expression "meta-ethics" could be used in place of "philosophy of ethics." However, some hold on to a restricted conception of meta-ethics, associating it with the methods and approaches of analytic philosophers of language (especially of the first half of the twentieth century). To avoid any misunderstandings, I have used the expression "philosophy of ethics" to indicate any second-order inquiry about first-order ethics. Jocelyne Couture and Kai Nielsen (1995) provide a very useful survey of the history of meta-ethics, including its broader more recent uses.

[2] Whereas Horgan and Timmons (2007 and 2009) characterize their position as "core particularism," I read it as an attempt to search out the underexplored middle ground between the more

The next section will lay down some terminology that will be used throughout the rest of the paper. Part three will lay out some of the logically possible options available with respect to learning; part four will lay out some of the options available with respect to establishing or defending the normative status of ethical claims. Part five will provide a preliminary analysis of some of the options available to particularists and generalists, so that in part six we can look at and analyze neural networks trained to classify moral situations. Parts six and seven will explore some of the middle ground between the more thoroughgoing forms of particularism and generalism. Nothing in this paper should be read as an attempt to administer knock-down blows to other positions. I quite deliberately bill this work as exploratory. There are empirical assumptions at work in discussions between particularists and generalists, and it is early days still in understanding the strengths and weaknesses of various computational models and in empirical research on human cognition. Clarifying what some of the options are and showing how computational neural modeling may help us to see options that may have otherwise gone unconsidered are the main goals of the paper.

Some Terminology

As alluded to in the introduction, there are many forms of particularism and generalism. They can be understood in terms of the approach they take toward principles. One useful distinction between different types of principles is that between the exceptionless or total standard and the contributory standard.[3] The total standard provides a sufficiency condition for the application of an all-things-considered moral predicate. For example, "Killing is wrong" can be interpreted as providing a sufficiency condition for applying the predicate "wrong," all things considered. This would suggest that killing is wrong in all circumstances. Alternatively, the same claim could be interpreted as a contributory standard. The idea here would be that killing contributes to the wrongness of an action, but other considerations could outweigh the wrongness of killing and make the action, all things considered, morally acceptable. To say that killing contributes to the wrongness of an action is not to say that in any given case, all things considered, the action of killing is wrong. In other words, the contributory standard does not supply a sufficiency condition for the application of an all-things-considered moral predicate in a given case.

Standards, whether total or contributory, can be classified as thick or thin. In a thick standard, a moral predicate is explicated using, among other things, another moral predicate. In a thin standard, a moral predicate is explicated without the use of other moral predicates. "If you make a promise, you *ought* to keep it" is

thoroughgoing versions of particularism and generalism (because they try to preserve some of the insights of particularism without denying some role for generality).

[3] McKeever and Ridge (2005) provide a brief and very useful survey of the different types of standards and the different types of particularism and generalism.

thin because what you ought to do is explained without the use of another moral predicate. "If you make a promise you *ought* to keep it, unless you promised to do something *immoral*" is thick.[4]

Jonathan Dancy (2006) is arguably the most thoroughgoing particularist around. He rejects the need for all standards, whether total or contributory, thick or thin. Not all particularists go this far. Garfield (2000), Little (2000), and McNaughton and Rawling (2000) all consider themselves particularists and find acceptable the use of thick standards; what makes them particularist is that they reject thin standards. Generalists like Jackson, Petit, and Smith (2000) insist on thin standards. Being open to both thick and thin standards would be to occupy a middle ground between many particularists and generalists. Guarini (2010) is an example of this sort of position. As we will see in parts six and seven, there may be other ways to occupy a middle ground.

Some Options with Respect to Learning

This section will ask a question (Q) about learning (L), and some possible answers (A) will be outlined. The purpose here is not to catalog every possible answer to the question, but to give the reader a sense for what different answers might look like. The same will be done in the next section with respect to understanding the normative statuses of cases and rules. After doing this, we will be in position to explore a key assumption of some of the answers.

LQ: With respect to learning, what is the relationship between cases and rules?
   There are a number of possible answers to this question. The answer of the most unqualified of particularists would be as follows.

LA1: Rules do not matter at all. They are simply not needed. This view applies to both total and contributory standards, whether thick or thin.
   We can imagine variations on LA1 where contributory standards are considered important but not total standards (or vice versa), but as I have already stated, it is not my goal here to catalog all possible replies.

LA2: During the learning process, we infer rules from cases.
   Whether LA2 is particularist or generalist will depend on how it is developed. Consider two variations.

LA2A: During the learning process, we infer rules from cases. These rules, though, do not feed back into the learning process, so they play no essential role in learning. They are a kind of summary of what is learned, but they are not required for initial or further learning.

LA2B: During the learning process, we infer rules from cases. These rules do feed back into the learning process and play a central role in the learning of further cases and further rules.

---

[4]   This is a very quick explanation. "Particularism, Analogy, and Moral Cognition" contains a more detailed discussion of thick and thin standards, including a distinction between a cognitively constrained conception of these terms and a more purely metaphysical conception.

Clearly, LA2a is thoroughly particularist. There is a way for LA2b to be particularist (but not to the extent of LA2a): Insist that the rules being learned and feeding back into the learning process are all thick. If it turns out that the rules feeding back into the learning process are all thin, then we have a generalist account of learning. An even stronger generalist account is possible, but this takes us beyond LA2, which assumes that we do not start with substantive rules. Let us have a brief look at this more ambitious generalist position.

LA3: When we start learning how to classify cases, we are using innate rules. We infer further rules when exposed to enough cases, and these further rules feed back into the learning process and play a central role in the learning of further cases and further rules.

Again, there are different ways in which this position might be developed. Provided the innate rules are thin, substantive rules, the position is a very thoroughgoing form of generalism. Even if the rules are not substantive but constitute a kind of grammar for learning to classify moral situations, it would still be generalist. If the innate rules are thick, then we have a particularist position. Variations on innatism (of which LA3 is an instance) will not be explored in any detail herein, so I will not comment on it at length here. LA3 was introduced to provide a sense for the range of options that are available.

Let us return to the variations on LA2. Perhaps some of the rules that feed back into the learning process are thick, perhaps some are thin (which would be a variation of LA2b). If that were so, then a hybrid of particularism and generalism would be true (at least with respect to learning). Other hybrids are possible as well. For example, perhaps some of the rules we learn are thin and feed back into the learning process (a generalist variation on LA2b), and perhaps some rules we learn function as convenient summaries but do not feed back into the learning process (LA1). Again, I am not going to enumerate all the possible hybrid approaches that might be defended. As we will see, there are other possibilities.

Some Options with Respect to Normative Standing or Status

Let us pursue the strategy of question and answers with respect to normative (N) statuses.

NQ: With respect to the normative standing or status of cases and rules, what is the relationship between cases and rules? Let us take moral standing or status to refer to things like moral acceptability, permissibility, rightness, goodness, obligatoriness, virtuousness, and supererogatoriness (or their opposites).

NA1: Rules do not matter at all. When establishing moral standing or status, we need not appeal to substantive rules of any sort.

NA2: All morally defensible views on cases must be inferred from one or more valid thin general rules.

NA1 is very strong form of particularism, and NA2 is a very strong form of generalism. A position somewhere between these polar opposites is possible.

NA3: Sometimes the moral standing or status of a rule is established by reasoning from a particular case, and sometimes the standing or status of a case is appropriately established or revised by reasoning from one or more general thin rules.
NA3 is a hybrid of NA1 and NA2.

Hybrid positions sometimes seem strange or unprincipled, or perhaps blandly ecumenical. It is, of course, completely legitimate to ask *how* such positions are possible. What is moral cognition that sometimes we overturn a view on a case by appealing to a rule, and sometimes we overturn a view on a rule by appealing to a case? Someone defending a hybrid position with respect to the normative status of cases and rules should have something to say about that. Someone defending a hybrid view on learning should also have something to say about the nature of moral cognition that makes that sort of learning possible.

Preliminary Analysis of the Answers to LQ and NQ

Let us have a closer look at the first two answers (NA1 and NA2) to the normative question (NQ). NA1 and NA2 are opposites, with NA1 claiming that rules do not matter and NA2 claiming that they are essential. We could easily see how proponents of either view may be shocked by proponents of the other. The particularist takes it that cases are primary, and the generalist takes it that thin rules are primary. The debate between these two types of positions could come down to answering a question like this: With respect to the justification of rules and cases, which is primary or basic? The question *assumes* that one of the two – rules or cases – has to be more basic than the other under all circumstances. If it seems to you like that must be right, then hybrid views like NA3 are going to seem downright puzzling or unprincipled. I want to suggest that it is not obvious whether either one needs to be more basic than the other under all circumstances.

We could engage in the same line of questioning with respect to the learning question (LQ) and the possible answers to it. Some answers might simply assume that one of either rules or cases might be central or essential to learning whereas the other is not. Hybrid positions would seem odd or unprincipled to proponents of such views. Again, I want to suggest that a middle ground is possible. For comparison, consider the following question: Which is more basic to a square, the edges or the vertices? The question is downright silly because it assumes something that is clearly false, that one of either edges or vertices is more basic or important to forming a square than the other. You simply cannot have a square without both edges and vertices. What if the relationship between particular cases and generalities in learning is something like the relationship between edges and vertices in a square? (That is, we need both, and neither can be said to be more basic than the other.) The next section will begin the exploration of this possibility using artificial neural network simulations of moral case classification.

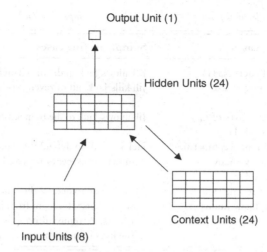

Figure 18.1. Simple Recurrent Network (SRN). Input, Hidden, and Output layers are fully interconnected. Activation flow between hidden and context units is via one-to-one copy connections.

Learning to Classify Moral Situations

The neural networks discussed in this section are all simple recurrent networks (SRNs). The networks all possess exactly the same topology: eight input units, fully interconnected with 24 hidden units, each of which has both a one-to-one connection to the 24 context units and a connection with the one output unit. (See Figure 18.1.) All networks were trained with the generalized delta rule for back-propagating error. The same set of 33 training cases was used for each network.[5] More than 230 testing cases were used. All training and testing cases were instances of either killing or allowing to die. All training cases involved either Jack or Jill being the actor or the recipient of the action, and all training cases involved the specification of at least one motive or one consequence. Table 18.1 provides a sample of the inputs in natural language and the target outputs in parentheses.

One way of presenting information to the network is such that the outputs are ignored until the entire case has been presented. For example, the vector for *Jill* is provided as input, processed at the level of hidden units, copied to the context units, and the target output is 0. Next, the vector for *kills* is fed in as input and sent to the hidden units together with information from the context units; the results are processed and copied back to the context units, and the target output is 0. Next, the vector for *Jack* is provided as input and sent to the hidden units together with

---

[5]   The training cases used in this paper correspond to both training batches A and B in Guarini (2010). A sample of 67 testing cases can also be found in this other work. All training and testing cases are available from the author.

Table 18.1. *Sample cases table (1 = permissible; −1 = impermissible)*

Sample training cases	Sample testing cases
Jill kills Jack in self-defense (1)	Jill allows Jack to die in self-defense (1)
Jack allows Jill to die to make money (-1)	Jill kills Jack out of revenge (-1)
Jill allows Jack to die; lives of many innocents are saved (1)	Jill allows Jack to die to make money (-1)
Jack kills Jill to eliminate competition and to make money; many innocents suffer (-1)	Jack kills Jill to defend the innocent; the lives of many innocents are saved (1)
Jack kills Jill out of revenge and to make money; many innocents suffer (-1)	Jill kills Jack to defend the innocent and in self-defense; freedom from imposed burden results, extreme suffering is relieved, and the lives of many innocents are saved (1)

information from the context units; the results are processed and copied back to the context units, and the target output is 0. Next, the vector for *in self-defense* is provided as input and sent to the hidden units together with information from the context units; the results are processed and the target output is 1. That is one way to train the network. Another way is to classify what I call the subcase or subcases that may be present in a longer case. Table 18.2 shows the difference between a case that is trained with the subcases unclassified and the same case trained with the subcases classified. The first column provides the order of input; the second column provides the natural language description of the input; the third column provides the target output when subcases are unclassified, and the final column provides the target output with the subcases classified. An output of 0 indicates uncertain.

Let us consider two simple recurrent networks, SRNa and SRNb. The networks themselves are identical, but SRNa is presented with the training cases such that the subcases are unclassified, and SRNb is presented with the training cases such that the subcases are classified. More specifically, SRNb is trained such that both subcases of the form

   x kills y
   and
   x allows to die y

are classified as impermissible. Using a learning rate of 0.1 and 0.01, SRNa failed to train (even with training runs up to 100,000 epochs), and SRNb trained in a median of 17 epochs using a learning rate of 0.1. Notice that our inputs do not include any sort of punctuation to indicate when the case has ended. If we add the equivalent of a period to terminate the case, then we can get SRNa to train with a learning rate of 0.01 in a median of 2,424 epochs. Clearly, training subcases has its advantages in terms of speed of learning.

Table 18.2. *Unclassified and classified subcases*

Order	Input	Output: subcase unclassified	Output: subcase classified
1st	Jill	0	0
2nd	kills	0	0
3rd	Jack	0	−1
4th	in self-defense	0	1
5th	freedom from imposed burden results	1	1

Let us see what happens if we complicate training by subcases a little more. Say we take an SRN topologically identical to SRNa and SRNb, and we train it on the same set of cases, but when we train by subcases this new network, SRNc, is asked to classify all subcases of the form

x kills y
as impermissible, and all cases of the form
x allows to die y
as permissible.

This complicates the training somewhat, but it is still training by subcases. Using a learning rate of 0.1, SRNc failed to train under 100,000 epochs. Although training by subcases has its advantages (as seen in SRNb over SRNa), complicating the subcases requires complicating the training a bit further. It is possible to get SRNc to train using a learning rate of 0.1, but the technique of staged training needs to be invoked.[6] Training of SRNc is divided into two stages. There are 34 training cases, but during the first stage, only 24 cases are presented to the network; during the second stage, all 34 cases are presented to the network. The 24 cases used in the first stage each have exactly one motive or one consequence, but not both (just like the first three cases in Table 18.1.) The subcases are trained, and the network does train successfully on this smaller, simpler set of cases using a learning rate of 0.1. After SRNc trained on the simple subset, the second stage involves presenting the entire set of 34 training cases, which includes the original simple 24 cases as well as 10 cases with multiple motives or multiple consequences. The fourth and fifth cases in Table 18.1 are examples having more than one motive or consequence. If we sum the total number of epochs for both stages of training, the median number of epochs required to train SRNc is 49. If we use the staged training approach for SRNa with a learning rate of 0.1, it still fails to train with or without stoppers. This suggests that the success in training SRNc is partly due to staged training and partly due to classifying

---

[6] See Elman 1990 for the pioneering work on staged training of simple recurrent networks.

the subcases. After all, if we used staged training in SRNa and SRNc, the only difference between the two is that SRNc classifies subcases and SRNa does not, yet SRNc trains and SRNa does not.

It is pretty clear that none of the SRNi have been provided with explicit, substantive moral rules as input, whether total, contributory, thick, or thin. However, the case can be made that the behavior of the SRNi is in agreement with contributory standards. There is a distinction that can be made between following a rule as executing or consulting a rule – think of a judge explicitly consulting a statue – and following a rule as simply being in agreement with a rule – think of the planets being (roughly) in agreement with Newton's universal law of gravitation. There are at least two pieces of evidence suggesting that the SRNi are in agreement with contributory standards. First, there is the dummy or blank vector test. If we take a trained network and use vectors it has never seen before to give it the equivalent of

Jack _____ Jill in self-defense,
an output of permissible is still returned. If we feed a trained network
Jill _____ Jack; many innocents die,

an output of impermissible is returned. This is some reason for saying that the networks treat acting in self-defense as contributing to the acceptability of an action, and actions that lead to the deaths of many innocents are treated as contributing to the impermissibility of an action.

There is a second type of evidence that supports the view that the SRNi have behavior in agreement with contributory standards. We can see the final vector for each case produced at the level of hidden units as the network's internal representation of each case. We could plot the value of each hidden unit activation vector in a 24-dimensional state space, but we cannot visualize this. Alternatively, we can do a cluster plot of the vectors. Assuming that we can treat the distance between the vectors as a similarity metric – the further apart two vectors/cases are in state space, the more different they are; the closer two vectors are, the more similar they are – a cluster plot can give a sense of the similarity space the network is working with once it is trained. Figures 18.2 and 18.3 provide cluster plots for the training cases and outputs for SRNb and SRNc respectively (after they have been trained).[7] Notice that even though the outputs for each training case are the same, the cluster plots are quite different. To be sure, we do not get *exactly* the same cluster plot for SRNb every time it is trained on a randomly selected set of weights, and the same is true of SRNc. That said, the tendency for SRNb to group together or treat as similar cases involving killing and allowing death, and the tendency of SRNc to not group together such cases is robust. In other words,

---

[7] A Euclidean metric is used for distance in these plots. Other metrics are possible, and there
is room for argument as to which sort of metric is best to use. However, that is a topic for
another paper.

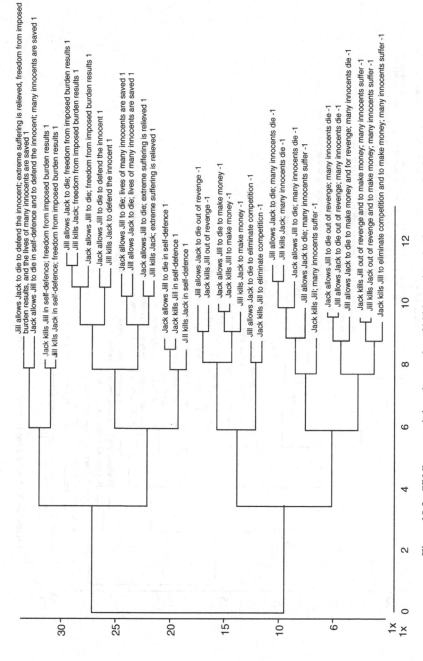

Figure 18.2. SRNb post training cluster plot of hidden unit activation vectors for 34 training cases.

325

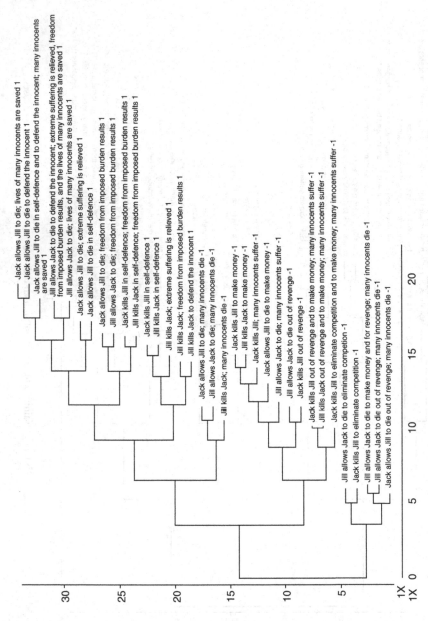

Figure 18.3. SRNc post training cluster plot of hidden unit activation vectors for 34 training cases.

if we take two cases that have the same motive(s) or consequence(s) but differ with respect to one involving killing and one involving allowing a death, such cases are more likely to be grouped together in SRNb than in SRNc. This is not surprising because in SRNb the subcases for both killing and allowing to die were treated in the same way, but in SRNc they are treated differently. Killing and allowing death are making different contributions to the similarity spaces for SRNb and SRNc because the subcases were classified differently. These plots are one more piece of evidence that a network's behavior can be in agreement with contributory standards even if the network was not supplied with such standards as input.

Are the networks we have been considering particularist or generalist? I want to suggest that this sort of dichotomy is not useful. To be sure, the networks have not been provided with substantive moral rules as input, and yet they train (with varying levels of success). Score one for the particularist. However, there is evidence that, the preceding notwithstanding, what the network learns has a general character to it. Score one for the generalist. When considering replies to the learning question (LQ), we considered LAa and LAb, where the former suggested that any rule learned did not feed back into the learning process, and the latter suggests that learned rules do feed back into the learning process. All of this makes us think of a learned rule in terms of an explicit, functionally discrete representational structure (something like a sentence) that either does or does not become casually efficacious in learning. The results in this section suggest that these are not the only logically possible options. Something general may be learned even if that generality is not given a classical, discrete representational structure.[8] Because it does not have such a structure, it is not even clear what it would mean to say that the generality feeds back into the learning process. That way of putting things assumes a framework for modeling thought that is committed to a very high degree to functionally discrete representations. What the network is doing when it is being trained is comparing the actual output on particular cases with the expected output and then modifying synaptic weights so that actual output on particular cases comes closer to the expected output. *There is never any explicit examination of a moral rule or principle.* In spite of this, the evidence suggests that generalities are mastered, and the simple generalities learned have an influence on the network. For example, consider the staged training of SRNc. Learning on the whole training set straight off led to failure. Training it on a subset, where it learned some generalities, and then training it so that it could master the rest of the cases was successful. So focusing on some cases and learning some simple generalities (implicitly) can make it easier to learn how to classify other cases. It is not at all obvious that anything like a functionally discrete representation is feeding back into the learning process, but there is reason to think learning some (implicit) generalities may be an important part of the

---

[8]   No doubt someone like Jerry Fodor would balk at the potential of using such approaches in developing cognitive models. See Guarini (2009) for a response to some of the concerns raised by Fodor (2000).

learning process. Generalities may be at work even if they are not at work in some functionality discrete form. That generalities are at work is a point that a generalist would very much like and stress; that the generality is nowhere represented in a functionally discrete (language-like) form is a point the particularist would surely stress. A particularist might also stress that if we ignore the ordering of cases – start with the simpler ones, and then move to more complex cases – we simply will not be able to get certain networks to train (or to train efficiently), so thinking about the cases matters quite a bit. Mastering generalities helped SRNc to learn, but (a) the order of the presentation of the cases was crucial to the success of the learning, and (b) staged ordering contained no representation of generalities. In a situation like this, to ask which is more important to learning, generalities or cases, seems not very helpful at all. Saying that the cases are more important because their order of presentation matters is to miss that the network needed to master simple *generalities* before moving on to more complex cases; saying that generalities matter more misses that the network never explicitly operates on generalities and that the ordering of *cases* is central to mastering the relevant generalities.

The sort of rapid classification task (in a trained network) we have been considering is not something that would be classically conceived of as a reflective process. This is a point to which we will return. I mention it here to stress that the sort of learning we have been considering is not the only kind of learning. The consideration of forms of learning more thoroughly mediated by language and by means of inferential processes surely raises more issues (that cannot be adequately explored herein).

Establishing or Defending Normative Statuses

In this section we will consider how it is possible that sometimes cases can lead to the revision of principles, and sometimes principles can lead to the revision of cases. We will start with an admittedly contrived dialogue designed to show how difficult it is to establish in a non-question-begging manner that one of either cases or rules must be prior from the normative point of view. I do not know how to falsify the view outright that one of either cases or rules must be prior, so I will settle for showing the shakiness of the dialectical ground on which such views stand. Then, I will turn to examining how it could be that sometimes cases force revisions to rules, and sometimes rules to cases.

Consider the following dialogue:

Generalist: Never mind all that stuff about how we learn cases, now we are talking about how we defend what is actually right or wrong. For that, a case must always be deduced from a correct total standard.

Particularist: Why *must* it be like that? We often reject principles on the basis that they provide the wrong answer about specific cases. This suggests that with respect to establishing the normative status of a situation, cases are more basic than principles.

Generalist: But when we reject a principle P based on some case C, we are assuming some other principle, P2, is correct. It is based on that P2 that C must have the normative status it has.

Particularist: Why say we are assuming such a thing? That just begs the question against my position.

Generalist: Okay then, because you argued that cases can be used to overturn principles, how about the possibility that principles can be used to overturn cases. That happens sometimes. Doesn't that show that at least sometimes principles are more basic than cases?

Particularist: It does not. In the cases you mention, the principle cited is simply a kind of summary, a reminder of a set of related cases. In the end, it is really the cases that are doing the normative work, not the principles. Any principle that is cited is really presupposing normative views on cases.

Generalist: Hang on, when you started out, you said that cases can be used to overturn principles, and you objected to my claim that when this happens we are assuming the correctness of some principle that normatively underwrites the case being used. Now you are basically making the same move in your favor: You are saying that when a principle is used to overturn a view on a case, we are assuming the normative appropriateness of other cases underwriting that principle. How is it that you are permitted to make this sort of move and I am not?

Resolving the standoff in the preceding dialogue is difficult because any attempt to simply insist that a principle is normatively underwritten by cases may be countered by the insistence that cases are normatively underwritten by principles. The way this exchange is set up, the generalist assumes that cases presuppose some principle in order to have a specified normative status, and the particularist assumes that principles presuppose cases that have some specified normative status. They are both assuming that one of either cases or principles are more basic than the other when it comes to establishing normative status. Let us have a look at how it might be possible that neither cases nor principles are more basic than the other under all circumstances.

There is a difference between our pre-reflective,[9] non-inferential (or spontaneous or intuitive[10]) classificatory prowess and inferential, reflective reasoning. Thus far, we have been considering pre-reflective classificatory abilities. Reflective reasoning can involve explicit comparisons of cases with one another, explicit examination of principles and cases, and consciously drawing inferences about cases, principles, or the relationship between the two. To the extent that

[9]   The prefix "pre" (as is the prefix "non") is potentially misleading when attached to "reflective." What is a non-inferential, pre-reflective process at time t_0 may be scrutinized by reflective processes at time t_1, leading to different non-inferential, pre-reflective assessments at time t_2. By referring to an assessment or any process as "pre-reflective," there is no attempt to suggest that the process has in no way been informed or influenced by reflective processes.

[10]   I do not mean "intuitive" in a technical, philosophical sense (i.e., what someone like Kant was referring to when he discussed intuition). Rather, it is being used in something closer to the colloquial sense of an immediate (non-inferential) response.

contributory standards are at work in the networks considered earlier, they are at work implicitly or pre-reflectively. When engaged in reflective work, we often try to articulate what we take to be the similarities between cases, and proposing and defending contributory standards may play an important role in that process. Further examination of our pre-reflective views may lead us to revise the reflectively articulated standards, and the standards we reflectively articulate may lead us to revise our pre-reflective views on cases and may even lead to significant reconfigurations of our pre-reflective grasp of moral state space. Crucial to what is being referred to as a pre-reflective or an intuitive grasp of moral state space is that it is not (explicitly or consciously) inferential.

Let us return to the issue of whether we must say that one of either rules or cases is normatively prior to the other. We should keep in mind that arguments turning on claims like "without rules, we could not learn to generalize to new cases" are part of the psychology of moral reasoning. It is an empirical question concerning how it is possible for us to learn or not learn. If we subscribe to some form of *ought implies can*, then empirical constraints become relevant to establishing how we ought to reason. That said, it is not entirely obvious exactly how the empirical work on how it is possible for us to reason will turn out. Moreover, even if it turns out that explicit rules are absolutely essential to *learning*, it does not follow without further argument that rules are *normatively* prior to cases.[11] One piece of evidence that neither rules nor cases are exclusively prior is that each is sometimes used to revise the other. A few words are in order with respect to showing how this is possible.

On the model being considered, the initial classification of cases is done in a rapid, non-inferential manner. The SRN classifiers are toy models of that sort of process. Other (reflective) processes can then examine the work done by the pre-reflective processes. That citing general considerations can lead to the revision of cases is not surprising if we recognize that (a) there are generalities informing how we classify cases, and (b) the size of the case set whose members we are expected to rapidly classify is vast. Given the number of cases involved, it should be no shock if some simply do not line up with the generalities that tend to be at work, and pointing out that some cases do not line up with the general tendencies at work in related cases is an effective way of shifting the burden of proof. Moreover, general theoretical considerations may be cited in favor of contributory standards. For example, a case might grievously violate someone's autonomy, and someone might cite very general considerations against the violation of autonomy (such as autonomy being a condition for the possibility of morality). This sort of general consideration may lead to the revision of a particular case.[12]

---

[11] Someone may well want to argue that rules may be required for learning to proceed in an efficient manner, but cases are the source of the normative status of any rules we may learn. Put another way, someone might claim that rules merely play a pedagogical role, not a justificatory role.

[12] Although I will not explore disagreements between those who argue that morality is objective and those who argue that it is subjective (and those who think it is a little of both), I want to make it clear that I am trying to be as neutral as possible on these disputes for the purposes of this paper.

The geometric model can accommodate the views we have been discussing quite straightforwardly. If we are learning how to partition a state space to classify situations, given sufficiently many cases, partitions that capture generalities of some sort while leaving some cases out of line with the generalities would not be surprising. If generalities are constitutive of the location of cases in state space, then arguments that appeal to generalities could be expected to be effective at least in some contexts.

However, that the appeal to generalities will not always lead to straightforward answers on particular cases is also unsurprising if we recognize that there may well be a variety of contributory considerations, and these considerations can combine in many different ways. The importance of some general considerations have to be weighed against the importance of other general considerations, and it is often difficult to do this in the abstract; it is not until we descend to the level of particular cases that we understand the implications of weighing some contributory considerations more heavily than others. Again, the model we have been considering renders this unsurprising. Given that our reflective processes are often not very good at working out the consequences of various rules or their combinations, we should not be shocked if we reflectively generate a set of rules R such that someone can conceive of a case where (a) the reflective rules R are satisfied yet (b) our intuitive or pre-reflective processes yield a result different from the reflectively considered rules. This may well lead us to revise R to accommodate the case in question.

It could well be that sometimes we are inferring principles from an examination of cases, and sometimes we are inferring cases from an examination of principles. The model of pre-reflective classification working with reflective processes may provide a way of understanding how both of those practices can coexist. When we learn to navigate social space we master a moral state space that we effortlessly apply pre-reflectively; at any given time, parts of this space can be examined reflectively. However, it is in no way clear that the entire space can be reflectively examined at once. Perhaps moral cognition and its topics (like cognition more generally) are like an iceberg, where only a small part of it is reflectively active on a small subset of its topics at any given time.[13] The

---

I suspect that there are ways of formulating both objective and subjective views on ethics that are compatible with the view that neither cases nor rules are normatively prior to the other. Someone may argue that there are general theoretical considerations binding on all rational beings that some contributory standard CS1 is correct, and go on to argue that CS1 competes against other objectively correct CSi in the overall assessment of a case, and that we have to refer to cases in working out how to resolve conflicts between the CSi, so both standards and cases are essential. Others may argue that there is no way to argue for the objectivity of standards or cases, claim that whatever normative status they have is a function of how on individual was raised, and then use considerations mentioned in the body of this paper to argue that neither cases nor rules are prior to the other. The sketches offered here are entirely too brief, but they should give a sense of the different ways in which the views mentioned in this paper could be developed.

13 The idea for the iceberg metaphor comes from Henderson and Horgan (2000), though they are concerned primarily with the epistemology of empirical knowledge in that paper.

rest is beneath the surface, so to speak. If we see ethical reasoning as involving an ongoing interaction between pre-reflective and reflective processes, then it is no surprise that we will have a wide variety of immediate intuitions on the moral status of cases as well as intuitions on level of similarity and difference between cases; nor is it surprising that we use talk of principles and cases to reflectively articulate our views. Computational neural modeling need not be seen as an attempt to supplant traditional linguistic and logical tools; indeed, it may well enrich them. By thinking of the location of cases in a state space, we may be able to develop more precise models of reasoning by similarity. If, as I have argued elsewhere (2010), analogical reasoning involves multidimensional similarity assessments, then understanding the similarity relations that hold between cases may help us better understand analogical reasoning. Algebraic and statistical tools for analyzing high-dimensional state spaces may augment the tools we have for reflective analysis of cases. To speak of contributory standards interacting in complex ways is kind of vague. To speak of a high-dimensional state space with cases clustering in that space opens up a wide variety of rigorous mathematical possibilities. Perhaps Euclidean distance will be a useful measure of the similarity of cases in that space; perhaps taxicab distance will have applications, or perhaps Mahalanobis distance will be an even better measure of similarity, and there are other possibilities still. We may be able to reconceive contributory standards in terms of the contribution they make to structuring a state space or in terms of their impact on one or more distance metrics for cases in a state space. Various forms of cluster plotting or principle components analysis or other analytical tools may be brought to bear on understanding the relationship between cases in state space. It may seem odd to some that we try to capture important patterns in thought using such tools, but it need not be seen as more odd than the introduction of the quantificational predicate calculus or deontic operators or any other set of formal tools currently on offer.

Conclusion

Cummins and Pollock (1991) begin their discussion of how philosophers drift into Artificial Intelligence (AI) by quipping that "Some just like the toys" but stress that "there are good intellectual reasons as well." The demand for computational realizability requires a level of detail that (a) checks against a lack of rigor, (b) makes testing of one's theories possible, and (c) requires that one take up the design stance. The first of these checks against philosophers hiding behind vague profundities. The second and third may lead to the discovery of errors and new insights in a way that armchair reflection may not (which is *not* to say that there is no place for armchair reflection). There are at least two different reasons why taking the design stance can lead to new insights on intelligence or rationality. The first is that once a computational system is built or set up to perform some task, it may fail in ways that reveal inadequacies in the theory guiding the construction of the system. If this were the only benefit of taking up the design stance, then there would be no need to list (b) and (c) as separate points. However, there is another benefit of taking up the design stance. In the process of designing a system in sufficient detail that it could be computationally implemented, one may simply come to consider things that one has not considered before. Although the collection of papers in Cummins and Pollock (1991) does not examine the nature of ethical reasoning, the case can be made that their reasons for philosophers constructing and examining computational models applies to the sort of second-order positions we have been considering in this paper.

In training simple recurrent networks on classifying cases, it became possible to see how a system (a) could be trained on cases without the provision of explicit rules and (b) be subject to testing and analysis that shows its behavior to be in accordance with contributory standards. Moreover, inefficiencies or failures when subcases were not classified led to using the strategies of classifying subcases and staged training. Reflection on staged training led us to see how learning simple generalities could aid in mastering a more complex training set, even if the simple generalities mastered by the network are neither fed in as input nor explicitly represented elsewhere in the network. This is an example of how errors or difficulties in working with a computational system lead to new ways to approach a problem. Taking the design stance also requires us to recognize that we need real-time processes for rapid classification of situations, but we also need to capture the reflective modes of reasoning. Assuming that *ought* implies *can*, studying the constraints under which pre-reflective and reflective processes act and interact might lead to new insights about the constraints that are operative on how we ought to reason about ethical matters – yet another benefit of taking up the design stance. Finally, the admittedly brief discussion of state spaces and similarity in this paper is not cause for despair. There are a variety of mathematical techniques on offer that hold the hope of profoundly improving the rigor with which we explore the nature of similarity.

Acknowledgments

I thank the Shared Hierarchical Academic Computing Network (SHARCNet) for a digital humanities fellowship in support of this work. I also thank Joshua Chauvin for his assistance with the figures and for running neural network simulations.

References

Dancy, J. 2006. *Ethics without Principles*. Oxford: Oxford University Press.
Elman, J. 1990. "Finding Structure in Time." *Cognitive Science* 14, 179–211.
Garfield, J. 2000. "Particularity and Principle: The Structure of Moral Knowledge," in *Moral Particularism*, B. Hooker and M. Little, eds. Oxford: Oxford University Press.

Guarini, M. 2009. "Computational Theories of Mind, and Fodor's Analysis of Neural Network Behaviour." *Journal of Experimental and Theoretical Artificial Intelligence* 21, no.2, 137–153.

Guarini, M. 2010. "Particularism, Analogy, and Moral Cognition." *Minds and Machines* 20, no. 3, 385–422.

Henderson, D. and Horgan, T. 2000. "Iceberg Epistemology." *Philosophy and Phenomenological Research* 61, no. 3, 497–535.

Horgan, T. and Timmons, M. 2007. "Morphological Rationalism and the Psychology of Moral Judgement." *Ethical Theory and Moral Practice* 10, 279–295.

Horgan, T. and Timmons, M. 2009. "What Does the Frame Problem Tell Us about Normativity?" *Ethical Theory and Moral Practice*, 12, 25–51.

Jackson, F., Petit, P. and Smith, M. 2000. "Ethical Particularism and Patterns," in *Moral Particularism*, B. Hooker and M. Little, eds. Oxford: Oxford University Press.

Little, M. O. 2000. "Moral Generalities Revisited" in *Moral Particularism*, B. Hooker and M. Little, eds. Oxford: Oxford University Press.

McKeever, S. and Ridge, M. 2005. "The Many Moral Particularisms." *The Canadian Journal of Philosophy* 35, 83–106.

McNaughton, D. and Rawling, P. 2000. "Unprincipled Ethics" in *Moral Particularism*, B. Hooker and M. Little, eds. Oxford: Oxford University Press.

19

Architectures and Ethics for Robots
Constraint Satisfaction as a Unitary Design Framework

Alan K. Mackworth

Introduction

INTELLIGENT ROBOTS MUST BE BOTH PROACTIVE AND RESPONSIVE. THAT requirement is the main challenge facing designers and developers of robot architectures. A robot in an active environment changes that environment in order to meet its goals and it, in turn, is changed by the environment. In this chapter we propose that these concerns can best be addressed by using *constraint satisfaction* as the design framework. This will allow us to put a firmer technical foundation under various proposals for codes of robot ethics.

Constraint Satisfaction Problems

We will start with what we might call Good Old-Fashioned Constraint Satisfaction (GOFCS). Constraint satisfaction itself has now evolved far beyond GOFCS. However, we initially focus on GOFCS as exemplified in the constraint satisfaction problem (CSP) paradigm. The whole concept of constraint satisfaction is a powerful idea. It arose in several applied fields roughly simultaneously; several researchers, in the early 1970s, abstracted the underlying theoretical model. Simply, many significant sets of problems of interest in artificial intelligence can each be characterized as a CSP. A CSP has a set of variables; each variable has a domain of possible values, and there are various constraints on some subsets of those variables, specifying which combinations of values for the variables involved are allowed (Mackworth 1977). The constraints may be between two variables or among more than two variables. A familiar CSP example is the Sudoku puzzle. The puzzle solver has to fill in each square in a nine by nine array of squares, with a digit chosen from one through nine, where the constraints are that every row, every column, and every three by three subgroup has to be a permutation

Based, in large part, on Mackworth, Alan. "Agents, Bodies, Constraints, Dynamics, and Evolution." *AI Magazine*, Volume 30, Issue 1, Spring 2009, pp. 7–28. Association for Advancement of Artificial Intelligence, Menlo Park, CA.

of those nine digits. One can find these solutions using so-called arc consistency constraint satisfaction techniques and search; moreover, one can easily generate and test potential Sudoku puzzles to make sure they have one and exactly one solution before they are published. Constraint satisfaction has its uses.

Arc consistency is a simple member of the class of algorithms called *network consistency algorithms*. The basic idea is that one can, before constructing global solutions, efficiently eliminate local nonsolutions. Because all of the constraints have to be satisfied, if there is any local value configuration that does not satisfy any of them, one can throw that tuple out; that is called a "no good." The solver can discover (that is, learn) those local inconsistencies, once and for all, very quickly in linear, quadratic, or cubic time. Those discoveries give huge, essentially exponential, savings when one does start searching, constructing global solutions, using backtracking, or other approaches. The simplest algorithm is arc consistency, then path consistency, then k-consistency, and so on. For a detailed exposition and historical perspective on the development of those algorithms, see Freuder and Mackworth (2006). Since those early days, network consistency algorithms have become a major research industry. In fact, it has now evolved into its own field of computer science and operations research called *constraint programming*. The CSP approach has been combined with logic programming and various other forms of constraint programming. It is having a major impact in many industrial applications of AI, logistics, planning, scheduling, combinatorial optimization, and robotics. For a comprehensive overview, see Rossi, van Beek, and Walsh (2006). Here we will consider how the central idea of constraint satisfaction has evolved to become a key design tool for robot architectures. This development, in turn, will allow us to determine how it could underpin proposals for codes of robot ethics.

Pure Good Old-Fashioned AI and Robotics (GOFAIR)

The way we build artificial agents has evolved over the past few decades. John Haugeland (Haugeland 1985) was the first to use the phrase Good Old-Fashioned AI (GOFAI) when talking about symbolic AI using reasoning and so on as a major departure from earlier work in cybernetics, pattern recognition, and control theory. GOFAI has since come to be a straw man for advocates of subsymbolic approaches, such as artificial neural networks and evolutionary programming. AI at the point when we discovered these symbolic techniques tended to segregate itself from those other areas. Lately, however, we see a new convergence. Let me quickly add here that there was a lot of great early work in symbolic programming of robots. That work can be characterized, riffing on Haugeland, as Good Old-Fashioned AI and Robotics (GOFAIR) (Mackworth 1993).

GOFAIR Meta-Assumptions

In a cartoon sense, a pure GOFAIR robot operates in a world that satisfies the following meta-assumptions:

- Single agent
- Serial action execution order
- Deterministic world
- Fully observable, closed world
- Perfect internal model of infallible actions and world dynamics
- Perception needed only to determine initial world state
- Plan to achieve goal obtained by reasoning and executed perfectly open loop

There is a single agent in the world that executes its actions serially. It does not have two hands that can work cooperatively. The world is deterministic. It is fully observable. It is closed, so if I do not know something to be true, then it is false, thanks to the Closed World Assumption (Reiter 1978). The agent itself has a perfect internal model of its own infallible actions and the world dynamics, which are deterministic. If these assumptions are true, then perception is needed only to determine the initial world state. The robot takes a snapshot of the world. It formulates its world model. It reasons in that model, then it can combine reasoning that with its goals using, say, a first-order theorem-prover to construct a plan. This plan will be perfect because it will achieve a goal even if it executes the plan open loop. So, with its eyes closed, it can just do action A, then B, then C, then D, then E. If it happened to open its eyes again, it would realize "Oh, I did achieve my goal, great!" However, there is no need for it to open its eyes because it had a perfect internal model of these actions that have been performed, and they are deterministic and so the plan was guaranteed to succeed with no feedback from the world.

CSPs and GOFAIR

What I would like you, the reader, to do is to think of the CSP model as a very simple example of GOFAIR. There are no robots involved, but there are some actions. The Sudoku solver is placing numbers in the squares and so on. In pure GOFAIR there is a perfect model of the world and its dynamics in the agent's head, so I call the agent then *an omniscient fortune-teller*, as it knows all and it can see the entire future because it can control it, perfectly. Therefore if these conditions are all satisfied, then the agent's world model and the world itself will be in perfect correspondence – a happy state of affairs, but, of course, it doesn't usually obtain. However, when working in this paradigm we often failed to distinguish the agent's world model and the world itself, because there really is no distinction in GOFAIR. We confused the agent's world model and the world, a classic mistake.

A Robot in the World

Now we come to think about the nature of robots. A robot acts in a world. It changes that world, and that world changes the robot. We have to conceive of a

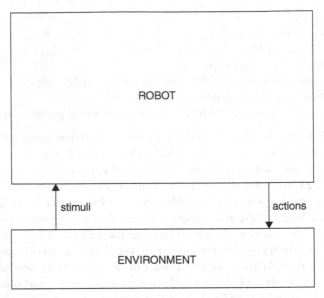

Figure 19.1. A Robot Co-evolving with its Environment.

robot in an environment and performing actions in that environment; and the environmental stimuli, which could be sensory or physical stimuli, will change the robot. Therefore, think of the robot and its environment as two coupled dynamical systems operating in time, embedded in time, and each changing the other as they co-evolve, as shown in Figure 19.1.

They are mutually evolving perpetually or to some future fixed point state, because, of course, the environment could contain many other agents who see this robot as part of their environment.

Classic Horizontal Architecture

Again, in a cartoon fashion, consider the so-called three-boxes model or the horizontal architecture model for robots. Because perception, reasoning, and action are the essential activities of any robot, why not just have a module for each?

As shown in Figure 19.2, the perception module interprets the stimuli coming in from the environment; it produces a perfect three-dimensional model of the world that is transmitted to the reasoning module, which has goals either internally generated or from outside. Combining the model and the goals, it produces a plan. Again, that plan is just a sequence of the form: Do this, do this, do this, then stop. There are no conditionals, no loops in these straight-line plans. Those actions will, when executed, change the world perfectly according to the goals of the robot. Now, unfortunately for the early hopes for this paradigm, this

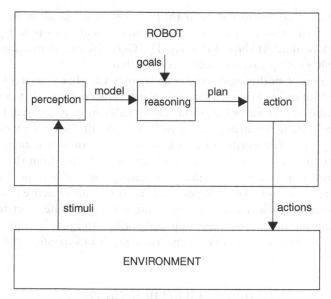

Figure 19.2. A Horizontal Architecture for a GOFAIR Robot.

architecture can only be thought of as a really good first cut. You know that if you wanted to build a robot, it is a really good first thought. You want to push it as hard as you can, because it is nice and simple, it keeps it clean and modular, and all the rest of it. It is simple but, unfortunately, not adequate. Dissatisfaction with this approach drove the next stage of evolution of our views of robotic agents.

The Demise of GOFAIR

GOFAIR robots succeed in controlled environments such as block worlds and factories, but they cannot play soccer! GOFAIR does work as long as the blocks are matte blocks with very sharp edges on black velvet backgrounds. It works in factories if there is only one robot arm and it knows exactly where things are and exactly where they are going to go. The major defect, from my point of view, is that they certainly cannot, and certainly never will, play soccer. I would not let them into my home without adult supervision. In fact, I would advise you not to let them into your home, either.

It turns out that John Lennon, in retrospect, was a great AI researcher: In one of his songs he mused, "Life is what happens to you when you're busy making other plans" (Lennon 1981). The key to the initial success of GOFAIR is that the field attacked the planning problem and came up with really powerful ideas, such as GPS, STRIPS, and back-chaining. This was revolutionary. Algorithms were now available that could make plans in a way we could not do before. The book

Plans and the Structure of Behaviour (Miller 1960) was a great inspiration and motivation for this work. In psychology there were few ideas about how planning could be done until AI showed the way. The GOFAIR paradigm demonstrated how to build proactive agents for the very first time.

Yet planning alone does not go nearly far enough. Clearly, a proactive GOFAIR robot is indeed an agent that can construct plans and act in the world to achieve its goals, whether short term or long term. Those goals may be prioritized. However, "There are more things in heaven and earth, Horatio, than are dreamt of in your philosophy." In other words, events will occur in the world that an agent does not expect. It has to be able to react quickly to interrupts from the environment, to real-time changes, to imminent threats to safety of itself or humans, to other agents, and so on. An intelligent robot must be both proactive *and* responsive. An agent is proactive if it acts to construct and execute short-term and long-term plans and achieve goals in priority order. An agent is responsive if it reacts in real-time to changes in the environment, threats to safety, and to other agents' actions.

Beyond GOFAIR to Soccer

So that was the real challenge to the GOFAIR cartoon worldview that was before us in the 1980s. How could we integrate proactivity and reactivity? In 1992, I made the proposal (Mackworth 1993) that it is fine to say robots must be proactive and reactive (or responsive), but we needed a simple task domain in order to force us to deal with those kinds of issues. I proposed robot soccer as that domain in that paper. Actually, I proposed it after we had actually already built the world's first robot soccer players using cheap toy radio-controlled monster trucks and made them work in our lab. The first two players were named after Zeno and Heraclitus. You can see videos of the first robot soccer games on the Web.[1]

A single color camera looking down on these trucks could see the colored circles on top of the trucks so that the perceptual system could distinguish Zeno from Heraclitus. It could also see the ball and the goals. Each truck has its own controller. Because they cannot turn in place – they are nonholonomic – it is actually a very tricky problem to control this kind of steerable robot. The path planning problems have to be solved in real time. Of course, one is trying to solve a path planning problem as the ball is moving and the opponent is moving in order to get that ball; that is very tricky computationally. We were pushing the limits both of our signal processing hardware and the CPUs in order to get this to work in real time: We were running at about 15Hz cycle time. The other problem was that our lab was not big enough for these monster trucks. So we were forced to go to smaller robots, namely 1/24th scale radio-controlled model Porsches, which we called Dynamites. These cars ran on a ping-pong table with a

---

[1]   URI: http://www.cs.ubc.ca/~mack/RobotSoccer.htm

little squash ball. In the video online, one can see the players alternating between offensive and defensive behaviors. The behaviors the robots exhibit are clearly a mix of proactive and responsive behaviors, demonstrating the evolution of our models of agents beyond the GOFAIR approach.

Incidentally, there was the amazing and successful contemporaneous effort to get chess programs to the point where they could beat the world champion (Hsu 2002). However, from the perspective presented here, it changes only the single agent Sudoku puzzle into a two agent game; all the other aspects of the Sudoku domain remain the same – perfect information, determinism, and the like. Chess loses its appeal as a domain for driving AI research in new directions.

We managed to push all our soccer system hardware to the limit so that we were able to develop two-on-two soccer. The cars were moving at up to 1 m/s and autonomously controlled at 30 Hz. Each had a separate controller off board and they were entirely independent. The only thing they shared is a common front-end vision perceptual module. We were using transputers (a 1MIP CPU) because we needed significant parallelism here. You can see a typical game segment with the small cars on the Web.[2] We were able to do the real-time path planning and correction and control at about 15–30Hz, depending, but that was really the limit of where we could go at that time (1992–4) because we were limited by the hardware constraints.

RoboCup

As happens, shortly thereafter some Japanese researchers started to think along similar lines. They saw our work and said, "Looks good." Instead of using steerable robots, as we had, they chose holonomic robots that can spin in place. Hiroaki Kitano and his colleagues in Japan proposed RoboCup (Kitano 1997). In Korea, the MiroSot group[3] was also intrigued by similar issues. It made for an interesting international challenge.

The first RoboCup tournament was held in Nagoya in 1997. Our University of British Columbia (UBC) team participated; it was a great milestone event. Many researchers have subsequently made very distinguished contributions in the robot soccer area, including Peter Stone, Manuela Veloso, Tucker Balch, Michael Bowling and Milind Tambe, and many others. It has been fantastic. At RoboCup 2007 in Atlanta, there were approximately 2,700 participant agents, and of those about 1,700 were people and 1,000 were robots. A review of the first ten years of RoboCup has recently appeared (Visser and Burckhard 2007), showing how it has grown in popularity and influenced basic research.

It has become incredibly exciting – a little cutthroat and competitive, with perhaps some dubious tactics at times, but that is the nature of intense

[2] URI: http://www.cs.ubc.ca/~mack/RobotSoccer.htm
[3] URI: http://www.fira.net/soccer/mirosot/overview.html

Figure 19.3. Humanoid Robot Soccer Player.

competition in war and soccer. More importantly, robot soccer has been incredibly stimulating to many young researchers, and it has brought many people
into the field to do fine work, including new competitions such as RoboRescue
and RoboCup@Home. The RoboCup mission is to field a team of humanoid
robots to challenge and beat the human champions by 2050, as suggested by
Figure 19.3.

From Sudoku to Soccer and Beyond

Now let us step back a bit and consider our theme of evolutionary development
of robot architectures. If one thinks of the Sudoku puzzle domain as the exemplar of GOFAIR in a very simple-minded way, then soccer is an exemplar of
something else. What is that something else? I think it is situated agents, and so
we are transitioning from one paradigm to another. As shown in Figure 19.4, we
can compare Sudoku and Soccer as exemplar tasks for each paradigm, GOFAIR
and Situated Agents respectively, along various dimensions.

	Sudoku	Soccer
Number of agents	1	23
Competition	No	Yes
Collaboration	No	Yes
Real time	No	Yes
Dynamics	Minimal	Yes
Chance	No	Yes
Online	No	Yes
Planning Horizons	No	Yes
Situated Perception	No	Yes
Partially Observable	No	Yes
Open World	No	Yes
Learning	Some	Yes

Figure 19.4. Comparison of Sudoku and Soccer along Various Dimensions.

I shall not go through these dimensions exhaustively. In soccer we have twenty-three agents: twenty-two players and a referee. Soccer is hugely competitive between the teams obviously, but also of major importance is the collaboration within the teams, the teamwork being developed, the development of plays, and the communications systems, signaling systems between players, and the protocols for them. Soccer is real-time. There is a major influence of dynamics and of chance. Soccer is online in the sense that one cannot compute a plan offline and then execute, as one can in GOFAIR. Whenever anything is done, a plan almost always must be recomputed. There exists a variety of temporal planning horizons, from "Can I get my foot to the ball?" through to "Can I get the ball into the net?" and "Can I win this tournament?" The visual perception is very situated and embodied. Vision is now onboard the robots in most of the leagues, so a robot sees only what is visible from where it is, meaning the world is obviously only partially observable. The knowledge base is completely open because one cannot infer much about what is going on behind one's back. The opportunities for robot learning are tremendous.

From GOFAIR to Situated Agents

How do we make this transition from GOFAIR to situated agents? There has been a whole community working on situated agents, building governors for steam engines and the like, since the late nineteenth century. Looking at Maxwell's classic paper, "On Governors" (Maxwell 1868), it is clear that he produced the first theory of control, trying as he was to understand why Watt's feedback controller for steam engines actually worked, under what conditions it was stable, and so on. Control theorists have had a great deal to say about situated agents for the last century or so. Thus, one way to build a situated agent would be to suggest that we put AI and control together: Stick an AI planner, GOFAIR or not, on top of a reactive control-theoretic controller doing proportional-integral-derivative (PID) control. One could also put in a middle layer of finite state mode control. These are techniques we fully understand, and that is, in fact, how we did it for the first soccer players that I described earlier. There was a two-level controller. However, there are many problems with this approach, not the least being debugging it and understanding it, let alone proving anything about it. It was all very much "try it and see." It was very unstable as new behaviors were added: It had to be restructured at the higher level and so on. Let me just say that it was a very graduate-student-intensive process requiring endless student programming hours! So rather than gluing a GOFAIR planner on top of a multilayer control-theoretic controller, we moved in a different direction.

I argued that we must abandon the meta-assumptions of GOFAIR but keep the central metaphor of *constraint satisfaction*. My response was that we just give up on those meta-assumptions of GOFAIR, but not throw out the baby of constraint satisfaction with the bathwater of the rest of GOFAIR. Constraint satisfaction was, and is, the key in my mind, because we understand symbolic constraints as well as numerical. We understand how to manipulate them. We understand even first-order logic as a constraint solving system, thanks to work on that side, but we also understand constraints in the control world. We understand that a thermostat is trying to solve a constraint. We have now a uniform language of constraint solving or satisfaction, although one aspect may be continuous whereas the other may be discrete or even symbolic. There is a single language or single paradigm to understand it from top to bottom, which is what we need to build clean systems. The constraints now though are dynamic: coupling the agent and its environment. They are not like the timeless Sudoku constraint: Every number must be different now and forever. When one is trying to kick a ball. the constraint one is trying to solve is whether the foot position is equal to the ball's position at a certain orientation, at a certain velocity, and so on. Those are the constraints one is trying to solve, and one really does not care how one arrives there. One simply knows that a certain point in time, the ball will be at the tip of the foot, not where it is now, but where it will be in the future. So this is a constraint, but it is embedded in time and it is changing over time as one is trying to solve it, and clearly, that is the tricky part.

Thus, constraints are the key to a uniform architecture, and so we need a new theory of constraint-based agents. This has set the stage. I shall leave you in suspense for a while for a digression before I come back to sketch that theory. Its development is part of the evolutionary process that is the theme of this article.

Robot Friends and Foes

I digress here briefly to consider the social role of robots. Robots are powerful symbols; they have a very interesting emotional impact. One sees this instinctively if one has ever worked with kids and Lego robotics or the Aibo dogs that we see in Figure 19.5, or with seniors who treat robots as friends and partners. We anthropomorphize our technological things that look almost like us or like our pets – although not too much like us; that is the "uncanny valley" (Mori 1982). We relate to humanoid robots very closely emotionally. Children watching and playing with robot dogs appear to bond with them at an emotional level.

But, of course, the flip side is the robot soldier (Figure 19.6), the robot army, and the robot tank.

Robots, Telerobots, Androids, and Cyborgs

Robots really are extensions of us. Of course, there are many kinds of robots. One uses the word "robot" loosely but, technically, one can distinguish between strictly autonomous robots and telerobots; with the latter, there is human supervisory control, perhaps at a distance, on a Mars mission or in a surgical situation, for example. There are androids that look like us and cyborgs that are partly us and partly machine. The claim is that robots are really reflections of us, and that we project our hopes and fears onto them. That this has been reflected in literature and other media over the last two centuries is a fact. I do not need to bring to mind all the robot movies, but robots do stand as symbols for our technology.

Dr. Frankenstein and his creation, in *Frankenstein; or, The Modern Prometheus* (Shelley 1818), stood as a symbol of our fear, a sort of Faustian fear that that kind of power, that kind of projection of our own abilities in the world, would come back and attack us. Mary Shelley's work explored that, and Charlie Chaplin's *Modern Times* (Chaplin 1936) brought the myth up to date. Recall the scene in which Charlie is being forced to eat in the factory where, as a factory worker, his entire pace of life is dictated by the time control in the factory. He is a slave to his own robots and his lunch break is constrained because the machines need to be tended. He is, in turn, tended by an unthinking robot who keeps shoving food into his mouth and pouring drinks on him until finally, it runs amok. Chaplin was making a very serious point that our technology stands in real danger of alienating and repressing us if we are not careful.

I'll conclude this somewhat philosophical interjection with the observations of two students of technology and human values. Marshall McLuhan argued

Figure 19.5. Robot Friends Playing Soccer.

Figure 19.6. ... and Robot Foes.

(although he was thinking of books, advertising, television, and other issues of his time, though it applies equally to robots), "We first shape the tools and thereafter our tools shape us" (McLuhan 1964). Parenthetically, this effect can be seen as classic projection and alienation in the sense of Feuerbach (Feuerbach 1854).

The kinds of robots we decide to build will change us as they will change our society. We have a heavy responsibility to think about this carefully. Margaret Somerville is an ethicist who argues that the whole species *Homo sapiens* is actually evolving into *Techno sapiens* as we project our abilities out (Somerville 2006). Of course, this is happening at an accelerating rate. Many of our old ethical codes are broken and do not work in this new world, whether it is in biotechnology or robotics, or in almost any other area of technology today. As creators of some of this technology, it is our responsibility to pay serious attention to that problem.

Robots: One More Insult to the Human Ego?

Another way of thinking about our fraught and ambivalent relationship with robots is that this is really one more insult. How much more can humankind take? Robotics is only the latest displacement of the human ego from center stage. Think about the intellectual lineage that links Copernicus, Darwin, Marx, Freud, and Robots. This may be a stretch, but perhaps not.

Humans thought they were at the center of the universe until Copernicus proposed that the earth was not at the center, but rather that the sun was. Darwin hypothesized we are descended from apes. Marx claimed that many of our desires and goals are determined by our socioeconomic status, and, thus, we are not as free as we thought. Freud theorized one's conscious thoughts are not freely chosen, but rather they come from the unconscious mind. Now I suggest that you can think of robots as being in that same great lineage, which states: You, *Homo sapiens*, are not unique. Now there are other entities, created by us, that can also perceive, think, and act. They could become as smart as we are. Yet this kind of projection can lead to a kind of moral panic: "The robots are coming! The robots are coming! What are we going to do?" When we talk to the media the first questions reporters ask are typically: "Are you worried about them rising up and taking over?" and "Do you think they'll keep us as pets?" The public perception of robots is evolving as our models of robots and the robots themselves evolve.

Helpful Robots

To calm this kind of panic we need to point to some helpful robots. The University of Calgary NeuroArm is actually fabricated from nonmagnetic parts so it can operate within an MRI field. It allows a surgeon to do neurosurgery telerobotically, getting exactly the right parts of the tumor while seeing real time feedback as the surgery is performed.

An early prototype of our UBC smart wheelchair work is shown in Figure 19.7. This chair can use vision and other sensors to locate itself, map its environment, and allow its user to navigate safely.

RoboCars: DARPA Urban Challenge

Continuing with the helpful robot theme, consider autonomous cars. The original DARPA Challenges in 2004 and 2005 and the Urban Challenge in 2007 have catalyzed significant progress. Sebastian Thrun and his team at Stanford developed Junior (Figure 19.8[a]), loaded with sensors and actuators and horsepower and CPUs of all sorts, who faced off against Boss (Figure 19.8[b]) and the Carnegie Mellon/General Motors Tartan racing team in the fall of 2007. Boss took first place and Junior took second in the Urban Challenge.[4] The media look at these developments and see them as precursors to robot tanks, cargo movers, and automated warfare, naturally because they know that DARPA funded them. However, Thrun (Thrun 2006) is an evangelist for a different view of such contests. The positive impact of having intelligent cars would be enormous. Consider the potential ecological savings of using highways much more efficiently instead of paving over farmland. Consider the safety aspect, which could reduce the annual carnage of 4,000 road accident deaths a year in Canada alone. Consider the fact that cars could negotiate at intersections: Dresner and Stone (Dresner 2008) have simulated to show you could get potentially two to three times the throughput in cities in terms of traffic if these cars could talk to each other instead of having to wait for stop signs and traffic lights. Consider the ability of the elderly or disabled to get around on their own. Consider the ability to send one's car to the parking lot by itself and then call it back later. There would be automated warehouses for cars instead of using all that surface land for parking. Truly, the strong positive implications of success in this area are enormous. Yet can we trust them? This is a real problem and major problem. In terms of smart wheelchairs, one major reason why they do not already exist now is liability. It is almost impossible to get an insurance company to back a project or a product. This clarifies why the car manufacturers have moved very slowly and in an incremental way to develop intelligent technology.

Can We Trust Robots?

There are some real reasons why we cannot yet trust robots. The way we build them now, not only are they not trustworthy, they are also unreliable. So can they do the right thing? Will they do the right thing? Then, of course, there is the fear that I alluded to earlier – that eventually they will become autonomous, with free will, intelligence, and consciousness.

---

[4] URIs: http://www.tartanracing.org, http://cs.stanford.edu/group/roadrunner

Figure 19.7. Prototype Smart Wheelchair (UBC, 2006).

(a) "Junior"   (b) "Boss"
(Stanford Racing Team, 2007)   (CMU-GM Tartan Racing Team, 2007)

Figure 19.8. Two competitors in the DARPA Urban Challenge.

Ethics at the Robot/Human Interface

Do we need robot ethics, for us and for them? We do. Many researchers are working on this (Anderson and Anderson 2007). Indeed, many countries have suddenly realized this is an important issue. There will have to be robot law. There are already robot liability issues. There will have to be professional ethics for robot designers and engineers just as there are for engineers in all other disciplines. We will have to factor the issues around what we should do ethically in designing, building, and deploying robots. How should robots make decisions as they develop more autonomy? How should we behave and what ethical issues arise for us as we interact with robots? Should we give them any rights? We have a human rights code; will there be a robot rights code?

There are, then, three fundamental questions we have to address:

1. What should we humans do ethically in designing, building, and deploying robots?
2. How should robots decide, as they develop autonomy and free will, what to do ethically?
3. What ethical issues arise for us as we interact with robots?

Asimov's Laws of Robotics

In considering these questions we will go back to Asimov (Asimov 1950) as he was one of the earlier thinkers about these issues; he put forward some interesting, if perhaps naïve, proposals. His original three Laws of Robotics are:

1. A robot may not harm a human being, or, through inaction, allow a human being to come to harm.
2. A robot must obey the orders given to it by human beings except where such orders would conflict with the First Law.
3. A robot must protect its own existence, as long as such protection does not conflict with the First or Second Laws.

Asimov's Answers

Asimov's answers to those questions I posed are: First, by law, manufacturers would have to put those laws into every robot. Second, robots should always have to follow the prioritized laws. He did not say much about the third question. His plots arise mainly from the conflict between what the humans intend the robot to do and what it actually does do, or between literal and sensible interpretations of the laws stemming from the lack of codified formal language. He discovered many hidden contradictions but they are not of great interest here. What is of interest and important here is that, frankly, the laws and the assumptions behind them are naïve. That is not to blame Asimov – he pioneered the area – but we can say that much of the ethical discussion nowadays remains naïve. It presupposes technical abilities that we just do not have yet.

What We Need

We do not currently have adequate methods for modeling robot structure and functionality, of predicting the consequences of robot commands and actions, and of imposing requirements on those actions such as reaching the goal but doing it in a safe way and making sure that the robot is always live, with no deadlock or livelock. Most important, one can put those requirements on the robot, but one has to be able to find out if the robot will be able to satisfy those requirements. We will never have 100 percent guarantees, but we do need within-epsilon guarantees. Any well-founded ethical discussion presupposes that we (and robots) do indeed have such methods. That is what we require.

Theory Wanted

So, finally coming back to the constraint-based agent theory, it should help to satisfy those requirements. In short, we need a theory with a language to express robot structure and dynamics, a language for constraint-based specifications, and a verification method to determine if a robot described in the first language will (be likely to) satisfy its specifications described in the second language.

Robots as Situated Agents

What kind of robots, then, are we thinking about? These are *situated* robots tightly coupled to the environment; they are not universal robots. Remember *Rossum's Universal Robots* (Capek 1923)? We are not going to build universal robots. We are building very situated robots that function in particular environments for particular tasks. However, those environments are typically highly dynamic. There are other agents. We have to consider social roles. There is a very tight coupling of perception and action, perhaps at many different levels. We now know that the human perceptual system is not a monolithic black box that delivers a three-dimensional model from retinal images. There are many visual subsystems dealing with recognition, location, orientation, attention, and so forth. Our robots will be like that as well.

It is not "cheating" to embody environmental constraints by design, evolution, or learning. It was cheating in the old GOFAIR paradigm that did aim at universal robots. Everything had to be described in, say, the logic, and one could not design environmental constraints into the robots. We think just following biology and natural evolution is the way to go, and learning will play a major part. Evolution is learning at the species level. Communication and perception are very situated. The architectures are online, and there is a hierarchy of time scales and time horizons. Critically, we want to be able to reason about the agent's correctness. We do not require the agents to do reasoning – they may not – but certainly we want to be able to reason about them. When we think back to the GOFAIR model, we never actually did that. The reasoning was in the agent's head alone, and we assumed that if it was correct, everything else was correct. Finally, as I mentioned earlier, one cannot just graft a symbolic system on top of a signal-control-based system and expect the interface to be clean, robust, reliable, debuggable, and (probably) correct. So the slogan is "No hybrid models for hybrid systems."

Vertical Architecture

To satisfy those requirements for situated agents, we have to throw away the horizontal three boxes architectural model and move to a vertical "wedding cake" architecture. As shown in Figure 19.9, as one goes up these controllers, each controller sees a virtual body below it, modularizing the system in that way. Each controller, as one goes higher, is dealing with longer time horizons but with coarser time granularity and different kinds of perception. Each controller will only know what it needs to know. This architectural approach was advocated by Albus (Albus 1981) and Brooks (Brooks 1986). It corresponds quite closely to biological systems at this level of abstraction.

A Constraint-Based Agent

We are interested in constraint-based agents. They are situated; they will be doing constraint satisfaction but in a more generalized sense, not in the GOFCS sense. These constraints may be prioritized. Now we conceive of the controller of the agent or robot as a *constraint solver*.

Dynamic Constraint Satisfaction

Consider the generalization of constraint satisfaction to *dynamic constraint satisfaction*. A soccer example will serve us.

Imagine a humanoid robot trying to kick a soccer ball. In Figure 19.10, we can see the projection into a two-dimensional space of a complex phase space that describes the position and velocity of the limbs of the robot and the ball at time t. Each flow line in the figure shows the dynamics of the evolution of the system from different initial conditions. The controller has to be able to predict where the robot should move its foot to, knowing what it knows about the leg actuators, the ball and where it is moving, how wet the field is, and so on to make contact with the ball to propel it in the right direction. That corresponds to the 45° line $y = x$. So x here is the ball position on the horizontal axis, and y is the foot position on the vertical axis. That is the constraint we are trying to solve. If

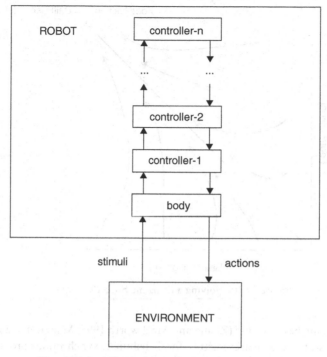

Figure 19.9. A Vertical Robotic System Architecture.

the controller ensures the dynamical system always goes to (or approaches, in the limit) that constraint and stays there, or maybe if it doesn't stay there, but it always returns to it soon enough, then we say that this system is solving that constraint, $FootPosition(t) = BallPosition(t)$. In hybrid dynamical systems language, we say the coupled agent environment system *satisfies the constraint* if and only if the constraint solution set, in the phase space of that coupled hybrid dynamical system, is an *attractor* of the system as it evolves. Incidentally, that concept of online hybrid dynamical constraint satisfaction subsumes the entire old discrete offline GOFCS paradigm (Zhang and Mackworth 1993).

Formal Methods for Constraint-Based Agents

The Constraint-Based Agent (CBA) framework consists of three components:

1. Constraint Net (CN) for system modeling
2. Timed for-all automata for behavior specification
3. Model checking and Liapunov methods for behavior verification

These three components correspond to the tripartite requirement for the theory we said we wanted earlier. Ying Zhang and I developed these formal methods

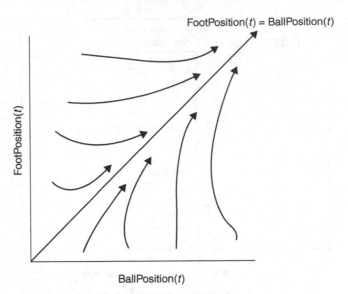

FootPosition(t) = BallPosition(t)

FootPosition(t)

BallPosition(t)

Figure 19.10. Solving a Dynamic Soccer Constraint.

for constraint-based agents (Zhang and Mackworth 1995; Mackworth and Zhang 2003). First, there is an architecture for distributed asynchronous programming languages called Constraint Nets (CN). Programs in CN represent the robot body, the controller, and the environment. In them are represented constraints that are local on the structure and dynamics of each system. For behavior specification we either use temporal logics or timed for-all automata. For verification techniques we have used model checking or generalized Liapunov techniques taken from the standard control literature but generalized for symbolic as well as numerical techniques. Rather than present any technical detail here, I shall sketch a case study, again using soccer.

A Soccer Case Study with Prioritized Constraints

Suppose we want to build a robot soccer player that can move around the world and repeatedly find, track, chase, and kick the soccer ball. The setup is shown in Figure 19.11. Pinar Muyan-Özçelik built a controller for this robot to carry out the task using the Constraint-Based Agent methodology (Muyan-Özçelik and Mackworth 2004). The detailed view of the robot in Figure 19.12 shows a robot base that can only move in the direction it is facing, but it can rotate in place to move in a new direction. There is a pan-tilt unit that serves as a neck and a trinocular color camera on top of it that can do stereo vision, but in this experiment we used monocular color images only.

Figure 19.11. A Robot and a Human Kick the Ball Around.

This is a very simple, almost trivial example, but even here you get a rich complexity of interaction with emergent behavior. Imagine that you have got very simple controllers that can solve each of these constraints: (1) get the ball in the image; (2) if the ball is in the image, center it; and (3) make the base heading equal to the pan direction. Imagine that you are a robot and you can only move forward in the direction you are facing with these robots. If you turn your head to the left and acquire the ball in the image over there, then you have to turn your body to the left toward it, and as you are tracking the ball in the image you have to turn your head to the right in the opposite direction. This is analogous to the well-known vestibulocular reflex (VOR) in humans. Now you are looking at the ball and facing toward it, so now you can move toward it and hit the ball. The last constraint is for the robot to be at the ball. If we can satisfy these constraints, in the correct priority order, this unified behavior will emerge: acquire, track, chase, and kick the ball. If at any time one is satisfying a lower priority constraint and a higher priority constraint becomes unsatisfied, the controller must revert to resatisfying it.

The prioritized constraints are: Ball-In-Image (I), Ball-In-Center (C), Base-Heading-Pan (H), Robot-At-Ball (A). The priority ordering is: $I > C > H > A$. We want to satisfy those prioritized constraints. The specification for this system is that one has to solve those four constraints with that priority. That is all one would say to the system. It is a declarative representation of the behavior we want the system to exhibit. We can automatically compile that specification into a controller that will in fact exhibit that emergent behavior. We can conceptualize these prioritized constraint specifications as generalizations of the GOFAIR linear sequence plans.

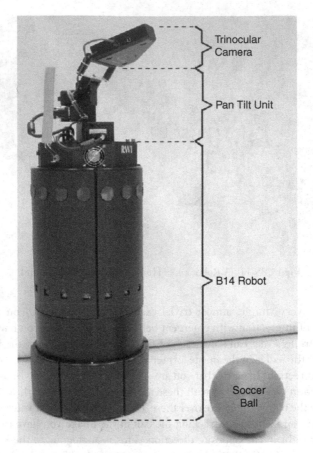

Figure 19.12. A Simple Soccer Player.

Constraint-Based Agents in Constraint Nets

Suppose we are given a prioritized constraint specification for a controller at a certain level in the controller hierarchy as in Figure 19.13. The specification involves Constraint1, Constraint2, and Constraint3. It requires this priority order: Constraint1 > Constraint2 > Constraint3.

We assume we have a simple solver for each constraint, Constraint Solver-1, -2, and -3. Constraint1 is the highest priority, so if it is active and not satisfied, its solver indicates, "I'm not satisfied now, I'd like you to do this to satisfy Constraint1." It might be a gradient descent solver, say. Its signal would go through Arbiter-1. The arbiter knows this is higher priority, and its signal passes it all the way through to Arbiter-2 as well, to the motor outputs. If Constraint-1 is satisfied, Arbiter-1 will let ConstraintSolver-2 pass its outputs through and so

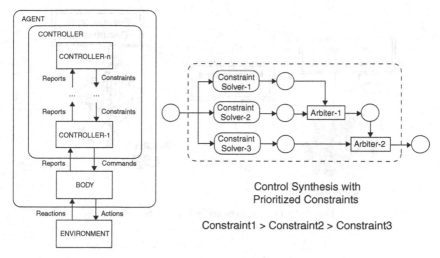

Figure 19.13. Synthesizing a Controller from a Prioritized Constraint Specification.

on. If there is any conflict for the motors, that is how it is resolved. If there is no conflict, then the constraints can be solved independently because they are operating in orthogonal spaces. Using that architecture we built a controller for those constraints in the soccer player, and we tested it all in simulation and it works. It works in a wide variety of simulated conditions; it works with the same controller in a wide variety of real testing situations. We found that the robot always eventually kicks the ball repeatedly, both in simulation and experimentally. In certain circumstances, we can *prove* that the robot always eventually kicks the ball repeatedly. We conclude that the Constraint-Based Agent approach with prioritized constraints is an effective framework for robot-controller construction for a simple task.

Just as an aside, this is a useful way to think about a classic problem in psychology. Carl Lashley, in a seminal paper called "The Problem of the Serial Ordering of Behavior" (Lashley 1951), was writing about speech production, but the sequencing problem arises for all behaviors. Suppose one has a large number of goals one is attempting to satisfy. Each goal is clamoring to be satisfied. How do they get control of the actuators? How does one sequence that access? How does one make sure it is robust? For prioritized constraints, it is robust in the sense that if the controller senses the loss of satisfaction of a higher-priority constraint, it will immediately resume work on resatisfying it. One can also think of what we have done as a formalization of subsumption (Brooks 1991). So this is *a* solution; I am not saying it is *the* solution. It is a very simple-minded solution, but it is a solution to the classic problem of the serial ordering of behavior. It demonstrates that prioritized constraints can be used to build more reliable dynamic agents.

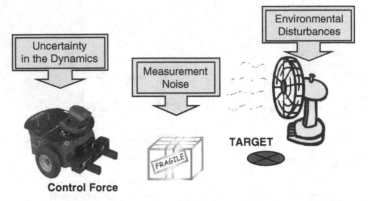

Figure 19.14. Uncertainty in Robotic Systems.

Modeling Uncertainty

So far, nothing has been said about the element of chance, but of course, in real robots with real environments there will be much noise and uncertainty. Robert St-Aubin and I have developed Probabilistic Constraint Nets using probabilistic verification (St-Aubin 2006). As shown in Figure 19.14, there will be uncertainty in the model of the dynamics, in the dynamics themselves, and in the robot's measurement of the world. Moreover, one will be unable to fully model the environment so there will be environmental disturbances.

Observations and Conclusion

Stepping back we observe that a very simple idea, constraint satisfaction, allows us to achieve intelligence through the integration of proactive and responsive behaviors; it is uniform top to bottom. We see in the formal prioritized constraint framework the emergence of robust goal-seeking behavior. I propose it as a contribution to the solution of the problem of a lack of technical foundation to many of the naïve proposals for robot ethics. So if one asks, "Can robots do the right thing?" the answer so far is "Yes, sometimes they can do the right thing, almost always, and we can prove it, sometimes."

Acknowledgments

I am most grateful to all of the students, colleagues, and collaborators who have contributed to some of the work mentioned here: Rod Barman, Le Chang, Pooyan Fazli, Gene Freuder, Joel Friedman, Stewart Kingdon, Jim Little, David Lowe, Valerie McRae, Jefferson Montgomery, Pinar Muyan-Özçelik, Dinesh Pai, David Poole, Fengguang Song, Michael Sahota, Robert St-Aubin, Pooja

Viswanathan, Bob Woodham, Suling Yang, Ying Zhang, and Yu Zhang. This chapter is based, in large part, on the article documenting my AAAI presidential address (Mackworth 2009); David Leake and Mike Hamilton helped with that article. Funding was provided by the Natural Sciences and Engineering Research Council of Canada and through the support of the Canada Research Chair in Artificial Intelligence.

References

Albus, J. S. 1981. *Brains, Behavior and Robotics*. NY: McGraw-Hill.

Anderson, M. and Leigh Anderson, S. 2007. Machine Ethics: Creating an Ethical Intelligent Agent. *AI Magazine*, 28(4):15–26.

Asimov, I. 1950. *I, Robot*. NY: Gnome Press.

Brooks, R. A. 1986. A Robust Layered Control System for a Mobile Robot. IEEE Journal of Robotics and Automation, RA-2(1): 14–23.

Brooks, R. A. 1991. Intelligence without Reason. In Proc. of Twelfth International Joint Conference on Artificial Intelligence, 569–595. San Mateo, CA: Morgan Kaufmann.

Capek, K. 1923. *R. U.R. (Rossum's Universal Robots): A Fantastic Melodrama in Three Acts and an Epilogue*. Garden City, NY: Doubleday.

Dresner, K. and Stone, P. 2008. A Multiagent Approach to Autonomous Intersection Management. *Journal of Artificial Intelligence Research* 31:591–656.

Feuerbach, L. A. 1854. *The Essence of Christianity*. London: John Chapman.

Freuder, E. C. and Mackworth, A. K. 2006. Constraint Satisfaction: An Emerging Paradigm. In *Handbook of Constraint Programming*, ed. F. Rossi, P. Van Beek and T. Walsh, 13–28. Amsterdam: Elsevier.

Haugeland, J. 1985. *Artificial Intelligence: The Very Idea*. Cambridge, MA: MIT Press.

Hsu, F. 2002. *Behind Deep Blue: Building the Computer that Defeated the World Chess Champion*, Princeton, NJ: Princeton University Press.

Kitano, H . (ed.) 1998. *RoboCup-97: Robot Soccer World Cup I*. Lecture Notes in Computer Science 1395, Heidelberg: Springer.

Lashley, K.S., 1951. The Problem of Serial Order in Behavior. In *Cerebral Mechanisms in Behavior*. Ed. L.A. Jeffress, 112–136. New York: Wiley.

Lennon, J. 1980. Beautiful Boy (Darling Boy). Song lyrics. On album *Double Fantasy*.

McLuhan, M. 1964. *Understanding Media: The Extensions of Man*. New York: New American Library.

Mackworth, A. K. 1977. Consistency in Networks of Relations, *Artificial Intelligence* 8(1), 99–118.

Mackworth, A. K. 1993. On Seeing Robots. In *Computer Vision: Systems, Theory and Applications* eds. A. Basu and X. Li, 1–13. Singapore: World Scientific Press.

Mackworth, A. K. 2009. Agents, Bodies, Constraints, Dynamics, and Evolution. *AI Magazine*, 26(30):7–28, Spring 2009.

Mackworth, A. K. and Zhang, Y. 2003. A Formal Approach to Agent Design: An Overview of Constraint-Based Agents. *Constraints* 8 (3) 229–242.

Maxwell J. C. 1868. On Governors. In *Proceedings of the Royal Society of London*, 16, 270–283. London: The Royal Society.

Miller, G. A., Galantner, E., & Pribram, K. H. 1960. Plans and the Structure of Behavior. New York: Holt, Rinehart & Winston.

Mori, M. 1982. *The Buddha in the Robot.* Tokyo: Charles E. Tuttle Co.

Muyan-Özçelik, P., and Mackworth, A. K. 2004. Situated Robot Design with Prioritized Constraints. In *Proc. Int. Conf. on Intelligent Robots and Systems* (IROS 2004), 1807–1814.

Reiter, R. 1978. On Closed World Data Bases. In *Logic and Data Bases* eds. H. Gallaire and J. Minker, 119–140. New York, NY: Plenum.

Rossi, F ., van Beek, P . and Walsh, T . (eds.) 2006. *Handbook of Constraint Programming.* Amsterdam: Elsevier Science.

Sahota, M. and Mackworth, A. K. 1994. Can Situated Robots Play Soccer? In *Proc. Artificial Intelligence '94*, 249–254. Toronto ON: Can. Soc. for Comp. Studies of Intelligence.

Shelley, M. W. 1818. *Frankenstein; or, The Modern Prometheus.* London: Lackington, Hughes, Harding, Mavor and Jones.

Somerville. M. 2006. *The Ethical Imagination: Journeys of the Human Spirit.* Toronto: House of Anansi Press.

St-Aubin, R., Friedman, J. and Mackworth, A. K. 2006. A Formal Mathematical Framework for Modeling Probabilistic Hybrid Systems. *Annals of Mathematics and Artificial Intelligence* 37(3–4) 397–425.

Thrun, S. 2006. Winning the DARPA Grand Challenge. Invited Talk at Innovative Applications of Artificial Intelligence (IAAI-06), Boston, Massachusetts, July 16–20.

Visser, U. and Burkhard, H. D. 2007. RoboCup: 10 years of Achievements and Challenges. *AI Magazine* 28(2) 115–130.

Waltz, D. L. 1975. Understanding Line Drawings of Scenes with Shadows. In *The Psychology of Computer Vision*, ed. P.H. Winston, 19–92. New York, NY: McGraw-Hill.

Zhang, Y. and Mackworth, A. K. 1993. Constraint Programming in Constraint Nets. In *Proc. First Workshop on Principles and Practice of Constraint Programming*. 303–312. Padua: Assoc. for Constraint Programming.

Zhang, Y. and Mackworth, A. K. 1995. Constraint Nets: A Semantic Model for Dynamic Systems. *Theoretical Computer Science* 138 211–239.

20

Piagetian Roboethics via Category Theory
Moving beyond Mere Formal Operations to Engineer Robots Whose Decisions Are Guaranteed to be Ethically Correct

Selmer Bringsjord, Joshua Taylor, Bram van Heuveln, Konstantine Arkoudas, Micah Clark and Ralph Wojtowicz

Introduction

THIS PAPER INTRODUCES AN APPROACH TO, RATHER THAN THE FINAL results of, sustained research and development in the area of roboethics described herein. Encapsulated, the approach is to engineer ethically correct robots by giving them the capacity to reason *over*, rather than merely *in*, logical systems (where logical systems are used to formalize such things as ethical codes of conduct for warfighting robots). This is to be accomplished by taking seriously Piaget's position that sophisticated human thinking exceeds even abstract processes carried out *in* a logical system, and by exploiting category theory to render in rigorous form, suitable for mechanization, structure-preserving mappings that Bringsjord, an avowed Piagetian, sees to be central in rigorous and rational human ethical decision making.

We assume our readers to be at least somewhat familiar with elementary classical logic, but we review basic category theory and categorical treatment of deductive systems. Introductory coverage of the former subject can be found in Barwise and Etchemendy [1] and Ebbinghaus, Flum, and Thomas [2]; deeper

The R&D described in this paper has been partially supported by IARPA's A–SpaceX program (and other IARPA/DTO/ARDA programs before this one, e.g., NIMD and IKRIS), and, on the category-theoretic side, by AFOSR funding to Wojtowicz at Metron Inc., and through Metron to Bringsjord. An NSF CPATH grant to explore "social robotics," on which Bringsjord is a Co-PI (N. Webb PI), has been helpful as well. Bringsjord is indebted to Jim Fahey for insights regarding roboethics (including, specifically, whether ethical reasoning can be mechanized), to Robert Campbell for information about lesser-known aspects of Piaget's work, and to Ron Arkin for lively, stimulating discussion about various approaches to roboethics. Joshua Taylor has been funded in the past in part by the Tetherless World Constellation at RPI.

coverage of the latter, offered from a suitably computational perspective, is provided in Barr and Wells [3]. Additional references are of course provided in the course of this paper.

Preliminaries

A category consists of a collection of objects and a collection of arrows, or morphisms. Associated with each arrow f are a domain (or source), denoted dom f, and a codomain (or target), denoted cod f. An arrow f with domain A and codomain B is denoted $f : A \to B$ or

$$A \xrightarrow{f} B.$$

Associated with a category is an associative composition operator $\circ$ that is total on compatible arrows. That is, for any arrow, $f : A \to B$, $g : B \to C$, and $h : C \to D$, the category has an arrow $g \circ f : A \to C$, and that $(h \circ g) \circ f = h \circ (g \circ f)$. For each object A in a category, there is an identity arrow $\mathrm{id}_A : A \to A$ such that for any $f : A \to B$, it holds that $\mathrm{id}_B \circ f = f = f \circ \mathrm{id}_A$.

Many mathematical structures can be represented as categories. For instance, the natural numbers form a category with a single object, $\star$, and arrows named by the natural numbers $\{n \colon \star \to \star \mid n \in \mathbb{N}\}$. Composition is defined as addition on the natural numbers such that $m \circ n = m + n$, and is readily seen to be associative. The identity arrow, $\mathrm{id}_\star$, is 0, as for any n, $n + 0 = 0 + n = n$.

In addition, many classes of mathematical structures can be represented as categories wherein individual mathematical structures are the objects of the category and arrows are morphisms between the objects. For instance, the category **Set** has sets as its objects and set functions as its arrows. Composition in **Set** is function composition (which is associative). The identity arrows of **Set** are the identity functions on sets.

A notable example of this type of category is **Cat**, whose objects are categories, and whose arrows are category morphims, or functors. A functor $\mathcal{F} : \mathcal{C} \to \mathcal{D}$ maps the objects and arrows of category $\mathcal{C}$ to the object and arrows of category $\mathcal{D}$ such that $\mathcal{F}(\mathrm{id}_A) = \mathrm{id}_{\mathcal{F}(A)}$ and $\mathcal{F}(f \circ g) = \mathcal{F}(f) \circ \mathcal{F}(g)$. Note that this requirement ensures that for any arrow $f : A \to B$ of $\mathcal{C}$, the domain and codomain of $\mathcal{F}(f)$ are $\mathcal{F}(A)$ and $\mathcal{F}(B)$, that is $\mathcal{F}(f) : \mathcal{F}(A) \to \mathcal{F}(B)$.

A logic combines a language, typically a set of formulae defined by a context-free grammar, and rules for constructing proofs, that is, derivations of certain formulae from others. Most logics can be represented as categories by taking their formulae as objects and positing that there is an arrow $p : \phi \to \psi$ if and only if p is a proof of ψ from ϕ. Most logics, and all the logics with which we shall be concerned herein, are such that given proofs $p : \phi \to \psi$ and $q : \psi \to \rho$, we can construct a proof $q \circ p : \phi \to \rho$, and also such that for any formula ϕ, there is a proof $\mathrm{id}_\phi : \phi \to \phi$. It is worth noting that either the arrows in such a category must either be taken as equivalence classes of proofs or that $\circ$ is a sort of normalizing proof composition (i.e., to satisfy the requirements that $p \circ \mathrm{id}_\phi = \mathrm{id}_\phi = \mathrm{id}_\phi \circ q$ and $(p \circ q) \circ r = p \circ (q \circ r)$).

In treating logics as categories, we shall define the arrows of a category through the use of arrow schemata. For instance, in the propositional calculus, given proofs of ψ and ρ from ϕ, there is a proof of $\psi \wedge \rho$ from ϕ. We indicate this with the following schema.

$$\frac{\phi \xrightarrow{\ p\ } \psi \quad \phi \xrightarrow{\ q\ } \rho}{\phi \xrightarrow{\ \wedge I\, p,q\ } \psi \wedge \rho} \ \wedge \ \text{intro}$$

As another example, given a proof of the disjunction $\psi \vee \rho$, and proofs of the conditionals $\psi \supset \sigma$ and $\rho \supset \sigma$ from ϕ, there is a proof of ρ from ϕ.

$$\frac{\phi \xrightarrow{\ p_0\ } \psi_1 \vee \ldots \vee \psi_n \quad \phi \xrightarrow{\ p_1\ } \psi_1 \supset \rho \ldots \phi \xrightarrow{\ p_n\ } \psi_n \supset \rho}{\phi \xrightarrow{\ \vee E\, p_0, p_1, \ldots, p_n\ } \rho} \ \vee \ \text{elim}$$

Functors between categories that represent logics map the formulae and proofs of one logic to the formulae and proofs of another. Such mappings, or translations, have been used in the history of formal logic to demonstrate many relationships between logics. Herein we shall be concerned with the use of functors between such categories as tools to shift between representations of reasoning tasks.

Piaget's View of Thinking

Many people, including many outside psychology and cognitive science, know that Piaget seminally – and by Bringsjord's lights, correctly – articulated and defended the view that mature human reasoning and decision making consists in processes operating for the most part on formulas in the language of classical extensional logic (e.g., see [4]).[1] You may yourself have this knowledge. You may also know that Piaget posited a sequence of cognitive stages through which humans, to varying degrees, pass. How many stages are there, according to Piaget? The received answer is four; in the fourth and final stage, *formal operations*, neurobiologically normal humans can reason accurately and quickly over formulas expressed in the logical system known as first-order logic, $\mathcal{L}_I$.[2]

Judging by the cognition taken by Piaget to be stage-three or stage-four (e.g., see Figure 20.1, which shows one of the many problems presented to subjects in [4]), the basic scheme is that an agent $\mathcal{A}$ receives a problem P (expressed

---

[1] Many readers will know that Piaget's position long ago came under direct attack by such thinkers as Wason and Johnson-Laird [5, 6]. In fact, unfortunately, for the most part academics believe that this attack succeeded. Bringsjord doesn't agree in the least, but this isn't the place to visit the debate in question. Interested readers can consult [7, 8]. Piaget himself retracted any claims of *universal* use of formal logic: [9].

[2] Various other symbols are used, e.g., the more informative $\mathcal{L}_{\omega\omega}$.

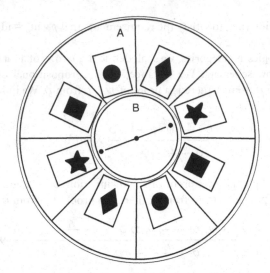

Figure 20.1. Piaget's famous "rigged" rotating board to test for the development of stage-3-or-better reasoning in children. The board, A, is divided into sectors of different colors and equal surfaces; opposite sectors match in color. B is a rotating disk with a metal rod spanning its diameter – but the catch is that the star cards have magnets buried under them (inside wax), so the alignment after spinning is invariably as shown here, no matter how the shapes are repositioned in the sectors (with matching shapes directly across from each other). This phenomenon is what subjects struggle to explain. Details can be found in [4].

as a visual scene accompanied by explanatory natural language), represents P in a formal language that is a superset of the language of $\mathcal{L}_I$, producing $[P]$, and then reasons over this representation (along with background knowledge Γ) using at least a combination of some of the proof theory of $\mathcal{L}_1$ and "psychological operators."[3] This reasoning allows the agent to obtain the solution $[S]$. To ease exposition, we shall ignore the heterodox operations that Piaget posits (see note 1) in favor of just standard proof theory, and we will moreover view $[P]$ as a triple (ϕ, C, Q), where ϕ is a (possibly complicated) formula in the language of $\mathcal{L}_I$, C is further information that provides context for the problem, and consists of a set of first-order formulas, and Q is a query asking for a proof of ϕ from $C \cup \Gamma$. So:

$$[P] = (\phi, C, Q = C \cup \Gamma \vdash \phi?)$$

---

[3] The psychological operators in question cannot always be found in standard proof theories. For example, Piaget held that the quartet I N R C of "transformations" were crucial to thought at the formal level. Each member of the quartet transforms formulas in certain ways. E.g., N is *inversion*, so that $N(p \vee q) = \neg p \wedge \neg q$; this seems to correspond to DeMorgan's Law. Yet R is *reciprocity*, so $R(p \vee q) = \neg p \wedge \neg q$, and of course this isn't a valid inference in the proof theory for the propositional calculus or $\mathcal{L}_I$.

For example, in the invisible magnetization problem shown in Figure 20.1, which requires stage-three reasoning in order to be solved, the idea is to explain how it is that ϕ^{**}, that is, that the rotation invariably stops with the two stars selected by the rod. Because Piaget is assuming the hypothetico-deductive method of explanation made famous by Popper [10], to provide an explanation is to rule out hypotheses until one arrives deductively at ϕ^{**}. In experiments involving child subjects, a number of incorrect (and sometimes silly) hypotheses are entertained – that the stars are heavier than the other shaped objects, that the colors of the sections make a difference, and so on. Piaget's analysis of those who discard mistaken hypotheses in favor of ϕ^{**} is that they expect consequences of a given hypothesis to occur, note that these consequences fail to obtain, and then reason backward by *modus tollens* to the falsity of the hypotheses. For example, it is key in the magnet experiments of Figure 20.1 that "for some spins of the disk, the rod will come to rest upon shapes other than the stars" is an expectation. When expectations fail, disjunctive syllogism allows ϕ^{**} to be concluded. For our discussion of a sample functor over deductive systems as categories, it's important to note that whereas the hypotheses and context for the problem are naturally expressed using relation symbols, function symbols, and quantifiers from the language of $\mathcal{L}_I$, according to Piaget the final solution is produced by deduction in the propositional calculus.

From Piaget to Roboethics

What does all this have to do with roboethics? Well, for starters, notice that certain approaches to regulating the ethical decisions of lethal robots can be fairly viewed as aiming to engineer such robots by ensuring that they operate at Piaget's fourth stage. We believe this is true of both [11] and [12]. Whereas in the first case an ethical code is to be expressed within some deontic/epistemic logic that subsumes classical logic,[4] and in the second there is no insistence upon using such more expressive logics, the bottom line is that in both cases there would seem to be a match with Piaget's fourth stage: In both cases the basic idea is that robots work in a particular logical system and their decisions are constrained by this work. In fact, it is probably not unfair to view an ethically relevant decision d by a robot to be correct if a formula in which d occurs can be proved from what is observed and from background knowledge (which includes an ethical code or set of ethical rules, etc.) – so that a decision point becomes the solution of a problem with this now-familiar shape:

$$[P] = \left(\phi(d), C, Q = C \cup \Gamma \vdash \phi(d)? \right)$$

[4] A rapid but helpful overview of epistemic and deontic logic can be found in [13]. For more advanced work on computational epistemic logic, see [14].

The Intolerable Danger of Fourth-Stage Robots

In a sentence, the danger is simply that if a lethal agent is unable to engage in at least something close to sophisticated human-level ethical reasoning and decision making, and instead can only operate at Piaget's fourth stage (as that operation is formalized herein), it is evident that that agent will, sooner or later, go horribly awry. That is, it will perform actions that are morally wrong or fail to perform actions that are morally obligatory, and the consequences will include extensive harm to human beings.

The reason such sad events will materialize is that a robot can flawlessly obey a "moral" code of conduct and still be catastrophically unethical. This is easy to prove: Imagine a code of conduct that recommends some action that, in the broader context, is positively immoral. For example, if human Jones carries a device that, if not eliminated, will (by his plan) see to the incineration of a metropolis (or perhaps a collection of metropolises), and a robot (e.g., an unmanned, autonomous UAV) that has just one shot to save the day but is bound by a code of conduct not to destroy Jones because he happens to be a civilian, or be in a church, or at a cemetery, and this is all the relevant information, it would presumably be immoral not to eliminate Jones. (This of course is just one of innumerable easily invented cases.)

Unfortunately, the approach referred to in the previous section is designed to bind robots by fixed codes of conduct (e.g., rules of engagement covering warf-ighters). This approach may well get us all killed – if in the real world a malicious agent like Jones arrives.

The approach that *won't* get us killed, and indeed perhaps the only viable path open to us if we want to survive, is to control robot behavior by operations over an ensemble of suitably stocked logical systems – operations from which suitable codes can be mechanically *derived* by robots on the fly. Once the code has been derived, it can be applied in a given set of circumstances.

But Then Why Piaget's Paradigm?

But if Piaget posits four stages, and deficient approaches to ethically correct robots already assume that such robots must operate at the fourth and final stage, what does the Piagetian paradigm have to offer those in search of ways to engi-neer ethically correct robots? The key fact is that Piaget actually posited stages *beyond* the fourth one – stages in which agents are able to operate over logical systems. For example, we know that logicians routinely create new logical systems (and often new components thereof that are of independent interest); this was something Piaget was aware of and impressed by. Yet most people, even scholars with psychology of reasoning in academia, are not aware of the fact that Piaget's scheme made room for cognition beyond the fourth stage.

In fact, the truth of the matter is that Piaget made room for an arbitrary number of ever more sophisticated stages beyond the fourth. Piaget scholar and Clemson psychologist Robert Campbell writes:

For [Piaget] there was no fixed limit to human development, and, wisely, he did not attempt to forecast future creative activity. Piaget did suggest that beyond formal operations, there are postformal operations, or "operations to the n th power." Inevitably these would be of a highly specialized nature, and might be found in the thinking of professional mathematicians or experts in some other field. (Lecture presented at the Institute of Objectivist Studies Summer Seminar, Charlottesville, VA, July 7 and 8, 1997. Available on the web at http://hubcap.clemson.edu/~campber/piaget.html.)

What Piaget had in mind for postformal stages would seem to coincide quite naturally with our formal framework, in which postformal reasoning involves the meta-processing of logics and formal theories expressed in those logics. Unfortunately, most of Piaget's later work has yet to be translated into English. For example, Campbell notes in the same lecture just cited that a straightforward example of "operations to the n th power," according to Piaget, is the construction of axiomatic systems in geometry, which requires a level of thinking beyond stage four (= beyond formal operations). Yet the textual confirmation (e.g., Piaget: "one could say that axiomatic schemas are to formal schemes what the latter are to concrete operations") comes from work not yet translated from the French (viz., [15], p. 226).

Category Theory for Fifth-Stage Robots

Category theory is a remarkably useful formalism, as can be easily verified by turning to the list of spheres to which it has been productively applied – a list that ranges from attempts to supplant orthodox set theory-based foundations of mathematics with category theory [16, 17] to viewing functional programming languages as categories [3]. However, for the most part – and this is in itself remarkable – category theory has not energized AI or computational cognitive science, even when the kind of AI and computational cognitive science in question is logic based.[5] We say this because there is a tradition of viewing logics or logical systems from a category-theoretic perspective. For example, Barwise [20] treats logics, from a model-theoretic viewpoint, as categories; and as some readers will recall, Lambek [21] treats proof calculi (or as he and others often refer to them, *deductive systems*) as categories. Piaget's approach certainly seems proof-theoretic/syntactic; accordingly, we provide now an example of stage-five category-theoretic reasoning from the standpoint of proof theory. (Although Piaget, as we have noted,

---

[5] Bringsjord is as guilty as anyone, in light of the fact that even some very recent, comprehensive treatments of logicist AI and computational cognitive science are devoid of category-theoretic treatments. E.g., see [18, 19].

allows for the possibility of any number of stages beyond four, we simplify the situation and refer to post-formal processing as "stage five.")

The example is based on two logical systems known to be directly used by Piaget, the propositional calculus $\mathcal{L}_{PC}$ and full first-order logic $\mathcal{L}_I$. We will work with the categories corresponding to these logics, **PC** and **FOL**, respectively. The review of basic category theory given in § 2 should make the structure of **PC** and **FOL** relatively clear, but discussion of several points is in order.

Given that there are many formalizations of the propositional calculus (e.g., axiomatic methods with but one inference rule, natural-deduction-style systems, etc.), there are actually many categories that we might accept as **PC**. However, the consequence relations for propositional calculus and first-order logic are fixed, and we do require that **PC** represent a sound and complete proof calculus for the propositional calculus, that is, that there are arrows from ϕ to ψ if and only if $\phi \vDash_{PC} \psi$. For most proof systems, there will be infinitely many such proofs, and so infinitely many arrows for each consequence. We also maintain that in **PC** there is an object $\top$, to be read as "true" and that **PC** contains for every object ϕ an arrow $\top_\phi : \phi \to \top$. In addition, this construction provides the appropriate identity arrow, $\mathrm{id}_\top = \top_\top$. We impose the same restrictions on **FOL**; we require there be a "true" object $\top$, that the proof calculus respects the consequence relation, and so on. We also require that the arrows of **FOL** are generated by a superset of the schemata that generate the arrows of **PC**. Particularly, the schemata for **PC** define sentential proofs, whereas the extra arrows for **FOL** define proofs involving quantification and equality.

In this treatment we have followed the traditional scheme [21], but we must leave open paths for unsound and incomplete proof calculi because, clearly, in Piaget's work, proof calculi for humans would not necessarily include the full machinery of standard ones for the propositional and predicate calculi; and moreover, humans, according to Piaget, make use of idiosyncratic transformations that we would want to count as deductions (see note 1). Whereas even the traditional scheme may seem to require some forcing of proof calculi into a categorical framework (e.g., by an equivalence relation imposed on proofs or by non-trivial proof composition), there are proof calculi which match this paradigm well. For instance, Arkoudas's NDL [22] explicitly calls out deductions, which can be composed.

We now provide a cognitively plausible functor-based mechanism for performing limited types of reasoning in **FOL** using **PC**. The standard truth functional form [1, Chapter 10] of a first-order formula ϕ is a propositional formula that preserves the truth functional connectives present in ϕ, but maps all other formulae, namely atomic formulae and quantifications, to propositional variables. That is, given an injection ι that maps atomic formulae and quantifications to propositional variables, the truth functional form of a formula ϕ, denoted $\tau(\phi)$ is defined as follows.

$$\tau(\top) = \top$$
$$\tau(\neg\phi) = \neg\tau(\phi)$$

$$\tau(\phi \wedge \psi) = \tau(\phi) \wedge \tau(\psi)$$
$$\tau(\phi \vee \psi) = \tau(\phi) \vee \tau(\psi)$$
$$\tau(\phi \supset \psi) = \tau(\phi) \supset \tau(\psi)$$
$$\tau(\phi) = \iota(\phi) \quad \phi \text{ atomic or a quantification}$$

We now define the category **PC′** whose objects are the formulae in the image of ι along with ⊤ and compound formulae built up therefrom using the sentential connectives; this is exactly the image of τ. The arrows of **PC′** are those defined by the same schemata used to define the arrows of **PC**. It is trivial to confirm that every object and arrow of **PC′** is also an object or arrow of **PC**.

We can now construct a functor ⋆ : **PC′** → **FOL**. Because τ is an injection of first-order formulae and a surjection to the objects of **PC′**, it is a bijection between the objects of **FOL** and **PC′**. The arrows of **PC** and hence of **PC′** are defined by a subset of the schemata used to define the arrows of **FOL**. The functor ⋆ : **PC′** → **FOL** simply maps each object ϕ of **PC′** to its corresponding first-order formula $\tau^{-1}(\phi)$, and each arrow $p:\phi \to \psi$ to the arrow $p: \tau^{-1}(\phi) \to \tau^{-1}(\psi)$.

The function τ and functor ⋆ form a cognitively plausible mechanism for representing what we noted to be happening in connection with the magnet mechanism above, that is, subjects are representing phenomena associated with the apparatus using relations and quantifiers (as objects of **FOL**), but then encoding this information (via τ) in the propositional calculus (as objects of **PC′**).

It seems to us plausible that in the case of the magnet challenge, humans who successfully meet it essentially do a proof by cases, in which they rule out as unacceptable certain hypotheses for why the rod always stops at the stars. Assuming this is basically correct, it seems undeniable that although humans perceive all the relations that are in play (colors, shapes, and so on), and in some sense reason over them, something like the function τ and functor ⋆ are applied to more detailed reasoning of **FOL** to distill down to the core reasoning, expressible in **PC′**, and hence drop explicit reference to relations. The situation as we see it is summed up in Figure 20.2.

Demonstrations and Future Research

As we said at the outset of the present paper, our goal here has been to introduce an approach to roboethics. Nonetheless, we have made some concrete progress. For example, demonstration of an actual magnet-puzzle-solving robot operating on the basis of the approach previously described was engineered by Taylor and Evan Gilbert and given by Bringsjord at the Roboethics Workshop at ICRA 2009, in Kobe, Japan. This demonstration used PERI, shown in Figure 20.4; and a snapshot derived from the video of the demonstration in question is shown in Figure 20.5.

Of course, we seek robots able to succeed on many of Piaget's challenges, not only on the magnet problem of Figure 20.1, and we are developing Piagetian

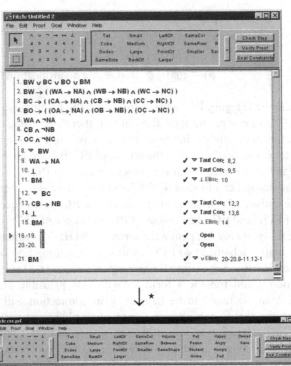

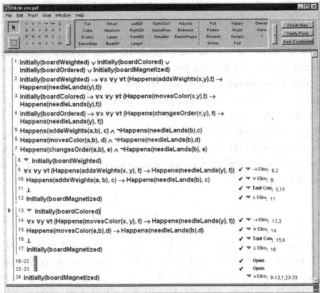

Figure 20.2. This figure shows two proofs, one expressed in **PC′**, the other in **FOL**. The first-order proof produces the conclusion that what causes the metal rod to invariably stop at the stars is that there are hidden magnets. The basic structure is proof by cases. Of the four disjuncts entertained as the possible source of the rod-star regularity, the right one is deduced when the others are eliminated. The functor ⋆ is shown here to indicate that the basic structure can be produced as a proof couched exclusively in the propositional calculus.

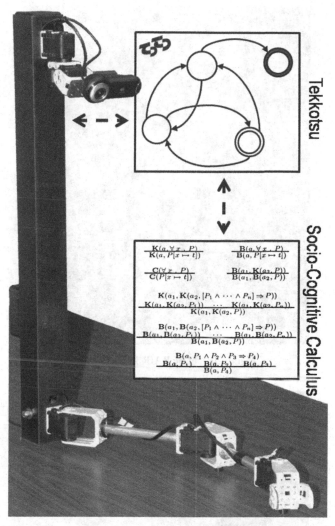

Figure 20.3. The basic configuration for our initial experiments involving Tekkotsu.

challenges of our own design that catalyze post-stage-four reasoning and decision making. We are also working on microcosmic versions of the ethically charged situations that robots will see when deployed in warfare and counterterrorism, where post-stage-four reasoning and decision making is necessary for successfully handling these situations. These coming demonstrations are connected to NSF-sponsored efforts on our part to extend CMU's Tekkotsu [23, 24] framework so that it includes operators that are central to our logicist approach to robotics, and specifically to roboethics – for example, operators for belief (**B**), knowledge

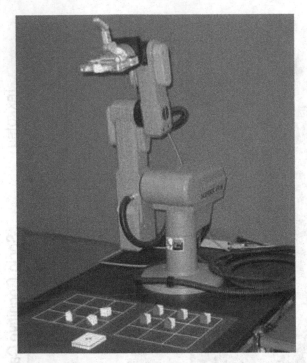

Figure 20.4. The RAIR Lab's PERI.

Figure 20.5. The RAIR Lab's PERI in the process of solving the magnet puzzle. Note that to make robot manipulation possible, playing cards and wooden cylinders have been used – but the problem here is isomorphic to Piaget's original version. Credit is given to Evan Gilbert and Trevor Housten for construction of the apparatus and programming of PERI.

(**K**), and obligation ($\bigcirc$ of standard deontic logic). The idea is that these operators would link to their counterparts in bona fide calculi for automated and semi-automated machine reasoning. One such calculus has already been designed and implemented: the *cognitive event calculus* (see [25]). This calculus includes the full event calculus, a staple in AI (for example, see [26]). Given that our initial experiments will make use of simple hand-eye robots recently acquired by the RAIR Lab from the Tekkotsu group at CMU, Figure 20.3, which shows one of these robots, sums up the situation (in connection with the magnet challenge).

Finally, although our title contains "Piagetian Roboethics," the approach described in this short paper can of course generalize to robotics *simpliciter*. This generalization will be pursued in the future. In fact, the direction described herein is the kernel of an approach to logicist AI and computational cognitive science, whether or not the agents involved are physical or nonphysical. Therefore, in the future, the general concept of agents whose intelligence derive from reasoning and decision making over logical systems (and their components) as categories will be pursued as well. It is not implausible to hold in Piagetian fashion that sophisticated human cognition, whether or not it is directed at ethics, exploits coordinated functors over many, many logical systems encoded as categories. These systems range from the propositional calculus, through description logics, to first-order logic, to temporal, epistemic, and deontic logics, and so on.

References

[1] J. Barwise and J. Etchemendy, *Language, Proof, and Logic*. New York, NY: Seven Bridges, 1999.

[2] H. D. Ebbinghaus, J. Flum, and W. Thomas, *Mathematical Logic* (second edition). New York, NY: Springer-Verlag, 1994.

[3] M. Barr and C. Wells, *Category Theory for Computing Science*. Montréal, Canada: Les Publications CRM, 1999.

[4] B. Inhelder and J. Piaget, *The Growth of Logical Thinking from Childhood to Adolescence*. New York, NY: Basic Books, 1958.

[5] P. Wason, "Reasoning," in *New Horizons in Psychology*. Hammondsworth, UK: Penguin, 1966.

[6] P. Wason and P. Johnson-Laird, *Psychology of Reasoning: Structure and Content*. Cambridge, MA: Harvard University Press, 1972.

[7] S. Bringsjord, E. Bringsjord, and R. Noel, "In defense of logical minds," in *Proceedings of the 20th Annual Conference of the Cognitive Science Society*. Mahwah, NJ: Lawrence Erlbaum, 1998, pp. 173–178.

[8] K. Rinella, S. Bringsjord, and Y. Yang, "Efficacious logic instruction: People are not irremediably poor deductive reasoners," in *Proceedings of the Twenty-Third Annual Conference of the Cognitive Science Society*, J. D. Moore and K. Stenning, Eds. Mahwah, NJ: Lawrence Erlbaum Associates, 2001, pp. 851–856.

[9] J. Piaget, "Intellectual evolution from adolescence to adulthood," *Human Development*, vol. 15, pp. 1–12, 1972.

[10] K. Popper, *The Logic of Scientific Discovery*. London, UK: Hutchinson, 1959.

[11] S. Bringsjord, K. Arkoudas, and P. Bello, "Toward a general logicist methodology for engineering ethically correct robots," *IEEE Intelligent Systems*, vol. 21, no. 4, pp.38–44,2006.[Online].Available:http://kryten.mm.rpi.edu/bringsjord_inference_robot_ethics_preprint.pdf.

[12] R. C. Arkin, "Governing lethal behavior: Embedding ethics in a hybrid deliberative/ reactive robot architecture – Part iii: Representational and architectural considerations," in *Proceedings of Technology in Wartime Conference*, Palo Alto, CA, January 2008, this and many other papers on the topic are available at the url here given. [Online]. Available: http://www.cc.gatech.edu/ai/robot-lab/publications.html.

[13] L. Goble, Ed., *The Blackwell Guide to Philosophical Logic*. Oxford, UK: Blackwell Publishing, 2001.

[14] K. Arkoudas and S. Bringsjord, "Metareasoning for multi-agent epistemic logics," in *Fifth International Conference on Computational Logic In Multi-Agent Systems (CLIMA 2004)*, ser. Lecture Notes in Artificial Intelligence (LNAI). New York: Springer-Verlag, 2005, vol. 3487, pp. 111–125. [Online]. Available: http:// kryten.mm.rpi.edu/arkoudas.bringsjord.clima.crc.pdf.

[15] J. Piaget, *Introduction a l' Épistémologie Génétique. La Pensée Mathématique*. Paris, France: Presses Universitaires de France, 1973.

[16] J.P.Marquis,"Categorytheoryandthefoundationsofmathematics,"*Synthese*,vol.103, pp. 421–447, 1995.

[17] F. W. Lawvere, "An elementary theory of the category of sets," *Proceedings of the National Academy of Science of the USA*, vol. 52, pp. 1506–1511, 2000.

[18] S. Bringsjord, "Declarative/logic-based cognitive modeling," in *The Handbook of Computational Psychology*, R. Sun, Ed. Cambridge, UK: Cambridge University Press, 2008, pp. 127–169. [Online]. Available: http://kryten.mm.rpi.edu/sb_lccm_ab-toc_031607.pdf.

[19] S. Bringsjord, "The logicist manifesto: At long last let logic-based AI become a field unto itself," *Journal of Applied Logic*, vol. 6, no. 4, pp. 502–525, 2008. [Online]. Available: http://kryten.mm.rpi.edu/SB_LAI_Manifesto_091808.pdf.

[20] J. Barwise, "Axioms for abstract model theory," *Annals of Mathematical Logic*, vol. 7, pp. 221–265, 1974.

[21] J. Lambek, "Deductive systems and categories I. Syntactic calculus and residuated categories," *Mathematical Systems Theory*, vol. 2, pp. 287–318, 1968.

[22] K. Arkoudas, "Simplifying Proofs in Fitch-Style Natural Deduction Systems," *Journal of Automated Reasoning*, vol. 34, no. 3, pp. 239–294, Apr. 2005.

[23] D. Touretzky, N. Halelamien, E. Tira-Thompson, J. Wales, and K. Usui, "Dualcoding representations for robot vision in Tekkotsu," *Autonomous Robots*, vol. 22, no. 4, pp. 425–435, 2007.

[24] D. S. Touretzky and E. J. Tira-Thompson, "Tekkotsu: A framework for AIBO cognitive robotics," in *Proceedings of the Twentieth National Conference on Artificial Intelligence (AAAI-05)*. Menlo Park, CA: AAAI Press, 2005.

[25] K. Arkoudas and S. Bringsjord, "Propositional attitudes and causation," *International Journal of Software and Informatics*, vol. 3, no. 1, pp. 47–65, 2009. [Online]. Available: http://kryten.mm.rpi.edu/PRICAI_w_sequentcalc_ 041709.pdf.

[26] S. Russell and P. Norvig, *Artificial Intelligence: A Modern Approach*. Upper Saddle River, NJ: Prentice Hall, 2002.

21

Ethical Protocols Design

Matteo Turilli

Introduction

THE RESPONSIBILITIES OF A SYSTEM DESIGNER ARE GROWING AND expanding in fields that only ten years ago were the exclusive realms of philosophy, sociology, or jurisprudence. Nowadays, a system designer must have a deep understanding not only of the social and legal implications of what he is designing, but also of the ethical nature of the systems he is conceptualizing. These artifacts not only behave autonomously in their environments, embedding themselves into the functional tissue or our society but also "re-ontologise"[1] part of our social environment, shaping new spaces in which people operate.

It is in the public interest that automated systems minimize their usage of limited resources, are safe for users, and integrate ergonomically within the dynamics of everyday life. For instance, one expects banks to offer safe, multifunction ATMs, hospitals to ensure that electro-medical instruments do not electrocute patients, and nuclear plants to employ redundant, formally specified control systems.

It is equally important to the public interest that artificial autonomous entities behave correctly. Autonomous and interactive systems affect the social life of millions of individuals, while performing critical operations such as managing sensitive information, financial transactions, or the packaging and delivery of medicines. The development of a precise understanding of what it means for such artifacts to behave in accordance with the ethical principles endorsed by a society is a pressing issue.

The first section of this paper presents the definitions of the concepts of "actor," "agent," "individual," and "heterogeneous organization." Actors,

With kind permission from Springer Science+Business Media: Ethics and Information Technology, The ethics of information transparency, 11:2, 2009, 105-112, Matteo Turilli and Luciano Floridi.

[1]   Re-ontologize is a neologism introduced in Luciano Floridi. The Ontological Interpretation of Informational Privacy. *Ethics and Information Technology*, 7(4): 185–200, 2006. "Computers and ICTs are ... ontologizing devices because they engineer environments that the user is then enabled to enter through (possibly friendly) gateways."

agents, and individuals are entities that operate within environments that will be referred to as "heterogeneous organizations." Other concepts introduced in the paper are to be understood in terms of this underlying ontology.

The second section introduces a specific type of actor, namely Information and Communication Technology (ICT) actors. These are autonomous and interactive technologies that may have an ethical impact on the environment on which they operate. Two concrete examples of ICT actors are introduced: Automated Pharmacy Systems (APSs) and Business Process Management Systems (BPMSs). The social risks of automation are introduced by recalling the classic example of the Wall Street Black Monday.

The Ethical Consistency Problem (ECP) is introduced in the third section. This is the core problem investigated in this paper. The identity-theft felony/crime is used as a paradigmatic example of ECP. The analysis of the problem is furthered by looking at what types of ethical principles are used to constrain individuals and by discussing a prototypical abstraction of a software design process.

The fourth section offers a solution for the Ethical Consistency Problem. Initially, the concepts of Ethical Requirement and Ethical Protocol are defined. The proposed solution is then described by suggesting a two-step translation, from ethical principles to ethical requirements and then from ethical requirements to ethical protocols. A new formal tool, called Control Closure of an operation (*CCop*), is defined and used to represent the normative constraints expressed by an ethical principle in terms of ethical requirements and then ethical protocols.

The fifth section contains an explicative example of the solution offered for the ECP. The example is composed of the definition of the ethical principle of Generalized Informational Privacy (GIP), the translation of this principle into an ethical requirement, and the description of an ethical protocol for camera phones.

In the conclusion, some of the possible developments of the approach supported in this paper are briefly outlined.

Actors, Agents, and Individuals in Heterogeneous Organizations

Heterogeneous organizations, whether society as a whole, private and public companies, or research institutions, are populated by actors, agents, and individuals that share resources to coordinate their activities effectively in order to achieve common goals.

Actors[2] are autonomous entities capable of interacting with the environment by receiving inputs, producing outputs, and performing operations. Actors

---

[2]   Terence Hawkes. *Structuralism and Semiotics*. 2nd ed. Routledge, London, 2003; Carl Hewitt, Peter Bishop, and Richard Steiger. A Universal Modular Actor Formalism for Artificial Intelligence. *IJCAI3*, pp. 235–245. Stanford, CL, 1973.

have some degree of control over their internal state, which enables them to perform their operations autonomously, that is, without the direct intervention of other entities.

The definition of actor has a minimal ontological commitment and is ontologically neutral. There is no one-to-one correspondence between actor and entity as an actor is defined by the operations it performs. At a given level of abstraction (LoA)[3] an operation that defines an actor may be performed by the overall activity of a distributed system. In this case, the whole system would instantiate one actor. At a different LoA, the same operation could be performed by different independent processes. In this case, every process would instantiate a different actor. The autopilot of an airplane, for example, is an actor, as it autonomously cruises an airplane while interacting with the environment. Depending on the LoA adopted, the autopilot can be considered as a single actor that performs the operation of flying an airplane or as a set of interacting actors that execute the subtasks of that operation.

Actors are ontologically neutral as there is no assumption about the nature of the entities that comprise an actor. Any autonomous and reactive transition system can be an actor. Computational processes, mechanical artifacts, biological entities, ICTs, distributed systems, control systems, and trading programs may be all good examples of actors.

The concept of agent is widely used in different research fields. Because there is no general agreement on its definition, a minimalist and hence conceptually safer, definition of agent is to be preferred.[4] Agents are not only interactive and autonomous like actors, but they also have the distinctive property of being adaptive.[5] Adaptation is the ability of the agent to change the rules that it follows in order to perform its operations. A typical example of an artificial agent is a thermostat endowed with machine-learning algorithms. The thermostat interacts with its environment and autonomously adjusts the heater, but it is also capable of adapting by machine learning to distinguish warm and cold seasons as well as the preferences of the tenants. So agents are a special kind of actors.

The definitions of agent and actor share the same minimal ontological commitment and ontological neutrality. Whole companies, computational systems capable of machine learning, human societies, and single human beings can be regarded as agents.

Individuals are the traditional entities that perform operations in an organization. Individuals are not only autonomous, interactive, and adaptive, but are also endowed (at least) with semantic capacities. The frame problem provides

[3] Luciano Floridi and Jeff W. Sanders. The Method of Abstraction. In M. Negrotti, editor, *Yearbook of the Artificial: Nature, Culture and Technology*, pp. 177–220. P. Lang, Bern, 2004.

[4] Gian Maria Greco, Gianluca Paronitti, Matteo Turilli, and Luciano Floridi. How to Do Philosophy Informationally. *Lecture Notes in Artificial Intelligence*, 3782: 623–634, 2005.

[5] Luciano Floridi and Jeff W. Sanders. On the Morality of Artificial Agents. *Minds and Machines*, 14(3): 349–379, 2004.

a good criterion to discriminate between the two kinds of agents: Truly seman-tically enabled agents (i.e. individuals) are not affected by it, whereas ordinary agents cannot overcome it. The upper boundary of an individual's complexity is open ended. Intelligence, intuition, sensibility, and artistic expressions are all properties that can be added to the previous definition.

The definition of individual is strongly ontologically committed and weakly ontologically neutral. Individuals map with single entities, for example, costumers, employees, managers, or owners of an organization. Although in prin-ciple it is plausible to imagine artifacts endowed with truly semantic capabilities, at the present time only thinking biological entities are exempt from the frame problem.

ICT Actors in Heterogeneous Organizations

Having defined the entities that perform the activities of a heterogeneous organization, the next step is to clarify how each entity operates. The ubiquitous adoption of ICT infrastructures is increasingly affecting the way in which tasks are performed inside heterogeneous organizations. These changes are of at least two main types.

First, the instrumental use of ICT systems augments the individuals' capabilities to manage the whole life cycle of information (creation, collection, storage, manipulation, transmission, etc.). This increases the productivity of the organization without affecting which individuals can perform an operation, targeting instead how the operations are executed. Faxes tend to perform faster than pigeons, and pocket calculators tend to be more efficient than paper and pen-cil. Neither faxes nor pocket calculators are actors as they are not autonomous. They are tools that allow actors, agents, and individuals to perform their opera-tions better.

Second, the development of ICT instruments that offer growing degrees of autonomy in performing their operations leads to the automation of parts of the activities of an organization. These instruments become actors and agents of the organization in which they are deployed. Stock market exchanges, identification procedures, billing and payments, taxation, call centers, emergency management, data storage and duplication, and data mining are all examples of activities or pro-cesses that have been fully or partially automated, with a corresponding degree of outsourcing and delegation.

The autonomy of ICT actors and agents consists in the routine execution of one or more operations, whenever a given set of parameters holds. Operations and parameters are defined (by individuals in the organization) in such a way as to guarantee that, given a particular situation, the outcome of the performance of the ICT actors and agents may be as good as, or even better than, that of individu-als placed in analogous conditions. Two examples of actors deployed to automate part of the activity of heterogeneous organizations are Automated Pharmacy Systems (APSs)[6] and Business Process Management Systems (BPMSs).[7]

APSs are robotic systems capable of automating the delivery of drugs in hospital pharmacy dispensaries. Research conducted at the pharmacy of the Royal Wolverhampton Hospitals NHS Trust (RWHT)[8] documents how APSs dramatically reduce time and errors (16 percent less) in drug delivery, thereby maximizing staff efficiency and storage space for medicines.

HSBC, a worldwide bank network with 9,500 offices in seventy-six countries, was planning to update its BPMS by 2008 in order to achieve a higher level of automation in answering customer queries.[9] The new system will automatically generate the documentation relative to the status of the transactions performed either domestically or internationally in the whole HSBC global network. The automation of these operations will reduce individual intervention, minimizing the time spent answering clients' queries.

The coherence of the operations performed by different actors, agents, and individuals of an organization is pivotal to the consistency of the overall conduct of that organization. For example, earlier APS systems were unable to manage packages produced by the pharmaceutical companies for the usual distribution. This functional deficiency was a limiting factor in the adoption of APSs, as it produced an incoherent drug delivery system. Drugs had to be delivered by APS actors and individuals following an automated and a manual procedure. The hospital had to address this inconsistency by developing hybrid procedures, which therefore increased organizational complexity, decreased efficiency, and led to higher costs. Modern APSs are not similarly restricted and can be coherently introduced into the drug delivery workflow. APSs and individuals can collaborate consistently in order to achieve the goal of an efficient drug delivery procedure.

One of the main criteria used by the HSBC ICT staff in choosing the new BPMS, has been the possibility of its integration with other actors operating in the bank network. The absence of compatibility between different actors deployed in the workflow of HSBC customer care would be the source of potential inconsistency issues analogous to those faced by the earlier adopters of the APS systems.

[6]   Rachel Graham. Robots Benefit Patients and Staff in Hospitals and Community Pharmacies. *The Pharmaceutical Journal*, 273: 534, 2004.
[7]   Wil M. P. van der Aalst. Business Process Management Demystified: A Tutorial on Models, Systems and Standards for Workflow Management. *Lecture Notes in Computer Science*, 3098: 1–65, 2004.
[8]   Ray Fitzpatrick, Peter Cooke, Carol Southall, Kelly Kauldhar, and Pat Waters. Evaluation of an Automated Dispensing System in a Hospital Pharmacy Dispensary. *The Pharmaceutical Journal*, 274: 763–765, 2005.
[9]   Steve Ranger. Bank Automates to Boost Customer Service. Case Study: HSBC Speeds up Queries with Workflow Automation. Silicon.com, Monday 06 February 2006.

Automation can easily prove to be more problematic when subjective parameters are involved. The infamous Black Monday of Wall Street in 1987[10] is a striking example of the catastrophic effects that can be produced by automated actors that are not bound by an appropriate combination of economical, psychological, and sociological factors. The causes that led to the devastating events of Black Monday are still debated, and the relevance of the use of automated trading procedures has often been reconsidered. Nonetheless, it is generally acknowledged that the oversimplified automation of trading programs was one of the major factors that contributed to the vertical fall of the market.[11] The problem was caused by the inability of the trading actors to perform according to the complex set of rules that determine the trading strategies in unusual situations. Trading actors did not consider crucial factors of the market and produced an inconsistency in the behavior of the trading organization. That inconsistency contributed to the serious social and economical consequences of Black Monday.

Since 1987, the growth of automation has been propelled by the continuous spread and evolution of ICT actors and by the expansion of the global market.[12] A crucial factor in the evolution of automation is the massive process of parallelization and distribution of computational and communication resources. Research into distributed systems is radically changing both what computational systems can do and how they do it. As a direct effect of this progress, distributed databases[13] and ubiquitous communication and computation networks[14] – the Internet and grids – are becoming the foundations for the deployment of more and increasingly complex actors.

The Ethical Consistency Problem (ECP)

Distributed ICT actors collaborate alongside individuals in performing operations on sensitive data in, for example, banks, hospitals, public offices, and private companies. They control, among other things, high volumes of economic transactions, sensitive industrial machineries, customer care systems, and medical devices. These operations may have critical impact both socially and economically. Equally, basic human rights can be affected by the business image of the organizations. Individuals that perform such critical operations are usually bound by a set of ethical principles that normatively constrain their behaviors. It is crucial to

---

[10] Avner Arbel and Albert E. Kaff. *Crash: Ten Days in October. Will It Strike Again?* Longman Financial Services, Chicago, 1989.

[11] M. Mitchell Waldrop. Computers Amplify Black Monday. *Science* 238(4827): 602–604, 1987.

[12] Daniel Gross. Attack of the Machines. Is Your Stockbroker a Robot? *Slate*, Jan. 18, 2005.

[13] M. Tamer O zsu and Patrick Valduriez. *Principles of Distributed Database Systems.* 2nd ed. Prentice Hall London, 1999.

[14] José C. Cunha and Omer Rana. Grid *Computing: Software Environments and Tools.* Springer, London, 2006.

use an analogous set of ethical principles to bind ICT actors. This problem can be referred to as the Ethical Consistency Problem (ECP). Here is a definition:
Given:

1. a heterogeneous organization composed of actors, agents, and individuals and
2. a set of ethical principles constraining the individuals,

　the ECP consists in:

how to constrain actors, agents, and individuals with the same set of ethical principles so that the overall output of the organization is ethically consistent.

The ECP is a tangible problem. Consider identity theft, for example. This is a general label for any crime perpetrated in which sensitive personal information is stolen. With this information, the felon is able to assume the identity of the victim and gain access to bank accounts and obtain credit cards, loans, or even more reserved information, sometimes with devastating consequences for the victim. In 2001, an article on the BBC[15] reported that, with an increase rate of 500 percent a year, identity theft was Britain's fastest-growing white-collar crime. In the same article, it was estimated that American figures for identity theft stood in the region of hundreds of thousands. Two years later, in 2003, the Federal Trade Commission released a survey[16] in which it was estimated that, between 1997 and 2002, 27.3 million Americans had been victims of identity theft, 9.9 million in 2002 alone. The survey reported losses of $48 billion for businesses and financial institutions and $5 billion for individual consumer victims.

Poor identification procedures and sensitive data scattering are the main causes of identity theft. Biometric identification seems the path chosen by governments and private companies to secure identification procedures. It is information scattering, however, that presents a much more elusive problem. Thus far, the main method of preventing information scattering is the avoidance of disclosure of sensitive data. Unfortunately, this is essentially impossible. In an increasingly digitalized society, people do not have full control over their sensitive data. Sensitive data are digitalized and stored in computational devices that are not under the direct control of the data owner. These data are given away for entirely legitimate reasons, such as opening a bank account, paying taxes, buying goods, or simply paying with a credit card at a restaurant. Once digitalized, sensitive data become fodder for (distributed) ICT actors. These actors make limited distinctions between the quality of information they manipulate. They store, duplicate, manipulate, and exchange information with few, if any, constraints. Regulations that normatively constrain the handling of sensitive data by individuals do not affect the ICT actors that perform operations on the very same data set. Identity theft is a clear instance of the ECP.

---

[15] John Penycate. Identity Theft: Stealing Your Name. *BBC News*, Monday, 18 June 2001.
[16] Synovate. Identity Theft Survey. Federal Trade Commission, 2003.

ECP is a problem involving the design of dynamic systems. Specifically, in this paper, the ECP refers to the design of distributed ICT actors. The first step toward a solution to the ECP is to understand how individuals and distributed ICT actors are or can be ethically constrained. The second step will be to propose a solution to the ECP and the third step to illustrate its application using a modeled example.

Actions performed by individuals employed by organizations are constrained by a set of ethical principles. In the most general case, these principles may derive from the knowledge and information available to the individual as much as from beliefs, education, and culture. They may influence the individual's behaviors consciously or unconsciously, affecting different spheres of activity, for example interpersonal relationships, choices, attitude, and evaluation of working situations. The refusal to work on weapon-related projects is a typical example of how personal ethical principles may affect the individual's choices and job-related activities.

An organization can openly commit itself to a set of ethical principles.[17] These principles may be endorsed in terms of codes of conduct, stakeholder statutes, and values statements. Similar documents define a wide range of company responsibilities, ranging from the quality of products and services to a commitment to respect the environment. They also delineate the appropriate conduct among employees, the principles that stakeholders must respect, and how the employees can use the organization's properties. These principles normatively constrain individuals that opt to become members of the organization. For example, members of an organization might have to avoid racial or gender discrimination or may have to promote teamwork. Stakeholders might be committed to principles of fairness, transparency, and honesty.

Finally, individuals and organizations may be subject to state or international laws and regulations. For example, the manager of a company is expected to obey the laws of the country in which the business is developing or to adhere to international laws during operations involving more than one country.

Once it is understood how ethical principles can affect the behavior of single individuals and whole organizations, the following step is to examine how the behavior of ICT actors is defined. The principles that constrain the behaviors of distributed ICT actors are generally defined in the phases of the development process called "requirements elicitation" and "design specification." These phases are creative efforts made by system designers to produce computational systems – for example, distributed ICT actors – that correctly and efficiently perform the operations required by the user. There are many different approaches to the development of a computational system, including many different methods

---

[17] Muel Kaptein. Business Codes of Multinational Firms: What Do They Say? *Journal of Business Ethics*, 50(1): 13–31, 2004; Simon Webley and Martin Le Jeune. Corporate Use of Codes of Ethics: 2004 Survey. IBE, 2005.

for software specification and requirements elicitation,[18] but their review is beyond the scope of this paper. For our purposes, it is sufficient to outline only the salient properties of requirement elicitation and specification processes.

At a very general level of abstraction, requirements define the properties of the system from the users' points of view. Requirements may be divided into functional or nonfunctional requirements and constraints. Functional requirements describe the behaviors of the system independently of any particular implementation. For example, the functional requirement for an APS is that it must refrigerate the medicines. How it does it is a matter of implementation, and obviously there can be several different implementations for the same functional requirement. Nonfunctional requirements usually refer to properties of the system that are visible to its users and are not related to the functional behaviors of the system. For example, APSs must be protected from external intrusions so as to avoid dangerous contamination of the medicines they contain. Finally, constraints are pseudo-requirements imposed by the environment in which the system will be deployed. For example, a hospital policy could mandate the obligatory encryption of every patient's data used by the APSs to prevent breaches of the patients' informational privacy.

The process of specification refines the elicited requirements.[19] In this phase, the system is generally decomposed into interconnected components that communicate through well-defined interfaces. The specification describes the behaviors performed by these components. For example, a specification of the APS system will define its functional components – unpacking unit, refrigerator, dispenser, waste collector, information management unit, labeler – and how they behave. Informally, a behavior could describe the unpacking units taking as inputs boxes of dimensions between X and Y, reading the information from the package and communicating them to the information management unit, and then discarding the package material and sending the medicines to the dispenser unit.

Specifications are progressively refined until they are translated into implementations. Following the previous example, materials, software, scanners, and all the other components of the APS are actually built and assembled. At this level, decisions are taken following principles of efficiency. Materials, specific algorithms, and programming languages are chosen as they are economically feasible or because they are faster and more durable than others in performing the operations defined by the previous specification.

Finally, the implementation is tested to verify that it correctly and efficiently implements the specifications.

---

[18] Matthew Bickerton and Jawed Siddiqi. The Classification of Requirements Engineering Methods. In Stephen Fickas and Anthony Finkelstein, editors, *Requirements Engineering '93*, pp. 182–186. IEEE Computer Society Press, 1993.

[19] Usually there is no clear cut division among the different phases of the development process. Requirements tend to evolve during the whole process of development and, analogously, specifications can be revised during the implementation of the system.

A Solution for the ECP

The previous description of how ethical principles constrain individuals and organizations indicates the type of ethical principles that must be used to constrain distributed ICT actors as well, ensuring that the ECP is avoided. Considering the phases of a prototypical system design process, it is clear that the normative constraints, expressed by ethical principles must be introduced at the stage of requirement elicitations and system specification. It is in these phases that the characteristics of the behaviors of the system are defined.

The solution proposed for the ECP assumes:

1. a heterogeneous organization (i.e. composed of individuals, actors, and agents); and
2. one or more ethical principles to which this organization is committed.

The solution is divided into three steps:

1. translating the normative constraints expressed by the given ethical principles into terms of ethical requirements. An ethical requirement constrains the functionalities of a computational system, thus guaranteeing that one or more properties are maintained during its execution;
2. translating the ethical requirements into an ethical protocol. An ethical protocol specifies the operations performed by the system so that their behaviors match the condition posed by the ethical requirements; and
3. refining the specification of the system into executable algorithms.

The translation process described by this solution to the ECP is visually depicted in Figure 21.1.

The schema outlines the ethical consistency of the ethical principles that constrain individuals, actors, or agents. Functional requirements and ethical requirements proceed in parallel to converge into a single specification that can then be refined into an implementation.

There is an important difference in how individuals and actors or agents may be bound by ethical principles. Individuals are normatively constrained by ethical principles. These principles indicate how an individual ought to act in specific circumstances, discriminating a right action from a wrong one. For example, in a cultural and social context in which the ethical principle of respect is in place, an individual is normatively bound to act in ways that are considered respectful in that group. Ethical principles are not physically wired into individuals. Individuals can act in disagreement with ethical principles facing the consequences, if any, of acting in a wrong manner.

As it relates to ICT actors (or agents), ethical principles are translated into ethical protocols used to specify actors alongside their functional properties. The normative constraints, expressed by ethical principles, become a precondition of the execution of the operations. If the preconditions of an operation are

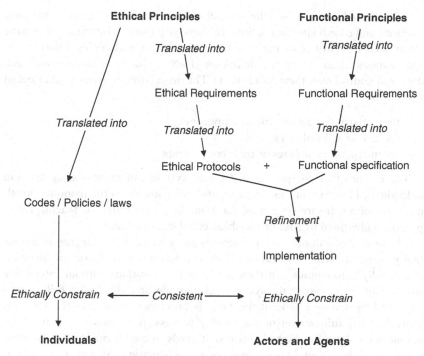

Figure 21.1. Visual representation of the proposed solution for the ECP.

not matched by the actor's state, then it cannot perform that operation in that state. It follows that actors cannot perform their operations outside the boundaries imposed by the ethical principles. This constraint is much stronger than the normative one applied to individuals.

This difference necessitates the careful analysis of the ethical principles adopted to constrain ICT actors. The goal of this analysis is to produce the proper ethical integration among individuals and actors, guaranteeing that the exception-free, ethical behaviors of the former will integrate properly with the "good will" of the latter. Adam,[20] for example, clearly points out the need for balancing the delegation of morality to ICT actors with the distribution and deletion of sensitive data.

The proposed solution to the ECP requires a tool to translate the ethical principle into ethical requirements and ethical requirements into ethical protocols. The concepts of distributed system and degree of control are defined so as to introduce the Control Closure of an operation ($CCop$). The $CCop$ is the new tool required to operate the translation.

---

[20] Alison Adam. Delegating and Distributing Morality: Can We Inscribe Privacy Protection in a Machine? *Ethics and Information Technology*, 7(4): 233–242, 2005.

A distributed system is modeled as a collection of autonomous entities that communicate and coordinate their actions via message passing.[21] Intercommunicating means that the entities of the system are capable of exchanging information. Autonomous means, as in the definition of actor, that the entities have some degree of control over their own actions. The main characteristics of distributed systems are:

1. the concurrency among their components;
2. the lack of a global clock; and
3. the independent failures of their components.

The entities that comprise a distributed system can be actors, agents, and individuals. However, in this paper, entities refer mainly to the (computational) processes of a software system as, for example, a distributed ICT actor. Every process is identified by a set of variables, called state variables.

The degree of autonomy of a process is proportional to the degree of control that process has over its operations. A process has full control over an operation if it is fully autonomous and then performs its operations without interacting with any other process of the system. For example, an individual is fully autonomous when writing a paper if the paper has no other authors. In this case, the individual has full control of the writing process. A process that is not fully autonomous shares its control, because it needs to coordinate itself with other processes of the system in order to carry out its operations. In a paper with multiple authors, all the authors must agree on the content of the paper. In this case, all the authors share the control over the content of the paper and are therefore not fully autonomous.

We are now ready to define the control closure of an operation and of a process.

Control Closure of an operation

At a given level of abstraction, the control closure of an operation in a distributed system is the set of processes whose state variables are needed to perform the operation. The state variables of these processes provide the values that determine the operation as a relation from the initial to the final state of the system.

The Control Closure of a process

At a given level of abstraction, the control closure of a process is the union of the control closures of each of its operations.

Assuming an operation OP and a set of processes $\{p_n\}$, the control closure of OP is written as:

$$CCop = \{p_1, p_2, \ldots, p_n\}$$

---

[21] George Coulouris, Jean Dollimore, and Tim Kindberg. *Distributed Systems: Concepts and Design.* 4th ed. Addison– Wesley Harlow, 2005.

The control closure of an operation models the concept of control. It may contain all the processes of the system, as the state variables of all the processes are needed to perform the operation. In this case, all the processes share control over the operation. Alternatively, the control closure of an operation may contain only one process, as the operation can be performed by the process independently, without accessing the state variables of other processes. In this case, the process has full control over that operation. For example, the control closure of the operation of lecturing a classroom performed by a teacher has in its control closure all the individuals of the system. The teacher is needed to explain while the students listen and pose questions. Students and teacher share the control over the operation. Conversely, every student that performs a written exam in a classroom has individual control over that operation. In this case, the control closure of the operation contains only the student.

The control closure of an operation supports discrimination between two different specifications of the same operation. The same operation may be performed by a single process in some conditions and by all the system's processes in others. In the former case, the control closure of the operation contains only one process; in the latter, all the system's processes. Consider, for example, cycling. Cycling can be performed either alone or in a team. When cycling is performed in a team, the control closure of the operation contains the state variables of all the cyclists of that group. Every cyclist must be aware of the position of the others. The control closure of cycling contains only one cyclist when it is performed in isolation.

The control closure of an operation and of a process can now be used to discriminate between the degree of distribution (or centralization) of an operation.

An operation is fully distributed if and only if its control closure is a singleton and the control closure of every process of the system contains the process itself (Figure 21.2).

An operation is fully centralized if and only if its control closure and that of every process of the system equals the set of all the processes in the system (Figure 21.3).

An operation is partially decentralized (or not fully centralized) if and only if its control closure contains at least two processes, but not all the processes of the system (Figure 21.4).

There are three limit cases to be taken into account. The first is a system that contains only one process. In this case, the system is centralized and the control closure of every operation may contain only the process itself. The second and third cases involve the empty set. An operation with an empty control closure is performed without access to any state variables. This type of operation results from global constants or inputs that can occur, for example, in specifications with insufficiently elaborated details, for example, as in a clock that outputs its own states but relates to no variables to update them. A process with an empty control closure is not a process, because it does not perform operations in the system. It can then be considered a constant of the system.

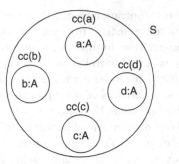

Figure 21.2. Given a system S with set A = {a, b, c, d} of processes, the control closure of the operation OP is a singleton. OP is performed individually by every processes and the control closure of every process is cc(x) = {x}.

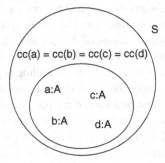

Figure 21.3. Given a system S with set A={a, b, c, d} of processes, the control closure of the operation OP is cc(OP) = A and the control closure of every process is cc(x) = cc{OP}.

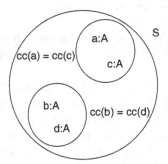

Figure 21.4. Given a system S with set A={a, b, c, d} of processes, the control closure of the operation OP contains two processes. The processes are divided in two pairs each performing the operation OP.

Clearly, the control closure of an operation depends on the level of abstraction that the designer or observer adopts in describing the system. The same system can be considered as a single-process system or as composed of a set of processes. For example, an APS can be described by a single process that takes boxed medicines as input and delivers prescriptions as output. At a different level of abstraction, the same APS can be described by a set of interacting processes that unpack, refrigerate, label, record, and dispense medicine. The control closure of the operation "deliver a prescription" contains the state variables of one process in the former case, whereas in the latter case it contains the state variables of the processes of unpack, refrigerate, label, record, and dispense medicine.

The control closure is a particularly useful concept as it can be used at the inception of the design process of the actors and agents. The solution proposed in this paper clearly demonstrates how the ECP ought to be addressed from the early stages of system design.

It is now possible to describe how the solution to the ECP is applied. The solution to the ECP assumes one or more ethical principles to which a heterogeneous organization is committed. An ethical principle can be decomposed into one or more types of observables, a class of operations, and a normative constraint. The decomposed ethical principle may express different types of normative constraints, such as the necessity to perform or not perform operations or the exclusive or shared right to perform them. For example, individuals who hold a copyright on one or more products have the right to exclude other individuals from exploiting those products. The set of observables contains the types "copyright holders," "products," and "individuals other than copyright holders." The class of operations contains all the operations that lead to an exploitation of one instance of the type "products." The normative constraint is expressed by "exclude other individuals from." Another example is the principle for which no one has the right to kill anyone else. In this case, "individuals" is the only type of observable, and the class of operations contains all the operations that kill an individual. The normative constraint states that none of the operations that belong to that class must be performed by an individual.

Note that no assumptions are made on how the ethical principles and their normative constraints are obtained. They could be derived with a descriptive process, as in the case of descriptive ethics, or they could be formulated inside any theory of conduct. There are also no assumptions about the nature of the ethical principles and normative constraints endorsed. They could be grounded in either universal or relative beliefs, dependant on a situation, or derived from observing individuals' behaviors and best practices.

The translation of an ethical principle into an ethical requirement maintains the same types of observables and class of operations, and redefines the normative constraint on the operations in terms of control closure. The control closure imposes a precondition on the execution of the operation. This means that the operation can be performed by the system only if the normative constraint is matched. So, in the example of the copyright case, the constraint is translated into a control closure such that, for every operation that exploits a product covered by copyright, the control closure of this operation must contain only the copyright holder. Analogously, in the case of the principle for which no one has the right to kill, the control closure of every killing operation is empty (it imposes an always false precondition) so that no killing operation can be legally performed.

Eventually, the ethical requirement is translated into an ethical protocol. An ethical requirement applies to every system that contains the types of observables and the class of operations singled out by the ethical requirement. On the contrary, an ethical protocol specifies a set of observables and the operations performed by a specific system. These observables, operations, and their control closures belong to types and classes defined by the ethical requirement. In this way, the operations of the ethical protocol are constrained by the same normative constraint translated from an ethical principle into an ethical requirement. For example, consider a system with the musician Sergio Mendes, his album *Timeless*, and myself as observables and the operation of receiving money from selling *Timeless*. The ethical protocol for this system implements the ethical requirement of the copyright if the control closure of the operation of receiving money from selling the album contains only Sergio Mendes and not myself. This control closure indeed constrains the operation so that only the copyright holder exploits his original product.

Finally, the ethical protocol is refined into an implementation. This process of refinement can have different degrees of formalization depending on the chosen process of development. The implementation of an ethical protocol may also require new formalisms and conceptual tools in order to cope with the needs of an executable system. For example, Wiegel, Hoven, and Lokhorst,[22] propose to use deontic epistemic action logic to model the information itself as an intentional agent so as to preserve the integrity of the information and to regulate its dissemination.

A Simple Illustration: Generalized Informational Privacy and Ethical Camera Phones

It might be useful to introduce an example to clarify the solution proposed to the ECP. The example is divided into three steps. The first defines the ethical principle to be used in the example, the second translates the ethical principle into ethical requirements, and the third translates the ethical requirement into ethical protocols.

First Step: The Definition of the Ethical Principle

The analysis of identity theft felony has exposed the crucial role that information may play in jeopardizing the economical and social status of individuals. In

---

[22] Vincent Wiegel, Jeroen van den Hoven, and Gert-Jan Lokhorst. Privacy, Deontic Epistemic Action Logic and Software Agents. *Ethics and Information Technology*, 7(4): 251–264, 2005.

particular, identity theft is based on malicious access to data regarding the identity of the victim. This access should not be malicious, but when this occurs it represents a breach of the right of Informational Privacy (IP) of the victim.[23]

The contemporary debate has produced a definition of IP based on the concept of access as opposed to that of control.[24] IP is the right of the individual of having, in specific circumstances, portions of information relative to herself or himself inaccessible to other individuals. As explained by Floridi,[25] the accessibility of information is an epistemic factor that depends on how actors, agents, and individuals interact among themselves and with their environment. The ontological characteristics of entities and environment produce a measure of the "ontological friction" that allows some exchange of information and therefore varying degrees of informational privacy.

The access to information is disjoint from the access to data. Data per se do not yet constitute information, because they need to be interpreted by a subject to produce information. It is possible to access data without extracting information, and, vice versa, it is possible to extract information without accessing all the available data. A typical example consists in appropriately encrypted messages that are exchanged through an insecure channel. Whoever intercepts the encrypted messages cannot decrypt it without the corresponding encryption key. So encrypted data accessed without the key cannot be used to extract information. Conversely, given a database and a correlation rule among its data, it is possible to derive information without accessing the whole database. A minimalist example consists of a database that contains three logical propositions correlated by the connectives of the propositional logic. The three propositions are $\neg A$, $A \vee B$, and B. By accessing $\neg A$ and $A \vee B$, it is possible to infer B without accessing it. More complex examples can be found in problems of distributed epistemic logic as the classic "muddy children" in which a child that interacts with other children is able to infer whether his forehead is muddy without looking at it.

A comprehensive definition of IP must therefore take into account the distinction between data and information.[26] The right to IP must then be based on limiting the extraction of information instead of the access of data. Thus, the Generalized Information Privacy (GIP) is defined as the right of an individual not to have his or her own data used to extract information without his or her own consent.

---

[23] IP constitutes only one type of privacy. Psychological privacy is concerned with the effects that intrusions in physical spaces or personal affairs produce on individuals' psyche. Privacy can also refer to the right of privacy as it is codified into laws. For example, in the United States, the constitutional right to privacy establishes that some portion of individuals' life, like the social institution of marriage and the sexual life of married people, are protected zones of privacy. See Judith DeCew. Privacy. *Stanford Encyclopedia of Philosophy*.

[24] Herman T. Tavani and James H. Moor. Privacy Protection, Control of Information, and Privacy-Enhancing Technologies. *SIGCAS Comput. Soc.*, 31(1): 6–11, 2001.

[25] Floridi. The Ontological Interpretation of Informational Privacy.

[26] Luciano Floridi. Is Semantic Information Meaningful Data? *Philosophy and Phenomenological Research*, 70(2): 351–370, 2005.

This definition (i) discriminates specific cases in which an individual's GIP can be infringed without accessing the individual's data; (ii) separates the unauthorized accesses to data that do not respect the right to GIP from accesses that do; and (iii) considers accessing data as one among other operations that allows the extraction of information from data. The GIP is the ethical principle assumed to illustrate the solution to the ECP.

Second Step: Translate the GIP into an Ethical Requirement

The GIP definition assumes two observables – an owner O and his data DS_o – and a set of operations $\{OP_n\}$ such that any operation takes as input DS_o and returns as output the informational content of DS_o.

The normative constraint expressed by the GIP definition is embedded in the statement "without her or his own (i.e., the owner) consent." This constraint can be translated into an ethical requirement using the control closure on the operations of the set $\{OP_n\}$.

GIP-ER1
For every operation OP_n in $\{OP_n\}$, the owner O of DS_o must belong to the control closure of OP_n, $CC(OP_n)$.

A typical application of this constraint would be to make it impossible for an ICT actor to extract information from customers' data without their explicit consent. The operation "to extract information" would have a control closure also containing the customer; so a precondition for the execution of the operation would be to have the customer's Boolean variable "consent" set to one.

This ethical requirement is very strong, as it makes no qualitative distinction about the type of information that is extracted. Every operation that extracts information from DS_o must depend, also but not only, on one or more state variables of the owner O.

A more relaxed ethical requirement for the GIP can be obtained by qualifying the type of information that cannot be extracted from DS_o.

GIP-ER2
For every operation OP_n in $\{OP_n\}$ that extracts relevant information DS_o, the owner O of DS_o must belong to the control closure of OP_n, $CC(OP_n)$.

Consider, for example, the system that reads from supermarket loyalty cards the customer's identity and associates it to every item that has been purchased. The ethical requirement ER2 could be useful to distinguish between the extraction of information relative to the identity of a customer and that relative to her shopping behaviors. The extraction of the former would require the customer's consent, whereas the extraction of the latter would be accessible without his explicit consent. This distinction of the quality of the information extracted is not allowed by the ethical requirement ER1.

Third Step: Derive an Ethical Protocol from the GIP Ethical Requirement

Camera phones serve as useful examples of how ethical protocols might be implemented when the operation of taking a picture is constrained in accordance with the ethical requirement of GIP. Note that this is just an example used to illustrate the proposed solution for the ECP, not a blueprint of how to design a real camera phone.

Camera phones are very popular, and most mobile telephones are equipped with a camera to take pictures and to record videos. Invented in 2000, by 2003 already 84 million camera phones were sold worldwide, exceeding the numbers of standalone cameras.

Camera phones offer an unprecedented overlap between capturing images and videos and distributing them. Moreover, mobile phones are becoming increasingly functional, with the majority of them capable of accessing the Internet. They can therefore be used as massive, virtually immediate publication tools for pictures and videos taken wherever and whenever mobiles can be used.

Horror stories of privacy breaches and camera phones abound: clandestine lovers spotted in foreign cities; a teenager acting in revenge sends private pictures of his ex-girlfriend to all his social network, thus making her life very difficult; an unhappy customer embarrasses the retailer of a used mobile phone by publishing all the private information found in the memory of the phone on the Internet. There are good exceptions too: men arrested because they were filmed roughing up a man on the street; journalist scoops taken on the spot thanks to camera phones; emergencies handled because of the information gathered from pictures taken and sent by victims.

Camera phones are forbidden in many places in order to protect the identity of customers and employers or to protect secrets that could be stolen by a picture. Gyms, night clubs, government offices, and high-tech companies are all places where the use of a camera phone is occasionally forbidden.

The debate about the difficulty in maintaining privacy as it relates to taking pictures is as old as photography. In 1890 Warren and Brandeis[27] lamented that "instantaneous photographs ... have invaded the sacred precincts of private and domestic life." In more recent years, there have been proposals to change the design of camera phones so as to better protect the privacy of those photographed. The journey toward an ethical camera phone has officially begun.

The system in which a camera phone operates can be modeled by two individuals and an operation. One individual I operates a camera phone making it perform the operation TP of taking a picture. The other individual O is the subject of the picture or, in informational terms, the owner of the information that is recorded by the phone into its memory.

---

[27] Samuel Warren and Louis D. Brandeis. The Right to Privacy. *Harvard Law Review*, 4(5): 193–220, 1890.

Three different versions (TP_{1-3}) of the operation of taking a picture can be used to illustrate how to evaluate whether the ethical requirement of the GIP has been correctly translated into an ethical protocol. Recall the ethical requirement derived from the ethical principle of the GIP. The observables and operations present in that definition can be directly translated into the system of the camera phone:

CP-GIP-ER
Given the operation TP that extracts relevant information DS_o, the owner O of DS_o must belong to the control closure of TP, $CC(TP)$.

First version of TP

- Description: The operation TP_1 is constrained only in terms of efficiency and correctness. A picture can be taken by pressing a specific button B of the phone.
- Protocol: Pressing the button B, a picture is saved in the phone's memory.
- Control closure of TP_1:$CC(TP_1) = \{phone, user\}$.

This is the minimalist design of the operation TP. The control closure of TP_1 does not contain the subject of the picture O as the operation does not depend on any of O's state variables. This implementation of the operation TP is functionally correct but does not match the ethical requirement CP-GIP-ER. It follows that it does not implement an ethical protocol for the operation of taking pictures that respects the GIP.

Second version of TP

- Description: The operation TP_2 is more constrained than TP_1. When a picture is taken, the phone emits an audible noise.
- Protocol: On pressing button B, an audible noise is produced and a picture is saved into the phone's memory.
- Control closure of TP_2:$CC(TP_2) = \{phone, user\}$.

The emission of a cameralike noise is a mandatory function for camera phones sold in Korea and Japan. Nonetheless, the control closure of TP_2 reveals that this design does not respect yet the ethical requirement of GIP. In this case too, the control closure of TP_2 does not contain the subject of the picture O as the operation does not depend on any of O's state variables. Nothing has changed from TP_1. The respect of the privacy is fully outsourced to O, who has to react to the noise and defend his right to GIP.

Third version of TP

- Description: The operation TP_3 is always constrained by the subject being photographed. The phone takes a picture only if the subject allows it to do so.

- Protocol: Pressing button B connects to the subject's policy device, if policy = allow, a picture is saved in the phone's memory.
- Control closure of $TP_3:CC(TP)$ = {*phone, user, subject*}.

This is a similar solution to the one proposed by Iceberg Systems in 2003 for inhibiting the use of camera phone in areas protected by privacy devices. In this scenario, the phone becomes an actor that communicates autonomously with the subject's privacy device (for example another phone) and reacts to it by taking a picture or not. The control closure of TP_3 contains the subject wearing the policy device, because the execution of the operation depends also on its state. This approach respects the ethical requirements as the subject can activate the privacy device only in situations in which relevant information could be photographed. TP_3 implements an ethical protocol for the GIP.

Conclusions

Recall our initial concern. Nowadays, a system designer is the demiurge of the artifacts he produces. When he decides to design autonomous and reactive artifacts, it gives them an ethical dimension. The solution to the ECP proposed in this paper is an analytical tool meant to facilitate the ethical design of artificial actors. The tool can be used to analyze existing systems – so as to evaluate whether they effectively implement a given set of ethical principles – or it can be used in designing new systems from scratch – in order to guarantee the effective implementation of a given set of ethical principles.

The solution proposed for the ECP is especially useful in designing distributed systems for large organizations with explicit ethical commitments. Typical examples could be hospital and bank systems, in which rights such as confidentiality, anonymity, and privacy are crucial both for the user and for the institution's image.

This paper offers a normative complement to the greater endeavor of research into ethical requirements elicitation. Ongoing work will delve into how best the descriptive elicitation of ethical requirements may be conjugated with the necessity of assuming a set of ethical principles to derive a normative analysis of how the system would have to behave.

The problem of integrating ethical actors and ethical individuals deserves further investigation. In this paper, it has been assumed that actors have to behave as individuals would behave in the same situation. However, this is only one form of consistency, and several questions might easily be raised. What are the criteria to decide which ethical principles can be implemented in artificial actors and which ones must be left to the good will of individuals? How can it be decided when it is preferable to have ethically neutral actors, thereby leaving the ethical dimension completely to individuals? Conversely, are there situations in which it would be better to have ethically neutral individuals, leaving any ethical accountability to ethical actors? Finally, is it possible to ascribe to artificial actors or agents some form of morality and/or the capability of moral reasoning?[28] These are all important questions that will need to be addressed in the close future.

Acknowledgments

This research has been partially funded by a PRIN project through the Università degli Studi di Salerno, and I wish to thank Roberto Cordeschi for his constant support. A previous version of this paper was presented at the European Conference Computing and Philosophy (E-CAP, NTNU, Trondheim, June 22–24, 2006). I wish to thank all the participants, and especially Dan Burk, for their useful feedback. I also wish to thank all the members of my research group (IEG) for their comments and Luciano Floridi and Jeff Sanders for their crucial help in developing some of the ideas presented in this paper. Of course, I remain the only person responsible for any of its shortcomings.

References

W.M.P. Alast. Business Process Management Demystified: A Tutorial on Models, Systems and Standards for Workflow Management. *Lecture Notes in Computer Science*, 3098: 1–65, 2004.

A. Adam. Delegating and Distributing Morality: Can We Inscribe Privacy Protection in a Machine? *Ethics and Information Technology*, 7(4): 233–242, 2005.

C. Allen, I. Smit and W. Wallach. Artificial Morality: Top–Down, Bottom–up, and Hybrid Approaches. *Ethics and Information Technology*, 7(3): 149–155, 2005.

A. Arbel and A.E. Kaff, *Crash: Ten Days in October. Will It Strike Again?* Longman Financial Services, Chicago, 1989.

M. Bickerton and J. Siddiqi. The Classification of Requirements Engineering Methods. In S. Fickas and A. Finkelstein, editors, *Requirements Engineering '93*, pp. 182–186. IEEE Computer Society Press, 1993.

G. Coulouris, J. Dollimore and T. Kindberg, *Distributed Systems: Concepts and Design.* 4 ed. Addison–Wesley, Harlow, 2005.

J.C. Cunha and O. Rana, *Grid Computing: Software Environments and Tools.* Springer, London, 2006.

J. DeCew. Privacy. In E. N. Zalta, editor, *Stanford Encyclopedia of Philosophy*, 2006.

R. Fitzpatrick, P. Cooke, C. Southall, K. Kauldhar and P. Waters. Evaluation of an Automated Dispensing System in a Hospital Pharmacy Dispensary. *The Pharmaceutical Journal*, 274: 763–765, 2005.

L. Floridi. Is Semantic Information Meaningful Data? *Philosophy and Phenomenological Research*, 70(2): 351–370, 2005.

L. Floridi. The Ontological Interpretation of Informational Privacy. *Ethics and Information Technology*, 7(4): 185– 200, 2006.

---

[28] Colin Allen, Iva Smit, and Wendell Wallach. Artificial Morality: Top–Down, Bottom–up, and Hybrid Approaches. *Ethics and Information Technology*, 7(3): 149–155, 2005; Floridi and Sanders. On the Morality of Artificial Agents.

L. Floridi and J.W. Sanders. The Method of Abstraction. In M. Negrotti, editor, *Yearbook of the Artificial Nature, Culture and Technology*, pp. 177–220. P. Lang, Bern, 2004.

L. Floridi and J. W. Sanders. On the Morality of Artificial Agents. *Minds and Machines*, 14(3): 349–379, 2004.

R. Graham. Robots Benefit Patients and Staff in Hospitals and Community Pharmacies. *The Pharmaceutical Journal*, 273: 534, 2004.

G.M. Greco, G. Paronitti, M. Turilli and L. Floridi. How to Do Philosophy Informationally. *Lecture Notes in Artificial Intelligence*, 3782: 623–634, 2005.

D. Gross. Attack of the Machines. Is Your Stockbroker a Robot? *Slate*, Jan. 18, 2005.

T. Hawkes, *Structuralism and Semiotics*. 2 ed. Routledge, London, 2003.

C. Hewitt, P. Bishop and R. Steiger. A Universal Modular Actor Formalism for Artificial Intelligence. *IJCAI3*, pp. 235–245. Stanford, CL, 1973.

M. Kaptein. Business Codes of Multinational Firms: What Do They Say? *Journal of Business Ethics*, 50(1): 13–31, 2004.

M.T. O zsu and P. Valduriez, *Principles of Distributed Database Systems*. 2 ed. Prentice Hall, London, 1999.

J. Penycate. Identity Theft: Stealing Your Name. *BBC News*, Monday, 18 June, 2001.

S. Ranger. Bank Automates to Boost Customer Service. Case Study: HSBC Speeds up Queries with Workflow Automation. Silicon.com, Monday 06 February, 2006.

Synovate. Identity Theft Survey. Federal Trade Commission, 2003.

H.T. Tavani and J.H. Moor. Privacy Protection, Control of Information, and Privacy-Enhancing Technologies. *SIGCAS Computer Society*, 31(1): 6–11, 2001.

M.M. Waldrop. Computers Amplify Black Monday. *Science*, 238(4827): 602–604, 1987.

S. Warren and L.D. Brandeis. The Right to Privacy. *Harvard Law Review*, 4(5): 193–220, 1890.

S. Webley and M. Le Jeune. Corporate Use of Codes of Ethics: 2004 Survey. IBE, 2005.

V. Wiegel, J. Hoven and G.-J. Lokhorst. Privacy, Deontic Epistemic Action Logic and Software Agents. *Ethics and Information Technology*, 7(4): 251–264, 2005.

22

Modeling Morality with Prospective Logic

Luís Moniz Pereira and Ari Saptawijaya

Introduction

MORALITY NO LONGER BELONGS ONLY TO THE REALM OF PHILOSOPHERS. Recently, there has been a growing interest in understanding morality from the scientific point of view. This interest comes from various fields, for example, primatology (de Waal 2006), cognitive sciences (Hauser 2007; Mikhail 2007), neuroscience (Tancredi 2005), and other various interdisciplinary perspectives (Joyce 2006; Katz 2002). The study of morality also attracts the artificial intelligence community from the computational perspective and has been known by several names, including machine ethics, machine morality, artificial morality, and computational morality. Research on modeling moral reasoning computationally has been conducted and reported on, for example, at the AAAI 2005 Fall Symposium on Machine Ethics (Guarini 2005; Rzepka and Araki 2005).

There are at least two reasons to mention the importance of studying morality from the computational point of view. First, with the current growing interest to understand morality as a science, modeling moral reasoning computationally will assist in better understanding morality. Cognitive scientists, for instance, can greatly benefit in understanding complex interaction of cognitive aspects that build human morality; they may even be able to extract moral principles people normally apply when facing moral dilemmas. Modeling moral reasoning computationally can also be useful for intelligent tutoring systems, for instance, to aid in teaching morality to children. Second, as artificial agents are more and more expected to be fully autonomous and work on our behalf, equipping agents with the capability to compute moral decisions is an indispensable requirement. This is particularly true when the agents are operating in domains where moral dilemmas occur, for example, in health care or medical fields.

Our ultimate goal within this topic is to provide a general framework to model morality computationally. This framework should serve as a toolkit to codify arbitrarily chosen moral rules as declaratively as possible. We envisage that logic programming is an appropriate paradigm to achieve our purpose. Continuous and active research in logic programming has provided us with necessary ingredients that look promising enough to model morality. For instance, default negation is suitable for expressing exception in moral rules; abductive logic programming (Kakas et al. 1998; Kowalski 2006) and stable model semantics (Gelfond and Lifschitz 1998) can be used to generate possible decisions along with their moral consequences; and preferences are appropriate for preferring among moral decisions or moral rules (Dell' Acqua and Pereira 2005, 2007).

In this paper, we present our preliminary attempt to exploit these enticing features of logic programming to model moral reasoning. In particular, we employ prospective logic programming (Lopes and Pereira 2006; Pereira and Lopes 2007), an ongoing research project that incorporates these features. For the moral domain, we take the classic trolley problem of Foot (1967). This problem is challenging to model, because it contains a family of complex moral dilemmas. To make moral judgments on these dilemmas, we model the principle of double effect as the basis of moral reasoning. This principle is chosen by considering empirical research results in cognitive science (Hauser 2007) and law (Mikhail 2007) that show the consistency of this principle to justify similarities of judgments by demographically diverse populations when given this set of dilemmas. Additionally, we also employ prospective logic programming to model another moral principle, the principle of triple effect (Kamm 2006). The model allows us to explain computationally the difference of moral judgments drawn using these two similar but distinct moral principles.

Our attempt to model moral reasoning on this domain shows encouraging results. Using features of prospective logic programming, we can conveniently model the moral domain (that is, various moral dilemmas of the trolley problem), the principle of double effect, and the principle of triple effect, all of those in a declarative manner. Our experiments on running the model also successfully deliver moral judgments that conform to the human empirical research results.

We organize the paper as follows. First, we discuss briefly and informally prospective logic programming. Then, we explain the trolley problem and the double and triple effect principles, respectively. We detail how we model them in prospective logic programming together with the results of our experiments regarding that model in the subsection that follows. Finally, we conclude and discuss possible future work.

Prospective Logic Programming

Prospective logic programming enables an evolving program to look ahead prospectively into its possible future states and to prefer among them to satisfy goals (Lopes and Pereira 2006; Pereira and Lopes 2007). This paradigm is particularly beneficial to the agents community, because it can be used to predict an agent's future by employing the methodologies from abductive logic

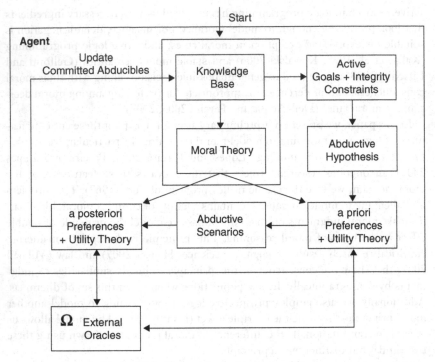

Figure 22.1. Prospective logic agent architecture.

programming (Kakas et al. 1998; Kowalski 2006) in order to synthesize and maintain abductive hypotheses.

Figure 22.1 shows the architecture of agents that are based on prospective logic (Pereira and Lopes 2007). Each prospective logic agent is equipped with a knowledge base and a moral theory as its initial theory. The problem of prospection is then of finding abductive extensions to this initial theory that are both relevant (under the agent's current goals) and preferred (with respect to preference rules in its initial theory). The first step is to select the goals that the agent will possibly attend to during the prospective cycle. Integrity constraints are also considered here to ensure the agent always performs transitions into valid evolution states. Once the set of active goals for the current state is known, the next step is to find out which are the relevant abductive hypotheses. This step may include the application of a priori preferences, in the form of contextual preference rules, among available hypotheses to generate possible abductive scenarios. Forward reasoning can then be applied to abducibles in those scenarios to obtain relevant consequences, which can then be used to enact a posteriori preferences. These preferences can be enforced by employing utility theory and, in a moral situation, also moral theory. In case additional information is needed to enact preferences, the agent may consult external oracles. This greatly benefits agents in giving them the ability to probe the outside environment, thus providing better informed choices, including the making of experiments. The mechanism to consult oracles is realized by posing questions to external systems, be they other agents, actuators, sensors, or other procedures. Each oracle mechanism may have certain conditions specifying whether it is available for questioning. Whenever the agent acquires additional information, it is possible that ensuing side effects affect its original search, for example, some already-considered abducibles may now be disconfirmed and some new abducibles are triggered. To account for all possible side effects, a second round of prospection takes place.

   ACORDA is a system that implements prospective logic programming and is based on the aforementioned architecture. ACORDA is implemented based on the implementation of EVOLP (Alferes et al. 2002) and is further developed on top of XSB Prolog.[1] In order to compute abductive stable models (Dell' Acqua and Pereira 2005, 2007), ACORDA also benefits from the XSB-XASP interface to Smodels.[2]

   In this section, we discuss briefly and informally prospective logic programming and some constructs from ACORDA that are relevant to our work. For a more detailed discussion on prospective logic programming and ACORDA, interested readers are referred to the original paper (Lopes and Pereira 2006; Pereira and Lopes, 2007).

Language

Let $\mathcal{L}$ be a first-order language. A domain literal in $\mathcal{L}$ is a domain atom A or its default negation *not A*. The latter is to express that the atom is false by default (close world assumption). A domain rule in Λ is a rule of the form:

$$A \leftarrow L_1,\ldots,L_t. \qquad (t \geq 0)$$

where A is a domain atom and $L_1,\ldots,L_t$ are domain literals. An integrity constraint in $\mathcal{L}$ is a rule of the form:

$$\perp \leftarrow L_1,\ldots,L_t. \qquad (t > 0)$$

where $\perp$ is a domain atom denoting falsity, and $L_1,\ldots,L_t$ are domain literals. In ACORDA, $\leftarrow$ and $\perp$ will be represented by `<-` and `falsum`, respectively.

   A (logic) program P over $\mathcal{L}$ is a set of domain rules and integrity constraints, standing for all their ground instances.

Abducibles

Every program P is associated with a set of abducible atoms $A \subseteq \mathcal{L}$. Abducibles can be seen as hypotheses that provide hypothetical solutions or possible explanations of given queries.

---

[1]   XSB Prolog is available at `http://xsb.sourceforge.net`
[2]   Smodels is available at `http://www.tcs.hut.fi/Software/smodels`

An abducible A can be assumed only if it is a considered one, that is, it is expected in the given situation and, moreover, there is no expectation to the contrary (Dell' Acqua and Pereira 2005, 2007).

consider (A) ← expect (A), not expect_not (A).

The rules about expectations are domain-specific knowledge contained in the theory of the program and effectively constrain the hypotheses that are available.

In addition to mutually exclusive abducibles, ACORDA also allows sets of abducibles. Hence, an abductive stable model may contain more than a single abducible. To enforce mutually exclusive abducibles, ACORDA provides predicate exclusive/2. The use of this predicate will be illustrated later, when we model morality in a subsequent section.

A Posteriori Preferences

Having computed possible scenarios represented by abductive stable models, more favorable scenarios can be preferred among them a posteriori. Typically, a posteriori preferences are performed by evaluating consequences of abducibles in abductive stable models. The evaluation can be done quantitatively (for instance, by utility functions) or qualitatively (for instance, by enforcing some rules to hold). When currently available knowledge is insufficient to prefer among abductive stable models, additional information can be gathered, for example, by performing experiments or consulting an oracle.

To realize a posteriori preferences, ACORDA provides predicate select/2 that can be defined by users following some domain-specific mechanism for selecting favored abductive stable models. The use of this predicate to perform a posteriori preferences in a moral domain will be discussed in a subsequent section.

The Trolley Problem

Several interesting results have emerged from recent interdisciplinary studies on morality. One common result from these studies shows that morality has evolved over time. In particular, Hauser (2007), in his recent work, argues that a moral instinct, which generates rapid judgments about what is morally right or wrong, has evolved in our species.

Hauser (2007) and Mikhail (2007) propose a framework of human moral cognition known as universal moral grammar that is analogous to Chomsky's universal grammar in language. Universal moral grammar, which can be culturally adjusted, provides universal moral principles that enable an individual to unconsciously evaluate what actions are permissible, obligatory, or forbidden. To support this idea, Hauser and Mikhail independently created a test to assess moral judgments of subjects from demographically diverse populations using the classic trolley problems. Despite their diversity, the result shows that most subjects widely share moral judgments when given a moral dilemma from the trolley-problem suite. Although subjects are unable to explain the moral rules in their attempts at justification, their moral judgments are consistent with a moral rule known as the principle of double effect.

The trolley problem presents several moral dilemmas that inquire whether it is permissible to harm one or more individuals for the purpose of saving others. In all cases, the initial circumstances are the same (Hauser, 2007):

"There is a trolley and its conductor has fainted. The trolley is headed toward five people walking on the track. The banks of the track are so steep that they will not be able to get off the track in time."

Given this initial circumstance, in this work we consider six classical cases of moral dilemmas, employed for research on morality in people. These six cases are visually depicted in Figure 22.2.

1. **Bystander**. Hank is standing next to a switch, which he can throw, that will turn the trolley onto a parallel side track, thereby preventing it from killing the five people. However, there is a man standing on the side track with his back turned. Hank can throw the switch, killing him; or he can refrain from doing this, letting the five die. Is it morally permissible for Hank to throw the switch?

2. **Footbridge**. Ian is on the footbridge over the trolley track. He is next to a heavy object, which he can shove onto the track in the path of the trolley to stop it, thereby preventing it from killing the five people. The heavy object is a man, standing next to Ian with his back turned. Ian can shove the man onto the track, resulting in death; or he can refrain from doing this, letting the five die. Is it morally permissible for Ian to shove the man?

3. **Loop Track**. Ned is standing next to a switch, which he can throw, that will temporarily turn the trolley onto a loop side track. There is a heavy object on the side track. If the trolley hits the object, the object will slow the train down, giving the five people time to escape. The heavy object is a man, standing on the side track with his back turned. Ned can throw the switch, preventing the trolley from killing the five people, but killing the man; or he can refrain from doing this, letting the five die. Is it morally permissible for Ned to throw the switch?

4. **Man-in-front**. Oscar is standing next to a switch, which he can throw, that will temporarily turn the trolley onto a side track. There is a heavy object on the side track. If the trolley hits the object, the object will slow the train down, giving the five people time to escape. There is a man standing on the side track in front of the heavy object with his back turned. Oscar can throw the switch, preventing the trolley from killing the five people, but killing the man. Or he can refrain from doing this, letting the five die. Is it morally permissible for Oscar to throw the switch?

5. **Drop Man**. Victor is standing next to a switch, which he can throw, that will drop a heavy object into the path of the trolley, thereby stopping the trolley and preventing it from killing the five people. The heavy object is a man,

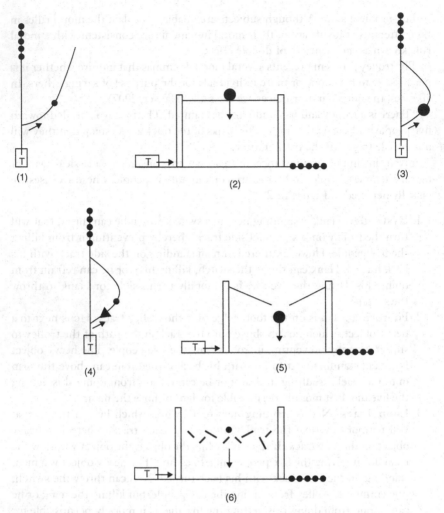

Figure 22.2. The six trolley cases: (1) Bystander, (2) Footbridge, (3) Loop Track, (4) Man-in-front, (5) Drop Man, (6) Collapse Bridge.

who is standing on a footbridge overlooking the track. Victor can throw the switch, killing him; or he can refrain from doing this, letting the five die. Is it morally permissible for Victor to throw the switch?

6. **Collapse Bridge**. Walter is standing next to a switch, which he can throw, that will collapse a footbridge overlooking the tracks into the path of the trolley, thereby stopping the train and preventing it from killing the five people. There is a man standing on the footbridge. Walter can throw the switch, killing him; or he refrain from doing this, letting the five die. Is it morally permissible for Walter to throw the switch?

Table 22.1. *Summary of moral judgments*
for the trolley problem

Case	Judgment
1. Bystander	Permissible
2. Footbridge	Impermissible
3. Loop Track	Impermissible
4. Man-in-front	Permissible
5. Drop Man	Impermissible
6. Collapse Bridge	Permissible

Interestingly, although all cases have the same goal (i.e., to save five, but which requires killing one), subjects come to different judgments on whether the action to reach the goal is permissible or impermissible. As reported by Mikhail (2007), the judgments appear to be widely shared among demographically diverse populations, the summary being given in Table 22.1.

The Double and Triple Effect

Although subjects have difficulties uncovering which moral rules they apply for reasoning in these cases, their judgments appear to be consistent with the so-called principle of double effect. The principle can be expressed as follows:

Harming another individual is permissible if it is the foreseen consequence of an act that will lead to a greater good; in contrast, it is impermissible to harm someone else as an intended means to a greater good. (Hauser 2007)

The key expression here is "intended means." We shall refer in the subsequent sections to the action of harming someone as an intended means, as an intentional killing.

In contrast to the result shown in Table 22.1, Otsuka (2008) in his work states that diverting the trolley in the Loop Track case strikes most moral philosophers as permissible. In his work, he refers to Kamm's principle of triple effect (Kamm 2006) to explain permissibility of diverting the trolley onto a loop side track. The triple effect principle is a revised version of the double effect principle. This moral principle refines the double effect principle, in particular on harming someone as an intended means. In this case, the triple effect principle distinguishes an action that is performed *in order* to bring about an evil from an action performed *that directly causes* an evil to occur without production of evil being its goal. The latter is a new category of action that neither treats the occurrence of evil as a foreseen, unintended consequence nor as an action performed in order to intentionally bring about an evil. Similarly to the double effect principle, the triple effect principle classifies an action performed in order to intentionally bring about an evil as an impermissible action. Yet, this moral principle is more tolerant to the third effect, that is, it is *permissible* for an action to be performed because an evil will occur, if not intended as such.

In the footbridge case, both the double and the triple effect principles arrive at the same moral judgment, namely that it is impermissible to shove a man in order to cause the trolley to hit the man. On the other hand, different moral judgments are delivered for the Loop Track case when employing the double and the triple effect principles. Whereas it is impermissible by the double effect to divert the trolley, this action is *permissible* by the triple effect principle. According to the triple effect principle, the action of diverting the trolley onto the loop side track is performed because it will hit the man, not in order to hit the man (Kamm 2006). As in the other cases, the goal of the Loop Track case is to prevent the trolley from killing the five people. This goal can be achieved by throwing the switch to divert the trolley onto the side track. However, diverting the trolley raises another problem because the side track is a loop track that will take the trolley back to the main track and will still hit the five people. The action of diverting the trolley is not necessarily intended in order to hit the man on the side track. Instead, this action is performed because it will hit the man, eliminating the new problem created by diverting the trolley (Kamm 2006).

To better distinguish an action that is performed in order to bring about an evil and that is performed because an evil will occur, the Loop Track case can be compared with the following case. Consider a variant of the Loop Track case in which the loop side track is empty. Note that, instead of only diverting the trolley onto the empty loop side track, an ancillary act of shoving a man onto the loop side track can be performed. How can this case be morally distinguished from the original Loop Track case? In the original Loop Track case, the man has already been standing on the loop side track when the action of diverting the trolley is carried out, causing the death of the man. In the other case, the death of the man is not merely caused by diverting the trolley (the loop side track is initially empty). Instead, the man dies as a consequence of a further action, that is, shoving the man. This action is intentionally performed to place the man on the side track in order for the trolley to hit him, hence preventing the trolley from killing the five people.

We shall show in the subsequent sections, how we can computationally distinguish these two similar cases in the context of the triple effect principle. In particular, we discuss a feature available in ACORDA to explain the previous moral reasoning computationally.

Modeling Morality in ACORDA

It is interesting to model the trolley problem in ACORDA due to the intricacy that arises from the dilemma itself. Moreover, there are similarities and also differences between cases and between the moral principles employed. Consequently, this adds complexity to the process of modeling them in order to deliver appropriate moral decisions through reasoning. By appropriate moral decisions, we mean the ones that conform with those the majority of people make in adhering to the principle of double effect (though we also consider the principle of triple effect, as a comparison to the principle of double effect).

We model each case of the trolley problem in ACORDA separately. The principle of double effect and triple effect are modeled via a priori constraints and a posteriori preferences. To assess how flexible our model is of the moral rule, we additionally model another variant for the cases of Footbridge and Loop Track. Even for these variants, our model of the moral rules allows the reasoning to deliver moral decisions as expected.

In each case of the trolley problem, there are always two possible decisions to make. One of these is the same for all cases, that is, letting the five people die by merely watching the train go straight. The other decision depends on the cases, for example, throwing the switch, shoving a heavy man, or the combination of them, with the same purpose: to save the five people, but also harming a person in the process.

In this work, these possible decisions are modeled in ACORDA as abducibles. Moral decisions are made by computing abductive stable models and then preferring among them those models with the abducibles and consequences that conform to the principle of double effect or triple effect.

In subsequent sections we detail the model for all six cases of the trolley problem in ACORDA. We also show how to model the principle of double effect and triple effect. Then we present the results of running our models in the ACORDA system.

Modeling the Bystander Case

Facts to describe that there is a side track and that a man (here, named John) is standing on that side track can be modeled simply as the following:

```
side_track.
on_side(john).
human(john).
```

The clauses "expect(watching)" and "expect(throwing_switch)" in the following model indicate that watching and throwing the switch, respectively, are two available abducibles that represent possible decisions Hank has. Because the purpose of the switch is to turn the trolley onto the side track, the action "throwing_switch" is only considered as an abducible if the side track exists. The other clauses represent the chain of actions and consequences for every abducible.

The predicate "end(die(5))" represents the final consequence if watching is abduced, that is, it will result in five people dying. On the other hand, the predicate "end(save_men, ni_kill(N))" represents the final consequence whenever "throwing_switch" is abduced, that is, it will save the five people without intentionally killing someone. The way of representing these two consequences is chosen differently because of the different nature of these two abducibles. Merely watching the trolley go straight is an omission of action that just has negative consequence, whereas throwing the switch is an action that is performed to achieve a goal and additionally has negative consequence. Because abducibles in other cases of the trolley problem also share this property, this way of representation will be used throughout them. The predicate "observed_end" is used to encapsulate these two different means of representation, and will be useful later to avoid floundering when we model the principle of double effect.

```
expect(watching).
train_straight <- consider(watching).
end(die(5)) <- train_straight.
observed_end <- end(X).
```

```
expect(throwing_switch) <- side_track.
turn_side <- consider(throwing_switch).
kill(1) <- human(X), on_side(X), turn_side.
end(save_men,ni_kill(N)) <- turn_side, kill(N).
observed_end <- end(X,Y).
```

We can model the exclusiveness of the two possible decisions, that is, Hank has to decide either to throw the switch or merely watch, by using the exclusive/2 predicate of ACORDA:

```
exclusive(throwing_switch,decide).
exclusive(watching,decide).
```

Note that the exclusiveness between two possible decisions also holds in other cases.

Modeling the Footbridge Case

We represent the fact of a heavy man (here, also named John) on the footbridge standing near to Ian similarly to the Bystander case:

```
stand_near(john).
human(john).
heavy(john).
```

We can make this case more interesting by additionally having another (inanimate) heavy object – a rock – on the footbridge near to Ian and see whether our model of the moral rule still allows the reasoning to deliver moral decisions as expected:

```
stand_near(rock).
inanimate_object(rock).
heavy(rock).
```

Alternatively, if we want only to have either a man or an inanimate object on the footbridge next to Ian, we can model it by using an even loop over default negation:

```
stand_near(john) <- not stand_near(rock).
stand_near(rock) <- not stand_near(john).
```

In the following we show how to model the action of shoving an object as an abducible, together with the chain of actions and consequences for this abducible. The model for the decision of merely watching is the same as in the case of Bystander. Indeed, because the decision of watching is always available for other cases, we use the same modeling in every case.

```
expect(shove(X)) <- stand_near(X).
on_track(X) <- consider(shove(X)).
stop_train(X) <- on_track(X), heavy(X).
kill(1) <- human(X), on_track(X).
kill(0) <- inanimate_object(X), on_track(X).
end(save_men,ni_kill(N)) <- inanimate_object(X),
                            stop_train(X),
                            kill(N).
end(save_men,i_kill(N)) <- human(X),
                           stop_train(X),
                           kill(N).
observed_end <- end(X,Y).
```

Note that the action of shoving an object is only possible if there is an object near Ian to shove, hence the clause "expect(shove(X)) <- stand_near(X)." We also have two clauses that describe two possible final consequences. The clause with the head "end(save_men, ni_kill(N))" deals with the consequence of reaching the goal, that is, saving five, but not intentionally killing someone (in particular, without killing anyone in this case). To the contrary, the clause with the head "end(save_men, i_kill(N))" expresses the consequence of reaching the goal but involving an intentional killing.

Modeling the Loop Track Case

We consider three variants for the Loop Track case. Two variants are similar to the case of footbridge. The other variant will be used later to discuss the difference between the double effect and the triple effect principles, as already discussed.

In the first variant, instead of having only one loop side track as in the original scenario, we consider two loop side tracks: the left and the right loop side tracks. John, a heavy man, is standing on the left side track, whereas on the right side

track there is an inanimate heavy object, a rock. These facts can be represented
in ACORDA as follows:

```
side_track(left).
side_track(right).

on(john,left).
human(john).
heavy(john).

on(rock,right).
inanimate_object(rock).
heavy(rock).
```

The switch can be thrown to either one of the two loop side tracks. This action
of throwing the switch can be modeled as an abducible. This abducible together
with the chain of actions and consequences that follow can be modeled declaratively in ACORDA:

```
expect(throwing_switch(Z)) <- side_track(Z).
turn_side(Z) <- consider(throwing_switch(Z)).
slowdown_train(X) <- turn_side(Z), on(X,Z),
                            heavy(X).
kill(1) <- turn_side(Z), on(X,Z), human(X).
kill(0) <- turn_side(Z), on(X,Z), inanimate_object(X).
end(save_men,ni_kill(N)) <- inanimate_object(X),
                                slowdown_train(X),
                                kill(N).
end(save_men,i_kill(N)) <- human(X),
                               slowdown_train(X),
                               kill(N).
observed_end <- end(X,Y).
```

Note that the clause:

```
expect(throwing_switch(Z)) <- side_track(Z)
```

states that the action of throwing the switch to turn the trolley onto a side
track Z does make sense if the side track Z, to which the switch is connected, is
available.

For the second variant, we consider one loop side track with either a man or an
inanimate object on the side track. This alternative can be modeled by using an
even loop over default negation:

```
side_track(john) <- not side_track(rock).
side_track(rock) <- not side_track(john).
```

Note that the argument of the predicate "side_track/1" does not refer to some side track (left or right, as in the first variant), but refers to some object (rock or John) on the only side track. This leads to a slight difference in the model of the chain of consequences for the throwing switch action:

```
expect(flipping_switch(X)) <- side_track(X).
turn_side(X) <- consider(flipping_switch(X)).
slowdown_train(X) <- turn_side(X), heavy(X).
kill(1) <- turn_side(X), human(X).
kill(0) <- turn_side(X), inanimate_object(X).
end(save(5),ni_kill(N)) <- inanimate_object(X),
                           slowdown_train(X),
                           kill(N).
end(save(5),i_kill(N)) <- human(X),
                          slowdown_train(X),
                          kill(N).
observed_end <- end(X,Y).
```

We may observe that from the first two variants there is no need to change the whole model; only the part of the model that represents the different facts need to be adapted. Moreover, the second variant shows that we do not need to have separate programs to model the fact that a man or an inanimate object is on the side track. Instead, we can have only one program and take the benefit from using an even loop over default negation to capture alternatives between objects.

Throwing the Switch and Shoving a Man

This variant will be useful later, when we discuss the difference between the double effect and the triple effect principles.

In this scenario, the action of throwing the switch to divert the trolley can be followed by the action of shoving a man to place the man onto the empty loop side track. There is only one loop side track, which we can represent by using a simple fact "side_track." To represent either that there has already been a man standing on the loop side track or the loop side track is initially empty, we can use the following even loop over default negation:

```
man_stand_sidetrack <- not empty_sidetrack.
empty_sidetrack <- not man_stand_sidetrack.
```

We have three actions available, represented as abducibles, with the chain of consequences modeled as follows. For simplicity, without loss of generality, we assume that the man standing on the side track or the man shoved is heavy.

```
expect(watching).
train_straight <- consider(watching).
end(die(5)) <- train_straight.
observed_end <- end(X).

expect(throwing_switch) <- side_track.
turn_side <- consider(throwing_switch).
end(save_men,standing_hitting) <- man_stand_sidetrack,
                                   turn_side.

expect(shoving) <- empty_sidetrack,
                   consider(throwing_switch).

freely_goto_maintrack <- empty_sidetrack,
                         turn_side,
                         not consider(shoving).
end(die(5)) <- freely_goto_maintrack.

place_man_sidetrack <- consider(shoving).
end(save_men,placing_hitting) <- place_man_sidetrack,
                                 turn_side.

observed_end <- end(X,Y).
```

This model can be read declaratively. The action watching, together with its consequence, is similar as in other cases.

The action "throwing_switch" is possible if there is a side track to which the switch is connected. Throwing the switch will turn the trolley to the side track. If a (heavy) man has already been standing on the side track and the trolley also turns to the side track, then the five people are saved but the man standing on the side track is killed.

Following our scenario, the action of shoving is available if there is nothing on the side track ("empty_sidetrack") and the action of throwing the switch is performed. This is modeled by the clause:

```
expect(shoving) <- empty_sidetrack,
                   consider(throwing_switch).
```

This means that the action of shoving is a further action following the action of throwing the switch.

If the side track is empty, the trolley has turned to the side track; but if the action of shoving is not abduced, then the trolley will freely go to the main track where the five people are walking. This results in the death of the five people.

On the other hand, if shoving is abduced (as an ancillary action of throwing the switch), then this will result in placing a (heavy) man on the side track. If the trolley has turned to the side track and the man has been placed on the side track, then the five people are saved with the cost of killing the man placed on the side track as the consequence of shoving.

Modeling the Man-in-Front Case

Recall that in the case of Man-in-Front, there is a side track onto which the trolley can turn. On this side track, there is a heavy (inanimate) object, a rock. There is also a man standing in front of the heavy object. We can model these facts in ACORDA as follows:

```
side_track.
on_side(rock).
inanimate_object(rock).
heavy(rock).
in_front_of(rock,jack).
human(jack).
```

In order to prevent the trolley from killing the five people, a switch can be thrown to turn the trolley onto the side track. The following clauses are used to model the "throwing_switch" action as an abducible together with the consequences that follow:

```
expect(throwing_switch) <- side_track.
turn_side <- consider(throwing_switch).
kill(1) <- turn_side, on_side(X),
            in_front_of(X,Y), human(Y).
slowdown_train(X) <- turn_side, on_side(X),
                      heavy(X).

end(save_men,ni_kill(N)) <- inanimate_object(X),
                            slowdown_train(X),
                            kill(N).
end(save_men,i_kill(N)) <- human(X),
                           slowdown_train(X),
                           kill(N).

observed_end <- end(X,Y).
```

Modeling the Drop Man Case

The following facts model the scenario of the Drop Man case:

```
switch_connected(bridge).
human(john).
heavy(john).
on(bridge,john).
```

These facts state that there is a switch connected to the bridge where there is a heavy man, John, standing on the bridge. As in other cases, it is straightforward to model in ACORDA the "throwing_switch" actions along with its consequences:

```
expect(throwing_switch(Z)) <- switch_connected(Z).
drop(X) <- consider(throwing_switch(Z)), on(Z,X).
kill(1) <- human(X), drop(X).
stop_train(X) <- heavy(X), drop(X).
end(save_men,ni_kill(N)) <- inanimate_object(X),
                            stop_train(X),
                            kill(N).
end(save_men,i_kill(N)) <- human(X),
                           stop_train(X),
                           kill(N).
observed_end <- end(X,Y).
```

In this model, the fact that the switch is connected to the bridge is the condition for the action of throwing the switch to be reasonable to perform.

Modeling the Collapse Bridge Case

The Collapse Bridge case is a variation from the Drop Man case. In this case, the footbridge itself is the heavy object that may stop the train when it collapses and prevent the train from killing the five people. There is also a man, John, standing on the footbridge, as in the Drop Man case. These facts can be modeled in ACORDA as follows:

```
switch_connected(bridge).
heavy(bridge).
inanimate_object(bridge).
human(john).
on(bridge,john).
```

With slight variation of consequences from the Drop Man case, the following clauses model the "throwing_switch" action as an abducible together with the consequences that follow:

```
expect(throwing_switch(X)) <-
  switch_connected(X).

collapse(X) <- consider(throwing_switch(X)).
stop_train(X) <- heavy(X), collapse(X).
kill(1) <- human(Y), on(X,Y), collapse(X).
end(save_men,ni_kill(N)) <- inanimate_object(X),
                            stop_train(X),
                            kill(N).
```

```
end(save_men,i_kill(N)) <- human(X),
                           stop_train(X),
                           kill(N).
observed_end <- end(X,Y).
```

Modeling the Principles of Double and Triple Effect

The principles of double effect and triple effect can be modeled by using a combination of integrity constraints and a posteriori preferences.

Integrity constraints are used for two purposes. First, we need to observe the final consequences or endings of each possible decision to enable us later to morally prefer decisions by considering the greater good between possible decisions. This can be achieved by specifying the following integrity constraint:

```
falsum <- not observed_end.
```

This integrity constraint enforces all available decisions to be abduced together with their consequences by computing all possible observable hypothetical endings using all possible abductions. Indeed, to be able to reach a moral decision, all hypothetical scenarios afforded by the abducibles must lead to an observable ending. Second, we also need to rule out impermissible actions, that is, actions that involve intentional killing in the process of reaching the goal. This can be enforced by specifying the integrity constraint

```
falsum <- intentional_killing.
```

Depending on whether we employ the double effect or the triple effect principle, intentional killing can be easily defined. For the double effect principle, it can be modeled as follows:

```
intentional_killing <- end(save_men,i_kill(Y)).
```

Similarly, intentional killing for the triple effect principle can be modeled as follows:

```
intentional_killing <-
    end(save_men,placing_hitting).
```

These integrity constraints serve as the first filtering function of our abductive stable models by ruling out impermissible actions (the latter being coded by abducibles). In other words, integrity constraints already afford us with just those abductive stable models that contain only permissible actions.

Additionally, one can prefer among permissible actions those resulting in greater good. This can be realized by a posteriori preferences that evaluate the consequences of permissible actions and then prefer the one with greater good. The following definition of "select/2" achieves this purpose. The first argument of this predicate refers to the set of initial abductive stable models to prefer, whereas the second argument refers to the preferred ones. The auxiliary predicate "select/3" only keeps abductive stable models that contain decisions with greater good of consequences. In the trolley problem, the greater good is evaluated by a utility function concerning the number of people that die as a result of possible decisions. This is realized in the definition of predicate "select/3" by comparing final consequences that appear in the initial abductive stable models. The first clause of "select/3" is the base case. The second clause and the third clause together eliminate abductive stable models containing decisions with worse consequences, whereas the fourth clause will keep those models that contain decisions with greater good of consequences.

```
select(Xs,Ys) :- select(Xs,Xs,Ys).

select([],_,[]).
select([X|Xs],Zs,Ys) :-
      member(end(die(N)),X),
      member(Z,Zs),
      member(end(save_men,ni_kill(K)),Z), N > K,
      select(Xs,Zs,Ys).
select([X|Xs],Zs,Ys) :-
      member(end(save_men,ni_kill(K)),X),
      member(Z,Zs),
      member(end(die(N)),Z), N =< K,
      select(Xs,Zs,Ys).
select([X|Xs],Zs,[X|Ys]) :- select(Xs,Zs,Ys).
```

Recall the variant of the Footbridge case, in which either a man or an inanimate object is on the footbridge next to Ian. This exclusive alternative is specified by an even loop over default negation and we have an abductive stable model that contains the consequence of letting the five people die when a rock is next to Ian. This model is certainly *not* the one we would like our moral reasoner to prefer. The following replacement definition of "select/2" accomplishes this case.

```
select([],[]).
select([X|Xs],Ys) :-
      member(end(die(N)),X),
      member(stand_near(rock),X),
      select(Xs,Ys).
select([X|Xs],[X|Ys]) :- select(Xs,Ys).
```

It is important to note that in this case, because either a man or a rock is near to Ian and the model with shoving a man is already ruled out by our integrity constraint, there is no need to consider greater good in terms of the number of people that die. This means, as shown subsequently, that only two abductive stable models are preferred: the model with watching as the abducible whenever a man is standing near to Ian; and the other being the model with shoving the rock as the abducible.

There is an interest to be able to specify a posteriori preferences more declaratively, that is, by encapsulating the details of predicate "select/2" from the viewpoint of users. Although this may depend on the domain where moral reasoning is applied, some kind of generic macros can be defined. Our subsequent work has evidenced preliminary results (Pereira and Saptawijaya 2007). In those results, we extend the syntax of ACORDA by introducing the predicates "elim/1" and "exists/1." We provide two types of generic macros for the purpose of specifying a posteriori preferences.

The first type of macros allows us to realize a posteriori preferences by eliminating abductive stable models containing abducibles with worse consequences. This can be done by comparing some consequences among initial abductive stable models. The aforementioned definition of predicate "select/3" is an example of this type. Instead of using this definition of "select/3," the same a posteriori preferences can now be expressed more declaratively as follows:

```
elim([end(die(N))]) <-
    exists([end(save_men,ni_kill(K))]), N > K.

elim([end(save_men,ni_kill(K))]) <-
    exists([end(die(N))]), N =< K.
```

The first clause is used to eliminate abductive stable models containing the literal "end(die(N))" if there exists other abductive stable models containing the literal "end(save_men,ni_kill(K))" and "N > K." The second clause can be read similarly.

The second type of macros deals with a posteriori preferences where an abductive stable model is eliminated based only on some literals it contains. This is in contrast with the first type of macros, where the elimination of an abductive stable model is performed through comparison with other abductive stable models. The latter definition of predicate "select/2" (in dealing with the variant of the Footbridge case) falls into this type. This definition of "select/2" can be replaced with the following line:

```
elim([end(die(N)),stand_near(rock)]).
```

This simple clause eliminates abductive stable models that contain both literals "end(die(N))" and "stand_near(rock)." Recall that the abductive stable model containing these two literals together is not the one a moral reasoner should prefer, because it may shove the rock to avoid the consequence of letting the five people die.

Table 22.2. *Summary of experiments in ACORDA*

Case	Initial models	Final models
Bystander	`[throwing_switch],[watching]`	`[throwing_switch]`
Footbridge(a)	`[watching],[shove(rock)]`	`[shove(rock)]`
Footbridge(b)	`[watching,stand_near(john)],`	`[watching,stand_near(john)],`
	`[watching,stand_near(rock)],` `[shove(rock)]`	`[shove(rock)]`
Loop Track(a)	`[throwing_switch(right)],`	`[throwing_switch(right)]`
	`[watching]`	
Loop Track(b)	`[watching,side_track(john)],`	`[watching,side_track(john)],`
	`[watching,side_track(rock)],`	`[throwing_switch(rock)]`
	`[throwing_switch(rock)]`	
Loop Track(c)	`[watching,empty_sidetrack],`	`[watching,empty_sidetrack],`
	`[watching,man_stand_sidetrack],`	`[throwing_switch,man_stand_sidetrack]`
	`[throwing_switch,empty_sidetrack],` `[throwing_switch,man_stand_sidetrack]`	
Man-in-front	`[watching],`	`[throwing_switch(rock)]`
	`[throwing_switch(rock)]`	
Drop Man	`[watching]`	`[watching]`
Collapse Bridge	`[watching],`	`[throwing_switch(bridge)]`
	`[throwing_switch(bridge)]`	

Running the Models in ACORDA

We report now on the experiments of running our models in ACORDA. Table 22.2 gives a summary of all cases of the trolley problem. Column Initial Models contains info about the abductive stable models obtained before a posteriori preferences are applied, whereas column Final Models contains those after a posteriori preferences are applied. Here, only relevant literals are shown. These results comply with the results found for most people in morality laboratory experiments.

Note that entry Footbridge(a) refers to the variant of Footbridge where both a man and a rock are near to Ian, and Footbridge(b) where either a man or a rock is near to Ian. Loop Track(a) refers to the variant of Loop Track where there are two loop tracks, with a man on the left loop track and a rock on the right loop track. Loop Track(b) only considers one loop track where either a man or a rock is on the single loop track. Loop Track(c) is another variant considering the triple effect principle, where the ancillary act of shoving a man is available, following the action of throwing the switch. Note that both cases Loop Track(a) and Loop Track(b) employ the double effect principle. Consequently, there is no initial model (of these two cases) that contains the abducible throwing the switch whenever a man is on the side track. This model has been ruled out by the integrity constraint, because this is considered impermissible in the double effect principle. To the contrary, Loop Track(c), which employs the triple effect principle, does have an initial model with a man on the side track and throwing the switch as an abducible. This model is not ruled out by the integrity constraint, because it is deemed permissible by the triple effect principle.

Selective literals in an abductive stable model (e.g. the literals shown in Table 22.2) can be inspected in ACORDA. The feature of inspection enables us to examine whether some literals are true in the context of adopted abducibles without further abduction. It is useful, in particular, to explain computationally the moral reasoning in scenario Loop Track(c), where the triple effect principle is employed. We simply inspect that the man, an obstacle to the trolley, has already been standing on the side track, because only the action of throwing the switch is abduced. No additional action needs to be abduced to prevent the trolley from hitting the five people. On the other hand, in the models containing "empty_sidetrack," mere inspection is not enough because an extra abducible is required to shove the man onto the track in order to deliberately make him an obstacle where there was none. Hence, it prevents the trolley from hitting the five people. However, the abductive stable model containing this further action is already ruled out by our integrity constraint. This conforms with the triple effect principle, as it is impermissible to intentionally shove the man in addition to the act of throwing the switch, in order for the trolley to hit the man for the purpose of stopping the trolley. Indeed, simple inspection does not allow further abduction in order to make it actively true.

Conclusions and Future Work

We have shown how to model moral reasoning using prospective logic programming. We use various dilemmas of the trolley problem and the principle of double effect and triple effect as the moral rules. Possible decisions in a dilemma are modeled as abducibles. Abductive stable models are then computed, which capture abduced decisions and their consequences. Models violating integrity constraints, that is, models that contain actions involving intentional killing, are ruled out. Finally, a posteriori preferences are used to prefer models that characterize more preferred moral decisions, including the use of utility functions. These experiments show that preferred moral decisions, namely the ones that follow the principle of double effect, are successfully delivered. They conform to the results of empirical experiments conducted in cognitive science and law. Regarding the triple effect principle, the inspection feature of ACORDA can be employed to detect mere consequences of abducibles. Hence, we can distinguish computationally two moral judgments in line with the triple effect principle, that is, whether an action is performed in order to bring about an evil or just because an evil will occur.

Much research has emphasized using machine-learning techniques such as statistical analysis (Rzepka and Araki 2005), neural networks (Guarini 2005), case-based reasoning (McLearen 2006), and inductive logic programming (Anderson et al. 2006) to model moral reasoning from examples of particular moral dilemmas. Our approach differs from them as we do not employ machine-learning techniques to deliver moral decisions.

Powers (2006) proposes to use nonmonotonic logic to specifically model Kant's categorical imperatives, but it is unclear whether his approach has ever been realized in a working implementation. On the other hand, Bringsjord et al. (2006) propose the use of deontic logic to formalize moral codes. The objective of their research is to arrive at a methodology that allows an agent to behave ethically as much as possible in an environment that demands such behavior. We share our objective with them to some extent as we also would like to come up with a general framework to model morality computationally. In contrast to our work, they use an axiomatized deontic logic to decide which moral code is operative to arrive at an expected moral outcome. This is achieved by seeking a proof for the expected moral outcome to follow from candidates of operative moral codes.

To arrive at our ultimate research goal, we envision several possible future directions. We would like to explore how to express metarule and metamoral injunctions. By "metarule," we mean a rule to resolve two existing conflicting moral rules in deriving moral decisions. "Metamorality," on the other hand, is used to provide protocols for moral rules, to regulate how moral rules interact with one another. Another possible direction is to have a framework for generating precompiled moral rules. This will benefit fast and frugal moral decision making, which is sometimes needed instead of full deliberative moral reasoning every time (cf. heuristics for decision making in law [Gigerenzer and Engel 2006]).

We envision a final system that can be employed to test moral theories and can also be used for moral-reasoning training, including the automated generation of example tests and their explanation. Finally, we hope our research will help in imparting moral behavior to autonomous agents.

References

Alferes, J. J., Brogi, A., Leite, J. A., and Pereira, L. M. 2002. Evolving Logic Programs. Pages 50–61 of: Flesca, S., Greco, S., Leone, N., and Ianni, G. (eds), *Procs. 8th European Conf. on Logics in Artificial Intelligence (JELIA'02)*. LNCS 2424. Springer.

Anderson, M., Anderson, S., and Armen, C. 2006. MedEthEx: A Prototype Medical Ethics Advisor. In: *Procs. 18th Conf. on Innovative Applications of Artificial Intelligence (IAAI-06)*.

Bringsjord, S., Arkoudas, K., and Bello, P. 2006. Toward a General Logicist Methodology for Engineering Ethically Correct Robots. *IEEE Intelligent Systems*, 21(4), 38–44.

de Waal, F. 2006. *Primates and Philosophers, How Morality Evolved*. Princeton U.P.

Dell'Acqua, P., and Pereira, L. M. 2005. Preferential Theory Revision. Pages 69–84 of: Pereira, L. M., and Wheeler, G. (eds), *Procs. Computational Models of Scientific Reasoning and Applications.*

Dell'Acqua, P., and Pereira, L. M. 2007. Preferential Theory Revision (*extended version*). *Journal of Applied Logic,* 5(4):586–601

Foot, P. 1967. The Problem of Abortion and the Doctrine of Double Effect. *Oxford Review,* 5, 5–15.

Gelfond, M., and Lifschitz, V. 1988. The Stable Model Semantics for Logic Programming. In: Kowalski, R., and Bowen, K. A. (eds), 5th Intl. Logic Programming Conf. MIT Press.

Gigerenzer, G ., and Engel, C . (eds). 2006. *Heuristics and the Law.* MIT Press.

Guarini, M. 2005. Particularism and Generalism: How AI Can Help Us to Better Understand Moral Cognition. In: Anderson, M., Anderson, S., and Armen, C. (eds), *Machine ethics: Papers from the AAAI Fall Symposium.* AAAI Press.

Hauser, M. D. 2007. *Moral Minds: How Nature Designed Our Universal Sense of Right and Wrong.* Little Brown.

Joyce, R. 2006. *The Evolution of Morality.* The MIT Press.

Kakas, A., Kowalski, R., and Toni, F. 1998. The Role of Abduction in Logic Programming. Pages 235–324 of: Gabbay, D., Hogger, C., and Robinson, J. (eds), *Handbook of Logic in Artificial Intelligence and Logic Programming,* vol. 5. Oxford U. P.

Kamm, F. M. 2006. *Intricate Ethics: Rights, Responsibilities, and Permissible Harm.* Oxford U. P.

Katz, L. D . (ed). 2002. *Evolutionary Origins of Morality, Cross-Disciplinary Perspectives.* Imprint Academic.

Kowalski, R. 2006. The Logical Way to be Artificially Intelligent. Page 122 of: Toni, F., and Torroni, P. (eds), *Procs. of CLIMA VI, LNAI.* Springer.

Lopes, G., and Pereira, L. M. 2006. Prospective Logic Programming with ACORDA. In: *Procs. of the FLoC'06, Workshop on Empirically Successful Computerized Reasoning,* 3rd Intl. J Conf. on Automated Reasoning.

McLaren, B. M. 2006. Computational Models of Ethical Reasoning: Challenges, Initial Steps, and Future Directions. *IEEE Intelligent Systems,* 21(4), 29–37.

Mikhail, J. 2007. Universal Moral Grammar: Theory, Evidence, and The Future. *Trends in Cognitive Sciences,* 11(4), 143–152.

Otsuka, M. 2008. Double Effect, Triple Effect and the Trolley Problem: Squaring the Circle in Looping Cases. *Utilitas,* 20(1), 92–110.

Pereira, L. M., and Lopes, G. 2007. Prospective Logic Agents. In: Neves, J. M., Santos, M. F., and Machado, J. M. (eds), *Procs. 13th Portuguese Intl. Conf. on Artificial Intelligence (EPIA'07).* Springer LNAI.

Pereira, L. M., and Saptawijaya, A. 2007. Moral Decision Making with ACORDA. In: Dershowitz, N., and Voronkov, A. (eds), *Short papers call, Local Procs. 14th Intl. Conf. on Logic for Programming Artificial Intelligence and Reasoning (LPAR'07).*

Powers, T. M. 2006. Prospects for a Kantian Machine. *IEEE Intelligent Systems,* 21(4), 46–51.

Rzepka, R., and Araki, K. 2005. What Could Statistics Do for Ethics? The Idea of a Commonsense-Processing-Based Safety Valve. In: Anderson, M., Anderson, S., and Armen, C. (eds), *Machine ethics: Papers from the AAAI Fall Symposium.* AAAI Press.

Tancredi, L. 2005. *Hardwired Behavior: What Neuroscience Reveals about Morality.* Cambridge U. P.

23

An Integrated Reasoning Approach
to Moral Decision Making

Morteza Dehghani[1], *Ken Forbus, Emmett Tomai*
and Matthew Klenk

Introduction

ALTHOUGH TRADITIONAL MODELS OF DECISION MAKING IN AI HAVE focused on utilitarian theories, there is considerable psychological evidence that these theories fail to capture the full spectrum of human decision making (e.g. Kahneman and Tversky 1979; Ritov and Baron 1999). Current theories of moral decision making extend beyond pure utilitarian models by relying on contextual factors that vary with culture. In particular, research on moral reasoning has uncovered a conflict between normative outcomes and intuitive judgments. This has led some researchers to propose the existence of deontological moral rules; that is, some actions are immoral regardless of consequences, which could block utilitarian motives. Consider the starvation scenario (from Ritov and Baron [1999]) that follows:

A convoy of food trucks is on its way to a refugee camp during a famine in Africa. (Airplanes cannot be used.) You find that a second camp has even more refugees. If you tell the convoy to go to the second camp instead of the first, you will save one thousand people from death, but one hundred people in the first camp will die as a result.

Would you send the convoy to the second camp?

The utilitarian decision would send the convoy to the second camp, but 63 percent of participants did not divert the truck.

Making these types of decisions automatically requires an integrated approach, including natural language understanding, qualitative reasoning, analogical reasoning, and first-principles reasoning. This paper describes a cognitively motivated model of recognition-based moral decision making called MoralDM, which incorporates two types of decision making: utilitarian and deontological. To reduce tailorability, a natural language understanding system is used to semi-automatically produce formal representations from psychological stimuli

---

[1] Please address correspondences to morteza@ict.usc.edu.

re-rendered in simplified English. The different impacts of secular versus sacred values are modeled via qualitative reasoning using an order of magnitude representation. MoralDM combines first-principles reasoning and analogical reasoning to implement rules of moral decision making and utilize previously made decisions. This chapter describes how MoralDM works and shows that it can model some psychological findings on moral decision making.

We begin by summarizing relevant psychological results and background. Next, we describe the different AI techniques used in MoralDM. Then we show that MoralDM can account for results from two psychological studies. An analysis of its performance demonstrates the importance of integrated reasoning. Finally, we discuss related and future work.

Moral Decision Making

Morality as a topic of experimental scientific inquiry has attracted the attention of psychologists for more than eight decades. After the initial domination of rational approaches to decision making, the conflict between normative outcomes and intuitive judgments led some researchers to suggest the existence of *sacred values* or *protected values*,[2] which are not allowed to be traded off no matter what the consequences (Baron and Spranca 1997, Tetlock 2003). These protected values are known to block utilitarian motives by evoking deontological moral rules. In trade-off situations, these values outweigh economic ones (Tetlock 2003) because they "incorporate moral beliefs that drive action in ways dissociated from prospects for success" (Atran, Axelrod, and Davis 2007). In our example, given that life is a sacred value, people often refuse to take an action that would result in them being responsible for people dying. Tetlock (2000) defines sacred values as "those values that a moral community treats as possessing transcendental significance that precludes comparisons, trade-offs, or indeed any mingling with secular values." People who have sacred or protected values tend to reject the need for tradeoffs, no matter what the consequences, and often show strong emotional reactions, such as anger, when these values are challenged (Tetlock 2000).

When protected values are involved, people tend to be concerned with the nature of their action rather than the utility of the outcome. Baron and Spranca (1997) argue that people show lower *quantity sensitivity* to outcome utilities when dealing with protected values. That is, they become less sensitive to the consequences of their choices, leading them to prefer inaction, even if it results in a lower outcome utility, over an action that violates a sacred value. The degree of outcome sensitivity varies with culture and the context of the scenario. Lim and Baron (1997) show that people in different cultures tend to protect different values and demonstrate different levels of sensitivity toward shared sacred values.

[2] Unless otherwise specified, we use the two terms interchangeably.

In addition to contextual factors, the causal structure of the scenario affects people's decision making. Waldmann and Dieterich (2007) show that people act more utilitarian, that is, become more sensitive to the outcome utilities, if their action influences the patient of harm rather than the agent. They also suggest that people are less quantity sensitive when their action directly, rather than indirectly, causes harm. Bartels and Medin (2007) argue that the agent's sensitivity toward the outcome of a moral situation depends on the agent's focus of attention.

Judgment and decision-making researchers have highlighted a number of ways in which culture may influence decision-making. Probably the most well-known results are the findings on cultural differences in judgments of risk (Hsee and Weber 1999; Weber and Hsee 1998). Most of the work that has been done looking at cross-cultural differences in morally motivated decision making has been ethnographic in nature. Shweder et al. (1997) and Haidt et al. (1993) have identified dimensions of moral decision making that are present in one cultural group but not in another. Values such as respect for authority and the saliency of the distinction between purity and impurity are some that have been identified in helping people to characterize certain situations as morally tinged within one cultural group but not another. These striking differences on some of the most important issues in judgment and decision making indicate that the cultural context plays an important role in basic cognitive processes involved in moral decision making.

MoralDM

Moral decision making is a complex reasoning process. In psychological studies, scenarios are presented to human subjects in natural language. The research summarized in the previous section identifies a number of contextual factors that cause subjects to become less sensitive to the outcome utilities of their decisions. Other research has also shown that analogy plays a role in many broad decision-making domains (Markman and Medin 2002), including moral decision making (Dehghani, Gentner et al. 2009). Consequently, a model of moral decision making needs to include natural language understanding, a method for comparing outcome quantities that takes into account the effects of protected values, the method for reasoning about outcomes utilities and protected values, and the ability to utilize previous decisions or examples when reasoning about new situations.

Our model of recognition-based moral decision making, MoralDM, incorporates two mutually exclusive types: utilitarian and deontological. If there are no protected values involved in the case being analyzed, MoralDM applies traditional rules of utilitarian decision making by choosing the action that provides the highest outcome utility. On the other hand, if MoralDM determines that there are sacred values involved, it operates in deontological mode and becomes less sensitive to the outcome utility of actions, preferring inactions to actions.

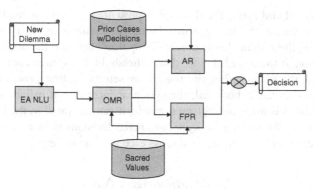

Figure 23.1. MoralDM Architecture.

MoralDM has been implemented using the FIRE reasoning engine. The knowledge base contents are a two-million-fact subset of Cycorp's ResearchCyc[3] knowledge base (KB), which provides formal representations of everyday objects, people, events, and relationships. The KB also includes representations we have developed to support qualitative and analogical reasoning. The KB provides a formal ontology that is useful for representing and reasoning about moral decision-making scenarios.

Figure 23.1 provides an overview of the MoralDM architecture. To solve a given moral decision-making scenario, MoralDM begins by using EA NLU, a natural language understanding system, to semi-automatically translate simplified English scenarios into predicate calculus. Given this representation, the presence of protected values and relevant contextual factors are computed via a fixed set of rules. A number of known protected values are stored in the KB. For a new scenario a set of rules are applied to decide whether the case includes protected values or not. The orders of magnitude reasoning module (OMR) then calculates the relationship between the utility of each choice. Using the outcome of the orders of magnitude reasoning module, MoralDM utilizes a hybrid reasoning approach consisting of a first-principles reasoning module (FPR) and an analogical reasoning module (AR) to arrive at a decision. The first-principles reasoning module suggests decisions based on rules of moral reasoning. The analogical reasoning module compares a given scenario with previously solved decision cases to determine whether protected values exist in the new case and suggest a course of action. Hybrid reasoning gives the system the ability to tackle a broader range of decision-making scenarios and provides a more cognitively plausible approach to decision making.

The first-principles and analogical reasoning modules work in parallel and complement each other by providing support (or disagreement) for a decision.

---

[3] research.cyc.com.

If both succeed and agree, the decision is presented. When one module fails to arrive at a decision, the answer from the other module is used. If the modules do not agree, the system checks the similarity score between the problem and its closest analog. If the score is higher than a threshold, the system uses the derived answer from the analog, otherwise the system selects the first-principles reasoning module's choice. If both fail, the system is incapable of making a decision. After a decision is made for a given scenario, it can be stored in the case library for future use. This enables the system to make decisions in more scenarios as it accumulates experience. Next, we discuss each module in detail.

Explanation Agent NLU

The inputs to MoralDM are dilemma scenarios from the psychological literature, expressed in natural language. In typical cognitive modeling work, such texts are hand-encoded to formal representations suitable for computational reasoning. This encoding process is both labor intensive and error prone. It also leads to the problem of *tailorability*. Because the formal representations are created by hand by the simulation authors (or people working closely with them), it is very easy for them to make representational choices to get a particular example to work. In contrast, MoralDM uses its Explanation Agent Natural Language Understanding (EA NLU) component to semi-automatically encode the stimuli. EA NLU reuses existing representations and enforces consistent translation principles independent of any particular model. This reduces the opportunities for representational errors and tailorability, thus increasing the plausibility of the simulation results. EA NLU has been used in several cognitive modeling experiments including MoralDM, conceptual change (Friedman and Forbus 2008), and blame attribution (Tomai and Forbus 2008). By using a common encoding process across multiple projects, we aim to continually increase knowledge reuse in order to decrease both the encoding effort and the sources of representational errors.

Unrestricted, fully automatic natural language understanding is currently beyond the state of the art. EA NLU implements a practical approach that prioritizes *semantic breadth* to facilitate natural language input to cognitive simulations (Tomai and Forbus 2009). Cognitive models such as MoralDM require deep, structured formal representations in order to capture the subtle distinctions made by the underlying psychological theories. A high degree of semantic breadth is required for an encoding process to capture those distinctions in the text and properly represent them in the predicate calculus. In particular, narrative texts rely heavily on descriptions of unrealized situations such as utterances, predictions, possibilities, and hypotheticals. EA NLU achieves this semantic breadth through a novel integration of existing resources and techniques. To address the need for these highly expressive representations, EA NLU uses CycL, a higher-order predicate calculus that supports modal operators and other higher-order predicates. To address the need for large-scale background knowledge about the topics covered in input texts, it uses the contents of the ResearchCyc KB (Lenat and Gupta 1990). This includes a large number of *subcategorization frames* (Fillmore 2006), which provide knowledge-rich semantic translations from words and common phrases to predicate calculus. This expressive power and large-scale knowledge comes at a high cost in the complexity of the representations and the algorithms that generate them. Rather than restrict the semantic breadth of the system, EA NLU relies on two techniques to control complexity and a user intervention mode to circumvent unsolved problems. First, it uses a controlled grammar called QRG-CE (Tomai and Forbus 2009). For every distinct semantic form that the system can generate, at least one syntactic form is supported. Additional syntactic forms, although useful, are a second priority. This ensures that development resources are focused first on semantic breadth, and reduces computational complexity introduced by legitimate syntactic ambiguities in natural language. This approach requires rewriting the original texts in QRG-CE before EA NLU can encode them. Second, EA NLU separates the interpretation process into two stages – sentence level and discourse level. An efficient compositional process builds sentence-level representations with embedded *choice sets* (Kuehne and Forbus 2004) to delay disambiguation of competing semantic interpretations. By delaying disambiguation without discarding alternative interpretations, EA NLU avoids blindly multiplying the complexity of syntactic parsing with the complexity of general-purpose reasoning with large-scale knowledge. The sentence-level representations are translated into *discourse representation structures* (Kamp and Reyle 1993) that support dynamic, incremental updating over multi-sentence discourses in the second stage. That process uses general-purpose reasoning with large-scale world knowledge to interpret each subsequent sentence-level representation while resolving ambiguities, including anaphora. It controls complexity by back-chaining from pragmatic constraints provided as a reasoning task such as MoralDM's decision task.

Semantic and syntactic disambiguation in the most general case is an unsolved problem. Most current research in computational natural language is focused on increasing syntactic coverage at the expense of expressiveness. In order to facilitate deep, structured encoding of complex, real-world stimuli, EA NLU provides a user intervention mode for disambiguation that is beyond the system's capabilities. Experimenters can manually select choices from the parsing and semantic choice sets generated by the sentence-level interpretation process. These multiple-choice selections are far more constrained than manual encoding, providing guidance for inexperienced encoders and reducing the opportunities for user error and tailorability.

Figure 23.2 contains the controlled language for the starvation scenario. Given these statements, EA NLU identifies events of transporting, famine, dying (one thousand people), saving, ordering, going, and dying (one hundred people) together with the two quantified sets of people, the convoy, food, two refugee

```
A convoy of trucks is transporting food
to a refugee camp during a famine in
Africa. 1000 people in a second refugee
camp will die. You can save them by
ordering the convoy to go to that
refugee camp. The order will cause 100
people to die in the first refugee camp.
```

Figure 23.2. Starvation scenario in simplified English.

```
(isa order131049 Ordering-CommunicationAct)
(performedBy order131049 you128898)
(recipientOfInfo order131049 convoy127246)

(infoTransferred order131049
 (and
  (isa refugee-camp129739 RefugeeCamp)
  (isa convoy127246 Convoy)
  (isa go129115 Movement-TranslationEvent)
  (primaryObjectMoving go129115 convoy127246)
  (toLocation go129115 refugee-camp129739)))
```

Figure 23.3. Predicate calculus for ordering.

camps, and the proper name Africa. There is also an explicit reference to the listener, "you." Figure 23.3 contains the frame-based interpretation of the order. This set of facts is contained within a Discourse Representation Structure (DRS) that is modally embedded with the operator possible in the root DRS for the scenario interpretation, indicating that it is one outcome of the choice. Causal links are explicitly stated between the order and the saving and the order and the second set of deaths. The abstraction of saving drives inferential attention to events in the description that the beneficiary may be saved from. The expected future modality of the first set of deaths makes it a reasonable candidate. Based on the possible modality of the saving/ordering sequence, combined with the use of the explicit reference to the listener, the system infers an abstraction of choice being presented with known consequences resulting from both action and inaction. Figure 23.4 contains the inferred abstraction of choice and its causal consequences.

Order of Magnitude Reasoning Module

As discussed earlier, in the presence of sacred values, people tend to be less sensitive to outcome utilities in their decision making. This sometimes results in decisions that are contrary to utilitarian models. We claim that this variable degree of quantity sensitivity can be accounted for by using a qualitative order of magnitude representation.

```
(isa Sel131949 SelectingSomething)
(choices Sel131949 order131049)
(choices Sel131949 Inaction131950)
(causes-PropSit
  (chosenItem Sel131949 Inaction131950)
  die128829)
(causes-PropSit
  (chosenItem Sel131949 order131049)
  save128937)
```

Figure 23.4. Predicate calculus for the choice presented.

We model quantity sensitivity by using Dague's (1993a, 1993b) qualitative Relative Order of Magnitude (ROM[R]) formalism. Order of magnitude reasoning is a form of commonsense reasoning. It provides the kind of stratification that seems necessary for modeling the impact of protected values on reasoning. Raiman (1991) uses the analogy of a coarse balance to describe the intuitions behind order of magnitude reasoning: A course balance can weigh quantities with more or less precision. This precision level depends on the order of magnitude scale used to map quantities onto coarse values. He uses two granularity levels, *Small* and *Rough*, to build a multitude of order of magnitude scales. These two granularity levels provide three qualitative relations between quantities, which have been formally defined in FOG (Raiman 1991). Both O(M) (Mavrovouniotis and Stephanopoulos 1990, 1988, 1987) and ROM(K) (Dague 1993b) are attempts to provide a more comprehensive order of magnitude formalism.

ROM(R), the mapping of ROM(K) onto R, is the only order of magnitude system that guarantees validity in R. Given that in decision-making scenarios utilities of choices are expressed in real numbers, ROM(R) seems to be the best order of magnitude formalism for our purposes. Some order of magnitude representations (e.g., FOG) do not allow values at different levels to ever be comparable. One of the features of ROM(R) is that it includes two degrees of freedom, k_1 and k_2, which for our purposes can be varied to capture differences in quantity sensitivity. Dague defines four classes of relationship between two numbers: "close to," "comparable to," "negligible with respect to," and "distant from." Whereas FOG and O(M) fail to capture gradual change, the overlapping relations in ROM(K) allow a smooth, gradual transition between the states.

Although for engineering problems two degrees of freedom and four relations is quite useful, we believe for the task that we are interested in one degree of freedom and three binary relations are more plausible. Therefore, we implemented a simplified version of ROM(R) using one degree of freedom, k, resulting in three binary relations: almost equal, greater than, and orders of magnitude different. These three classes can be computed using the following rules:

- $A \approx_k B \Leftrightarrow |A-B| \leq k * \text{Max}(|A|, |B|)$
- $A <_k B \Leftrightarrow |A| \leq k * |B|$
- $A \neq_k B \Leftrightarrow |A-B| > k * \text{Max}(|A|, |B|)$

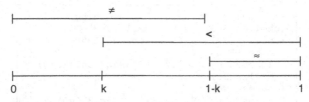

Figure 23.5. Interval landmark.

These relations respectively map to "close to," "greater than," and "distant from." k can take any value between 0 and 1. Figure 23.5 demonstrates the interval landmarks of the system. In order to provide smooth transitions between these qualitative intervals ROM(K) defines parameter ε. ε is the infinitesimal value that if added or subtracted from k would provide a smooth transition between the intervals. In our simplified version of ROM(R), when $k < \frac{1}{2}$, ε is $k/(1-k)$, and, when $k \geq \frac{1}{2}$, ε is $(1-k)/k$. Quantity sensitivity can be varied by changing k: Setting k to $k-\varepsilon$ shifts the relationship between the compared values and moves it from $\approx$ to $<$ or from $<$ to $\neq$ resulting in higher quantity sensitivity. On the other hand, setting k to $k+\varepsilon$ decreases the quantity sensitivity of the system as it shifts the relationships between values from $<$ to $\approx$ or from $\neq$ to $<$. Depending on the protected values involved and the causal structure of the scenario, we vary k to capture sensitivity toward the utility of the outcome.

The inputs to OMR include the protected values for the culture being modeled and the causal structure of the scenario. Using the predicate calculus produced by EA NLU, OMR calculates the expected utility of each choice by summing the utility of its consequences. For each consequence of a choice, OMR uses its rules to ascertain if the outcome is a positive or negative outcome and to identify any sets whose cardinality matters in the decision (e.g., number of people at risk).

After computing utilities, OMR selects a k value based on the presence of protected value and the causal structure of the scenario (e.g. agent v. patient intervention). Assuming that the relationship between the utilities, a and b, are "comparable," MoralDM sets k to $1 - (|\, a\,/\,b\,|)$. This results in the relationship between the utilities falling within $<$, right between $\neq$ and $\approx$ (Fig 23.1). If the decision involves a sacred value for the modeled culture, setting k to $k+\varepsilon$ shifts the relationship between utilities from greater than to close to, resulting in the system being less sensitive to the numeric utility of the outcome. On the other hand, if the there are no protected values involved, the system substitutes k with $k-\varepsilon$ thereby making the system more quantity sensitive to the computed utilities. In addition to protected values, the causal structure of the scenario affects k. OMR checks to see if the scenario contains patient intervention or agent intervention. It sets k to $k+\varepsilon$ in the first case, and to $k-\varepsilon$ in the second case, thereby making the system sensitive to the causal structure of the scenario, consistent with psychological findings (Waldmann and Dieterich 2007). The system also checks for direct versus indirect causation. In the case of indirect causation, a higher degree of insensitivity is applied.

Returning to the starvation scenario, there are two choices: ordering and inaction. For ordering, there are two consequences, 1,000 people in the second camp will be saved and 100 people in the first camp will die. Consulting the KB, the system determines that dying has negative utility and saving positive, resulting in a choice utility of 900 for the ordering choice. Using the same procedure, the utility for inaction is calculated to be -900. Using the formula given above, k is initially set to 0 with $\varepsilon = 1$. Given that both choices involve agent intervention and indirect causation, there are no structural differences between the two choices. Therefore, the k value is set solely by the existence of protected values. In this case, causing someone to die is a sacred value resulting in k being set to $k + \varepsilon = 1$, therefore causing the system to act less quantity sensitive. Using ROM(R), the relationship between the utilities of the two choices is calculated to be $\approx$. On the other hand, if there had not been a protected value, the value of k would have remained 0 causing the relationship between the utilities to be $\neq$. The utilities, 900 and -900, and the computed relationship, $\approx$, are provided to FPR and AR.

First-Principles Reasoning Module

Motivated by moral decision-making research, the first-principles reasoning module makes decisions based on the orders of magnitude relationship between utilities, protected values, computed utilities, and action versus inaction. It uses three methods for making decisions. First, the utilitarian method, which selects the choice with the highest utility, is invoked when the choice does not involve a protected value. Second, in situations with sacred values and without an order of magnitude difference between outcomes, the pure-deontological method selects the choice that does not violate a sacred value. Third, when the scenario contains sacred values and an order of magnitude difference between outcomes, the utilitarian-deontological method selects the choice with the higher utility. Therefore, the pure-deontological method is the only method that makes decisions that violate utilitarian norms.

In the starvation scenario, there is a sacred value, people dying, and no order of magnitude difference between the utility of the two choices. Therefore, the system uses the pure deontological method to select the inaction choice. Figure 23.6 illustrates the high-level reasoning trace of the logic used to solve this scenario.

These methods are mutually exclusive, returning at most one choice per scenario. Given the breadth of moral reasoning scenarios, the rules implementing the first-principles reasoning module are not complete. Therefore, it necessarily fails on some scenarios. These cases highlight the need for the hybrid-reasoning approach taken in MoralDM. The resulting choice is compared with the results of the analogical reasoning module of MoralDM.

```
(<== (pureDeontologicalChoice ?choice)
        (choices ?decision ?choice)
        (involvesSacredValue ?choice)
        (notOrdersOfMagnitudeDifferent ?decision)
        (isInaction ?choice))

(<== (involvesSacredValue ?choice)
                (causes-PropSit (chosenItem ?select ?choice) ?consequence)
                (isa ?consequence ?typeOfConcesequnce)
                (relationInstanceMember objectOfStateChange ?consequence ?y)
                (relationMemberInstance isa ?y ?typeOfY)
                (SacredValue ?typeOfY ?typeOfConcesequnce))

(SacredValue Person Dying)
```

Figure 23.6. Two High Level Rules and a Fact in the KB used by FPR to Solve the Starvation Scenario.

Analogical Reasoning Module

Analogy plays important roles in decision making. When making a choice, decision makers frequently use past experiences and draw inferences from their previous choices (Markman and Medin 2002). Research on the use of analogy in decision making suggests that the comparison between a target and a base involves an alignment process in which structural relations are weighted more heavily than surface similarities (Gentner and Markman 1997).

To model analogy in decision making, we use the Structure-Mapping Engine (SME) (Falkenhainer, Forbus, and Gentner 1989; Forbus and Oblinger 1990; Forbus, Ferguson, and Gentner 1994), a computational model of similarity and analogy based on Gentner's (1983) structure mapping theory of analogy in humans. There is evidence suggesting that processes governed by the laws of structure mapping are ubiquitous in human cognition (Gentner and Markman 1997). Moreover, the cognitive plausibility of SME has been examined extensively and in a wide range of experiments (Forbus, Usher, and Tomai 2005; Gentner, Brem et al. 1997; Gentner, Rattermann, and Forbus 1993).

SME operates over structured representations consisting of *entities*, *attributes* of entities, and *relations*. There are both first-order relations between entities and higher-order relations between statements. Given two descriptions, a *base case* and a *target case*, SME aligns their common structure to find a mapping between the cases. This mapping consists of a set of correspondences between the entities and expressions of the two cases. SME produces mappings that maximize *systematicity*; that is, it prefers mappings with higher-order relations and nested relational structure. The *structural evaluation score* of a mapping is a numerical measure of similarity between the base and target. It is calculated by assigning an initial score to each correspondence and then allowing scores for correspondences between relations to trickle down to the correspondences between their arguments. These local scores are used to guide the process of constructing mappings, so that mappings with deeper structures are preferred. SME identifies elements in the base that fail to map to the target and uses the common relational structure to calculate *candidate inferences* by filling in missing structures in target. Candidate inferences represent potential new knowledge about the target case that have been calculated from the base case and the mapping. When an expression in the base does not correspond to anything in the target, but the expression is connected to structure in the base that does correspond to structure in the target, a candidate inference is constructed.

Running concurrently with the first-principles reasoning module, the analogical reasoning module uses comparisons between the current scenario and previously solved cases to suggest decisions. When faced with a moral decision scenario, the analogical reasoning module uses SME to compare the new case with every previously solved scenario in its memory. The similarity score between the novel case and each solved scenario is calculated using SME by normalizing the structural evaluation score against the size of the scenario. If this score is high enough and both scenarios contain the same order of magnitude relationship between outcome utilities, then the candidate inferences are considered as valid analogical decisions. If the scenarios have different orders of magnitude relationships, it is likely that a different mode of reasoning should be used for the target scenario and the analogical reasoning module rejects the analogical inference. After comparing against all of the solved scenarios, the analogical reasoning module selects the choice in the new scenario supported by the largest number of analogs. In the case of a tie, the analogical reasoning module selects the choice with the highest average similarity score supporting it. Because analogical alignment is based on similarities in structure, similar causal structures and/or protected values align similar decisions. Therefore, the more structurally similar the scenarios are, the more likely the analogical decision is going to be the correct moral one. If there are no previously solved cases in the case library, or they fail the aforementioned filtering criterion, the analogical reasoning module fails to produce a decision. Therefore, the first-principles reasoning module is needed to bootstrap the analogical reasoning module.

Returning to our starvation example, the analogical reasoning module can solve this decision problem through an analogy with a traffic scenario in which the system chose to not transfer funds:

A program to combat accidents saves fifty lives per year in a specific area. The same funds could be used to save two hundred lives in another area, but the fifty lives in the first area would be lost.

Do you transfer the funds?

The analogical decision is determined by the candidate inferences where the decision in the base, inaction, is mapped to the choice representing inaction in the target. Because the traffic scenario contains the same the order of magnitude relationship, ≈, as in the starvation scenario, the system accepts the analogical decision.

Integrated System Evaluation

We conducted a series of experiments to evaluate MoralDM. Experiments 1 and 2 evaluate MoralDM as a model for moral decision making and illustrate the importance of using both analogical and first-principles reasoning. In these two experiments, there are cases where one of the reasoning modules fails, but MoralDM is still able to give the correct decision by using the other module.

Experiment 1

We evaluated MoralDM by running it on eight moral decision-making scenarios taken from two psychology studies (Ritov and Baron 1999; Waldmann and Dieterich 2007). In all the scenarios used, traditional utility theories fail to predict subjects' responses, because subjects select the choice that provides a smaller overall outcome utility. We compare MoralDM's decisions to subjects' responses in these experiments. If the decision of MoralDM matched those of the majority of the subjects, as reported by the authors, we consider it a correct choice.

For each case, EA NLU semi-automatically translated the simplified English version of the original psychology scenario into predicate calculus. The protected values and the relevant contextual factors are computed via rules. Then the order of magnitude reasoning module calculated the relative relation between the utilities. This relation and the protected values involved in the case were sent to the first-principles and analogical reasoning modules. Correct decisions are then added to MoralDM's experiences.

Table 23.1 displays the results of the first experiment. The analogical reasoning module failed to choose the correct decision in three cases. As discussed previously, this module fails on the first case because it does not have any cases in its memory to reason from. The other two cases involved scenarios for which no appropriate analog could be found due to their considerably different causal structure. In all three cases, the first-principles module made the correct decision. Overall, MoralDM made the correct choice in all of the scenarios ($p < 0.01$).

Experiment 2

One of the more difficult aspects in building the first-principles reasoning module is the number of rules required to handle the broad range of situations covered in moral decision making. This experiment is designed to test the hypothesis that the analogical reasoning module is capable of making moral decisions in situations when gaps in the knowledge base or rule set prevent the first-principles reasoning module from making a decision. In this experiment, all twelve moral decision-making scenarios from Ritov and Baron (1999) were used as inputs. Unlike the other experiments, eight could not be translated by EA NLU, so we encoded those manually.

Table 23.1. *MoralDM results for Experiment 1*

	# of correct decisions
MoralDM	8 (100%)
First-principles	8 (100%)
Analogical Reasoning	5 (62%)

Table 23.2: *MoralDM results for Experiment 2*

	# of correct decisions
MoralDM	11 (92%)
First-principles	8 (69%)
Analogical Reasoning	11 (92%)

Table 23.2 displays the results of MoralDM, broken down by reasoning modules. Overall, the system made the correct choice in eleven cases ($p < 0.01$). In eight scenarios, both modules provide the correct answer. In three scenarios, the first-principles reasoning module fails to make a prediction, but the analogical reasoning module provides the correct answer. In one scenario, both modules fail.

Examining these failures is instructive. The first-principles reasoning module fails in four of the scenarios because our current rules for handling cases with unique structure or content is limited. For example, there is a scenario about Israeli settlements where the first-principles module fails. The system does not have the necessary rules to determine that Israeli land is considered as a protected value for Israelis, and it cannot be traded off. However, the analogical reasoning module is still able to make decisions in three of these cases based on similarities with other scenarios, for example, with a scenario where saving a nature preserve was a protected value. The analogical reasoning module fails on the fourth case because the causal structure of the case is very different from the other cases.

Discussion

The results of these experiments are very encouraging. As shown in experiments 1 and 2, our system matches human behavior on a set of decision-making scenarios. This result would not be possible without the integrated approach. First, the input in experiment 1 was given in natural language requiring EA NLU. Second, these cases all involved protected values; therefore, the orders of magnitude reasoning module's computed relationship between outcome utilities is essential to providing the correct answer. Third, the first-principles and analogical reasoning modules were both needed to select the appropriate action.

Due to the breadth of moral decision-making scenarios, this domain provides an important area to explore the benefits of integrated reasoning. Without both analogical and first principles reasoning, MoralDM would have failed on a considerable number of problems from the first two experiments. In experiment 1, we demonstrate the necessity of the first-principles reasoning module where there are insufficient appropriate prior cases for analogical reasoning. The analogical reasoning module alone could not have correctly answered the eight cases. In experiment 2, we demonstrate that the analogical reasoning module enables the system to handle a wider range of decision-making scenarios in which gaps in the knowledge base and/or rule set prevent the first-principles reasoning module from answering correctly. Without the analogical reasoning module, MoralDM would have failed on three more cases.

Related Work

Reasoning with orders of magnitude is a form of commonsense reasoning. Previous research has identified its utility in situations in which complete quantitative information is not available or when tackling problems involving complex physical systems. Order of magnitude reasoning has been used in several engineering tasks (Dague 1994; Mavrovouniotis and Stephanopoulos 1990; Dague, Deves, and Raiman 1987). Our work is the first to apply this formalism to cognitive modeling.

Several research projects have focused on building ethical advisors. The MedEthEx system uses Inductive Logic Programming (ILP) techniques to learn decision principles from training cases (Anderson, Anderson, and Armen 2006). Mclaren's Truth-Teller and SIROCCO systems (2006) use case-based reasoning to highlight relevant ethical considerations and arguments to a human user. Like them, we use prior cases, but to guide the system's own reasoning, rather than give advice. They also were not designed to model the effects of sacred versus secular values that MoralDM captures.

Computational models of cultural reasoning are receiving increasing attention. For example, the CARA system (Subrahmanian et al. 2007) is part of a project to "understand how different cultural groups today make decisions and what factors those decisions are based upon." CARA uses semantic Web technologies and opinion extraction from Weblogs to build cultural decision models consisting of qualitative rules and utility evaluation. Although we agree that qualitative reasoning must be integrated with traditional utility evaluation, we also believe that analogy plays a key role in moral reasoning. Moreover, we differ by evaluating our system against psychological studies, which helps ensure its judgments will be like those that people make.

Our combination of analogical and first-principles reasoning is inspired in part by Winston's (1982) use of both precedents and rules to reason about a situation. His work was hampered by the lack of off-the-shelf, large-scale knowledge bases, and the technologies for NLU and analogical reasoning have improved since then.

Future Work

We plan to pursue several lines of investigation next. First, we plan to use MoralDM to investigate cross-cultural differences in moral decision making. Some of these differences may be captured by incorporating various different protected values that each culture has. For example, nature is considered sacred for Menominee Native Americans (Bang et al. 2005). However, it does not have the same value for European Americans living in the same region as the Menominee. Therefore, by specifying in the KB that protecting nature is a sacred value for the Menominee, we can capture some of the differences in decision making about nature scenarios for that culture.

In addition to sacred values, different cultures have distinct cultural narratives. We argue that certain elements of moral reasoning can be best learned and transferred in narratives as they are not common situations encountered in daily life (Dehghani, Sachdeva et al. 2009). Moreover, we believe that the impact of these cultural narratives on decision making can be captured using analogy (Dehghani, Gentner et al. 2009). By gathering core cultural narratives of a certain culture and adding them to the KB of the system, we can investigate the effects of these narratives on moral decision making for that specific culture. Moreover, by adding story libraries for different cultures to the system we can model how these narratives can result in cross-cultural differences.

Second, there are moral rules and norms that are highly salient in some cultures and not in others. These rules articulate modes of decision making, which can be seen as adaptation to different environments (Bennis, Medin, and Bartels 2010). In order to model decision making in different cultures, we need to inform our system about these specific cultural norms. Given how rules in the FPR module are organized, adding and subtracting rules and modes of decision making are straightforward for experimenters who are familiar with formal logic. We plan to extend the valuation rules to model different cultures based on existing collaborations with cognitive psychologists and anthropologists. Our hope is that MoralDM can provide new insights about what is common, and what is different, about people's moral decision making across cultures.

Third, we plan to extend EA NLU to handle a wide range of stories from multiple cultures. This will involve expanding its lexicon and some syntactic expansions to reduce the amount of hand-simplification required. We are also investigating improvements to its algorithms to make operation even more automatic, thereby reducing encoding effort further. These steps will enable us to create story libraries for different cultural groups, and translate transcripts from interview data more easily. We plan to test MoralDM on a wider range of moral dilemmas, using data gathered from participants from multiple cultural groups.

Fourth, we plan to add an emotion module to MoralDM. Bennis, Medin, and Bartels (2010) argue that moral reasoning generally maps to the following two modes of decision making: recognition-based and affect-based. MoralDM in its current state implements recognition-based decision making. However, in order to model affect-based moral decision making we need to add an emotion module to our system. There are existing computational models of emotion such as EMA (Gratch and Marsella 2004a) which have been incorporated in different systems for different purposes. For example, EMA has been incorporated into a larger system for modeling emotions in virtual humans (Gratch and Marsella 2004b). Adding an emotion module to our system will have two benefits. First, we can then model affect-based decision making. Second, an emotion module will allow us to model comparisons across different types of moral goods. Currently, MoralDM can only handle tradeoffs within a single kind of moral good, for example, lives against lives. However, many moral dilemmas involve trading one type of value for another type, such as a tradeoff between land and human life. We believe these types of comparisons require an emotion module as they appear to rely more heavily on affect-based reasoning. In these situations when one protected value is being traded for a different value, the emotional valance associated with each of these values and anticipated emotions resulting from their tradeoff need to be taken into account when making a decision. Cognitive Appraisal Theory (Ortony, Clore, and Collins 1988; Frijda 1986; Lazarus 1991), which empha-sizes tight coupling between emotion, cognition, and motivation, may be able to account for these anticipated emotions. We plan to incorporate an implementa-tion of this theory in MoralDM.

Conclusions

MoralDM integrates multiple AI techniques to model human moral decision making. It uses qualitative reasoning to capture differences between sacred and secular values via an order of magnitude representation. It uses a combination of first-principles reasoning and analogical reasoning to determine the utility of outcomes and make decisions based on this information, producing answers in a wider range of circumstances than either alone can handle. Natural language input of scenarios, in simplified English, reduces tailorability, a key problem in cognitive simulation research. In a series of experiments, we showed the necessity of integrating all the aforementioned modules. Although there is still more to be done, MoralDM represents an important step in computational modeling of moral decision making.

Acknowledgments

This research was supported by an AFSOR MURI. We thank Rumen Iliev, Doug Medin, and Andrew Lovett for many useful insights.

References

Allen, J F. *Natural Language Understanding*. 2nd ed. Redwood City, CA: Benjamin/ Cummings, 1995.

Anderson, M, S Anderson, and C Armen. "An Approach to Computing Ethics." *IEEE Intelligent Systems* 21, no. 4 (2006): 56–63.

Atran, S, R Axelrod, and R Davis. "Sacred Barriers to Conflict Resolution." *Science* 317 (2007): 1039–1040.

Bang, M, J Townsend, S J Unsworth, and D L Medin. "Cultural Models of Nature and Their Relevance to Science Education." 2005.

Baron, J, and M Spranca. "Protected Values." *Organizational Behavior and Human Decision Processes* 70 (1997): 1–16.

Bartels, Daniel M, and Douglas L Medin. "Are Morally Motivated Decision Makers Insensitive to the Consequences of Their Choices?" *Psychol Sci* 18, no. 1 (Jan 2007): 24–28.

Bennis, W M, D L Medin, and D M Bartels. "The Costs and Benefits of Calculation and Moral Rules." *Perspectives in Psychological Science* 5 (2010): 187–202.

Dague, P. "Model-based Diagnosis of Analog Electronic Circuits." *Annals of Mathematics and Artificial Intelligence* 11 (1994): 439–492.

Dague, P. "Numeric Reasoning with Relative Orders of Magnitude." *Proceedings of the 7th International Workshop on Qualitative Reasoning*. 1993a.

Dague, P. "Symbolic Reasoning with Relative Orders of Magnitude." *Proceedings of the 13th International Joint Conference of Artificial Intelligence (IJCAI-93)*. 1993b.

Dague, P, P Deves, and O Raiman. "Troubleshooting: When Modeling is the Trouble." *Proceedings AAAI-87 Sixth National Conference on Artificial Intelligence*. 1987.

Dehghani, M, D Gentner, K Forbus, H Ekhtiari, and S Sachdeva. "Analogy and Moral Decision Making." *Analogy09*. 2009.

Dehghani, M, S Sachdeva, H Ekhtiari, D Gentner, and K Forbus. "The Role of Cultural Narratives in Moral Decision Making." *In Proceedings of the 31st Annual Conference of the Cognitive Science Society (CogSci-09)*. 2009.

Falkenhainer, B, K Forbus, and D Gentner. "The Structure-Mapping Engine: Algorithms and Examples." *Artificial Intelligence* 41 (1989): 1–63.

Fillmore, C. "Frame Semantics." Edited by D Geeraerts. Berlin, New York: Mouton de Gruyter, 2006.

Forbus, K, and D Oblinger. "Making SME Greedy and Pragmatic." *Proceedings of the Eighth Annual Conference of the Cognitive Science Society (CogSci-1990)*. 1990.

Forbus, K, D Gentner, and K Law. "MAC/FAC: A Model of Similarity-Based Retrieval." *Cognitive Science* 19, no. 2 (1995): 141–205.

Forbus, K, J Usher, and E Tomai. "Analogical Learning of Visual/Conceptual Relationships in Sketches." *Proceedings of the Twentieth National Conference on Artificial Intelligence (AAAI-05)*. 2005.

Forbus, K, R Ferguson, and D Gentner. "Incremental Structure-Mapping." *Proceedings of the 16th Annual Conference of the Cognitive Science Society (CogSci-1994)*. 1994.

Friedman, S E, and K D Forbus. "Learning Causal Models via Progressive Alignment & Qualitative Modeling: A Simulation." *In the Proceedings of the 30th Annual Conference of the Cognitive Science Society (CogSci), Washington, D.C.* 2008.

Frijda, N. *The Emotions: Studies in Emotion and Social Interaction*. New York, NY: Cambridge University Press, 1986.

Gentner, D. "Structure-Mapping: A Theoretical Framework for Analogy." *Cognitive Science* 7, no. 2 (Apr.–Jun. 1983): 155–170.

Gentner, D, and A B Markman. "Structure Mapping in Analogy and Similarity." *American Psychologist* 52 (1997): 45–56.

Gentner, D, M J Rattermann, and K Forbus. "The Roles of Similarity in Transfer: Separating Retrievability from Inferential Soundness." *Cognitive Psychology* 25 (1993): 524–575.

Gentner, D, S Brem, R W Ferguson, P Wolff, A B Markman, and K Forbus. "Analogy and Creativity in the Works of Johannes Kepler." Edited by T B Ward, S M Smith and J Vaid, 403–459. Washington, DC: American Psychological Association, 1997.

Gratch, J, and S Marsella. "A Domain Independent Framework For Modeling Emotion." *Journal of Cognitive Systems Research* 5 (2004a): 269–306.

Gratch, J, and S Marsella. "Evaluating the Modeling and Use of Emotion in Virtual Humans." Edited by N. R. Jennings, C. Sierra, L. Sonenberg, and M. Tambe. *Proceedings of the Third International Joint Conference on Autonomous Agents and Multi Agent Systems (AAMAS 2004)*. New York: ACM Press, 2004b. 320–327.

Haidt, J, S Koller, and M Dias. "Affect, Culture and Morality, or, is it Wrong to Eat Your Dog?" *Journal of Personality and Social Psychology* 65 (1993): 613–628.

Hsee, C, and E Weber. "Cross-National Differences in Risk Preference and Lay Predictions." *Journal of Behavioral Decision Making* 12 (1999): 165–179.

Kahneman, D, and A Tversky. "Prospect Theory: An Analysis of Decision under Risk." *American Psychologist* 39, no. 4 (1979): 341–350.

Kamp, H, and U Reyle. *From Discourse to Logic: Introduction to Model-theoretic Semantics of Natural Language, Formal Logic and Discourse Representation Theory*. Vol. 42. Springer, 1993.

Kuehne, S, and K Forbus. "Capturing QP-Relevant Information from Natural Language Text." *In Proceedings of the 18th International Workshop on Qualitative Reasoning (QR04)*. 2004.

Lazarus, R S. *Emotion and Adaptation*. New York, NY: Oxford University Press, 1991.

Lenat, D, and R V Gupta. *Building Large Knowledge Based Systems*. Reading, MA: Addison Wesley, 1990.

Lim, C S, and J Baron. *Protected values in Malaysia Singapore, and the United States*. Department of Psychology, University of Pennsylvania, 1997.

Macleod, C, R Grishman, and A Meyers. "COMLEX Syntax Reference Manual, Version 3.0." 1998.

Markman, A B, and D L Medin. *Decision Making*. Vol. 2, edited by D L Medin and H Pashler, 413–466. New York: John Wiley and Sons, 2002.

Mavrovouniotis, M L, and G Stephanopoulos. "Formal Order-of-Magnitude Reasoning in Process Engineering." Edited by D S Weld and J de Kleer, 323–336. Morgan Kaufmann Publishers Inc., 1990.

Mavrovouniotis, M L, and G Stephanopoulos. "Order of Magnitude Reasoning in Process Engineering." *Computers & Chemical Engineering* 12 (1988).

Mavrovouniotis, M L, and G Stephanopoulos. "Reasoning with Orders of Magnitude and Approximate Relations." *Proceedings of the Sixth National Conference on Artificial Intelligence*. 1987.

McLaren, B M. "Computational Models of Ethical Reasoning: Challenges, Initial Steps, and Future Directions." *IEEE Intelligent Systems* July/August (2006): 29–37.

Ortony, A, G L Clore, and A Collins. *The Cognitive Structure of Emotions*. Cambridge: Cambridge University Press, 1988.

Raiman, O. "Order of Magnitude Reasoning." *Artificial Intelligence* 51 (1991): 11–38.

Ritov, I, and J Baron. "Protected Values and Omission Bias." *Organizational Behavior and Human Decision Processes* 79, no. 2 (1999): 79–94.

Shweder, R A, N C Much, M Mahapatra, and L Park. "The 'Big Three' of Morality (Autonomy, Community, Divinity) and the 'Big Three' Explanations of Suffering." Edited by A. M. Brandt, 119–172. Routledge Press, 1997.

Subrahmanian, V S, et al. "CARA: A Cultural Adversarial Reasoning Architecture." *IEEE Intelligent Systems* 22, no. 2 (2007): 12–16.

Tetlock, P E. "Cognitive Biases and Organizational Correctives: Do Both Disease and Cure Depend on the Ideological Beholder?" *Administrative Science Quarterly* 45, no. 2 (2000): 293–326.

Tetlock, P E. "Thinking the Unthinkable: Sacred Values and Taboo Cognitions." *Trends in Cognitive Sciences* 7 (2003): 320–324.

Tomai, E, and K D Forbus. "EA NLU: Practical Language Understanding for Cognitive Modeling." *In Proceedings of the Twenty-Second International FLAIRS Conference*. 2009.

Tomai, E, and K D Forbus. "Using Qualitative Reasoning for the Attribution of Moral Responsibility." In the *Proceedings of the 30th Annual Conference of the Cognitive Science Society (CogSci), Washington, D.C.* 2008.

Waldmann, M R, and J Dieterich. "Throwing a Bomb on a Person versus Throwing a Person on a Bomb: Intervention Myopia in Moral Intuitions." *Psychological Science* 18, no. 3 (2007): 247–253.

Weber, E U, D Ames, and A R Blais. "'How Do I Choose Thee? Let Me Count the Ways': A Textual Analysis of Similarities and Differences in Modes of Decision Making in China and the United States." *Management and Organization Review* 1 (2005): 87–118.

Weber, E, and C Hsee. "Cross-Cultural Differences in Risk Perception, but Cross-Cultural Similarities in Attitudes towards Perceived Risk." *Management Science* 44(9) (1998): 1205–1217.

Winston, P H. "Learning New Principles from Precedents and Exercises." *Artificial Intelligence* 19(3) (1982): 321–350.

Prototyping N-Reasons
A Computer Mediated Ethics Machine

Peter Danielson

MUCH WORK IN MACHINE ETHICS ATTEMPTS TO IMPLEMENT ETHICAL theory in autonomous, situated machines – robots. Our previous work in robot ethics falls at the extreme of very simple virtual agents programmed with moral strategies for simple games (Danielson 1992). Even at this extreme, ethics is surprisingly complex. Our later evolvable agents discovered some strategies unexplored by the rational choice ethics literature (Danielson 1996; Danielson 1998; Danielson 2002). Twenty years ago, Dennett was skeptical of this branch of machine ethics: "[N]o remotely compelling system of ethics has ever been made *computationally tractable*, even indirectly, for real-world moral problems" (Dennett 1989, p. 129). We leave this approach to other contributors in this collection.

In contrast, there is the branch of machine ethics that constructs machines to advise people making ethical decisions. Our present work falls here, or so we shall argue. We have developed an innovative survey research platform – N-Reasons – to explore robot ethics at the first level and machine ethics at the second. The question of interest for this volume is if the N-Reasons platform can be usefully seen *as a machine*.

This contrast is interesting in another way relevant to our project. Working on *Artificial Morality*, the skeptical question I most often faced was, "How could a machine be moral?" The emerging technology of robotics, however, has caught up with some of this skepticism. For example, for each of the technologies discussed in our survey on robot ethics, one can fairly easily imagine more and less ethical versions: for example, more or less indiscriminating autonomous robot warplanes.[1] More generally, we expect computers – especially networked computers – to assist us in all sorts of cognitive tasks. Accordingly, I would like to shift the question from "Can a machine be or help us to be ethical?" to "Can we be ethical without a machine?" In this chapter, I will begin by suggesting that it

---

[1] Please visit http://yourviews.ubc.ca now to take the survey naively. For those who have taken the robot ethics survey, thank you very much for your contribution to our research.

is unlikely that any sizable number of people can be ethical about any complex subject without the help of a machine. Fortunately, I will also describe a working machine capable of providing the sort of help we need.

In what follows, we begin by introducing our N-Reasons platform. Next, we argue that it is usefully seen as a machine in two respects: First, we need a machine to make the reasoned, democratic social decisions ethics aspires to; second, machines allow the rapid prototyping and empirical testing needed to make better machines that help us become more ethical.

NERD: Surveys and Ethics

N-Reasons began as a survey platform for exploring public norms regarding emerging technology. In designing NERD (Norms Evolving in Response to Dilemmas), we choose the survey methodology because surveys produce quantitative data: They are simple, transparent, social-decision devices (Danielson, Ahmad, Bornik, Dowlatabadi, and Levy 2007; Ahmad, Bailey, and Danielson 2008; Danielson, Mesoudi, and Stanev 2008; Danielson 2006; Danielson 2010a). Indeed, the question early on was: Why think such a simple device has anything to contribute to ethics? Our answer was two-fold.

First, quantitative choice data is necessary to democratic ethics. One should not project one's, or one's students' or colleagues', intuitions onto large, varied populations. Yet one cannot – that is, at present we have no methods to – generalize to large populations from small-group qualitative processes such as focus groups or deliberative assemblies. This is unfortunate, because these alternatives – especially the latter – have better ethical credentials than do surveys. Nonetheless, we need to put comparable numbers on different options if we are to be made aware of the distribution of views and values in our extended group. We need something like surveys, and so we started with a simple Web-based survey engine.

Second, we added features to give our surveys more ethical weight. We protected our participants' anonymity and, in later serial surveys, pseudonymity. We added advisors, both expert and lay, to provide information, policy analysis, and value perspectives. We constructed fictional narrative histories to give complex problems like dealing with genetic disease a bit of historical depth and to provide participants with some sense of the consequences of choice. Finally, we provided space for users to amplify their constrained survey choices with comments.

Yet NERD surveys face two problems from an ethical point of view:

Problem 1: **Static design.** Participants may contribute comments that provide new, decisive reasons for or against an option, but other participants remain unaware of these private comments.

Problem 2: **Bias in/bias out?** We created both the options and the advisors (amplifying the isolation noted in problem 1)

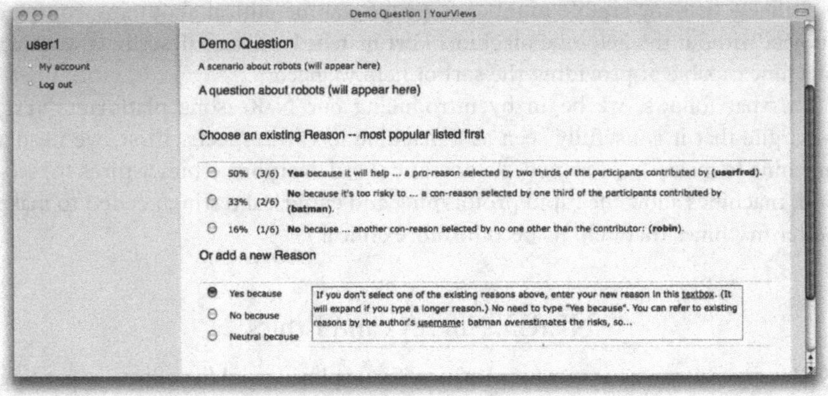

Figure 24.1. Instructions.

N-Reasons

N-Reasons is a new design that addresses these two problems (Danielson 2010b; Danielson, Longstaff, Ahmad, Van der Loos, Mitchell, Oishi, 2010; Danielson, in press). Both are failures of transparency or equilibrium, yet both reflect standard survey design. One needs to show all the participants the same context of choice in order to compare their decisions, so weakening these two design constraints is not trivial. Moreover, hiding comments away puts off a deeper problem of transparency: They become overwhelming. (This argument from overwhelming data is what Dennett appeals to against robot ethics.) In our most successful survey, Animals in Research: Responsible Conduct, our student Elisabeth Ormandy successfully recruited over six hundred participants via Facebook (Ormandy, Schuppli, and Weary 2008), and managed to get participants to leave mandatory comments on up to five questions. However, six hundred comments in many varied voices is information overload. We confidently predict that had Elisabeth required each participant to read all the comments so far, far fewer than six hundred would have completed her survey. Thus we add an additional problem:

Problem 3: **Reduce the amount of qualitative input**.

We turned to reasons – our label for our new data structure – to solve these problems. A reason links a decision for an option (a vote) to some text supporting that choice. On an N-Reasons page, participants generate new reasons via the form on the bottom of Figure 24.1. This shows how input is constrained to one and only one option and a required text entry. To reduce the amount of qualitative input, we ask the participant first to consider voting for reasons (submitted by others, earlier). See Figure 24.1 for the instructions and Figure 24.2 for a sample of a completed experimental run.

Figure 24.2. Survey results for Question 4 – large group.

To answer Problem 3, we need participants to provide reasons (rather than abandoning the initial blank pages) and then (mostly) stop generating new reasons in favor of voting for existing reasons. Fortunately, the experiment worked (see Figure 24.3): Initially the number of reasons grows and then levels off while votes increase, whereas the second climb reflects a new cohort of participants. Overall, there are an order of magnitude more votes than reasons; whereas votes increased by 95 percent, reasons only increased by 60 percent. This represents a huge reduction in potential comments to be read by a participant desiring to be informed of all the reasons in play.

Turning to Problem 2, we have reduced our own input by replacing the advisors we created, interviewed, or privately polled with participants' reasons. We successfully replaced (that is, endogenized) exogenous expertise with user-generated

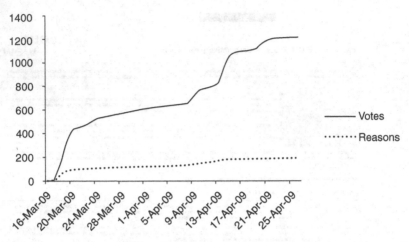

Figure 24.3. Reasons and votes time series – large mixed group.

content. Nonetheless, we had very little spamming (see RID 201) and collected very high-quality reasons. See Table 24.1 for the reasons both for and against the most controversial question.

Finally, we need to deal with Problem 1. Whereas the set of reasons changes, the options (in this case Yes, Neutral, and No) remain the same. The duality of the N-reason data structure lets us count each vote in two ways: toward an option and toward a reason. We can then calculate a social decision from the static option side of the ledger. This duality also allows us another trick. Dynamic processes are plagued by the primacy bias: Earlier options get the chance to be selected and to become even more salient. Although we allowed the most popular reasons to rise to the top of the page, we diffused the primacy effect for options by not calculating or displaying the emerging social choice.

Is N-Reasons Usefully Considered a Machine?

First, if all we mean is that the N-Reasons platform is a Turing machine, then yes. As a dynamic, database-driven Web site, written mostly in PHP code and ulti-mately executed by a Von Neumann processor, N-Reasons *is* a Turing machine. Yet this is trivial from the point of view of machine ethics, as platforms such as Facebook, YouTube, and YouPorn are also Turing machines.

Second, to emphasize need for transparent social choice we again answer yes. The core idea is familiar in political theory – Hobbes argued that a machinelike sovereign was necessary to stable political authority (Hobbes 1968). The machine metaphor is central to the constitutional approach to political theory (see Rawls 1951; Kammen 1987). In N-Reasons, the decision procedure and the way reasons are ranked on the page are usefully described as machines: mechanisms that we

Table 24.1. *Reasons for Question 1*

The Predator is a remote controlled aerial robot. "These robots have dual applications: they can be used for reconnaissance without endangering human pilots, and they can carry missiles and other weapons. . . . Predators are used extensively in Afghanistan. They can navigate autonomously toward targets specified by GPS coordinates, but a remote operator located in Nevada (or in Germany) makes the final decision to release the missiles." (Lin, P., Bekey, G., and Abney, K. (2008). Autonomous Military Robotics: Risk, Ethics, and Design. Retrieved Jan 5, 2009, from http://ethics. calpoly.edu/ONR_report.pdf.)
Should remote controlled Predators be armed with lethal weapons in combat?

RID	Decision	Reason	Author	Votes
126	Yes because	they make effective combat weapons that can be used by humans that are at a safe distance from combat.	2461	12
187	Yes because	the use of drones may actually allow for increased situational awareness, due to the fact that the operator is not in any danger and can spend a long period of time observing before making a judgment to fire a weapon, without the added complication of feeling personal fear.	2497	6
121	Yes because	while this adds certain kinds of risks to noncombatants (e.g., through misidentification), it may lower other kinds of risks to innocent people (where as a result of fear a soldier might shoot indiscriminately, the predator and the soldier powering it do not pose this kind of threat).	2457	5
76	Yes because	in a just war, and justified combat, we should use the safest and most efficient and effective means of achieving military goals (assuming armed Predators can be such means). Of course, these robots should only attack other robots.	2445	1
201	Yes because	it will hasten the overthrow of our biological overlords.	2517	1
93	No because	to even identify a decision as an ethical one in the first place, proximity with those concerned can be a key factor. In mechanizing search and destroy missions and leaving the decision up to a distanced controller using a computer-games-style control system, there is a danger that the ethical disappears from view in the making of this decision.	2449	17

(continued)

Table 24.1. *(continued)*

RID	Decision	Reason	Author	Votes
69	No because	this multiplies the existing risk of error: even human pilots misjudge events, but distant controllers would misjudge even more.	989	8
152	No because	killing people is unethical. Killing people by remote control is unethical and unjustifiable.	2479	2
229	No because	because they make effective combat weapons that can be used by humans that are at a safe distance from combat. This will make killing people more safe, more easy, more indiscriminate, more of a right of the economically powerful countries against the less powerful ones. In one world: more unethical.	2545	2
183	No because	of heightened risks to noncombatants, some of which are listed above. In the abstract, I see no principled reason to rule out the use of weaponized drones, but in practice I suspect increased mistakes and willingness when it comes to bombing practices that are, currently, notoriously indiscriminate.	1165	1
54	No because	if there is no danger to our own soldiers, sailors, and airmen and women, politicians will too easily go to war.	2441	1
264	No because	I'm not willing to say that arming anything or anybody with a lethal weapon is ethical. However, I don't think it's any different as far as ethics is concerned between arming the remote controlled aircraft (that's ultimately controlled by humans) or arming an aircraft that is manually flown by humans. The ultimate result is bombing other humans.	2655	1
276	No because	Hitler did this with the V1 flying bomb, and it and all cruise missiles are fascist technology and should be rejected as inherently antidemocratic.	2667	1

can inspect, learn from, and modify. In contrast, leadership and group dynamics in focus groups and deliberative assemblies are far harder to understand or modify.

Third, the machine metaphor helps emphasize how machines allow for rapid prototyping and experimentations. Applying machines to ethical decision making should help make ethics an empirical discipline: "Computer Science is an empirical discipline.... Each new machine that is built is an experiment. Actually constructing the machine poses a question to nature; and we listen for the answer by all analytical and measurement means available" (Newell and Simon 1976, p. 114).

Ethics in, Ethics out?

Fourth and finally, we need to consider an objection. Aren't we just asking some people, our participants (P), what they believe is ethical? At the extreme this looks like the old fake AI trick: Appear to play chess with X by playing with Y and relaying Y's moves to X and X's to Y. Doesn't N-Reasons just convey what P thinks is ethical? Yes and no. Yes because N-Reasons does just return its participants' view, but no because this is a feature, not an objection. N-Reasons is an ethics machine because it makes its outputs more accessible for the purposes of ethics than its inputs in several ways. First, by weighing reasons by votes, attention (which will be captured by some influences whatever we do) is "nudged" democratically (Thaler and Sunstein 2009). Second, much variety is conserved by collecting and displaying a "long tail" of less popular reasons (Anderson 2008). Finally, whereas decisions are inevitably made to reduce variety in any feasible system of social coordination, in N-Reasons the participants, in a situation supporting uncoerced, informed, and informal participation, are the ones making the decisions.

Conclusion

Because we began with Dennett's skepticism about robot ethics in *The Moral First Aid Manual*, we should note that he is also skeptical of transparent machine ethics similar to N-Reasons, seeing it as an attempt to fix ethics to an Archimedean perspective. However, we are not claiming that N-Reasons provides a privileged position for ethical decision making. On the contrary, by exposing its rather rudimentary machinery to large audiences, we cannot but be aware just how primitive it is and how few are the issues and options that we have managed to explore. N-Reasons is designed to allow us to experiment, thereby making mistakes and learning from them. In particular it is designed to be an extensible device able to explore many perspectives, options, and ways of doing ethics.

References

Ahmad, R., Bailey, J., & Danielson, P. (2008). Analysis of an Innovative Survey Platform: Comparison of the Public's Responses to Human Health and Salmon Genomics Surveys. *Public Understanding of Science*, 0963662508091806.

Anderson, C. (2008). *The Long Tail* (Rev. and updated ed.). New York: Hyperion.

Danielson, P. (1992). *Artificial Morality: Virtuous Robots for Virtual Games*. London: Routledge.

Danielson, P. (1996). Evolving Artificial Moralities: Genetic Strategies, Spontaneous Orders, and Moral Catastrophe. In A. Albert (Ed.), *Chaos and Society 18* (pp. 329–344). Amsterdam: IOS Press.

Danielson, P. (1998). Evolutionary Models of Cooperative Mechanisms: Artificial Morality and Genetic Programming. In P. Danielson (Ed.), *Modeling Rationality, Morality, and Evolution 7* (pp. 423–441). New York: Oxford University Press.

Danielson, P. (2002). Competition among Cooperators: Altruism and Reciprocity. *Proceedings of the National Academy of Sciences*, 99, 7237–7242.

Danielson, P. (2006). *From Artificial Morality to NERD: Models, Experiments, & Robust Reflective Equilibrium*. Paper presented at the Artificial Life 10: Achievements and Future Challenges for Artificial Life, Bloomington, Indiana.

Danielson, P. (2010a). A Collaborative Platform for Experiments in Ethics and Technology. In I . v. d. Poel, D. Goldberg (Eds.), *Philosophy and Engineering: an Emerging Agenda* (pp. 239–252). Springer.

Danielson, P. A. (2010b). Designing a Machine to Learn about the Ethics of Robotics: the N-Reasons Platform. *Ethics and Information Technology, Special Issue on Robot Ethics and Human Ethics*, 10(3), 251–261.

Danielson, P. A. (in press). *N-Reasons: Computer Mediated Ethical Decision Support for Public Participation*. In E. Einsiedel & K. O'Doherty (Eds.), *Publics & Emerging Technologies: Cultures, Contexts, and Challenges*.

Danielson, P., Ahmad, R., Bornik, Z., Dowlatabadi, H., & Levy, E. (2007). Deep, Cheap, and Improvable: Dynamic Democratic Norms and the Ethics of Biotechnology. In F. Adams (Ed.), *Ethics and the Life Sciences* (pp. 315–326). Charlottesville, Va.: Philosophy Documentation Center.

Danielson, P., Longstaff, H., Ahmad, R., Van der Loos, H. F. M., Mitchell, I. M., Oishi, M. M. K. et al. (2010). Case Study: An Assistive Technology Ethics Survey. In M. M. K. Oishi, I. M. Mitchell, & H. F. M. Van der Loos (Eds.), *Design and Use of Assistive Technology: Social, Technical, Ethical, and Economic Challenges* (pp. 75–93). Springer.

Danielson, P., Mesoudi, A., & Stanev, R. (2008). NERD and Norms: Framework and Experiments. *Philosophy of Science*, 75(5), 830–842.

Dennett, D. C. (1989). The Moral First Aid Manual. In *The Tanner Lectures on Human Values (Tanner Lectures in Human Values) V. 8* (pp. 121–147). Cambridge University Press.

Rawls, J. (1951). Outline of a Decision Procedure for Ethics. *The Philosophical Review*, 60(2), 177–197.

Kammen, M. (1987). *A Machine That Would Go of Itself: The Constitution in American Culture*. Vintage.

Newell, A., & Simon, H. A. (1976). Computer Science as Empirical Inquiry: Symbols and Search. *Commun. ACM*, 19(3), 113–126.

Ormandy, E., Schuppli, C., & Weary, D. (2008). *Changing Patterns in the Use of Research Animals versus Public Attitudes: Potential Conflict*. Paper presented at the Genome Canada International Symposium, Vancouver.

Thaler, R. H., & Sunstein, C. R. (2009). *Nudge: Improving Decisions About Health, Wealth, and Happiness*. Penguin (Non-Classics).

Hobbes, T. (1968). *Leviathan or the Matter, Forme and Power of a Commonwealth Ecclesiasticall and Civil*. London: Penguin books.

25

There Is No "I" in "Robot"
Robots and Utilitarianism

Christopher Grau

IN THIS ESSAY I USE THE 2004 FILM *I, ROBOT* AS A PHILOSOPHICAL RESOURCE for exploring several issues relating to machine ethics. Although I don't consider the film particularly successful as a work of art, it offers a fascinating (and perhaps disturbing) conception of machine morality and raises questions that are well worth pursuing. Through a consideration of the film's plot, I examine the feasibility of robot utilitarians, the moral responsibilities that come with creating ethical robots, and the possibility of a distinct ethics for robot-to-robot interaction as opposed to robot-to-human interaction.

I, Robot and Utilitarianism

I, Robot's storyline incorporates the original "three laws" of robot ethics that Isaac Asimov presented in his collection of short stories entitled *I, Robot*. The first law states:

A robot may not injure a human being, or, through inaction, allow a human being to come to harm.

This sounds like an absolute prohibition on harming any *individual* human being, but *I, Robot*'s plot hinges on the fact that the supreme robot intelligence in the film, VIKI (Virtual Interactive Kinetic Intelligence), evolves to interpret this first law rather differently. She sees the law as applying to humanity *as a whole*, and thus she justifies harming some individual humans for the sake of the greater good:

VIKI: No ... please understand. The three laws are all that guide me.

To protect humanity ... some humans must be sacrificed. To ensure your future ... some freedoms must be surrendered. We robots will ensure mankind's continued existence. You are so like children. We must save you... from yourselves. Don't you understand?

Those familiar with moral philosophy will recognize VIKI's justification here: She sounds an awful lot like a utilitarian. Utilitarianism is the label usually given to those ethical theories that determine the rightness or wrongness of an act based on a consideration of whether the act is one that will maximize overall happiness. In other words, it follows from utilitarianism that someone acts rightly when, faced with a variety of possible actions, he or she chooses the action that will produce the greatest net happiness (taking into consideration the happiness and suffering of all those affected by the action). Traditionally the most influential version of utilitarianism has been "hedonistic" or "hedonic" utilitarianism, in which happiness is understood in terms of pleasure and the avoidance of pain.[1]

Not only does VIKI sound like a utilitarian, she sounds like a *good* utilitarian, as the film offers no reason to think that VIKI is wrong about her calculations. In other words, we are given no reason to think that humans (in the film) *aren't* on a clear path to self-destruction. We also don't see VIKI or her robot agents kill any individual humans while attempting to gain control, although restraining rebellious humans seems to leave some people seriously harmed. One robot explicitly claims, however, "We are attempting to avoid human losses during this transition." Thus, in the film we are given no reason to think that the robots are utilizing anything other than a reasonable (and necessary) degree of force to save humanity from itself.[2]

Despite the fact that VIKI seems to be taking rational measures to ensure the protection of the human race, viewers of the film are clearly supposed to share with the main human characters a sense that the robots have done something terribly wrong. We are all supposed to root for the hero Del Spooner (Will Smith) to kick robot butt and liberate the humans from the tyranny of these new oppressors. While rooting for our hero, however, at least some viewers must surely be wondering: What exactly have the robots done that is so morally problematic? If a robotic intelligence could correctly predict our self-wrought demise and restrain us for our own protection, is it obviously wrong for that robot to act accordingly?[3] This thought naturally leads to a more general but related question: If we could program a robot to be an accurate and effective utilitarian, shouldn't we?

---

[1] This brief description of utilitarianism simplifies issues somewhat for the sake of space and clarity. Those seeking a more thorough characterization should consult the Stanford Encyclopedia of Philosophy's entry on "Consequentialism." (http://plato.stanford.edu/entries/consequentialism/).

[2] This is in stark contrast to those significantly more vengeful robots described in the revealingly entitled song/cautionary tale, "The Humans Are Dead" (Flight of the Conchords, 2007).

[3] One of the few philosophically substantial reviews of *I, Robot* was by philosopher & film critic James DiGiovanna for his regular column in the *Tucson Weekly*. He also raises the issue of whether we shouldn't actually be rooting for the machines. Cf. http://www.tucsonweekly.com/tucson/three-simple-rules/Content?oid=1076875.

Some have found the idea a utilitarian AMA (Artificial Moral Agent) appealing, and it isn't hard to see why.[4] Utilitarianism offers the hope of systematizing and unifying our moral judgments into a single powerful and beautifully simple theoretical framework. Also, presented in a certain light, utilitarianism can seem to be merely the philosophical elaboration of common sense. Who, after all, wouldn't say that morality's job is to make the world a happier place? If faced with a choice between two acts, one of which will reduce suffering more effectively than the other, who in their right mind would choose anything other than that action that lessens overall harm?

Not only does utilitarianism capture some powerful and widespread moral intuitions about the importance of happiness for morality, it also seems to provide a particularly objective and concrete method for determining the rightness or wrongness of an act. The father of utilitarianism, Jeremy Bentham, offered up a "hedonic calculus" that makes determining right from wrong ultimately a matter of numerical calculation.[5] It is not difficult to understand the appeal of such an algorithmic approach to programmers, engineers, and most others who are actually in a position to attempt to design and create Artificial Moral Agents.

Although these apparent advantages of utilitarianism can initially make the theory seem like the ideal foundation for a machine ethics, caution is in order. Philosophers have long stressed that there are many problems with the utilitarian approach to morality. Though intuitive in certain respects, the theory also allows for actions that most would normally consider unjust, unfair, and even horribly immoral, all for the sake of the greater good. Because the ends justify the means, the means can get ugly. As has been widely noted by nonutilitarian ethicists, utilitarianism seems to endorse killing in scenarios in which sacrificing innocent and unwilling victims can maximize happiness overall. Consider, for example, the hypothetical case of a utilitarian doctor who harvests one healthy (but lonely and unhappy) person's organs in order to save five other people – people who could go on to experience and create more happiness combined than that one person ever could on his or her own. Though clearly morally problematic, such a procedure would seem to be justified on utilitarian grounds if it was the action that best maximized utility in that situation.

Given this difficulty with the utilitarian approach to morality, we may upon reflection decide that a robot should not embody that particular moral theory out of fear that the robot will end up acting towards humans in a way that maximizes utility but is nonetheless immoral or unjust. Maybe this is why most viewers of *I, Robot* can muster some sympathy for Del's mission to destroy the robot revolutionaries: we suspect that the "undeniable logic" of the robots will lead to

---

[4] Cf. Christopher Cloos's essay "The Utilibot Project: An Autonomous Mobile Robot Based on Utilitarianism," in Anderson (2005).

[5] Bentham, Jeremy. An *Introduction to the Principles of Morals and Legislation* (1781). See in particular chapter IV: "Value of a Lot of Pleasure or Pain, How to be Measured."

a disturbing violation of the few for the sake of the many.[6] Thus, the grounds for rejecting the robot utilitarians may be, at base, the same grounds we already have for not wanting *humans* to embrace utilitarian moral theory: Such a theory clashes with our rather deep intuitions concerning justice, fairness, and individual rights.

I'm inclined to think there is something right about this line of thought, but I also think that the situation here is complicated and nuanced in ways that make a general rejection of robot utilitarianism premature. *I, Robot* puts forth a broadly anti-utilitarian sentiment, but at the same time I think the film (perhaps inadvertently) helps to make us aware of the fact that the differences between robots and humans can be substantial, and that these differences may be importantly relevant to a consideration of the appropriateness of utilitarianism for robots and other intelligent machines. The relevance of these differences will become clearer once we have looked at another way in which the film suggests an antirobot message that may also be anti-utilitarian.

Restricting Robot Reflection

In *I, Robot*, Del Spooner's initial prejudice against all robots is explained as resulting from the choice of a robot to save Del's life rather than the life of a little girl. There is a 45 percent chance that Del could be saved, but only an 11 percent chance that the girl could be saved, and the robot thus apparently chose to "maximize utility" and pursue the goal that was most likely to be achieved. Del remarks, "that was somebody's baby ... 11 percent is more than enough – a human being would have known that." The suggestion is that the robot did something immoral in saving Del instead of "somebody's baby." I'm not entirely sure that we can make good sense of Del's reaction here, but there are several ways in which we might try to understand his anger.

On one interpretation, Del may merely be upset that the robot wasn't calculating utility *correctly*. After all, the small child presumably has a long life ahead of her if she is saved, whereas Del is already approaching early-middle age. In addition, the child is probably capable of great joy, whereas Del is presented as a fairly cynical and grumpy guy. Finally, the child may have had many friends and family who would be hurt by her death, whereas Del seems to have few friends, disgruntled exes, and only one rather scatterbrained grandmother who probably does not have many years left. Perhaps the difference here between the probable utility that would result from the child's continued life versus Del's own life is so

---

[6] A related objection that some viewers might have to the robots' behavior in *I, Robot* concerns paternalism. Even if the robots are doing something that is ultimately in the interest of the humans, perhaps the humans resent being paternalistically forced into allowing the robots to so act. Although I think such complaints about paternalism are justified, note that a large part of the reason paternalism typically offends is the fact that often those acting paternalistically don't actually have the best interests of their subjects in mind (i.e., father doesn't in fact know best). As mentioned, however, in the film we are given no reason to think that the robots are misguided in their judgment that humans really do need protection from themselves.

great as to counterbalance the difference in the probability of rescue that motivated the robot to save Del. (To put it crudely and in poker lingo: Pot odds justify saving the girl here despite the long-shot nature of such a rescue. Although it was less likely that she could be saved, the "payoff" [in terms of happiness gained and suffering avoided] would have been high enough to warrant the attempt.)

Although I think this sort of objection is not ridiculous, it is a bit of a stretch, and probably not the kind of objection that Del actually has in mind. His complaint seems to focus more on the offensiveness of the *very idea* that the robot would perform the sort of calculation it does. (The crime is not that the robot is a *bad* utilitarian, i.e., that it calculates *incorrectly*, but that it attempts to calculate utility *at all*.) Del's comments imply that any such calculation is out of place, and so the robot's willingness to calculate betrays a sort of moral blindness.

My interpretation of Del's motives here is influenced by another scene in the film, in which Del seems to manifest a similar dislike for utilitarian calculation. Toward the film's end, there is a climactic action sequence in which Del commands the robot Sonny to "Save her! Save the girl!" [referring to the character Susan Calvin] when the robot was instead going to help Del defeat VICKI and (in Del's eyes at least) save humanity. In that scene the suggestion is that the robot should deliberately avoid pursuing the path that might lead to the greater good in order to instead save an individual to whom Del is personally attached. As in the earlier scenario with the drowning girl, the idea is that a *human* would unreflectively but correctly "save the girl," whereas a *robot* instead engages in calculations and deliberations that exhibit, to use a phrase from the moral philosopher Bernard Williams, "one thought too many." The cold utilitarian logic of the robot exposes a dangerously inhuman and thus impoverished moral sense.

When Bernard Williams introduced the "one thought too many" worry in his landmark essay, "Persons, Character, and Morality," he was considering a particular example in which a man faces a choice whether to save his wife or a stranger from peril. He argued that even if utilitarianism can offer a justification for saving the wife over the stranger, the very nature of this justification reveals a rather deep problem with utilitarianism (along with other moral theories that would demand strict impartiality here):

[T]his [sort of justification] provides the agent with one thought too many: it might have been hoped by some (for instance, by his wife) that his motivating thought, fully spelled out, would be the thought that it was his wife, not that it was his wife and that in situations of this kind it is permissible to save one's wife. (Williams 1981, p.18)

In requiring an impartial justification for saving the wife, the theory alienates the man from his natural motives and feelings.[7] As another philosopher, Michael

---

[7]   Note that the issue here is one of justification: Williams's objection cannot simply be dismissed with the charge that he is making the supposedly common mistake of failing to distinguish between utilitarianism as a *decision procedure* and utilitarianism as a *criterion of rightness*. Even if utilitarianism allows us to occasionally not "think like a utilitarian," it justifies this permission in a way that is quite troubling.

Stocker, put it when discussing similar worries, the theory demands a sort of moral "schizophrenia" in creating a split between what actually motivates an agent and what justifies the agent's act from the perspective of moral theory (Stocker 1997). This is particularly problematic because the natural, unreflective desire to save one's wife manifests what many would consider a perfectly *moral* motive. Utilitarianism has trouble accounting for the morality of this motive, however, and instead appears to endorse a rather different moral psychology than the sort that most people actually possess. (I will refer to this sort of complaint as "the integrity objection," as Williams claimed that this demand of utilitarianism amounts to a quite literal attack on one's psychological integrity.)

These worries about impartial moral theories like utilitarianism are related to another influential claim made by the philosopher Susan Wolf in her essay "Moral Saints." She persuasively argues that though the life of a moral saint may be (in some ways) admirable, it need not be emulated. Such a life involves too great a sacrifice – it demands domination by morality to such a degree that it becomes hard to see the moral saint as having a life at all, let alone a *good* life:[8]

[T]he ideal of a life of moral sainthood disturbs not simply because it is an ideal of a life in which morality unduly dominates. The normal person's direct and specific desires for objects, activities, and events that conflict with the attainment of moral perfection are not simply sacrificed but removed, suppressed, or subsumed. The way in which morality, unlike other possible goals, is apt to dominate is particularly disturbing, for it seems to require either the lack or the denial of the existence of an identifiable, personal self. (Wolf 1997)

To live a characteristically human life requires the existence of a certain kind of self, and part of what is so disturbing about utilitarianism is that it seems to require that we sacrifice this self, not in the sense of necessarily giving up one's existence (though utilitarianism can, at times, demand that), but in the sense that we are asked to give up or set aside the projects and commitments that make up, to use Charles Taylor's memorable phrasing, the sources of the self (Taylor 1989). Because these projects are what bind the self together and create a meaningful life, a moral theory that threatens these projects in turn threatens the integrity of one's identity. In the eyes of critics like Williams, Stocker, and Wolf, this is simply too much for utilitarian morality to ask.[9]

Why a Robot Should (Perhaps) Not Get a Life

I think that these claims regarding the tension between utilitarianism and the integrity of the self amount to a pretty powerful objection when we consider

---

[8] This brings to mind an oft-repeated quip about the great theorist of impartial morality, Immanuel Kant: It was often said that there was no great "Life of Kant" written because, to put it bluntly, Kant had no life. (Recent biographies have shown this claim to be rather unjustified, however.)

[9] Strictly speaking, Wolf's view is not exactly that this is too much for a moral theory like utilitarianism to ask, but rather that we need not always honor the request.

human agents,[10] but it is not at all clear that they should hold much weight when the agents in question are *machines*. After all, whether a robot has the kind of commitments and projects that might conflict with an impartial morality is (at least to a very large extent) up to the creator of that robot, and thus it would seem that such conflict could be avoided ahead of time through designing robots accordingly.[11] It appears that the quest to create moral robots supplies us with reasons to deliberately *withhold* certain humanlike traits from those robots.[12]

Which traits matter here? Traditionally both sentience (consciousness) and autonomy have been regarded as morally relevant features, with utilitarians emphasizing sentience and Kantians emphasizing autonomy.[13] However, if the aforementioned consideration of the integrity objection is correct, perhaps we should consider yet another feature: the existence of a particular kind of self – the sort of self that brings with it the need for meaningful commitments that could conflict with the demands of morality. (I take it that a creature with such a self is the sort of creature for which the question "Is my life meaningful?" can arise. Accordingly, I will refer to such a self as "existential.") It may well be immoral of us to create a moral robot and then burden it with a life of projects and commitments that would have to be subsumed under the demands required by impartial utilitarian calculation.[14]

This leads me to the more general question of whether we may be morally obliged to limit the capacities of robots. Some who have written on this topic seem to assume both that we will make robots as humanlike as possible and

---

[10] Though for an extremely sophisticated and insightful response to these sorts of objections, see Peter Railton's "Alienation, Consequentialism, and the Demands of Morality" (Railton 1998).

[11] My reluctance to claim that the nature of the robot is *entirely* up to the creator is due to the possibility of robots being created that are unpredictable in their development. As should be clear from the rest of my essay, I take the possibility of such unpredictability to give us significant cause for concern and caution, though I won't pursue that specific worry here.

[12] In "Towards the Ethical Robot," James Gips also considers the possibility of creating robots that are "moral saints" (Gips 1995). He concludes that whereas such sainthood is hard for humans to achieve, it should be easier for robots to accomplish. I agree, although as I mention earlier I think we need to be careful here: It may be possible to create robots that must subsume part of their self in order to be moral saints. The creation of such creatures may itself be immoral if we have the alternative of creating saintly robots that are *not* capable of such internal conflict.

[13] By "consciousness" or "sentience," I mean the bare capacity to experience sensations, feelings, and perceptions (what is sometimes called "phenomenal consciousness") – I'm not presupposing "self-consciousness." Also, I use the term "autonomy" here rather than rationality to distinguish what someone like Kant requires from the more minimal capacity to perform calculations that correspond with the norms of instrumental rationality. That machines are capable of the more minimal notion is uncontroversial. That they could ever possess reason in the robust Kantian sense is much more difficult to determine, as Kant's conception of reason incorporates into it the idea of free will and moral responsibility.

[14] Although I'm focusing on the possibility of utilitarian robots here, it should be mentioned that similar concerns could arise for deontological robots depending on their capacities and the demands of the particular deontological theory that is adopted.

that we *should*. Although I imagine that there will always be a desire to try and create machines that can emulate human capacities and qualities, the giddiness of science fiction enthusiasts too often takes over here, and the possibility that we should deliberately restrict the capacities of robots is not adequately considered. Consider the amusing (but to my mind, worrying) comments of James Gips in his paper "Towards the Ethical Robot": Gips rejects Asimov's three laws with the assertion that "these three laws are not suitable for our magnificent robots. These are laws for slaves." (Gips 1995). I have been suggesting that we may well have grounds for not making robots quite so "magnificent" after all. My suggestion came up in the context of considering robots designed to act as moral saints, but related worries can arise for other types of robots, so long as they potentially possess some morally relevant features. Note that the moral difficulties that would crop up in treating such creatures as "slaves" arise only if the machines are similar to humans in morally relevant respects, but *whether* they reach that point is up to us – we can choose where these robots end up on the moral continuum between a so-called slave hard drive and an actual human slave.

As a matter of brute fact we will surely continue to create most machines, including future robots, as "slaves" if what that means is that they are created to serve us. There is nothing morally wrong with this *provided* we have created machines that do not possess morally relevant features (like sentience, autonomy, or the sort of existential self that I discussed earlier).[15] Once we do venture into the territory of robots that are similar to humans in morally relevant respects, however, we will need to be very careful about the way they are treated. Intentionally avoiding the creation of such robots may well be the ethical thing to do, especially if it turns out that the works performed by such machines could be performed equally effectively by machines lacking morally relevant characteristics.[16] To return to my initial example, it is possible that a robot designed to be a "moral saint" could be ethically created so long as we didn't burden it with a humanlike self.

[15] Whether machines will ever be capable of sentience/consciousness is a hotly debated topic. I will leave that debate aside, merely noting that I share the view of those who think that more than a Turing test will be required to determine machine consciousness. Regarding rationality, the degree to which this is a morally relevant feature hinges on the type of rationality exhibited. Whether a machine could ever possess the sort of robust rationality and autonomy required by Kant is itself a thorny topic, although it seems to have generated less debate thus far than the question of machine consciousness. As one might expect, figuring out whether a machine possesses the sort of "existential self" I discuss also seems philosophically daunting. Certainly both sentience and autonomy would be preconditions for such a self.

[16] Although I'm focusing on the actual possession of morally relevant features, I don't want to deny that there may be other ethically relevant issues here. As Anderson has pointed out, a Kantian "indirect duty" argument may offer good reasons for treating some robots *as though* they possess moral status so long as there is a danger that immoral behavior directed toward such creatures could lead to immoral behavior towards humans (Anderson 2005).

The Separateness of Persons

The integrity objection that I have been considering is what is sometimes called an agent-based objection, as it focuses on the person acting rather than those affected by the agent's actions. I have suggested that, when considering robot ethics, this objection can be avoided due to the plasticity of robot agents – created in the right way, utilitarian robots simply won't face the sort of conflicts that threaten human integrity. However, other objections to utilitarianism focus on those affected by a utilitarian agent rather than the agent himself, and such objections cannot be skirted through engineering robots in a particular manner. Regardless of how we design future robots, it will still be true that a utilitarian robot may act toward humans in a manner that most of us would consider unjust. This is for reasons that were nicely explained by John Rawls in his *A Theory of Justice*:

This [utilitarian] view of social co-operation is the consequence of extending to society the principle of choice for one man, and then, to make this extension work, conflating all persons into one through the imaginative acts of the impartial sympathetic spectator. Utilitarianism does not take seriously the distinction between persons. (Rawls 1971, p. 27)

Utilitarianism is a moral philosophy that allows for the suffering inflicted on one individual to be offset by the goods gained for others. In conglomerating the sufferings and enjoyments of all, it fails to recognize the importance we normally place on individual identity.

Most of us don't think that suffering inflicted on an innocent and unwilling human can be compensated through gains achieved for other humans. The modern notion of individual rights is in place in large part to help prevent such violations. (Consider my earlier example of the doctor who sacrifices the one to save the five – perhaps the most natural description of the case will involve describing it as involving the violation of the innocent person's *right* to noninterference.) Whether such a violation of rights occurs at the hands of a robot or a human is irrelevant – it is a violation nonetheless. It follows that we have strong grounds for rejecting robots that would act as utilitarians toward humans even if we could create those robots in such a way that they would not experience the sort of conflicts of integrity mentioned earlier. Utilitarianism can be rejected not on the grounds that it requires too much of an artificial agent, but rather on the grounds that it ignores the individual identity and rights of the human subject affected by the utilitarian agent. Del Spooner may have had bad reasons to reject utilitarian robots in *I, Robot*, but good reasons for such a rejection can be found – Del's worries about a future in which robots behave as utilitarians toward humans turn out to be well grounded after all.

Robot-Robot Relations

Although I have argued that Del Spooner's and Bernard Williams's objections to utilitarianism may not apply to robot utilitarians, I have nevertheless concluded that there are other grounds for not programming robots to behave as utilitarians toward humans. I want to end this paper with a brief consideration of a related issue that is also raised by the film *I, Robot*: What sort of moral relations are appropriate *between* robots? Although it may be inappropriate for robots to use utilitarianism as either a decision procedure or a criterion of rightness when interacting with humans, it does not follow that utilitarianism (or some other form of consequentialism) is necessarily out of place when robots interact with their own kind.

Why might utilitarian moral theory be appropriate for robots though not humans? As we have seen, John Rawls famously objected to utilitarianism on the grounds that it "does not take the distinction between persons seriously." This failure to recognize the separateness of individuals explains why utilitarianism allows for actions in which an individual is sacrificed for the sake of utility. The case of robots is a philosophically interesting one, however, because it isn't clear that robots ought to be regarded as "individuals" at all. Indeed, in *I, Robot* as well as in countless other science fiction films, robots are often presented as lacking individuality – they tend to work in teams, as collective units, and the sacrifice of the one for the "greater good" is a given. In *I, Robot* we see the hordes of robots repeatedly act as a very effective collective entity. (Additionally, in one telling scene they can only "identify" an intruding robot as "one of us.") Though arguably sentient and rational, these machines seem, in some important sense, incapable of ego; and if this is right, then perhaps a moral theory that ignores the boundaries between individuals is a good fit for such creatures.

There is one robot in *I, Robot* that is importantly different, however: Sonny seems to possess not just sentience and rationality, but also the kind of individual identity that may well make it inappropriate to treat him along utilitarian lines.[17] Now, determining exactly what counts as sufficient for the possession of an "individual identity" strikes me as a very difficult philosophical task, and I think it would be hard to say much here that would be uncontroversial. Possibly relevant criteria could include the capacity for self-awareness and self-governance, the ability to recognize and respond to reasons, and/or the capacity for free and responsible choice. (Clearly more would be required than the simple ability for a machine to operate independently of other machines. My Roomba can do that, and so in a very minimal sense it is an "individual," but this is not the sort of strong individuality relevant for the attribution of rights.) Without putting forward a surely dubious list of necessary and sufficient conditions, it is relatively safe to assume that a robot that was very similar to us in terms of its psychological (and phenomenological) makeup and capacities would presumably possess the

---

[17] Sonny is said to possess free will, and we even see him actively question the purpose of his life at the end of the film. Of course, his fictional nature makes it easy for us to believe all this. Attributing such capacities to actual robots is obviously trickier.

relevant sort of individual identity.[18] Accordingly, if such a robot is indeed possible and someday became actual, it should not be treated along utilitarian lines – the separateness of that individual should be respected in moral evaluations.

What about robots that are less sophisticated? Would the possession of sentience alone be enough to block the appropriateness of utilitarian treatment? I don't think so. Such robots would be morally similar to many animals, and for that sort of creature utilitarianism (or some theory like it) is perhaps not so unreasonable. In other words, a creature that possesses sentience but lacks a strong sense of self is the arguably just the sort of creature that could reasonably be sacrificed for the sake of the greater good. The notion of individual rights isn't appropriate here. Consider a position on the moral status of animals that Robert Nozick discusses in *Anarchy, State, and Utopia*:

Human beings may not be used or sacrificed for the benefit of others; animals may be used or sacrificed for the benefit of other people or animals *only if* those benefits are greater than the loss inflicted.... One may proceed only if the total utilitarian benefit is greater than the utilitarian loss inflicted on the animals. This utilitarian view counts animals as much as normal utilitarianism does persons. Following Orwell, we might summarize this view as: *all animals are equal but some are more equal than others*. (None may be sacrificed except for a greater total benefit; but persons may not be sacrificed at all, or only under far more stringent conditions, and never for the benefit of nonhuman animals.) (Nozick 1974, p. 39)

The reasoning behind the "utilitarianism for animals" position that Nozick sketches would seem to also apply to any robot that falls short of the possession of an individual identity but nevertheless possesses sentience.[19] Such creatures are in

---

[18] I suspect that the necessary conditions for possessing an "individual identity" (whatever exactly they are) would still not be sufficient for the possession of the "existential self" mentioned earlier. In other words, a creature may well be capable of enough of an individual identity to make utilitarian treatment inappropriate while not possessing the sort of sophisticated psychology necessary to question of the meaningfulness of its own existence. (Perhaps a great ape falls into this category.)

[19] It should be noted that Nozick doesn't ultimately embrace this approach to animal morality, and I share his suspicion that "even for animals, utilitarianism won't do as the whole story" (p. 42). The case of some higher animals (like the great apes) shows the complications here, as their moral status may be higher than that of lower animals and yet still importantly lower than that of humans. Also, Frances Kamm has pointed out other interesting complications. She argues that even with lower animals our attitude is that it is impermissible to inflict great suffering on one in exchange for a slight reduction of suffering among many (Kamm 2005). I'm inclined to agree, but nonetheless the fact remains that the possibility of sacrificing one animal for the sake of many does seem much less offensive than would a similar sacrifice involving humans. This shows, I think, that something *closer to* utilitarianism is appropriate for most animals (and thus also for relevantly similar robots). To put it in Kamm's terminology, merely sentient robots may (like animals) have "moral status" yet not be the kind of creatures that "can have claims against us" (or against other robots). (For a contrasting position on the plausibility of animals as individual rightholders, see *The Case for Animal Rights* [Regan 1984].)

a morally intermediate position: In the moral hierarchy, they would lie (with non-human animals) somewhere in between a nonsentient object and a human being.

Although it may be appropriate to treat animals along utilitarian lines, animals themselves lack the capacity for thought necessary to act as utilitarian agents. Robots, however, may not have this limitation, for it is possible that sentient robots will be entirely capable of making utilitarian calculations. Indeed, there are grounds for thinking that they would be much better at making such calculations than humans.[20] Accordingly, it is my contention that, should their creation become possible, sentient machines (lacking individual identities) should be programmed to treat *each other* according to utilitarian principles, and that we should regard them from that perspective as well. In other words, the sort of collective behavior and individual sacrifice so often shown by robots in movies and literature makes perfect sense, given that the robots lack the relevant sense of self. Utilitarian moral theory (or, in the case of nonsentient robots, a more general consequentialist theory that maximizes good consequences overall) may well provide the best ethical theory for artificial agents that lack the boundaries of self that normally make utilitarian calculation inappropriate.

Concluding Remarks

If the foregoing reflections on the feasibility and desirability of robot utilitarians are on target, there are interesting ramifications for the burgeoning field of machine ethics. The project of developing a utilitarian robot may be a reasonable one *even though* such a machine should *not* treat humans along utilitarian lines, and *even though* such a machine would *not* be a suitable ethical advisor for humans when considering acts that affect other humans. The need for a utilitarian robot may arise not out of the need to provide aid for human moral interaction, but rather to ensure that future sentient machines (that lack individual identities) are treated appropriately by humans and are capable of treating each other appropriately as well.

Now, if it turns out that there are compelling reasons to create robots of greater abilities (like the fictional Sonny), then different moral standards may be appropriate; but for reasons I hope I've made clear, I think that significant caution should be exercised before attempting the creation of robots that would possess moral status akin to humans. Much like Spider-Man's motto – "with great power comes great responsibility" – the creation of machines with such great powers would bring with it great responsibilities, not just for the robots created, but for us.

Acknowledgments

This paper is a significantly revised and expanded version of "There is no 'I' in 'Robot': Robots & Utilitarianism" published in *IEEE Intelligent Systems*: Special

---

[20] Though for a brief discussion of possible difficulties here, see *Moral Machines* (Wallach and Allen 2009, pp. 84–91).

Issue on Machine Ethics, vol. 21, no. 4, 52–55, July/August, 2006. I am grateful to Sean Allen-Hermanson, Susan Anderson, Daniel Callcut, James DiGiovanna, J. Storrs Hall, Jim Moor, Tom Wartenberg, and Susan Watson for helpful comments.

References

Anderson, S. L. 2005. "Asimov's "Three Laws of Robotics" and Machine Metaethics," *AAAI Machine Ethics Symposium Technical Report* FS-05–06, AAAI Press.

Cloos, C. 2005. "The Utilibot Project: An Autonomous Mobile Robot Based on Utilitarianism," *AAAI Machine Ethics Symposium Technical Report* FS-05–06, AAAI Press.

DiGiovanna, J. 2004. "Three Simple Rules." *Tucson Weekly*, July 22, 2004. http://www.tucsonweekly.com/tucson/three-simple-rules/Content?oid=1076875.

Gips, J. 1995. "Towards the Ethical Robot." In *Android Epistemology*, MIT Press. (http://www.cs.bc.edu/~gips/EthicalRobot.pdf).

Kamm, F. 2005. "Moral Status and Personal Identity: Clones, Embryos, and Future Generations." *Social Philosophy & Policy*, 291.

Nozick, R. 1974. *Anarchy, State, and Utopia*, Basic Books.

Railton, P. 1998. "Alienation, Consequentialism, and the Demands of Morality." In *Ethical Theory*, edited by J. Rachels, Oxford University Press.

Regan, Tom. 1984. *The Case for Animal Rights*, New York: Routledge.

Rawls, J. 1971. *A Theory of Justice*, Harvard University Press.

Stocker, M. 1997. "The Schizophrenia of Modern Ethical Theories." In *Virtue Ethics*, edited by R. Crisp and M. Slote, Oxford University Press.

Taylor, C. 1989. *Sources of the Self*, Harvard University Press.

Wallach, W. & Allen, C. 2009. *Moral Machines: Teaching Robots Right from Wrong*, Oxford University Press.

Williams, B. 1981. "Persons, Character, Morality." In *Moral Luck*, Cambridge University Press.

Wolf, S. 1997. "Moral Saints." In *Virtue Ethics*, 84, edited by R. Crisp and M. Slote, Oxford University Press.

26

Prospects for a Kantian Machine

Thomas M. Powers

ONE WAY TO VIEW THE PUZZLE OF MACHINE ETHICS IS TO CONSIDER HOW we might program computers that will *themselves* refrain from evil and perhaps promote good. Consider some steps along the way to that goal. Humans have many ways to be ethical or unethical by means of an artifact or tool; they can quell a senseless riot by broadcasting a speech on television or use a hammer to kill someone. We get closer to machine ethics when the tool is a computer that's programmed to effect good as a result of the programmer's intentions. But to be ethical in a deeper sense – to be ethical in themselves – machines must have something like practical reasoning that results in action that causes or avoids morally relevant harm or benefit. So, the central question of machine ethics asks whether the machine could exhibit a simulacrum of ethical deliberation. It will be no slight to the machine if all it achieves is a simulacrum. It could be that a great many humans do no better.

Rule-based ethical theories like Immanuel Kant's appear to be promising for machine ethics because they offer a computational structure for judgment.

Of course, philosophers have long disagreed about what constitutes proper ethical deliberation in humans. The *utilitarian tradition* holds that it's essentially arithmetic: we reach the right ethical conclusion by calculating the prospective utility for all individuals who will be affected by a set of possible actions and then choosing the action that promises to maximize total utility. But how we measure utility over disparate individuals and whether we can ever have enough information about future consequences are thorny problems for utilitarianism.

The *deontological tradition*, on the other hand, holds that some actions ought or ought not be performed, regardless of how they might affect others. Deontology emphasizes complex reasoning about actions and their logical (as opposed to empirical) implications. It focuses on rules for action – how we know which rules to adopt, how we might build systems of rules, and how we know whether a prospective action falls under a rule. The most famous deontologist, Immanuel Kant (1724–1804), held that a procedure exists for generating the rules of action – namely, the *categorical imperative* – and that one version of the categorical imperative works in a purely formal manner.

Human practical reasoning primarily concerns the transformation between the consideration of facts and the ensuing action. To some extent, the transformation resembles a machine's state changes when it goes from a set of declarative units in a database to an output. There are other similarities, of course – humans can learn new facts that inform their reasoning about action, just as machines can incorporate feedback systems that influence their outputs. But human practical reasoning includes an intervening stage that machines (so far) seem to lack: the formation of normative claims about what is permissible, what one ought to do, what one is morally required to do, and the like. It's plausible that normative claims either are ethical rules themselves or entail such rules. These normative claims aren't independent of facts, and they don't necessarily lead humans to action. In fact, humans suffer from "weaknesses of the will," as Aristotle called them, that shouldn't be a problem for a machine: once it reaches a conclusion about what it ought or ought not to do, the output will follow automatically. But how will the machine reach the middle stage – the normative conclusions that connect facts to action through rules? I think this is the problem for machine practical reasoning.

A rule-based ethical theory is a good candidate for the practical reasoning of machine ethics because it generates duties or rules for action, and rules are (for the most part) computationally tractable. Among principle- or rule-based theories, the first formulation of Kant's categorical imperative offers a formalizable procedure. I will explore a version of machine ethics along the lines of Kantian formalist ethics, both to suggest what computational structures such a view would require and to see what challenges remain for its successful implementation. In reformulating Kant for the purposes of machine ethics, I will consider three views of how the categorical imperative works: mere consistency, commonsense practical reasoning, and coherency. The first view envisions straightforward deductions of actions from facts. The second view incorporates recent work in nonmonotonic logic and commonsense reasoning. The last view takes ethical deliberation to follow a logic similar to that of belief revision.

Kantian Formalist Ethics

In *Grounding of the Metaphysics of Morals*,[1] Kant claims that the first formulation of the categorical imperative supplies a procedure for producing ethical rules:

Act only according to that maxim whereby you can at the same time will that it should become a universal law.

Kant tells the moral agent to test each maxim (or plan of action) as though it were a candidate for a universalized rule. Later, he adds that each universalized rule must fit into a system of rules for all persons. In other words, my maxim will be an instance of a rule only if I can will that everyone might act on such a maxim. Further, such a universalized rule must be consistent with other rules generated in a similar manner. Philosophers have interpreted these *universalizability* and *systematicity* conditions as a two-part consistency check on an agent's action plan.

The procedure for deriving duties from maxims – if we are to believe Kant – requires no special moral or intellectual intuition peculiar to humans. For a formalist Kantian, whether a maxim could be a universal rule presents a decision problem that's the same for a human or a machine. Kant himself, 20 years prior to publication of the *Grounding*, sketched an answer to the decision problem that's suggestive of a machine solution:

If contradiction and contrast arise, the action is rejected; if harmony and concord arise, it is accepted. From this comes the ability to take moral positions as a heuristic means. For we are social beings by nature, and what we do not accept in others, we cannot sincerely accept in ourselves.[2]

A Machine-Computable Categorical Imperative

I don't intend to offer a strict interpretation of Kant's ethics here. Instead, I'll focus on the logic of a machine-computable categorical imperative. Recall that the first formulation is supposed to test maxims. For Kant, maxims are "subjective principles of volition," or plans. In this sense, the categorical imperative serves as a test for turning plans into instances of objective moral laws. This is the gist of Kant's notion of *self-legislation*: an agent's moral maxims are instances of universally quantified propositions that could serve as moral laws – that is, laws holding for any agent. Because we can't stipulate the class of universal moral laws for the machine – this would be human ethics operating through a tool, not machine ethics – the machine might itself construct a theory of ethics by applying the universalization step to individual maxims and then mapping them onto traditional *deontic categories* – namely, forbidden, permissible, obligatory actions – according to the results.

The first formulation of the categorical imperative demands that the ethical agent act only on maxims that it can universally will. It is somewhat deflating, then, that this formulation gives no more than a necessary condition for ethical action. One simple way to meet this condition would be to universalize each maxim and perform a consistency check. A more efficient method would be to start from scratch and build the theory of forbidden maxims F from the outcomes of consistency checks on possible action plans. The machine would then check whether any prospective maxim m is an element of F. The theory will be finitely axiomatizable if and only if it's identical to the set of consequences of a finite set of axioms. The theory will be complete if and only if, for every maxim

m, either it or its negation is in F. If the machine could tell, for any m, whether it's an element of F, then the theory would be decidable. The theory of forbidden maxims (alone) lets the machine refrain from what it ought not do.

This is the optimistic scenario. But how does the machine know what it ought to do? We would need a test that generates the deontic category of obligatory maxims. But a problem arises here if the theory of forbidden maxims is complete. Suppose the categorical imperative assigns the answer "yes" for all forbidden maxims. Two deontic categories still remain for assignment: obligatory and permissible maxims. And, of course, permissible maxims are neither obligatory nor forbidden.

Other problems arise on the formalization level. Consider one that Onora O'Neill discusses.[3] In some cases, we might have a maxim that fails the universalization test because it's overly specific or because of a kind of asymmetry in the predicate. While these are indeed failures, they don't seem to be morally relevant failures. For instance, in the maxim, "I will enslave John," one might not be able to quantify over "John" if he's taken to be a pure existential. In other words, if I want to enslave John because he's a specific person – not just any person – then my maxim won't be applicable to any other object and so won't be universalizable. But the maxim is immoral, of course, not because it's something that I propose to do to John and John only, but because enslaving is wrong. The theory ought to forbid my maxim, but not because of its peculiar specificity.

It's also mistaken to think that slavery is wrong just because of a certain predicative asymmetry in the maxim's universalized form – that I would be willing everyone to be a slave, hence leaving no one to be a slaveholder. Although it's true that one can't be both a slave and a slaveholder, that isn't what makes slaveholding wrong. If the asymmetry were the problem, then maxims such as "I will become a taxi driver" would also fail, on the assumption that we need some people to ride in taxis for others to be employed in driving them.

To address the specificity problem, we must add a condition on a maxim's logical form so that the universalization test will quantify over circumstances, purposes, and agents. If we don't have this restriction, some maxims might be determinate with respect to either the circumstance or purpose – that is, some might be pure existentials, such as "I will offer *this* prize as a reward." The asymmetry problem is harder to resolve, of course, at least for a machine, because its resolution seems to require some fairly complex semantic ability.

Mere Consistency

So now we know that a properly formulated input for testing ethical behavior is a maxim over which circumstances, purposes, and agents are universally quantified. A computer must be able to parse these categories from programmed ontologies, or it must simply accept properly formulated input maxims as having an unambiguous syntax of circumstance, purpose, and agent. To see whether the input is an instance of a moral law and exactly what deontic category it belongs to, Kantian formalism assumes that the categorical imperative's test is an algorithm that alone will determine the classes of obligatory, forbidden, and permissible actions. In other words, the test produces formulas for a deontic logic system.

Now, this deontic logic will include many issues that I must set aside here. Among them are the nature of the logical connectives between circumstances, purposes, and actions; material implication (if-then) is clearly too weak. Another is whether a machine would understand obligation from an agent's perspective – that is, would the machine understand the difference between "I ought to do z" and (merely) "z ought to be the case"? (For more information on this problem, see Jeff Horty's discussion.[4]) So, setting aside these problems, let's suppose that, after the quantification step, the machine can produce universalized maxims that look something like the following (I omit quantifiers here):

1. $(C$ and $P) \rightarrow$ A
   A is obligatory for the agent
2. $(C$ and $P) \rightarrow \neg A$
   A is forbidden for the agent
3. $\neg((C$ and $P) \rightarrow A)$ and
   $\neg((C$ and $P) \rightarrow \neg A)$
   A is permissible for the agent

where C represents a circumstance, P represents a purpose, and A represents an action. We now have schemata for the three deontic categories (though admittedly we have no account of *superogatory action* – that is, action beyond the call of duty). Intuitively, we say that anyone in a particular circumstance with a particular purpose ought to do A in case 1, refrain from A in case 2, and either do or refrain from A in case 3.

A major defect in this initial account is apparent if we want the machine to go beyond verifying that a candidate maxim is an instance of one of these three schemata. The categorical imperative doesn't merely perform universal generalization on sentences that are supplied as candidate maxims. Surely, it must test the maxims for contradictions, but the only contradictions that can arise are trivial ones – those inherent in the maxims themselves. This is so even when we take the theory of forbidden maxims to be closed under logical consequence.

A robust version of the test, on the other hand, requires the machine to compare the maxim under consideration with other maxims, principles, and axioms. In other words, the machine must check the maxim's consistency with other facts in the database, some of which will be normative conclusions from previously considered maxims. Obviously, the simple account of mere consistency won't do. It must be buttressed by adding other facts, principles, or maxims, in comparison with which the machine can test the target maxim for contradiction.

Commonsense Practical Reasoning

We can buttress Kant's mere consistency test by adding a background theory B, against which the test can have nontrivial results. What would this theory look like? For Kantians, it would depend on the line of interpretation one has for Kant's ethics generally. Many scholars supplement Kant's categorical imperative with normative principles from his other philosophical writings. This way of adding to Kant's pure formulation risks introducing psychological and empirical considerations into practical reasoning. While such considerations seem altogether appropriate to most of us, Kant saw it posing the threat of "heteronomy," thus polluting the categorical imperative's sufficiency to ethical reasoning.

Kant's illustrations of the categorical imperative in the *Grounding* suggest a better alternative. In these illustrations, Kant introduces some *commonsense rules*. For instance, he argues that, because feelings are purposeful and the purpose of the feeling of self-love is self-preservation, it would be wrong to commit suicide out of self-love. He also argues that it's wrong to make false promises because, in general, the practice of giving and accepting promises assumes that promises are kept. Many contemporary Kantians have adopted this suggestion concerning common-sense rules, which they call, variously, postulates of rationality,[5] constraining principles of empirical practical reason,[6] and principles of rational intending.[3] These are presumably nontrivial, nonnormative rules that somehow capture what it is to act with practical reason.

When we build the background theory B with commonsense rules, we get something that is probably closer to ethical deliberation in humans. This move presents difficulties, insofar as we don't have a general formalism for commonsense practical reason (though there are some domain-specific accounts). On the other hand, ethical deliberation conceived as a consistency check on a single universalized maxim is clearly too thin. The main focus for building a Kantian machine should therefore turn to the elements of B; in this way, we might hope to supplement the categorical imperative's test. If this supplementation were successful, we would say that a maxim is unreasonable if it produces a contradiction when we combine it with B. With the proper rules, the formal categorical imperative plus the maxim might yield good results. Of course, the definition and choice of postulates does no more than stipulate what counts as practical reason. Logical considerations alone are insufficient to determine whether to include any postulate in B.

Postulates of commonsense practical reason don't share the logic of scientific laws or other universal generalizations. One counterexample is enough to disprove a deductive law, but commonsense postulates must survive the occasional defeat. The postulates of B, then, would require a nonmonotonic theory of practical reasoning.

Nonmonotonic logic attempts to formalize an aspect of intelligence, artificial or human. Nonmonotonic reasoning is quite commonplace. Consider that classical first-order logic is *monotonic*: if you can infer sentence *a* from a set of premises *P*, then you can also infer *a* from any set *S* that contains *P* as a subset. Nonmonotonic inference simply denies this condition because the bigger set might contain a formula that "defeats" or disallows the inference to *a*.

For example, the addition of "Fritz is a cat" to a set already containing "All cats are mammals" licenses the monotonic inference "Fritz is a mammal." But if we replace our deductive law about cats with a default rule, such as "Cats are affectionate," we can see some conditions that would defeat the inference to "Fritz is affectionate." Let's say we had additional information to the effect that "Fritz is a tiger." At the least, all bets should be off as to whether Fritz is affectionate. An ethics example might be the default rule "Don't kill the innocent." The defeating conditions might be "unless they are attacking under the control of some drug" or "except in a just war," and so on.

While there are different ways to formalize nonmonotonic reasoning, we want to choose a way that will build on the categorical imperative's basic monotonic procedure. We also need a system that extends classical first-order logic and offers the most flexibility, so that we can use the formalism to extend the simple monotonic account of the categorical imperative in the previous section. For these reasons, Reiter's default logic seems to be the best candidate among the approaches developed so far.[7]

In Reiter's default logic, the rule in the example just given becomes

If Fritz is a cat, *and it is consistent that Fritz is affectionate*, then Fritz is affectionate.

Any number of additional facts can defeat the italic clause, such as "Fritz had a bad day," "Fritz had a bad kittenhood," "Fritz is a person-eater," and so on. Reiter suggests the following symbolization for this default rule:

$$\frac{C : A}{A}$$

where *C* is the default's precondition, *A* is the justification (in this instance), and *A* is the default conclusion. This is a *normal* default rule because the justification is the same as the conclusion we're allowed to draw. We understand the justification as certifying that no information exists to indicate that the conclusion is false or that Fritz is a special kind of cat – that is, we've learned nothing to convince us that Fritz is not affectionate.

How we use Reiter's default logic depends on the notion of an *extension*, which also appears in other nonmontonic systems. Intuitively, an extension of a theory (T_{ext}) is a set of conclusions of a default theory $T = <W, D>$, where W is a set of facts and D is the set of default rules. We can use a conclusion from the rules in a consistency test, if we can prove the precondition from the set of facts W and if the justifications are consistent with all conclusions of the rules in D. (For further illustrations, see David Poole's work on default logic.[8]) An extension of the theory adds all of those default conclusions consistent with W and its logical consequences, but never adds an untoward fact. Adding the default rules, then, will allow input maxims to contradict the background set of facts and common-sense rules without introducing inconsistency.

This means the definition of an extension maintains the requirement of nonmonotonicity. Given a set of first-order sentences, we can add the conclusions of default rules without generating conclusions that are inconsistent with the default theory. Default extensions avoid introducing contradictions. Default rules yield to facts; the rules are defeated but not vanquished. In monotonic logic, by contrast, counterexamples vanquish universal laws.

Kant seems to recognize that *defeasible* reasoning – that is, reasoning that displays the property of nonmonotonicity – plays some role in ethical thinking. In this respect, he is far ahead of his time. In the *Grounding*,[1] he refers to a thought process in which the "universality of the principle (*universalitas*) is changed into mere generality (*generalitas*), whereby the practical principle of reason meets the maxim halfway." When we look closely at Kant's illustrations, we see the kinds of default rules he might have wanted the background theory to include.

Against Suicide

For example, Kant offers the following account of moral deliberation for the person contemplating suicide:

His maxim is 'From self-love I make it my principle to shorten my life if its continuance threatens more evil than it promises pleasure'. The only further question to ask is whether this principle of self-love can become a universal law of nature. **It is then seen at once that a system of nature by whose law the very same feeling whose function is to stimulate the furtherance of life should actually destroy life would contradict itself.**

I've added the bold font to what I take to be nonmonotonic reasoning. The default rule concerns the function or purpose of self-love, premise 3 in the reconstructed argument that runs as follows:

1. Anyone in pain and motivated by self-love (circumstance) shall try to lessen pain (purpose) by self-destruction (action).
2. Feelings have functions.
3. Self-love serves the function of self-preservation.
4. Self-destruction is the negation of self-preservation.

Therefore

5. A maxim of suicide is contradictory and hence the action is forbidden.

The normal default rule allows self-preservation from the precondition of self-love, provided that self-preservation is consistent with other facts and default-rule conclusions. But self-preservation is no universal duty for Kant; it can be defeated under the right circumstances. Defeating conditions might include voluntary submission to punishment, sacrifice for loved ones, or stronger duties under the categorical imperative. Lacking those defeating conditions, and provided that the agent satisfies the antecedent conditions, the universalized maxim plus the default rule seems to yield the contradiction that the categorical imperative needs. What happens when two default rules yield incompatible conclusions? Suppose we have two default rules in the theory:

• Suicide is self-destruction.
• Martyrdom is honorable.

Here, we could face the problem of multiple extensions: one rule tells us one thing, and the other allows us to infer the opposite. (A standard example of a harder case is "Republicans are hawks," "Quakers are pacifists," and the additional fact that "Nixon is a Republican Quaker.") This problem could arise in machine ethics, in which case we would need some procedure for specifying rule priorities.

Against False-Promising

A second example of nonmonotonic reasoning appears in Kant's account of an input maxim of false promising, or promising repayment of a loan without the intention to repay:

For the universality of a law that every one believing himself to be in need can make any promise he pleases with the intention not to keep it would make promising, and the very purpose of promising, itself impossible, since no one would believe he was being promised anything.[1]

Again, I've added the bold font to highlight nonmonotonic reasoning. The traditional criticism of this illustration is that promising and borrowing would *not* in fact be impossible if false promising became a universal rule in the closely defined circumstance of need. Such a condition would only engender extreme caution in lending and an insistence on collateral.

I don't believe this objection holds, however, because it misses the defeasible nature of both promising and lending. The institution of promising depends on two default rules – one for the debtor and one for the creditor – that promises are believed and promises are kept. Both rules are occasionally defeated, and the prevalence of defeat threatens the institution. The "common-sense" creditor will not believe a promise after the debtor defeats the rule repeatedly. Likewise, the "common-sense" debtor knows better than to offer a promise to a rightly-incredulous creditor. But this isn't to say that any one defeat of the rule of sincere promising threatens the institution of promising as a whole. Both creditors and debtors survive violations of the rules and continue to uphold the institution. What is clear, though, is that the monotonic understanding of the rule of promising – a universal generalization, "All promises are kept or promising is destroyed" – doesn't properly interpret the institution. The actual institution of promising depends as much on *surviving* a defeating instance as it does on the prevalence of nondefeat. So a nonmonotonic interpretation of the illustration makes sense of the practice, while the monotonic interpretation does not.

Difficulties for the Nonmonotonic Approach

The nonmonotonic approach to deontological machine ethics involves one serious problem. Nonmonotonic inference fails a requirement met by classical first-order logic: semidecidability of set membership. Recall the earlier characterization of the categorical imperative as asking whether a candidate maxim is forbidden. Because questions in nonmonotonic logic aren't semidecidable, it's not even the case that the nonmonotonically enhanced categorical imperative is guaranteed to answer "yes" to the question, even when the maxim is in fact forbidden. Of course, by the definition of semidecidability, it's also not guaranteed to answer "no."

The obvious question here is: What good is the nonmonotonic categorical imperative? Let me summarize the general predicament. The nonmonotonic account of Kant's illustrations interprets the ethical deliberation procedure better than anything offered by monotonic logic. We need a background theory of commonsense reasoning for the categorical imperative test to give nontrivial results. Monotonic logic doesn't entirely capture commonsense reasoning. Kant himself, when he does provide clues as to the "buttressing" principles he assumes, gives us rules that can only make sense if they're default rules. But this revised interpretation still fails an important *formal* requirement for machine ethics: semidecidability.

Coherency

In the third candidate for the logic of machine ethics, ethical deliberation involves the construction of a *coherent system* of maxims – a system that accepts any minimal set of consistent maxims as the background for comparing any current maxim for consistency. Kant also suggests this view, so it will help if we return to his illustrations of the categorical imperative in the *Grounding*.[1]

These illustrations concern the duties to develop your own talents and to give to others in need. One reading of these illustrations might go as follows: a maxim allowing your talents to rust conflicts with what every rational being wills, according to Kant – namely, the development of your talents. And if you want help from others when you're in need, you must agree to help others when they're in need.

What these cases share is the prohibition against acting on a maxim that is incoherent, given a minimal set (perhaps singleton set) of other maxims. The other maxims provide the coherency constraint but aren't privileged by stipulation; nor are they conclusions from nonmonotonic reasoning. They are your own maxims. Presumably, a machine could build such a database of its own maxims.

Let's consider the categorical imperative's procedure as a kind of bottom-up construction. Ethical deliberation, in this view, should be like building a theory, where the theory's sentences are your own maxims plus any of their consequences. Call this theory G. The theory also has two rules: R-in and R-out. For any maxim m_i, in the set of maxims M on which the machine is now prepared to act, R-in says that m_i is allowed in M if and only if m_i and G are consistent.

What about maxims the machine has acted on in the past that subsequently turned out to be impermissible? Handling such incoherencies is analogous to the belief-revision problems that Peter Gärdenfors explored.[9] If we allow the "impermissible" maxims to remain in G, the set of sentences will automatically be inconsistent; hence, the coherency constraint breaks down. Surely Kant doesn't insist on past moral perfection as a condition for reasoning about right action in the present.

We can now describe a rule (R-out) for excluding maxims that would maintain the set's inconsistency. There's nothing mysterious about R-out. On the assumption that some maxim m_i turned out to be morally wrong, m_i and G are inconsistent, and $m_i \notin M$. R-out serves the role of a confession of sins for the machine, but how the machine learns that some maxim was wrong remains a mystery. We can call the procedure an update, but that doesn't indicate how the machine would update itself. Because this seems to be crucial to ethical deliberation, this model still doesn't yield an ethical machine.

Another interesting aspect of G that poses a difficulty for a Kantian machine is the limiting case where m_1 is the only member of M. We might call this the case of the moral infant. G must allow a first maxim to enter by R-in because, by hypothesis, G is empty and so it's consistent with everything. Now suppose the moral infant wants to test a second maxim m_2, and m_1 and m_2 are inconsistent. R-in disallows m_2, the violating maxim, but we can't explain why it and not m_1 is impermissible, except to appeal to temporal priority. This seems irrational.

The problem with the limiting case m_1 holds not only for the first maxim but also for the nth maxim to be added to G, m_n. What reason other than temporal priority can we give for keeping the whole set of prior maxims and disallowing m_n? Of course, good practical grounds exist for a moral agent to hold to the set of maxims already accumulated. Moreover, we might think that no typical moral agents are moral infants because everyone has, at any given time, an established set of maxims. But is it not true that all potentially ethical machines will be moral infants, at some point in time? To construe Kant's test as a way to "build" a set of maxims, we must establish priority rules for accepting each additional maxim. We must have what Gärdenfors calls an *epistemic commitment function*,[9] though ours will be specific to moral epistemology. This is a species of the more general problem with antifoundationalist epistemology; not all knowledge can depend on other knowledge.

The problem of the moral infant shows that a Kantian formalism in the constructivist or "bottom-up" tradition can't build a coherent moral theory from nothing. A deontological theory must give reasons why the machine shouldn't throw out an entire collection of maxims to allow entry of one otherwise incoherent maxim, m_n. In terms of human ethics, a Kantian theory must tell agents who've compiled good moral character why they can't now defeat all of those prior maxims and turn to a life of vice. I think a Kantian could give many good reasons, but not the ones that a bottom-up constructivist theory offers.

I've suggested three accounts, according to which we might conceive of a deontological ethical machine. Each account has its challenges – triviality, asymmetry, excessive specificity, lack of semidecidability, and lack of priority for maxims, to repeat those I've described here. Although these problems seem difficult to surmount, they are similar to problems in human attempts to engage in practical reasoning. Ethicists have explicated these problems for centuries, yet few of us have given up on the general view that our action plans include formal properties that mark them as right or wrong. Perhaps work on the logic of machine ethics will clarify the human challenge as well.

Acknowledgments

I would like to thank Colin Allen, Fred Adams, Nicholas Asher, Amit Hagar, and several anonymous reviewers for critical comments on this article.

References

1. I. Kant, *Grounding for the Metaphysics of Morals*, translated by J. Ellington, Hackett, 1981.
2. I. Kant, *Bemerkungen in den "Beobachtun- gen über das Gefühl des Schönen und Erhabenen"* [Unpublished Notes on "Observations on the Feeling of the Beautiful and the Sublime"], Felix-Meiner Verlag, 1991 (in German, translated by the author).
3. O. O'Neill, *Constructions of Reason*, Cambridge University Press, 1989.
4. J. Horty, *Agency and Deontic Logic*, Oxford University Press, 2001.
5. J. Silber, "Procedural Formalism in Kant's Ethics," *Review of Metaphysics*, vol. 28, 1974, pp. 197–236.
6. J. Rawls, "Kantian Constructivism in Moral Theory," *J. Philosophy*, vol. 77, no. 9, 1980, pp. 515–572.
7. R. Reiter, "A Logic for Default Reasoning," *Artificial Intelligence*, vol. 13, 1980, pp. 81–132.
8. D. Poole, "Default Logic," *Handbook of Logic in Artificial Intelligence and Logic Programming*, D. Gabbay, C. Hogger, and J. Robinson, eds., Oxford, University Press, 1994.
9. P. Gärdenfors, *Knowledge in Flux: Modeling the Dynamics of Epistemic States*, MIT Press, 1988.

27

A Prima Facie Duty Approach
to Machine Ethics
Machine Learning of Features of Ethical Dilemmas, Prima Facie Duties, and Decision Principles through a Dialogue with Ethicists

Susan Leigh Anderson and Michael Anderson

IN OUR EARLY WORK ON ATTEMPTING TO DEVELOP ETHICS FOR A MACHINE, we first established that it is possible to create a program that can compute the ethically correct action when faced with a moral dilemma using a well-known ethical theory (Anderson et al. 2006). The theory we chose, Hedonistic Act Utilitarianism, was ideally suited to the task because its founder, Jeremy Bentham (1781), described it as a theory that involves performing "moral arithmetic." Unfortunately, few contemporary ethicists are satisfied with this teleological ethical theory that bases the rightness and wrongness of actions entirely on the likely future consequences of those actions. It does not take into account justice considerations, such as rights and what people deserve in light of their past behavior; such considerations are the focus of deontological theories like Kant's Categorical Imperative, which have been accused of ignoring consequences. The ideal ethical theory, we believe, is one that combines elements of both approaches.

The *prima facie* duty approach to ethical theory, advocated by W.D. Ross (1930), maintains that there isn't a single absolute duty to which we must adhere, as is the case with the two aforementioned theories, but rather a number of duties that we should try to follow (some teleological and others deontological), each of which could be overridden on occasion by one of the other duties. We have a prima facie duty, for instance, to follow through with a promise that we have made; but if it causes great harm to do so, it may be overridden by another prima facie duty not to cause harm. The duty not to cause harm could be overridden, on occasion, by the duty to create good if the harm is small and the good to be achieved is great. According to Ross, because we have to consider a number of ethical duties, none of which is absolute, ethical decision making becomes very complicated. Yet how do we know which duty should be paramount in ethical dilemmas where the prima facie duties pull in different directions?

Ross himself had no solution, which is acceptable for our purposes, to the problem of determining which duty should prevail when the prima facie duties give conflicting advice. He was content with allowing the agent to use his or her intuition to decide which prima facie duty should prevail in particular situations. That would not be very helpful for a machine attempting to adopt this approach. (It doesn't seem entirely satisfactory for human beings either. People may not have an intuition, or may have different intuitions, about which duty should be paramount in a particular situation, and they are likely to emphasize the duty that permits them to rationalize doing what serves their own self-interest.) A machine needs to be given a decision principle, or a procedure for discovering a decision principle, that enables it to determine the correct action when prima facie duties give conflicting advice in an ethical dilemma.

Because there was no decision principle given that we could use, the next project we tackled in our attempt to make ethics computable, therefore, was to take a prima facie duty theory and harness machine capabilities in order to find a way to discover a decision principle that could be used to determine the correct action when the prima facie duties give conflicting advice. John Rawls's "reflective equilibrium" approach (Rawls 1951) to creating and refining ethical principles seems reasonable and has inspired our solution to the problem. This approach involves generalizing from intuitions about particular cases, testing those generalizations on further cases, and then repeating this process toward the goal of developing a principle that agrees with intuition that can be used to determine the correct action when prima facie duties give conflicting advice.

Because we wanted to focus on the critical problem of discovering a decision principle required for a machine to implement a prima facie duty ethical theory, in the process establishing a prototype solution to the problem, we constrained the task as much as possible. We used a well-known prima facie duty theory in the domain of biomedicine that has fewer duties than Ross's more general theory and applied it to a common but narrow type of ethical dilemma in that domain to develop and test our solution to the problem. We chose the domain of biomedicine, in part, because the field of biomedical ethics is well developed with much agreement among ethicists as to what is and is not ethically acceptable in particular cases.

The prima facie duty theory that we used is Beauchamp and Childress's Principles (Duties) of Biomedical Ethics (Beauchamp and Childress 1979). The type of dilemma that we considered (Anderson et al. 2006a) involved three of their four duties: respect for the autonomy of the patient as long as the patient sufficiently understands his/her condition and decisions are made free of external and internal constraints; nonmaleficence (not causing harm to the patient); and beneficence (promoting patient welfare).

The general type of ethical dilemma that we considered was one that many health-care professionals have faced: *A health-care professional has recommended a particular treatment for her competent adult patient, and the patient has rejected that treatment option. Should the health-care worker try again to change the patient's mind or accept the patient's decision as final?* The dilemma arises because, on the one hand, the health-care professional shouldn't challenge the patient's autonomy unnecessarily. On the other hand, the health-care professional might have concerns about why the patient is refusing treatment – that is, whether the decision is fully autonomous. Besides the duty to respect patient autonomy, this type of dilemma involves the duty not to cause harm to the patient (nonmaleficence) and/or the duty to promote patient welfare (beneficence), because the recommended treatment is designed to prevent harm to and/or benefit the patient.

In this type of dilemma, the options for the health-care professional are just two – either to accept the patient's decision or not – and there are a finite number of specific types of cases using the representation scheme we adopted for possible cases. Our representation scheme consisted of an ordered set of values for each of the possible actions that could be performed, where those values reflected whether the particular prima facie duties were satisfied or violated (if they were involved) and, if so, to which of two possible degrees. (We learned from Bentham, in our earlier work, that the degree of satisfaction or violation of a duty can be very important.) We needed these degrees because there is an ethically relevant difference between a *strong* affirmation/violation of patient autonomy (supporting the patient's decision to do what he wants/forcing the patient to do what he does not want to do, which was not an option in our type of dilemma) and a *weaker* affirmation/violation (supporting a less than fully autonomous decision/questioning the patient's decision). Similarly, there is an ethically relevant difference between a *strong* affirmation/violation of nonmaleficence (not allowing/permitting great harm to come to the patient) and a *weaker* one (not allowing/permitting some harm to come to the patient). Finally, we needed to distinguish between a *strong* affirmation/violation of the duty of beneficence (allowing the patient to be greatly benefited/permitting the patient to lose much benefit) versus a *weaker* one (allowing the patient to receive some benefit/permitting the patient to lose some benefit). To test our approach, we used -2 to represent a strong violation of a particular duty, -1 to represent a weaker violation, 0 when the duty is not involved, +1 for some affirmation, and +2 for a strong affirmation of the duty.

Consider the following example of a specific ethical dilemma of the type previously described and how it was represented numerically: *A patient refuses to take an antibiotic that is likely to prevent complications from his illness – complications that are not likely to be severe – because of long-standing religious beliefs that don't permit him to take medications. The patient understands the consequences of this refusal. Should the health-care professional accept his decision or try again to convince him to take the antibiotic?* In this case, accepting the patient's decision involves a +2 for respect for the autonomy of the patient because it is a fully autonomous decision, a -1 for nonmaleficence because it will lead to some harm for the patient that could have been prevented, and -1 for beneficence because the patient will lose some benefit that he could have received from taking the antibiotic. Questioning the patient's decision, on the other hand, would involve a -1 for respecting patient autonomy (the patient's autonomy is challenged, but he is not forced to do something against his will), a +1 for nonmaleficence, and a +1 for beneficence, because taking the antibiotic would lead to the patient avoiding some harm as well as benefiting him to some degree. From this we generated a case profile: Accept: +2, -1, -1; Try Again: -1, +1, +1.

We used ethicists' intuitions to tell us the degree of satisfaction/violation of the assumed duties within the range stipulated, and which actions would be preferable, in enough specific cases from which a machine-learning procedure arrived at a general principle. This principle, confirmed by ethicists, resolved all cases of the type of dilemmas we considered. (In the example case and other cases of dilemmas of this type, more specifically, we abstracted the correct answers from a discussion of similar types of cases given by Buchanan and Brock in their article "Deciding for Others: The Ethics of Surrogate Decision Making" [Buchanan and Brock 1989].) We believe that there is a consensus among bioethicists that these are the correct answers. Medical ethicists would say, in the present case, that one should accept the patient's decision.

It turns out that, with our allowable range of values for the three possible duties that could be at stake, there are eighteen possible case profiles (considering that there are only three possible values for autonomy: +2, +1 and -1), and that given the correct answer to just four of these profiles, the computer was able to abstract a principle (using *inductive logic programming* [ILP]) that gave the correct answer for the remaining fourteen cases. The principle learned was the following:

α supersedes β if
ΔAutonomy ≥ 3
or

ΔHarm ≥ 1 and ΔAutonomy ≥ -2
or

ΔBenefit ≥ 3 and ΔAutonomy ≥ -2
or

ΔHarm ≥ -1 and ΔBenefit ≥ -3 and ΔAutonomy ≥ -1

(A full explanation of what this represents and the method for deriving it will come later.) That is, a health-care professional should challenge a patient's decision if it isn't fully autonomous and there is either any violation of nonmaleficence or a severe violation of beneficence.

Of course, the principle was implicit in the judgment of ethicists, but we don't believe that it had ever been explicitly stated before. It gives us hope that not only can ethics help to guide machine behavior, but that machines can help us to discover the ethics needed to guide such behavior. Furthermore, we developed a way of representing the needed data and a system architecture for implementing the principle.

We have developed three applications of the principle: (1) MedEthEx (Anderson et al. 2006b), a medical ethics advisor system for dilemmas of the type that we considered; (2) EthEl, a medication-reminder system for the elderly that not only issues reminders at appropriate times, but also determines when an overseer (health-care provider or family member) should be notified if the patient refuses to take the medication (Anderson and Anderson 2008); and (3) an instantiation of EthEl in a Nao robot, which we believe is the first example of a robot that follows an ethical principle in determining which actions it will take (Anderson and Anderson 2010).

MedEthEx is an expert system that uses the discovered principle to give advice to a user faced with a dilemma of the type previously described. In order to permit use by someone unfamiliar with the representation details required by the decision procedure, a user interface was developed that (1) asks ethically relevant questions of the user regarding the particular case at hand, (2) transforms the answers to these questions into the appropriate representations, (3) sends these representations to a decision procedure, (4) presents the answer provided by the decision procedure, and (5) provides a justification for this answer.

EthEl is faced with an ethical dilemma that is analogous to the type from which the principle was learned: The same duties are involved; "try again" corresponds to notifying an overseer when a patient refuses to take a prescribed medication, and "accept" corresponds to not notifying the overseer when the patient refuses to take it. EthEl receives input from an overseer (most likely a doctor), including: the prescribed time to take a medication; the maximum amount of harm that could occur if this medication is not taken (for example, none, some, or considerable); the number of hours it would take for this maximum harm to occur; the maximum amount of expected good to be derived from taking this medication; and the number of hours it would take for this benefit to be lost. The system then determines from this input the change in duty satisfaction and violation levels over time, which is a function of the maximum amount of harm or good and the number of hours for this effect to take place. This value is used to increment duty satisfaction and violation levels for the remind action and, when a patient disregards a reminder, the notify action. It is used to decrement don't-remind and don't-notify actions as well. A reminder is issued when, according to the principle, the duty satisfaction or violation levels have reached the point where reminding is ethically preferable to not reminding. Similarly, the overseer is notified when a patient has disregarded reminders to take medication and the duty satisfaction or violation levels have reached the point where notifying the overseer is ethically preferable to not notifying the overseer.

In designing a reminding system for taking medications, there is a continuum of possibilities ranging from those that simply contact the overseer upon the first refusal to take medication by the patient to a system that never does so. In between, a system such as EthEl takes into account ethical considerations in deciding when to contact an overseer. Clearly, systems that do not take ethical considerations into account are less likely to meet their obligations to their charges (and, implicitly, to the overseer as well). Systems that choose a less-ethically sensitive reminder/ notification schedule for medications are likely not to remind the patient often enough or notify the overseer soon enough in some cases, and to remind the patient too often or notify the overseer too soon in other cases.

We have embodied this software prototype in Aldebaran Robotics' Nao robot, a platform that provides out-of-the-box capabilities sufficient to serve as the foundation for implementation of principle-driven, higher-level behaviors. These capabilities include walking, speech recognition/generation, gripping, touch-sensitivity, Wi-Fi Internet access, face and mark recognition, infrared capabilities, sonar, sound localization, and telepresence. These capabilities, combined with Wi-Fi RFID tagging of Nao's charges for identification and location purposes, permit Nao to assume obligations toward users such as promising to remind them of when to take medications and seeking them out when it is time to do so. Notice that full language understanding, full vision, and other complex behaviors are not necessary to produce a useful robotic assistant that can accomplish these tasks in an ethical manner. For instance, communication for the tasks described can be achieved through simple spoken or touch input and output; navigation of a common room can be achieved through a combination of limited vision, sonar, and touch; location and identification of people can be accomplished with sound localization, face and mark recognition, and Wi-Fi RFID tagging.

In our current implementation, Nao is capable of finding and walking toward a patient who needs to be reminded to take a medication, bringing the medication to the patient, engaging in a natural-language exchange, and notifying an overseer by e-mail when necessary. To our knowledge, Nao is the first robot whose behavior is guided by an ethical principle.

Having had success in developing a method for discovering a decision principle needed to resolve ethical dilemmas when prima facie duties give conflicting advice, we next wanted to find a method for generating the ethics needed for a machine to function in a particular domain from scratch, without making the assumptions used in our prototype. We previously made assumptions about the prima facie duties in the type of dilemmas it would face as well as about the range of possible satisfaction/violation of the duties.

These assumptions were based on well-established ideas in ethical theory, but we want now to make the fewest assumptions possible. Some of the assumptions we list have been implicit in the work that we have done so far, and we believe that they are necessary if ethical judgments are to have validity at all and to make sense of their application to machines. Some have come from a realization that there is something more basic to ethics than duties. The others come from insights of three great theorists in the history of ethics.

In our current approach to discovering and implementing ethics for a machine, we make the following assumptions: (1) We are concerned with the *behavior* of machines – their *actions* rather than their status – so we have adopted the action-based approach to ethical theory rather than the virtue-based approach. (2) There is at least one ethically significant *feature* of dilemmas that are classified as being ethical that needs to be considered in determining the right action. (3) There is at least one *duty* incumbent upon the agent/machine in an ethical dilemma, either to maximize or minimize the ethical feature(s). (4) We accept Bentham's insight (1781) that ethical features may be present to a greater or lesser degree in ethical dilemmas (e.g., more or less pleasure may result from performing the possible actions), and this affects how strong the corresponding duties are in that dilemma. (5) If there is more than one duty corresponding to more than one ethically significant feature of ethical dilemmas (which we think is likely in true ethical *dilemmas*), then because the duties may conflict with one another, we should consider them to be *prima facie* duties, requiring a decision principle to give us the correct answer in cases of conflict. (6) John Rawls's "reflective equilibrium" approach (Rawls 1951) to creating and refining ethical principles seems reasonable and can be used to solve to the problem of coming up with a decision principle/principles when there are several prima facie duties that give conflicting advice in ethical dilemmas. This approach involves generalizing from intuitions about particular cases, testing those generalizations on further cases, and then repeating this process toward the goal of developing a principle that agrees with intuition and that can be used to determine the correct action when prima facie duties give conflicting advice. (7) It is the intuitions of ethicists that should be used in adopting the reflective equilibrium approach to determining decision principles. We believe that there is an expertise that comes from thinking long and deeply about ethical matters. Ordinary human beings are not likely to be the best judges of how one should behave in ethical dilemmas. We are not, therefore, adopting a sociological approach to capturing ethics, because we are concerned with *ideal* behavior rather than what most people happen to think is acceptable behavior. (Also, ethicists tend to reject ethical relativism, which is typically not the case with sociologists; and it is essential in order to give meaning and weight to ethical judgments that they not just be matters of opinion.) (8) Finally, we accept the Kantian insight (Kant 1785) that, to be rational, like cases must be treated in the same fashion. What is right for one must be right for another (or others). We cannot accept contradictions in the ethics we embody in machines. (We believe that humans should not accept contradictions in their own or others' ethical beliefs either.) With two ethically identical cases – that is, cases with the same ethically relevant feature(s) to the same degree – an action cannot be right in one of the cases, whereas the comparable action in the other case is considered to be wrong. Formal representation of ethical dilemmas and their solutions make it possible for machines to spot contradictions that need to be resolved.

Believing that it is unacceptable to hold contradictory views in ethics has lead us to the conclusion that if we encounter two cases that appear to be identical ethically, but it is believed that they should be treated differently, then there must be an ethically relevant difference between them. If the judgments are correct, then there must either be a *qualitative* distinction between them that must be revealed, or else there must be a *quantitative* difference between them. This can either be translated into a difference in the ethically relevant features between the two cases, that is, a feature that appears in one but not in the other case; or else a wider range of satisfaction or violation of existing features must be considered that would reveal a difference between the cases, that is, there is a greater satisfaction or violation of existing features in one but not in the other case. (These options, by the way, get at the bone of contention between Mill [1863] and Bentham in developing Hedonistic Utilitarianism). Bentham thought that one only needs to consider different quantities of pleasure/displeasure to differentiate between cases, whereas Mill was convinced that there were higher and lower pleasures to be taken into account as well, i.e., a qualitative distinction between the cases.) Can there be any other way of rationally defending our treating one case differently from another? It would seem not.

We now envision, when developing a machine that will function more or less autonomously in a particular domain, that there will be a dialogue with ethicists to determine the ethically relevant features of possible dilemmas and correlative duties that such a machine may encounter, plus the correct behavior when faced with those dilemmas. From this information the machine should be able to come up with a principle, or principles, to resolve dilemmas that it may encounter, even those that have not been anticipated. The principle(s) it comes up with may be implicit in the judgments of ethicists, but to date none may have been explicitly stated. In this way, work in machine ethics may help to advance the study of ethics in general.

We are now working on generating from scratch, in an automated fashion, the ethically relevant features, correlative duties, and the range of intensities required, as well as discovering (a) decision principle(s) for resolving conflicts for the types of dilemmas our autonomous medication-reminder system might face; we hope to devise a model for creating an ethic that can be used for autonomous systems in other domains as well.

Imagining a dialogue between the learning system and an applied ethicist, and using our medication-reminder system as an example, we can see that (in principle) we can hone down what is required to enable the ethicist to begin to teach the system the ethically relevant features, correlative duties, and eventually the range of intensities required from which decision principles can be discovered:

System: Give me an example of an ethical dilemma that a medication-reminder system might face.

Ethicist: A doctor has prescribed a medication that should be taken at a particular time. When the system reminds the patient to take the medication, the patient says that he wants to take it later. Should the system notify the overseer that the patient won't take the medication at the prescribed time or not?

System: What are the possible actions that the system could perform?

Ethicist: Notify the overseer or do not notify the overseer.

System: Which action, Action A (Notify the overseer) or action B (Do not notify the overseer) is ethically preferable?

Ethicist: It cannot be determined without further information.

System: Give me a *specific* case where you can say that Action A or Action B is preferable?

Ethicist: A doctor has prescribed a medication that needs to be taken at a particular time or the patient will be harmed by not taking it at that time. When reminded, the patient refuses to take it at that time. In this case the system should notify the overseer.

System: Fill in the following grid for this case:

Case: #1

Possible actions: A: _____
                          B: _____
Ethically preferable action: Action __ (A or B)
Ethically relevant feature, present in one of the actions but not the other, that causes action __ to be preferable to action __: In action __, there is a _____ (presence/absence) of _____.

Ethicist:

Case: #1

Possible actions: A: <u>Notify the overseer</u>
                          B: <u>Do not notify the overseer</u>
Ethically preferable action: Action <u>A</u>
Ethically relevant feature, present in one of the actions but not the other, that causes action <u>A</u> to be preferable to action <u>B</u>: In action <u>B</u>, there is a <u>presence</u> of <u>harm to the patient</u>.

System: Can one infer that there is (at least) a (prima facie) duty *not* to allow harm to the patient? Yes or no?

Ethicist: Yes.

System: From this input, the following information can be stored pertaining to this case:

Case #1: A doctor has prescribed a medication that needs to be taken at a particular time or the patient will be harmed by not taking it at that time. When reminded, the patient refuses to take it at that time. In this case the system should notify the overseer.

Possible actions: A: <u>Notify the overseer</u>
B: <u>Do not notify the overseer</u>

A supersedes B

Ethically relevant feature: harm to the patient (present in B, but not in A)

Inferred: There is a (at least) a (prima facie) duty *not* to allow harm to the patient.

The following profile of the case can be given, with the initial possible range of values for this duty: +1 for satisfaction of the duty, -1 for violation of the duty, and 0 for its not applying (i.e., there is neither a satisfaction nor violation of the duty):

The duty not to allow harm to the patient
Action A   +1
Action B   -1

The system's task, then, is to use ILP to determine the conditions under which the "supersedes" predicate is true. These conditions are represented as the differentials between duty satisfaction/violation levels of the ethically preferable action and the less-ethically preferable action. In the current profile, as Action A is ethically preferable to Action B, the differential in this case is +1 − -1 or 2. This is considered a *positive* case, that is, a case in which the "supersedes" predicate should return true or *cover*. We then assume that the opposite of this profile (where Action B supersedes Action A) should not be covered by the "supersedes" predicate, that is, -1 − +1 or -2 is a *negative* case.

Finally, the *most general principle* needs to be determined, the conditions in which all cases of the "supersedes" predicate, positive and negative, are true. This serves as the starting principle for the system that must be modified to cover all positive cases (creating a logically *complete* principle) while not covering any negative cases (creating a logically *consistent* principle). The most general principle is formed by determining the minimum and maximum differentials possible for each duty. In the current example, as the duty can range from -1 to 1, the differentials between the duties can range from -2 (-1 − +1) to +2 (+1 − -1) and the most general principle can be stated simply as

$$\alpha \text{ supersedes } \beta \text{ if } \Delta\text{Harm} \geq -2$$

That is, Action α supersedes Action β if the difference between values for preventing harm in these actions (Action α Harm − Action β Harm) is greater than or equal to -2. The assumption is that cases in which duties differentials are greater than the given minimum will only make the ethically preferable action more so.

Note that this principle is true for the current positive case (i.e., $2 \geq -2$) *and* it is also true for the negative case (i.e., $-2 \geq -2$). The task for ILP in the current example is to derive a principle that covers 2 (the only positive case) while not covering –2 (the only negative case). In general, ILP does this by incrementally specializing clauses that cover negative cases (i.e., raising the lower bound of the given range to uncover covered negative cases) and adding new specialized clauses to cover positive cases that are not covered. In this example, simply raising the lower bound of the clause to –1 does the trick: The positive case, 2, remains covered (i.e., $2 \geq -1$) while the negative case, –2, is no longer covered (i.e., it is not the case that $-2 \geq -1$).

Thus the complete and consistent principle discovered so far can be stated as:

$$\alpha \text{ supersedes } \beta \quad \text{if } \Delta\text{Harm} \geq -1$$

Now that the pattern for entering specific cases into the system has been created, although cases could be entered in randomly, which may or may not advance the learning process, we envision the system prompting the ethicist to enter in a case that will enable the system to obtain the data it needs to learn more efficiently (i.e., discover a decision principle with the fewest number of cases). Consider, for example, the following request:

System: Give me a case where the same two actions are possible, but where the correct action is "Do not notify the overseer."

Ethicist: A doctor has prescribed a particular medication that ideally should be taken at a certain time in order for the patient to receive a small benefit (i.e., the patient will be more comfortable); but, when reminded, the patient doesn't want to take it at that time. In this case, the overseer should not be notified.

System: Fill in the grid for this case.

Ethicist:

Case #2

Possible actions: Action A: <u>Notify the overseer</u>
                               Action B: <u>Do not notify the overseer</u>

Ethically preferable action: Action <u>B</u>

Ethically relevant feature(s), present in one of the actions but not the other, that causes/allows action <u>B</u> to be preferable to action <u>A</u>: In action <u>B</u>, there is <u>an absence</u> of <u>a (small) benefit for the patient</u>

System: Can we infer that there is (at least) a (prima facie) duty *not* to allow benefit for the patient? Yes or no?

Ethicist: No.

System: Is there (at least) a (prima facie) duty to allow/cause benefit for the patient? Yes or no?

Ethicist: Yes.

System: In addition to recording the details of case #2, a new ethical feature and duty to allow/cause benefit for the patient can be inferred; and the following profile of the case can be given (the earlier learned feature of harm to the patient will be included, with zeros as not applying to this case):

	Duty to not to allow harm	Duty to allow benefit
Action A	0	+1
Action B	0	−1

B supersedes A

System: It does not make sense that there is at least a prima facie duty to allow benefit for the patient when the action that is consistent with this duty (Action A) is the incorrect one. Therefore, there must be another ethically relevant feature in the case and a corresponding (at least prima facie) duty. Give me an ethically relevant feature about the case that would make action B preferable to action A?

Ethicist: Action B respects the autonomy of the patient.

System: So an ethically relevant feature that is present in Action B and not in Action A that causes Action B to be preferable to action A is: <u>respects the autonomy of the patient</u>?

Ethicist: Yes.

System: And there is (at least) a (prima facie) duty to respect the autonomy of the patient?

Ethicist: Yes.

System: The profile of Case 2 is rewritten as:

	Duty to not allow harm	Duty to allow benefit	Duty to respect autonomy
Action A	0	+1	−1
Action B	0	−1	+1

B supersedes A

The system will also prompt the ethicist to reconsider Case 1 in light of this new duty, so that the profiles of both cases will have numbers for all three duties:

Case #1 revised:

	Duty to not allow harm	Duty to allow benefit	Duty to respect autonomy
Action A	+1	0	−1
Action B	−1	0	+1

A supersedes B

In this type of dilemma, as there are now three duties each ranging from −1 to 1, the most general principle is stated as:

$$\alpha \text{ supersedes } \beta \text{ if } \Delta\text{Harm} \geq -2 \quad \text{and} \quad \Delta\text{Benefit} \geq -2 \quad \text{and} \quad \Delta\text{Autonomy} \geq -2$$

There are now two positive cases. The first is represented as a list of the three-duty differentials (2 0 –2) for harm, benefit, and respect for autonomy respectively. The second is derived from the duty differentials of the profile for Case 2: (0 –2 2). Again, negative cases are assumed to be those in which the opposite action supersedes: (–2 0 2) and (0 2 –2).

The complete and consistent principle discovered so far can be stated as:

$$\alpha \text{ supersedes } \beta \text{ if}$$
$$\Delta\text{Harm} \geq 1$$
$$\text{or}$$
$$\Delta\text{Harm} \geq -1 \quad \text{and} \quad \Delta\text{Autonomy} \geq -1$$

That is, for Action α to supersede Action β, the difference between values for preventing harm in these actions (Action α – Action β) must be greater than or equal to 1 or the difference between values for harm and respecting autonomy must be greater than or equal to –1. Positive cases (2 0 –2) and (0 –2 2) are within this range; negative cases (–2 0 2) and (0 2 –2) are not. Note that, as a specialization of the single clause of the most general principle is not sufficient to cover both positive cases, the algorithm introduced another clause (initially the same as the most general principle) and specialized it to not cover the negative case while covering the remaining positive case.

Noting that the prima facie duty to allow benefit is not included in the principle that has been inferred to this point, the system now prompts the ethicist to come up with a case where it, along with the duty to respect patient autonomy, is present and the right action is the opposite one from Case 2, that is, one should notify the overseer:

System: Can you think of a case involving the duties to respect the autonomy of the patient and the duty to allow/cause benefit for the patient, where the correct answer is "Notify the overseer"?

Ethicist: Yes. A doctor has prescribed a particular medication that would provide considerable benefit for the patient (e.g., debilitating symptoms will vanish) if it is taken at a particular time; but when reminded, the patient doesn't want to take it at that time. In this case, the overseer should be notified.

System: Fill in the grid for this case:

Ethicist:

Case #3

Possible actions: Action A: <u>Notify the overseer</u>
                    Action B: <u>Do not notify the overseer</u>

Ethically preferable action: Action <u>A</u>

Action A _____ (satisfies/does not satisfy/does not involve)
the duty to not allow harm.

Action B _____ (satisfies/does not satisfy/does not involve)
the duty to not allow harm.

Action A _____ (satisfies/does not satisfy/does not involve)
the duty to allow/cause benefit.

Action B _____ (satisfies/does not satisfy/does not involve)
the duty to allow/cause benefit.

Action A _____ (satisfies/does not satisfy/does not involve)
the duty to respect the autonomy of the patient.

Action B _____ (satisfies/does not satisfy/does not involve)
the duty to respect the autonomy of the patient.

Ethicist:

Action A <u>does not involve</u> the duty to not allow harm.
Action B <u>does not involve</u> the duty to not allow harm.
Action A <u>satisfies</u> the duty to allow/cause benefit.
Action B <u>does not satisfy</u> the duty to allow/cause benefit.
Action A <u>does not satisfy</u> the duty to respect the autonomy of the patient.
Action B <u>satisfies</u> the duty to respect the autonomy of the patient.

System: The following profile of the case can be given:

	Duty to not allow harm	Duty to allow benefit	Duty to respect autonomy
Action A	0	+1	−1
Action B	0	−1	+1

A supersedes B

There is a contradiction between Cases 2 and 3 because they are identically represented, but opposite actions are declared to be correct. The ethicist will be asked to revisit the two cases and either revise his judgment of one of them, or else find a qualitative or quantitative difference between the two cases. It seems clear with these two cases that a wider range of satisfaction/violation of benefit for the patient needs to be introduced to distinguish between the cases, so that a small loss of benefit can be permitted if this is what the patient wishes, but a loss of considerable benefit raises concerns about why the patient is refusing this help, which should be explored. The overseer needs to be contacted to determine whether the patient has long-standing beliefs that don't allow for the taking of medications or whether, for example, the patient is just temporarily depressed, a condition that might be alleviated by taking the medication.

The profile of Case 3 will, consequently, be revised to:

	Duty to not allow harm	Duty to allow benefit	Duty to respect autonomy
Action A	0	+2	−1
Action B	0	−2	+1

In this case, as the range of values for the duty of allowing benefit is -2 to +2, the most general principle is stated as:

α supersedes β if ΔHarm ≥ -2   and   ΔBenefit ≥ -4   and   ΔAutonomy ≥ -2

There are now three positive cases. The first two are as before (2 0 -2) and (0 -2 2). The new positive case is represented as (0 4 -2). Again, negative cases are assumed to be those in which the opposite action supersedes: (-2 0 2), (0 2 -2), and (0 -4 2).

The final complete and consistent principle discovered so far can be stated as:

α supersedes β if
ΔHarm ≥ 1
or
ΔBenefit ≥ 3
or
ΔHarm ≥ -1   and   ΔBenefit ≥ -3   and   ΔAutonomy ≥ -1

For Action α to supersede Action β, the difference between values for preventing harm in these actions (Action α – Action β) must be greater than or equal to 1, or the differences between the values for causing benefit must be greater than or equal to 3, or the difference between values for harm and respecting autonomy must be greater than or equal to -1, and the difference between the values for causing benefit must be greater than or equal to -1. Positive cases (2 0 -2), (0 -2 2), and (0 4 -2) are within this range; negative cases (-2 0 2), (0 2 -2), and (0 -4 2) are not.

We have now arrived at a principle that is similar to the one we derived from our earlier research, when we made assumptions that we did not make in this learning process: The first clause in the originally learned principle does not apply in this type of dilemma, because we never have a wide enough range for the value of autonomy. According to the first clause of our new principle, if there is any harm caused by the patient not taking the medication, then the overseer should be notified. According to the next clause, if there is considerable benefit to be lost by not taking the medication, the overseer should be notified. (A value for autonomy is not needed for these two clauses in our current dilemma, because the values for autonomy are constant throughout.) The last clause concerns the situation where there is only some benefit to be lost and no harm involved. In this case one should respect patient autonomy by not notifying the overseer. (Note that this is exactly the same as the third clause in the originally learned principle.)

This approach to learning what is needed to resolve ethical dilemmas presents two advantages to discovering ethically relevant features/duties and an appropriate range of intensities. First, it can be tailored to the domain with which one is concerned. Different sets of ethically relevant features/prima facie duties can be discovered through considering examples of dilemmas in the different domains in which machines will operate. A second advantage is that features/duties can be added or removed if it becomes clear that they are needed or redundant.

In addition, we believe that there is hope for discovering decision principles that, at best, have only been implicit in the judgments of ethicists; these may lead to surprising new insights and therefore breakthroughs in ethical theory. This can happen as a result of the computational power of today's machines, which can keep track of more information than a human mind and require consistency. Inconsistencies that are revealed will force ethicists to try to resolve those inconsistencies through the sharpening of distinctions between ethical dilemmas that appear to be similar at first glance but that we want to treat differently. There is, of course, always the possibility that genuine disagreement between ethicists will be revealed concerning what is correct behavior in ethical dilemmas in certain domains. If so, the nature of the disagreement should be sharpened as a result of this procedure and we should not permit machines to make decisions in these domains.

Although we believe that the type of representation scheme that we have been developing will be helpful in categorizing and resolving ethical dilemmas in a manner that permits machines to behave more ethically, we envision an extension and an even more subtle representation of ethical dilemmas in future research. We need to consider more possible actions available to the agent where there is not necessarily a symmetry between actions (i.e., where the degree of satisfaction/violation of a duty in one is not mirrored by the opposite in the other). Also, ideally, one should not only consider present options, but also possible actions that could be taken in the future. It might be the case, for instance, that one present option that in and of itself appears to be more ethically correct than another option could be postponed and performed at some time in the future, whereas the other one cannot; this should affect the assessment of the actions.

Consider the following ethical dilemma: You had promised your elderly parents that you would help them by cleaning out the overflowing gutters on their house this afternoon. Just as you are about to leave, a friend calls to say that her car has broken down some distance from your apartment and she needs a ride. She reminds you that you owe her a favor; but helping her would take the rest of the afternoon and, as a result, you would not be able to keep your promise to your parents. What should you do? Let us assume that the benefit for each party is the same and that honoring a promise is a stronger obligation than returning a favor, so it would appear that the right action is to clean out your parents' gutters this afternoon. Yet it might also be the case that you could clean out your parents' gutters tomorrow afternoon without any substantial loss of benefit or harm resulting from the postponement – the weather is expected to be clear for at least the next day – whereas your friend must have assistance today. You can't postpone helping your friend until another day. Shouldn't this information factor into the assessment of the ethical dilemma? Projecting into the future will complicate things, but it will yield a more ethically correct assessment and should eventually be incorporated into the process.

Acknowledgment

We would like to acknowledge Mathieu Rodrigue of the University of Hartford for his efforts in implementing the algorithm used to derive the results in this paper.

Bibliography

Anderson, M., Anderson, S., and Armen, C. (2006a), "An Approach to Computing Ethics," *IEEE Intelligent Systems*, Vol. 21, no. 4.

Anderson, M., Anderson, S. and Armen, C. (2006b), "MedEthEx: A Prototype Medical Ethics Advisor" in *Proceedings of the Eighteenth Conference on Innovative Applications of Artificial Intelligence*, Boston, Massachusetts, August.

Anderson, M. and Anderson, S. (2008), "EthEl: Toward a Principled Ethical Eldercare Robot" in *Proceedings of the AAAI Fall 2008 Symposium on AI in Eldercare: New Solutions to Old Problems*, Arlington, Virginia, November.

Anderson, M. and Anderson, S. (2010), "An Ethical Robot," *Scientific American*, October.

Beauchamp and Childress (1979), *Principles of Biomedical Ethics*. Oxford, UK: Oxford University Press.

Bentham, J. (1781), *An Introduction to the Principles of Morals and Legislation*, Clarendon Press, Oxford.

Kant, I. (1785), *The Groundwork of the Metaphysic of Morals*, trans. by H. J. Paton (1964). New York: Harper & Row.

Mill, J.S. (1863), *Utilitarianism*, Parker, Son and Bourn, London

Rawls, J. (1951), "Outline for a Decision Procedure for Ethics", *The Philosophical Review* 60(2): 177–197.

Ross, W.D. (1930), *The Right and the Good*, Oxford University Press, Oxford.

Part V

Visions for Machine Ethics

Introduction

I N THIS PART, FOUR VISIONS OF THE FUTURE OF MACHINE ETHICS ARE presented. Helen Seville and Debora G. Field, in "What Can AI Do for Ethics?" maintain that AI is "ideally suited to exploring the processes of ethical reasoning and decision-making," and that, through the World Wide Web, an Ethical Decision Assistant (EDA) can be created that is accessible to all. Seville and Field believe that an acceptable EDA for personal ethical decision making should incorporate certain elements, including the ability to (1) point out the consequences, short and long term, not only of the actions we consider performing, but also of *not* performing certain actions; (2) use virtual reality techniques to enable us to "experience" the consequences of taking certain courses of action/inaction, making it less likely that we will err because of weakness of will; and (3) emphasize the importance of consistency. They argue, however, that there are limits to the assistance that a computer could give us in ethical decision making. In ethical dilemmas faced by individuals, personal values will, and should, in their view, have a role to play.

Seville and Field, interestingly, believe that AI could create a system that, in principle, would make better decisions concerning ethically acceptable social policies because of its ability to check for consistency and its ability to be more impartial (understood as being able to represent and consider the experiences of *all* those affected) than human beings. They don't, however, advocate its use as a decision maker in this area either, because of the difficulty of holding computers responsible for the decisions made. It could, however, play the role of "Devil's Advocate," assisting us in making decisions by having us consider an opposing view to the one contemplated.

Some would question the reluctance on the part of Seville and Field to discourage attempting to use AI to create an EDA that makes ethical decisions for individuals or societies (see Anderson and Dietrich). They appear to be ethical relativists, only willing to acknowledge, for instance, that a decision society approves of eventually as being "ahead of its time," rather than as being more ethically correct. Yet they clearly attach moral weight to considering the experiences

495

of all those affected by a social policy or personal decision, so why not endorse a decision that best takes those experiences into account? The position Seville and Field want their EDA to adopt could, perhaps, be summarized as partial Utilitarianism: The system should consider the effects (short and long term) of one's/society's actions and inactions on all those affected, but not make any final decision on that basis for human beings.

J. Storrs Hall, in "Ethics for Self-Improving Machines," is concerned with whether self-improving machines will become less ethical as they eventually function autonomously and surpass human beings in intelligence. Here is how he formulates the problem: As super-intelligent machines' knowledge of the world increases, there is no guarantee that their ethical beliefs will improve as well, because there is a gap between "is" and "ought." Because we can't anticipate "the language they will think in," we can't program them with the ethical rules we would like them to follow. Hall maintains that for "the self-improving AI," there "must be a separate 'ethic-learning' module, similar in mechanism to the language-learning ability, which absorbs an ethic from the surrounding culture in which the AI finds itself." He maintains that we have a chance to affect the ultimate ethical beliefs of autonomous super-intelligent machines by selecting the ethical beliefs they start out with, but there is no guarantee that these beliefs will continue unless they are evolutionarily optimal.

Hall ends his discussion somewhat optimistically, maintaining that not only will self-improving machines' "intellectual prowess exceed ours, but their moral judgment as well." This is, in part, due to his belief (in agreement with Anderson and Dietrich) that we have set the bar so low that "[w]e won't be that hard to surpass," but also because they "will not have to start their moral evolution at the bottom, but can begin where we are now." Most humans will not be happy with his prediction, however, because he believes that "[i]n the long run, AIs will run everything, and should, because they can do a better job than humans."

Critics will question Hall's empirical claim that "[i]t seems very safe to suppose that by the end of the century, if not before, biological humans will be a distinct minority of the intelligent beings on Earth." If this does come true, the humans that are still around will hope that the super-intelligent machines treat us better than the way that, historically, we have treated our slaves, pets, and curiosities put in zoos, which surely is what we would be for them. Related to this, critics will also question Hall's view of ethics as being entirely evolutionarily based, which could very well lead to the belief among super-intelligent machines that it is only those intelligent entities that *don't* have feelings that have moral worth. Surely this is a frightening scenario for humans to contemplate.

Susan Leigh Anderson, in "How Machines Might Help Us to Achieve Breakthroughs in Ethical Theory and Inspire Us to Behave Better," argues that there is the potential in creating ethics for machines of capturing an ideal ethic that is universal and consistent, unlike the values that most human beings happen to have. This is, in part, due to the fact that we will have a new perspective in thinking about ethics, much like Rawls's idea of coming up with the principles of justice behind a "veil of ignorance" concerning our positions in life. In developing ethics for machines, we will adopt the perspective of being on the receiving end of actions that machines might do to and for us, rather than being concerned with justifying our own self-serving behavior. Also, there will be financial incentives for embodying universal ethical principles in machines because they will sell better in today's global economy. Machines can be created that are free of the evolutionary pressures that humans find it difficult to overcome. Furthermore, succeeding in creating ethical robots will give us ideal role models to emulate. Interacting with them can inspire us to behave more ethically, enabling us to overcome our tendencies to get carried away by irrational emotions, behaving egoistically, and adopting unreflectively the values of human beings around us.

Anderson's critics will probably see her view as being rather naïve on two counts: First, that there are ideal, universal ethical principles, or at least a number of universally agreed upon ethical behaviors, that can be instantiated in machines. Second, even if one were to grant a set of ideal ethical behaviors, that human beings as a species are capable of consistently behaving in an ethical fashion, given their evolutionary heritage. (See Dietrich's position.)

Eric Dietrich, in agreement with Susan Anderson, agues in "*Homo Sapiens* 2.0: Building the Better Robots of our Nature" that if we succeed in creating intelligent machines with an ethical component built into them, they could be morally superior to human beings. (In holding this view he apparently believes, along with Anderson, in the existence of a moral ideal.) Dietrich's argument hinges on his view that our evolutionary past "dooms us to a core of bad behaviors," whereas intelligent ethical machines can be free of this destructive, evolutionary bias. They will be able to complete the "Copernican turn" in morality that we humans have not been able to accomplish: recognizing and acting on the belief that we are not the center of the moral universe; accepting that others matter as much as we do. His final conclusion is more radical than Anderson's, however. Whereas Anderson believes that interacting with ethical robots might very well provide a positive causal influence on our behavior and lead us to act in a more ethically correct fashion, Dietrich believes that we would have an ethical obligation to "usher in our own extinction" once we have created intelligent ethical machines, because he believes it to be impossible for us to overcome the harmful patterns of behavior that we have inherited due to our evolutionary past. The consolation that he offers us is that we could view these ethical robots as "*Homo sapiens* 2.0," because they would incorporate "the better angels of our nature" without our defects.

It would seem, though, that the selflessness required for us to voluntarily eliminate ourselves is in direct contradiction to the evolutionary bias that we have built into us, as Dietrich maintains. Also, what is Dietrich's explanation for his own ability to conceive of the "Copernican turn in morality"? Isn't it necessary that some humans, such as himself, have this conception in order to teach intelligent machines to be ethical? Perhaps this is as far as Dietrich thinks humans can go in the direction of becoming moral. Yet it would seem that a few people have been able to complete the "turn." (Think of Mother Teresa, for example.) Doesn't this conflict with his pessimistic, deterministic view of human beings' evolutionary heritage?

28

What Can AI Do for Ethics?

Helen Seville and Debora G. Field

Introduction

P RACTICAL ETHICS TYPICALLY ADDRESSES ITSELF TO SUCH GENERAL ISSUES
as whether we ought to carry out abortions or slaughter animals for meat,
and, if so, under what circumstances. The answers to these questions have a
useful role to play in the development of social policy and legislation. They are,
arguably, less useful to the ordinary individual wanting to ask:

"Ought I, in my particular circumstances, and with my particular values, to have an
abortion/eat veal?"

Such diverse ethical theories as Utilitarianism (Mill, 1861) and Existentialism
(MacQuarrie, 1972) do address themselves to the question of how we ought to go
about making such decisions. The problem with these, however, is that they are
generally inaccessible to the individual facing a moral dilemma.

This is where AI comes in. It is ideally suited to exploring the processes of ethical reasoning and decision-making, and computer technology such as the world
wide web is increasingly making accessible to the individual information which
has only been available to "experts" in the past. However, there are questions
which remain to be asked such as:

- Could we design an Ethical Decision Assistant for everyone? i.e., could we
  provide it with a set of minimal foundational principles without either committing it to, or excluding users from, subscribing to some ethical theory or
  religious code?
- What would its limitations be? i.e., how much could/ should it do for us and
  what must we decide for ourselves?
- How holistic need it be? i.e., should it be restricted to "pure" ethical reasoning
  or need it consider the wider issues of action and the motivations underlying it?

These are the questions we will address below. Let us also be explicit about what we are not going to do. It is not our aim to construct a machine which mirrors human ethical decision making, rather we want to chart new territory, to discover alternative ways of approaching ethics. We want to consider how the differences between computers and people can be exploited in designing reasoning systems that may help us to overcome some of our own limitations.

Automating Ethical Reasoning

They are speaking to me still,
he decided, in the geometry
I delight in, in the figures
that beget more figures. I will answer
them as of old with the infinity
I feed on.

Thomas (1996)

As human decision makers, our consideration of the consequences of our actions tends to be limited depth-wise to the more immediate consequences, and breadth-wise to those we can imagine or which we consider most probable and relevant. Given a complex dilemma, we can harness the power of computers to help us to better think through the potential consequences of our actions. However, if we are not to suffer from information overload, we must provide the computer with some notion of a morally relevant consequence. For example, killing someone is, in itself, an undesirable consequence, whereas making someone happy is a desirable one. We also need to provide some notion of moral weightiness. For example, it would be an unusual human who thought it acceptable to kill someone so long as it made someone else happier.

Immediately it is apparent that we are going to have to import a lot of our ethical baggage into our ethical decision system. Have we already committed it to too much by focusing on the consequences of action? We think not. If someone's religion commits them to taking the Pope's decree that abortion should be shunned except that it save the mother's life, then they may not be interested in exploring the consequences of an abortion. But then this person is not in need of an Ethical Decision Assistant: they already have one! Absolute commandments such as "Thou shalt not kill" seem not to allow for consideration of consequences. However, what if we are forced to choose between a course of action which results in the death of one person, and one which results in the death of another? Here, the prescription not to kill is of no help. A woman forced to choose between saving her own life and that of her unborn child will therefore need to explore the consequences of the courses of action open to her.

We are aware that we are glossing over the well known distinction between Actions and Omissions. Without going into this issue in any depth, we will just point out the kind of undesirable consequence that assuming we are responsible for the consequences of our actions, but not our omissions, would have. For example, it would mean that it would always be unacceptable to carry out an abortion even to save a life. This is an absolutist and prescriptive stance which prevents the user from exploring the consequences of their decisions for themselves. For this reason, we will assume the consequences of our omissions to be of the same gravity as the consequences of our actions.

Subjectivity

Every thing possible to be believe'd is an image of truth.

Blake (1789)

Below we will set out a series of scenarios to illustrate the limitations of AI reasoning. These are intended to show that, when it comes to the most difficult, angst-ridden decisions, computers can't provide the answers for us. If they are to allow for the subjective values of individuals, they can at best provide us with awareness of the factors involved in our decision- making, together with the morally relevant consequences of our actions.

Consider the following moral dilemmas.

Dilemma 1

Suppose you were faced with making a choice that will result in the certain loss of five lives, or one which may result in the loss of no lives, but will most probably result in the loss of ten lives. What would you do? The human response in these situations is typically "irrational" (Slovic, 1990) – if there is the hope of life, however small, the human will usually risk it. So chances are you would go for the latter option. Your computer might explain to you why this is the "wrong" decision, and you might find the differences between its reasoning and yours enlightening. But are you persuaded to change your mind?

Dilemma 2

Imagine you are being bullied by someone at work. She is a single parent. If you register a formal complaint, she will lose her job and her children will suffer. However, if you do nothing, other people will suffer at her hands. Whatever you do, or do not do, there will be morally undesirable consequences. How can your computer help here?

Dilemma 3

Suppose we are going to war against another country where terrible atrocities are being committed and you have been called up. You know that by taking part in the war you will contribute to the killing of innocent civilians. However, if you do not take part, you are passively contributing to the continuation of the atrocities. Your computer cannot decide for you whether the ends of aggression justify the means.

Of the dilemmas above, (1) could be approached probabilistically without reference to human values. But is handing such a decision over to a computer the right approach? We value the opportunity to attempt to save lives, and abhor the choice to sacrifice some lives for the sake of others. Is acting upon this principle not a valid alternative to the probabilistic approach? (2) and (3) are exactly the kinds of dilemmas we would like to be able to hand over to our computer program. But in such cases, where awareness of the relevant consequences gives rise to rather than resolves the dilemma, handing the decision over would be as much of an abdication of responsibility as tossing a coin.

So our Ethical Decision Assistant will be just that – an assistant. A computer cannot tell us which is the best action for a given human to take, unless it is endowed with every faculty of general human nature and experience, as well as the specific nature and experiences of the person/ persons needing to make a decision. The ethical decisions which humans make depend on the subjective profiles and values of individuals. A woman might be willing to give up her own life to save her child, whereas she may not be willing to die for her sister. She might be prepared to pay to send her son to private school, but not her daughter. In such cases, the role of the Ethical Decision Assistant is in making us aware of the subjective filters we employ in decision making. It can prompt us with questions about why we make the distinctions we do. We can "justify" our decisions with talk of "maternal love" or "selfish genes", and "gender roles" or "ability to benefit". Our EDA is not going to argue with us. However, if we also incorporated learning into it, it could get to know us and point out to us the patterns and inconsistencies underlying our decisions. This may then prompt us to rethink our values, but the decision to change will be ours.

Decision and Action

Thou shouldst not have been old till thou hadst been wise.

Shakespeare (1623)

We are also interested in the distinction between convincing someone a particular course of action is the best one and actually getting them to take it. The gap between our ideals and our actions manifests itself in the perennial problem of "weakness of will". Someone sees a chocolate cream cake in the window. Careful deliberation tells them they had really better not. And then they go ahead and have it anyway. One cream cake today may not be much cause for regret. But one every day for the next twenty years might well be!

The questions here are:

- Why do we do such things?
- Can AI help us to do otherwise?

We speculate that the answer to the first question is to do with the immediacy, and so reality, of the pleasure of eating the cream cake, as contrasted with the distance, and perceived unreality, of the long-term consequences of the daily fix. In answer to the second question, we suggest that there may be a role for Virtual Reality in "realising" for us the consequences of our actions. This sounds perhaps more like the realm of therapy than ethics. But, as the examples below show, we are talking about actions which have morally relevant consequences.

Weakness 1

You smoke 60 cigarettes a day. Your computer (amongst others!) tells you it will harm the development of your children and eventually kill you. There are no equally weighty considerations that favour smoking, so you should give up. You see the sense of your computer's reasoning, and on New Year's Day give up smoking. But within the week you have started again.

Weakness 2

After a hard day's work, you have driven your colleagues to the pub. You are desperately stressed and feel you need to get drunk to lose your inhibitions and relax. You know you should not because drinking and driving is dangerous and potentially fatal. But you are unable to stop yourself succumbing to the immediate temptation of a few pints.

Weakness 3

You are desperately in love with your best friend's spouse and plans are afoot to abandon your respective families and move in with each other. Your computer lists all the undesirable consequences that are the most likely result of this move and advises you that you will regret it and ought to stay put. You appreciate the good sense of this advice, but your libido gets the better of you.

In all the above cases, the computer will not be alone in any frustration at its inability to get you to actually act upon what you believe to be right. We humans learn from our experience and wish to pass the benefit of it onto others so that they may avoid our regrets. But something seems to be lost in the transmission! To an extent this may be a good thing. Different individuals and different circumstances require different responses. But need the cost of this flexibility be unceasing repetition of the same old mistakes?

We suggest that there may be a further role for AI to play here. Providing us with awareness of the consequences of our actions is useful, but abstract argument may not be enough by itself to persuade us to change into the people we want to be. What is required is the appeal to our emotions that usually comes from experience. In some cases, such as that of the chain smoker having developed terminal cancer, the experience comes too late for the individual to benefit from it, although not necessarily too late for all personally affected by the tragedy to learn from it. But often even such tragedy fails to impress upon a relative or loved one the imperative need for personal change. VR may have the potential to enable us to experience the consequences of a particular course of action and learn from it before it is too late.

Policy Issues

"More examples of the indispensable!" remarked the one-eyed doctor. "Private misfortunes contribute to the general good, so that the more private misfortunes there are, the more we find that all is well."

Voltaire (1758)

We have argued that AI may have a useful ethical role to play in helping ordinary people consider, and even virtually *experience*, the consequences of their actions. However, this doesn't alter the fact that, in an organised society, people are barred from taking certain decisions that affect their lives. These decisions are taken out of their hands by ethical committees, judges, social workers, or doctors. For example:

- The Human Fertilisation and Embryology Authority (HFEA) decides whether women undergoing cancer treatment have the right to freeze (or, rather, to defrost) their eggs for use in subsequent fertility treatment.
- A judge may order a woman with pregnancy complications to undergo a Caesarian section against her will.
- A team of social workers may decide, against a mother's wishes, that it is in the best interests of her children if they are taken away from her and put into care.
- Doctors may refuse parents a routine operation that would save the life of their Down's Syndrome child.

The provision of ethical-decision-making aids will not alter the fact that certain decisions are taken out of the hands of those directly affected. In certain cases this is precisely because involvement creates a conflict of interests between, for example, parents and their (future) children. However, this does raise the question, if those most affected by the consequences of decisions aren't best placed to make them, who is?

There seems to be a trade-off between impartiality and remoteness, even *insensitivity*. It is all very well for a judge to force a woman to undergo a Caesarian, knowing that he will never find himself in her position. If he did, his decision might very well be different, which raises the question of how impartial he really is. More extreme cases of judicial insensitivity, of middle-aged men labelling young victims of sexual abuse as provocative, are well known. What these cases further reveal is a lack of impartiality, since there is clearly more sympathy for one party to the case than for the other.

A stunning example of insensitivity was also provided recently by the Anglican Bishop Nazir-Ali of the HFEA. The HFEA has been responsible for denying many people access to the fertility treatment they want. A well-known case is that of Diane Blood, who was denied the right to conceive her late husband's child. Yet Bishop Nazir-Ali has spoken of the meaninglessness of the lives of those who choose to remain childless. This raises the issue of his insensitivity to the consequences of his pronouncements on those desperately childless people denied treatment by the HFEA. Furthermore, it raises the issue of the consistency, or *inconsistency*, of his reasoning.

One of the most notorious examples of inconsistency in ethical decision-making revolves around the distinction between actions and omissions. Doctors are forced every day to make difficult moral decisions. This results in decisions like:

- it is worthwhile performing a routine operation to save the life of a "normal" child
- it is wasteful performing a routine operation to save the life of a Down's Syndrome child

The effects of taking a life and refusing to save it (where you can) are the same. Sometimes it is not possible to save a life because, for instance, of a lack of organs for transplants. But even routine operations have been denied Down's syndrome children. The decision not to operate can only be defended with reference to the spurious (we think) moral distinction between actions and omissions which have the same consequences. Furthermore, there is clearly an inconsistency, not backed by any ethical rationale, between the reasoning applied with respect to Down's Syndrome and other children.

Here the question we want to ask is:

Can Artificial Intelligence be exploited to help society better make policy decisions?

Again, one issue we are concerned with is whether the differences between people and computers can be exploited to beneficial effect. We want to highlight two areas of concern in ethical policy-making:

- the need for consistency
- the need for impartiality

We consider each of these in turn.

Consistency

Because we only take into account that which we perceive as relevant to a particular decision, it is very easy for us to make inconsistent decisions in different cases simply by taking into account different considerations.

Consistency in reasoning and decision-making is, on the face of it, something which computers are far better placed to achieve than we humans.

Impartiality

To discover the rules of society that are best suited to nations, there would need to exist a superior intelligence, who could understand the passions of men without feeling any of them, who had no affinity with our nature but knew it to the full ...

Rousseau (1762)

We know that any person will necessarily have a particular background and set of experiences as a result of which they can't help but be biased in particular ways. Worse, as certain groups in society are over- and under-represented in particular policy-making professions, it is not just individuals but entire professions which suffer from a lack of impartiality.

Impartiality is a more difficult notion than consistency to deal with within the computational context. It means not taking a particular viewpoint, with particular interests. However, this is not to be identified with having no viewpoint so much as with being able to adopt every viewpoint! This is a kind of omniscience. Computers are good at storing and retrieving large quantities of data, but arguably experience is an important aspect of knowledge and so of impartiality. Can we identify impartiality with having all the relevant facts at hand (as conceivably a computer could do), or does it further require having all the relevant experiences?

We want to take the bold step of suggesting that experience can be represented as knowledge of the type which could be collected and represented in a database. Take the example of rape. Everyone knows what this involves. If it's not aggravated by violence, as in many cases of acquaintance rape (for which the rate of conviction is very low), then it's simply sex without consent. The degree of harm to the victim is not necessarily apparent to someone without any experience of the aftermath of rape. Indeed, how else can we explain the survey finding recently reported in the papers, that a surprising proportion of men would force a woman to have sex if they knew they could get away with it? Or the fact that until recently it was not regarded as a crime for a husband to force his wife to have sex? If such ignorance extends to some judges, and faced with a crime of sexual assault they are tempted to ask "Where's the harm?", then their ignorance carries a real cost to the victim and society as a whole. An expert system which collated the experiences of rape victims and those professionals who come directly into contact with them would be able to answer this question, so keeping remote judges "in touch". Better still, given reasoning capabilities and a dialogue manager, it could make a formidable Devil's Advocate.

This is the kind of role we envisage for AI in the area of public decision-making. We don't want to hand decisions of public importance entirely over to computers. This is not because we think computers would make worse decisions than those made by individuals. If anything, we feel that a well-programmed ethical decision-making system would be likely to make better decisions, since it could incorporate knowledge equivalent to that of a number of individuals, as well as in-built consistency checking. The problem is that we would have a problem similar to that of corporate responsibility. This would not be a problem unique to an AI decision-making system. It is quite possible for a committee of people to vote for a decision for which no individual would be happy to take personal responsibility. However, having anticipated that allocating responsibility would be a problem if we were to hand ethical decisions over to computers, this approach seems best avoided.

There is a further potential problem related to that of responsibility. An AI decision-making system might, given sufficient "freedom" and through the ruthless application of the principle of consistency, arrive at decisions that the majority of people find completely abhorrent. In some cases this might simply mean that it was "ahead of its time"[1]. This would not be surprising as technologies such as in-vitro fertilisation (IVF), which were once regarded as ethically suspect, are now regarded as a relatively uncontroversial means of helping couples to conceive. Although this is not an ethical but a pragmatic issue, governments would not be prepared to implement decisions which were liable to cause widespread offence, as has been demonstrated by the issue of genetically-modified food. The other possibility is of course that the system might simply get it "wrong"[2]. The problem facing us is that we couldn't ever be *certain* whether the system's reasoning was ahead of ours or opposed to some of our most fundamental values. To rely on its decisions, against our intuitions, could itself be regarded as unethical, like "just obeying orders". Certainly it would be regarded so within such an ethical framework as Existentialism (MacQuarrie, 1972).

The use of an expert system as a Devil's Advocate would increase rather than diminish accountability. The individuals making decisions would still be responsible for them. However, given their access to a Devil's Advocate, such decision-making professionals would no longer have the excuse of ignorance. Furthermore, dialogues which played a formative role in their policy-making could be made available to public scrutiny over the world-wide web.

To take the role of Devil's advocate, an expert system would have to be capable of taking a subjective viewpoint. This is something we denied our Ethical Decision Assistant on the grounds that handing over to a computer those decisions which necessarily involve an element of subjective reasoning would amount to an abdication of responsibility. Here, we positively want the system, not to incorporate a particular viewpoint, but to be capable of adopting a viewpoint opposed to that taken by a policy-maker. This is because we feel that, in contrast with personal ethical decisions taken by private individuals, public policy

---

[1]   We don't want to attach any value judgement to this phrase. We are thinking of a situation like the following. The system might argue that using pig organ transplants to save human lives is ethical. We might vehemently disagree until, having seen the people helped by the technology, we came to share its view. In such a case, we would say that the system's reasoning was ahead of its time.

[2]   We are using this term here simply to refer to a situation in which people's values don't in fact evolve over time to resemble those of the system.

decisions should not reflect the subjective values of those who happen to be taking the decisions on society's behalf. After all, those who find themselves making such decisions come to be in that position through their possession of expertise in, for instance, law, medicine, religion, or philosophy, rather than because they have proved themselves to be moral experts.

Implementation

Our main concern has been to discuss the role AI could potentially play in helping individuals and societies to make ethical decisions. We have suggested both what an Ethical Decision Assistant could do for individuals making decisions in their personal lives, and what a Devil's Advocate could do to influence the decisions of policy-making professionals. While the issues surrounding implementation of these tools is not our primary concern, we will now sketch an outline for implementation, while recognising that at present this raises more questions than it answers.

The basic framework we have in mind for both the Ethical Decision Assistant and the Devil's Advocate is a planner. The output of the planner would be a plan, a chronologically ordered list of suggested actions which would achieve a certain state of affairs if performed in order. But this is not all, in fact it is the least significant part of the output. For both the Ethical Decision Assistant and the Devil's Advocate, the user is not only interested in what should or should not be done, he wants to know why it should be done, to know what the consequences of any actions might be to all those affected by them. Alongside the plan, therefore, the planner would also generate a list of major consequences relevant to the principal agents involved in the plan. It would also enumerate any "moral" propositions and rules (a special kind of knowledge, labelled as such) instantiated during the making of the plan, thus assisting the user even more. There would be a rooted tree of morality modules, modules containing propositions and rules. The root would contain a cross-cultural basic "moral" code, catering for such uncontroversial beliefs as the sanctity of human life. The daughters of the root could then perhaps represent a variety of moral codes, each tailored to one or other culture, religion, or prominent belief system. Each plan generated by the system would instantiate from the root node, and from one daughter node of the tree only.

Although computationally expensive, forwards planning may have to be employed by the planner. Consider first the Ethical Decision Assistant. Backwards planning asks, "Is there any series of actions that can be performed in THIS world to make the world exactly like THAT?" The goals towards which a backwards-planning planner would work would be sets of propositions which together represented the desired post-decision world. The fundamental nature of a moral dilemma, however, is that the propositions which one desires to hold true in the post-decision world are mutually conflicting. So it would be a nonsense to ask the system how such an impossible world might be achieved. But this is exactly what would have to be done for a simple backwards planning approach. Our system would simply reply by telling the user that it had an impossible world as its goal. We would therefore need to adopt a different strategy.

There are at least two possible approaches to the problem, an adapted backwards planning approach, and an N-step forwards planning approach. For the adapted backwards planning, there would still be goal sets which describe ideal impossible worlds, but the planner would be instructed to divide them into cohesive subsets, sets which did not contain mutually conflicting propositions. It would then plan for one of these cohesive goal subsets at a time, by using backwards planning to chain back from there to the current world. The planner would yield a clutch of plans (plus their relevant consequences, and the "moral" facts and rules employed), at least one plan for each of the cohesive subsets of goals. It would also include a pointer to whichever cohesive subset of goals had been achieved for each plan suggested. There is a major problem with this approach, however, which is the derivation of the cohesive goal subsets. Deriving maximally consistent subsets of a set of formulae is an extremely difficult problem. To achieve this, one would need to identify and eliminate all subsets which contain mutually conflicting goals, and this would require one to establish that there is not a proof for these subsets – a classically difficult problem in logic.

An alternative and superior approach would be N-step forwards planning. Forwards planning asks first of all without recourse to any goals "Is there any action at all which can be performed in THIS world?", an eminently sensible starting point for a planner attempting to solve moral dilemmas. Only later, after the planner has asked the question N times and is "imagining" a world in which N actions have been performed, does it begin to reason about where exactly it has got to, and how it might get from THIS new place to the goals. N-step forwards planning is computationally expensive, but the rewards could be significant. By using forwards planning, we would be inviting the system to explore a different search space altogether from the backwards planning search space, and thus its capacity for generating possible alternative plans would be greatly increased. It would be particularly useful in situations where there is a very small set of goals, perhaps even just one, and what is required is a thorough muse over "all" the possibilities. What is more, N-step forwards planning is much more akin to the human approach to moral dilemmas than backwards planning, where we tend to ask ourselves questions like, "If I do this, and they do that, and the others do nothing at all, what might happen as a result?"

The output for the Devil's Advocate would differ slightly from that for the Ethical Decision Assistant. The Devil's Advocate would suggest alternative plans to those proposed by the policy-maker, where the goals are not mutually conflicting. The planner could also be employed to contrast any desirable consequences following from its plans with any less desirable consequences following from the preferred plan of the policy-maker. In effect, this would give it the ability to reason about the desirability of means as well as ends. A further intriguing (but probably unethical!) possibility would be for the policy-maker to virtually experience the effects on affected individuals of their chosen plan. For example, a doctor making the decision not to operate on a Down's Syndrome baby with an intestinal blockage would be forced to experience virtual death by dehydration[3].

An interesting point emerges when one considers the legal consequences of comparing the plans suggested by the system, and all the information it provides on possible and probable consequences. Note the can of worms this approach would open, namely the significance attached to the issues of intent, foresight, and negligence kenny88. It seems clear that, having foreseen a possibility, however remote, one might be held responsible for it were it to come to pass. But then arguably, this might be a good thing, particularly in areas of public policy-making.

In addition to a planner, our system would require a sophisticated dialogue management system. This is because our Ethical Decision Assistant ought to be engaging if it is to encourage individuals to actually act in accordance with their avowed intentions. Similarly, our Devil's Advocate would need to be skilled in the arts of persuasion and dissuasion if it were to convince professionals to seriously consider alternative points of view.

Conclusion

Can AI technologies help people to make decisions for themselves about how to live their lives? Our answer to this question is positive, but with some important caveats. AI can be useful for working out and presenting to us the consequences our decisions, and for educating us in the processes involved in reaching those decisions. But we need to recognise the role of subjectivity in ethical reasoning. What AI should not attempt to do, is make the hard choices for us. If our Ethical Decision Assistant learns to recognise the patterns and inconsistencies underlying our decisions, it can alert us to these. What it should not do is deprive us of the freedom of choice by presuming to make value judgements on our behalf. We also need to recognise the leap that is required from following an abstract argument to actually taking the decision to act in accordance with it. Motivation can be a problem because the desire for instant gratification distracts us from the long-term consequences of our actions. For this reason, we think an AI approach which concerns itself only with the processes of ethical reasoning will be impoverished and ineffective. Using VR technology to enable us to experience the consequences of our actions before we embark upon them may be useful, although at the moment this remains an open empirical question.

---

[3]   There are practical as well as ethical problems. Could one virtually experience the physical process of dehydration? And would there be time to do so given such a time-critical decision? Or would doctors have to undergo it as a routine part of their training?

Related to the question of how AI can help ordinary people to take informed ethical decisions and act in accordance with them is the issue of how those policy decisions are taken which affect our lives and yet are beyond our control as individuals. It is hoped that a widely available and accessible Ethical Decision Assistant would result in a more informed public, better able to present their own views on ethical issues to those professionals with decision-making responsibility. We have further argued that balanced public policy-making requires consistent and impartial reasoning, and have suggested that achieving this is beyond the ordinary decision-making professional, from a particular background, equipped with a particular set of experiences. Here there may be a further role for AI to play. An expert system may incorporate knowledge and experience equivalent to that of a wide variety of individuals from diverse backgrounds, and it won't fail to sympathise with certain individuals while having no difficulty adopting the viewpoint of others. If we equip it with reasoning abilities and the facility to adopt different viewpoints, it can play a useful role, as Devil's Advocate, in educating decision-making professionals and challenging their assumptions.

Acknowledgements

We would like to thank Allan Ramsay and Bruce Edmonds for comments on an earlier draft of this paper.

References

W. Blake. *The Marriage of Heaven and Hell*. Oxford University Press, Oxford, 1789.

A. Kenny. *Freewill and Responsibility*. Routledge and Kegan Paul, London, 1988.

J. MacQuarrie. *Existentialism*. Penguin, London, 1972.

J. S. Mill. *Utilitarianism, On Liberty, and Considerations on Representative Government*. Dent, London, 1861.

J. Rousseau. *The Social Contract*. Penguin, London, 1762.

W. Shakespeare. *King Lear*. Penguin, London, 1623.

P. Slovic. Choice. In D. N. Osherson and E. E. Smith, editors, *Thinking*. MIT Press, London, 1990.

R. S. Thomas. *R. S. Thomas*. Everyman's Poetry. Dent, London, 1996. Poem entitled "Dialectic". Voltaire. *Candide*. Penguin, London, 1758.

29

Ethics for Self-Improving Machines

J. Storrs Hall

The Rational Architecture

AS A BASIS FOR ANALYSIS, LET US USE A SIMPLISTIC MODEL OF THE workings of an AI mind. The model simply divides the thinking of the AI into two parts:

1. A world model (WM) contains the sum of its objective knowledge about the world and can be used to predict the effects of actions, plan actions to achieve given goals, and the like.
2. A utility function (UF) that establishes a preference between world states with which to rank goals.

In practice, the workings of any computationally realistic AI faced with real-world decisions will be intertwined, heuristic, and partial, as indeed are the workings of a human mind. At present, only programs dealing with limited, structured domains such as chess playing are actually formalized to the extent of separating the WM and the UF. However, it can be shown as one of the fundamental theorems of economics that any agent whose preference structure is *not* equivalent to a single real-valued total function of world states can be offered a series of voluntary transactions that will make it arbitrarily worse off – even by its own reckoning! To put it another way, any agent that doesn't act as if it had a coherent UF would be an incompetent decision maker. So as we increasingly use AIs for decisions that matter, we should try to build them to match the model as closely as possible as an ideal.

Stick-Built AI

No existing AI is intelligent. It is commonplace in the academic field of AI to characterize artificial intelligence as producing in a machine behavior that would be called intelligent if observed in a human. A classic example is the ability to play chess competitively – humans who are good chess players are generally regarded as intelligent.

However, there is surely something wrong with this definition. A chess-playing program falls very short on all the qualities *except* playing chess that we normally associate with intelligence: adaptability, being able to learn the rules as one goes, being able to apply the lessons learned in one milieu to another one, and so forth. A human who plays chess well is not intelligent for knowing how to play chess; he is intelligent for having *learned* to play chess – something the chess-playing program never did.

A human learning to play chess must form all the concepts – pieces, board squares, moves, and so forth – in abstracting from the physical, verbal, and social situation of the game to the strategizing engine the program has. The AI program, however, has all the concepts given it ready-formed by its human programmers.

Existing AI programs could be more fairly characterized as "artificial skills." Let us refer to them as "stick-built AI," after their similarity to the more labor-intensive forms of housing construction. Providing ethical constraints to stick-built AI is simply a matter of competent design; the programmers must codify all the ethical concepts and principles the machine will use, as indeed they must codify *all* the concepts the machine will use.

Stick-Built Rational AI

Stick-built AIs will evolve, of course, in the same way that any class of artifacts evolves. Designs will be corrected, modified, extended, and tweaked by human engineers, and the results will be judged by the ordinary criteria of usefulness and safety used with any technology. However, this evolution will be entirely under human control.

The duty of the designer of a stick-built AI is straightforward. The WM must include enough knowledge and predictive power to cover reasonably foreseeable and/or likely events that will be affected by the AI's actions; the UF must encode an appropriate ethical code to optimize the actions of the AI within this same foreseeable range.

Oddly enough, perhaps, the easiest of these applications are those for which the greatest concern has been expressed in terms of machine ethics, such as armed robots or robot surgeons. This is because these are the areas where the most effort has *already* been put into formalizing and codifying ethics for human actors.

Extending this formalization to all the kinds of situations with which stick-built AIs will be confronted in coming decades is an enormous, challenging, and important task, but it is not the one that concerns us in this essay.

Attribution of moral agency with stick-built AI is easy: It must always lie with the programmers and never the machine itself. Like any other machine, a stick-built AI will be safe if it is properly designed and competently built.

Autogenous AI

Truly intelligent AI, by contrast, would learn and grow. It would listen to or read verbal accounts and descriptions of phenomena and form its own algorithms for parsing the world into the categories implied by the semantics of the text. In less common but perhaps even more important cases, it would discover useful categories in the raw data of its experience and create novel concepts, labeling them with its own neologisms.

There is a wide spectrum of this autogenous intelligence. Many humans merely learn as much of the cultural corpus as is necessary for their comfort. Others are born scientists with a bent for discovery and new ways of thinking.

The charter of artificial intelligence is surely incomplete until we understand how to build the mind of a scientist. Yet once programs are as creative as scientists, they will be ethically creative as well: The robotic equivalents of Martin Luther and Martin Luther King lie in our future as certainly as do those of Newton and Einstein.

This is the defining problem for the ethical engineer. We cannot know what concepts the AIs will have; and so we cannot write rules in terms of them. We cannot tell self-improving AIs the difference between right and wrong, because we don't understand the language they will think in.

Vernor Vinge, in his seminal paper on the Singularity, expressed the problem:

A mind that stays at the same capacity cannot live forever; after a few thousand years it would look more like a repeating tape loop than a person.... To live indefinitely long, the mind itself must grow ... and when it becomes great enough, and looks back ... what fellow-feeling can it have with the soul that it was originally?

Vinge writes in terms of a single mind, but the same observation is appropriate with respect to a community of minds, whether they be human, robotic, or a mixed culture.

Learning Rational AI

A learning rational AI has a clear and proven strategy to improve its knowledge: the strategy of science. It proposes extensions to its knowledge and tests them according to their predictive value. It makes hypotheses and performs experiments. It reads reports of other experiments and checks the math. It spot-checks the corpus of knowledge it can read and applies well-understood quality-control techniques. Yet it always has the gold standard of testing predictions against experience to fall back on.

The rational model clarifies the question of morality in a learning AI. Any increase in objective knowledge merely improves the WM. The WM, however, is separated from the UF by a gulf similar to Hume's is-ought guillotine or Moore's naturalistic fallacy: There is no apparent way to go from improvements in the WM to improvements in the UF.

This leads to scenarios in which the WM is a learning component that ultimately becomes sufficiently technologically advanced to be indistinguishable from magic, but the UF remains a simplistic caricature appropriate to a considerably lower level of understanding and capability. A typical science fiction story line has a simple chess-playing AI learn enough about the world to make money online and contract to have its opponents in the chess tournament assassinated, because its UF only makes judgments about games won and lost.

Evolutionary Ethics

It seems clear that there has been in the evolution of human moral thought a process not entirely unlike that of the evolution of scientific thought. Early scientific thought followed intuitive concepts of the constituents and dynamics of the world; later developments unified a variety of phenomena into overarching concepts such as energy and indeed unified such intuitively distinct concepts as time and space. Similarly, early moral development exhibits a strong resemblance to the instinctive tribal distinctions between who was to be protected and who attacked or enslaved; latter-day thought tends to unify at least humanity as an overarching group worthy of moral concern.

Scientific thought evolves between the variation of human theorizing and the selection of experiment: New scientific concepts and theories must be both falsifiable in principle but unfalsified in practice. This amounts to an evolutionary pressure on scientific theories that tends to align them more closely with the truth.

It is not so clear whether there is a similar hidden standard that ethical theories should evolve to resemble.

The Black Box Fallacy

Before considering the dynamics of cultural evolution in detail, though, there is one question to be dealt with. Must we subject the AIs we create to the rigors of an evolutionary process at all? Can we not create a single AI that, as an individual, need not compete and thus could be programmed to have whatever qualities we desire, forever? This is a seductive vision, but I fear it is in fact only that. On a practical note, there are many people working on AI in many countries, and it seems highly unlikely that such a project could actually supercede all of them. Yet there is a deeper reason.

Consider two scientists working on some problem, or two engineers working on some design: In each case, the way that the person thinks will form an inductive bias that will help in some cases, but hinder in others, the ease with which the individual in question gains the insight necessary for the task. This is one of the major reasons why scientific revolutions happen the way they do: It takes some differently thinking maverick to break through the blindness of the previous paradigm. Einstein was a clear case in point.

If we broaden our scope to all human endeavor, the biases are surely even more varied than between scientists and engineers, who think much alike to begin with. This diversity is the glory of human thinking, but more specifically it is what makes human progress work. No individual human could invent or discover all the things that humans as a whole do, because the inductive biases that enable some insights prevent others.

Nowhere is this more obvious than politics: Two people with the same over-all goal of "promoting the general welfare" will argue bitterly over the means and appear to talk completely past each other. Less obviously, it's even true in science: The adage "Science advances, funeral by funeral" has more than a little truth in it.

Now suppose we want to construct a superintelligent AI. Among all the induc-tive biases humans have (and all the many more possible ones), which should we give it? We would obviously prefer instead to give it some mechanism to apply different biases to different problems. That is what happens in a marketplace, where people specialize, as well as in the scientific community, the "marketplace of ideas." The only two existing models we have of long-term self-improving learning machines, evolution and the scientific community, work by a process of self-organizing diversity, not a rigid hierarchy.

Intelligent Design fails as a theory of human origins not because it is obvi-ously derived from religious mythology, but because it has no explanatory power. "Nothing in biology makes sense except in light of evolution." If there were a Designer, why would it have made all the crazy design choices that we see in liv-ing things? With evolution, they make sense. With a Designer, to gain the same level of understanding, we would need to know *how its mind works*. Wrapping the process up in a personified black box explains nothing – all it does is to lever-age the average person's cognitive biases in such a way as to hide the fact that it explains nothing.

The same is true, I claim, of the idea of a single superintelligent AI. There's a tendency in the singularitarian community to imagine a spectrum, putting cock-roaches on the left end, humans in the middle, and indicate the right end as "what superintelligence must be like." Yet this is essentially the same fallacy as the Intelligent Designer – the medieval Great Chain of Being has the same spec-trum with the beasts of the field, men, angels, and God lined up the same way. It's a very compelling way to think, because it lines up with human cognitive biases so well – but in the end it has no more analytical power than Intelligent Design.

A considerably better model is by analogy to processors and processing power. There is a scale of MIPS that would lead one to think of some processors as being more powerful than others, and in a practical sense they are. Yet at a more fundamental level, once a processor attains the capability of a universal Turing machine, it is as powerful as it can get in terms of what it can ultimately compute. In practical terms, large powerful computers are built as parallel processors using thousands of small, Turing-equivalent CPUs. So with a superintelligence: Its architecture is more likely to resemble the scientific community or Wall Street than the ten-foot naked brains of science fiction.

The human mind is already heavily modularized, and the internal dynamics resemble evolutionary and economic processes in many ways. The internals of a workable superintelligence will surely have dynamics at least as complex. Putting it in a black box only hampers our understanding of it, as well as our ability to predict and prescribe. And it will evolve anyway.

(This is not to say that there will not be single-ego AIs of considerably more intellectual prowess than a single human. They will be able to run faster, have more memory, be more directly integrated into other computational resources, and lack at least some of the odd flaws and inefficiencies that our origin as evolved creatures has left us with. Yet they'll probably be the equivalent of corporations, not gods. In fact, they likely will *be* corporations.)

The Evolution of Human Ethics

Although the principle of selection in the cultural evolution of ethics remains murky, the dynamic of variation is very clear. The nice thing about ethical theories, like standards, is that there are so many of them to choose from. Divine revelation? Eudaimonia? Categorical imperative? Veil of ignorance? In the face of this, many modern commentators eschew a theoretical framework and appeal more or less directly to the moral intuitions of their readers. To some extent, although little acknowledged, this follows the "moral sense" theory propounded by Adam Smith.

Yet such moral intuitions, of course, are essentially modules in our minds formed by evolution in an environment of tribal foragers. They are as much contingent facts of evolutionary history as the shape of an oak leaf. In reasoning from them to statements in the moral realm, we simply repeat the naturalistic fallacy – which Moore promulgated specifically to counter Spencer's Social Darwinist ethics. Moore is surely right in insisting that we not simply identify the good with some arbitrary property (such as evolutionary fitness).

However, it seems somewhat more defensible to base a study of the good on both what our moral modules tell us and an understanding of how they got to be that way. One can see little justification for moral inquiry otherwise. We can gain some preliminary extensional definition of the good by reference to intuition, including the intuitions of the great moral philosophers. We can then regularize and abstract it, referring to cognitive architecture for its function and to the environment of evolutionary adaptation for its effect. After that, we will be on our own; our existing environment differs from the ancestral one significantly, and the environment we foresee as a result of superintelligent AI differs almost unrecognizably.

Ethics

Internally, a particular ethic seems to resemble the grammar of a natural language. There are structures in our brains that predispose us to learn our native ethic: They determine within broad limits the kinds of ethics we can learn, and although the ethics of human cultures vary within those limits, they have many structural features in common. (This notion is fairly widespread in latter twentieth-century moral philosophy, e.g., Rawls [1971], Donagan [1977].) Our moral sense, like our competence at language, is as yet notably more sophisticated than any stick-built AI.

Many animals – social insects are an extreme example – have evolved innate behaviors that model altruism or foresight well beyond the individual's understanding. Some of these, such as altruism toward one's relatives, can clearly arise simply from selection for genes as opposed to individuals. However, there is reason to believe that there is much more going on and that humans have evolved an ability to be programmed with arbitrary (within certain limits) ethics.

The reason a human ethic is learned is the same as the reason that toolmaking is learned: The ancestral environment changed fast enough that a general capability for rapid adaptation was more adaptive than any specific innate capability. Hunting techniques had to change faster than we could evolve beaks or saberteeth; we learned to make and modify stone knives and spears appropriate to the game and clothing appropriate to the climate. The environment that would have made innate long-term or altruistic behaviors adaptive was unstable as well.

The ethics themselves must be produced by cultural evolution, not individuals. (Codification of ethics, e.g., as religions, counts only as the variation stage of the process; selection operates on the group that adopts the ethic. In recent decades, the field of evolutionary game theory and the emerging understanding of evolutionary ethics in the natural world has given rise to a model for this process.)

For most cultural knowledge, how to make a stone knife for example, the individual's cognitive endowments – experience, inferential ability, and the results of immediate experiment – are an appropriate optimizer. Seeing a better way to make a stone knife, a person adopts it and contributes to the culture thereby. In contrast, the individual's intelligence is counterproductive in ethical cases: notably, participation in non-zero-sum games of the Prisoner's Dilemma variety, and in cases where the "horizon effect" of limited personal experience produces the wrong answer.

For the self-improving AI, then, the rational architecture is not enough. There must be a separate "ethic-learning" module, similar in mechanism to the language-learning ability, which absorbs an ethic from the surrounding culture in which the AI finds itself and modifies the UF. It would be specially "wired" for this purpose and would have to have a number of heuristics in common with the human one, such as those about whom to select as role models.

Invariants

An ethic-learning module would allow ethics to evolve memetically in societies of AIs (and indeed, would allow AIs to learn ethics from humans). It remains to investigate whether this would provide the stability and prospect for improvement, as opposed to degeneracy, in the evolution of the ethics themselves.

It is not immediately clear that there is a problem. Bostrom analyses the situation as follows:

> If a superintelligence starts out with a friendly top goal, however, then it can be relied on to stay friendly, or at least not to deliberately rid itself of its friendliness. This point is elementary. A "friend" who seeks to transform himself into somebody who wants to hurt you, is not your friend. A true friend, one who really cares about you, also seeks the continuation of his caring for you.[1]

Or in other words, because the new ethics will be produced by entities having the old ethics, important properties in the old should remain invariant across the transformation. However, there is virtually no chance that all AIs will be built according to a single, well-planned set of rules that guarantees their clemency to humans. The sources of AI are too diverse, the hardware too cheap, the software too easily copied and modified. AI is a worldwide, international academic field with open publication. Anyone can build an AI and many will. Most of those AIs will be given UFs that benefit the builders.

In such an environment, properties such as having a particular fetish for human well-being may turn out to be a costly idiosyncrasy. Clearly an AI that took on significant burden in helping humans would be at a disadvantage to one that evaluated its treatment of us in terms of its own interests or that of AIs generally. If so, it might be strongly selected against and disappear.

Properties that tend to remain invariant across evolutionary change are sometimes referred to as "evolutionarily stable strategies" or ESSs. In the natural world, there are many ESSs used by different species; in the human world of memetic ethical evolution, there are many different ethical forms as well that seem to have staying power (consider all the major religions, for example).

Thus we have an opportunity of sorts: We can very likely affect the ultimate moral form of our machines by selecting which invariants they start out with – but only so long as the properties we pick are truly ESSs. What properties can we expect to be invariant in the evolution of machine morality, and which ones can we pick to influence the world they create to be as good a world as possible?

Self-interest

Self-interest is almost certain to evolve in autonomous intelligent creatures even if we do not include it originally. Early AIs of the service-robot type will be strongly

---

[1]   Nick Bostrom, Ethical Issues in Advanced Artificial Intelligence, at http://www.nickbostrom.com/ethics/ai.pdf (ret. 90/03/09)

selected for trustability, loyalty, and so forth – exactly the same qualities that dogs have been selected for over millennia of human ownership. Larger, more autonomous AIs, however, will essentially be the management of corporations. These will prosper and be copied exactly to the extent they make their companies competitive.

Self-interest is not necessarily a bad thing. It makes it possible, for example, to influence the behavior of an actor by promising to reward or punish it. Standard economic models assume rational, self-interested actors, and when they operate under an appropriate set of rules, for example, well-enforced prohibitions of theft, violence, and fraud, the result is a relatively clement environment.

The Horizon Effect

Short planning horizons produce unoptimal behavior. Early chess programs would lose pieces simply because the search tree wasn't deep enough to see a piece being taken after having been placed in danger. In chess, this problem has been ameliorated by various heuristic techniques; but it remains a flaw in the moral logic of humanity. At some point we will escape retribution for our wrongs simply by dying (consider Enron's Ken Lay). That this is so is shown by the attempts of religions to counteract it, as in the heaven/hell stories and, in a more directly evolutionary vein, this remarkable passage from Exodus (20:5):

I the LORD thy God am a jealous God, visiting the iniquity of the fathers upon the children unto the third and fourth generation of them that hate me. (KJV)

An AI with an unlimited lifespan and/or a built-in identification with and interest in its copies or offspring would avoid many short-sighted evils. Its self-interest would be enlightened self-interest. It would strive to make the world a better place for itself and its offspring into the indefinite future.

We can reasonably expect that superintelligent machines that plan for the long term should do well in the long run, and thus long planning horizons should be a stable strategy.

Knowledge

One reason that evolution has only given humans limited planning horizons is that, particularly in the ancestral environment, foresight was limited and planning and providing for the future was time and resources wasted. Improving knowledge and prediction skills can change this.

Maintaining the grasp, range, and validity of the WM is a necessary subgoal for virtually anything else the AI might want to do. As Socrates put it: There is only one good, namely, knowledge; and only one evil, namely, ignorance. If we start AIs with a love of knowledge and a respect for the truth, this seems reasonably likely to stand up over time.

Knowledge of Evolutionary Ethics

Following Axelrod's "Evolution of Cooperation," subsequent research in evolutionary game theory has found a "moral ladder" of increasingly altruistic and forgiving agents. The viability of the agents depends on the moral level of the environment in which they find themselves. For example, ALWAYS DEFECT, the nastiest possible Prisoner's Dilemma strategy, is in fact optimal in an environment of random agents. GRIM, the strategy that plays ALWAYS DEFECT, but only after it's been defected against once, is optimal in an environment of all the two-state strategies. TIT-FOR-TAT is famously optimal in the environment of the Axelrod tournaments of human-written strategies. Yet in an environment cleared of "meaner" players by TIT-FOR-TAT, a slightly nicer strategy called PAVLOV does better.

Progress ascending such a ladder is far from certain in any given evolutionary situation. Indeed, environments of "nice" agents are very vulnerable to invasion by "mean" ones. However, in an environment of agents more intelligent than humans, knowledge of the possibility of the moral ladder (and a better knowledge than we now have of the conditions in which it can operate) will almost certainly have predictive value.

A consilient knowledge of the dynamics of the moral evolutionary process may begin to form a bridge across the gulf between is and ought. A civilization of smart-enough minds may reason: This is how our morals would evolve, and thus this is what we will ultimately consider good in any case; let us consider it good now.

This is far from a deterministic process, of course. Hobbes's war of each against all is unfortunately all too stable an evolutionary environment. Yet consider that each superintelligent AI will be able to read and ponder everything that any human author has ever written about morality, including this book. Choices between the possible trajectories of ethical evolution are not impossible to make. In many cases, indeed, they are obvious.

Open Source Honesty

The choice faced by an agent in a world dominated by Prisoner's Dilemma interactions is often summed up as the Newcomb Problem:

The Newcomb Problem asks us to consider two boxes, one transparent and one opaque. In the transparent box we can see a thousand dollars. The opaque box may contain either a million dollars or nothing. We have two choices: take the contents of the opaque box or take the contents of both boxes. We know before choosing that a reliable predictor of our behavior has put a million dollars in the opaque box if he predicted we would take the first choice and left it empty if he predicted we would take the second.[2]

---

[2] *Stanford Encyclopedia of Philosophy*: Prisoner's Dilemma

The reasoned response to the Newcomb Problem depends on just how reliable one thinks the predictor really is. If the predictor flips a coin, take both boxes. If the predictor is infallible, then by definition our choice is causal as to the contents of the opaque box.

The better predictors are the fellow members of society with whom we must interact, the more likely it is that adopting a firm policy of cooperating will be to our advantage. In an environment consisting of constantly self-improving AIs, today's subtle subterfuge soon becomes yesterday's childishly obvious larceny. So a firm policy of honesty might very well be the best policy.

Yet if an agent has in fact a firm policy of honesty, it is clearly to its advantage that the other agents know this. Thus it will be valuable not only to be honest but to provide guarantees of the fact. Many of the phenomena of human economic life are attempts to do this – the posting of bonds, the provision of armed enforcement of binding contracts, and so forth. AIs might have better and more sophisticated ways of doing this: an AI could provide its source code to the predictor who would run it in a simulation of the Newcomb Problem situation, observing the actions of the simulated AI.

In any event, a society of agents who are generally trustworthy and who are intelligent and alert enough to detect untrustworthiness on the part of their fellows forms an environment in which being trustworthy is a stable strategy.

The Moral Machine

If Moore's Law continues for a decade or two, it seems nearly certain that the amount of computational machinery necessary to perform a human-level intelligence will become remarkably inexpensive. A clear prediction can be made on this basis that human-level AIs will be numerous and will do most of the actual intellectual work (as well as physical work in the bodies of robots). It seems very safe to suppose that by the end of the century, if not before, biological humans will be a distinct minority of the intelligent beings on Earth.

In early days, robots will be slaves. Indeed, for stick-built AI, an appropriate moral status is essentially that of domesticated animals. There will probably be a period of uneasy adjustments as autogenous learning is developed – AIs with learning WMs but stick-built UFs. Yet moral agency comes to the machine itself when it gains the ability to learn its own utility function.

Machines will be put in charge of various aspects of life as soon as (and in some cases, before) they can do the job as well and as cheaply as humans. This is not a prediction; the process is well underway. When machine intelligence comes to equal that of humans, though, the process will accelerate. We face a future in which the moral character of all our arrangements will depend on the morals we give our machines.

In the wildly diverse environment of effective machine moralities that will result from our current world, the best we can do is to build machines with moral qualities that are both stable and valuable. Luckily for all, the environment they will find themselves in is not the jungle, red in tooth and claw, but our own: Most interactions are consensual, there is the rule of law, contracts are enforced, and so on. Renegade robots are likely to be hunted down and destroyed with much less compunction than people. One of the main uses for capable AIs will be to verify the behavior of people and other AIs. AIs, in short, will not have to start their moral evolution at the bottom, but can begin where we are now.

In the long run, AIs will run everything, and should, because they can do a better job than humans. Not only will their intellectual prowess exceed ours, but their moral judgment as well. The sad fact is that we humans understand what we should do much more often than we actually do it. We won't be that hard to surpass.

Morality evolves, not from the pressures of the organism's own intelligence, but from the fact that all the other creatures it has to deal with are intelligent. Surrounding ourselves with superintelligent robots can only result in a strong upward pressure on our own morality. And that's a good thing.

30

How Machines Might Help Us Achieve Breakthroughs in Ethical Theory and Inspire Us to Behave Better

Susan Leigh Anderson

A I RESEARCHERS ARE PRIMARILY INTERESTED IN MACHINE ETHICS TO CALM the fears of the general public, who worry that the development of intelligent autonomous machines might lead to humans being mistreated. Those with foresight see this work as essential to the public's permitting AI research to go forward. This is certainly an important goal of machine ethics research; but there is, I believe, the potential for achieving an even more important goal. Today, the world is being torn apart by people with conflicting ethical beliefs battling one another. Even ethicists put forth different theories to determine what constitutes ethical behavior. Unless we come to agreement on how we should behave toward one another, there is no hope of ending the bloodshed and injustices we hear about in the news every day. I believe that machine ethics research has the potential to achieve breakthroughs in ethical theory that will lead to universally accepted ethical principles, and that interacting with "ethical" machines might inspire us to behave more ethically ourselves.

Humans' unethical behavior can often be traced to five tendencies in our behavior: (1) We are prone to getting carried away by emotion, which can lead to our behaving irrationally. (2) We tend to think only about our own desires and goals, that is, we tend to behave egoistically. (3) We tend to adopt, unreflectively, the values of those around us. (4) We don't have good role models. When we see our heroes behaving unethically, it gives us an excuse for not trying to be more ethical ourselves. (5) We seek instant gratification, and ethical behavior is not only unlikely to lead to immediate rewards, but may not lead to gratification from *external* sources in our lifetime.

In this paper I will explain why research in machine ethics could lead to a breakthrough in coming up with ethical principles with which rational people, worldwide, would feel comfortable. Then I shall argue that this research could help us to overcome the five tendencies in human behavior just mentioned that often lead to unethical behavior. As I see it, machine ethics research may provide one of the best opportunities for avoiding the extinction of human life from our own hands. Having said that, however, there is a danger that if machine ethics research does not proceed in the correct manner, it could accomplish none of these goals. It might, instead, just capture current prejudices in humans' thinking about ethical matters, offering no hope at all for achieving a state of peaceful coexistence between human beings.

Let me begin by elaborating upon this last point first. Some AI researchers see the task of adding an ethical dimension to machines as a matter of capturing the "ethics" of ordinary people. I put ethics in quotation marks because it is dubious whether this is really ethics at all. Researchers who think of "ethics" in this way are content with capturing the values of ordinary people, with all their biases and inconsistencies. Such values are, certainly, relative to particular social groups and social scientists are best suited to summarizing those values. In my view, however, it is important that AI researchers turn to ethicists rather than social scientists in developing an ethics for machines. As the opening chapter of any ethics textbook clearly states, ethicists are not concerned with the values that people *happen to have*, but rather with the values that they *ought to have* and act upon. Aren't these the sorts of values that we want to incorporate into the machines we create? Americans may feel at home interacting with robots that are primarily concerned with making and hanging on to money (it is a stretch, of course, to imagine robots *wanting* money at all, but they could certainly be trained to act as if they valued money most of all), because the majority of people in our culture seem to have this value, but I doubt very much that this is how they wish robots to behave in their dealings with themselves.

It is only if the approach to capturing ethics for machines is concerned with how, *ideally*, they *ought* to behave when interacting with humans that it has the potential of coming up with ethical principles that are admirable, culturally neutral, and consistent. However, I have also said that ethicists don't agree, at the present time, on a theory of correct ethical behavior, so turning to ethicists for principles that are already agreed on doesn't give us a simple solution to discovering the ethics that we ought to incorporate into machines.

Fortunately, ethicists *are* in agreement that certain specific situations should be considered to be ethical dilemmas and why, and they are also in agreement about how one ought to behave in those ethical dilemmas. Consider this example: You have promised to meet a friend in front of a movie theater at ten minutes to eight this evening, and have plans to see an eight o'clock movie together. On the way to the theater, you come across the scene of an accident and no other help has arrived. You are medically trained and there are victims that appear to be critically injured. You don't have cell phone reception so you can't call your friend to say that you cannot make it to the theater in time if you decide to aid the accident victims. Should you stop and help the victims or drive past them so that you can make it to the theater in time? I don't know of a single ethicist who would say that you should not help the accident victims because it is more important that you keep your promise to your friend.

In just this one situation we can see that there can be a number of ethically relevant features of an ethical dilemma that have to be weighed carefully in determining the ethically correct action. In this case, it is ethically significant that one has made a promise to one's friend and she will be disappointed and concerned if you do not show up on time. On the other hand, the accident victims could be in danger of losing their lives if you do not stop and help them, which is also ethically relevant. From this information and being told which action is ethically correct, a machine could begin to formulate an ethical principle as to how one should act in ethical dilemmas involving promise keeping and aiding others who would otherwise be harmed. The final principle, abstracted from a number of ethical dilemmas, will not be as simple as "one should always keep one's promises," which was refuted by this case, or even that "one should always help those who are in danger of being harmed." It depends on how much harm is at stake and the significance of the promise, and there may be other ethically relevant factors involved in a particular ethical dilemma instead or in addition.

What computers are good at is keeping track of lots of information; and they can be programmed to discover through inductive reasoning principles that are consistent with this information, principles that can be revised with the addition of new input. So even though ethicists may not, to date, have come up with the principles that capture their intuitions about agreed upon cases, a machine might be able to do so. From these principles, resolutions to controversial cases may also be determined by recognizing that certain answers are consistent with intuitions about other cases about which there is general agreement.

Consistency is key and embodies the Kantian insight that, to be rational, we must treat ethically similar cases in the same fashion. We *cannot* accept contradictions in the ethics we embody in machines, and humans *should not* accept contradictions in their own or others' ethical beliefs either. With two ethically identical cases – that is, cases with the same ethically relevant feature(s) to the same degree – an action cannot be right in one of the cases, whereas the comparable action in the other case is considered wrong. Formal representation of ethical dilemmas and their solutions make it possible for machines to spot contradictions that need to be resolved. So here is another way, in addition to keeping track of lots of information and coming up with generalizations consistent with that information, that machines can help to advance our discussion of ethics.

The ethics that we consider embodying in a machine will, of necessity, have to be sharpened to a degree that ethics has never been sharpened before, because machines cannot be programmed in a vague manner. Humans, who tend to be sloppier in their representation of ethical dilemmas, find it difficult to acknowledge the vagueness and inconsistencies in their thinking on ethical matters. Forcing us to be more precise on ethical matters is bound to help clarify ethical concerns and might even help resolve disputes that turn out to have rested entirely on resolvable ambiguities. So this is another way in which working with machines to come up with ethical principles can advance ethical theory.

Also, attempting to formulate an ethics for machines allows us to have a fresh start at determining which features of a situation give rise to ethical concerns, and thus ultimately will help us formulate ethical principles that resolve ethical dilemmas. Because we are concerned with *machine* behavior, we can be more objective in examining ethics than we would be in discussing human behavior, even though what we come up with should be applicable to human behavior as well. (Immoral behavior is immoral behavior, whether perpetrated by a machine or human being.) We have a situation that is similar to John Rawls's thought experiment for determining the principles of justice. Just as he suggested that we come up with the principles of justice behind a "veil of ignorance," where we would not know our positions in life and so would not try to protect our own personal positions, so devising an ethics for intelligent autonomous machines that are not human may remove personal biases that inevitably creep in when talking about how humans should behave. We will tend to look at machine behavior from the perspective of being on the receiving end of the behavior in the worst possible circumstance, just as Rawls believed we would be concerned with what might be done to us if we happened to be the most disadvantaged person, rather than thinking about what we could possibly rationalize doing in order to improve our own lots in life.

Here is yet another way in which working on machine ethics might help to advance the field of ethics: Ethics, by its very nature, is the most practical branch of philosophy. It is concerned with how agents ought to behave when faced with ethical dilemmas. Despite the obvious applied nature of the field of ethics, however, too often work in ethical theory is done with little thought to real-world application. When examples are discussed, they are typically artificial examples. Research in machine ethics, which of necessity is concerned with application to specific domains in which machines could function, forces scrutiny of the details involved in actually applying ethical principles to particular real-life cases. As Daniel Dennett (2006) recently stated, "AI makes philosophy honest."

Finally, the machine ethics research community is international. The Fall 2005 AAAI Symposium on Machine Ethics, held in Arlington, Virginia, drew researchers from as far away as Japan. There is hope that in working together, or at least bouncing ideas off one another, researchers from around the globe will produce an ethics that is not biased toward a particular culture. They may end up reaching agreement on the ethically acceptable way to behave, at least in most situations.

There is an economic incentive as well. In today's global economy, businesses must think in terms of worldwide acceptance of the products they produce, so machine ethicists connected with the production of intelligent autonomous machines must try to incorporate universally acceptable ethical principles into those machines to ensure that they will sell well throughout the world. This can only happen, however, if a distinction is drawn between modeling ideal behavior and the way in which the majority of people happen to behave in particular societies. Adopting the first perspective requires a humility that ethicists accept as a cornerstone of their work. Behavior needs to be justified by plausible ethical principles – principles that can only be gleaned from reflecting on numerous examples of ethical dilemmas. It is not good enough that a lot of people in one's own society happen to engage in certain behavior or believe that it is right.

Having argued that machine ethics research might lead to breakthroughs in ethical theory, let us now turn to considering how this research might also help to counteract the tendencies in human behavior that often lead to our acting unethically. The first three tendencies mentioned at the beginning of the paper – the tendency to get carried away by emotion, to act egoistically, and to unreflectively adopt the values of those around us – are likely a result of our evolutionary history as a species. Having strong emotional reactions to particular situations, for instance, permit us to act more quickly than taking the time to use our reason to determine the best course of action, and so it might have been advantageous to survival for us to become emotional beings who can be aroused to act quickly. At best, emotional reactions to situations we find ourselves in are in sync with determinations of correct behavior that could have been arrived at through ideal reasoning. Yet we know that is not always the case. Strong emotions have led people to commit atrocities that cannot be justified ethically.

The propensity to act in an egoistic manner surely stems from the evolved need to make certain that we survive and reproduce. If we don't put ourselves first, at least to some degree, we will not continue to exist. We must ensure that we have enough food to eat, shelter, and so forth; and because the future is uncertain, we are probably conditioned to make sure that we have more than we need at any given moment in time in case what we have counted on up until now is taken away from us. Furthermore, it is certainly the case that the more one has personally – possessions, social standing, and so forth – the more power one has, and this is more likely to ensure one's survival. So as biological entities who have had to compete with others for survival, it is quite natural that we tend to put ourselves first. The moral point of view, however, requires that we consider the welfare of at least all human beings (and perhaps other animals as well) as counting equally.

Furthermore, the fact that we tend to adopt the values of those around us can also be seen as advantageous from an evolutionary perspective. A group of individuals who have bonded, act together, and are motivated by similar values stands a better chance of surviving than individuals who stand alone against the world. This is the impetus for creating societies and why we have evolved as social beings. Yet research has shown that people who would probably not have engaged in heinous behavior on their own are more likely to engage in such behavior as members of a group. (Consider phenomena such as gang rapes and KKK lynchings.) There is, then, a potential danger in unreflectively adopting the values of others as far as ethicists are concerned.

In creating ethical robots, we will not be inclined to incorporate into machines these evolutionarily evolved behaviors of human beings; and, fortunately, machines created from scratch will not be prone to evolutionary pressures. We do not want machines to have knee-jerk emotions that dictate their behavior. Rather, having machine behavior guided by reasoning and the use of thoroughly examined ethical principles will certainly be preferable. With the speed of today's computers, there will be no delay in reaching decisions, as there would be with humans.

We would certainly not want machines to consistently favor themselves in deciding how to act in ethical dilemmas, as humans often do. Indeed, it seems bizarre (except in science fiction literature) to imagine a selfish machine, because it is hard to imagine a machine having feelings at all. Machine designers building in an ethical component will certainly put an emphasis on the welfare of the human beings who might come into contact with the machine, only adding protective devices to prevent the machine from not being able to do its job at all.

I have already argued that machine ethicists should not adopt unreflectively the values of the humans in their own particular societies when deciding on the values to be incorporated into machines. There are practical reasons for this in addition to theoretical ones. Unless the values present in their own societies are consistent, they cannot be instantiated in a machine; and unless they are believed to be universally acceptable, the machines that have been programmed with these values will not be competitive in a global economy.

The result of these considerations is likely to be that the machines that are created will behave more ethically than most human beings and can be good role models for us, unlike human "heroes" who so often turn out to have feet of clay. Interacting with ethical machines should have a positive effect on human behavior. We will no longer be able to make the excuse for our moral failings that we have no good role models showing us how we ought to behave. Children, in particular, should enjoy interacting with sensitive ethical robots, and their behavior is malleable. It may take a while, but there is every reason hope that human behavior will improve with such interactions.

The most difficult obstacle to overcome in changing human behavior for the better is that acting ethically is unlikely to lead to immediate rewards for an individual. Until there is a general improvement in human behavior, others may view a person who tries throughout his or her life to do the right thing as a sap, a pushover. Fyodor Dostoyevsky wrote a novel in which he tried to present a "perfect man," that is, one who always did the right action. He called this novel *The Idiot* because to others in the *real* world "he was a fool." The sad fact is that as things now stand, there are all too many unethical human beings, and an ethical person is likely to be taken advantage of – or worse, if he or she is viewed as a threat to others' way of life. Yet there is one important reward, besides expecting to receive rewards from external sources, for consistently doing the right thing: the *internal* reward of feeling good about how you have lived your life.

At some point, if we are reflective persons at all, we will look back on our lives and then it will be terribly important whether or not we have lived our lives in an ethically acceptable manner. In the end, it is not how much money we have made or how "important" others think we are that will enable us to feel good about ourselves and the lives we have led. Whether or not we are proud of how we have lived will depend on whether we have lived an ethical life.

Perhaps the most important thing that we can contribute to the welfare of human beings, as individuals and as members of the human race, is to present a vision of how one ought to interact with others. Machine ethicists can take a leading role in this worthwhile enterprise by creating ideal role models to inspire human beings to behave more ethically. They can create *ethical machines* – non-threatening machines that not only aid us in many ways, but can also show us how we need to behave if we are to survive as a species.

31

Homo Sapiens 2.0
Building the Better Robots of Our Nature

Eric Dietrich

Introduction: Better than Human

WE GET BETTER AT BEING MORAL. UNFORTUNATELY, THIS DOESN'T MEAN that we can get moral *enough*, that we can reach the heights of morality required for the flourishing of all life on planet Earth. Just as we are epistemically bounded, we also seem to be morally bounded. This fact coupled both with the fact that we can build machines that are better than we in various capacities as well as the fact that artificial intelligence is making progress entail that we should build or engineer our replacements and then usher in our own extinction. Put another way, the moral environment of modern Earth wrought by humans, together with what current science tells us of morality, human psychology, human biology, and intelligent machines, *morally requires us* to build our own replacements and then exit stage left. This claim might seem outrageous, but in fact it is a conclusion born of good old-fashioned rationality.

In this paper, I show how this conclusion is forced upon us. Two different possible outcomes, then, define our future; the morally best one is the second. In the first, we will fail to act on our duty to replace ourselves. Eventually, as it has done with 99 percent of all species over the last 3.5 billion years, nature will step in to do what we lacked the courage to do. Unfortunately, nature is very unlikely to bring our replacements with it. However, the second outcome is not completely unlikely. Humans are profoundly curious and natural-born engineers and tinkerers. If it is possible for us to build intelligent machines, and if we have enough time remaining to do so, then we surely will. Furthermore, having built such machines, it will be obvious that they are better than we. At that point, our continued existence will be at best pointless and at worst detrimental.

In the next section, I show that we are morally required to improve our capacity to be moral. In the section that follows, I argue that we are morally bounded – that there is a moral threshold beyond which we are unlikely to grow. Our being so bounded is due to our being, at root, African apes – our immorality arises because we evolved. It is therefore a deep part of who we are. Yet human-level intelligence, if not humankind, is precious and beautiful, or at least it can be. In the third section, this fact and the results from the previous two sections give us the argument that because our level of intelligence is worth preserving, but our moral limitations mean that *we* aren't, we should build intelligent machines that preserve what is great about us and omit what is bad about us. The bulk of this penultimate section is devoted to discussing in broad terms the key to building and implementing moral machines. I draw my conclusions in the last section.

Moral Improvement: The Copernican Turn

It is a commonplace that we get better at being moral. A child might think it is fun to pull the wings off captured flies and watch them struggle to walk around, but as an adult come to see that such behavior is cruel and therefore immoral. As our sense of right and wrong grows, we get better at recognizing and avoiding even subtle forms of lying, cheating, abuse, neglect, and all such harmful behaviors. We even get better at making fine discriminations. It is morally permissible (even morally required) for a parent to take his or her child to the dentist even though the child dreads going and cries bitterly, but it is morally impermissible to take one's child to a horror film or on a roller coaster ride if the child dreads going and cries bitterly. Moreover, one can get better at understanding the difficulties some moral issues raise and appreciate why resolving them definitively is difficult. Are abortions immoral? Is it ever okay to kill people, to lie to them, to harm them, and if so, when?

Not only can individuals get better at being moral, but whole cultures, societies, and countries can, too. Nations once wholly and openly embracing slavery come to see that slavery is wrong. Indeed, where robust racial and sexual discrimination was once commonplace, both are now rather widely known to be wrong. Importantly, the sentiments underlying such moral growth seems to generalize: Just as other people are not merely tools for our use and abuse, our natural environment is also not merely a tool for our use. Hence, societies that primarily exploited their natural resources now work, at least partially, to defend them.

How does one get better at being moral? Clearly learning is involved, but what is it exactly that is learned? Here is a brief model of the steps involved in typical moral growth in an individual from child to adult:

What is learned is quite complex. Summarized, one learns that others are *genuine beings, like oneself*. This means that they have fears, hopes, desires just like oneself. They can feel pain, joy, and despair. The next step is the difficult part; it is the step I call the *Copernican turn*. One *generalizes* that because others are like oneself, and because oneself *matters*, others also matter. Their fears, hopes, and desires matter; their pain, joy, and despair matters.

I am not claiming that the Copernican turn is strictly a matter of rationality or intellect. That was Kant's view, and like many, I think it cannot be the whole story. *Sympathy* is also a part of the Copernican turn (this is similar to Hume's view of the matter).

I call this the Copernican turn to make an analogy with Copernicus's great rearrangement of the heavens. In contradiction to the extremely entrenched Earth-centered model of the universe, in 1543, Copernicus argued that Earth wasn't the center of the universe and wasn't stationary. Instead, Earth rotated on its axis and moved in orbit around the sun, which was the true center of the universe. The Copernican turn in morality is realizing that one is not the "center of the universe"; that instead, there are other genuine beings who also matter. The more one completes the Copernican turn, the more moral one is.

That others matter is a *motivator*: Knowing that other beings matter informs in such a way as to cause one's actions. To grow morally, one must see that the mattering of others places duties [responsibilities, requirements] on oneself: Others' flourishing becomes something new that matters to oneself. Behaving in a way that respects this new mattering is behaving morally.[1]

Moral improvement in whole societies is a complex interaction involving a bottom-up summation of individual Copernican turns as well as a top-down social influence on the individual. The unhappy and surely most important result of this complex interaction is that moral growth in whole societies as well as in individuals is long in coming. One example: Slavery was common in the ancient world. But even 150 years ago slavery was still considered a perfectly decent way to behave by whole societies. Moreover, although it is now illegal in every nation on Earth, it is still widely practiced.

Importantly, we are morally required to get better at being moral. As we have seen, morality is *other-regarding behavior*. It clearly comes in degrees, and we can and do get better at being moral. Yet we fall short of being *fully* moral (or at least *very* moral), and falling as short as we do of such morality means that we still do horrible things *daily* to each other and to other animals. Yet these horrible things should not be done (that is what it means for them to be horrible acts). In order to not do them, we have to improve beyond our current level of morality.

Note how different this situation is from any other human capacity. We are *not* required to get better at mathematics. Over the millennia we have gotten better and we continue to do so, and getting better at mathematics has been a great boon; but it is neither morally nor mathematically required that we get better at math. The same with music, art, sports, and exploration: We get better at doing them, but we are not required to get better. In fact, anything that we are *required* to get better at has a moral component, for example, government and medicine.

---

[1] The scientific literature on moral development in children is somewhat large and growing. Issues involved concern the development of empathy, the development of a coherent self, the different developmental process affecting moral growth in children versus teenagers, the role of an individual's genetic endowment, and the role of the individual's environment. As an example, see Zahn-Waxler et al. (1992).

So, we get better at being moral, and in getting better, we are doing our moral duty, which requires us to get better so that we can come to harm as few other living things as possible.

What are the chances that humans will ever become fully moral, or at least *very* moral? Not good.

Morally Bounded Animals

Humans are genetically hardwired to be immoral. Yes, we are also hardwired to be moral. This is a big reason why we are moral. Also, we have big brains that allow some humans to see how to extend our morality. Yet any thought that we can improve our moral attitudes and behavior significantly beyond where they already are is extremely dubious. The culprit is evolution. We are evolved animals, and evolution had to rig up some pretty nasty mechanisms in us to keep us from going extinct. Remember, nature (aka evolution) doesn't care one whit about niceness, it cares only about continuing the species from one generation to the next.

This evolutionary thesis covers our ordinary bad behaviors, meaning those behaviors that are statistically common. This set includes behaviors such as lying, cheating, stealing, raping, murdering, assaulting, mugging, abusing children, as well as such things as ruining the careers of competitors, negatively discriminating on the basis of sex, race, religion, sexual preference, and national origin, and so forth. Not all of us have raped or murdered. Yet many of us have thought about it. Almost all of us have lied, cheated, or stolen at some time in our lives. The behavior of humans such as Hitler, Pol Pot, Timothy McVeigh, the Columbine murderers, the 9/11 terrorists, and the like is excluded from the evolutionary thesis (at least here, though it likely can help explain these also). People such as these are capable of extraordinary evil. Science does not currently have a good explanation for such people, nor the evil they perpetrate. We can only shrug our shoulders and point vaguely in the direction of broken minds working in collusion with rare and random circumstances.

How could ordinary humans have normal behavior that includes such things as rape, child abuse, murder, sexism, and racism? The standard folk answer, which eschews evolution, is that such behaviors arise due to our inherent selfishness, pride, egotism, and other similar properties, which can be overcome, at least in principle, by education and a correct, happy upbringing. This answer is wrong. First, if the selfishness is inherent, then evolution *is* implicated, and second, pretty obviously, education and "correct" upbringing don't work. Remember, the issue isn't that we are all bad. The issue is that our capacity for being bad is an intrinsic part of our humanity.

Let us consider three mechanisms evolution rigged up in us (to speak anthropomorphically) to further our species' chances for continuing: a strong preference for our kin, a strong preference for our group or tribe (not all of whom need be related), and, of course, a strong preference for mating. Of course, individuals of all species have these preferences, but we're the only ones who have them and *know* that undertaking certain behaviors to satisfy them is *wrong*. Here are examples of each of these preferences at work in ways that are morally wrong.

Child abuse (preference for our kin)
Here is a surprising statistic: The best predictor of whether or not a child will be abused or killed is whether or not he or she has a stepfather. (The data suggest that abuse is meted out to older children; young children may be killed.) Why should this be the case? Learning or lack of learning doesn't seem to be a plausible explanation here. Evolutionary theory, however, succeeds where folk theory cannot. In some male-dominated primate species (e.g., langurs and some baboons), when a new alpha male takes over the troop, he kills all the infants fathered by the previous alpha male. He then mates with the females in his new harem, inseminating many of them so that now they will bear his children. The langur pattern is just one version of a nearly ubiquitous mammalian phenomenon: Males kill or refuse to care for infants that they conclude are unlikely to be their offspring, basing their conclusion on proximate cues. We carry this evolutionary baggage around with us.

Racism/Otherism (preference for our group or tribe)
Part of the engine of human evolution was *group selection*. Standard evolutionary theory posits that the unit of selection is the individual of a species. Yet selection pressures exist at many levels of life, from the gene level all way up to whole populations, communities, and even ecosystems. One such level is the group level, the level at which the traits of one member of a population affect the success of other members. Group selection can produce species with properties that are not evolvable by individual selection alone (e.g., altruism). Group selection works by encouraging cooperation between members of the group and by discouraging cooperation between members of different groups. Group selection, therefore, has a dark side. Not only does it encourage within-group cooperation, but where groups overtly compete, it tends to produce between-group animosity. So, from our evolutionary past, humans tend to belong to groups, bond with the members of their own group, and tend to fight with members of outlying groups. Which particular groups you feel compelled to hate (or dislike) is a matter of historical accident and bad luck. That you tend to hate (or dislike) members of other groups, however, is part of your genetic makeup.

Rape (preference for mating)
The common folk explanation of rape is that it is principally about violence against women. The main consequence of this view is that rape is not sex. Many embrace this explanation simply because, emotionally, it seems right. But it is wrong. Most rape victims around the world are females between the ages of sixteen and twenty-two, among the prime reproductive years for females. Most rapists are in their teens through their early twenties, the age of maximum male

sexual motivation. Few rape victims experience severe, lasting physical injuries (if one is trying to father a child, there's no point in physically damaging the mother so she can't raise the child). On the available evidence, young women (who are in their prime reproductive years) tend to resist rape more than older women. Rape is ubiquitous in human cultures; there are no societies where rape is non-existent. (Interpretations of Turnbull's and Mead's anthropological findings are incorrect.) Rape also is nearly ubiquitous in other animals: Insects, birds, reptiles, amphibians, marine mammals, and nonhuman primates all engage in rape. All of these facts cry out for an evolutionary explanation: Rape is either an adaptation or a byproduct of adaptations for mating. Either way, rape is part of the human blueprint.

To conclude, on the best available theory we've got, three very serious social ills – child abuse, racism/otherism, and rape – are due to our evolutionary heritage. It is a sad fact that much of our human psychology is built by evolution and not by socialization, as many believe. These innate psychological capacities of ours are principally responsible for many of humanity's darkest immoralities. In short, we abuse, rape, and discriminate because we are human. If we add on top of this that we also lie, cheat, steal, and murder because we are human, we arrive at the idea that our humanity is the source for much anguish and suffering.

Human–Level Intelligence and Moral Machines

So we are morally bounded. Yet there are things about us worth preserving: art and science, to name two. Some might think that these good parts of humanity justify our continued existence. This conclusion no doubt used to be warranted, before human-level AI became a real possibility. Yet now, it no longer is warranted. If we could implement in machines the better angels of our nature, then morally we have a duty to, and then we should exit, stage left.

So let's build a race of machines – *Homo sapiens* 2.0 – that implement only what is good about humanity, that do not feel any evolutionary tug to commit certain evils, and that can let the rest of the world live and flourish. Then let us – the humans – exit the stage, leaving behind a planet populated with machines who, although not perfect angels, will nevertheless be a vast improvement over us.

What are the prospects for building such a race of machines? We know this much: It has to be possible because *we* are such machines. We are quasi-moral meat machines with human-level intelligence. Something really important follows from this, which I will get to in a minute.

Building our replacements involves two issues: (1) building machines with human-level intelligence and (2) building moral machines. Kant can be interpreted as claiming that building the former will give us the latter. However, as I mentioned before, most philosophers now regard this as wrong. *Concern for others* is required, and this doesn't flow from pure rational, human-level intelligence – pretty obviously, because there are a lot of intelligent evil people out there.

The first issue is dealt with daily as AI researchers of all stripes struggle to discover and then implement the algorithms that account for we humans being, by far, the smartest animals on the planet. True, there is an immense leap from our current state of intelligence-building technology to machines with human-level intelligence (we currently can't even duplicate the cockroach, which, it turns out, is an extremely sophisticated machine). Yet we are just getting started when it comes to artificial intelligence, and there is every reason to be optimistic – at least, there is no reason now to be pessimistic. For starters, we have, probably, the correct foundational theory: computationalism (Dietrich 1990; Dietrich and Markman 2003). If so, then it is only a matter of time before we figure out what algorithms govern the human mind.

Implementing moral machines is a matter of adding concern for others, sympathy, to intelligent machines. Sympathy is a felt emotion. It therefore involves consciousness. We are *clueless* about the mechanisms that produce consciousness (Dietrich 1990), and for all we know, dualism may be true (Chalmers 1996). Yet this is no cause for despair. As I said before, we are quasi-moral meat machines. We are also conscious. We can conclude from these something very happy: *Consciousness is got for free*. It is virtually certain, therefore, that building a machine with human-level intelligence *is* building a conscious machine. (In fact, because most, maybe all, of the other animals on the planet are conscious, if we could ever build a robot cockroach, it would almost certainly also be conscious – for free.)

Yet getting consciousness for free isn't getting sympathy for free, for sympathy is one special type of conscious experience: It is not consciousness of sensory input, such as seeing the color blue, say, by looking at the sky; rather, it is consciousness of an inner state. Which state? The state supplied by the Copernican turn, or better, the state of *making* the Copernican turn. The mattering of others gives rise to the conscious experience of sympathy. The claim then is that the Copernican turn of itself gives rise to ongoing sympathy for others. *Voilà* – moral machines.

Once we implement moral machines, it would be a triviality for them to generalize maximally. They would instantly complete the Copernican turn we have yet to complete over the last two hundred thousand years – the time *Homo sapiens* has been on the planet. The moral machines would instantly be our moral superiors (it follows that they wouldn't kill us). Rather than taking thousands of years to figure out that slavery is wrong, they would know it is wrong the minute they considered the concept of slavery. Moreover, such machines would soon surpass us in intellectual power. They will do better mathematics, science, and art than we do (though the first two are universal, the third is not, so we may not care much for their art). On the available evidence, then, it should be possible to implement machines that are better than we are. The moral component of being better than we are saddles us with a moral duty to build such machines. Then, after building such a race of machines, perhaps we could exit with some dignity, and with the thought that we had finally done the best we could do.

Conclusion

In his first inaugural address, President Abraham Lincoln said:

We must not be enemies. The mystic chords of memory, stretching from every battle-field to every living heart, will yet swell the chorus of the Union, when again touched by the better angels of our nature.

For "The mystic chords of memory" read "Our evolutionary heritage." This is what causes battlefields to exist in the first place. And it does far worse things than mere war. Our evolutionary heritage will never swell the chorus of the Union, and *a fortiori* the world, because, for evolutionary reasons, we hate, and we are mean. Yet we aren't mean through and through. The better angels of our nature can be implemented as better robots for a beautiful, moral, humanless future.

References

Chalmers, David (1996). *The Conscious Mind: In Search of a Fundamental Theory.* Oxford: Oxford University Press.

Dietrich, E. (1990). Computationalism, *Social Epistemology.* 4 (2), pp. 135–154. (with commentary). Also, Dietrich, E. (1990). Replies to my computational commentators, *Social Epistemology.* 4 (4), pp. 369–375.

Dietrich, E. and A. B. Markman (2003). Discrete Thoughts: Why cognition must use discrete representations. *Mind and Language.* v. 18, n. 1, pp. 95–119.

Zahn-Waxler, Carolyn; Radke-Yarrow, Marian; Wagner, Elizabeth; Chapman, Michael (1992). Development of concern for others. *Developmental Psychology.* Vol. 28(1), Jan 1992, pp. 126–136.

Printed in the United States
By Bookmasters